THE LEVIATHAN FACTOR

THE LEVIATHAN FACTOR

Lawrence E. Burkholder

WIPF & STOCK · Eugene, Oregon

THE LEVIATHAN FACTOR

Copyright © 2017 Lawrence E. Burkholder. All rights reserved. Except for brief quotations in critical publications or reviews, no part of this book may be reproduced in any manner without prior written permission from the publisher. Write: Permissions, Wipf and Stock Publishers, 199 W. 8th Ave., Suite 3, Eugene, OR 97401.

Wipf & Stock
An Imprint of Wipf and Stock Publishers
199 W. 8th Ave., Suite 3
Eugene, OR 97401

www.wipfandstock.com

PAPERBACK ISBN: 978-1-4982-9995-4
HARDCOVER ISBN: 978-1-4982-9997-8
EBOOK ISBN: 978-1-4982-9996-1

Manufactured in the U.S.A.   01/06/17

All scripture quotations are from the NRSV unless otherwise noted. 'New Revised Standard Version Bible, copyright 1989, Division of Christian Education of the National Council of the Churches of Christ in the United States of America. Used by permission. All rights reserved.'

To Jesus of Nazareth
in whom are hidden
all the treasures of wisdom and knowledge

CONTENTS

Acknowledgments | ix
Table of Psi *Illustrations* | xi

    PROLOGUE | 1
 1 WINDOWS INTO REALITY | 12
 2 THE NEW PARADIGM | 36
 3 DEATH | 58
 4 THE SIXTH DAY | 79
 5 EDEN | 100
 6 THE UNIVERSAL COVENANT | 122
 7 LEVIATHAN AND NATURE | 147
 8 THE DISORDERED MIND | 169
 9 THE TRANSCENDENT LIGHT | 193
10 ECSTASY | 215
11 THE FINAL FRONTIER | 239
12 FROM ETERNITY TO ETERNITY | 261

Glossary | 293
Bibliography | 297
Index | 347

ACKNOWLEDGMENTS

First of all, I thank Wipf and Stock Publishers and their many editors and staff people who have helped bring *The Leviathan Factor* to the finish line. They have collectively assumed some risk to the Press' reputation; may their heavenly reward be great!

Though I have worked independently of all academic institutions, I appreciate very deeply the willingness of Gregory A. Boyd and E. Janet Warren to lend their kind words to the book's back cover. I trust that they will not have cause to regret their affirmation of this work.

There are several people from my personal circle who deserve heartfelt thanks.

My prayer support team stayed faithful even though they didn't really know what I was writing about! They include Anne Ashton, Judy Bergen, Art Burkholder, Lois Burkholder, Evelyn Burkholder, Earl Davey, Marion Davey, Pieter Niemeyer, Susie Niemeyer, Bruce Twining, and Martha Twining. Ralph Garbe wasn't a part of this team but formed his own one-man support group over coffee. He also read every chapter at the first draft stage.

Several friends influenced and supported me, sometimes unwittingly on their part. Early on Judy Bergen most clearly realized the demands and risk of doing cutting-edge thinking. In that regard Bruce Twining and Martha Twining, and Evelyn Burkholder raised a spiritual bulwark for me when the battle was especially intense. Bruce also told me I could ask God any question I wanted to—so I did! You can judge the results of my listening for yourself. I have enjoyed many personal conversations and e-mail discussions with my nephew Charles Bakker. His unique knowledge of the issues enabled him to offer constructive feedback. Finally, thanks to various other people who inquired regularly about my progress and more or less held my feet to the fire.

I am blessed that my wife, Lois, never once objected to having an extra financial and emotional load due to this work. Her willingness to carry heavy responsibilities freed me to write. She was especially supportive during the several hospitalizations and other medical detours I suffered that threatened to derail the whole thing. Lois, for fifteen years of love, patience, endurance, and lack of complaint you have truly been the ideal woman of Proverbs 31.

Early on when I began to realize the magnitude of the job and my inability to do it, I asked Jesus Christ of Nazareth to be my divine editor. He responded by telling me that the Holy Spirit would make me more than I am; by instilling in me what it takes to run a marathon against great opposition from the forces of darkness; by leading me many times to library, internet, and other sources I didn't even know I needed; and by directing me to many conceptual breakthroughs. These include creation's foundational automaton, the ubiquitous nature of chaoplexic laws, the dynamic yet irrevocably fractured covenant relationship between Leviathan (Satan) and God, the identity of the trees of life and knowledge, and the transhistorical persistence of the gnostic program of ascent to the throne of God. Even though I understand these things and their interconnections only in part, I thank Jesus Christ for teaching me.

I ask the readers' forbearance for any remaining errors of fact or interpretation which are, of course, my responsibility.

Gormley, Ontario, June 15, 2016

TABLE OF *PSI* ILLUSTRATIONS

No.	Pg.	*Psi* Illustrations
1	10	Joseph of Cupertino levitates during Eucharist
2	10	Sir George McKenzie observes tactile (non-Braille) reading
3	10	2,000 individual poltergeist events in an Enfield, England, household
4	10	Possession, ESP, déjà vu, ghosts, etc., in 502-person Winnipeg study
5	12	"Exorcism" of Mother Teresa
6	12	Mother Teresa's vision/voice of Jesus
7	15	Élise-Catherine Müller and materialization and apports
8	23	Charles Leadbeater's vision during mass
9	28	Hubbard hears "Jesus'" voice about coming gnostic planetary evolution
10	116	A medieval nun describes erotic sex with "Jesus"
11	120	Self-divinization, *Epic of Gilgamesh*
12	120	Self-divinization, *Brhadaranyaka Upanishad*
13	120	Self-divinization, *Poimandres*
14	120	Self-divinization, *Sufi Abu Yazid Bistami*
15	120	Self-divinization, *Sufi Abu Hamid al-Ghazali*
16	120	Self-divinization, *Hadewijch of Brabant*
17	120	Self-divinization, *John Custance*
18	148	Psychic Ted Owens causes a lightning strike in Philadelphia
19	149	Hildegarde Schaefer sees spirit images materialize on bicameral TV loop
20	149	Carol Herkimer takes a shamanic journey and her metal chair burns the floor
21	149	Jordanian sufi has self-inflicted cheek punctures heal within hours
22	156	Anna Schmidt levitates during exorcism
23	159	Haunting and geomagnetism at Hampton Court Palace
24	159	Nina Kulagina emits strong electromagnetic force fields
25	160	Shanghai man ballooned to seven men's weight during Taoist exorcism
26	160	Prayer promotes plant growth
27	160	Uri Geller regresses a plant to its seed

Table of *Psi* Illustrations

No.	Pg.	*Psi* Illustrations
28	162	Wolfgang Pauli explodes equipment by entering the room
29	164	Ted Owens called up Hurricane David
30	166	Agnes Sanford stops hurricanes
40	169	John Forbes Nash Jr.: aliens' voices and messages help him win Nobel
41	190	David Berkowitz (Son of Sam) hears Satanic voices which led to his murders
42	193	Mystical light attends Christian healer William Branham's birth
43	194	Emanuel Swedenborg describes his vision of the mystical heavenly light
44	194	Joseph Smith encounters the "angel" Moroni
45	195	John, a doctor, sees a glowing golden halo given off by a Satsung guru
46	195	Hiroshi Motoyama sees an intense light during meditation and is levitated
47	195	The radiant light enables Timothy Leary to see inside people's bodies
48	195	Rita Klaus sees incredible light which heals her MS and transforms her spiritually
49	201	Vicki Umipeg had a classic NDE although her optic nerves were destroyed at birth
50	201	Pam Reynolds sees her surgery while brain dead with her body drained of blood
51	203	Mrs. A. sees her doppelgänger with misty and transparent legs
52	204	Swami Dadaji bilocates 400 miles between Allahabad and Calcutta
53	206	A cardiac survivor sees "Jesus": jet-black hair and beard, white teeth, nail scars
54	207	Agnes Sanford experiences "Jesus" sending her to earth on a messianic mission
55	208	Sundar Singh has multiple visions of "Jesus" sitting on the center throne in heaven
56	209	Participant in a holotropic altered state sees Mother Goddess and then Brahma
57	211	The Light tells Jayne Smith there's no sin; she's eternal, immortal, indestructible
58	213	A missionary sees "Jesus," who promises to wash off her sins externally like dust
59	215	"Holy" laughter produces catatonic and uncontrolled people
60	215	Rodney Howard-Browne: three days of uncontrollable tongues, laughter, weeping
61	217	Huguenot preliterate infants preached repentance
62	218	Brigham Young spoke an unlearned Native American language
63	219	Mr. Le Baron experiences "psycho-automatism" (inner voice) from spiritist camp
64	224	J. S. Slotkin heard a song sung in Winnebago in his Fox tongue
65	225	Under hypnosis Dolores Jay spoke unlearned German from Bismarck's time
66	227	Wesley brothers' Psalm-singing was shut down by uncontrolled laughter
67	234	Unbeliever Mick Brown overcome with laughter at John Arnott's touch in Toronto
68	235	Claire Myers Owens experiences total repentance at Zendo and sees through walls
69	243	Blumhardt identifies demon as deceased human by conversation during exorcism
70	251	A linguist identifies a regressed client's babbling as 7th-century BCE Assyrian
71	252	In regression trance Bob spoke unlearned languages and wrote hieroglyphics
72	282	Celeste had a vision of "Jesus" healing her ancestors after death due to her prayers
73	284	Drythelm's medieval vision was a forerunner of purgatory

PROLOGUE

IN 1710 GOTTFRIED WILHELM von Leibniz published a book whose translated title was *Theodicy: Essay on the Goodness of God, the Liberty of Man and the Origin of Evil.* In *The Leviathan Factor* I argue that a cosmic being traditionally called Satan is the origin of evil and therefore of moral dualism in creation.

This is a minority view in much of the modern world. While a subset of people still believe in his ontological reality more folks believe in Satan as an ideal or archetype of evil. For instance, a 1991 survey of eighteen legacy Christian countries reported belief in an ontological Satan ranging from just 3.6 percent in the former East Germany to 45.4 percent in the United States.[1] A more recent 2009 Barna poll clarified US opinions. Slightly more than a third of American respondents believe in a personal devil but roughly three-fifths define Satan as a mere symbol of evil.[2]

Nonetheless, the name Satan has significant recognition value. Consequently it may seem counterintuitive to have chosen the term Leviathan for this book. The main reason for doing this is to embrace the wider ancient Near Eastern (ANE) theological environment. This allows us to blend biblical allusions to Leviathan—and Satan—with other accounts of a rebellious celestial creature. For example, an ancient Ugaritic source referred to the prideful junior god Ashtar, whose "legs were too short for the throne."[3] While my usage is predominantly Leviathan I have employed the labels Satan, Lucifer (as morning star), and Leviathan according to the sense and source of particular points.

The specific name Leviathan appears in archeology as early as 2400 BCE on an Akkadian vase. He's depicted as the serpent from the deep (chaos) in battle with human warriors who have killed four of its heads while the other three are alive and

---

1. Robinson, "Satan." Robinson lists percentages for seventeen countries: United States, 45.4; Northern Ireland, 43.1; Philippines, 28.3; Ireland, 24.8; New Zealand, 21.4; Italy, 20.4; Poland, 15.4; Netherlands, 13.3; Norway, 13.1; Great Britain, 12.7; Israel, 12.6; Russia, 12.5; Austria, 11.1; West Germany, 9.5; Slovenia, 6.9; Hungary, 4.2; East Germany, 3.6.

2. Barna, "Most American Christians."

3. Biti-Anat, "Ba'al Battles Mot," lines 54–65.

fighting.[4] These dead-and-living heads are an apt metaphor for the human experience of an adversary who is only partially defeated in history. Leviathan appears alone in the OT (Job, Ps, Isa), OT apocryphal (Add Esth 11:6), intertestamental (1 En. 60:7–8), ANE and NT (Rev 13:1, 11) sources. He also is paired with Behemoth in a two-beast water-and-land monster typology in Job and 1 Enoch. Overall, the OT shows him as the first of God's created works who has become the implacable enemy.

Before we can begin to address the many questions raised by attributing evil's origin and operation to Leviathan, we must first deal with the even more fundamental issue of God's existence. After all, theodicy assumes God and if God is not, then evil takes on a drastically different coloration.

Consequently I begin below with a defense of God's reality as prelude to explaining moral reality. As doubtless with the disputants at Plato's Academy, the nature of the present-day audience will have a major influence on a discussion of God's existence. In recognition of the modern materialistic mind-set, I will focus here on creation and natural theology as pointers to God's existence.

The question of Leviathan's (Satan's) existence and role as the cosmic origin of evil and death is similar. I propose here that Leviathan's true ontological existence is signaled by two primary data: as the originator of death and by *psi* phenomena.

I. CREATION AND GOD'S EXISTENCE

Classical materialism assumes that all reality is essentially physical, that no supernatural or immaterial reality can exist and that all organic life arises from and returns to inorganic matter.[5] This is the milieu out of which arose the dogmatic rejection of a spirit realm.

Based on chaos, complexity, and information a dramatic new scientific environment has emerged in postmodernity. Though the quantum vacuum is believed by many to be reality's bottom floor, others are already speculating about subquantum thermodynamic creational processes. These more serious investigations are paralleled by metaphysical speculations which try to link the physical realm to a spiritual or immaterial realm from which creation has been launched. This has spawned a wide range of proposals, including self-eternal platonic forms, a consciousness-bearing Zero Point Field in the vacuum, the gnostic All, Brahmin, an Akashic Field with archetypes (similar to Jung's collective unconscious), chaos, a demiurge or demiurgic field, and a revitalized ether.

In contrast to this mélange of pseudoscientific and warmed-over esoteric doctrines, I will touch on three areas in which creation unreservedly points to a maker. These are God as: attractor, information source, and life-giver.

---

4. Gordon, "Leviathan," 4.
5. Vitzthum, "Philosophical Materialism."

PROLOGUE

God as Attractor

In December 2014, with over three billion users worldwide,[6] the internet was by far the best-known dynamic system in peoples' daily experience. Probably few internet users were aware, though, of how ubiquitous network processes are in creation. They function all the way from human mind/brain modules to the stock market to the cosmic forces which seek equilibrium between vacuum matter creation and black hole matter destruction. In formal terms, a dynamic network is designed to process information through interconnected junctions (nodes). As input data is processed its output is compared to the target output and an error is computed. This error can be fed backward or forward in the network and used to adjust performance.

Of the various features of networks, we're particularly interested here in self-organizing systems (SOS) and attractor basins. SOSs are nonlinear systems whose control rules have the capacity to produce new configurations of greater complexity if one or more of their control parameters are changed or augmented by external input. When SOS information is tabulated in a visible graphical form, the patterns being traced in abstract logic or phase space are represented as trajectories which orient around a location called an attractor.

Creation's network systems function as hierarchies conceptually operating both within horizontal and vertical causation levels.[7] The human visual cortex is a good example of these network processes in conventional operation. "Areas of the [viewed] image with high contrast are processed in a feed-forward fashion, while areas of low-contrast rely more on contextual influences (driven by lateral interactions) and top-down predictions."[8] The subquantum vacuum illustrates a more enigmatic network. The vacuum harbors an immense quantity of energetic potential called the zero point field (ZPF). This energy field drives particle motion and in turn the sum of particle motions throughout the universe generates the ZPF fields. Physicist Harold E. Puthoff likened this feedback cycle to a cat chasing its own tail and labeled the network cycle the grand ground state of the universe.[9]

The ultimate cosmic network is GUT, the grand unified theory, aka the holy grail of physics. The GUT may be described as "a common mathematical scheme, preferably deriving from an elegant and simple underlying principle, which would provide a unified description of all forces and particles, as well as space and time."[10] In a creation where dynamic networks are ubiquitous a GUT theory therefore will be a network relationship. From a basement level out of which all further development in the universe occurred, the GUT began as a core algorithm. Since at this stage neither an open nor

---

6. Beal, "Internet."
7. Ellis, "Top-Down Causation," 126–40.
8. Ringach, "Spontaneous and Driven Cortical Activity," 439–44.
9. Puthoff, "Energetic Vacuum," 251.
10. Davies, "Where Do the Laws of Physics Come From," 689–708.

a closed system would have had access to external environmental input, neither type could complexify. Therefore at system start-up all SOSs were dependent on an outside dynamic attractor in company with which the universe's laws and phenomena could develop.

This attractor function was supplied by God, not as metaphor but via literal synchronization with the GUT self-organizing network system. The divine attractor can be further specified in light of Heb 1:3. The preexistent Second Person of the Trinity, later to be incarnate as Jesus of Nazareth, upholds all things by his powerful word. The Word (Gr. *logos*) means "rational principle" and so we understand that it was in and through the Son that the Trinity synchronized with GUT. More generally, the Trinity's synchronization with dynamic systems is the way in which God may interact with creation at any level.

In dynamic terms, though the GUT system could compute it couldn't complexify until the God-GUT synchronization generated novel input. By judicious use of network control techniques, the GUT dynamics were nudged toward a division. The result was two new stable systems—ZPF and energetic particles—synchronized with each other in place of the original GUT. This explains how the enigmatic loop mentioned by Puthoff was created as the necessary precursor to all other material instantiation.

God as Information Source

The Trinity may enter creation informationally at the level of dynamic systems. What, though, is information? Paul Davies says that a physicist ultimately "interrogates nature" in such a way as to elicit a "yes/no" answer.[11] The technical definition for this answer in our computer age is a "bit," short for binary digit. A single bit can hold only one of two values, 0 or 1 (or yes/no). If the universe itself is considered as a physical computer where every elementary particle functions as a bit, then during its history the universe can have performed no more than 10^{120} operations using 10^{90} bits.[12]

However, creation's information processes are ultimately taking place in higher-dimensional logical or phase space. As various authors have observed—John Polkinghorne,[13] M. A. Marais,[14] and Arthur Peacocke,[15] to name three—God's entry at the phase space level doesn't involve any direct manipulation of energy. Polkinghorne put it this way, "Since the paths through the strange attractor all correspond to the same energy, we are not concerned with a new kind of energetic causality. The energy content is unaffected whatever happens. What is different for the different paths through

---

11. Davies, "Universe from Bit," 65.
12. Lloyd, "Computational Capacity," 237901.1.
13. Polkinghorne, *Reason and Reality*, 45.
14. Marais, "Information Concepts," 51.
15. Peacocke, *Sciences of Complexity*, 274–75.

phase space is the unfolding pattern of dynamical development they represent."[16] This information/energy distinction answers science's concern that physical law is inviolate and cannot be arbitrarily manipulated even by God.

It's not just to preserve the laws of physics that makes God's informational synchronization with networks so crucial. The origin of information in creation represents the frontline in the contest between naturalism and supernaturalism. For instance, it's been calculated that in the first micro-second of the big bang the initial growth rate of information was about 10^{44} bits per second.[17] If so, what triggered this exponential information explosion? Conventional cosmology merely asserts that a quantum fluctuation in the vacuum was responsible but the reality is that outside information injection is the only mechanism which allows a system to increase its organization and complexity. Naturalism acknowledges this: "The fundamental question [is] of the initial, spontaneous priming of the [feedback] cycle."[18] Though the quote refers to life's requirements, it applies equally well to early cosmology since both the creation of the universe and of life were singularities unanswerable by naturalism.

Physicist John Wheeler coined the phrase "it from bit" to indicate that the universe is ultimately computational. "It from bit symbolizes the idea that every item of the physical world has at bottom—at a very deep bottom, in most instances—an immaterial source and explanation; that what we call reality arises in the last analysis from the posing of yes-no questions."[19] So, if the physical world is the hardware, what or where's the software? When the Trinity synchronizes with a given network, is there a frantic rummaging through infinite numbers of divine filing cabinets and post-it notes to find out where to plug in?

Konrad Zuse and Edward Fredkin had already pointed to the answer in the 1960s with their proposal that creation's lowest-level mechanism is a cellular automaton. This is a multidimensional grid intersected by logical nodes or cells which contain algorithms. These rule-sets drive all of creation's processes. As outside information source, whom Fredkin called the *Other*,[20] God had spoken these rule-sets into existence prior to triggering the big bang. Therefore when the universe began and grew it had a complete algorithmic map to follow, being pulled by preset goals in a teleological fashion. This isn't a watchmaker model where the system was wound up and left to run by itself. Rather it should be construed as a system with continuous built-in choices similar to computer if/then or yes/no logic where discretionary divine intervention in response to creational action is natural.

---

16. Polkinghorne, *Belief in God*, 62.
17. Treumann, "Evolution of Information," 141.
18. Michel, "Life Is a Self-Organizing Machine," 147.
19. Wheeler, "Information, Physics, Quantum," 311.
20. Fredkin, "New Cosmogony," 116–21, italics original.

God as Life-Giver

Our universe is proceeding toward heat death. This condition, called complete entropy, is an unavoidable outcome of the movement from initial energy availability to energy unavailability when no further creative action is possible. To explain the appearance of life in direct contradiction of the universe's death movement, conventional science postulates a very specific fine-tuning sequence. Energy ripples or fluctuations in the vacuum which underlays all physical reality manifested as the big bang. This explosion is conjectured to have inflated space-time exponentially during the first 10^{-35} of a second before settling down to the present rate of expansion. Inflation allowed for matter to be homogenous, smooth or unclumped throughout space. Gravitational collapse of this smooth matter released energy in the form of galaxies, stars, and planets. The fine-tuning which life required also included the laws and constants of physics, and various properties of the chemical elements. So constituted, the universe's free energy ultimately powered all dissipative structures and activities (energy in/entropy out) required by life to swim uphill against the second law of thermodynamics and entropy.[21]

The issue raised by the fine-tuning sequence is the origin of the novel information which life required to begin and develop. In 1953 Stanley Miller designed an experiment to simulate a possible chance process for prebiotic amino acid creation in an early earth atmosphere. He discharged an electric spark in a mixture of methane, ammonia, water, and hydrogen. The process created glycine, a-alanine, b-alanine, and two other possible acids,[22] or five of the twenty amino acids used by the human body to build proteins. More recent work, though, has shown the immense gulf between Miller's results and reality. For instance, the cytochrome c protein is a chain of 110 amino acid components which functions as an electron carrier involved in food oxidation. The random chance of finding a functional cytochrome c protein in a Miller-style prebiotic soup would be 1.14×10^{-75}, which Walter Bradley of the Discovery Institute calls "an exercise in futility."[23]

Recognizing this reality, scientists replaced Darwinism's reliance on chance with neo-Darwinism's dependence on random mutation. This too was unworkable since natural selection could not randomly "pre-know" survival fitness but needed functional entities from which to select. Origin-of-life tautology is even more obvious given that selection would be needed for these operational organisms but there were none prior to life itself being created. In light of all these factors origin-of-life theorists contend that a new paradigm is needed. Life, it's argued, was triggered neither by chance nor natural selection but by algorithmic information gaining "direct, context-dependent, causal efficacy over matter."[24]

---

21. Lineweaver and Egan, "Life, Gravity and the Second Law," 227–29.
22. Miller, "Amino Acids," 528–29.
23. Bradley, "Information, Entropy, and the Origin of Life," 336.
24. Walker and Davies, "Algorithmic Origins."

Here we must carefully distinguish between self-ordering and self-organizing processes. Nature has many examples of spontaneous self-ordering: a water vortex at a bathtub drain, the behavior of a sand pile, the shape of a candle flame, the formation of a tornado or hurricane, snowflakes, the spherical shaping of an oil droplet in water, and crystals. Such processes develop out of the interacting forces of inanimate nature. They don't result from programming which allows system choice. On the other hand, self-organization is designed for precisely that, relying on decision nodes, configurable switches, logic gates, and steering toward algorithmic optimization.

These features of digital programming are unique to life[25] so the quest for life's origin must be a quest for the algorithmic programmer. Citing an eclectic and sometimes mutually contradictory set of scientific authorities, we can synopsize some key characteristics of such a code-writer. This programmer—and let us call this being God—will be outside creation (Fredkin),[26] personal (Harkavy),[27] intelligent (Ostoma and Trushyk),[28] purposeful (O'Keefe),[29] master of all logically possible universes (Schmidhuber),[30] concerned for human life (Weinberg),[31] and self-existent (Kelly).[32] Last but not least God will be a modeler able to simulate all life probabilities (Hoyle and Wickramasinghe).[33] Acknowledging God to have these qualities we may ask how the two big issues in creating life were handled. First, how did God localize free energy and inject it into earth to enable life to counteract the universe's general drag of entropy? Second, how did God actually perform the information input and complexification which transitioned inorganic non-life into organic life?

Creation functions within a logical grid (automaton) whose nodes contain algorithmic statements. Not every node contains identical statements, but, analogous to the human mind, the grid is modular. Borrowing from the mind analogy, the grid can be described as "a domain-specific innately-specified processing system."[34] Therefore particular clusters of algorithms are networked together for functional cooperation. As required God can synchronize with these modules at the informational level. For example, to counteract entropy and input free energy to earth, in the early history of the universe God synchronized with the galactic formation module(s) and fine-tuned operations via noise (usually network timing delay in SOCs). Some nine billion years later the eventual sun was born in the Milky Way as an anomalous star peculiarly

---

25. Abel and Trevors, "Self-Organization vs. Self-Ordering Events," 212–14.
26. Fredkin, "Digital Mechanics," 260.
27. Harkavy, *Human Will*, 71.
28. Ostoma and Trushyk, "Hidden Quantum Processes."
29. Deem, "Quotes from Scientists."
30. Schmidhuber, "In the Beginning."
31. Weinberg, "Designer Universe?"
32. Kelly, "God Is the Machine."
33. Hoyle and Wickramasinghe, "Evolution from Space," 139.
34. Carruthers, "Massively Modular Models of Mind," 205–25.

suited in mass, temperature, radiation emission, life cycle, and galactic positioning to support life on an inner planet.

Similarly, after several hundred million years of solar history, God synchronized with the life-building module to create organic life. As recent studies note, life results from algorithmic instructions.[35] However, the coding required for the singularity that was the first living cell was many orders of magnitude beyond the algorithms which control inorganic nature. Life algorithms in fact needed to constitute a three-part linguistic system. "Each specific genetic message from DNA to RNA to protein can only be decoded if the coding/decoding apparatus and operating system preexist the message."[36] Inorganic chemistry and physics did not, do not, and cannot program the symbolic semantics and syntax of genetic languages.

II. CREATION, HISTORY AND LEVIATHAN'S EXISTENCE

I began this prologue with von Leibniz's question of how a good God can countenance evil. In this section I contend that the existence of an ontologically real Leviathan is inferred in two ways. First, in opposition to God's crowning achievement of offering eternal life to humans, Leviathan initiated death as the overpowering feature of evil in creation. Second, as a corollary, Leviathan is the source of genuine paranormal activities in which natural law is employed for unnatural purposes. I will look at each of these evidences in the following remarks.

Death

As I showed earlier, creation is in a network relationship with God. This network, which from creation's side may be labeled as the grand unified theory (GUT), explains how God can input information at any level. If God desired, the network connection would allow a balancing of the universe's energy budget between entropy and negentropy so that there would be no death. In light of theodicy's assertion that a just God would be both willing and able to eradicate evil, why is creation death-driven? Conventional wisdom merely accepts the entropic universe as a given and focuses on the paradox that life originated in the midst of death. Thus Ludwig von Bertalanffy wrote, "What is at present quite inexplicable is why and how organic substances, nucleoproteins, or coacervates should have formed against the second principle [of thermodynamics]."[37]

Let's begin our answer by positing a Satanic warping of fundamental laws' operation prior to creation of the physical universe. To avoid the Manichaean doctrine

---

35. Abel, "Is Life Reducible to Complexity?"; Walker and Davies, "Algorithmic Origins of Life"; Trevors and Abel, "Chance and Necessity."

36. Trevors and Abel, "Chance and Necessity," 734.

37. Bertalanffy, "Chance or Law," 73–74.

of granting equal powers to Leviathan as the evil principle and to God as the good principle, we'll define Leviathan in his traditional role as a cherubim. Leviathan as Lucifer self-created a dynamic system bifurcation designed to break his dependence on God without suffering personal dissolution. This goal was consistent with F. D. Abraham's remark:

> All living and psychological systems are self-organizational. That is, they can control their own control parameters, giving them the capacity to make bifurcations [forced splits] within their own dynamical schemes and complex dynamical systems. Sentient beings can thus learn their own response diagrams, so to speak, can learn to navigate them, and can imagine extrapolations of those diagrams and test a new universe of self.[38]

Leviathan's actions didn't literally rewrite deep-level laws but redirected some of their outcomes so that they were effectively reprogrammed. Though he wasn't referring to Leviathan, Karl Svozil has noted that "any attempt to render, manipulate and change certain [creational] phenomena could be interpreted as 'reprogramming.' In fact, reprogramming or 'tuning' reality may be a powerful new metaphor hitherto foreign to theoretical physics."[39] In Leviathan's case, his reprogramming introduced death and defined it as an irreversible system bifurcation at the most fundamental level of creation. More specifically, he replaced his covenant relationship with God with a self-referential process which could only produce internal paradox because God's feedback input was compromised. Leviathan tweaked lawful structures' operation and threw himself and the system into formlessness, a more-than-adequate working definition of death. Consequently when God created the physical universe, death was already present in self-organizing systems.

Paranormal Phenomena

While the preceding reconstruction is based on cosmological considerations, we can assess within human experience how Leviathan uses natural law in our world. Even as Leviathan illicitly redirected pre-physical law to introduce death, he illicitly uses present physical law as manifested in *psi*. Three specific examples of arguably demonic phenomena are levitation, bilocation, and telekinesis, which operate in the physical realm as *psi-kappa*.

Consider the following.

Joseph of Cupertino (1603–1663) entered a trance state during the Eucharist and levitated to the ceiling so often that church authorities even tied him down with lead boots. More than once another priest hanging onto him was lifted along with Joseph.

---

38. Abraham, "Introduction to Dynamics," 46.
39. Svozil, "Computational Universes," 855.

This happened in front of many hostile witnesses who knew that it was scientifically impossible,[40] as well as before a stunned Pope Urban VIII.

A different *psi* power was observed in 1846 by Sir George McKenzie, president of the Edinburgh Phrenological Society. He reported on a woman who when blindfolded could distinguish colors with her hands and other parts of her body. In addition, she could read the contents of any printing or manuscript by merely laying her hand on the page without tracing the lines or letters. It didn't matter whether it was day or night, nor whether the medium was cloth, silk, muslin, wax, or even glass. The sole variable was that her ability came on a twelve-hour rotation.[41]

Poltergeist activities like that of the 1977 case of eleven-year-old Janet Hodgson and her sister in Enfield, England, are usually dismissed as young girls' puberty-triggered fraud. They did acknowledge faking a small number of events, estimated at 2 percent, as a way of testing the investigators. However, more than thirty people witnessed two thousand logged incidents. "Heavy furniture would amble across the room. Huge fireplaces would be ripped from their fittings. Fires were lit spontaneously and pools of water would appear. . . . American paranormal investigator Ed Warren concluded that the children were the subject of demonic possession."[42]

Other paranormal phenomena manifest within peoples' bodies and minds as *psi-gamma*. For instance, two-thirds of a general population sample of 502 persons in Winnipeg, Manitoba, reported that they had experienced at least one paranormal event and nearly 10 percent had had four or more. Paranormal events listed included mental telepathy, precognition, telekinesis, precognitive dreams, déjà vu, possession by a demon, possession by a dead person, possession by a living person, possession by some other power or force, contact with ghosts, contact with poltergeists, contact with spirits of any kind, knowledge of past lives, and trance channeling.[43] Other studies highlight mediumistic ability, the ability to contort the body, blasphemy, consistency across cultures, face and eyes which manifest an alien ego, incredible physical strength, physical voice change, rejection of Christian symbols, and rejection of Jesus' name.[44]

The assertion that *psi* exists and that it points to demonism is controversial for some. The skeptic who rejects the data's objective factuality might try treating it theoretically. "If these accounts do contain substantial truth, what would it mean for our views of reality?" Conversely, other readers have already crossed a worldview Rubicon. Their counseling work, research projects, and personal experiences have convinced them that there are evil cosmic powers. For both kinds of readers, though, paranormal events raise profound questions about the creation in which we live and our role in it.

40. Etzold, "Does Psi Exist," 368.
41. Esdaile, *Mesmerism in India*, 124–25.
42. Clarke, "Amityville Haunting."
43. Ross and Joshi, "Paranormal Experiences," 358.
44. Gregory, introduction to *Possession*; Isaacs, "Possessive States Disorder"; Lechler, "Occult Bondage"; MacNutt, *Deliverance from Evil Spirits*, 76–78; Oesterreich, *Possession*, 7–21.

Prologue

The beginning of an answer for von Leibniz's question about evil is that creation has a basic moral dualism. God is creation's attractor, information source, and life-giver, and Leviathan is creation's death-monger and destroyer. This dualistic theodicy explains the contradiction of why death—ultimate evil—is foundational in a universe so obviously fine-tuned to produce life. It also responds to God's apparent powerlessness (i.e., "why didn't God eradicate death?") by presenting God's voluntary kenosis (self-emptying) as a form of power. To avoid immediately destroying the Satanically skewed lawful creation God chose to create the physical universe with death inbuilt and reserve the option to re-create in future. Finally, God didn't ignore the catastrophe initiated by Leviathan but gave the entropic universe a stopwatch whose ticking moves inexorably toward final heat death, thereby ending the Satanic influence.

The physical creation's inheritance of death didn't destroy creation's networking with the Trinity. Therefore all laws in the universe, whether physical or moral, were and are dualistic in design, scope, and action. In theological language, this means that all laws are covenantal and God-referential, not self-referential.

In the big picture, Leviathan's story is the story of creation and redemption. This book shows how Leviathan was created as the cherub Lucifer who "walked among stones of fire" but rebelled and was transformed into Leviathan the serpent. It explains how he fits within nature and is able to influence both natural and especially spiritual and psychological phenomena in people. Theodicy's concern for evil zeroes in on Leviathan's success in convincing humans to also break covenant with God. This rupture ultimately was reparable only by Jesus incarnating as creation's kinsman redeemer. The old creation's story will end when history is terminated, creation is renewed, and Leviathan's destruction will be completed. "On that day the LORD with his cruel and great and strong sword will punish Leviathan the fleeing serpent, Leviathan the twisting serpent, and he will kill the dragon that is in the sea" (Isa 27:1).

1

WINDOWS INTO REALITY

MANY PEOPLE WERE SURPRISED in 2001 when news media reported that late in life Mother Teresa had received the ministry of exorcism. Journalists quoted Henry D'Souza, Roman Catholic Archbishop of Calcutta, as saying that Teresa had experienced disturbed sleep during hospitalization for heart problems in 1996. Doctors found no medical reason for this, so she agreed with D'Souza's proposal to have Fr. Rosario Stroscio come and pray for her. D'Souza told him, "'Please say the prayer of exorcism over Mother Teresa.' And he got a shock and said, 'Shall I pray and should I drive out the devil if it's there?' I said, 'Yes, you do.' But he says, 'What will the devil do to me?' I said to him, 'You command the devil to go if he's there. In the name of the church, as archbishop, I command you to go and do it.'"[1] Along with Stroscio, Teresa participated in a "prayer of protection" and "slept peacefully after that."[2] D'Souza clarified that "I did not think she was possessed by an evil spirit" and what was done for her was not "real exorcism." As it turned out, Stroscio had not performed the full rite of exorcism, but merely led a short prayer which they read from the ritual.[3]

However, the story really started years before when Teresa heard a voice which she believed to be Jesus. In one vision she saw herself as a little child standing at the foot of the cross talking with the dying Jesus. Four years after vowing to give God anything he asked, in 1946 she was told to serve the poor. For the next fifty years the voice was silent; but while the public saw her smiling and talking about joy, Teresa in actuality suffered from a "cold darkness." Calling her incessant public smile a "big cloak which covers a multitude of pains,"[4] she agonized in 1959:

1. Bindra, "Archbishop: Mother Teresa Underwent Exorcism."
2. Banerjee, "Mother Teresa Had Exorcism."
3. "Mother Teresa Was Not Exorcised, Archbishop Says," Zenit.org, Sept. 10, 2001.
4. Kolodiejchuk, "Mother Teresa to Archbishop Périer, July 15, 1958," in *Mother Teresa*, 176.

> Lord, my God, who am I that You should forsake me? The child of your love—and now become as the most hated one—the one You have thrown away as unwanted—unloved. . . . The darkness is so dark—and I am alone. —Unwanted, forsaken. . . . It pains without ceasing. —I have no faith. . . . —I am told God loves me—and yet the reality of darkness & coldness & emptiness is so great.[5]

"Darkness and coldness and emptiness" may be understood as emotional depression or as traditional spiritual testing. Throughout history, though, these terms have also referred to demonic affliction,[6] gnostic self-death[7] and a descent into blackness, spiritual death, and hell.[8] Obviously in hindsight we cannot absolutely identify Mother Teresa's voices, visions, and darkness as of demonic origin. The odds are strong though, that in our assessment of what we think happened in the hospital prayers we will mostly call upon one of three belief systems.

Scientific materialists will ask why the doctors didn't relieve Teresa's anxiety by prescribing twenty mgs of diazepam (Valium) and/or by calling for the hospital staff psychologist. Neognostics will be inclined to treat Teresa's event as the marker of a transformative spiritual experience which had the potential to integrate her ego with her divine transpersonal Self. On the other hand, biblical realists with an awareness of the historical attribution of inner voices to demons may choose to include such affliction in their analysis.

In each case, it's important to recognize that the labels "scientific materialism," "neognosticism," and "biblical realism" are metaconcepts. In technical terms, they are overarching theories of knowledge. Practically speaking, by transcending particular theologies and philosophical schools they indicate how a person truly looks upon the world. For instance, someone who says mind and spirit are epiphenomena of electrochemical processes is a philosophical materialist whether or not they claim other theological commitments. Similarly, the *psi* so central to neognosticism grants voices, visions, and other paranormal phenomena preeminence regardless of the formal spiritual system.

To illustrate, *psi* body heat is ubiquitous, burning and/or peeling the skin of medieval saints,[9] Sufi mystics,[10] Pennsylvania Dutch magic healers,[11] Holiness Pentecostals,[12] therapeutic touch practitioners,[13] spiritualist healers,[14] Kingdom Now

---

5. Kolodiejchuk, *Mother Teresa*, 186–87.
6. Desert Father Dorotheus, in Van Beeck, "Unanticipated Inner Experiences," 13–14.
7. Voss, "Spiritual Alchemy," 157.
8. Eliade, *Forge and the Crucible*, 161.
9. Leuba, *Psychology of Religious Mysticism*, 72.
10. Sanella, *Kundalini*, 21.
11. Dluge, "My Interview with a Powwower," 39–42.
12. Synan, *Holiness-Pentecostal Movement*, 52.
13. Fuller, "Unorthodox Medicine," 56, 60, 63.
14. Edwards, *Healing Intelligence*, 120.

revivalists,[15] "Christian" kundalini experiencers,[16] and others. Finally, biblical realism as a metaconcept is really just an updated label for the traditional designation of nature and scripture as authoritative disclosures of God's existence, purposes and character.

The rest of the chapter is devoted to examining these three metaconcepts in turn.

I. SCIENTIFIC MATERIALISM

Modern science operates according to memes. Richard Dawkins originally coined this term to refer to psychosocial equivalents to biological genes. As such, memes are the intellectual contents which give to theories, worldviews, or cultures the glue which holds them together and keeps them firmly in our minds. Just as genes give structure to the DNA sequence, so memes are almost unshakable once established in our minds.[17] I suggest that three memes operate within science as root principles: truth is reductionist, the universe is self-existing, and creation is computational.

Truth Is Reductionist

Hard-core scientific materialism's presuppositions are: methodological reductionism, in which only science can formulate statements about reality; determinism, where knowledge of initial conditions fixes the future; and ontological reductionism, in which knowledge of elementary constituents like atoms is sufficient to determine the organism.[18]

These principles lead to a problem, though. For example, consider how research is done. Apparatuses generate output-numbers so that the number is said to stand for or symbolize the thing. Statements about reality require that these numbers be connected by a corresponding syntax called equations.[19] The issue is that too much data in human experience refuses to fit this reductionist slot. In terms of this book's focus on Leviathan, *psi* events across cultures and centuries are pervasive and don't fit within the materialist consensus. This confronts reductionist science with an intractable problem. Either its philosophical foundation is wrong or sound empirical data indicating preternatural *psi*, which I have argued in the prologue are actually demonic phenomena, must be dismissed. This dialectic can't be avoided by any serious student of human affairs.

I have chosen to focus on paranormal phenomena witnessed by Théodore Flournoy to demonstrate the dilemma.

---

15. Tillin, "Toronto Phenomenon."
16. Bodri, "Kundalini and Samadhi Cultivation."
17. Dawkins, *Selfish Gene*, 192.
18. Arecchi, "Why Science Is an Open System," 108.
19. Ibid., 110–11.

During the 1890s, Flournoy conducted sessions with the medium Hélène Smith, née Élise-Catherine Müller. The book based on his session notes, *Des Indes a la Planète Mars*, became famous and was acclaimed for bringing "subliminal psychology" out of the dark ages. This was a term coined in the later nineteenth century by Frederic W. H. Myers to refer to a supposed higher self which was the source of altered states and *psi* phenomena.[20] The modern historian Henri Ellenberger has written that Flournoy rescued the unconscious from "epidemics of demonism, collective psychoses among witches, revelations of spiritualists, the so-called reincarnation of mediums, automatic writing ... unfortunately neither Freud nor Jung became aware of the role of the mythopoetic unconscious."[21]

These intriguing words prompt one to wonder if Ellenberger actually read Flournoy's later chapters where he discussed the incomprehensible events associated with Hélène's sessions. For instance, in midwinter Geneva, roses, as well as handfuls of violets, lilacs, green branches, and an ivy leaf with the engraved name of one of the disincarnate spirits involved all materialized upon the séance table. During "tropical and Chinese visions" shells turned up "that were still shining and covered with sand." There were Chinese coins, a little vase with water and a superb rose. Flournoy recounts a great many other *psi* events as well.[22]

Flournoy's reaction was ambiguous. As to certain paranormal séance information, he disbelieved spiritism's claim to contact the dead, saying that Christ was not a perpetual undertaker. That is, the dead are really dead, not hanging around in some ethereal realm interacting with the living. Telekinesis and materialization were more problematic. Flournoy thought that the objects were truly apported. However, since he saw no adequate mechanistic explanation for these things, he wondered whether there might be a body in the ether conceived as a system of movements.[23]

Although from our perspective this sounds vaguely theosophical, given Flournoy's largely negative attitude toward spiritualism, it's unlikely that he really was touting multileveled theosophical bodies. We might rather credit him with a fairly sophisticated comment on the age-old debate involving form and object. It's worth noting that in 1891, just nine years before Flournoy published *Des Indes à la Planète Mars*, Hans Driesch had discovered that when fertilized sea urchin ova (blastomeres) were separated at the two-cell stage, each one developed into a smaller but complete blastula. What controlled this duplication? Ultimately Driesch opted for a vitalistic force or law that flowed through inorganic material to vivify it and give physicality to the underlying form.

For his part, it seems that Flournoy supposed that during Hélène's séances an analogous set of laws which he called ethereal movements came into play. They were

20. Myers, *Human Personality*, 78.
21. Mousseau, "Freud in Perspective," 56.
22. Flournoy, *From India to the Planet Mars*, 230.
23. Ibid., 254.

responsible for manifesting objects like Chinese coins from their underlying forms. Even so, Flournoy was left with two interrelated and unresolved issues. None of this speculation told him where the form came from in the first place. In turn, Flournoy was forced to relinquish traditional materialist exclusivism without knowing exactly what paradigm could replace it.

Reductionist science has been responsible for enormous gifts to humankind of understanding nature and applying these insights to the common good. On the negative side, its philosophy spurs rejection of data which uses but exists outside nature's four fundamental forces. Ironically, it seems like the more reductionism holds fast to its principles, the further its goal of finding creation's underlying unifying laws recedes into the distance. In the words of physicist Harold E. Puthoff, "Mainstream physics reductionism is leading to . . . the possibility of yet more 'fundamental' forces . . . in spite of efforts to develop a grand unified theory to simplify our picture of nature, the actual day-to-day work on this effort is complexifying faster than the hoped-for simplification."[24]

The Universe Is Self-Existent

Modern cosmology has largely committed itself to a hot big bang one-time origin of the universe, a view we'll examine further in chapter 2. Nonetheless, since at least Aristotle a self-existent eternal universe has been proposed as the alternative to God as creator. There are two modern versions—plus various permutations—of an eternal universe. One theory is oscillation in which universes cycle between expansion and contraction, and the second theory is a quasi steady-state universe which self-renews and maintains entropic equilibrium.[25]

Cosmologists handle "eternal" implicitly by speculating about metaphysical causation and explicitly by making dogmatic assertions. Examples of metaphysical speculations include an eternal cosmic egg which breaks open to start an emergent universe;[26] the eternal existence of immanent universals;[27] and mathematics which eternally underlie physics as ultimate reality.[28]

In dogmatic terms Richard C. Vitzthum commented that all across history materialist philosophers have held "that material or natural reality form an unbroken material continuum that is eternal and infinite."[29] Victor Stenger zeroed in on multiverse ideology: "The multiverse is eternal. So, since it always was, it didn't have to come

---

24. Puthoff, "Searching for the Universal Matrix," 22.
25. Kragh, "Quasi-Steady-State."
26. Mithani and Vilenkin, "Did the Universe Have a Beginning?"
27. Lewis, *On the Plurality of Worlds*, 2.
28. Davies, "Universe from Bit," 67.
29. Vitzthum, "Philosophical Materialism."

from anything."[30] Adolf Grünbaum merely fell back on infinite regression: defending a self-existent universe without any beginning; refuting the idea that causal chains require first or final causes; and finally arguing that causal chains can extend infinitely into the past.[31] Others argue that such questions merely reflect the separate and mutually exclusive realms in which religion and science operate. This was the stance of the US National Academy of Sciences in a 1981 statement. On this basis, ultimate causation questions are outside scientific cosmology's purview.[32]

A self-existent eternal universe is one that's self-referential. This means that systems reenter themselves via feed-forward and/or feed-backward propagation. Reentry introduces into the algorithm either memory-based or new environmental information for its next computation. Self-reference has been deployed in a wide range of analyses: form, hypercycles, catastrophism, eigenbehavior, spontaneous social orders, communication, dissipative structures, synergetics, complexity, fractals, living systems, autopoeisis and tangled hierarchies.[33]

The problem arises when self-referencing is ramped up for the universe as a whole. We saw in the prologue that the grand unified theory (GUT) is creation's ultimate network in which the master attractor is the triune God. Accordingly all creation and the physical universe within it are ultimately not closed but open to provide relationship with God. However, if creation were closed, it would fall into self-reference paradox. This reentry issue is clear in the pioneering work of Kurt Gödel, George Spencer-Brown, and Francisco Varela.

In 1931 Gödel set the scientific world on its ear by creating a technique for mapping syntactic statements onto arithmetic and then reentering the formula into itself. This made the formula self-referential, as in: "The statement that 'the statement that [the statement is false] is false' is false."[34] Based on this logical paradox, Gödel's first theorem asserted that "every axiomatic system S large enough to contain arithmetic contains statements which are not provable in S, and, if S is consistent, they are not decidable in S."[35] These have been debated at length but if we accept that the universe may be described mathematically, the ultimate logical statements expressing this (i.e., GUT) cannot be self-referential.

Gödel himself recognized that to avoid the problem of infinite regression of sets a meta-mathematical realm is necessary. His solution to this was a higher realm of platonic ideal mathematical models.[36] Since Gödel's work in 1931 several other proofs

---

30. Stenger, "Nuthin' to Explain."
31. Grünbaum, "Pseudo-Problem of Creation," 376, 381.
32. Davies, *Mind of God*, 57.
33. Winiwarter, "Autognosis."
34. Robertson, *Jungian Archetypes*, 224.
35. Cundy, "Gödel's Theorem in Perspective," 40.
36. Feferman, "Are There Absolutely Unsolvable Problems?," 135.

of his theorems have been demonstrated and, in fact, recent information theory suggests that the Gödel limitation is a natural structure.[37]

With Spencer-Brown[38] we see the self-referential issue from a different perspective. He invented a base calculus starting with two values consisting of a marked and unmarked state. (Interestingly enough, it's been calculated that at the initial Planck time, 5.4×10^{-44} sec, the amount of information present in the universe was about one bit. This would only permit a simple "yes/no," "the world exists or does not exist"[39] or more fundamentally yet, God's self-reference in Exodus as "I Am.") At any rate, much like Gödel had done Spencer-Brown reentered a variable into itself. He discovered the same paradox as had Gödel: "Anomalies appeared; reentry of equations back into themselves sometimes resulted in paradox. This occurred when marked states became equated with unmarked ones."[40]

In yet another variation, Francisco Varela expressed reentry in terms of well-established neural network system feedback principles. A neural network consists of a series of interconnected neurons in the brain or nodes in electronics arranged in various configurations for the transmission of signals from one to another. This input is counterbalanced by a return or feedback circuit so that a loop is formed. As the input and feedback signals are varied in amplitude, frequency and phase, their interaction allows choice in the system. However, Varela then made a blanket metaphysical claim. Perhaps because he practiced Buddhism, he chose the uroborus (snake eating its tail) to symbolize the "ceaseless circular process" representing the (re)creation of everything "since time immemorial."[41]

The paradox integral to self-referential systems denies the claim that creation coevolved controlling laws and even logic itself along with the instantiation of such laws. Lee Smolin, whom I'm citing here, based this contention on a Spencer-Brown type of argument that nature's structures and objects allow basic distinctions to be made. "We do this whenever we separate one part of the world from another, or when we define a set that contains only certain things and not others."[42] Smolin went on to say that quantum theory, general relativity, natural selection, and complexity theory "describe a world that is whole unto itself, without any need of an external intelligence to serve as its inventor, organizer, or external observer."[43]

Contrary to Smolin's assertion, though, emergent systems do not reenter themselves in order to generate their own rules unless their design includes agents who are in turn created with the necessary rules. These rules are literally called "god

37. Chaitin, "Gödel's Theorem and Information," 950.
38. Spencer-Brown, *Laws of Form*, 69–76.
39. Treumann, "Evolution of Information," 136.
40. Marks-Tarlow, "Observer in the Observed."
41. Varela, "Calculus for Self-Reference," 23.
42. Smolin, *Life of the Cosmos*, 189.
43. Ibid., 194.

parameters" in recognition of their design indispensability. Thus novel law always originates in a lawgiver from outside the system. Such cosmological speculations as eternal universes, infinite progressions, multiverses which result from cosmic natural selection, and the emergence of natural law from matter—all of these fail the self-reference test.

Finally, the self-referencing limitation means that there can't be an ultimate theory for a closed universe. Since we are part of nature, we fall prey to Gödel's limitation that arithmetic statements made within nature are unprovable. The fact is that only an observer outside the system is positioned to make ultimate pronouncements. Therefore in the very first sentence of his algebraic-set formulation of the universe, Fotini Markopoulou says, "In general, an entire spacetime, or an entire spatial slice in canonical gravity, can only be seen by an observer either in the infinite future or outside the universe."[44]

Creation Is Computational

Alexander Pope's poem *Essay on Man* (1733–34) defined creation as a downward emanation from the Infinite to nothing.[45] By the dawn of the nineteenth century, however, in a radical reversal of the Great Chain of Being, nature had been revisioned from an emanational top-down to an evolutionary bottom-up process. The new hierarchy was captured by Friedrich Schelling: "That from which development proceeds is lower than that which is developed."[46] Conceptually speaking, this revolution is responsible for the confusion over whether we visualize creational law as top down, bottom up or bidirectionally.

Two more centuries have passed and now evolution is theorized in terms of physical systems which self-organize. Chaoplexity refers to the many aspects of complexity theory and law: attractors, chaos, nonlinearity, fractals, neural networks, agents, cellular automata, dynamic systems, etc. In his chart of agent models Benyamin Lichtenstein has noted that these are part of the same conceptual family of fourteen members in a "matrix of complexity."[47] While we must acknowledge the merits of this family analogy, it will become clear as we go along that the various terms address somewhat different aspects. Nonetheless, because chaoplexity is such a useful and inclusive label it will appear frequently throughout the book.

The rules which operate self-organizing systems permit them to jump abruptly and spontaneously into new, more complex, and/or highly ordered states. In this brave new world, the mathematical laws which drive evolution are not the simple linear statistical models of Darwinian selection. They are rather nonlinear networks

---

44. Markopoulou, "Internal Description of a Causal Set," 559.
45. Pope, *Essay on Man*, epistle I, VIII, lines 237–41.
46. Lovejoy, *Great Chain of Being*, 325.
47. Lichtenstein, "Matrix of Complexity," ch. 15.

which are seemingly programmed to produce increasingly complex order. The laws of physics preclude cosmic anarchy but are not so restrictive that there's no openness in how the system evolves.[48]

As we shall see in chapter 2, neo-Darwinism is in tatters, in part because it has failed on crucial technical levels. More fundamentally, though, it has failed because it's a Newtonian ideology in a post-Newtonian world. Darwin's proposed law of selection was viewed as an analogue of the law of gravity where selection pressure checks inherent tendencies of species to vary just like gravity prevents planetary wandering. Within this paradigm, natural selection was unitary. It was never meant to be merely one cause among many.

Today, the cellular automaton, quantum mechanics, the molecular revolution, and chaos and complexity theory have led all but the most hidebound of old-school thinkers to give up on the idea of a universal law of natural selection.[49] There is no doubt that, to the extent that evolution as a term can be used, it must refer to self-organizing systems. Though these systems are characterized by the fact that they never trace the same dynamic pathway,[50] they are deterministic and in nature nonreversible. Consequently, they carry only the appearance of randomness, making them the exact antithesis of neo-Darwinism. In light of chaoplexity's role in evolution, it's particularly perplexing to see cosmologists explain earth's evident design for life by appeal to a Darwinian cosmic natural selection.[51]

The question of randomness is highlighted further when we view creation according to a cellular automaton model of computation. Leibniz with his monads may have visualized an early version of such a creation,[52] but the modern idea was proposed first by Edward Fredkin in 1960 and then by Konrad Zuse in 1967, who actually published first.[53] Since then various computer scientists and physicists have taken up a computational model, including Marvin Minsky, John Wheeler, Stephen Wolfram, David Deutsch, Seth Lloyd, Anton Zeilinger, Gerard 't Hooft, Lee Smolin, Paola Zizzi, Jarmo Makela, Ted Jacobson, and many others. The automaton postulates that creation operates within a structural grid that looks something like a multidimensional checker board. Each grid intersection is a logical cell or node containing the numerical information necessary for physical reality as well as mental and spiritual life. Clusters of logical rules called Deterministic Finite Automata (DFAs) in each cell govern how cell contents interact with neighboring nodes. The rules specify that the new state of the cell will be based both on the cell's current numerical state and on

---

48. This paragraph derives from Davies, "Intelligibility of Nature," 148, 154–55.
49. Baker, "Theology and the Crisis in Darwinism," 183.
50. Quenette and Gerard, "Why Biologists Do Not Think like Newtonian Physicists," 361.
51. Smolin, "Scientific Alternatives," 341–44.
52. Steinhart, "Digital Metaphysics," 118.
53. Zuse, "Rechnender Raum," 336–44.

that of all the cell's immediate neighbors.[54] The automaton is massively parallel so that at every tick of the master clock, the whole of creation recalculates instantaneously. Low-level system operation is absolutely deterministic, although we will see in chapter 2 that apparent randomness can be built into the governing algorithms (rules) to permit free will.

Estimates of the number of cells in creation's automaton vary according to the comparison volume and philosophical assumption used. Estimates list this value as ten thousand nodes within the radius of the electron,[55] or 10^{30} monads across a single atomic nucleus,[56] or 10^{99} cells per cubic cm,[57] or as 10^{184} cells in the universe.[58] Since the cells would not correspond to anything which is spatially extended[59] this effectively defines them as logical information way-stations in a higher dimensional realm. In this case, says Karl Svozil, "the field nodes or phase space are more fundamental than the frames of space and time that we use to define those fields. In this idealistic picture, space and time may be convenient constructions of our minds to sort out the evolution of field modes."[60] A phase space definition of the automaton is enhanced by data such as superluminal (faster-than-light) speed which we'll consider in chapter 7.

What or who built the automaton? In the prologue I merely said that God had spoken algorithmic rule-sets into existence prior to triggering the big bang. Scientists' reactions to the possibility of divine causation range from outright rejection to prevarication to carefully worded acceptance.

Those who desire to divorce God from a designed creation are very explicit. According to Maya Paczuski and Per Bak, "A few ideas have been proposed that begin to address this problem, which can be characterised as, 'how do we take God out of the equations.'"[61] Lee Smolin plaintively agreed that a grand unified theory demanded an outside observer, which is a problem for "those of us" who prefer a scientific to a religious view of the world. "Must science in this way always lead back to the religion of its inventors and first practitioners?"[62]

As to the automaton specifically, Tom Ostoma and Mike Trushyk exemplify prevaricators. "The design of the cellular automaton must have required intelligence, which was applied to the cellular automaton in the form of the mathematical rules for the cells."[63] With Edward Fredkin we see a progression. In likening the universe to

---

54. Ostoma and Trushyk, "What Are the Hidden Quantum Processes?"
55. Kurucz, "Elementary Physics."
56. Steinhart, "Digital Metaphysics," 119.
57. Smolin, "Atoms of Space and Time," 71.
58. Fredkin, "New Cosmogony," 121.
59. Svozil, "Computational Universes," 850.
60. Ibid., 855.
61. Paczuski and Bak, "Self-Organization of Complex Systems."
62. Smolin, *Life of the Cosmos*, 199–200.
63. Ostoma and Trushyk, "What Are the Hidden Quantum Processes?"

a massive parallel computer, he says that to model it would require its array to exist outside creation.[64] Elsewhere he states that the informational process and its engine are not to be found in this universe.[65] In later musings, though, he explicitly discusses a god, who, as the automaton's programmer, is outside creation in a place Fredkin calls the *Other*.[66] Karl Svozil is more explicitly religious and calls on ancient gnostic theology in his suggestion, "It is for instance quite likely that a demiurge would create an 'atomistic' world such as ours, in which an immense (to us) number of discrete gaming pieces come together to form a universe and which are constantly rearranged to form rich and varied and seemingly complex patterns."[67]

Scholars may dither but a rule-driven creation demands a rule-maker.

The cellular automaton paradigm has several revolutionary implications. Here I will note three which impact very directly on the scientific realm and reserve comment on several metaphysical issues until chapter 2.

To begin with, the cellular automaton forces us to recast our perspective on how reality is constituted. If creation is built on an automaton, then information and not matter and energy is paramount. In fact, motion is illusory, being merely the transfer of information from one particle pattern to another in an adjoining cell.[68] According to Edward Fredkin, "An information process runs what we think of as physics. At the much higher level of complexity, life, DNA—you know, the biochemical functions—are controlled by a digital information process. Then, at another level, our thought processes are basically information processing."[69] The ultimate result of the computational model would be to discover the grand rule or equation that is the foundation of everything.[70]

As a second related point, the cellular model not only allows for Einstein's unified field theory, it renders it straightforward. All physical phenomena—particles, energy, forces and motion—are the manifestations of a vast amount of numerical information that is being processed on the universal computer. Since, as Princeton's John Wheeler puts it, all "reality arises in the last analysis from the posing of yes/no questions,"[71] the four forces of nature logically cohere in their rule-sets. As we shall discover in chapter 7, this has been proven by real-world application of Einstein's unified field equations linking gravity and electromagnetics.

---

64. Fredkin, "Digital Mechanics," 260.
65. Fredkin, "Finite Nature."
66. Fredkin, "New Cosmogony," italics original.
67. Karl Svozil, "Computational Universes," 855–56.
68. Ostoma and Trushyk, "What Are the Hidden Quantum Processes?" Also see Fredkin, "Digital Mechanics," 261.
69. Quoted in Wright, "Did the Universe Just Happen?," 31.
70. Fredkin, "Digital Mechanics," 258.
71. Quoted in Kelly, "God Is the Machine."

Third, the automaton offers a reasonable place to lodge the big bang. Conventional cosmology supposes that the quantum vacuum generates fluctuations, one of which manifested eons ago as the big bang. However, given that the automaton subsists the vacuum then the big bang is merely a yes/no decision in a single logical cell which triggered a cascading sequence of rule execution throughout the automaton. At the gross physical level, science calls this process the inflationary universe.

Summary

Several significant points emerge from this assessment of scientific materialism's memes. First, the universe at every point indicates an external creator. Fredkin, Gödel, Penrose, and many others all agree that the laws which govern the universe imply a source external to the system. Second, an honest evaluation of neo-Darwinism will reveal a well-advanced Kuhnian collapse from imploding paradigms.[72] Third, the origin of cohering law is the crucial aspect of all debates about the structure of reality. Again and again the question will arise, "From whence was promulgated the law which so beautifully and necessarily operates the creational realities we observe?" The God-answer is not anti-scientific. Indeed, it's worth quoting Taner Edis—writing in the *Sceptical Inquirer*, no less—on this point. "A theoretically sophisticated, empirically well-anchored [intelligent design] hypothesis can be a serious scientific proposal."[73] I shall pursue these issues further in chapter 2.

To sum up, there can be no doubt about scientific materialism's claims as a philosophical framework. Its commitment to a fully naturalized definition of reality is both its strength and weakness. On one hand its naturalism guards against naive credulity when viewing creation but at the same time it is blind to empirical data which lays outside its purview.

II. NEOGNOSTICISM

We are familiar with reason and revelation as avenues to truth. Knowledge (Gr. *gnosis*), intuitive inner unveiling, is a third road. The power of this inwardness rests on the gnostic conviction that reality is essentially spiritual and is therefore perceived through spiritual faculties. These faculties include intellectual reflection but even more they embrace visions, dreams, voices, and pictorial images. Theosophist Charles W. Leadbeater, founder of the Liberal Catholic Church, offers a simple illustration of low-level gnosis. During mass, he saw "a large spiritual bubble rising like a dome over the chapel and . . . colorful rays streaming forth from the Eucharistic elements."[74]

---

72. Baker, "Theology and the Crisis in Darwinism," 195–99.
73. Edis, "Darwin in Mind," 35.
74. Smith, "Revival of Ancient Gnosis," 205.

Western history carries a gnostic subtext which has been labeled "perennial philosophy," "prisca theologia," "prisca philosophia," and the "primordial tradition." These all refer to the belief that there's really only one underlying spiritual stream which expresses itself through the different sets of symbols unique to the various religions. Matthew Fox used poetic language in making the point, "There is only one great underground river, though there are numerous wells into it—Buddhist wells and Taoist wells, Native American wells and Christian wells, Islamic wells and Judaic wells."[75]

The gnostic conviction that reality is unified is an apt segue to the term "neognosticism" or new gnosticism, and its virtual synonymy, the term "holistic." This latter term, which was coined by the South African physicist-politician Jan Smuts, adds two modern ideas.

First, neognosticism incorporates Jung's theory of the collective unconscious. Jung conceptualized human personality as a vertical strata connecting the individual with subterranean memories shared by all people.[76] The imaginal world and its mental phenomena function as translators between everyday reality and this alleged collective unconscious. Jung legitimized the process of inner unveiling through his own experiences[77] and by basing his active imagination psychotherapy on it. He said that his "archetypal motifs of the unconscious are the psychic source of Gnostic ideas, of delusional ideas (especially of the paranoid schizophrenic forms), of symbol-formation in dreams, and of active imagination in the course of an analytical treatment of neurosis."[78]

Second, neognosticism uses selected parts of quantum physics to give a scientific veneer to its concept of an interactive, energetic universe. Non-locality is mustered to show that there's a nonphysical intertwining of energy particles and/or fields across interstellar distances. An energetically connected universe contains a continuum of energy fields presumed to range from the pre-quantum to supposed subtle, higher levels.[79] According to best-selling author Richard Gerber, subtle energy literally moves faster than the speed of light, "Etheric energy or substance vibrates at speeds beyond light velocity and has a magnetic character."[80] Pierre Teilhard de Chardin described the holistic universe in these words: "Without the slightest doubt there is *something* through which material and spiritual energy hold together and are complementary. In the last analysis, *somehow or other*, there must be a single energy operating in the

---

75. Fox, *Coming of the Cosmic Christ*, 230.
76. Jung, *Notes of the Seminar*, 133.
77. Jung, *Memories, Dreams, Reflections*, 171–78.
78. Jung, "Foreword to Quispel," 652.
79. Albanese, "Magical Staff," 73.
80. Gerber, *Vibrational Medicine*, 33.

world." He continued, "To avoid a fundamental dualism, at once impossible and anti-scientific . . . we shall assume that, essentially, all energy is psychic in nature."[81]

For Teilhard, the physical energy known to science ("tangential energy") is converting to psychic energy ("radial energy") as evolution progresses. This conversion process is teleological, drawing the universe "towards even greater complexity and centricity—in other words forwards." "Tangential" and "radial" are roughly equivalent to modern holistic use of "electromagnetic" and "subtle." Jung similarly argued that psychic energy possesses quantity and mass just like physical energies. He affirmed the two energies can be transformed into each other, being converted by physiological processes.[82] Like Teilhard, he visualized energy as having an inner and outer aspect, which led Jung to label energy as "psychoid" in nature. In the last resort psyche and matter are to be seen as the two poles of one and the same reality.[83]

This blend of holistic energetics and Jungian psychology amounts to the yin and yang of the neognostic worldview. Each perspective encourages its advocates to introduce Eastern philosophies into their framework as well. For instance, physicist Fritjof Capra likened quantum concepts to the core of the Buddhist scripture *Avatamsaka Sutra*. It's a "description of the world as a perfect network of mutual relations where all things and events interact with each other in an infinitely complicated way."[84]

The doctrine of an energetic, connected universe contains God (or the Absolute), who is the ultimate energy being. This God "is the creative energy that is the cause of all visible things," and "man is the last and highest manifestation of divine energy."[85] Psychic Eva Pierrakos, who channeled 258 Pathway lectures from "The Guide," said, "Think of God as being, among so many other things, life and life force. Think of God as of an electric current, endowed with supreme intelligence. This 'electric current' is there, in you, around you, outside of yourself."[86] According to healer Barbara Ann Brennan, "All is composed of the same energy. The Goddess/God force is both black and white, both masculine and feminine. It contains both the white light and the velvet black void."[87] An advocate of "Christian" kundalini stated that there is a First Cause Creator who is "composed of Spirit, the highest Light form and frequency of Universal Energy, described as being composed of Creative, Discerning, Intelligent Energy . . . [all beings are] composed of Spirit-Energy, fragments at one frequency or another of the Light-Energy which at its apex is our Creator."[88] And finally, Sir George Trevelyan, a New Age founding father, claimed, "We each form part of a universe of living energy,

---

81. Chardin, *Phenomenon of Man*, 69–70, italics original.
82. Jung, "On Psychic Energy," 8.
83. Jung, *Atom and Archetype*, 126.
84. Capra, *Tao of Physics*, 139.
85. Albanese, "Subtle Energies of Spirit," 309.
86. Hanegraaff, *New Age Religion*, 184.
87. Brennan, *Hands of Light*, 25.
88. Holcombe, "Christ-Consciousness," 90–91.

an immense, unified field of living, pulsating energy. If we are to speak of God, then God must comprise the totality of this universal life energy."[89]

With this overview of neognosticism's foundations before us, we may ask whether it offers a dependable path to truth. I will consider three aspects of the question.

First of all, neognosticism tends toward holography rather than hierarchy. To claim that the universe is seamlessly interconnected means that any given small snippet mirrors the larger whole. If this is so, by definition sentient beings are contiguous with energy/matter. This logic explains why holistic theoreticians spend so much intellectual capital trying to develop models of consciousness based on quantum physics.[90]

However, dissidents like transpersonal psychologist Ken Wilber resist the all-is-interconnected worldview. In contrast to the unitary model, Wilber theorizes six levels of reality. They are physical, biological, psychological, subtle (the transpersonal), causal (perfect transcendence), and ultimate (pure consciousness).[91] He succinctly calls the unitary model "category confusion" and asks, "What relationship does ionic plasma have with, say, egoic goals and drives?"[92] Using a building metaphor, in which mystical experience resides in the penthouse and quantum physics in the basement, Wilber says:

> The new physics has simply discovered the one-dimensional interpenetration of its own level (nonsentient mass/energy) . . . the study of physics is on the first floor, describing the interactions of its elements; the mystics are on the sixth floor describing the interactions of all six floors . . . physics and mysticism are not two different approaches to the same reality. They are different approaches to two quite different levels of reality.[93]

So, is neognostic creation unitary? Or does it have four reality levels like Huston Smith suggested[94] or six like Wilber says or even 365 as Basilides the gnostic of old believed? Ironically this conflict between inner and outer truth apparently needs science to act as the judge. To take a simple case, the laws of physics currently seem to operate in a layered fashion (not unitary) so that quantum effects are subatomic, Newtonian are planetary, and Einsteinian are galactic. Presently—the automaton excepted—the bridge connecting quantum and general relativity levels is otherwise unknown. Nonetheless neognosticism theorizes a yet higher subtle realm. In real life, this realm has never been perceived by instrument but only ever by clairvoyance, a fact candidly admitted by holistic theoreticians.[95] Therefore from a hermeneutical point of view,

---

89. Hanegraaff, *New Age Religion*, 187.
90. Hameroff, "Funda-Mentality," 119–27.
91. Wilber, *Eye to Eye*, 128–29.
92. Ibid., 134–35.
93. Ibid., 135–37.
94. Smith, *Forgotten Truth*, 37–56.
95. Quinn, "Therapeutic Touch," 44, 48.

neognosticism really is an internal faith dependent on a preternatural power exercised by a minority of people, and not knowledge in the usual sense.

This leads to another issue. We have already seen that mathematics is the core language for scientific materialism. Is there a parallel core language for neognosticism? Jungian Schuyler Brown proposed a starting point with his observation that Christian orthodoxy and gnosticism are founded in different root metaphors. In orthodoxy, the Word speaks both in Genesis and in John's Prologue and consequently the Word assumes precedence over Sophia. For gnostics, though, Sophia is protagonist. "She is given the epithet *prouneikos* [lustful] . . . which suggests impetuosity, wantonness, libido . . . any form of psychic energy." Sophia is the connecting principle between the deity and creation.[96]

Brown is wrong in this distinction. Orthodox Christianity has no such clash as he asserts because Sophia (Wisdom) in the OT is seen as the pre-incarnation of Jesus Christ the Logos (Word) in the NT. Therefore we must inquire what, in its use of language, leads neognosticism into elevating Sophia over Logos. I think that the answer is rooted in a defining feature of postmodernism, namely the cultural movement from mimesis to semiosis.

In linguistics, mimesis describes a literal relationship between sign-word and object. For example, the word "pony" always stands for the same four-legged equine animal. One might refer to ponying up money to a loan shark, or to frontier mail delivered by pony express, or to playing the ponies at the track, but each of these phrases ultimately uses imagery involving the same four-legged animal.

On the other hand, semiosis is the technique of using sign-symbols to translate an original term into a universal meaning. As we shall see in detail in the final section, semiosis can be a valid technique if properly used. To make the point in a preliminary way here, let's consider the World Tree. The Christian cosmological cross took two forms in history with one being Greek, and the other Semitic and biblical. The Greek tree in its six-armed version has immeasurable scope, with arms extending to encompass the world; the post reaches up to heaven and down into the abyss. The Semitic, biblical tree is a great fruit-bearing tree whose top touches heaven, whose branches cover the earth, and whose roots are watered by a marvelous fountain.[97] However, both signs, whether six-armed cross or fruit tree, say the same thing: earth is joined to heaven and vivified by a vertical divine principle signified by post and tree. The mimetic connection is retained between earth-heaven linkage and treeness.

However, what happens when we symbolize external objects in such a way that they are divorced from their mimetic roots? When Jung wrote "Christ, a Symbol of the Self," he did not use the word "Christ" to mean a Jewish messiah-figure put on trial by Herod Antipas and Pontius Pilate. He meant that Christ is a symbol standing for a tiny segment of divinity called the Self within the core of every person. For Jung,

---

96. Brown, "Begotten, Not Created," 72–73.
97. Greenhill, "Child in the Tree," 331.

Christ is a principle or a thread, that is, an archetypal symbol, operating in the person's unconscious to reveal the essential divinity of their Self.[98]

Christology is a truly powerful theological flash point in the shift away from mimesis. A couple of illustrations are enough to show that Jung is merely one marcher in an intellectual parade. Former NT scholar Tom Harpur is another. In his best-selling book *The Pagan Christ*, he rejected Jesus' sacrificial death on the cross. This rejection is common enough but what's intriguing is the language used. "The way to go is to understand the complete account as a 'divine drama where Jesus, as the persona representing the Christ of the universal myth' does and says the same things all ancient saviour figures in the various mystery rituals did and said."[99] Elsewhere Harpur stated, "There is no way that a literally understood self-sacrifice by a literal, historical person, however pure, holy or even divine can 'wash away' the terrible crimes, errors and stupidities of such evolving humans."[100] Thus does Harpur shift from mimesis to semiosis.

Another parade exemplar is Barbara Marx Hubbard. She's noted for launching the Foundation for Conscious Evolution and for being a confidante of celebrities like Dwight Eisenhower, Abraham Maslow, and Buckminster Fuller. In her earlier years, she had tried the Episcopalian Church but she "could not tolerate the emphasis on guilt, pain, suffering and sin. Where, I asked, was the celebration of our power, goodness, glory and future?"[101] After what she called her planetary birth, she began hearing an inner voice which in due course approached her in the guise of Jesus, "*I, Jesus, the man, was able to manifest Christ consciousness in one lifetime; and exert it to transform my physical body. . . . You are not to become martyrs, saints or crazy fools. You are to become evolved humans, normal, good.*"[102]

Then, finally, Hubbard experienced the voice's presence as "an omnipresent Being that I felt from within as the resurrected Christ. . . . It was both within me, and beyond me, it was my Self and yet far more than myself."[103]

Now, we are impelled to ask whether there is evidence from pre-Christian Greek or Jewish thought to show that *christós*, meaning "Christ," "the anointed one," and "messiah" ever meant "divine fragment of the human personality"? Homer and the Greek dramatists used *chrio* as a verb, "to anoint," as in oiling weapons or whitewashing. The OT uses anointing and rubbing as helps for physical health, and as a legal/religious symbol of conferred strength and majesty. As a noun *christos* never related to persons in a nonbiblical setting. To the contrary, anointing conveyed the sense of God's election and a special relationship to God. The high point for "anointed one" is

---

98. Jung, "Christ, a Symbol of the Self," 36–40.
99. Harpur, "Symbols Are about Reality," F-7.
100. Harpur, "Bible's Literal Interpretation Is Outdated," F7.
101. Hubbard, *Revelation*, 73.
102. Ibid., 62, italics original.
103. Ibid., 63.

reached with the vision of the Davidic king who will be God's ruler on earth.[104] The LXX, Apocrypha, and Pseudepigrapha of later Judaism follow these conventions. So to the question, "Does the data support the symbolizing of Christ as Self?" the answer is "no."

Finally, we must make more explicit previous hints about neognosticism's view of history. The unitary principle incorporates correspondences by which one may see the universe and history as a huge theater of mirrors. Correspondences exist between the planets and the human body, forming the basis of astrology's New Age popularity. Other correspondences between nature, the cosmos or history, and revealed texts are the basis of the Jewish and Christian Kabbalah. History can never be conceptualized in typical linear or even nonlinear terms but is a mystical process of sign, concealment, and mystery.[105]

Since purity is found only in higher emanations of spirit, this leaves human history as the realm of darkness and ignorance from which we must escape. The upshot is that atonement cannot literally mean that sin must be discharged (Heb., *kipper*, cover) through Jesus' historical death. Atonement must be understood through our symbolic death during a psychic recapitulation function. From the neognostic perspective, in Jesus' physical death he visibly demonstrated the way that each of us must die symbolically in the course of our inward journey of self-transformation. In short, the neognostic hermeneutic supports a worldview wherein each of us by ourselves is able to start over and eradicate sin and evil in our lives through the inner transformations available through gnostic experience.

In the larger picture, it's clear that the semiotic hermeneutic is today no longer alternative or underground, but has become a major player in the cultural mainstream. The nature of hermeneutics is crucial, for, as Karl Pribram reminds us, we all choose our truth.[106]

III. BIBLICAL REALISM

When Flournoy witnessed levitation of objects, what did he see? Or, perhaps, more accurately, how did he see? The scientific answer describes a photon path from the object to the cornea and lens, then onto the rod and cone receptors of the retina. They are converted there into electrical signals and transmitted through the optic nerves to the brain where the eyes' two sets of signals are correlated in the optic chiasma. Eventually, after further processing, the information arrives at the visual cortex.[107]

In philosophy, this explanation is called naive realism and in neognostic thought consensus reality. Cognitive psychology labels it experientialism and biblical

---

104. Hesse, "*Chriō*," 1322–24.
105. Faivre, *Access to Western Esotericism*, 10.
106. Pribram, "Brain and the Composition," 39.
107. Abramowitz et al., "Human Vision and Color Perception."

hermeneutics, common sense literalism. These all agree that the apprehended sensory datum is directly related to and dependent on external reality. This is in contrast to idealism, which holds that we cannot see the real world but only mental representations or symbols which stand for what is "out there." Bishop Berkeley is famous for his defense of such idealism, but the modern version says that nothing—even, in the extreme case, the existence of the universe—may be called real until it's internally perceived in the mind of the viewer.

This brings us back to the discipline of semiotics which I introduced in the previous section. Rather than merely stating that all reality is translated through symbols which are integral form-structures in the brain/mind complex, semiotics regards nature and life as sign languages in themselves. Consequently the world is seen as a universal language rather than a giant clockwork. Life is a sign-relation network and not an information-processing machine.[108]

However, as we shall see in future chapters, the mind and its brain agent operate according to chaoplexic mathematical principles. There's a constant bidirectional translation process between mathematical mind objects and external sensory inputs. The brain and mind complex is uniquely structured to perform this transduction between interior and exterior worlds. Every symbol must be rooted in an external reality since it otherwise doesn't exist in the person. The nonnegotiable truth of this statement is borne out by the experiences of sensory-deprived people like Helen Keller. With the use of three of five physical senses, she wrote that "before my teacher came to me, I did not know that I am. I lived in a world that was a no-world. I cannot hope to describe adequately that unconscious, yet conscious time of nothingness."[109] Psychologist Stevan Harnad is correct in saying that ungrounded personal interpretations can skew symbol meaning.[110] The primary fact, though, is that without sensory input there's no grounding, symbol formation, and interpretation to skew at all.

Symbol grounding is demanding. We know that mere looking around at the world will not reveal the four fundamental forces in physics, because there is a genuine hiddenness in nature. Through self-limitation (*kenosis*) God chooses to hide so that human freedom is preserved, a process resulting in "epistemic distance."[111] G. F. R. Ellis points out that both science and theology face the problem of hiddenness. The difference between them is that science appeals to strong statistical results and Christianity to scripture, tradition, personal experience, prophecy, and prediction—all the constituents of historical revelation.[112]

---

108. Marais, "Information Concepts," 34.
109. Keller, *World I Live In*, 142–43.
110. Harnad, "Artificial Life," 547.
111. Ellis, "Theology of the Anthropic Principle," 390, citing John Hick.
112. Ibid., 369.

Science's mathematical (statistical) foundation reflects the powerful, indeed "unreasonable effectiveness"[113] by which mathematics predicts the laws which govern creation's external reality. R. W. Hamming noted how Maxwell, to some extent for reasons of symmetry in his equations, "put in a certain term, and in time the radio waves that the theory predicted were found by Hertz." From his own experience, Hamming described how "the numbers we so patiently computed on the primitive relay computers agreed so well with what happened on the first [atomic] test shot at Almagordo." He points out too that Einstein is well-known for discovering relativity through mathematical reasoning and not experiment. "When experiments were done to check them, he was not much interested in the outcomes, saying that they had to come out that way or else the experiments were wrong."[114] More such illustrations could be given, but suffice to say that as science penetrates the hiddenness, general lawful patterns are left revealed in their glory.

Theology also faces a grounding challenge in uncovering moral and spiritual law. In Ellis' words, "The test of the validity of the exercise of theological investigation will lie in its ability to discern pattern, to offer coherent understanding of human experience at its most profound."[115] In other words, to uncover divine law theology must be grounded in the external realities of creation and history and transcend the temptation to relapse into mere symbolism, metaphor, and inner intuition. Ellis' warning cuts to the heart of modern hermeneutics.[116] Postmodern analysis is less concerned about science versus theology as avenues to truth and more concerned with whether the symbols used in every human discipline and activity are socially constructed.

This merits further comment.

Ferdinand de Saussure said that a linguistic symbol is constructed in the mind and is composed of the concept and its sound. He further argued that the connection between the concept and its sound is theoretically arbitrary but that in any language, a society's present symbol-sense depends on its inheritance from the past. That is, signs are arbitrary and follow no law but that of tradition.[117] Postmodernism has interpreted de Saussure as justifying a radical disconnection of sensory symbol from object. It asserts that there's no inherent association between a word, say "dog," and its object but that all symbol-associations for objects are socially created. Western intellectual circles drew the even broader inference that to enforce symbol association is an act of power. Postmodernists assume that the ability to name external things as Adam did the animals is in fact a power by which personal reality is constructed. This justifies a rejection of convention.[118]

113. Wigner, "Unreasonable Effectiveness," 1–14.
114. Hamming, "Unreasonable Effectiveness," 81–90.
115. Ellis, "Theology of the Anthropic Principle," 370.
116. Touryan, "From Objective-Realism," 188.
117. Saussure, *Course in General Linguistics*, 66–73.
118. Zimmer, "Possible Natural Complement," 162–63.

But is postmodernism right in this radical disconnection of the sensory symbol from the object? Take the instance of polysemy, which identifies adjectives which may be used to modify two very different nouns, such as "soft pillow" and "soft voice." Another case is the use of the word "hot" to describe both chilli peppers and the stove top. Are these usages just social construction?

It transpires that a specific brain receptor responds to both capsaicin (the "hot" ingredient in chili peppers) and to painful heat. The sensation of "hot" encoded as a neurological function applies to very different sensory sources.[119] This lawful brain-mind coding is replicated worldwide in various sensory modalities. If we illustrate this with visual terms, we find that words for "light" and "dark" always hold precedence, followed by "red," "yellow or green," then "blue," and so on.[120] Or how about glossolalia (tongues speaking). We'll return to glossolalia in chapter 10, but for now I will simply note Felicitas Goodman's argument that the tonal structure of glossolalist utterances is maintained across cultures and languages.[121] This is consistent with Noam Chomsky's theories of universal language systems. These ideas in turn are supported by studies showing the universal mathematical techniques by which infants extract words and their meanings from sound sequences.[122] The mind and its brain use universal structures to ground symbol associations in the physical reality of the external world. Associations are not mere social constructions but develop out of sophisticated controlling laws.

Many of this book's key themes are rooted in Genesis. Consequently, it's helpful to ask how the relationship between symbols and external reality plays out in it. Suppose we began constructing a symbol scheme with Hegel's view that history unfolds according to an evolutionary progressivist dialectic. Then take a belief that early Israelite religion advanced from polytheism to monotheism, and add a Eurocentric conviction that the sources of Homer's poetry and the OT developed in exactly parallel fragmented fashion. When we blend all three together, what would our symbol system look like? You may already have guessed the answer—in this case we actually would have constructed the Graf-Wellhausen symbol set, complete with the acronymic letters JEPD. In light of our preceding discussion, the big question is whether this symbol set reflects a true grounding in ancient Near Eastern culture and history.

Already in the 1920s, some fifty years after Julius Wellhausen's book *Prolegomena to the History of Ancient Israel*, Umberto Cassuto had identified and demolished the source theory's "five pillars."[123] He identified them as the use of different names for the Deity, variations of language and style, contradictions and divergences of views, duplications and repetitions, and signs of composite structure in the sections. Twenty

---

119. Rakova, *Extent of the Literal*, 22.
120. Ibid., 35.
121. Goodman, "Phonetic Analysis of Glossolalia," 227.
122. Jusczyk, "How Infants Begin to Extract Words," 323–28.
123. Cassuto, *Documentary Hypothesis*, 14.

years after that, Frank M. Cross Jr. wrote that "Israelite history can no longer be made to climb the three-flight staircases of Wellhausen's Hegelian reconstruction."[124]

Nevertheless, traditional source criticism has lurched along fixated on atomistic and genetic premises. By "atomistic," I mean an extravagant focus on minutiae, and by "genetic," the assumption that the text is best interpreted if its sources can be reconstructed and its prehistory determined. David Clines, from whom I have borrowed these terms and ideas, observes that the presumed OT sources and prehistory are "for the most part hypothetical" and an art work.[125] In fact, shortly after Clines' critique, a statistical study of the purported JEPD strands concluded that "J and E alternate at random as if they never existed."[126] Though this conclusion was subsequently contested[127] the Graf-Wellhausen model in general doesn't adequately reflect reality.

What happens if we use the neognostic hermeneutic? It holds that all external ("consensus") reality is just the iceberg tip pointing to unseen realms of knowledge and supernatural beings. The paranormal information and powers obtained through the mind's doorway to these realms are translated to consensus reality by using symbols encoded in normal language and culture. To examine neognosis and symbol grounding in a Genesis setting, we will use the well-known Tree of Life metaphor.

Psi healer Carolyn Myss offered an intriguing illustration of symbols-as-universal-language in a chart where she combined the ten signs of the Jewish kabbalistic Sefirot (Tree of Life) with those of the seven chakras, and the seven Christian sacraments.[128] For instance, she integrated the tribal chakra muladhara with baptism and the shekinah. The combined symbolic sign "transmits into our energy and biological systems the sacred truth [that] All is One."[129] Any specific historical meaning, say of Christian baptism's signification of forgiveness of sins through Jesus Christ, which formerly would have been inherent in baptism, is subsumed in this conjectured universal sign language.

Myss' confident conflation of symbols camouflages the incoherence that is inescapable at the dogmatic level. In doctrinal terms, world religions clearly are in hopeless conflict with each other. Buddhism has no god, Hinduism has many gods and goddesses; Islam regards the Qur'an as the final revelation of God, but Christianity says it is Jesus; Moses is Judaism's law-giver, while Jesus is Christianity's sin-bearer. Since there is no logical process to meld these at the dogmatic level, the only way to claim their inherent unity of meaning is to divorce symbol meaning from grounding object. However, we have already shown that creation and history prove this divorce to be impossible.

124. Cross, "Tabernacle," 47–48.
125. Clines, *Theme of the Pentateuch*, 7–9.
126. Radday et al., "Genesis, Wellhausen and the Computer," 469.
127. Portnoy and Petersen, "Genesis, Wellhausen and the Computer," 421–25.
128. Myss, *Anatomy of the Spirit*, 70.
129. Ibid., 80.

On the other hand, suppose we root our symbol system in the belief that the Genesis text factually corresponds to observed reality. This doesn't require a literalist perspective, but it does recognize that extremely ancient historical records were extant when Genesis was committed to writing. A reference to such ancient materials derives from King Ashurbanipal of Assyria (ca. 669–630 BCE), who states that he had read preflood stone tablets.[130] Placing Genesis in its ANE culture shows that its underlying source documents, whether those referred to by Ashurbanipal or not, are in fact extremely early toledoth family histories.[131] These eleven family chronicles in Gen 1–37:2 are each well-marked by the colophon phrase, "These are the generations of..."

Furthermore, the Genesis materials likely reflect an ancient chiastic structure. Chiasm is the technique of inverting sets of two parallel thoughts around a bridging core idea. It dates at least back to Ugaritic and Sumero/Akkadian texts from the third millennium BCE and appears in virtually every ancient literature.[132] Normally biblical scholars identify chiasm in fairly short segments of text, but there's been an increasing recognition that whole books or even sections of scripture are probably chiastic in form. Complete books thought to reflect this form include Ruth, Amos, Mark, John, Philemon, Hebrews, Jude, and Revelation. At least one scholar suggests that Genesis to Joshua is a hexateuch structured chiastically around the Sinai covenant.[133] In the case of Genesis, Terry J. Prewitt has argued that the kinship stories have been arranged in a series of chiastic reversals based on seven-chapter blocks.[134] His schematic result looks rather like a sine wave.

As well, there are series of heptads (sevens) in the syntax of the Genesis text. These were first seen by Cassuto and noted by others. Various key words in Gen 1—"God," "heaven," "earth," "living thing," and "that it was good"—occur in multiples of seven.[135] In his summary of these heptads, Jon Levenson states that Genesis reflects a style primarily based on internal linguistic structures and not on atomized source documents.

The biblical grounding question is far from new. By Jesus' day, Jewish hermeneutics employed literalism, midrash (less apparent interpretations), pesher (prophetic revelation), and allegory. Church Father John Cassian (ca. 360–435 CE) created a multilayered system for interpreting scripture which echoed the four Jewish techniques. His Four Senses hermeneutic allowed for historical, allegorical, tropological, and anagogical levels of meaning. These terms—referring to a text's objective, spiritual, moral, and eschatological meanings—permitted a nuanced way to accommodate various

---

130. Luckinbill, *Ancient Records*, 379.
131. Wiseman, *Ancient Records and the Structure of Genesis*.
132. McCoy, "Chiasmus," 18.
133. Dorsey, *Literary Structure of the Old Testament*, 97–102.
134. Prewitt, *Elusive Covenant*, 76–78.
135. Levenson, *Creation and the Persistence of Evil*, 67.

genres of literature.[136] This preserved externalized symbol grounding yet also allowed for nonliteral interpretations. With some terminological fine-tuning this hermeneutic passed through Tyconius and Augustine into mainstream medieval biblical interpretation. According to Gerhard Ebeling, Luther was still using the fourfold-sense method in his earlier lectures on Psalms.[137]

I think that there's good reason to like this approach. We have been using Genesis to test the various grounding schemes, and Cassian lets us continue this focus, though somewhat obliquely. He illustrates his method in Gal 4:22–31, where Paul speaks of Abraham's two sons through a series of four contrasts—law and grace, flesh and promise, slavery and freedom, and Mt. Sinai and Jerusalem. Commenting on the text, Cassian says, "And if we wish it, these four modes of representation flow into a unity so that the one Jerusalem can be understood in four different ways, in the historical sense as the city of the Jews, in allegory as the church of Christ, in anagoge as the heavenly city of God . . . [and] in the tropological sense as the human soul."[138]

In Cassian's hands, language retains its mimetic core and allows for suitable semiosis. The words which are used to represent the concepts under discussion mirror life so that whatever one's point of view, the text is a skillful copy of the original being imitated. According to Cassian's methodology, we might then read Gal 4 as follows. Mt. Sinai is a real historical mountain somewhere in the Arabian peninsula. However, as the idealized moral mountain of ancient Near Eastern mythology where the gods meet humans, Sinai is more—it's where YHWH gave Moses the law. For Jesus, Sinai served as the backdrop to both the spiritual-ethical Sermon on the Mount and the eschatological transfiguration. Whether one is interpreting Sinai in historical, moral, spiritual or eschatological terms though, there is always an objectively real mountain in Arabia.

In summary, the phrase "biblical realism" is an umbrella under which we may delve into ancient Near Eastern documents, historical materials, scientific theories of the beginning of the universe, the literature of human personality, and various other sources. All of these are to be regarded as valid avenues to truth. All are disciplined by the conviction that because creation is coherent, its underlying patterns may be discovered. Creation, seen to be orderly and lawful, validates a sequence of conclusions into the being and nature of God. As the authoritative account of God's actions in history, the biblical record for its part warrants its role as the absolute revelatory standard of the nature and destiny of humans.

---

136. Cassian, "Conference 14, 8," 160–61.
137. Ebeling, "New Hermeneutics," 40.
138. Cassian, "Conference 14, 8," 160–61.

2

THE NEW PARADIGM

Nobel physicist Steven Weinberg should have been a professional comedian.

In his concluding remarks at a cosmology conference at Cambridge, he noted that the idea of a multiverse was controversial. Martin Rees, he remarked, "was sufficiently confident about the multiverse to bet his dog's life on it." Andrei Linde was even more certain, said Weinberg, "he would bet his own life." Then Weinberg added, "As for me, I have just enough confidence about the multiverse to bet the lives of both Andrei Linde and Martin Rees' dog."[1]

When we stop laughing we are left pondering the uncertain nature of paradigms. One generation's truth is a later one's heresy; and the journey from one to the other is often perilous. It's a frightening feeling when the intellectual tectonic plates on which we've built careers and reputations suddenly undergo a cataclysmic paroxysm. It's one thing when the terrain is at least clearly within the physical realm, as for instance the mysteries of quantum physics. In his 1966 Nobel lecture, Richard Feynman told the audience not to be dismayed by quantum physics. "You see my physics students don't understand it.... That is because I don't understand it. Nobody does."[2] It's something else again when the data takes us into borderline territory. In considering the evidence for the paranormal, Russell Targ and H. E. Puthoff ask us in their book *Mind-Reach*, "Where do you want to be standing when the paradigm shifts?"[3]

But what about unfamiliar terrain?

In this chapter I explore the central intellectual transformation of our time. It's not the multiverse, quantum physics, nor, contrary to Targ and Puthoff, the normalizing of the paranormal. It is instead the transition from the old Newtonian Darwinism

---

1. Weinberg, "Living in the Multiverse," 40.
2. Feynman, "Strange Theory of Light and Matter," Nobel lecture, 1966.
3. Targ and Puthoff, *Mind-Reach*, 17.

to the new chaoplexity paradigm. Like a winding lowland river cutting new channels, this shift is reshaping our familiar landscapes. In the following sections we will look at several of these new contours: the automaton and the big bang, universe versus multiverse, why neo-Darwinism has failed and chaoplexity is succeeding, and finally how creation reveals certain key metaphysical truths.

I. CREATION'S STANDARD MODEL

How did the universe come to be? Current cosmology generally accepts the hot big bang as its standard creation model. The following description is about as succinct as one can get, "In an instant, the nothing becomes something. In an enormous flash of energy, the big bang creates space and time."[4] The "something" was a very hot gas which expanded through space, condensing into stars and galaxies as it cooled. This general picture, which supplanted continuous creation (steady state) theories,[5] receives support from three lines of evidence. First, the universe is indeed flying apart and the further reaches are moving fastest. Second, the residual early-phase microwave radiation which was predicted was found at the expected wavelengths. Third, the theory accurately predicts the amounts of light elements (hydrogen, deuterium, helium three and four, and lithium) which resulted from the early hot phase of expansion.

Initially cosmologists regarded the big bang as a spontaneous "seeming miracle."[6] This was primarily because in Einsteinian mechanics the moment just prior to the big bang would have had infinite heat, zero size, and total lawlessness.[7] With the apparent cessation of the laws of physics, there seemed to be no avenue for further investigation. Then in 1973 Edward Tryon proposed that the big bang was really a kind of energy bubble which emerged from a preexisting quantum vacuum. He hypothesized that the vacuum contained an energy potential field which through quantum mechanics' inherent probabilistic fluctuations actualized as real energy.[8] Cosmologists weighed in and pointed out that modern accelerator experiments show that particles do spontaneously come into and flash out of existence. Therefore a bubble process could be scaled up to explain the universe. If the big bang actually was triggered by such a sequence, then the massive hot expansion is merely a stage in a vacuum-launched creational event.

Quantum inflation theory is virtually mainstream now but its core question remains unresolved. Namely, how can the universe's far reaches be increasing their acceleration from each other and from us so dramatically? The answer seems to involve something called dark energy in the vacuum. At the present time, it's believed that the

---

4. Seife, *Alpha & Omega*, 65.
5. Hoyle and Narlikar, "Radical Departure," 162–76.
6. Davies, *Cosmic Blueprint*, 5.
7. Davies, *Edge of Infinity*, 156, 161.
8. Tryon, "Is the Universe a Vacuum Fluctuation?," 396–97.

universe is composed of 26.8 percent dark matter, 68.3 percent dark energy, and 4.9 percent ordinary matter.[9] The dark energy, often equated with Einstein's cosmological constant, is hypothesized to apply negative pressure on matter while gravity applies positive pressure. This interaction establishes a delicate balancing act in which nature must choose among a collapsing (closed), balanced (flat), or expanding (open) universe.

Manasse Mbonye has proposed that the dark energy/gravitation balancing act is controlled by a dynamic network system designed to maintain equilibrium over the course of very long time-cycles.[10] Whether or not his model is right in details, Mbonye renders great service in pointing to the same type of feedback system which is ubiquitous throughout creation. This model introduces lawful controlling processes which are subterranean to the quantum and gravitational levels. Therefore the latter are not themselves first principles in what is often labeled as creation's fundamental rule book.

What triggering process might produce a vacuum-based inflation bubble? Several classes of theory have been proposed to account for this event but I will focus on creation ex nihilo and the string theory–based multiverse.

In cosmology, creation ex nihilo doesn't carry the literal meaning that something was made from nothing, as theology teaches. Ex nihilo still presupposes the primordial vacuum but it asserts that a vacuum truly empty of matter overlays a deeper-level field of energy potential.[11] The idea is that quantum fluctuations in this field created a tiny bubble of non-gravitational energy. Though the amount of energy was almost zero, it had a high density which was maintained during inflation. As the density grew to occupy a large volume, energy was created from nothing.[12]

One specific formulation of the "tiny bubble that could" is the instanton concept described by Stephen Hawking and Neil Turok.[13] This is an object whose size has been likened to "a millionth of a trillionth of a trillionth as big as a pea." It combined gravity, space, time, and matter for an infinitesimal moment and then turned itself into an inflating open universe. Nonetheless, such ex nihilo models leave untouched the questions of the origin of the primordial vacuum and potential energy field, along with the necessary governing laws. Scientific ex nihilo really ends up being a misnomer since it still requires other first principles, for, as Heinz Pagels notes, "even the void is subject to law."[14]

String theory was developed to unite quantum mechanics with general relativity. It proposes that fundamental particles like quarks are actually loops of energy which under the universe's currently cooler conditions have shrunk to infinitely thin

9. Francis, "First Planck Results."
10. Mbonye, "Cosmology with Interacting Dark Energy," 117–34.
11. McCabe, "Structure and Interpretation of Cosmology," 68–70.
12. Ibid., 73.
13. Hawking and Turok, "Open Inflation Without False Vacua," 25–32.
14. Pagels, *Perfect Symmetry*, 347.

one-dimensional objects. These strings have a finite size of no smaller than about 10^{-35} meter, so this value becomes a new constant in nature, paralleling Planck's constant and the speed of light.[15] Because the hypothesized strings have a finite irreducible size, a creation singularity cannot be zero in radius as the standard big bang model says. The extraordinary consequence is that, contrary to what Einstein's equations show, the singularity is really a transition from a previous state. The theory can be constructed to include an eternal prehistory of the universe so that even if it recollapses one day, it will never end.[16]

String theory requires at least six or seven dimensions beyond the four dimensions of space-time and postulates many new elementary particles. Furthermore, cosmologists say that string theory's parameters offer up to 10^{500} or more configurations of possible universes.[17] However, there is no experimental evidence for string theory,[18] a fact to be borne in mind when using it as the foundation for multiverse ideology.

In examining these theories, we see that part of the automaton's great appeal is the ease with which various cosmologies find homes within it. For instance, ex nihilo is redefined so that the universe's bottom floor isn't a void with potential but an automaton driven by rules. Similarly, the Hawking-Turok instanton would be the single specific automaton logic node in which a yes/no decision triggered the rule execution sequence called the big bang. Finally, the automaton's code would be the previous informational state out of which primordial energetic strings emerged.

II. UNIVERSE OR MULTIVERSE?

The God-as-creator view rests heavily on the design argument. Our universe's congeniality to carbon life, to humans and, many argue, to consciousness, is the driving idea behind the principle of divine design. The argument draws on a variety of fine-tuning data.

For starters, mathematician Roger Penrose stated that for the universe to have by chance an initial singularity which looks like it presently does is so infinitesimal as to not really exist. With a certain awe Penrose says, "The Creator has to locate that [initial] point in phase space to an accuracy to one part in 10^{124}. If I were to put one zero on each elementary particle in the Universe, I still could not write the number down in full. It is a stupendous number."[19] Lee Smolin, who argued that cosmic natural selection explains the universe's fine-tuning, puts the likelihood of the universe's present numerical parameters at one in 10^{240}.[20]

15. Veneziano, "Myth of the Beginning of Time," 58.
16. Ibid., 64.
17. Barrow and Webb, "Inconstant Constants," 58.
18. Vaas, "Time Before Time."
19. Penrose, *The Large, the Small*, 47–48.
20. Smolin, "Self-Organization of Space and Time," 1085.

Though design advocates list dozens of finely tuned parameters which must be just so to allow life, the most powerful are the numbers used to describe cosmology's standard model.[21] The omega value is one example of this fine-tuning. Omega is the ratio between the universe's average density and the density that would halt inflation. If, after the big bang, this ratio had differed from its actual value by about one-quadrillionth of 1 percent the universe-to-be "would have collapsed back on itself or experienced runaway-relativity effects that would render the fabric of time-space weirdly distorted."[22] Astrophysicist Trinh Xuan Thuan comments that "the precision of the fine-tuning of the physical constants and of the initial conditions is astonishing. It is similar to the precision that a marksman has to exercise in order to put a bullet through a square target of one centimeter on a side located at the edge of the observable universe some 15 billion light-years away."[23]

Fine-tuning appears even more impressively in human life processes. For instance, Templeton Prize winner G. F. R. Ellis points out how 10^{13} human brain cells work purposefully as one to control organization, growth, and ecosystem issues.[24] A specific case is the computation required for typical object recognition. This demands about 100 trillion multiplications per eye per second.[25] From a genetic informational perspective Stephen C. Meyer states:

> The coding regions of DNA have the very same property of sequence specificity, or information content, that computer codes and linguistic texts do. Though DNA does not possess all the properties of natural language or semantic information, that is, information that is subjectively meaningful to human agents, it does have precisely those properties that jointly implicate a prior intelligence.[26]

A design advocate might think that even agnostic scientists would accept such finely tuned life parameters as conclusive evidence for a divine creation paradigm. Not so. In asking if the universe has a blueprint to explain such a fortuitous state of affairs, Paul Davies says that many cosmologists like the terms "predestiny" and "predisposition."[27] By this they mean that matter and energy may have inherent tendencies to self-organize even to the point of producing life under the right conditions. In Davies' case, he believes that life and mind are fundamental rather than incidental in the universe; therefore a teleological principle must be at work. Davies calls this principle "directional evolution," meaning that "the general trend from simple to com-

---

21. Donoghue, "Fine-Tuning Problems," 233.
22. Easterbrook, "New Convergence," 3.
23. Thuan, "Cosmic Design from a Buddhist Perspective," 212.
24. Ellis, "Theology of the Anthropic Principle," 377.
25. Kurzweil, *Age of Intelligent Machines*, 227.
26. Meyer, "Return of the God Hypothesis," 8.
27. Davies, *Cosmic Blueprint*, 200–202.

plex and from mindless to mental is lawlike."[28] As is typical of non-theistic programs, the origin of the first constituent, whether law or matter, is left unspecified.

Davies' impersonal principle is a belief metaphysic offered as an alternative to God as creator. However, for design advocates the evidence is overwhelming that cosmology requires a lawgiver who is outside the system. All proposals of self-referencing creation, eternal universes, multiverses, and the like are religious in nature and should be so identified. We are left to choose which of these faith options is the more reasonable.

Still, naturalism argues that at least in the abstract a God-tuned universe need not necessarily be the only choice. Several other options have been suggested, including pure chance with no explanation; pure chance in a multitude of universes where every parameter combination will be realized as a probability; a teleological pull where the observed parameters are needed for humans to exist; a final theory of everything which requires these; the universe's values are the result of cosmological natural selection in a multiverse cosmos; and—reluctantly—the universe is supernaturally designed to have these parameters.[29] A bit of reflection shows that modern cosmological options boil down to two opposing camps.[30]

On the one hand are those who think that a supernatural creator has carefully designed this universe to result in humans and a suitable environment for us. Supernatural creation means that our universe is absolutely unique. Suggestions that the universe may result from a series of predecessor big bang-collapse cycles are ruled out since each universe in such a sequence inherits its predecessor's entropy. Eventually, as one extrapolates backward, there will be a zero-length big bang-collapse cycle, which automatically requires an absolutely initial singularity.[31] Therefore the model states that God has created our universe to have the exact conditions required for us to be here.

Multiverse proponents are convinced that the theory stick-handles around a creator entirely. The idea that the cosmos might contain many universes has been around for many centuries. According to Simplicius, the presocratic philosopher Anaximander believed that worlds come to be and pass away without end.[32] Millennia later, in 1779, David Hume wrote, "Many worlds might have been botched and bungled, throughout an eternity, ere this system was struck out: Much labour lost: Many fruitless trials made: And a slow, but continued improvement carried on during infinite ages in the art of world-making."[33] In the mid-nineteenth century, poet Edgar Allen Poe referred to "clusters of clusters" and to "universes" which have no commonality

28. Davies, "Multiverse or Design?"
29. Vaas, "Is There a Darwinian Evolution?"
30. Bettini, "Anthropic Reasoning in Cosmology," 1069.
31. Mann, "Inconstant Multiverse," 306.
32. Wheelwright, *Presocratics*, 57, 59.
33. Smith, *Hume's Dialogues on Natural Religion*, 167.

with ours. He thought that these are totally unrelated to our universe in their laws, their material and even their gods.[34]

The modern impetus for multiverse ideology has been the scientific urge to find naturalistic alternatives to divine design of our universe. Whereas those who champion design suppose that God conceptually modeled all possible universes, multiverse advocates suppose that all possible universes really exist as an ensemble. Therefore our universe with all its fine-tuning is inevitable. This belief not only relies on string theory's enormous number of possible universes but is rooted in Plato's principle of plenitude. Plato's version stated that God is obligated to create everything of which he can conceive; the multiverse version simply replaces "God" with "Nature." If one adds the premise that the universe is eternal[35] and that it instantiates first-principle laws, then God is rendered logically unnecessary. According to Occam's razor, one chooses the simplest solution, so why insert a creator into the mix when a multiverse explains everything?

In answering this question, we'll consider three issues: theory testability, naturalness, and metaphysical rationality.

Because it's primarily historical science, cosmology argues from effects to causes on the basis of traces or artifacts of the past.[36] All the radiation which is studied now originated at some time in the past; the more distant the source, the further into the past one peers. It's true that statistical probability can be a tool, but in the end it can't replace phenomena. So, for instance, when we consider Stephano Bettini's impressive list of multiverse-origin theories—instantons, brane bounces, eternal inflation, oscillations, quantum world-splitting, symmetry-breaking bubbles, chaotic distributed scalar fields, inflaton fields, wormholes, Smolin's black holes, super-symmetric M-theory, primordial antimatter domains at high redshifts, and other similarly exotic ideas[37]—we need more than mathematical models to judge which, if any, is right. Even experts label quantum cosmology and string theory—let alone the multiverse—as "quite speculative, controversial, and almost without any empirical footing yet."[38] So to move beyond theory, we need some traces or artifacts, that is, hard data.

However, physicists acknowledge that the multiverse theory may well remain forever directly untestable.[39] Even if a multiverse existed, we could never observe it since it would lay beyond the boundary (the horizon) at which electromagnetic radiation could ever reach us. Indeed, given that other universes would have constants with different values, it's unlikely that they'd be visible even if they were within range. Such

---

34. Poe, *Eureka*, 77, para. 187.
35. Grünbaum, "Pseudo-Problem of Creation," 376.
36. Cleland, "Methodological and Epistemic Differences," 480–81.
37. Bettini, "Cosmic Archipelago."
38. Vaas, "Time Before Time."
39. Carr, "Introduction and Overview," 14.

factors mean that no experimental test of other universes can be devised which we can falsify. Therefore it fails the test of being a scientific theory.[40]

Untestability feeds into the problem of naturalness.

Naturalness is an evaluation by which physics' theories and values are deemed consistent with the deep-seated belief that the laws of nature are harmonious. One practical definition is that a natural theory is one in which entropy increases and its parameters do not vary overmuch from what experience implies one might anticipate.[41] Physicist Paul Steinhardt commented, "On the macroscopic scale, the latest measurements show our observable universe to be remarkably simple, described by very few parameters, obeying the same physical laws throughout and exhibiting remarkably uniform structure in all directions."[42]

Some physicists who advocate for a multiverse point to the Higgs boson and the cosmological constant as cases in which our universe has unnatural values. According to naturalness, the Higgs boson is ten to one hundred times too light. In addition, the cosmological constant is almost unimaginably smaller than what is calculated to be its natural value.[43] The advocates' view is that either there are some missing factors in these values or there's a multiverse where the calculated values exist as naturalness in another universe.

Enthusiasm for the multiverse is rooted in its presumed ability to solve the improbabilities of inflation and to use string theory's near-infinite possible configurations. However, many critics note that neither of these theories is well-founded. Virtually all inflation scenarios lead to eternal, run-away inflation.[44] To avoid such an outcome, inflation would have to be fine-tuned every bit as much as the already-known fine-tuning that we observe in our universe. String theory is designed to unite gravity and quantum mechanics in a theory of all four physical forces, and perhaps one day may do so. In the here and now, there's never been an experiment performed confirming it and theorist Brian Greene wrote that he doubted "that string theory will 'confront data' in his lifetime."[45]

In multiverse arguments naturalness is in the eye of the beholder, both advocate and critic, because the theory really is about metaphysics. Lack of experimental evidence hasn't prevented the multiverse vision from capturing a significant chunk of both scientific and cultural acceptance. For instance, journalist Gregg Easterbrook noted that tenured professors at Stanford now casually discuss entire unobservable universes.[46] One might ask why tenured professors would treat as real things that can

40. Smolin, "Scientific Alternatives."
41. Carroll, "Is Our Universe Natural?," 1132.
42. Steinhardt, "Theories of Anything."
43. Wolchover, "Is Nature Unnatural?"
44. Steinhardt, "Inflation Debate," 41–42.
45. Greene, "Why String Theory Still Offers Hope."
46. Easterbrook, "New Convergence," 4.

never be detected? Perhaps Paul Davies has the answer. He noted how the multiverse appeals "to an infinite unknown, invisible, and unknowable system." This, he said, makes it deism dressed up in scientific language.[47] In other words, the multiverse isn't science but religious mythology. According to Easterbrook, "The multiverse idea rests on assumptions that would be laughed out of town if they came from a religious text. [Nobel physicist Charles] Townes has said that speculation about billions of invisible universes 'strikes me as much more freewheeling than any of the church's claims.'" The short answer to why the multiverse fascinates so many folks is that it's a religious belief system just as much as is traditional Christian theism.

In summary, a God-designed multiverse is possible. However, taking into account theory testability, naturalness, and metaphysical rationality the multiverse as presently conceived isn't natural. It's speculation inside conjecture inside surmisal inside poetic abstraction.

III. FROM DARWINISM TO CHAOPLEXITY

Evolution is science's primary explanatory myth of existence, being called upon to describe the beginning and growth of the universe, the arrival of life, and the emergence of *Homo sapiens spiritus*, thinking spiritual man. As in modern cosmology, Darwin's goal was to offer a natural mechanistic law which would explain apparent design. To do this, he focused on three assumptions: random hereditary variation, struggle for survival, and survival of the best adapted individual. Neo-Darwinism has moved on and instead of these its principles are random mutation, a differential reproduction which selects those mutants which produce the most offspring, and continuous gene pool change.[48]

Neo-Darwinists continue to believe that the second set of mechanisms is sufficient to account for the evolutionary tree of life.[49] However, Darwinism of every form—and evolution itself—have been shaken to the core by the revolution imposed by information theory and chaoplexic systems. Here's why.

Let's suppose we are writing what Steven Weinberg calls "the fundamental principles, the final laws of nature, the book of rules that govern all natural phenomena."[50] How must the rule-book be written so that we can communicate the most information as accurately and efficiently as possible? To illustrate the difficulties, let's begin with the following three sets of letters.[51]

(a) THE END THE END THE END

---

47. Davies, "Multiverse or Design?"
48. Bertalanffy, "Chance or Law," 64.
49. Pigliucci, "Design Yes, Intelligent No."
50. Weinberg, "Designer Universe?"
51. Thaxton et al., *Mystery of Life's Origin*, 130.

(b) AGDCBFE GBCAFED ACEDFBG

(c) THIS SEQUENCE OF LETTERS CONTAINS A MESSAGE!

Each of these sets contains information, but the useful amount in them differs widely. To start with, the more improbable the sequence, then the more complex is its information.[52] At the same time, complexity requires randomness. Therefore statement (a) has great order but a book full of its content would convey little meaning. There needs to be less order and more randomness. THE END is like a crystal which has an extremely orderly structure but very little information. Statement (b) is completely random and therefore complex. However, though it is present in nature—for instance, as chains of amino acids—it has limited information too. It's not stymied by excessive order, but by a random complexity which lacks a specified sequence that conveys meaning. Statement (c) is the ideal information-carrier, being both random/complex and specified. William Dembski terms this "Complex Specified Information";[53] an alternative label is Ervin Laszlo's "Organized Complexity,"[54] but regardless of phrasing, it's what is needed for DNA or proteins. The set of instructions to form a crystal might be as short as a couple of sentences, specifying the substance to be used, the way to package it, and the instruction to keep on doing this over and over. Such an instruction set is an algorithm. In contrast, to communicate the instructions for a chemist to synthesize the DNA of E. coli, sequence is all important. This sequence has to be specified letter-by-letter in a series totalling about four million instructions, which would be, not a few short sentences, but a book.[55]

Complex specified information has been key in forcing neo-Darwinism into a progressive retreat from classic mutation-natural selection beliefs. This retreat may be followed through several stages involving the collapse of chance mechanisms, the breakdown of the postulate of gradual change, and the substitution of self-organization for natural selection. Let's consider these in turn.

In chapter 1, I cited odds on the ordering of the universe in its presently observed form. The same approach may be followed with the origin of life. As a test case, Fred Hoyle and Chandra Wickramasinghe calculated the probabilities which operate during the reactions by which the enzyme hexokinase helps break down glucose and release energy. Enzyme surface shape is crucial, and in the case of hexokinase, involves a particular sequence of some ten to twenty amino acids in the structure, along with about one hundred others which perform fine-tuning jobs. The problem is to gauge the probability of the main acids randomly assuming the exact required sequence. Since there are some two thousand enzymes, Hoyle and Wickramasinghe calculate that the probability of obtaining them all by chance is $10^{40,000}$ (20 acids x 2,000 enzymes). They

---

52. Meyer, "Origin of Biological Information," 216.
53. Dembski, *No Free Lunch*, 145–56.
54. Laszlo, "Systems and Structures," 177–78.
55. Thaxton et al., *Mystery of Life's Origin*, 131.

term this an "outrageously small probability that could not be faced even if the whole universe consisted of organic soup." In a memorable metaphor they write, "Troops of monkeys thundering away at random on typewriters could not produce the works of Shakespeare, for the practical reason that the whole observable universe is not large enough to contain the necessary monkey hordes, the necessary typewriters, and certainly the waste baskets required for the deposition of wrong attempts."[56]

William Dembski's calculations flesh out why Hoyle and Wickramasinghe deny the role of chance in life formation. When deciding if an event is due to chance or design, its probability must be calculated with all relevant resources factored in. The physical universe has about 10^{80} elementary particles, and matter cannot change states at a rate faster than 10^{45} times per second. Assuming an age for the universe of 10^{25} seconds, we sum these three powers to get the total number of subatomic particle events in the history of the universe. The total of 10^{150} is called the universal probability bound (UPB) and Dembski notes that it's a built-in barrier that is absolutely impervious to circumvention. He states further that the US National Security Council uses one in 10^{94} as the safety ceiling to prevent code-breaking while the French mathematician Borel suggested only one in 10^{50}.[57] When traditional evolutionists—stuck in their meme—appeal to random chance over time, the argument inevitably founders on the UPB. There simply isn't enough time in the history of the universe for such evolutionary processes to occur. In fact, for nature to satisfy by chance Hoyle's and Wickramasinghe's probability of $10^{40,000}$ would require countless universes. As we have seen, this sort of probability requirement is the main impetus for the multiverse cosmological hypothesis. Perhaps the renowned erstwhile atheist philosopher Antony Flew deserves the last word on this. Saying he's now best labeled a deist like Thomas Jefferson, Flew stated:

> A super-intelligence is the only good explanation for the origin of life and the complexity of nature. . . . [DNA] has shown, by the almost unbelievable complexity of the arrangements which are needed to produce (life) that intelligence must have been involved.
>
> It has become inordinately difficult even to begin to think about constructing a naturalistic theory of the evolution of that first reproducing organism.[58]

There's another critical factor in this discussion of randomness. The human genome is not arbitrarily thrown together but has a modular hierarchical structure.[59] What happens if randomness is applied to hierarchical structures? The answer is that as randomness increases hierarchical modularity decreases. As a matter of fact, if a

---

56. Hoyle and Wickramasinghe, *Evolution from Space*, 23–24, 148.
57. Dembski, *No Free Lunch*, 21.
58. Ostling, "There Is a God," A18; see also Flew and Habermas, "My Pilgrimage," 201.
59. Shaw and Shapshak, "Fractal Genomics Modeling," 9–17.

sufficient amount of randomness is applied, the hierarchical modularity disappears.[60] In light of this, we obviously can't have it both ways, defending random genetic development when such a process would destroy the modular hierarchy that's the genome's structural reality. The genetic evidence forces us to abandon randomness ideology.

So much for the operation of chance in evolution. What about the role of gradual change?

Darwin called his theory "descent with modification" to indicate that life had common ancestry. He postulated that as life evolves, genetic modification based on survival fitness would produce a new form. In this Darwinian model, novelty was the result of chance operating through gradual random development of functional gene structures. However, science has learned that much of the novelty in genetics instead reflects change in the pattern and timing of gene activity. "Evolutionary change seems to result not from changes in the number or structure of genes but from changes in their regulation," say Neil H. Shubin and Charles R. Marshall. They note that there has been a large measure of gene conservation (continuity) over the last two billion years, and that evolutionists have been surprised by how "major patterning genes and regulatory interactions are deeply conserved across vast expanses of time and phylogeny [sets of organisms]."[61]

Furthermore, present indications are that "gross differences" between body plans correlate "with major changes in the action and/or number of a few regulatory genes." So this seems to affirm that large-scale evolution is due to macromutation, that is, large change through manipulation of several genes at once.[62]

This brings us to Michael Behe's (in)famous mouse trap. According to Behe, a system is irreducibly complex if it consists "of several mutually adapted and interacting parts that contribute to the basic function," such that removing even a single part completely destroys the system's function.[63] Behe points to the ordinary mouse trap, where removal of any one component renders the whole thing useless. By comparison, a system is cumulatively complex if components can be arranged sequentially so that successive removal never leads to total loss of function. An example of this is the human brain, where sequential removal of neural connections causes gradual degradation, as in Alzheimer's disease.

In contrast to cumulative complexity, Behe cites the bacterium flagellum as a case study in irreducible complexity. The flagellum is an "acid-powered rotary motor with a whip-like tail whose rotating motion enables a bacterium to navigate through its watery environment." The rotor, stator, O-rings, bushings, and drive shaft require

---

60. Nagy et al., "Effect of Disorder," 101–10.
61. Shubin and Marshall, "Fossils, Genes," 325, 331.
62. Ibid., 336.
63. Behe, *Darwin's Black Box*, 39–45.

about thirty proteins to operate and another twenty or more to assemble. The absence of any of these would cause complete failure of the motor.[64]

Here's the central problem for natural selection. It believes in sequential development but the flagellum had to be produced all at once.[65] The bacterium flagellum in E. coli has 4,639,221 base pairs and codes for 4,289 proteins. Using conservative assumptions which together inflate the probability of chance as causation, Dembski shows the odds of the flagellum acquiring by chance the right building blocks of proteins as one in 10^{234}. This is much less than the UPB of 10^{150}. The necessity of simultaneous genetic manipulation is strong evidence for the infusion of critical information which enables genuine novelty to occur. How did this amazing infusion occur?

One answer is that systems can self-create information by following operator-supplied sets of instructions called genetic algorithms. It's helpful to illustrate the idea with several examples.

NetTalk was a 1987 speech synthesizer[66] which had 203 input "neurons," a middle layer of eighty, and an output set of twenty-six, one for each letter of the alphabet. This neural-style network gave about four thousand connectors to change. The network was fed sets of seven letters and was programmed to deal with the middle letter. No sound prompts were given, but it was given a rule which enabled the program to learn to handle errors. *NetTalk* successfully learned to pronounce English text by itself, and what impressed observers was how much it sounded like a child as it progressed. It started out babbling, then early on distinguished vowels and consonants, and then found boundaries and spoke pseudo words. "After being presented 50,000 times with a selection of 1,024 words, *NetTalk* was correct ninety-five percent of the time when tested on that training set. When presented with words it had never before seen, its pronunciation was eighty percent correct."[67]

A close reading of the account shows the various places where outside rule-makers set boundary conditions which directed the algorithm. These rules included the number of neurons available, their placement in a hierarchy of levels, the number of input letters and the instruction to use the middle one, and an error correction protocol (technically called back propagation).

Likewise, Richard Dawkins produced METHINKS•IT•IS•LIKE•A•WEASEL through a very specific algorithm. He preselected the word size and division, and randomly altered all letters and spaces that didn't agree with the target sequence. After this, it's no surprise that the message was obtained after forty-three steps.[68] Similar rule-dominance shows up in an algorithm created by Thomas Schneider. Its goal was to let random selection model how DNA evolves the sites where the DNA's proteins

---

64. Ibid., 69–72.
65. Dembski, *No Free Lunch*, 292–93.
66. Satinover, *Quantum Brain*, 76–78.
67. Ibid., 41–43.
68. Dembski, *No Free Lunch*, 181–82.

attach. According to protocol, the algorithm was told to take the best one-half of results and use them for the program's next iteration or cycle. Schneider stated that the algorithm found the ideal binding locations in only 704 generations (repetitions). But when the complete test conditions are examined, one sees quickly that he gave the algorithm numerical floors and ceilings so that it would know what to consider a good or bad result.[69]

In every one of the preceding cases, iteration rules were externally designed to select greater proximity to future function rather than to actual present function. However, Stephen Meyer points out that "such foresighted selection has no analogue in nature. . . . In biology, where differential survival depends upon maintaining function, selection cannot occur before new functional sequences arise."[70] Genetic algorithms are teleological in preselecting according to future goals. These operate with god parameters and it is the job of the engineer designing the evolutionary algorithm to set them to reasonably optimal values. The process is run for many thousands of generations of simulated evolution, and at the end of the process, one is likely to find solutions that are of a distinctly higher order than the starting conditions."[71] On the other hand, Darwinism (and evolution generally) assumes post-selection.

Rule specification can be directly transposed to other real-life biological systems. It turns out that protein folding occurs very restrictively according to some one thousand designed patterns. In each case, the final form represents a natural free energy minimum toward which the organic fold is drawn. Researcher Michael Denton categorically states, "The role of selection in shaping this vast and rapidly growing inventory of forms is clearly trivial and secondary."[72] The obvious conclusion is that creational processes precisely follow their laws. As systems theorist Donella Meadows puts it, "The divine creator does not have to produce miracles. He, she, or it just has to write clever rules."[73]

So to the question "How does information infusion occur?" we can affirm that neo-Darwinian ideology has no solution. Former US Major League Baseball commissioner Faye Vincent once said that baseball is about rules. If there are none, there is no game. Creation is no different. Physical laws instantiate as matter but matter does not create laws any more than a baseball game creates the rules by which it's played. The issue of law-maker is crucial to understanding both baseball and creation. The sum of the matter is that neo-Darwinian principles are unworkable and conferred algorithms, rules, and laws are crucial.

69. Bracht, "Natural Selection as an Algorithm," 265.
70. Meyer, "Origin of Biological Information," 229.
71. Kurzweil, "Reflections on Stephen Wolfram."
72. Denton et al., "Physical Law Not Natural Selection," 310.
73. Meadows, "Places to Intervene in a System."

It's at this precise juncture that chaoplexity theory claims that the various data which have destroyed Darwinism as a legitimate theory[74] can be overcome by self-organizing or emergent phenomena.[75] Dynamic systems are those with nonconstant rates of change over time which are described by nonlinear differential equations. In street language, nonlinearity is the butterfly effect where a tiny change in initial conditions can magnify into immense change later. A. J. Lotka and V. Volterra pioneered the use of nonlinear analysis in the 1920s. Using just two differential equations, they modeled predator and prey numbers. They found that initial values controlled how the numbers varied but that regardless of these nonlinear values the cycles were endlessly repetitive. Furthermore, if the initial values were set at the central equilibrium point, there would be no population swings. By adding what they termed an "ecological friction" constant, the cycles could be made to swing about the equilibrium point but never quite reach it.[76] Recent research has found nonlinear functions in the human body, brain, and mind. These include blood cell production,[77] cerebral blood flow,[78] cardiopulmonary rhythms and tasks,[79] walking stride intervals,[80] complex learning,[81] language acquisition[82] and music appreciation,[83] among others.

At about the same time that Lotka and Volterra were modeling predator-prey interactions, other scholars were applying the idea to life itself. They noted that although life is more than physics and chemistry there was yet no resolution of how higher qualities emerge from lower.[84] A generation later, Michael Polyani agreed, "It is obvious, therefore, that the rise of man can be accounted for only by other principles than those known today to physics and chemistry. . . . Evolution can only be understood as a feat of emergence." Polyani specifically targeted consciousness, saying that men think but acids don't.[85] Emergent evolution's answer to these puzzles is that the universe is progressing according to the principle of complexification rooted in nonlinearity.

Complex emergent systems assume a loop in which an emergent quality materializes as a new higher level and then is available to exert downward causation

---

74. Thaxton et al., *Mystery of Life's Origin*, 146.
75. Kaneko, "Chaos as a Source of Complexity and Diversity."
76. Bechtel and Abrahamsen, "Phenomena and Mechanisms," 174.
77. Perazzo et al., "Large Scale-Invariant Fluctuations."
78. West et al., "Multifractality of Cerebral Blood Flow."
79. Suki et al., "Fluctuations, Noise and Scaling."
80. Hausdorff et al., "Is Walking a Random Walk?"
81. Mayer-Kress et al., "What Can We Learn from Learning Curves?"
82. Bechtel and Abrahamsen, "Phenomena and Mechanisms," 174.
83. Bhattacharya and Petsche, "Universality in the Brain."
84. Alexander, *Space, Time, and Deity*, 46–47.
85. Polyani, *Personal Knowledge*, 389–90.

on lower levels.[86] By this means it is supposed that novel information and natural law are co-created.[87] Applying the loop to biology, Rupert Sheldrake coined the term "morphogenetic forms." He regards these patterns as equivalent to Plato's forms or Jung's collective unconscious, but with the specific function of pre-modeling biological organisms. Life develops according to downward causation by existing forms. The feedback mechanism allows evolutionary adaptations to upward-propogate so that the pre-patterns change over time.[88]

Paul Davies utilizes this type of endless loop in cosmology. He maintains that when matter goes through phase changes, as when the vacuum's potential energy converts to the bubble's real energy, laws change. Because such an emergent process still implies design, Davies then says that there's a teleological principle in the universe which produces "life and mind, laws and universes." He eventually ends up in the panentheistic camp where nature is equivalent to God's body.[89]

Nonetheless, the enthusiasm over complexity and self-organization overlooks a critical fact. The systems involved follow equations which are so complicated that at present it's mathematically impossible for humans to design chaotic sources which produce signals with specific properties.[90] In spite of this, emergent theory credits nature with producing these complex systems although we've already seen that even simple genetic algorithms must be externally programmed. Just calling a system emergent, complex, dynamic, or nonlinear doesn't change the need for external operator input. Nature cannot defeat Gödel any more than can mathematicians because emergent philosophy is self-referential. The conclusion to which we are inexorably drawn is that to exalt self-organization without a concomitant emphasis on its conferred rules subjugates chaoplexity to the evolutionary religious myth.[91]

IV. CREATION AND THE CHARACTER OF GOD

In light of the preceding discussion, what may we say about the creator's character and relationship to the universe?

God Is "The Other"

The universe cannot be self-referential and therefore demands a creative source who is outside the system. As I noted in chapter 1, the work of Gödel, Spencer-Brown, Varela, Fredkin, Markopoulou, and other scholars demonstrate this fact even if they

---

86. Emmeche et al., "Levels, Emergence, and Three Versions," 13–14.
87. Kirilyuk, "Universal Symmetry of Complexity," 827.
88. Sheldrake, *New Science of Life*, 127, 132–33, 149.
89. Davies, "Multiverse or Design?"
90. Abarbanel et al., "Blending Chaotic Attractors," 214.
91. Ruse, "Is Evolution a Secular Religion?," 1523–24.

personally reject it. However, the evidence doesn't lie. Evolution is not random, genetic selection is teleological (goal-directed), and a computational creation requires a programmer and rule-giver. All of these are indicators of a guiding hand.

The philosophical implication is clear. All theories which place the creator inside the universe, in panpsychic relationship with it, or ontologically identical to it are falsified by the self-reference principle. Early emergentists, writing before Gödel, failed to understand this. C. Lloyd Morgan said, "Deity is an emergent quality of the highest natural systems that we know.... God as actually possessing deity does not exist but is an ideal, is always becoming; but God as the whole universe tending towards deity does exist."[92] Samuel Alexander echoed him: "Deity is thus the next higher empirical quality to mind, which the universe is engaged in bringing to birth."[93] The doctrine that God was created by or is co-evolving with nature is echoed by anthropologists (Teilhard),[94] cosmologists (Hoyle and Wickramasinghe),[95] philosophers (Alfred North Whitehead),[96] clerics (Anthony Freeman),[97] and theologians (Karl Rahner).[98]

However, in contrast to emergent pan(en)psychism, the universe reveals a God who stands outside of nature and whose hiddenness is gradually unveiled just like a negative of a photograph materializes in the dark room.

Of course, if God is "The Other" who lives in outer darkness then immediately we must ask how such a being could interact with creation and specifically with people. One approach is to define this interaction as information input, not energy.[99] This is consistent with the fact that God and creation are in a dualistic feedback network relationship which theology calls covenant. As we have shown, in this framework God is outside creation and enters as the Holy Spirit becomes a parameter (especially through human agents) in a given self-organizing system. But Christian doctrine historically has taken the issue further by asserting that one aspect of divine personality became flesh and blood in Jesus of Nazareth.

It's true that many people look askance at the Trinity. However, I think that modern psychology gives us a model for a God who is multitarian. The human ability to dissociate and produce alter personalities demonstrates a genuine way in which God could have more than one personality yet still be one.[100] Such a psychological model assumes God's voluntary dissociation as compared to human trauma-based splitting.

---

92. Morgan, *Emergent Evolution*, 25, 34.

93. Alexander, *Space, Time, and Deity*, 347.

94. Chardin, *Phenomenon of Man*, 284–97.

95. Hoyle and Wickramasinghe, *Evolution from Space*, 33, 143–50.

96. Whitehead, *Process and Reality*, 519–33.

97. Freeman, "God as an Emergent Property," 147–59.

98. Rahner, *Theological Investigations*, 5:160.

99. Polkinghorne, "Creatio Continua," 105.

100. This concept occurred to me independently in December 2003. I later discovered a similar proposal in Duane Mullner, "Dissociation and Trinity," *Gestalt Institute of the Rockies*, now a dead link.

Its strength is that because it uses analogical categories rooted in personality it far surpasses the usual God-like-water (solid, fluid, vapor) metaphors.

God Is Personal

In the prologue I cited a number of authorities' collective opinions about the characteristics of a code-writing God. Such a being, they said, would be outside creation, personal, intelligent, purposeful, master of all logically possible universes, concerned for human life, self-existent, and able to simulate all life probabilities. A grasp of these features is possible because humans can use mathematics to penetrate creation's fundamental structures. Such understanding would be impossible if God had not created this language to be capable of bridging the gap between the Trinity and created beings. Though Christians accept the Bible as inspired revelation from God in history, mathematics is revelation in nature and accessible to anyone.

More than one observer has been struck by the elegance, mystery, power and accessibility of mathematics as the language which interprets the universe. Consider a simple example like the Golden Ratio, *Phi*, wherein A is to B, as B is to C, and A plus B equals C. These ratios, which have been calculated to one and a half million decimal places, yield a rounded-off value of about 1:1.62. *Phi* has fascinated many for millennia: the ratios are found in plants, the human body, the design of the Egyptian pyramids, Notre Dame Cathedral, and much more. "The miracle of the appropriateness of the language of mathematics for the formulation of the laws of physics," says Nobel winner Eugene Wigner, "is a wonderful gift which we neither understand nor deserve."[101]

However, while mathematics is objective, much of our real-world experience is subjective. R. W. Hamming is blunt: "So far as I can see, science has contributed nothing to the answers . . . [of what] Truth, Beauty, and Justice are." He says further than human experience in the real world does not fall under the domain of science and mathematics. Indeed, these disciplines take on faith that they can explain the world by mathematics.[102] This prompts us to ask how an impersonal generative principle could create a universe suitable for creatures who "know that they know" or in formal terms, are self-conscious observers of the universe in which they live.[103] Indeed, could such an impersonal principle even conceive of the subjectivities of ethics, aesthetics, and morality?

Stephen Weinberg stated that when we use the term "God" to specify a designer, either we mean something definite or we don't. "You may tell me that you are thinking of something much more abstract, some cosmic spirit of order and harmony, as

---

101. Wigner, "Unreasonable Effectiveness of Mathematics," 14.
102. Hamming, "Unreasonable Effectiveness," 6.
103. Barrow and Tippler, *Anthropic Cosmological Principle*, 1–6.

Einstein did . . . but then I don't know why you use words like 'designer' or 'God.'"[104] Weinberg has put his finger on the core psychological issue. Design means purpose and purpose points to personality.

Alan Harkavy typifies those who position themselves between god within matter (panpsychism or panentheism) and God the creator of matter. This leaves him professing faith in a local god but not one who made the laws of the universe. Harkavy's god "arose naturally with the creation of matter from the will which is in all matter and from the awareness which is in all matter." It used information, knowledge, and will and worked through evolution to create the earth as a viable place for humans. Most importantly, he affirms that this god "is a personal God. This God has a very powerful will."[105] But this god is not what anthropology calls a "high god." Harkavy's creator god is more or less analogous to the early gnostic creative demiurge who was an inferior angelic being.

As we have found, the law-giver must be external to the cosmos, so Harkavy's demiurge is a nonstarter. What's interesting, though, is his demand that a god be personal. I think this reflects an instinctive realization that human subjectivity implies a parallel quality of creator subjectivity. Let us then be explicit about this.

God and Free Will

A crucial metaphysical issue is whether a computational creation permits free will. For God or anyone else to exercise free will in the universe means that there must be a way for personal choice to occur. The question is how this is accomplished if creation's foundational structure is a constantly computing cellular automaton. There are basically four ideas on the table.

First, with materialists we might simply say that free will is an illusion. Steven Weinberg commented, "Free will to me means only that we sometimes decide what we do . . . but we have no mental experience that tells us that our decisions are not inevitable consequences of past conditions and the laws of nature."[106]

Second, quantum theorists argue that the uncertainty principle allows for free will. According to the Copenhagen interpretation, an observer creates reality out of uncertainty by choosing to study matter as a wave or particle function. However, an important objection is that if particles are quantized in terms of their various properties, the particle and data views of reality are essentially equivalent.[107] This also means that if space-time really is computing, then it's impossible to have a truly random

---

104. Weinberg, "Designer Universe?"
105. Harkavy, *Human Will*, 93.
106. Weinberg, "Is the Universe a Computer?"
107. Kurzweil, *Age of Intelligent Machines*, 195.

quantum number that is independent (Fredkin, "othogonal"[108]) of everything in the creational computer.

Therefore, a creature within the system never really knows much about its states, not because they are random, but because of space-time's enormous computational speed, size, and complexity. In such a universe, a human observer confronted with quantum uncertainty doesn't create reality through observation but simply chooses which cellular output to watch. Quantum uncertainty ends up being what Fredkin calls the system's "unknowable determinism."[109] There's no need to presuppose infinite numbers of universes in which all quantum probabilities are realized. Being a logical, non-spatial construct the automaton is so vast—effectively infinite—that quantum possibilities which do not manifest simply exist as informational memory in the mass of cells. On the other hand, a sufficiently competent outside creator would know the system's initial state and all subsequent states—both realized and non-realized—in exhaustive detail.

A third option is that the automaton might actually combine discrete and continuous processes. For example, even though light and matter have been quantized and are discrete, many physicists still regard space and time as continuous. Konrad Zuse raised this same point in 1968. He argued that, given that classical and relativistic physics have no limits and continuous values while quantum mechanics is discrete, one might define nature as a hybrid.[110]

While this sounds possible, there are problems with it. In aesthetic terms, it offends against the principle of symmetry. Second, even if nature is hybrid, it's not clear how this provides for free choice. Merely to say that part of nature is not computing doesn't mean that it is nondeterministic. Finally, the apparent hybridization might just be optics. That is, at a fine scale, creation looks and is grainy while at a large scale it looks continuous but isn't. In different language, we would say that nature is fully deterministic but is so complicated that to human inside observers it's operationally random. For example, in Stephen Wolfram's book *A New Kind of Science*, cellular automaton rule 110 is completely deterministic yet produces phenomena that passes every statistical test for randomness.[111] In this regard, we recall that Einstein refused to accept quantum mechanical indeterminacy as anything more than apparent randomness.[112]

In contrast to all these proposals, I think the real solution to the free will question involves autonomous agents who function with their own rules and decision-making within the larger structure. In particular, creaturely agents and their wills become

---

108. Fredkin, "Finite Nature."
109. Fredkin, "Digital Mechanics," 260.
110. Zuse, "Rechnender Raum," 337.
111. Kurzweil, "Reflections on Stephen Wolfram."
112. Aaronson, review of *New Kind of Science*, 415.

parts of self-organizing processes of all kinds, systems in which by nature agents are parameters which influence how the system develops.

A decade ago Stan Franklin and Art Graesser of IBM defined an autonomous software agent as a system which can sense its own environment, pursue its own agenda, and bring this about in the future.[113] In addition to carrying out their own purposes, agents "carry out some set of operations on behalf of a user or another program with some degree of independence or autonomy, and in so doing, employ some knowledge or representation of the user's goals or desires."[114]

One thing is instantly crystal clear. Franklin's and Graesser's agents must function with at least some rules which extend beyond those which control the software program itself in order for them to exercise choice. Although these agents "live" within their micro automaton they have purposes and choices which are analogous to Wolfram's rule 110. This ability is dependent on the programmer who must write the necessary rules. The IBM analogy also shows that agents are designed to execute purposes which represent the values of the programmer. Applied to humans, this means that our agent rule-sets have externally given components which provide for free will in all the personal subjective realms of morals, ethics, aesthetics, justice, theology, love, and truth.

Therefore the structural provision for free will is agent participation in self-organizing systems. Philosopher Karl Popper distinguished three worlds: nature (the realm of physics, chemistry, biology, and the other natural sciences), mind (states of consciousness), and culture (knowledge in its objective sense). Popper's world three is particularly relevant since it includes languages; tales, stories and religious myths; scientific conjectures or theories; and mathematical constructions.[115] All three worlds use self-organization but humans do not have equal access to all three. The primary boundary is that humans may not synchronize our minds—as do demonic and angelic beings—with the information patterns in the automaton's nodes. This is why I shall argue in chapter 5 that the primal sin was the human attempt to use demonic power to directly control nature's rudimentary elements. On the other hand, the worlds of mind and cultural self-organization are where one's free will is exercised as an autonomous agent participating in systems. We become one parameter among many. An excellent illustration of this is our everyday participation in the market economy. People remark on the mysterious hand that seems to control economic relationships. The answer is easy; the unseen hand of a self-organizing system driven by numerous agent-parameters is at work.[116]

If creatures are autonomous agents within the larger automaton, how does God relate to such beings? Since the Jesuit Luis de Molina (1535–1600), God's ability to

113. Franklin and Graesser, "Is It an Agent," 26.
114. Ibid., 23.
115. Popper, *Three Worlds*, 144.
116. Rosser, "On the Complexities," 180.

foreknow creaturely choice and make divine decisions based on this information has been referred to as middle knowledge. This knowledge is "between" God's knowledge of all that is and all that's logically possible. This is also referred to as the counterfactuals of creaturely freedom. That is, God knows "what free creatures would do if they were created in other possible worlds."[117] Nonetheless, such creatures will, if created, enjoy freedom of choice. It's a powerful way of resolving the conundrum of God's sovereignty and creaturely choice.

Since I began the chapter by quoting Richard Feynman's self-professed ignorance about the mysteries of quantum physics, it seems fair to give him the last word. In his *Messenger Lectures* at Cornell University two years before his Nobel comments, he was a bit more optimistic about creation's intelligibility. With reference to the law of gravity, he commented, "I am interested not so much in the human mind as in the marvel of a nature which can obey such an elegant and simple law."[118] Were Feynman alive to read this chapter, I would hope that he could agree with me that the elegant and simple laws we find in nature reveal the grandeur of the mind of the person who wrote them.

---

117. Boyd, *Satan and the Problem of Evil*, 124.
118. Feynman, *Character of Physical Law*, 14.

3

DEATH

CONTRARY TO MARK TWAIN's joke that reports of his passing were premature, reports of creation's death are all too accurate.

In the big picture the presenting culprit is entropy. Because the universe began with a large amount of heat differential, it had a capacity for work. However, the universe is irreversibly flowing toward heat equilibrium. This process may be measured as the amount of energy which is unavailable for useful work.[1] Such a decrease in ability to do work is called an increase in entropy. When no further work can be done, the universe has reached equilibrium, its final state of maximum entropy, or heat death.

Death creates a three-part intellectual challenge.

To begin with, life's appearance ought to have been precluded in a universe controlled by entropy. This contradiction led physicists Shahar Dolev and Avshalom Elitzur to remark on life's negentropic complexity. "Living systems control the operation of single molecules, guiding minuscule amounts of energy and matter into an enormously ordered, macroscopic system." Though they leave a possibility fudge factor they add, "Statistically, it seems, the odds for such a transition are nearly zero. Yet, the very fact that this statement is made by living creatures means that, long ago, the next-to-impossible *has* happened."[2]

The second conundrum is that logically, the miracle of life ought to have resulted in immortality. According to Leonid A. Gavrilov and Natalia S. Gavrilova:

> [It's] difficult to understand why natural selection seemed to result in such bizarrely injurious features as senescence and late-life degenerative diseases instead of eternal youth and immortality. How does it happen that, after having accomplished the miraculous success that led us from a single cell at

---

1. Corning and Kline, "Thermodynamics, Information and Life Revisited," 276–77.
2. Dolev and Elitzur, "Biology and Thermodynamics," 24–33.

conception through birth and then to sexual maturity and productive adulthood . . . the developmental program formed by biological evolution fails even to maintain the accomplishments of its own work?[3]

Finally, given the incredibility of the sheer existence of creation and life, why is death present in the first place? That is the major question I will address in this chapter. There are four classes of answers; I will give brief overviews for three of these and then focus in detail on the fourth for the rest of the chapter.

The first answer to death is that it's simply a given. For example, Buddhism holds that there is no first cause. Matter and consciousness coexist in an endlessly cycling universe[4] which therefore will always include death as a foundational structure. The Hindu argument is that infinite numbers of universes may be required for reincarnation to be completed and death overcome.[5] The multiverse, which we encountered earlier, has a built-in contradiction around death. The same logic that says, given 10^{500} possible universes, one with death like ours is inevitable, also leads to the conclusion that a universe with immortality must exist somewhere. In this case, death is a cosmic roll of the dice: in this universe you die, in that one you live. Each of these metaphysical theories is unsupported by anything other than wishful thinking.

A second answer comes from those Christian creationists who assert that human sin caused death. The problem is that both the universe and terrestrial ecology have been designed around death's reality. For example, we're familiar with the maxim that nature is red in tooth and claw. This proverb is well-captured in Howard Bloom's remarks that the peaceful pride of lions will kill this afternoon; female bees will chase an overage queen through the hive and bite it to death; myxobacteria will form wolf packs that gang up on prey and male dolphins will fight like street gangs.[6]

In fact, earth's present ecology would collapse without death in the biological chain.[7] Forest fires destroy so that new growth may follow, predators dispatch the weak who can't reproduce, and human white blood cells kill disease bacteria. Modern biomedical life-extension models are understandably silent about the irony that sustainable population health requires a certain death and replacement rate.[8] In short, it's absurd to claim that terrestrial ecology, let alone the universe's entropic heat death, can be explained as the consequence of human action.

Theistic evolutionists comprise a third set of interpreters. They feel the question of death keenly, acknowledging that it's the reality of suffering, disease, death, and extinction which is a genuine challenge to Christian theology. It unavoidably "leads to the recognition that underlying human, moral evil are forms of natural evil which, in

---

3. Gavrilov and Gavrilova, "Evolutionary Theories," 340–41.
4. Thuan, "Cosmic Design," 210–11, 213.
5. Ram and Achari, *Cosmic Game*, 23–28.
6. Bloom, *Lucifer Principle*, 24.
7. Terborgh et al., "Ecological Meltdown," 1923–26.
8. Waltner-Toews, "Ecosystem Approach to Health."

an implicitly Manichaean way, characterize the universe as a whole."[9] Since God is the external law-giver, God indeed has embedded death in creation's structures. Could not a competent creator have done better?

Another way of putting this is to say that if God is directly responsible for Manichaean-like structural evil in creation, then Carl Jung was correct in his doctrine of the quaternity. In describing his psychological construction of the godhead, Jung is unequivocal on God's amorality. "Our quaternity formula confirms the rightness of their [gnostic] claims; for the Holy Ghost, as the synthesis of the original One which then became split, issues from a source that is both light and dark."[10] He continues, "Satan is one whose origin needs no inquiry since the OT shows YHWH as moral and immoral at the same time; YHWH behaves immorally though he is the guardian of law and order; He is unjust and unreliable according to the O.T."[11]

In assessing whether God really is amoral, incompetent, or both, we must ask first whether natural death is evil. With one exception, all Christian interpreters agree that it is. Young earth creationism argues that human sin introduced carnivorous death into the world. Creation-gap theorists add that the original perfect creation was corrupted by Satan, who is thus the cause of prehistoric animal death. Evolution-as-kenosis says that God self-limits so that, being immanently within natural processes, God suffers along with those who die. The Promethean Determinism[12] of utopian evolution expects existing organisms to transcend death by replacing themselves with new models into which they've designed perfection.[13] Though unsuccessful, a pioneering instance of Promethean Determinism was reported in 2015 with the first-ever editing of an embryonic human genome.[14]

The minority view is evolution-as-progress, which regards death as the cost of life. Nature ends up producing the shark, a perfectly designed killing machine, and, as Job 39:30 says, God takes credit for the eagle, whose babies suck up blood. In milder language, "cancer in creation is not something that a more competent or compassionate creator could easily have eliminated, but is the necessary cost of a creation allowed to make itself."[15] The outcome of the Christian explanations for death is twofold. Theistic evolution holds God responsible for death due to creation's design. Conversely theistic creationists hold humans responsible due to sin after the universe's formation.

I shall urge the fourth alternative in which cosmic angelic powers rebelled against their proper places in creation prior to the formation of the physical universe. This cosmic mutiny skewed the automaton's operations resulting in what the ancient texts

---

9. Russell, "Eschatology and Scientific Cosmology," 9.
10. Jung, "Psychological Approach," 177.
11. Jung, "Jung and Religious Belief," 709.
12. Peters, *Playing God*, 6–7.
13. Rifkin, *Algeny*, 17.
14. Cyranoski and Reardon, "Chinese Scientists Genetically Modify Human Embryos."
15. Polkinghorne, *Science and the Trinity*, 72.

call chaos. There are several aspects to this structural disorder which bear directly on why death is in creation.

In the first place, creation is structured as a feedback network with God acting as downward causation. In biblical terms, this relationship is labeled as a covenant (Jer 33:20). The network cannot be annulled but this doesn't mean that it can't be thrown into disorder. Indeed, the concern for order is fundamental in ancient Near Eastern (ANE) doctrines of creation. As a case in point, the Egyptian term *ma'at* meant world order, correctness, truth, and righteousness.[16] *Ma'at* is an axis, "below being the infernal sea of chaos, above being the supernal ocean of bliss." If people don't perform their ritual and responsibilities, thus staying aligned with the axis—in biblical language, the covenant—they fall into the hands of Yamm, king of death. In this case they are "lost, fragmented, disordered."[17]

Second, a disordered creation is one in which the automaton's rules have not been rewritten but have been manipulated to throw creation off course. Since the automaton merrily computes its next states without regard for consequences, the most startling aspect of an angelic revolt was its capacity to actually change creation's outcome. In technical terms, this happens most readily in the feedback loop of network processes running in the automaton. We will examine this further in later chapters but suffice to say here that if feedback input is delayed or blocked then neither noise nor new information is available to use in computing the next state. It's worth repeating Karl Svozil's statement that reprogramming the automaton would be (re)tuning reality.[18]

Consequently, the rebellion by cosmic beings was actually a struggle with God for control of creation. If demonic beings were reprogramming creation prior to the formation of the universe, God faced a macrocosm progressively succumbing to disorder. Therefore the reason that heat death marks the end of the physical universe is to delimit the universe's vulnerability to Satanic reverse engineering which ultimately could destroy the overarching moral, ethical, and spiritual realms. Assuming the present creation originally to be the best that God could devise, post-angelic rebellion God had to integrate death into nature. The alternative would have been annihilation of the demonically skewed creation with no re-formation. However, by self-limitation (*kenosis*) God chose not to destroy creation and instead to offer it future redemption. This is neither amorality nor implicit Manichaeism but eschatological hope. All of this stands in sharp contrast with G. F. R. Ellis' idea that God created through trial and error.[19]

Finally, to say that God had to design death into the universe because of angelic revolt assumes that such cosmic demonic beings really exist. Otherwise the whole

16. Knight, "Cosmogony and Order," 139–40.
17. Versluis, *Egyptian Mysteries*, 15.
18. Svozil, "Computational Universes," 855.
19. Ellis, "Theology of the Anthropic Principle," 393.

argument crumbles. In the remainder of this chapter, we'll survey ANE materials which describe the fall of the cosmos into demonic disorder and death.

I. LUCIFER

A prime concern for ANE theologians was cosmic order. This is exemplified by the Egyptian *ma'at*, which is itself a reasonable facsimile of Isa 24. In Isaiah God warns idolatrous Israel that it is in danger of being reduced to a bleak wasteland because the eternal covenant has been broken. The perpetrators of covenant fracture are both cosmic and earthly: the host of heaven in heaven, and on earth the kings of the earth. By exploring the roots of disorder in human culture, Isaiah uses Israel's history to point to deeper cosmic realities.

The same combination of cosmic and terrestrial powers is found in Isa 14:12–21. The text refers historically to Babylon, though the king is unknown. (No king of Babylon fits the story line properly, and the matter is confused because kings of Assyria styled themselves as kings of Babylon. Examples of this are Tiglath-Pileser, Sargon, and Sennacherib.[20]) Deeper interpretive levels involve, (1) a moral warning about pride, (2) a strong cosmic inference that the fallen priest-king was originally Lucifer the Day Star, and (3) a futurist indication of Lucifer's ultimate destruction in the eschaton. In what follows, I will focus on the fallen priest-king Lucifer, Day Star, Son of Dawn (14:12).

Both the Bible and other ANE sources identify a god named Dawn (*Shachar*). Shachar is personified in Job 3:9 with eyelashes, in Ps 139:9 with wings, and in Song 6:10 with vision. A Ugaritic text says El fathered Shachar, who is seen as a parallel to Shalem, the god of twilight.[21] In Isa 14:4, the Day Star or morning star is the king of Babylon, but by v. 12 the scene has switched to the cosmic level. This is particularly evident in the exclamation, "How you are fallen from heaven, O Day Star son of Dawn!" The term Day Star translates the Hebrew *helel*, "shining one," and reflects equivalent renderings of *Eosphorus* in the Septuagint and *Lucifer* in the Latin Vulgate. The celestial image is that of Venus rising at dawn as the brightest star in the sky before being fully eclipsed by the sun.

Later rabbinic commentaries talked about a supernatural character who had a "celestial glory. His eyes are great orbs of light and his fins can dim the light of the sun with their brilliance."[22] These qualities rendered this creature comparable to the primordial light which "emanated from the mantle donned by God at the time of creation." In the Babylonian creation epic, their dragon monsters also have apparel, "a

---

20. Oswalt, *Book of Isaiah*, 314, 321.
21. Watts, *Isaiah 1–33*, 209.
22. Jacobs, "Elements of Near-Eastern Mythology," 6.

pulhu, the awesome, fiery garment of the gods, and are crowned with a *melammu*, a dazzling, divine aureole."[23]

Ezekiel's heavenly priest-figure adds another dimension to the story. The historical context is an oracle against the king of Tyre (28:11). The king in this passage was called a signet ring, *hotam*, that is, one empowered to authenticate documents and wield royal authority. The same word is used of King Coniah (Jer 22:24) and Zerubbabel (Hag 2:23), as well as describing the vestments of Israel's high priest. Isaiah 14:13 informs us that the priest/king was adorned with precious jewels since the day of his creation. The verb used is *bara*, a word reserved for God's creative actions rather than for human birth, thus pointing us toward a suprahistorical figure. Scholars disagree over whether the king *was* a guardian cherub (Masoretes Text) or was *with* a guardian cherub (LXX) in the garden of God (14:14). Katheryn Pfisterer Darr elects the Masoretes Text version, saying the king is cast "in the guise of a primeval, celestial king/priest."[24] It's entirely plausible to see Lucifer as a priestly guardian cherub who in some sense functioned on behalf of the angelic realm before God's altar and throne.

Let's take as our operating thesis, then, that Lucifer was created to mirror God's glory and to function as the dawn star for the rising sun, God's Word. Consequently, Lucifer merits the title angel of light, even recognizing that in his use of this phrase in 2 Cor 11:14 Paul is speaking of a now false and fallen light. However, in distinction to Lucifer's secondhand reflected glory, Jesus the Word shares God's glory as the exact imprint of God's very being (Heb 1:3).

Lucifer's light-bearing character as cherubim forms the backdrop for his transformation into Leviathan the serpent. This transformation plays out in several ways.

To begin with, ANE mythology and biblical accounts point to a cosmic rebellion by a low god against the High God. We earlier met Shachar, a lower god of Dawn charged with preparing the way for the Day Star (High God). In a Ugaritic version, the junior god was Ashtar who rebelled and wanted to rule on Baal's throne. However, he was too small: "His feet did not reach the footstool, His head did not reach the top."[25] A similar Akkadian story involves Zu, a seraphim-like lion/bird god who sought to displace the Great God Enlil. Zu said, "I will take the divine tablets of destinies, I, and the decrees of all the gods I will rule. I will make firm my throne and be the master of the norms. I will direct the totality of all the Igigi [gods]."[26] Likely Isaiah had such myths in mind which he collated as a statement of suprahistorical creaturely hubris, "I will ascend to heaven; I will raise my throne above the stars of God. . . . I will make myself like the Most High" (Isa 14:13–14).

This Canaanite low god-High God conflict is mirrored in a series of parallelisms in Isa 14. These are Emperor-Heaven, Day Star-Sun and, by inference, Lucifer-YHWH.

23. Ibid., 6–7.
24. Darr, *Book of Ezekiel*, 1393.
25. Biti-Anat, "Ba'al Battles Mot," lines 54–65.
26. Pritchard, "Myth of Zu," lines 12–15.

The conflict principle is captured very well by John J. Collins' comments on light and darkness themes in the ANE. Antimonies are present "on a series of distinct levels—the individual heart, the political and social order, and the cosmic level, embracing heaven and earth. The cosmic conflict of the two spirits may be used to express this dualism on any other level."[27]

Second, Genesis tells us that the serpent was cursed for its role in primeval human sin.

On the one hand, we learn in Gen 3:14 that the wise serpent (*nahash*) is punished for its part in Eden's tragedy by being reduced to undulating travel. Given that this is analogical language, we ask, "How did it move beforehand?" The likely answer is that it was one of the flying creatures who attend God's throne. A surprising number of angelic beings are identified in the OT: *Malach* (messenger/angel), *Irinim* (watchers/high angels), *Cherubim* (mighty ones), *Sarim* (princes), *Seraphim* (fiery ones), *Chayyot* ([holy] creatures), *Ophanim* (wheels), and several others. We especially note that the winged seraphim exercised a purifying ministry with Isaiah in ch. 6 and a healing function for the Israelites in the wilderness in Num 21:6. *Seraphim* is translated as "fiery flying serpent" in Isa 14:29 and as "flying serpent" in Isa 30:6.

On the other hand, God's curse on the serpent also specified that it would henceforth eat dust. A similar phrase, to put one's mouth to the dust, occurs in Lam 3:29. What does dust-eating mean? Walter Brueggemann has shown that elevation from the dust is a central metaphor in OT enthronement theology. For example, God tells King Jehu, "I exalted you out of the dust" (1 Kgs 16:2). In Brueggemann's words, "To be taken 'from the dust' means to be elevated from obscurity to royal office and to return to dust means to be deprived of that office and returned to obscurity."[28] Thus God's pronouncement that the serpent will henceforth eat dust amounts to a radical judgment on its status. Its exalted prerogatives were stripped away as it was "returned to the dust."

A third aspect of Lucifer's transformation into Leviathan is revealed in the book of Job. Here we encounter traditions of not one but two cosmic monsters, Leviathan and Behemoth. Since the sources probably derive from the early second millennium BCE,[29] we are in touch with very old cosmic theodicies. The two-monster tradition was very powerful and even in the NT period, the beast and dragon still appear together in Rev 13:1–4 as manifestations of Satan, the serpent of old. Job 40–41 treats these monsters separately but with an intent to link them to each other and also with the *ha-satan* (adversary) of the first two chapters.

We learn that Behemoth was the first of the great acts of God (40:19a), that is, the first thing created. Commentators often see Behemoth historically as the hippopotamus but in Ugarit it was referred to as El's Bullock. Although Behemoth was not

27. Collins, "Patterns of Eschatology," 365.
28. Brueggemann, "From Dust to Kingship," 2.
29. Harrison, *Introduction to the Old Testament*, 1040.

necessarily serpentine, it was a supernatural cosmic being[30] just as Leviathan is.[31] For its part, Leviathan is depicted as "king over all that are proud" (41:34), perhaps referring to the heavenly rebels who followed Lucifer. The descriptions of each monster extend far beyond anything that could apply to even the greatest creatures in the animal kingdom. Of Behemoth, God tells Job, "Only [I] can approach it with the sword" (40:19b). As to Leviathan, God says, "Were not even the gods overwhelmed at the sight of it?" (41:9b).

It has been suggested that these dual monsters with their intertwined identity represent Hebrew poetic repetition.[32] However, modern science combined with ancient mythology opens the door to a very different meaning. Hebrew, Mesopotamian, Chinese, Indian, Egyptian, Greek, and Roman sources all describe dragon pairs and their cosmic conflicts, though often in poetic language. These include such twosomes as the Babylonian Apsu and Tiamat, the Indian Vritra and Danu, Greece's Zeus and Typhon, the Egyptian Horus and Seth, and of course, Leviathan and Behemoth. The dragons are identified as such in Job and elsewhere in the Bible. The non-canonical Additions to Esther (11:6) simply says, "Then two great dragons came forward, both ready to fight, and they roared terribly. . . . It was a day of darkness and gloom, of tribulation and distress, affliction and great tumult on the earth!" Astronomers Victor Cluba and Bill Napier have reconstructed a plausible historical scenario to account for this unanimous ancient testimony. They argue that a large comet, whose remnants are present today as Comet Emcke, sequentially broke apart producing the cosmic clashes of mythology as well as earth impacts on both land (Behemoth) and sea (Leviathan).[33]

Fourth, the dualism implicit in Lucifer's catastrophic and irreversible plummet from his original glory into a serpentine dust-eater is depicted in the wider ANE context. The sources portray the serpent at one and the same time as self-proclaimed creator, life-giver, and image of immortality, but also as the demonic enemy of God.

The Egyptian *Pyramid Texts* illustrate this serpent duality. These describe the serpent taking form in the darkness of the primeval waters (World Ocean) before any definite thing existed. The serpent claimed divinity: "I extended everywhere. . . . I knew, as the One, alone, majestic, the Indwelling Soul, the most potent of the gods. He [I, the Indwelling Soul] it was who made the universe."[34] The Egyptian *Book of the Dead* "prophesies that at the end of time the world will revert to the primary state of undifferentiated chaos and Atum will become a serpent once more." There is reference to "that great surviving serpent, when all mankind has reverted to the slime."[35] This serpent went under various names—Atum, Khoprer, Horus, and others—and being

30. Smick, *Job*, 1050.
31. Pope, *Job*, 331.
32. Smick, *Job*, 1050.
33. Clube and Napier, *Cosmic Serpent*, 198–211.
34. Clark, *Myth and Symbol in Ancient Egypt*, 50–51.
35. Ibid., 52.

bisexual it self-procreated and gave birth to Shu and Tefnut. Shu is significant since he became the separator of earth and sky as well as the mediator between the High God and all other creatures.[36] Nonetheless, Egyptian theology has an ambivalent aspect wherein the serpent is sometimes regarded as supreme creator and other times as the High God's enemy.[37]

Semitic and Sumerian cultures also had double-sided serpent metaphysics. On the one hand, the serpent was the metaphor for immortality. The common Semitic word for serpent is *hawwa*, which is from the same root as the word for life. Thus Karen Joines remarks that "the serpent cult is the fundamental expression of the desire, inherent in man, for immortality."[38] On the other hand though, the serpent is a figure of chaos, and especially represents the Babylonian chaotic sea-serpent Tiamat. For example, the Assyrian word for serpent, *ai-ub-ilu*, is from *aibu*, enemy, and means enemy of God. The god Honoru of Ugarit was seen as the antipole of the creator-god. He also was regarded as the originator of the forces of evil. The snake is clearly a demon, called a devourer, a common Ugaritic designation of monstrous demons.[39] In the ANE in general, Joines says, the serpent is a figure of chaos, evil and destruction.[40]

The conclusion is that in both Egypt and the wider ANE the serpent is not amoral but bimoral. In Spencer-Brown terms, the serpent is a creature who is totally self-referencing and compromised by paradoxical double-marking. In biblical language, the serpent has eaten of the tree of the knowledge of good and evil so that it knows good but has lost the capacity to do it.

He is a creature who had had several functions. As Lucifer, Leviathan had been a seraphim or cherubim who attended God's throne; reflected the glory of the Word; in some sense prepared the way for the Word; and perhaps had a purifying heavenly ministry. Pride destroyed all of these. This catastrophic event is captured by Jesus' words that he saw Satan fall from heaven (Luke 10:18). This descent is strongly implied by the serpent-seraphim's loss of flight, restriction to crawling, and return to the dust in Gen 3. Lucifer was transformed from his original light-bearing splendor into serpentine darkness. All of these themes are historicized through reference to astronomical events which in the Bible are portrayed via Venus, the sun, dawn, wisdom, and divine throne attendants. Lucifer had become God's adversary by aspiring to the throne of God. Creational law was broken and Lucifer became Leviathan the serpent who inhabits the lawless chaos.

Finally, we must ask the meaning of Leviathan for the doctrine of creation. The following remarks are intended as backdrop to a more detailed exploration of the relationship between natural law and the demonic in chapter 7.

36. Ibid., 38–45.
37. Joines, "Serpent in Gen 3," 9.
38. Ibid., 2–3.
39. Moor, "East of Eden," 107.
40. Joines, "Serpent in Gen 3," 8

A fundamental principle is that creational law is the actual spoken word of God which Leviathan could not annul. Scripture reads, "But I the Lord will speak the word that I speak, and it will be fulfilled. . . . I will speak the word and fulfil it, says the Lord God" (Ezek 12:25); "Long ago I learned from your decrees that you have established them forever" (Ps 119:152); "Heaven and earth will pass away but my words will not pass away" (Matt 24:35). However, Leviathan could resist the proper unfolding of law merely by being insubordinate within creation's self-organizing systems (SOSs). This is because even one disturbance (network noise) in an SOS can move the whole system outside its properly bounded behavior(s).[41]

The principle of system sensitivity to a single variable may be extrapolated to primal angelic life. Deep-level chaoplexic law is a necessary structural condition in creation to allow volitional choice since it permits non-repeating behavior which still is constrained by boundaries. When Lucifer chose to rebel, the lawful operations of these chaoplexic systems gradually became adulterated with Luciferian noise. As other angels also rebelled, the systems moved even faster toward chaos in both a mathematical and theological sense (see below). Eventually the disorder became general and formed the deep, over which God's Spirit blew in Genesis as a preamble to creation of the universe. In terms of Jesus' parable, an enemy came by night and sowed weeds in the good wheat so that the field yielded a mixed crop.[42]

II. CHAOS AND THE DEEP

The struggle between YHWH and Lucifer was for control of creation and resulted in chaos. But what is chaotic disorder?

Old Testament chaos derives from the Hebrew term *tohu wabohu*, without form and void (or waste and void in Jer 4:23). Other ANE languages carry meanings like desolation, emptiness, formlessness (Aramaic/Arabic), and heaviness, unconsciousness, and lifelessness (Syriac).[43] In the Septuagint (LXX) *tohu wabohu* was transposed as *chaos*, "a place of misty darkness before creation."[44] In the previous section, I stated that this chaos was a deep-level angelic disorder and lawlessness resulting from Lucifer's rebellion. The consequence was that demonically caused chaos preexisted formation of the universe.

This perspective differs from two other commonly held views of Gen 1:1–3. One opinion, labeled the gap theory, asserts that Gen 1:1 describes God's creation of a fully formed and perfect universe. Before v. 2 there's an angelic rebellion which led God to reduce creation to chaos and after a gap lasting perhaps eons, the present re-creation followed in v. 3. A second opinion says that chaos was an integral and necessary

41. Fradkov and Evans, "Control of Chaos."
42. Matt 13:1–8 and 13–23; Mark 4:1–9 and 13–20; Luke 8:4–15.
43. Delitzsch, *New Commentary on Genesis*, 78.
44. Maahs, "Chaos," 633.

building block of the original creation. We must evaluate these two opinions in light of the view for which I am arguing.

In the gap theory, creation in Genesis 1:1–3 is a restitution. Satan was the ruler of the preprimeval world in Gen 1:1 but because of his rebellion (Isa 14:12–17), sin entered creation. Consequently, God judged the world and reduced it to the chaotic status of Gen 1:2. Later God re-created according to 1:3–31, leaving a gap of unknown time between vv. 1 and 2. The gap theory appears as early as Simeon ben Jochai (early second century CE) and was popularized by Cyrus Scofield as an explanation for the challenge of geology: "[The gap] refers to the dateless past, and gives scope to all the geological ages."[45] Scofield cited Jer 4:23–26, Isa 24:1, and Isa 45:18 as support for a cataclysmic past for earth due to divine judgment.

There are several reasons why an eclectic cross section of scholars has maintained the restitution theory through the centuries. First, it's true that *tohu wabohu* could be construed as God's judgment laying waste to creation in texts like Jer 4:23 and Isa 34:11. Also, restitution theory gives a believable career summary for Satan, assuming Satan to be the figure in Isa 14:12, "How you have fallen from heaven, O Lucifer." Furthermore, a creation-destruction-re-creation progression offers a reason for chaos to be present in Gen 1:1–3.

However, the gap theory may be criticized on various counts. If Jer 4:23 and Isa 34:11 refer to God's historical judgments on Israel, there's no reason why the same phrase in the Genesis creation account ought to mean preprimeval judgment. The restitutional approach has also prompted scholarly debates over the grammatical and theological minutiae.[46] In Gen 1:1–3, for example, linguists doubt that the Hebrew word "and" may be translated as "and then" ("And then the earth was a formless void"). Fundamental theories ought not to rest on one word! Perhaps thinking along similar lines, Franz Delitzsch called the restitution theory a "theologumen," meaning that it's an opinion and not a doctrine.[47] Finally, restitutionalism turns God into a trial-and-error creator. There's no real logical distinction between Rabbi Simeon ben Jochai's series of creations and physicist G. R. F. Ellis' speculation that God may actually be limited and forced to experiment to find the right universe.[48]

A second standard interpretation of chaos defines it as the first stage in the creation of the universe.[49] To begin with, this interpretation is flatly contradicted by Isa 45:18, which explicitly denies that God created chaos. Since mathematical chaos is a definite creation, this prompts us to wonder, are there perhaps two different flavors of chaos, one created by God and one not? As we saw above, both biblical and other ANE sources use terms for chaos like misty darkness, formless waste, watery depths,

---

45. Waltke, "Creation Account," 136–38.
46. Waltke, *Creation and Chaos*, 20–21.
47. Delitzsch, *New Commentary on Genesis*, 79.
48. Ellis, "Theology of the Anthropic Principle," 392–94.
49. Simpson, *Genesis*, 468.

abyss, primeval darkness, the infinity, the nothingness, and the nowhere. Are these descriptors of apparent complete formlessness applicable to modern mathematical chaos? Here we must digress a moment into the cultural context of chaos theory.

Sets of information (systems) with many interacting input variables create a control point called an attractor. Over time, the system evolves toward this point regardless of the starting conditions of the system boundaries. Depending on the variables, the attractor may produce oscillations between rigid and unpredictable behaviors (chaos). In the latter case, there is still form; the system is deterministic although humanly unpredictable. To an ancient commentator who simply saw disorder at the core of creation, chaos would be the formless *tohu wabohu*. To a modern scientist who knows something about the structure of chaos, it would be mathematical although no more predictable. It's probable that this sort of culturally modified distinction is part of the issue in Genesis 1.

We can take this a step further. Although there are multiple types of bifurcations (splits) in chaotic systems, at this stage we're especially interested in two of them. On the one hand, bifurcations can result in constructive new attractors in the system.[50] In fact, just such a bifurcation process may have been employed to create the tree of life. The crucial precondition for such formative chaos is the injection of network noise or fluctuations (i.e., information) from an outside source. No one but God can provide noise from outside creation such that novelty inside creation results.

Conversely, systems can experience catastrophic splits which are destructive. If components reenter themselves along the lines of Spencer-Brown's and Varela's closed models, internal double-marking or paradox results which leads to systemic dead-ends. In fact, a catastrophic bifurcation can destroy the original attractor so that there's nothing to which to return.[51] The split is irreversible and this is what Leviathan's revolt produced. Consequently, in Genesis 1 the Spirit of God moved across this second kind of chaos, the *tohu wabohu* dead-end left in the wake of Leviathan's actions. Tohu wabohu could not be the substrate of the universe because it followed a new dead-end attractor.

Bruce Waltke's assessment is typical of theologians who wrestle with the problem of OT chaos. He acknowledges Isa 45:18 and its contention that God did not create the earth a chaos but formed it to be inhabited. Waltke adds, "God does not contend with a living hostile chaotic force but hovers over the primordial mass awaiting the appropriate time for history to begin. How can the chaos be hostile when it is not living but inanimate?" He continues, "Though not called good at first, it is called good later. We need not fear it. It is all part of His plan. According to His own sovereign purposes, however, in due time He has said that He will eliminate it from His organized universe altogether."[52]

---

50. Abraham, "Chaos, Bifurcations, & Self-Organization," 90.
51. Ibid., 90.
52. Waltke, *Creation and Chaos*, 27, 48, 52.

Here's a case where dogmatic premises paint us into a corner. The God-is-sovereign assumption holds that chaos begins as a not-good substrate, becomes part of God's plan, and then is obliterated. All of this is due to God. But as Jon Levenson reminds us, biblical chaos is more than not-good. It is, in fact, a "sinister force that, left to its own, would submerge the world and forestall the ordered reality we call creation."[53] To attribute this evil to God is to rehash the untenable demonic-in-YHWH theory;[54] but to allow chaos to somehow appear on the scene uninvited, uncreated, and unascribed to any creational entity is either impossible or Manichaean. All of these are equally objectionable and must be avoided.

Nor is chaos the logical device that Karl Barth's nothingness (*das nichtige*) makes it out to be. Barth sets chaos within enantiodromia, a construct derived from the Greek philosopher Heraclitus. Enantiodromia states that all phenomena need their opposites and tend toward them. Night requires day, cold demands hot, good offsets evil. Therefore according to Barth, enantiodromia means that God's creational "Yes" demanded that God at the same time have willed a "No"—a negative intention to not create.[55] For Barth, the nothingness of Gen 1:2 is that which God passed over, that which God "set behind him as chaos, not giving it existence or meaning." Nonetheless, it's still the place of the devil, demons, sin, evil, death as annihilator of life, guilt, calamity, and suffering.[56]

This road leads to a theological cul-de-sac. First, enantiodromia implies that God's sheer existence itself generates a negation (not-God), since God wills self-existence. Such a not-God would be Manichaean. Second, it puts Jesus in the curious situation of dying simply because God's positive decision to create a good universe automatically generated a necessary negative and evil offset, nothingness, or chaos. Third, it ignores Jesus' direct statement that he came to destroy Satan and his works (1 John 3:8).

In assessing Barth's approach to blending modern cosmology and biblical language, R. J. Russell repeats the charge that neoorthodox theology involves a basic contradiction. "[The Bible] is a book of the acts Hebrews believed God might have done and the words he might have said had he done and said them—but of course we recognize that he did not."[57] It's better that we dispense with Barth's enantiodromia and its importation of Greek philosophy into the theology of creation.

To summarize primordial chaos, we can confidently claim that it was not formed by God either as judgment of Lucifer or as a creational substrate. The hypothesis that best fits the empirical data is that chaos was caused by Lucifer and that it is the logical outcome of an irreversible system bifurcation. It therefore preexisted the universe as

---

53. Levenson, *Creation and the Persistence of Evil*, 15.
54. Boyd, *God at War*, 144–47.
55. Barth, *Church Dogmatics*, III, 3, 74, 351.
56. Ibid., 74, 291.
57. Russell, introduction to *Quantum Cosmology*, 7.

the sea which had to be rolled back by the breath of the Spirit of God in Gen 1:2. This is echoed by the later *Prayer of Manasseh* 3 which says that God "shackled the sea . . . [and] confined the deep and sealed it" by the power of his name.

Finally, we must consider the relationship between the terms chaos and the deep.

Immediately in Gen 1:2b the deep appears: "The earth was a formless void and darkness covered the face of the deep, while a wind from God swept over the face of the waters." In the ANE worldview the waters were the world-ocean on which earth rests. Consequently Genesis presupposes a layered structure with the deep at the core, then the land, and the lighter envelope of waters over the earth. Umberto Cassuto suggested a rephrasing which places the deep at the core, lighter waters floating to the top and darkness spreading over everything.[58] The whole formed a chaotic, "undifferentiated, unorganized, confused and lifeless agglomeration."

The deep is personified in a positive light in Gen 49:25 and Deut 33:13. In each case, it lies beneath and is a source of blessing.[59] However, virtually all other biblical personifications negatively portray the ocean or primeval sea as the realm of the serpent/dragon and of opposition to God. David Neiman lists several OT serpent monster titles: *Leviathan* (Isa 27:1; Ps 74:14), *Rahab* (Isa 51:9), *Tannin* (Isa 51:9; Ps 74:13; Job 7:12), *Nahash Bariah* ("slithering serpent," Isa 27:1) and *Nahash Aqalathon* ("twisting serpent," Isa 27:1).[60] In addition, the Babylonian *Enuma Elish* creation story uses the name *Tiamat* which is likely an equivalent term for *tehom* in Gen 1:2. By the NT, the LXX term abyss (*abyssos*) was the equivalent of *tehom* and was regarded as the home of demons. The implication is that the negative aspects of chaos are indistinguishable from the deep. In fact, Franz Delitzsch asserts this, noting that in the Babylonian myth, chaos is identical with the primeval deep (*apsu*, ocean) and "is the producing mother of all things."[61]

ANE theologians clearly were of one mind that regardless of these local name variations, chaos or the deep was essentially bad and was the home of evil supernatural creatures who are to be feared. As I mentioned in the prologue, an Akkadian seal cylinder from about the twenty-fourth century BCE depicts heroes destroying the seven-headed dragon Leviathan. Four of its heads are already dead, with the other three alive and fighting.[62] The Canaanite god Baal, which Israel reinstated with the Asherah poles on the high places, was conceived to be in a struggle with the Sea (*Yamm*) and Death (*Mot*), "Yamm embodies the chaos that threatens the life of the world. Mot is Death incarnate."[63]

---

58. Cassuto, *Commentary on the Book of Genesis*, 21–23.
59. Clifford, *Cosmic Mountain*, 17.
60. Neiman, "Gihon and Pishon," 326.
61. Delitzsch, *New Commentary on Genesis*, 79.
62. Gordon, "Leviathan," 4.
63. Smith, *Ugaritic Baal Cycle*, 59.

Demons also are pictured on bowls inscribed with protective curses. An Aramaic inscription reads, "I have gone [and] confronted the evil satans and mighty foes. I say to them: 'Woe unto you if you do anything to them.... I am enchanting you with the great spell of the Sea and with the spell of Leviathan the dragon.... I am bringing down upon you the decree of the heavens and the excommunication.'"[64] Such citations demonstrate how denizens of the deep were not mere cultural myths but were feared purveyors of disorder and death, and, as the Jews accused Jesus of doing (Matt 12:24), worthy of being called upon to control other demons. In short, chaos was conceived as the home of demonic beings whose influence extended into nature and human affairs.

I have shown that God's purposes were sabotaged by Leviathan. The question then becomes one of working out how God proceeded with creation of the universe in the face of this fifth columnist action.

III. CONFLICT IN CREATION

Given this backdrop of the fracturing of the eternal covenant we can begin to unravel the environment in which God created the physical realm. Some of the best-kept secrets in Christian theology are the stories of the creation of the universe. The idyllic and majestic cadences of the seven days in Genesis are normative for many people. However, when we examine the whole of the biblical witness, a startlingly different story emerges. It is a story marked by God's engagement with powers determined to thwart the purposes for which creation was designed. In the nineteenth century, Hermann Gunkel labeled this contest *chaoskampf*, "conflict with chaos." He noted how frequently God is portrayed in battle with various enemies who resist the completion of creation. The inference is inescapable; the cosmic foes have somehow brought confusion and malfunction into creational law and stand in opposition to God's purposes. We know the "by whom" part and now we seek to uncover "how."

In the ANE creation myths, a pre-creation monster blocks the primeval waters, a heroic god destroys the monster and releases the waters, and the god then regulates that which he has made. Bruce Waltke, citing Mary Wakeman, shows this battle sequence in Sumerian, Indian, and Akkadian myths. He notes that few "Christians are aware that at least in a dozen texts of the Old Testament, reference is made to the LORD's conflict with a dragon or sea monster.... Moreover, at least five of these texts are in a context pertaining to the creation of the world."[65] In a powerful passage, Herbert May also points to cosmic dualism:

> There is a suggestion of a cosmic dualism, for there continues throughout history the kind of conflict which is posited at creation when YHWH's wind blew over the watery abyss, or at the time when, in the distant past, YHWH slew the

---

64. Gordon, "Leviathan," 8.
65. Waltke, *Creation and Chaos*, 6–9.

dragon Leviathan or Rahab, or conquered the rivers and the sea. In this sense, YHWH's conquest over the enemies of Israel, whether at the Red Sea, or in the present, or at the beginning of the new age (cf. Isa 27:1) is a victory over cosmic evil and wickedness, over the demonic, or more properly the dragonic.[66]

May mentions Leviathan (Seven-Headed Serpent) and Rahab (Proud One). They are part of a now-familiar family of ANE monsters in scripture which also includes Tiamat (Deep), Yamm (Raging Seas), and Behemoth.[67] In Ugaritic, the god Mot (Death) speaks of Baal's battle with Yamm, "When you smote L[o]t[a]n the writhing serpent, [you] made an end of the slippery serpent, the tyrant with seven heads."[68] All of these sources show that creation was and is a battle-ground where God alone proves to be the warrior powerful enough to subdue the chaos/deep and its inhabitants, and to preserve order.[69] Various creation texts indicate that this conflict was present at the point when God was calling the physical universe into being. Several are found in Job,[70] one example being when Job asks how a mortal can be just before a God who orders the constellations into being and in so doing defeated Rahab and its helpers. Job acknowledges God, "who alone stretched out the heavens and trampled the waves of the Sea, who made the Bear and Orion, the Pleiades and the chambers of the south; . . . God will not turn back his anger; the helpers of Rahab bowed before him" (Job 9:8, 9, 13).

Similarly, Psalms and Isaiah link God's rulership of the raging sea/deep with an ability to bring creation into being.

> Who in the skies can be compared to the Lord? Who among the heavenly beings is like the Lord, a God feared in the council of the holy ones. . . . You rule the raging of the sea; when its waves rise, you still them. You crushed Rahab like a carcass; you scattered your enemies with your mighty arm. The heavens are yours, the earth also is yours; the world and all that is in it—you have founded them. (Ps 89:6–11)

> Yet God my King is from of old, working salvation in the earth. You divided the sea by your might; you broke the heads of the dragons in the waters. You crushed the heads of Leviathan. . . . Yours is the day, yours also the night; you established the luminaries and the sun. (Ps 74:12–16)

> Was it not you who cut Rahab in pieces, who pierced the dragon? Was it not you who dried up the sea, the waters of the great deep? (Isa 51:9b, 10a)

---

66. May, "Some Cosmic Connotations," 11–12.
67. Boyd, *God at War*, chs. 2 and 3.
68. Curtis, "Subjugation of the Waters," 246.
69. Waltke, *Creation and Chaos*, 5.
70. Day discusses 3:8; 7:12; 9:5–14; 26:5–14; 38:8–11. See Day, *God's Conflict*, 38–46.

Sigmund Mowinkel points out that the Psalms portray YHWH as victor over many levels of opposition. YHWH defeated the primeval dragon, the sea, and its monsters, as well as the other gods (who are terror-stricken) at creation. In forming Israel, God was victor over the heathen [Mowinkel's word], including Egypt, which becomes Rahab in Ps 87:4, and Canaan. This manifests especially in the Exodus and the Red Sea, identified as the primeval sea in Exod 15:5, 8.[71]

At this stage, we might as well clear away any misconceptions that dualistic theologies began with Persia and Zoroastrianism. The name Satan is not Persian; and further, Talmudic Babylonian incantation bowls used as magical defenses against demons show continuity with bowls from Knossos (Minoa)—not Persia—from two thousand years earlier. Cyrus Gordon stated, "Long before the rise of Zoroastrianism, dualism is attested to in the art of Mesopotamia and in the texts of Ugarit. Therefore we cannot attribute Jewish, Christian and Muslim dualistic trends to Iranian influence. Dualism is embedded in the Semitic world before there is any evidence of it in Iran."[72]

This dualistic conflict in creation presents a problem for interpreters who ignore the cosmic dimensions involved. An illustration of the difficulty is found in Rom 8:19–22 and its description of creation in bondage. William Hendriksen argues that God subjected the natural creation by pronouncing the curse on the ground.[73] C. E. B. Cranfield says God subjected the creation by denying it the opportunity to reach its potential as long as humans fail to contribute our part.[74] Joseph Fitzmyer disagrees with both, saying humans have subjected the creation to chaos and the ineffectiveness of something which doesn't attain its goal.[75] Douglas Moo agrees that human sin has caused creation's frustration at not realizing its potential. Conversely, he also thinks that God, being the only one with authority to do so, is the one who subjects creation.[76] Nowhere is there a hint that creation's bondage antedates humanity by eons and is rooted in the biblical and ANE serpent-data which I have been citing.

The confusion is a direct result of relocating the origins of primordial chaos within history. John Oswalt's comments on Rahab and the dragon in Isa 51:9–10 offer an excellent illustration of this shift. Oswalt puts the creation conflict texts into history on the assumption that a sovereign God can have no real opponent capable of initiating primordial evil. He first notes the parallelism between Rahab and the dragon on one hand, and *yamm* (sea) and the *tehom rabba* (great deep) on the other. Oswalt says, "The author is suggesting that either poetically or literally that YHWH's parting of the Red Sea was analogous to the defeat of the chaos monster."

---

71. Mowinkel, *Psalms in Israel's Worship*, 108.
72. Gordon, "Leviathan," 4–5.
73. Hendriksen, *Romans*, 269.
74. Cranfield, *Epistle to the Romans*, 413–14.
75. Fitzmyer, *Romans*, 507.
76. Moo, *Epistle to the Romans*, 515–16.

Then the shift appears. Because Oswalt assumes that the evil personified by the dragon results from human sin, Rahab must be a mere artistic device. Consequently these primordial chaos monsters actually are myths whose purpose is to show that YHWH conquers evil and chaos in history. The conflict metaphor in Isa 51 only teaches that YHWH fully controls all nature. This is a sovereignty which "was not won as a result of some 'do or die' cosmic battle."[77]

Brevard Childs' understanding of chaos is more balanced as evidenced in his discussion of Gog in Ezek 38. Childs sees both a historical and eschatological application to the text. "Gog has become the representative of the cosmic powers of the returned chaos which YHWH destroys in the latter days, powers which cannot be described as historical, though presented partly in historical dress."[78] Because Childs is using—perhaps unconsciously—a version of the Four Senses method here, he is better able to penetrate to deeper meanings. He is more in tune with the rabbinic commentators, who never questioned the supernatural character of Leviathan.[79]

What about Oswalt's proposition that evil and disorder are not inherent in cosmic stuff? He understandably wishes to avoid ending up in Jung's destination where God contains good and evil within himself and produces a similarly mixed created order. This would be aligning oneself with the demonic-in-YHWH theory. Middle knowledge says in response that God knew all possible creaturely choices, including evil ones, before speaking creational law. There must be potential for genuine choice and hence there is true potential within the cosmos for rebelling against creational law. There can be no alternative. This does not mean that creation is evil, nor that God is the author of angelic evil, nor that God was the cause of evil in Eden by giving Adam and Eve two trees from which to choose. Much as we might find it distasteful, for God to extend choice means the possibility of evil. The necessity for choice really is a case where one cannot be half-pregnant!

IV. SUMMARY

Our argument leads to three sets of observations.

First, death has a conceptual core which is captured by several interrelated words. In this chapter I have analyzed death in terms of chaoplexic processes and ANE chaos and the deep. Madeleine L'Engle has contemporized these terms with her use of un-Naming, a dissolution into nothingness. In her novel *The Wind in the Door*, six-year-old Charles Wallace Murry is dying from a mysterious attack on his mitochondria, the cells' energy factories. It transpires that the villains are the *Echthroi*,[80] who kill not only mitochondria and their human hosts, but obliterate stars in the cosmos. (*Echthroi*,

---

77. Oswalt, "Myth of the Dragon," 164–65.
78. Childs, "Enemy from the North," 169.
79. Jacobs, "Elements of Near-Eastern Mythology," 1–11.
80. Foerster, "*Echthrós* [hostile]," 285–86.

singular *echthros*, is a Greek word which in the LXX means "enemies of righteousness" or "enemies of God." In the NT it stands for personal enemies, all forces hostile to God, and in Matt 13:39 and Luke 10:19, specifically the devil.) The cherubim Proginoskes tries to explain the *Echthroi* to Charles' sister Meg, "I think your mythology would call them fallen angels. War and hate are their business, and one of their chief weapons is un-Naming—making people not know who they are.... There is war in heaven and we need all the help we can get. The Echthroi are spreading throughout the universe."[81]

To chaos, the deep, and un-Naming we may tack on Spencer-Brown's concept of double-marking. This returns us explicitly into the realm of chaoplexic processes and especially the breakdown of the creational covenant as a sustainable network relationship. In covenant terms, Spencer-Brown's logical first distinction was not performed by drawing a boundary between a human observer and his/her environment but between God the creator and creation. In due course Leviathan replaced the covenant relationship which sustained him with a self-referential process which could only produce internal paradox. Formless waste became a literal description of how he misused self-organizing systems to initiate reprogramming in the automaton. The ground-level rules continued working but their feedback input from God was compromised. The lawful structures didn't lose their fundamental design but Leviathan tweaked their operation and threw himself and the system into formlessness. This is precisely what we saw in the Egyptian idea of *ma'at*. Sentient creatures who fail to perform their covenant obligations fall into the hands of Yamm, king of death, and become lost, fragmented, and disordered.

The upshot is that Egypt's fragmenting *ma'at*, the Bible's *tohu wabohu* (chaos) and *tehom* (the deep), Spencer Brown's double-marking, and L'Engle's un-Naming are different descriptions of one and the same thing, death.

Second, death as it really is denies all theories that the universe operates as a continuous life-death-life loop of self re-creation. The idea is ancient but Francisco Varela has given it a modern form. Using Spencer-Brown's laws of form he hypothesized that life is a self-referencing, self-perpetuating closed process which he called autopoiesis. Even on its own terms, though, autopoiesis fails. Critics note that this theory really deals with the organization of existing systems and is silent about the underlying structures which create them.[82]

We saw in chapter 2 that on quite other grounds, eternal or self-creating universes simply don't fly. To those earlier arguments we now add the principle that death is not the prelude to a new formative phase but a dead end. The uroborus is not joined head-to-tail but its ends dangle ephemerally in a philosophical nowhere. We are forced to conclude that belief in an eternal structure which expresses itself in an endless formation-dissolution-formation cycle is simply fantastical.

---

81. L'Engle, *Wind in the Door*, 97–98.
82. Goldstein, "Construction of Emergent Order," 302.

Finally, although cosmic history is unidirectional and God is creator, death blocked God's work of creating the universe. Assuming that Karl Svozil is right that an automaton-based creation might be reprogrammable, then when God's spirit blew over the *tohu wabohu* in Gen 1:2 the situation was doubly desperate. As I showed above, the formless waste, far from being the primordial stuff of creation, was the detritus of Lucifer's revolt. This blocked the two key divine goals: that of creating the universe as a dynamic system whose chaoplexic laws produce equilibrium;[83] and that of creating the universe as a home for immortal human life. From a structural point of view, the general disorder caused by Leviathan had forced the pre-universe system into a new irreversible basin of operation. No laws were changed but their arena of activity was reconfigured through the addition of serpentine noise. Therefore, the ensemble of potential parameters available to God for use in our universe would have been limited by Leviathan's pre-universe deviation.

Even though I have argued that multiverse cosmology is unfounded, its use of probability does illustrate the effect of parameter shift. Multiverse theorists calculate the likelihood of our universe by assuming that all potential universes actually exist, estimating the probability of ours, and finally expressing the results as a wave function.[84] Even a slight parameter shift will yield a very different universe. Parameter shift can be easily illustrated with human mortality. It's been suggested that one reason we die is because cells have a built-in counter that puts a ceiling on replications.[85] Make that ceiling number limitless as in cancer and you have human immortals.

So, it's imperative for us to grasp the radical nature of death. It leads nowhere and has no potential for renewal or restoration within it. In spite of this, physical eschatology postulates that humans could survive through local outposts of re-creation as the universe at large dies,[86] or through development of virtual software human personalities.[87] The former is acknowledged to be only a temporary oasis pending absolute heat death, while the latter is technological utopianism which is still dependent on a physical substratum. Either scenario reads like the science fiction it is. It's therefore perplexing to encounter theologies which denigrate the biblical hope of a new creation that trumps the death card.[88]

For its part, the neognostic New Age myth is that we are even now in a macrohistorical transition from the Age of Pisces to the Age of Aquarius. Wouter Hanegraaff points out that few New Agers speak about what comes after Aquarius in the Age of

---

83. Mbonye, "Cosmology with Interacting Dark Energy," 117–34.
84. Hartle and Hawking, "Wave Function of the Universe," 2960–75.
85. Aviv et al., "Growth, Telomere Dynamics," 830.
86. Schwartz, "Modern Scientific Theories," 475n7, citing Peters, "Eschatology in Light of Contemporary Science."
87. Tipler, *Physics of Immortality*, 221–22.
88. Schwartz, "Modern Scientific Theories," 475n7, citing Peters.

Capricorn[89]—let alone after the full 26,400-year cycle—as the zodiac moves to its next astronomical region. Since even this macrohistory is irrelevant in a dead universe, the usual solution is to transcend death either through reincarnation (see ch. 11) or by an evolutionary transition to a spiritual creation. Teilhard is the preeminent prophet of such evolutionary completion. His scheme of cosmic history runs from the cosmosphere, via biosphere and noosphere, to the Christosphere. In simple language, this refers to the sequential appearances of the universe, life, human culture, and panentheistic union with God. The union is Teilhard's famous Omega point which represents a final joining of matured humans and descended divinity.[90]

In this summary I will raise only a single, basic objection to neognosticism's view of death. Obviously anyone can believe anything they want, but, as we have seen in our discussion of grounding, for that belief to be valid it must be rooted in creation as it really is. What, then, is the evidence in creation that, to use Barbara Marx Hubbard's words, our "mammalian bodies will soon perish"[91] as we undergo the planetization of spirit? What is the evidence for Teilhard's assertion that the evolutionary ascent will result in a "still unnamed Thing which the gradual combination of individuals, peoples and races will bring into existence, [which] must needs be *supra-physical*?" Or that the stuff of the universe will complete its evolution by becoming "a harmonised collectivity of consciousnesses equivalent to a sort of super-consciousness"?[92]

I think that the answer to both Marx Hubbard and Teilhard is "nil." There's no evidence of a coming post-physical planetization let alone an Omega point. Nonetheless, such proposals raise fundamental issues about what it means to be human. Consequently we take up the core questions of human personality in chapter 4.

---

89. Hanegraaff, *New Age Religion*, 102.
90. Chardin, *Future of Man*, 122–23.
91. Hubbard, *Revelation: Our Crisis is a Birth*, 69.
92. Chardin, *Phenomenon of Man*, 275–76.

4

THE SIXTH DAY

IMAGINE THAT SOMETIME IN the twenty-first century researchers manage to create humanzees. In the best science-fiction tradition of H. G. Wells, these genetically engineered human-chimpanzee chimeras are speech-empowered and learning-enhanced. This qualifies them to be psychiatric drug trial subjects, coal miners, and caregivers for patients with lethal communicable diseases. Now, the question I want to ask here has nothing to do with the technological feasibility of hybrids or the ethical propriety of using humanzees in high-risk jobs, as interesting as these issues are. The more fundamental question turns on what it means to be human.

Contemporary questions about human identity flow from two interlocking issues.

The primary question is whether humans are more than organic matter, and if so, in what way. Comments from Stanford law professor and ethicist Henry Greely flag this. He warned that the use of human brain cells in an animal produces "a nontrivial risk of conferring some significant aspects of humanity" on the animal. Greely's concern was illustrated by cross-species cell and organ transplant experiments. For instance, quail neural cells were transplanted into chick brains. The resulting chickens exhibited vocal trills and head bobs unique to quails,[1] thus showing that the mind control codes moved over along with the organic cells. The point is, of course, that a mind, whether animal or human, is more than a physical epiphenomenon or emergent property.

Therefore, if we wish to argue that personhood is more than organic matter we must give an account of what that more is. In other words, what does it mean to be a chimpanzee or a human or, as Thomas Nagel so famously put it, a bat.[2]

---

1. Weiss, "Of Mice, Men and In-Between."
2. Nagel, "What Is It Like to Be a Bat?," 435–50.

The second issue is methodology. Nagel writes elsewhere that no current concepts of either consciousness or the brain show how they are related. Therefore a radical and scientifically unprecedented conceptual breakthrough is needed to reveal the underlying necessary connection between mental and physical concepts.[3] Since science has failed so far to describe mind, spirit, and their interrelationship, Nagel argues that we can settle for nothing less than a brand new conceptualization and a new methodology to break the impasse.

The idea of yet-unknown deep-level rule-sets in creation is not a novel idea. More than one researcher says that new organizing principles or laws are needed, since the present ones are inadequate. Of the many who assert this,[4] the following few examples give the lay of the land. John Polkinghorne thinks there may be holistic laws of nature driving the evolution of complexity.[5] To the question, how can consciousness be added to the already closed laws of physics, Henry Stapp, a retired but still active staff member at the Lawrence Berkeley Laboratory, answers, "It can't." "Nothing efficacious could be added if the laws were already complete! But the quantum laws are grossly incomplete before consciousness, or some stand-in for consciousness, is added."[6] In an especially interesting opinion because of *psi* data's relevance to demonic phenomena, Charles Tart hypothesizes a new class of law to account for *psi* events.[7] Perhaps the most acerbic critique of the present state of personality research comes from John McCrone. He writes that "there is almost no cohesion to the mind sciences and certainly no track record of solid, cumulative progress. Instead of a Standard Model for the mind, there is a theoretical vacuum, a conceptual void filled only by stale philosophical arguments and creaking computer metaphors."[8] McCrone's diagnosis is particularly apt in light of our efforts to formulate a new model of mind.

I will fill this conceptual void by arguing that human personality is a tripartite composition of body, mind, and spirit. These are multileveled manifestations of a series of rule-sets lodged in the automaton's logic nodes. The operations include algorithmic rule-sets, nonlinearity, neural networks, self-organizing systems, and covenant with God. Such a trail will take us throughout the realms of psychology, neurology, cultural anthropology, and theology. We begin with the basic issue of how our intellectual mind-sets frame our understanding of human consciousness.

---

3. Nagel, "Psychophysical Nexus," 208.
4. See a listing in Thaxton et al., *Mystery of Life's Origin*, 152.
5. Polkinghorne, "Theological Notions of Creation," 236.
6. Stapp, "Hard Problem," 23.
7. Tart, "Transpersonal Realities or Neurophysiological Illusions."
8. McCrone, "Theory Vacuum."

THE SIXTH DAY

I. APPROACHES TO CONSCIOUSNESS

Western thought regards consciousness as a central feature of human personality. Consciousness refers to the capacity for psychological identity, mindness, and selfhood. Helen Keller's description of her preconscious state helps us to define what these terms mean: "I did not know that I am. I lived in a world that was a no-world. I cannot hope to describe adequately that unconscious, yet conscious time of nothingness. I did not know that I knew aught, or that I lived or acted or desired. I had neither will nor intellect."[9]

Human self-reflection, including awareness of time—having eternity in our heart (Eccl 3:11 AV)—has been called the hard problem[10] of modern psychology, neurology, and philosophy. The challenge is to explain how it is that subjective qualities like self-awareness and time can be experienced by creatures composed of dust. We can begin to appreciate the scope of the problem as we consider how a memory frame is created.

In memory formation, interconnected neurons process and distribute incoming and outgoing electrochemical signals at varying strengths. At the beginning, these strengths are randomized so that they initially scramble any incoming signal and put out noise. However, their controlling rules have the capacity to modify the connection strengths through experience. Strong connections are strengthened and those carrying weaker or infrequent signals are themselves weakened. Eventually the underlying neural network control logic memorizes the incoming pattern as a specific distribution of varying signal strengths.[11] This data is expressed mathematically in a memory template or frame.

When a memory is generated or recalled, neurons all over the brain in the various physical and emotional sensory areas fire simultaneously like Christmas tree lights.[12] The metaphor may be refined even more to say that a memory template looks like multidimensional science fiction virtual reality—think the *Star Trek* holodeck here—rather than a two-dimensional still photo. The end result is that neurons, association areas, local and distant interrelated hierarchies, and underlying rules all interact to create a mathematical memory object every 100^{-300} msec.[13] Somehow, consciousness results as these math objects are interpreted as a consecutive stream experience.

Well and good. However, this explanation resolves nothing. Such a model fails to explain how electrochemical processes and their allied math objects or forms generate conscious experience, mind, and spirit. As we shall see, materialism, physicalism

---

9. Keller, *World I Live In*, 142–43.
10. Rosenberg, "Rethinking Nature," 76.
11. Varela et al., "Brainweb," 235–36.
12. Blakeslee, "Christmas Tree in Your Brain."
13. Varela et al., "Brainweb," 237.

(both emergent and panpsychic), and trichotomism take very different paths in answering this question.

Materialist views of consciousness are thoroughly grounded in brain physiology. Indeed, there's no doubt that the brain is a marvel of engineering. Considered as a bodily organ, an adult brain weighing about three pounds (roughly 2 percent of body weight), consumes 20 to 30 percent of the body's energy. The brain's grey matter consists of some 100 billion densely packed bodies of neurons. The total of these neurons' synaptic connections is greater than the number of stars in the universe.[14] In addition, the neurons' capacity for varying their signal strength means that their effective number inflates to an incredible $10^{11(10)}$ "individuals."[15] Neural cell bodies are surrounded by branches called dendrites which enable short-distance communication with other neurons. Axons resemble long wires and are used in longer-distance neural communication. They make up about 90 percent of the cell's volume. Fetal brain cell formation is controlled by DNA coding whose blueprint is itself shaped and modified by the person's life experiences. Since DNA is its ultimate authority, materialism remains rather quiet about the metaprogram which runs deep underneath and controls DNA expression.[16]

All of the preceding factoids have been determined by scientific research procedures.

However, to take the next step and regard consciousness research as real science causes neurology to tread warily. John Searle writes, "A legitimate brain science can study the micro anatomy of the Purkinje cell, or attempt to discover new neurotransmitters, but consciousness seems too airy-fairy and touchy-feely to be a real scientific subject."[17] This reflects the assumption that human consciousness is an epiphenomenon (by-product) of neural activity. Searle continues, "In the end I think that is the right way to think of the problem of consciousness—it is a biological problem like any other, because consciousness is a biological phenomenon in exactly the same sense as digestion, growth, or photosynthesis."[18] Nancy Andreason, past editor of the *American Journal of Psychiatry*, agrees: "The mind is the expression of the activity of the brain" and these are separable for analysis but not in actuality.[19] That is, brain equals mind. When a materialist says, "I know that I know," she simply means that self-awareness, memories, and the ability to think abstractly are all just electrochemical transfers along neural pathways.

Therefore, if we ask how we see the color red, the materialist can only focus on the visual association process in the brain. As with the brain generally, the truly awesome

14. Amen, *Healing the Hardware of the Soul*, 19.
15. Mainzer, *Thinking in Complexity*, 166.
16. Dewar, *Second Tree*, 68.
17. Searle, "Consciousness," 558.
18. Ibid., 559.
19. Andreason, "Linking Mind and Brain," 1586.

magnitude of this visual process leaves even the most jaundiced observer speechless. In this regard, it's worth repeating a quote from chapter 2 that typical object recognition computation demands about 100 trillion multiplications per eye per second.[20] During the sequence, the retina receives external radiation which follow pathways, creating a visual field. For the color red, cones in the retina are sensitive to radiation of 590 nanometer wavelength (one-billionth of a meter) and from then on the image is converted to electrical signals which the brain processes. Although the optic nerve sends signals which end up in the visual cortex and causes neurons to fire, in the end no one has any idea how the brain sees the retina's picture. Signals are perceived as the color red but since the brain cannot see a picture or color, the conundrum is, why is red, red? According to contrarian Nobel neuroscientist John Eccles:

> All you get out of all this is just cells responding specifically to lines or angles or . . . geometrical shapes . . . you may think you can see color, but there's no color in the world, only wavelengths. The color is created, not in my brain, but in my mind . . . there's no color until the message gets through to the mind, only just wavelengths and firings of cells in the brain. Nowhere are there neurons which reconstitute the picture.[21]

With these words, Eccles forces the materialist to explain how electrochemical signals are perceived subjectively as red, or sharp, or loud, or sweet. As I noted earlier, Michael Polyani—yet another Nobel laureate—summed up the issue with the pungent comment, "Acids don't think."[22] We may impute to Eccles an equally biting comment, that neuronal discharges don't see red! In the end, materialism actually has no explanation for consciousness.

The second model, physicalism, has two main camps, emergentism and panpsychism.[23]

In the first case, theoreticians argue that there really is a human mind but it is an emergent property of physical processes. Nancey Murphy is a current advocate of this stance. She described the matter-to-mind process this way:

> The version of physicalism I espouse argues that, just as life appears as a result of complex organization, so too sentience and consciousness appear as nonreducible products of biological organization. To conceive of how it is possible to get "mind" out of matter one needs to appreciate not only the development from inorganic to organic, but also from mere homeostasis, through goal-directedness, information processing, goal evaluation, consciousness, and sociality to self-consciousness.[24]

---

20. Kurzweil, *Age of Intelligent Machines*, 227.
21. Eccles, "Human Person," 254–55.
22. Polyani, *Personal Knowledge*, 390.
23. Seager and Allen-Hermanson, "Panpsychism."
24. Murphy, "Scientific Perspectives," 92.

Murphy is merely repeating in her own words what earlier philosophers first asserted. Pioneer emergentist Samuel Alexander wrote, "Life is at once a physico-chemical complex... [but it] is not merely physical and chemical... it emerges therefrom, and it... constitutes its possessor a new order of existent with its special laws of behaviour.... It admits no explanation."[25]

Alexander's last clause highlights emergent philosophy's fundamentally mystical nature. For emergent processes to create mind novelty out of physico-chemical interactions there must be an internal qualitative change from matter to more-than-matter. Theoreticians address this demand by postulating a transition to a higher level of reality complete with self-evolved controlling laws. Roger Sperry, a pioneer in split-brain neurology, is typical of those who hold that "new forces and new laws of the universe emerge at higher levels."[26] Therefore emergence answers the question "What is consciousness?" by postulating that biological reality—which means electrochemical processes—jumps to a new nonphysical mind level. This is exactly what Teilhard asserted.

Is emergence a reliable road map to consciousness?

Modern philosophy labels our internal experiences of pain, color, sound, and so forth as qualia (Lat. *qualis*, "what kind of"). To return to the problem of seeing red, the visual association area's discharges are transduced (converted) into neural network equations. The mind is coded to interpret the resulting mathematical logic space objects. In formal terms, these objects have a syntactic (logical) and semantic (meaning) aspect expressed by ascending hierarchies of the controlling laws.

This description can be illustrated by qualia's feedback loop systems. At the sensory stage, input data (upward causation) have been shown experimentally to follow a mathematical formulation known as Fechner's law.[27] The output side of the qualia-consciousness system may be tracked by the mind's downward causation of body functions (see below). So biblical realism answers the question "Why is red, red?" by invoking a rule-centered translation between syntactic and semantic dimensions. The crucial aspect in all of this is that the integrated upward and downward causations require input from feed-forward and feed-backward network processes which instantiate fundamental algorithms.

In section 2 I will examine upward and downward causation more fully but for the moment, let's use Klaus Mainzer's conception of consciousness law as a starting-point for a trichotomic model. Although he didn't make his remarks in the context of body/mind/spirit personhood, some essential elements of such a paradigm are present. He writes, "In the framework of complex systems the emergence of consciousness is no epiphenomenon [by-product] of evolution. It is a lawful occurrence of global states according to the dynamics of complex systems which produce macroscopic

---

25. Alexander, *Space, Time, and Deity*, 46–47.
26. Sperry, "Changed Concepts of Brain and Consciousness," 47.
27. Norwich and Wong, "Unification of Psychophysical Phenomena," 929–40.

order patterns by microscopic interactions of their elements if certain critical conditions are satisfied."[28]

Mainzer's emphasis on lawful global states, dynamics, and order patterns is on target but what are the "certain critical conditions" which must be satisfied?

First, without noise (information) from outside the system, the feedback loops in complex systems lead to illogic and inconsistency as outlined in Gödel's self-reference theorems. Evolutionary apologists themselves acknowledge the crucial nature of this point, "[Gödel] reveals how any rule-bound system has blind spots because it is unable to step outside of a predefined framework."[29] All closed emergent systems are blind, restricted, and predestined to paradox.

Second, creation both reveals and is dependent on a true—and not merely apparent—teleological arrow of development. In the words of Einstein's famous dictum, God did not throw dice when planning the universe. Purpose does not emerge from within the dynamic system but is assigned by God. Systems labeled emergent are actually following their inbuilt codes.

The third point is directly related and rests on the multiple streams of evidence that the universe is a complex system of rule-driven computation reliant on an outside instructional engine. This engine may be relabeled as God's intelligent agency.

Together these factors mean that Mainzer's order patterns originate in divinely conferred laws. Consequently, human personhood is a function of lawful substructures. Otherwise, without these lawful mind and spirit substructures the human body is just a lump of purposeless organic material. Now, in order for these substructures to become mind and spirit, they must be actuated or instantiated by environmental relationships. In this process, the brain functions as a transducer by which external environmental sensory data are converted into the mathematical language of mind. Then this higher-dimensional mathematical mind language is interpreted as conscious experience, a process which I examine further in chapter 8. Finally, the mind transduces data between the body and spirit.

So much for emergent consciousness.

Panpsychism takes us into mystical territory as well with its claim that spirit is inherent in matter as opposite sides of the same coin.[30] The doctrine is ancient; Plato held that "we must declare that this Cosmos has verily come into existence as a Living Creature endowed with soul and reason owing to the providence of God. But we shall affirm that the Cosmos, more than aught else, resembles most closely that Living Creature of which all other living creatures, severally and generically, are portions."[31] Throughout history many prominent people have espoused panpsychism but we're especially interested in two twentieth-century figures.

28. Mainzer, *Thinking in Complexity*, 173.
29. Edis, "Darwin in Mind," 38.
30. Van Cleve, "Mind-Dust or Magic?," 215–26.
31. Plato, "Timaeus," sec. 30b, 30c.

Teilhard de Chardin invoked panpsychism to explain each jump in novelty in the tree of life. He labeled the human transition into consciousness as the hominization of humans. "Hominization can be accepted in the first place as the individual and instantaneous leap from instinct to thought, the progressive phyletic spiritualisation in human civilisation of all forces contained in the animal world."[32] By hominization of humans, Teilhard meant the abrupt appearance of consciousness where access to thought involved a threshold which was crossed in one leap.

According to Teilhard, "*Spiritual perfection (or conscious 'centricity') and material synthesis (or complexity) are but the two aspects or connected parts of one and the same phenomenon.*" He stated further, "We shall assume that, essentially, all energy is psychic in nature."[33] Elsewhere he wrote that all "corpuscles" (matter) in the universe are conscious depending only on their relative complexity for the degree of consciousness.[34] The duality of matter and spirit meant that matter doesn't acquire new properties but merely expresses its obverse creational character as spirit.

The second key modern prophet of panpsychism was Jung. He coined the term "psychoid" to point to the same inherent spirit-matter dualism. Jung used psychoid as a way to define archetypes as essentially transcendental junctions, "where psychic processes and their physical substrate touch." For Jung, synchronous phenomena are prime examples of psychoid duality, since they are real and yet not subject to scientific validation.[35] This paradox stirred Jung and Nobel physicist Wolfgang Pauli into discussions of the psychoid nature of spirit and matter. Pauli looked for a standard language which could "describe an invisible, potential form of reality that is only indirectly inferable through its effects."[36] (With these words Pauli unwittingly offered a bang-on definition of demonic *psi-kappa*!)

At the end of the day, both emergence and panpsychism lead to the conclusion that matter has an inherent capacity for consciousness. Most objective critics would recognize this is a classic instance of circular reasoning: because we're conscious creatures though composed of matter, matter therefore has inherent consciousness.

II. MIND, CONSCIOUSNESS, AND BIDIRECTIONAL CAUSATION

In chapter 2 I showed that downward causation in dynamic systems relies on externally imposed rule-sets. In the mind-brain duality, downward causation is one-half of a network in which upward causation is the offsetting component. Another way of defining this system is in terms of input and feedback loops. Such systems are essential in understanding and modeling mind structures and processes and are, in fact, at the

---

32. Chardin, *Phenomenon of Man*, 189–200; quote on 200.
33. Ibid., 66, 70, italics original.
34. Chardin, *Future of Man*, 131.
35. Jung, *Letters 2: 1951–1961*, 22n5.
36. Jung, *Atom and Archetype*, 81–82.

core of the human mind-brain duality. In this section I will provide an overview of how this dynamic system works, while chapter 8 will describe the mind itself in more detail. In the ensuing remarks, I have chosen child isolation to illustrate bottom-up environmental inputs. Top-down feedback processes are most clearly seen in various psychosomatic functions which I consider later.

The following case studies show three types of child isolation. Victor, a feral child grew up in the wild. Helen Keller was isolated by becoming deaf and blind at a young age. Genie's isolation from human contact was due to physical confinement. In each of these cases, there was isolation from people at the critical stages of childhood and adolescence. For each child, this isolation stunted and prevented normal human mental, emotional, and spiritual development.

Victor, a boy about twelve years old, was captured near Aveyron, France, in January 1812. He moved mostly on all fours; there were scars and burns on much of his body; he was insensitive to hot and cold; he was mute, being only able to make sounds when provoked but he couldn't communicate using them. On the other hand, he had learned to cook potatoes that he had stolen during forays from the forest. When he was found, he was brought to the Institute National des Sourds-Muets in Paris where the scientists named him Victor.[37] Modern-day psychologist Harlan Lane picks up the story. "Victor walked into the middle of a raging debate. His timing was incredible. The question was, what makes us human? What separates man from the beasts?" In a TV interview done at the Institute, Lane continues:

> We're at the National Institute for the Deaf, and it happened right here.... Sicard [the director] comes out, and what does he see? Not a nice little bourgeois deaf kid in the school uniform, his new pupil, but a raging, spitting, snarling, filthy savage, defecating where he is, urinating where he is, biting, covered with scars, long hair, wadded, yellow teeth, long fingernails, a savage. Sicard had never seen anything like that in his life.[38]

About the most that Victor's doctor, twenty-six-year-old Jean-Marc Itard, could do was to get Victor to acquire a few word associations. For example, he learned to bring milk when he was shown wooden letters spelling out *lait*.

Helen Keller was rendered blind and deaf by fever in her eighteenth month. She lost the words she knew (perhaps a dozen) and added about the same number of gestures. Around the ages five to six years old, her family saw her becoming distant, wild, and stubborn. In speaking of this period, Keller later testified that "she was a shadowy 'phantom,' a 'no-one.'"[39]

> Phantom did not seek a solution for her chaos because she knew not what it was. Nor did she seek death because she had no conception of it. All she

---

37. Leiber, "Nature's Experiments," 327.
38. PBS, "Secret of the Wild Child."
39. Shattuck, "Afterword: A Mind of One's Own," 452.

touched was a blur without wonder or anticipation, curiosity or conscience. Nothing was part of anything, and there blazed up in her frequent, fierce anger which I remember not by the emotion but by a tactual memory of a kick or blow she dealt to the object of that anger. In the same way I remember tears rolling down her cheeks but not the grief. There were no words for that emotion or any other, and consequently they did not register.[40]

Then there's Genie, whose mentally challenged mother brought her to social agencies on November 4, 1970. Then thirteen years old, Genie had been locked up by her father in a back room in straitjackets since she was twenty months old. Genie had a strange bunny walk and other almost inhuman characteristics like constant spitting, sniffing, and clawing. She weighed fifty pounds, was fifty-four inches tall, was incontinent, couldn't chew solid food, could hardly swallow, couldn't focus her eyes beyond twelve feet, and some accounts said she couldn't cry.[41] Genie could understand less than two dozen words and the only ones she could say were "stopit," "nomore," and two shorter negatives. Though during the first year in special care she acquired scores of words, she plateaued after that and failed to acquire grammar.

These stories lead to several conclusions.

First, interaction with the human environment is absolutely crucial for the brain/mind duality to develop self-awareness. The brain and mind function as a reciprocal system and if one component fails the other cannot function properly. Our examples show two failures and one success, with the critical factor being the child's age when helpers intervened. In fact, isolated children confirm in spades the role of critical periods and activity-dependent learning[42] for which David Hubbel and Torsten Wiesel won the Nobel Prize for their work on the developing visual cortex.

Second, we see that timing is crucial, especially for language acquisition. In spite of intense efforts by Itard, Victor never really learned to speak. Genie was also past the critical stage for language acquisition when found. Eventually she was institutionalized and became silent, depressed, and withdrawn. Neurological tests showed that the language ability she had was in her right hemisphere and that substantial portions of the left seemed to be shut down. The simplest theory was that she didn't acquire language before the critical age of puberty. "In some ways, she resembled adults with extensive left brain stroke damage, particularly Broca's area, who talk like telegrams . . . though Genie lacked their sense of self and personal history."[43]

Likewise, Keller says that prior to language she was a phantom "without wonder or anticipation, curiosity or conscience. . . . I shall never forget the surprise and delight I felt when I uttered my first connected sentence, 'It is warm.' My soul, conscious of

---

40. Keller, *Teacher: Anne Sullivan Macy*, 42.
41. Leiber, "Nature's Experiments," 328.
42. Andreason, *Brave New Brain*, 47.
43. Leiber, "Nature's Experiments, Society's Closures," 329.

new strength, came out of bondage."[44] As we saw previously, Keller referred to her pre-vocabulary self as the "Phantom." Next, until she acquired sentence structure, she was "Helen"; and with full-fledged language, she became "I."[45] The progression in pronouns is striking: it, she, I. It's worth giving a fuller version of the earlier Keller quote concerning her complete lack of soulness,

> Before my teacher came to me, I did not know that I am. I lived in a world that was a no-world. I cannot hope to describe adequately that unconscious, yet conscious time of nothingness. I did not know that I knew aught, or that I lived or acted or desired. I had neither will nor intellect. I was carried along to objects and acts by a certain natural impetus. . . . I can remember all this, not because I knew that it was so, but because I have tactual memory. It enables me to remember that I never contracted my forehead in the act of thinking. . . . I also recall tactually the fact that never in a start of the body or a heart-beat did I feel that I loved or cared for anything. My inner life, then, was a blank without past, present, or future, without hope or anticipation, without wonder or joy or faith. My dormant being had no idea of God or immortality, no fear of death.[46]

In the Keller quotations, words of voidness leap out at us: "Nothing was part of anything," "no-world," "nothingness," "neither will nor intellect," "inner life . . . a blank." The generation of mind self-awareness demanded environmental input at the critical time. The brain/mind duo go through no self-organizing phase changes by themselves but require outside informational input.

Third, the human spirit is dependent on the personality growth supplied by environmental inputs and language acquisition. Keller's testimony supports the argument that language is a prerequisite for spiritual maturity. She lacked all sense of eternity in her heart—God, immortality, fear or awareness of death, time past, and time future—until language acquisition. The evidence implies that the human spirit is not an eternal, conscious entity parachuted from heaven into the newly conceived fetus. Rather the spirit is a lawful framework which when suitably prompted has the ability to become. In the next section I will develop this view of the human spirit in greater detail.

So much for the bottom-up input loop of the network. What do we find when we consider top-down feedback, otherwise known in the brain-mind system as psychosomatic functioning?

To begin with, pure mental activity (ideation) produces express, measurable neural responses. P. E. Roland and colleagues showed that regional brain blood flow increases 20 percent in the supplementary motor area and nowhere else while a subject

---

44. Keller, *Story of My Life*, 53.
45. Leiber, "Nature's Experiments, Society's Closures," 335.
46. Keller, *World I Live In*, 142–43.

carried out a learned motor task mentally but not physically.[47][48] The mental intention activated an immense number of neurons which would have been essential to cause the desired movement. L. Deecke and H. H. Kornhuber confirm the supplementary motor area as the site of strong activation by mental intention.[49] Along the same lines, positron emission tomography scans demonstrate widespread patchy activity in the neocortex during specific mental operations in selective attention.[50] Of special interest is Benjamin Libet's important work in which he observed and tabulated intent-to-act time lags which precede specific motor actions. He found that "the cerebral processes which precede a voluntary motor act begin at least 350 msec *before* the subject is aware of his/her intention or wish to 'act-now.'" This awareness happens about 150–200 msec before activation of the muscles involved. Thus there is an observable though unconscious cerebral process of at least 500 msec prior to performing a voluntary act.[51]

Second, the existence of a nonphysical self is forcefully implied by more powerful psychosomatic events. An example was induced heart stoppage performed by three Indian yogis who agreed to undergo clinical testing of their claim to be able to stop their heart beats. By using controlled deep breathing, the yogis produced what the researchers called "strongly contracted" chest and abdominal muscles. The subjects were continuously monitored by EKG, pulse, respiration, and tape recorder for heart sounds. There were also chest X-rays at certain points. The test phase evoked "marked engorgement of the neck veins," at which time no heart sounds could be heard. There was instead a "faint murmurish sound" which the researchers attributed to chest muscle contraction. "The radial pulse was also not felt during these periods in most of the experiments." "These findings were confirmed by playing back the tape-recordings of heart sounds as well as by the disappearance of arterial pulse oscillations from the records of the finger volume." One subject did display a feeble pulse during some tests. When the stoppage concluded, loud and banging heart sounds could be heard right away. These were initially "at a fast rate, but later on the heart rate was slower than normal for sometime. Similarly, higher amplitude arterial pulse was felt and recorded immediately after the experiment was stopped."[52]

In their chapter, "Somatic consequences of consciousness," Anees A. Sheikh, Robert G. Kunzendorf, and Katharina S. Sheikh list 205 books or research studies which depict an astonishing variety of mind-based controls of the body.[53] In addition to the cardiopulmonary effects seen in the yogi test above, other results of meditation-type techniques include increased total urinary protein, decreased reaction time, and the

---

47 Roland et al., "Supplementary Motor Area," 118–36.
48 Ingvar, "On Ideation and 'Ideography,'" 433–53.
49. Deecke and Kornhuber, "Electrical Sign," 473–76.
50. Posner et al., "Localization of Cognitive Operations," 1627–31.
51. Libet, "Cerebral Processes," 194, italics original.
52. Anand and Chhina, "Investigations of Yogis," 90–91.
53. Sheikh et al., "Somatic Consequences of Consciousness," 140–61.

amelioration of asthma, insomnia, severe migraines and cluster headaches, muscular dysfunction, cancer, and abuse of non-prescribed drugs.[54] When mental imagery is applied to blood pressure, diastolic pressure rises due to images of anger but not to fear; systolic rises due to both of them; both pressures rise as a result of imagined exercise, and clinical research with relaxing images shows long-lasting reductions of both pressures.[55] Breast size can be increased by repeated imaging of pulsation and warm feelings in the breast area. Redness of skin and skin blistering results from imaginary burns.[56] Many more of the authors' data could be cited, but the pattern is clear.

A third sphere exemplifying the mind's downward causation is dissociative identity disorder (DID). This hysteric reaction typically results from radical trauma like extreme abuse, and cult and coven terrorization. In these situations, the victim cannot integrate real-life events into existing memory frames. Personality splits then occur as a defense mechanism to insulate the person from the trauma and the new unprocessed memories.

Researchers are well aware of the fact that different alters in one body can express wildly divergent physiological features. Bennett Braun has reported on several cases of this phenomenon. In one, a woman abused by cigarette and whip burns as a child developed red dots the shape of the burns. These would last six to ten hours and return each time that alter did. One of her alters developed whip welts on both arms, shoulders and across the back of her neck.[57] Another patient had psychogenic (mind induced) epilepsy. This produced spastic seizures and paralysis of the larynx, which became cyanotic and required a Heimlich Manoeuvre to open it. She also suffered headaches. Braun says, "The seizures were triggered by alternate personalities in an attempt to gain control through the use of pain." The object was an attempt to prevent violence, and to keep the patient from disclosing abuse secrets.[58]

Personality parts within the same individual will differ from each other in the widest ways possible. Some wear glasses and others don't; some are physically blind and others retain perfect sight;[59] some feel post-surgical pain and others don't; some are diabetic and others not. Some have higher IQs and others lower IQs; some speak with North Carolina accents and others in the same person speak Québecois French; some will seizures to happen and others resist them. I have encountered counselee alters whose induced seizures the medical profession had regarded as genuine epileptic activity but which stopped when the trauma was resolved. My point is simply that personality splitting happens at the level of the human mind, and through downward causation manifests in brain and body physiology.

54. Ibid., 145.
55. Ibid., 146.
56. Ibid., 147.
57. Braun, "Psychophysiologic Phenomena," 127.
58. Ibid., 131.
59. Strasburger and Waldvogel, "Sight and Blindness," 180.

III. THE HUMAN SPIRIT

For some while now, many scholars have interpreted the OT view of human personality in non-dualistic terms. Nancey Murphy illustrates such a contemporary view, "It is widely agreed among current Christian and Jewish scholars that early Hebraic accounts of the person were holistic and physicalist."[60] A moderate form of the argument states that while people have different aspects which we perceive as body, soul, and spirit, it's wrong to elevate these to actual explicit partitions within the person.[61] In a variation of this position, dualists—who hold that the body *is* partitioned from the soul—argue that trichotomists mistakenly think that a similar partition exists between soul and spirit.[62]

Rejections of body-soul or body-mind-spirit models are rooted in the physicalist assumptions of modern neuropsychology. However, I have already shown that the brain-mind duality is not merely matter with new emergent properties. Mind is a transducer between body and spirit and exists as a vast and complex cluster of logic space mathematical forms, or more specifically, agents. These are created through the interaction of laws of algorithmic rule-sets, nonlinear equations, neural networks, logic, dynamic systems, and qualia. In its turn, then, the human spirit is to be conceptualized as a distinct lawful entity which functions as a transducer between the mind and God. I will develop this model of spirit in arguments from ANE, OT, and NT anthropology.

The Human Spirit and ANE Anthropology

A significant source of ANE anthropology is to be found in Egyptian and Mesopotamian temple design. These structures included conventional temples and also, since ANE royalty was deemed to be God's physical presence, royal burial chambers and palaces.

Temple architecture symbolized three increasing zones of holiness,[63] a movement which has been termed a successive ascension to heaven.[64] An early example of this temple design comes from third century BCE Egypt at Edfu. It had an outer court, then a main hall, and finally an inner sanctuary with a raised floor.[65] The attempt to separate the outer mundane from the inner holy may be seen as well in the Ramses II

---

60. Murphy, "Scientific Perspectives on Christian Anthropology," 84.
61. Ibid., 85.
62. Boyd, "One's Self-Concept and Biblical Theology," 212.
63. Barker, *Gate of Heaven*, 26.
64. Lindquist, "What Is a Temple?," 211.
65. Baines, "Temple Symbolism," 10.

mortuary temple at Thebes. It had eighty meters of pylons, courts, staircases, and halls before one reached the sanctuary.[66]

ANE temples combined community and individual levels of meaning. On the one hand, temples were designed to express cultural convictions about the chaotic deep, earth and heaven, and their interconnections along the world axis.[67] Jewish legend said in this regard that Solomon's temple was built on Mt. Moriah, the cosmic high mountain. The holy of holies sealed shut the abyss which lay beneath it, threatening to break forth and overwhelm humans again.[68]

However, temples were also meant to depict beliefs about the individual and his/her relationship to God. Thus the twelfth-century BCE Egyptian *Book of the Earth* from the burial chamber of Ramses VI demonstrates an individual-cosmic interactive schematic based on birth. Commenting on this, Franz Renggli writes, "Cosmology and embryology, macrocosm and microcosm are compared at will. In other words, *individual ontogeny is a recapitulation of the creation of the world*."[69]

It's true that the OT rejected the ANE mythology of God as the mother-birther of creation. However, this doesn't negate the idea that a temple's theological motifs mirrored beliefs about how human personality is structured. Thus the Egyptian temple's tripartite structure and its focus on the sacred inner core is echoed by a similar psychology. The tripartite person was composed of a core soul particle from God, a subordinate soul particle from the human male, and matter from the human female.[70] These psychological aspects, known as the *ba*, *ka*, and *khat* respectively,[71] anticipated the later biblical tripartism, though the biblical elements were different.

Turning to Mesopotamia, the basic tripartite temple design is repeated in northern Syrian structures at 'Ain Dara, Hazor, and Tell Ta' yinat. 'Ain Dara was contemporaneous with Solomon's temple and shared some thirty-three of sixty-five features listed by the Bible for Solomon's temple.[72] Both buildings stood on the city's highest point, were built on a platform, had a front courtyard with a monumental staircase, and had a portico supported by two massive pillars.[73] Similar to Solomon's temple, 'Ain Dara had a tripartite combination of porch, antechamber and the main hall with the shrine.[74] 'Ain Dara's raised holy of holies paralleled the ten foot elevation of Solomon's holy of holies. In each temple, the holy of holies was separated from the inner hall by

---

66. McCullough, "Dimensions of the Temple," 28.
67. Levenson, "Temple and the World," 282–85.
68. Terrien, "Omphalos Myth," 322–23.
69. Renggli, "Sunrise as the Birth," 218, italics original.
70. Ibid., 224.
71. Mohit, "Mental Health and Psychiatry," 338.
72. Monson, "New 'Ain Dara Temple," 33.
73. Ibid., 30.
74. Ibid., 22.

a wooden wall. All of these features symbolized both cosmological and psychological meanings.

At this point there's a crucial caveat. Lest we stumble into esoteric theology, I hasten to say that the temple motif in general and Solomon's in particular is a template for dualistic covenant theology expressed in mimetic (symbol-grounded) language. In drastic contrast, esoteric ideology views Solomon's temple as part of the system of semiotic (sign) correspondences by which all of creation is connected monistically to God.[75] Therefore, while both I and esotericists appeal to Solomon's three-part structure as a basis for human personality, our underlying logic and use of language is completely antithetical.

In summary, the holy of holies is the place of deity. The human spirit as the seat of covenant with God is expressed in Jas 4:5: "Do you suppose that it is for nothing that the scripture says, 'God yearns jealously for the spirit that he has made to dwell in us'?" Consequently, the question before us is how to conceptualize the human spirit as the seat of God's covenant presence.

The Human Spirit and Biblical Anthropology

Four Hebrew words are key to OT anthropology. These are *aphar* (dust), *basar* (animated flesh), *nephesh* (soul), and *ruah* (wind or spirit). In modern terms, these words depict four layers of creational law. Hence *aphar* refers to the laws of physics and chemistry, *basar* to the laws sustaining organic life, *nephesh* to laws of emotions and mind, and *ruah* to laws which constitute the seat of covenant with God. *Aphar* is foundational but it's also lifeless even though it's involved in such quantum processes as neural firing probabilities.[76] Of the remaining three, *basar* law controls the low-level vivification of the body's organic life. Therefore the critical issue in modeling the tripartite human has to do with the relationship between *nephesh* and *ruah*.

The body-mind-spirit view of personality begins with the fact that on the surface *nephesh* and *ruah* seem to be interchangeable. For instance, a person's *nephesh* can feel emotions, appetites, and desires, as exemplified by Shechem's *nephesh* bonding to Dinah's (Gen 34:3). However, the men of Ephraim were emotionally vexed in their *ruah* by Gideon's handling of the battle against Midian (Judg 8:3). Josiah made a covenant to keep God's commandments with all his *nephesh* (2 Kgs 9:15), while after his healing, Hezekiah says that knowledge of life and death is the life of his *ruah* (Isa 38:16). We read in Ezek 21:12 that every *ruah* grows dim and in Jer 4:31 that our *nephesh* faints before the slayers. Prov 15:4 says, "A gentle tongue is a tree of life but perverseness in it breaks the spirit [*ruah*]." On the other hand, Prov 16:24 says the *nephesh* is invigorated by pleasant words as by a honeycomb.

---

75. Faivre, *Access to Western Esotericism*, 158.
76. Eccles, *How the Self Controls Its Brain*, 73–74.

Even in these few examples we can already see how conceptual confusion arises. It appears that emotions, thought processes, willfulness, and even spiritual commitments can be described by each term. Fortunately, though, certain distinctions are possible. To begin with, the fact that many *ruah* texts refer to God but few *nephesh* texts do[77] argues against a direct equivalence of their meanings. Second, when the terms refer specifically to people, the *nephesh* is the center of all actuating forces but it's the *ruah* which puts those forces into effect. "One may do things with his *nephesh*, but one's *ruah* does things with him."[78] The *ruah* is the seat of covenant purposes and goals while the *nephesh* carries these out. In a spiritual sense, our *ruah* directs our life either in accordance with or contrary to the words of YHWH. One's *ruah* receives God's words and passes them to the *nephesh* to enjoy.[79] Finally, while *nephesh* can refer to the person as a whole, *ruah* never carries this sense. They function together as parameters in the self-organizing system of human personality. Sven Tengström notes that this is the precise point on which monism errs. "Linguistically and conceptually, therefore, the ancient Israelites were in a position to differentiate between individual persons and their constituent elements, as well as between the inward spiritual core of a person and the various outward manifestations of that person's life . . . it would be wrong to overemphasize the 'synthetic' thought or the 'monism' of the OT."[80]

On linguistic grounds, therefore, Tengström denies monists' core argument that in Hebrew anthropology the person is unitary and not segmented in any real way.

This linguistic evidence is the backdrop for the theological import of the human spirit as God's sanctuary. To further understand the instantiation of God's character within the human spirit, let's revisit Solomon's temple. In it the ark was a two-part object consisting of the chest and the cover (*kapporet*). The *kapporet* was the mercy seat and was covered by the cherubim's outstretched wings which touched each other at their tips. The cover symbolized God's throne while the ark proper contained the law-tablets given at Sinai. This arrangement paralleled ANE practice in which documents, oaths, covenants, and the like were buried in special cases under the images of gods.[81]

All of this is analogy for the relationship between the Holy Spirit as divine agent and the human spirit. In Solomon's temple, God dwelt on the *kapporet* and his law with its eternal goals and purposes was written on tablets within the ark-structure. For the person in covenant with God, the divine law combined with the human spirit's goals and purposes is inscribed in the spirit's structure (i.e., the OT ark, see Ezek 36:27). Meanwhile, the Holy Spirit is separate from and enthroned above the system but in connection with it.

---

77. Tengström, "רוּחַ *rûah*," 375.
78. Staples, "'Soul' in the Old Testament," 156.
79. Ibid., 167.
80. Tengström, "רוּחַ *rûah*," 379.
81. Haran, "Ark and the Cherubim."

For its part, the NT maintains and expands this OT tripartite psychological structure. The NT writers followed the LXX and used *sarx* for flesh 151 times and *soma* 129 times, *psyche* for mind 105 times, and *pneuma* for spirit 385 times, of which 80 refer to the human spirit.[82] S. V. McCasland refers to "Paul's triangle of personality," and cites Rom 7:7–25 and Gal 5:16–24 as primary texts which show a threefold structure of human anthropology. In the first, the three terms are flesh, mind, and ego. In the second text, "mind" is replaced by "spirit."[83] Either series points to tripartism. Similarly Paul wrote in 1 Thess 5:23, "May the God of peace himself sanctify you entirely; and may your spirit [*pneuma*] and soul [*psyche*] and body [*soma*] be kept sound and blameless at the coming of our Lord Jesus Christ."

That the body is the temple of the Holy Spirit is clear from 1 Cor 6:19, "Or do you not know that your body is a temple of the Holy Spirit within you, which you have from God, and that you are not your own?" However, as we have seen from ANE and Solomon's temple design, divinity doesn't meet with humanity in the outer "body" court but in the inner holy of holies. The human spirit grows both as it interacts with the environment via sequential transduction through mind and body and also as it develops via its God-attachment. This linked development capacity is fortunate indeed for the many followers of Christ who are developmentally or otherwise disabled, genetically damaged, contending with degenerative illnesses, suffering from diseases of old age, and generally "wasting away." Such people often have a deep faith that transcends their circumstances and which illustrates 2 Cor 4:16, "So we do not lose heart. Even though our outer nature is wasting away, our inner nature is being renewed day by day."

The Human Spirit and Imago Dei

The preceding discussion leads us to consider the ultimate issue: how does creation in God's image relate to the nature of the human spirit?

In Gen 1:27 we read that humans have been created in God's image. The Latin term, *imago Dei*, is usually defined in ethical, moral, psychological, or even political categories. An example of this is the idea that just as a statue represents an absent ruler, so a human carries dignity and authority as God's representative on earth.[84] Such analogies may clarify some aspects of *imago Dei* but they barely touch the surface of the foundational issues. In keeping with the model of spirit which I have been developing, I propose another approach entirely.

As a wholistic hierarchy of autonomous agents the human spirit is created within history according to lawful processes. Adam's spirit-structure was divine law which Jesus the Word spoke in creation (Heb 1:2) and its instantiation was human.

82. Good, "Parts of Man in Translation," 47.
83. McCasland, "Spirit," 434.
84. Porteous, "Image of God," 683.

Conversely Jesus' spirit-structure was his preexistent divine being which he shared with the Father and Holy Spirit. However, its instantiation was also human. The *imago dei* premise is that if any person's lawful spirit framework were perfectly instantiated, it would produce an absolutely accurate reflection of God's personality and character. This was Adam's original condition. In that sense the perfectly instantiated spirit-agent could be considered a clone of God. Jesus, the second Adam, perfectly instantiated the framework throughout his whole life until his death. He therefore could tell Philip, "Whoever has seen me has seen the Father" (John 14:9).

The term clone of God is perhaps unusual language but it's merely a contemporary restatement of the traditional doctrine of theosis[85] (divinization). The fourth-century church father Athanasius coined the classic deification statements. He wrote that Jesus was made man "that he might deify us in himself"[86] and also that Christ "was made man that we might be made God."[87] Western theologians have preferred to rephrase this as becoming like God rather than becoming God, while Orthodox (Eastern) Christianity has stressed that redemption means that Christ is formed within us.[88]

The model of spirit that I am developing offers a new perspective on Jesus' God-human duality. For more than fifteen centuries since the Council of Chalcedon (451 CE), Christian orthodoxy has affirmed that Jesus is one person with two natures. Chalcedon called Jesus the God-bearer who was "recognized in two natures, without confusion, without change, without division, without separation; the distinction of natures being in no way annulled by the union."[89]

As we read the definition today, we see more clearly the mix of biblical theology, Greek philosophy, and even gnostic terminology. For example, to call God immutable (without change) reflects the platonic vision of the unchanging Absolute. Similarly, when saying that Jesus was "of one substance with the Father," the term used was *homoousios*. This word was coined by second-century gnostics[90] and in its original meaning was used to overcome the radical emanation which separated the All from the demiurge. "The Nous-Father and the Logos-Son, who are two distinct beings, share the same perfection of the divine nature."[91]

As in the church's early history the issue today still is how the preexistent Word could become incarnate. In its general form, the question is how the creator can become the creature. That is, how can God become both God and not-God? I suggest that the answer rests on two imperatives.

---

85. Rakestraw, "Becoming Like God," 257.
86. "Athanasius to Adelphius," 1320, letter 60, para. 4.
87. Athanasius, "On the Incarnation," 328, sec. 54.
88. Rakestraw, "Becoming Like God," 265, 267.
89. Bettenson, "Council of Chalcedon, Actio V," 51.
90. Beatrice, "Word 'Homoousios,'" 248.
91. Ibid., 243.

First, there had to be psychological continuity between the preexistent Word and the historical Jesus.[92] This means that his complete personal history had to be explanatorily connected by personal memories. When Jesus told the Pharisees that "before Abraham was, I am" (John 8:58) he was remembering. The memory principle thereby disallows a radical break between Jesus' divine and human natures of the sort which has been used to explain his ignorance of the timing of his second coming (Mark 13:32). Since the church fathers such a radical break has been a favorite way of rationalizing this text. A typical example is Athanasius' comment that Jesus was ignorant of his return in his human nature even though he was omniscient in his divine nature.[93] If I made a similar remark about a splitness in your personality, I would in effect be saying that you suffered from either hysteric conversion syndrome or DID. In a moment we shall see that such logical and psychological subterfuges are both unnecessary and wrong when applied to Jesus.

Second, the Trinity is economic, meaning that each member has specified roles. In Jesus' case, he's the creative Word but his roles also include redemption and restoration.[94] These latter functions require him to enter creation which in turn demands that he be fully subject to the laws of creation. As the incarnate Word, Jesus' subjection to these laws from inside the system leads us to a conclusion startling to Christian orthodoxy. Namely, he entered creation without the famous omni attributes whose subsequent divestiture present such immense problems for two-nature christology. As preexistent Word or incarnated Jesus, though one with the Father Christ never did have omnipotence, omnipresence, and omniscience. These would have road blocked his redemptive role and in any event are reserved for the Father's rulership functions. As Son of Man, therefore, Jesus didn't need to mysteriously divest so-called "disposable"[95] omni attributes.

This economic restriction echoes the doctrinal form of Phil 2:6–7 which teaches Jesus' self-emptying (*kenosis*, "without content"[96]). Rather than snatching the Father's rulership role over us or the Holy Spirit's immanence role in us, Jesus took the form (Gr. *morphe*) of a servant under us. In practical terms, this means, for instance, that his miracles were performed not by his divine power but by the Holy Spirit's. It also explains why Jesus could say that his followers would do even greater works than he had done (John 14:12) because we too will do them by the Holy Spirit.

The stakes in this matter are incredibly high. We shall discover later in the book that the broken eternal covenant can be redressed only by a full member of the community to be redeemed. Jesus had to make atonement as a full-blooded human. This criterion is met since his personality makeup is exactly like ours except that his

---

92. Forrest, "Incarnation," 134–35.
93. Athanasius, "Four Discourses Against the Arians," 1001.
94. Kovach and Schemm, "Defense of the Doctrine," 472.
95. Feenstra, "Reconsidering Kenotic Christology," 130–32.
96. Oepke, "κενὸν," 659.

spirit-structure is the preexistent eternal form he shares with the Father and Holy Spirit.

In sum, Chalcedon was twice wrong. On the one hand, Jesus does not have two natures but one. In his exaltation to the right hand of God as the preexistent Second Person of the Trinity, his hands, feet, and side are still scarred; he retains his earthly history; and he still doesn't know the time of his return. On the other hand, Jesus isn't unchanging. He now has a history he did not have when he proceeded from the Father in the mists of eternity. It's quite true that in his spirit-structure he's the same yesterday, today, and forever. But his instantiation of that structure has varied: Wisdom with God at creation, pre-incarnate Word in the OT, flesh-and-blood Son of Man in history, and the glorified Second Adam at the Father's right hand. He is the first fruits of the resurrection; he is what we shall be; and according to 2 Cor 15:47 he is nothing less than the man from heaven.

5

EDEN

Humanity was to be a gardener—with specific restrictions on hubris, known as the forbidden tree. Overreaching dominion resulted in paradise lost. That should instill fear in all of us to not take our dominion reach beyond our grasp of creation's rules.

—JOEL SALATIN[1]

THE STORY OF ADAM, Eve, and the serpent in the garden of Eden (Gen 1–3) has been iconic for millennia. Traditional interpreters believe that it's a historical account of the descent of the first humans into original sin. Evolutionary revisionists see the story as a symbolic tale of human ascent into new knowledge and maturity. These competing assessments are crucial: do humans need salvation or knowledge? In Reinhold Niebuhr's words, what is the nature and destiny of man [sic]?

In this chapter I will examine the annals of ancient Near Eastern (ANE) thought with two objectives in mind. The first goal is to show that the traditional view of a divine image-bearer falling into irreversible and catastrophic sin is widespread in the ANE data. A second aim is to identify the actual primal sin that was committed. To these ends, I will begin with a brief survey of transcendence in human prehistory. Then I will consider Eden's historicity, its identity as God's sanctuary, the trees of life and the knowledge of good and evil in the garden, and the nature of primal sin. I will conclude by placing Eden in the context of God's ongoing struggle with chaos.

---

1. Salatin, *Folks, This Ain't Normal*, 16.

Eden

I. TRANSCENDENCE IN HUMAN PREHISTORY

Mitochondrial DNA are small energy-producing organelles outside the cell nucleus which are transmitted only through the female. They can be used to date humans by multiplying presently observed mutation rates by the number of mutations. Accuracy can be cross-referenced to archaeology, carbon fourteen, luminescence, and electron spin rates.[2] These facts are important for dating early humans. Although Bishop James Ussher (1581–1656) calculated the date of creation as Sunday, October 23, 4004 BCE,[3] modern science dates mitochondrial Eve—the mother of all humankind—at about 130,000 years ago.[4]

Presently it's believed that modern humans migrated from central and east Africa about 54,000 years ago[5] and that these peoples were thinking symbolically.[6] By about 30,000 years ago, the European Upper Paleolithic period furnishes new artifacts which reflect human creativity and abstract thought. Cro-Magnon people invented tools like punches, edge-retouched blades, needles, sewn clothes, beaded clothing, and other personal adornments which imply self-consciousness.[7] The art of the period especially signals cultural development and increased self-understanding and creativity. Cave paintings at Chauver, France, rivaled any to come for more than 15,000 years. One painting is of a half-man, half-bison figure, while a similar painting at the Höhlenstein-Stadel cave in south Germany features a lion-headed human being done on a mammoth ivory.[8] In passing we may note that in folklore such chimeric art figures often reproduce peoples' experiences of genuine evil spirits.

This is a natural segue to other pointers to transcendence dating from 22–24,000 years ago. The *Venus of Willendorf*, which comes from that period, is a mother goddess figurine discovered in Austria. By 15,000 years ago, there are hints of shamanic rituals and altered states of consciousness in Non Nak Tha, Thailand.[9] Somewhere around 11,500 years ago, Çatalhöyük in Anatolia was already a town of about two thousand houses and eight thousand people. It too yielded a mother goddess figurine, this one found in a grain storage bin. Scholars conjecture that it was meant to enhance fertility through sympathetic magic.[10] All of these cultural data suggest that humans have had an "I-Thou" awareness of a transcendent God for many millennia before Adam.

2. Stringer, "Dating the Origin of Modern Humans," 265.
3. Barr, "Pre-scientific Chronology," 380.
4. Forster, "Ice Ages," 257.
5. Ibid., 260.
6. Wilcox, "Establishing Adam," 52.
7. Jordan, *Neanderthal*, 217–18.
8. Ibid., 231.
9. McKenna, *Food of the Gods*, 37.
10. Hodder, "Women and Men at Çatalhöyük," 78–79.

In light of these background data, I suggest that we formulate human origins and destiny as follows. Over the course of tens of thousands of years the laws required for *Homo sapiens* to become *Homo sapiens spiritus* were instantiated by God. Late in this prehistoric timeline, Adam and Eve appear as two real, specific, physical specimens taken from the preexisting human population.[11] They were formed to be, not the first humans, but the first humans with conditional immortality. Consequently, they represented the next stage in human creation. This interpretation not only integrates scientific and biblical data, but it reflects the ancient stories of immortals, of descent from heaven in Greek and other mythologies, and the widespread ANE accounts of the theft of immortality by the serpent.

A late Paleolithic date is implied since Adam's offspring immediately began farming and livestock production (Gen 4:2, 20). These practices fit with the use of tools, death and burial, aesthetics, art, domesticated sheep herding, and cereal production found at Jericho and Çatalhöyük. If the celestially triggered global catastrophe of 11,500 years ago[12] was indeed the Deluge, this places Adam and Eve somewhat earlier than that time. Conversely, the copper required for bronze was discovered about ten millennia ago, but it wasn't annealed until around 4000 BCE. This dates Adam's descendant Tubal-cain, who "made all kinds of bronze and iron tools" (Gen 4:22).

How does the preceding reconstruction integrate pre-Adamic transcendence with Adam's appearance in God's image? In particular, what about pre-Adamic sinfulness?[13] There are a few possible responses. For starters, wherever and whenever spirit-structure humans have lived without knowledge of God's covenant, they still are accountable to God and the universal moral law. Accountability, however, includes the principle that God has overlooked the times of human ignorance (Acts 17:30). In addition, we might suppose that pre-Adamic humans were placed under the spiritual tutelage of angels even as Israel later received the law from angels. Finally, it seems that the Adamic line led the preexisting human population to cross a spiritual threshold in their knowledge of God. Such a transition is implied in Gen 4:15 where we are told that in the second generation after Adam, "people began to invoke the name of the Lord."

In summary, Eden is the story of initial and conditional human immortalization, and its loss. This garden had two trees, Adam and Eve, a serpent, the breaking of true covenant and the contracting of a second illicit one, and God. These threads coalesced in a series of fateful events in which Adam and Eve met Leviathan (Satan), the seven-headed serpent of myth. This encounter changed the direction of human history. In the remainder of the chapter I will unravel the various historical, psychological, and spiritual levels of this story.

---

11. Wilcox, "Establishing Adam," 52.
12. Alland and Delair, *Cataclysm!*, 169.
13. Day, "Adam, Anthropology and the Genesis Record."

II. EDEN AS A PHYSICAL LOCATION

A decision on Eden's geographical location must begin with the meaning of the word itself. The term correlates with biblical Hebrew, which has several words with *dn* as the base and a common idea of pleasure or luxury. There are parallel Assyrian texts which describe Hadad as the god of life-giving water, and in which a verb *dn* means to enrich or make abundant.[14] In light of early texts which translate garden as paradise it's been suggested that Eden was a park surrounded by a hedge.[15]

Where could such a place have been?

Excluding ancient fanciful identifications of the Indus and Nile as rivers of Eden,[16] there are only two realistic possibilities for Eden's setting in the ANE. The first is an Armenian location advocated by C. F. Keil and F. Delitzsch,[17] and its modern Iranian variation championed by David Rohl.[18] Keil and Delitzsch argued that the headwaters of the Euphrates and Tigris rise only two thousand paces apart, and since the four rivers of Eden begin as one (Gen 2:10), the Pishon and Gihon must also be nearby. This leads them to identify the Pishon as the Cyrus River, and the Gihon as the Araxes. The two join shortly before they enter the Caspian Sea just below modern Baku.

British archaeologist David Rohl proposed a modernized version of this inland setting. He was led to the Adji Chay Valley in Iran by following a route described in the Sumerian epic *Enmerkar and the Lord of Aratta*. Rohl cites a number of local geographical, cultural, and historical data in favor of the valley, which is about ten miles northwest of modern Tabriz. This puts him some four hundred kms east of the Armenian site favored by Keil and Delitzsch. He identifies three of the same rivers as Keil and Delitzsch, but for the Pishon he replaces the Cyrus with the Uizhun.

The major problem with these Armenian or Iranian solutions is that the four rivers don't actually rise as one nor are they ever one. They are separate from the beginning, with the Armenian pair discharging into the Caspian Sea and the Mesopotamian pair into the Persian Gulf. The most that can be said is that each originates in the same general regional watershed.

The second possible location for Eden is at the mouth of the Persian Gulf. Several issues bear on the exact location. For starters, there have been large-scale shifts in regional geography and topology which reflect glaciation and/or planetary crustal dislocations. Around 18000 BCE, sea levels were 350–400 feet lower than today and the entire Persian Gulf to the Strait of Hormuz was a dry river valley. With the return of a warmer and moister climate, sea levels began rising about 8000 BCE. This means that at the time I have proposed for the creation of Adam and Eve, the river channels

---

14. Millard, "Etymology of Eden," 105.
15. Wenham, *Genesis 1–15*, 61.
16. See Childs, "Garden of Eden," 23; also Westermann, *Genesis 1–11*, 216–17.
17. Keil and Delitzsch, *Genesis to Judges* 6:32, 62–64.
18. Rohl, *Legend*, 54–68, 75.

at the head of the Persian Gulf still extended out into what is today open water. By the peak of the warmer climate around 3500 BCE, the Arabian empty quarter had lakes and the head of the Gulf was 240 kms inland from where it is today.[19] As late as 325 BCE, Nearchus, an important sea captain during Alexander the Great's Asian campaign, recorded a coastal position which even then was 190 kms inland from the current coast.[20]

In addition, modern satellite imagery and some basic linguistic analysis enables identification of two other rivers which merged with the Euphrates and Tigris in a now-inundated river delta. The Pishon is almost certainly the Wadi al Batin, a dry riverbed which formerly drained 112,400 square kms of Saudi Arabia and Kuwait.[21] During the warm moist climate at the proposed time for Eden, the Pishon was at places three miles wide. It now enters the Persian Gulf at Umm Qasr in Kuwait, but when sea levels were lower, it entered the Gulf north of Umm Qasr in the Euphrates-Tigris river basin. As one tracks the wadi upstream, satellite imagery follows it under sand dunes, after which it splits in two. One branch, known as the Wadi al Jarir, enters the region of the Mahd adh Dhahab gold mine.[22] This correlates with Gen 2:11, which states the Pishon flows around the land of Havilah "where there is gold." Carol Hill makes similar arguments in locating Eden's other precious jewels and spices in the Persian Gulf region. She states that "the trees from which myrrh and bdellium [Gen 2:12] are extracted grew during ancient times only in southern Arabia and northern Somaliland."[23] Clearly, as she says, this in itself rules out an Armenian or Iranian locale for Eden.

Our pursuit of the river Gihon ("turbulent one" or the "bursting or bubbling forth one"—it's so rendered in Job 38:8 and 40:23, and also may lend its name to the fountain in Jerusalem) leads us "around the land of Cush" (Gen 2:13)—but where is that? The KJV rendered Cush (Heb. *kush*) as Ethiopia, which would force the river to be in neither of the places suggested for Eden. Conversely, if *kush* corresponds with the Old Babylonian *kussu*,[24] it points to the Kassites who lived in eastern Mesopotamia. This would imply the Karkheh or Karun Rivers, neither of which is turbulent. In fact, the Karun—Hill's choice as the Gihon—is a meandering river with great bends. However, the Karun rises in the Zagros mountains and these upstream flows might be described as bubbling. Hill also comments that the KJV "compasseth" ("around the whole land," NRSV, Gen 2:13) means "to pursue a roundabout course, to twist and turn." This brings the Karun and its eight hundred-plus km length back into the picture as the Gihon.

19. Hill, "Garden of Eden," 39.
20. Munday, "Eden's Geography," 145.
21. Sauer, "River Runs Dry," 64.
22. Ibid., 57.
23. Hill, "Garden of Eden," 36–37.
24. Speiser, *Genesis*, 20.

There's one final consideration before we leave the theme of rivers. Gen 2:10 says that a stream rises (present tense) in Eden to water the garden, "and from there it divides and becomes four branches" (NRSV, but "heads" in KJV). In Hebrew usage, the river's mouth is the "end" (Josh 15:5) while "head" is the upper course or source. Thus in Genesis 2, four upstream heads join to become one river either before or within Eden.[25] As to the stream which "rises," Hill points out that "the Dammam Formation is the principal aquifer (water-bearing rock) for all of Kuwait, Saudi Arabia, and Bahrain. . . . The formation is known to crop out only a few miles southwest of Eridu."[26] If Eridu (some 160 kms north-west of present-day Basra in Iraq), was Eden's original site, then the limestone formation would have been a source for a spring out of which flowed Eden's stream.

This reconstruction is enhanced by cuneiform evidence which places Eridu near a garden. The scene depicts a holy place and a sacred palm tree which has been interpreted as a reference to Eden.[27] Similarly, the Sumerian list of preflood kings mentioned Eridu as the site of the first humans. "[When the . . .] of kingship had come down from heaven, After the lofty crown and the throne of kingship had come down from heaven, . . . Gave them their names, apportioned their capitals; The first of these cities, Eridu, he gave to the leader Nudimmud."[28]

Along the same lines, Babylonian mythology identified Adapa as the priest-sage of Eridu. The god Ea gave Adapa vast understanding, "that he might give names to all concepts in the earth," including the origin of all nouns in human speech.[29] This echoes the account in Gen 2:19 in which YHWH assigned Adam the task of naming the animals. Additional intriguing parallels to biblical Eden are these two quotes from Sumerian sources. The first is a text with an Akkadian interlinear translation and it relates the tree of life to paradise:

> In Eridu there is a black *kiskanu*-tree,
>   growing in a pure place,
>   its appearance is lapis-lazuli,
>   erected on the *Apsu* [the Deep].
> Enki, when walking there, filleth Eridu with abundance.
>   In the foundation thereof is the place of the underworld,
>   in the restingplace is the chamber of Nammu.
> In its holy temple there is a grove, casting its shadow,
>   therein no man goeth to enter.
> In the midst are the Sun god and the Sovereign of heaven,
>   in between the river with the two mouths.

---

25. Ibid., 17.
26. Hill, "Garden of Eden," 42.
27. Munday, "Eden's Geography," 144.
28. Civil, "Sumerian Flood Story," 141.
29. Langdon, *Semitic*, 175.

The *Epic of Gilgamesh* records of the tree:
Carnelian it bears as its fruit,
  Vine-grapes are hanging there, sweet to look at.
Lapis lazuli the foliage is,
  fruit it bears, wonderful to behold.[30]

Therefore geographic, climatic, and cultural data agree that Eridu is the likely site of the original Eden.[31]

II. EDEN AS SANCTUARY

We saw previously that the Four Senses hermeneutic allows biblical interpretation according to historical, allegorical, tropological, and anagogical levels of meaning. These terms refer to a text's objective, spiritual, moral, and eschatological significance. In section 1, I considered Eden's historicity; now we focus on its moral and spiritual meaning.

ANE and the Cosmic Mountain

The sanctuary of the gods is a central motif in ANE theology. Various symbols convey this idea, including those of the cosmic mountain, mound, or hill; the world axis (*axis mundi*), tower, or pole; the world or cosmic tree; and the vine of the gods. These various images all describe the link between earth and heaven, the individual, and God. This link may be conceptualized for any spot on earth as going through the centers of the earth, the sanctuary, the priest/worshipper, the cosmos, and God. One might visualize a shishkebob where each of these cosmic centers takes the place of the meat and vegetables and the shishkebob stick represents the world axis.

As cosmic mountain, the sanctuary of the gods emerged from the deep to reach up to heaven. In Sumer, the cosmic mountain was called "the bond of Heaven and Earth," in Egypt, "the holy places of the first time,"[32] and in Babylon, the "house of the foundation of heaven and earth."[33] The Ugaritic parallel equates the name Tyre with the word *gr*, mountain, which is applied to the home of the Canaanite gods. It's also instructive to note Canaanite usage which designated the abode of El as "the source of the two rivers amid the channels of the two deeps."[34] The Mesopotamian ziggurat, or staircase temple, also meant "mountaintop." Thus the sanctuary at Kish bore the name "exalted house of Zababa and Ininna, whose head is as high as the heavens." At

---

30. Widengren, "King and the Tree of Life," 5–7.
31. Hill, "Garden of Eden," 40.
32. Clifford, *Cosmic Mountain*, 14, 26.
33. Keel, *Symbolism of the Biblical World*, 113.
34. Habel, "Ezekiel 28," 517.

Nippur, it was called the "house of the mountain" and at Assur, the "house of the great mountain of the nations."[35] In the case of Israel, Mount Zion was the holy mountain of YHWH[36] even though the surrounding summits are higher. Its height wasn't the point though. The point was that even as the tabernacle was fashioned on the heavenly pattern (Exod 25:9, 40),[37] so too was the temple in Jerusalem.

The Sanctuary and Priest-King

The sacral king is at the heart of ANE theology and represents the tree of life. Geo. Widengren is quite explicit in summing up this priestly role. He writes that "the guardian and waterer, the gardener and libation priest at once, is the king. He performs certain acts of libation with the view of revivifying this tree."[38] Widengren's point is borne out in several illustrations. Sulgi, king of Ur's Third Dynasty (2094–2047 BCE), is called "the graceful lord, [who] is a datepalm planted by the waterditch."[39] Adapa, Eridu's Adam, was labeled a priest of lustrations, superintending the rituals and guarding the god Ea's sanctuary.[40] A Phoenician sarcophagus bas-relief shows the king on a cherubim throne,[41] indicating a priestly function since cherubim were the traditional guardians of ANE holy places. Akkadian bas-reliefs show the king performing rites with a stylized tree.[42] L. Yardin sums up these motifs, "The temple came to represent the deity's 'heavenly dwelling,' the temple grove with the sacred tree the legendary Paradise, and the sacral King as the deity's representative its Gardener."[43]

Biblical interpreters have had conflicting opinions about the priest-king motif. Erich Sauer regarded Adam as God's kingly point-man in the divine reconquest of creation. Sauer argued that Satan's cosmic rebellion *ipso facto* gave the devil legal rights to earth. In God's larger strategic plan to deal with evil, earth was therefore the battleground. Sauer said that the reconquest

> could only be effected through a moral confrontation between the power of God and the power of the devil. This demanded a free, moral being to carry this out as God's representative. His task involved both his remaining subject to God as an act of free self-decision and his spreading over the earth as ruler. . . . The practical accomplishment of such a double task, to be both servant of

---

35. Keel, *Symbolism of the Biblical World*, 113–15.
36. Ps 2:6; 3:4; 15:1; 24:3; 43:3; 48:1–2, 11; 74:2; 78:68; 99:9; 125:1; 133:3.
37. Also Num 8:4; Acts 7:44; Heb 8:5–6; 9:23; 10:1.
38. Widengren, "King and the Tree of Life," 19.
39. Ibid., 42.
40. Langdon, *Semitic*, 176.
41. Cross, "Tabernacle," 63, fig. 7.
42. Watson, "Tree of Life," 233.
43. Yardin, *Tree of Light*, 35.

the Lord and ruler of the earth, involved the actual deliverance of the earth from Satan's power.[44]

According to Sauer, humans were originally morally neutral, uncommitted to either God or Satan. With Satan already holding a legal right to earth, Adam was commanded to guard the garden lest the legal right became one of possession. Consequently Adam's sin became the door for cosmic sin to enter the world. Sauer summed up, "Only so can one explain the appearance of the 'subtle' serpent and the story of the temptation as a whole."[45] Sauer is right about Adam's involvement in the cosmic battle. His assertion that Adam was morally neutral is wrong.

The reason hinges on Adam's identity as the priestly First Man. As such, he is the prototypical human in Eden, a perfect and wise mortal. His rulership was signaled by his identity as a royal signet ring (Ezek 28:12), just as were King Coniah (Jer 22:24) and Zerubbabel (Hag 2:23). The superhuman glory of the first man in Ezek 28 corresponds to "the divine *doxa* [glory and honor] of the Son of Man of later ages."[46]

Esoteric theologians co-opted this first man language for their own purposes. Their claim is that the first man was the *anthropos*, the *Homo maximus*, or primordial man, that is, the Adam Kadmon of alchemy. He is the origin and spiritual substance of the world who links the macro and micro cosmos. Since this Adam is spiritual and androgynous,[47] the Genesis fall was a splitting of the original psychic unity into two.

As is the case generally with theological disagreement between orthodoxy and gnosticism, the decision about the meaning of the First Adam depends on our use of mimesis (realism) and semiosis (symbolism). I think it's conclusive, though, that when we ground the discussion in the OT data, even from a semiotic perspective we are not led toward Adam Kadmon but toward Adam as priest of the universal covenant.

This priestly interpretation is rooted in Eden's correlations to various sanctuary motifs. For instance, ANE temple entrances always faced east to the rising sun. Though not due to sun worship, Jewish architecture followed the ANE pattern. Eden's entrance faced the east (Gen 2:8), as did the tabernacle (Exod 27:13–16), Solomon's temple (Ezek 8:16), and Herod's temple sanctuaries. Other parallelisms exist between Eden's jewels and the high priestly vestments,[48] the tree of life and the tabernacle menorah,[49] God walking in the garden and moving with the tabernacle (2 Sam 7:6), the cherubim who guarded Eden's entrance and those who guarded the tabernacle's mercy seat, and between Adam as priest and the Levitical priesthood.

---

44. Sauer, *King of the Earth*, 73.
45. Ibid., 71.
46. Bentzen, *King and Messiah*, 42.
47. Jung, "To Hélène Kiener," 304.
48. Wenham, "Sanctuary Symbolism," 20.
49. Myers, *Tabernacle Menorah*, 119.

God, by clothing the genitals of Adam and Eve with skin tunics (Gen 3:7, 21), implies an Adamic priesthood.[50] Consequently, they prefigured the Levites, who also were required to have covered genitals (Exod 28:42). Levite duties are also prefigured in Gen 2:15 where Adam and Eve are told "to till it and keep" the garden. The only other OT occurrences where the verbs are used together are in Num 3:7–8; 8:26; and 18:5–6. In these, they refer to the Levites' duties of guarding and serving in the sanctuary.

Adam's priestly function is also described in Ezekiel's prophetic oracle against the king of Tyre (28:11–19). The text has as many as fifteen content parallels with the Genesis account of Eden.[51] Several of these are of the moral (tropological) type: he was the signet of perfection, full of wisdom and perfect in beauty, covered with every precious stone, on God's holy mountain, walking among the stones of fire, and blameless in his ways from the day of his creation.

In summary, Eden as sanctuary points us to two important concepts.

First of all, we note that the garden is located on the cosmic mountain of God. For Erich Sauer, Adamic earth was a spiritual type in which Paradise was the holy of holies, Eden the holy place, and the whole earth the vestibule and court.[52] (Note the obvious parallels with the tripartite discussion in ch. 4.) Gordon Wenham is more restrained, merely saying that Eden "is symbolic of a place where God dwells. Indeed, there are many other features of the garden that suggest it is seen as an archetypal sanctuary, prefiguring the later tabernacle and temples."[53] Throughout biblical history, we encounter the unfolding series of tabernacles: the tent of meeting, the wilderness tabernacle, Solomon's temple, Ezekiel's ideal temple, Herod's temple, Jesus Christ, and finally the New Jerusalem.

One important tabernacle is still missing from this list. The climactic shrine is the person's spirit-structure which here is equivalent to Eden as Garden sanctuary. In his commentary on Mary's Magnificat, Martin Luther described tabernacle typology and tripartite human psychology:

> In this tabernacle we have a figure of the Christian man. His spirit is the holy of holies, where God dwells in the darkness of faith, where no light is; for he believes that which he neither sees nor feels nor comprehends. His soul is the holy place, with its seven lamps, that is, all manner of reason, discrimination, knowledge and understanding of visible and bodily things. His body is the forecourt, open to all, so that men may see his works and manner of life.[54]

---

50. Wenham, "Sanctuary Symbolism," 21.
51. Habel, "Ezekiel 28 and the Fall of the First Man," 522.
52. Sauer, *Dawn of World Redemption*, 45.
53. Wenham, *Genesis 1–15*, 61.
54. Luther, "Magnificat."

Second, Eden is where the priest-king mediates before God and dispenses the water of life. This figure has a sinless, godlike nature and is wearing precious stones analogous to the high priest's breastplate.[55] We learn that even as Moses literally and spiritually walked among Mt. Sinai's thunder, fire, smoke, and trumpet (Exod 19:18), Eden's priest-king also walked among stones of fire. Adam as created was evidently high priest of earth and was intended by God to have a representational ministry for all humans.[56] The fact that Adam's sin produced death for his immortal line (Rom 5:12f.) implies that his obedience would have allowed a continuing priestly ministry for him for earth's earlier humans who were still in the realm of death.

III. THE TWO TREES IN EDEN

Like the cosmic mountain, the ANE world tree, pole, or tree of life stands at the center of sacred places[57] to reflect its identity as the *hieros topos*, the place of the marriage of earth and heaven.[58] The earth's astronomical sign—an orb with a cross emerging upwards from it—is a symbol of the tree of life growing at the center of the earth.[59]

The sacred tree or its branches appear on the oldest archaeological finds such as cylinder seals, vases, and bowls. One such stone vase from Khafaje in Mesopotamia (ca. 3000 BCE) depicts a seven-branched tree which is flanked by animals. Another famous one, known as the Cylinder of Temptation, is in the British Museum. The seven-branched tree is flanked by a man and woman with a snake in the background. Temple and tree motifs appear as far east as Japan.

Since the sacred tree embodies the life principle and the ultimate source of life is divine, then "trees become imbued with the divine power that has deigned to impart life and regeneration within the mundane sphere."[60] Tree deities are depicted either as trees with human arms or as humans with tree branches. A noteworthy aspect of ANE iconography is the portrayal of paired shoulder emanations. Akkad represents this with three stalks of grain or three rays of sun (with the head as the central seventh element) or a stream of water. In Ur, Ishtar was pictured with three or four weapons coming from each shoulder. One seal shows both streams and stalks emanating from the god Enki. Another has a solar deity with flames emanating from the shoulders.[61] In a variation, a Canaanite mountain god is shown holding a vessel from which four streams flow, reminiscent of the four rivers of paradise in Gen 2:10.[62] The goddess

---

55. Block, *Book of Ezekiel Chapters 25–48*, 105.
56. Wilcox, "Establishing Adam," 53.
57. Guénon, *Symbolism of the Cross*, 46.
58. Myers, *Tabernacle Menorah*, 95–96.
59. Yardin, *Tree of Light*, 37–38.
60. Myers, *Tabernacle Menorah*, 95.
61. Ibid., 96, 100, 101.
62. Keel, *Symbolism of the Biblical World*, 118, plate 153a.

aspect echoes these motifs. As an example, a fresco from Mari shows two female figures facing each other. Each goddess has a vase from which flow four streams and in which a branch or small plant is growing. A side panels depicts griffins and other animals together with date palms in fruit.[63] However, unlike all other ANE theologies, Eden was inhabited by two trees, each of which was created by God. The tree of life (Gen 2:16–17) has been physically identified as the cedar (Ezek 31:3), fir and plane (Ezek 31:8), date palm,[64] tamarisk,[65] grapevine (or the raspberry or gooseberry bush),[66] almond,[67] and sycamore.[68] The tree of the knowledge of good and evil is unnamed but we are told that it was in the middle of the garden (Gen 3:3). These two trees confronted Adam with a basic dilemma. As the priest-king charged with tending the garden and mediating before God, which tree would he use to carry out his responsibilities?

The key part of this is the question of immortality. Adam and Eve were created with conditional immortality and put in a world of natural death. In the midst of death all around them, Adam and Eve were commanded by God to be fruitful and fill the earth (Gen 1:28). How were they to do this? God's answer was that they were to eat from the tree of life (Gen 2:9). So we must determine what the trees actually were.

Tree of Life

To begin with, the Bible refers to the cosmic world tree. A generic example is Ezek 31:3–9 which mentions the Assyrian cedar. Its description makes obvious that the world tree is in mind, "Consider Assyria, a cedar of Lebanon . . . the deep made it grow tall . . . no tree in the garden of God was like it in beauty." An explicit statement of the cosmic tree is in Dan 4:10–27. Daniel (Belteshazzar) interprets Nebuchadnezzar's dream, which begins in v. 10, "Upon my bed this is what I saw; there was a tree at the center of the earth . . ."

In addition, there are scattered references to the tree of life,[69] though not all name it as such. This tree is a symbol of well-being, health, and fullness of life. In a wider sense, the tree of life metamorphosed into a well-known symbol of good life in the OT. In Proverbs, a tree is wisdom (3:18), the fruit of the righteous (11:30), a desire fulfilled (13:12), and a gentle tongue (15:4). Trees are regarded as symbolic of the life of God (Ps 1:3; Jer 17:8) because they remain green throughout the summer drought.

---

63. Wallace, *Eden Narrative*, 76.
64. Moor, "East of Eden," 109.
65. Widengren, "King and the Tree of Life," 43, 50, 56.
66. Albright, "Goddess of Life and Wisdom," 281, 283.
67. Yardin, *Tree of Light*, 40–42.
68. Childs, "Tree of Knowledge, Tree of Life," 695.

69. Prov 3:18; 11:30; 13:12; 15:4; Ezek 31:3–9; 47:12; Dan 4:10–12; Rev 2:7; 22:2, 14, 19. Non-canonical texts include 1 Enoch 24:4–6; 25:1–6; 30:2; 2 Enoch 8:3, 5 (the shorter recension of the Slavonic apocalypse); 2 Esd 8:52; Test Levi 18:11.

Furthermore, it's likely that the golden candlestick (menorah) which shone on the twelve loaves of the bread of the Presence symbolized God's life sustaining Israel's tribes.[70] Other ANE motifs related to the tree of life are picked up frequently in the Bible. Prominent themes include the water of life, which runs throughout scripture and reaches its peak in Jesus' promise to give this water to any who thirst (John 4:10, 13, 14). Another is Jesus' teaching that he is the vine, which we now see to be deeply rooted in ANE theology of the tree of life which connects humans and God.

I suggest that the common thread linking these various ideas is that the tree of life is intimate covenant relationship between God and humans. A contemporary label is dynamic attachment. In terms of psychological theory, attachment describes the intimate human social relationship which has a major developmental influence from the cradle to the grave. In psycho-babble, such a two-person relationship is a dyad. This attachment is not a relationship of equals but one where one member of the dyad is "wiser, stronger, and can provide protection, care and comfort."[71] The relationship is a long-term tie with a unique and non-interchangeable partner from whom "inexplicable, involuntary separation would cause grief."[72] The dynamic aspect of human-divine attachment refers to the fact that it's a system built on covenant (network) reciprocity and thus on error-correcting feedback.

In applying attachment theory to the God-human relationship, it's necessary to make a couple of clarifications.

First, there's the problem of God's physical absence. Some evidence suggests that certain human attachments—for example, those with overseas family members—can form without there being direct contact. Consequently we might conclude that it's the willingness to be present rather than actual presence that results in felt security. Nonetheless, such attachments still presuppose a prior direct contact in human terms. On the other hand, God as the attachment partner stands "forever outside the domain of observation."[73]

Somewhat surprisingly, it turns out that, given many choices to describe God, survey respondents focus precisely on relationships. God "is someone with whom you can talk; He is a friend; a father; a support; He loves you; is near to you, is a compassionate God. . . . He forgives us."[74] So it appears that lack of physical presence doesn't derail attachment with God in and of itself.

Anthropomorphism is a related issue. If God is outside our observation, how can God's personality be described in anything apart from human categories? Taken to the extreme, if the emergentists are right that everything arises from nothing and eventually produces God, then yes, God would be anthropomorphic. In this regard Anthony

---

70. Wenham, *Genesis 1–15*, 42.
71. Buchheim et al., "Measuring Adult Attachment," 136–37.
72. Coleman and Watson, "Infant attachment," 297.
73. Proctor, "God Attachment Interview," 61–62.
74. Ibid., 73.

Freeman tells us to conceive "of God as organically one with humanity, both emerging from it and also inspiring it to greater and 'higher' achievements."[75]

However, I have shown that creation testifies that God is outside the system. A creature inside the system who generates God concepts must do so in the first instance according to observation of creation. Since creation reflects design and purpose, we are led to infer that subjective aspects of human personality and culture—truth, justice, beauty—could not arise from an impersonal creative principle. Instead, God must be personal; creation has been deliberately formed to allow creaturely bounded choices; and God's existence outside creation means that God's intent to also enter creation requires God to be a person with multiple personalities. These data trigger a logical sequence which ends with the doctrine of *imago Dei*. In short, our God ideas arise according to God's self-disclosure in both creation as we observe it and in our higher moral, aesthetic, and ethical qualities. Emergentist views like Freeman's are the ones which are anthropomorphic. In dynamic terms, true God-qualities result from top-down causation while emergent God-qualities are hypothesized as bottom-up causation.

Practically speaking, attachment with God provided for conditional immortality. As long as Adam and Eve exercised their designated rulership (vicegerency[76]) of nature and priestly ministry to God, they would preserve their immortality. On the other hand, failure to do these things would turn their immortality into mortality.

Consequently the ANE sources testify that the serpent robbed the first man of immortality. We observe that in Egypt, a serpent biting its tail (*uraborus*) was a common emblem for eternity and the cobra was the ideograph for immortal.[77] In Sumer, Gilgamesh was directed to go to the bottom of the sea (*apsu*, chaos) and retrieve a plant named "Man Becomes Young in Old Age," which the serpent has stolen. "I [Gilgamesh] myself shall eat (it) and thus return to the state of my youth."[78] Similarly, the king begged the god Ishme-Dagon for prolonged life "that in the 'House of Heaven' [the sanctuary] the serpent rob me not."[79] A Ugaritic fragment says of the first man, "He did not know how to bind the Biter, he did not understand how to stop the poison . . . the destructive venom made him twist. [The fle]sh of Sharrughazizu fell."[80] In the end, of course, the serpent also destroyed humanity's benign connection with nature, an event the Gilgamesh epic likewise describes.[81]

The OT substantiates this loss of immortality with the record of the decreasing ages of the antediluvian Adamic line (Gen 5). This has often embarrassed interpreters,

75. Freeman, "God as an Emergent Property," 158.
76. McCartney, "*Ecco Homo*," 3–6.
77. Joines, "Serpent in Gen. 3," 3.
78. Heidel, "Epic of Gilgamesh," tablet XI, lines 278–82.
79. Langdon, *Sumerian Liturgical Texts*, 148, col. 2, line 12.
80. De Moor, "East of Eden," 109.
81. Heidel, "Epic of Gilgamesh," tablet 1, col. 4, lines 24–27.

but current scientific energies directed to aging reversal suggest that the historical biblical memory is accurate.

Tree of the Knowledge of Good and Evil

What was the tree of the knowledge of good and evil? The fact that interpreters cannot agree on the answer tells us immediately that something basic has been left out of the equation. Before I try to fill that vacuum, we need to briefly state the theories which have been put forward. I shall not argue the merits and deficiencies of the proposals in detail but rather draw out of them ideas which together can become part of the solution.

Moral Knowledge[82]

This is often couched as a merismus, a term which describes how polar opposites indicate a totality. When God created and the text says, "And there was evening and there was morning," we encounter language designed to capture the idea of the complete day. Therefore the tree of knowledge means the totality of moral knowledge, both good and evil. A synonym might be moral omniscience. In this model humans attempted to acquire a totality of moral understanding that is only possible for God.

A Probationary Test of Obedience[83]

By breaking probation Adam and Eve became aware of what it is to be disobedient sinners and to know what it is to be evil. Many expositors choose this, some even allowing for a literal fruit tree whose prohibition against eating was designed to test obedience. However, the destruction of immortality is an incredible result for merely eating fruit.[84] In addition, we may well ask, what of those who were to come after Adam and Eve? Would every person in turn need to pass the test? Though probationary test appeals to the concept of maturation, the idea founders on illogic.

Sexual Consciousness

To "know" in the OT can mean sexual intimacy. Therefore some texts say or imply that knowledge of good and evil arrives after development of the sexual urge and disappears when the urge fades. For instance, Deut 1:39 refers to children who do not yet know good and evil, meaning they lack sexual maturity, not reasoning ability. Louis

---

82. Gordon, "(*Twb*)," 354.
83. Walker, "Tree of the Knowledge of Good and Evil," 1259–60.
84. Hartman, "Sin in Paradise," 32–33.

Hartman cites Isa 7:15 and 2 Sam 19:35 for the only additional uses of the specific phrasing. He notes that Qumran Cave I, "The Customs of the Congregation," regards twenty as the age of marriage for a male, "when he knows good and evil" by becoming sexually mature.[85] In other words, it represents sexual potency.

A different version of sexuality focuses on immortality. In this scenario, the two trees are two roads to immortality. The tree of life conferred personal immortality on the person, while the tree of knowledge conferred vicarious immortality through the procreation of children.[86] Given that Adam and Eve were told to fill the earth (Gen 1:28), though, how is that necessary sexual urge—which even today parents see as extending their lives past death—rendered illicit?

I think the more basic meaning of sexual consciousness is rooted in the enigmatic allusion to nakedness in Gen 3:7. This comment stands in sharp juxtaposition with Gen 2:25 where we find that Adam and Eve "were both naked, and were not ashamed" (NRSV). Louis Hartman notes that the Hebrew here really means that "they did not consider themselves to be disgraced."[87] That is, the shame was not sexual but moral and spiritual. This reflects the general OT use of genital uncovering as a metaphor for personal and social moral shame, as we see in Jer 13:26 where women were put naked into the pillory as a sign of disgrace.

Therefore in Gen 3:7 Adam and Eve were ashamed. Why?

Around the world, a central feature of the human relationship with nature-gods is *hieros gamos*, literally heavenly marriage. This typically is a ritual sexual union between a ruler or priest(ess) and the temple hierodule (sacred prostitute) in which heavenly powers are released to earthly realms. Several of the motifs appear in an early Babylonian hymn celebrating King Iddin-Dagan (1974–1954 BCE). In this hymn we read greetings to "the hierodule, to the one who ascends above. Let me say 'hail' to the great lady of heaven, Inana."[88] Also known as the Lady of Heaven or queen of heaven,[89] she was the Sumerian Great Goddess. Other ANE names were Siduri, Ishtar (Assyria), Ba'alat (Phoenicia), Hathor (Byblos), Isis (Egypt), Astarte (Ugarit), and much later Kalypso (Greek).

The Iddin-Dagan hymn is quite explicit in depicting the sexual union which unites heavenly powers with humans. "The king goes proudly to the holy loins. He goes proudly to the loins of Inana."[90] *Hieros gamos* doesn't even require two humans; sexual union with demonic incubi (male) or succubi (female) spirits symbolizes and seals the covenant with demons. During the sexual impersonation the person experiences all the sensations of intercourse with another human.

---

85. Ibid., 37.
86. Gordis, "Knowledge of Good and Evil," 130.
87. Hartman, "Sin in Paradise," 34.
88. Jones, "Embracing Inana," 294–95, lines 1–9.
89. Deut 4:19; Amos 5:26; Jer 7:18; Jer 44:17–19.
90. Jones, "Embracing Inana," 293, line 187.

In Christian history, *hieros gamos* appears in alchemy and the beatific vision, the latter including Christian mystics who described erotic sexual experiences. One nun testified, "My beloved Saviour . . . pressed his lips over mine, giving me the most ravishing kiss of a divine spouse, and sending a delicious thrill through my entire body."[91] Sister Juana Asensi, a Franciscan nun, was executed in 1649 after describing in considerable anatomical detail mystical sexual intercourse with 'Christ'.[92] Such human-demonic sexual union continues to be reported today in shamanism,[93] syncretistic folk religion,[94] counselees, and even in Fourth Wave Christianity (see ch. 12).

Taking all this into account, we are justified in seeing in Gen 3:7 a reference to the covenant with Leviathan having been sealed with ritual sexuality.

Illicit Wisdom

It's implausible that Adam and Eve would be judged for acquiring wisdom *per se*, since Proverbs calls for us to obtain it.[95] The usual answer is that there's a wisdom which is God's alone.[96] Therefore, to pursue wisdom without revelation is to assert human autonomy and to neglect the fear of the Lord. The conclusion is that the tree of good and evil is the pursuit of that wisdom which is reserved for God alone, an overreaching depicted in Ezek 28:2 in the first man's claim to be wise as a god. The notion of overreaching is on target, but we are left still not knowing what wisdom is deadly.

Control of Nature

This is the prime candidate for "deadly wisdom." Nature control has been an imperative since the earliest humans, a point emphasized recently by Craig Venter in announcing his lab's synthesis of the first computer-generated DNA code able to operate a replicating cell.[97] Though nature control is amply demonstrated throughout history generally, we're especially interested in the OT's concern with it.

The garden of Eden account features the serpent. In the ANE it was the symbol and personification of idolatrous practices aimed at controlling key aspects of nature: weather, fertility, illness, and especially immortality.[98] Commentators point out that the Hebrew word for serpent in Gen 3:1 employs the common term *nahas*. Just one

---

91. Nisbet, *Insanity of Genius*, 248.
92. Sluhovsky, "Devil in the Convent," 1399.
93. Eliade, *Shamanism*, 74.
94. León, "El Duende," 159.
95. Wenham, *Genesis 1–15*, 63.
96. Ibid., 63. See also Job 15:7–9; Prov 30:4.
97. Coghlan, "Craig Venter Close to Creating Synthetic Life."
98. Joines, "Serpent in Gen 3," 2–3.

vowel point separates this word from the verb "to practice divination or to observe signs," a parallel which has been called a "sinister nuance."[99]

Consequently, a central feature of the OT is its continuing warnings about recourse to the nature control gods. God's prohibition of asherah worship "on every high hill and under every green tree" appears sixteen times in the OT.[100] By using the words "tree," "pole," and "pillar" Deut 16:21 describes a threefold use of asherah. "You shall not plant any tree as a sacred pole [*asherah*, a world tree or axis] beside the altar that you make for the Lord your God, nor shall you set up a stone pillar." First Kgs 15:13 calls the asherah a *mipleset* (abominable image, NRSV) of the goddess, which apparently comes from the root *pls*, "to shudder."

Although it's from a much later period, evidence from Pergamum refers to the god Stheno as "the one who brings shivers."[101] That was precisely the case with the prophets of Baal when they tried to access demonic powers to bring the rains during their confrontation with Elijah (1 Kgs 18:28–29). By overstimulating their central nervous systems, they tried to generate bodily excitations like St. Vitus' Dance which are conducive to demonic linkage. These excitatory phenomena occur within the chaotic regime of the SOS attractor basins, allowing entryway to demonic spirits.

The biblical view of nature control is captured in the temptations experienced by Adam and Jesus. In common, each man was challenged to subvert creational boundaries in his relationship to God and nature, but from there the paths diverge. Adam was tempted to thwart physical human death by invoking demonic powers while Jesus was urged to call on holy angelic powers to protect him from death during a temple jump. Adam was condemned to compete with thistles for his daily bread, inferring that he had previously used Leviathan's powers to produce fertility. Jesus was tempted to spurn his submission to creational law and turn rocks—metaphoric thistles—into bread. Finally, each man's understanding of God's limits was tested. Satan challenged Adam, "Did God really say?" but Jesus refuted Satan with the text that man is not to test God. In short, unlike Adam, Jesus refused to illicitly exercise nature control.

To sum up, we have seen that prominent ANE themes at the core of the garden story include attachment to God, human immortality, and the serpent from the deep who stole the water of life. God-attachment and immortality came through the tree of life, located in the human spirit. Conversely, the tree of good and evil resides in the mind. It's the attempt to achieve immortality directly through demonic powers or indirectly via technology. In either case covenant dependence on God is rejected. Although both trees can be said to be in the middle of the spirit/mind garden, in the trichotomic personality spirit is hierarchically superior to mind. In the OT this hierarchy was demonstrated by YHWH's position above the ark in which resided the tablets with his life-giving words inscribed on it.

99. Hamilton, *Book of Genesis*, 187.
100. Myers, *Tabernacle Menorah*, 142.
101. Arnold, *Colossian Syncretism*, 63.

IV. EDEN AND THE RETURN OF CHAOS

Although this section title may sound a bit melodramatic, I think that the following summary comments will bear out its truthfulness. I want to focus particularly on three outcomes of the human decision to break covenant with God and form an alliance with Leviathan.

The Loss of Sole Vicegerency

Adam abdicated his vicegerent role in terrestrial creation. This blunt assertion needs to be carefully nuanced, though. Philosopher Karl Popper proposed three worlds or spheres in which human existence occurs. These are physical states and objects, states of consciousness, and knowledge in its objective sense. They represent the realms of physics, chemistry, biology, and the other natural sciences; the world of the mind; and human culture. What within these three realms did humans relinquish to Leviathan? Certainly *something* changed hands to account for the later NT assessment. For instance, 2 Cor 4:4 labels Satan as the god of this age; John 12:31 calls him the prince of this world; and in Luke 4:5–6 Satan's contention that he controls the kingdoms of the world is uncontested by Jesus.

What about Popper's world one? I have argued that the tree of knowledge is the attempt to control natural law supernaturally (reprogram the automaton) in order to overcome the barrier of death. While that breaks covenant with God, it doesn't transfer control from humans to demons for the simple reason that humans never had control of nature. In fact Leviathan's core lie is precisely that with his help we can control nature.

Popper's worlds two and three are different, though. Commenting on John 12:31, Leon Morris identifies Satan's world as the realm of human minds.[102] Looked at structurally, the mind is the location for the tree of knowledge while the tree of life is in the spirit. In functional terms, all humans from Adam onwards are mental chimeras (hybrids) whose minds combine creational design with chaos. This infiltration of chaos generates a deadly mix as though, says Jay Williams, we're on a mind-altering substance.[103] Through his demonic minions, Leviathan, being an inhabitant of chaos, continuously threatens every person's mind. This leads to strongholds of spiritual darkness, manifestations of mental disorders, and bodily afflictions. When Adam as representational head of the human race did the deal in Eden all human minds were henceforth rendered open to chaos and its denizens. The only question is the degree of penetration.

Human culture broadly understood is Popper's world three. This is particularly relevant here because it includes languages, tales, stories, religious myths, scientific

---

102. Morris, *Gospel according to John*, 598.
103. Williams, "Genesis 3," 276–77.

conjectures or theories, and mathematical constructions.[104] Once we granted Leviathan access to our minds then his entree to culture follows automatically. An example may help to clarify how demons salt culture with chaos. In his classic analysis of Christ and culture, Richard Niebuhr listed several reasons why critics across the centuries have exculpated Christianity. His very first point is a quote from Gibbon's *The Decline and Fall of the Roman Empire*. Gibbon stated that the Empire was threatened by Christianity's contempt for present existence and by its confidence in immortality.[105] These core values of Christianity were seen to conflict fundamentally with the values driving culture, namely this-world preservation and future-world nihilism. With the barbarians at the gates, Christians were accused of being cultural draft dodgers.

However, history and culture are self-organizing systems[106] and so the real problem is to determine which parameters in cultural systems are truly preservative: military force? political control? economic justice? personal righteousness? The truth is that history demonstrates that our Leviathan-driven choices result in cultural dilemmas which are always Janus-faced. Nuclear energy diagnoses organic illness and produces centuries-long radioactive waste. Petroleum extraction powers civilization and destroys the environment. Ever-increasing GDP guarantees contemporary pensions and robs future generations of earth's resources. Examples like these illustrate how chaos manifests its double-marking nature in the very structures of culture. In spite of advances, the goal of preservation is always receding. These dilemmas all emanate from the chimeric human mind caused by Leviathan.

The Delusion of Self-Divinization

In chapter 3 I demonstrated Lucifer's abortive ascent to the throne of God, but the scope of self-divinization also extended to humans after Adam's choices. The ANE lament witnessing to the serpent's theft of human immortality is a half-truth. The rest of the story revolves around the biblical view of Adam-as-transgressor: "You were blameless in your ways from the day that you were created until iniquity was found in you" (Ezek 28:15). This iniquity is described as violent behavior and a proud heart, which ultimately defined Adam's stance toward God. In Isa 14:13, the prideful king of Babylon, serving as a type of Adam, said, "I will ascend to heaven . . . I will sit on the mount of assembly." The similarly typological king of Tyre, claiming a godlike mind (Ezek 28:2b, 6) followed suit: "I am a god; I sit in the seat of the gods" (Ezek 28:2).

The following quotations across many historical periods demonstrate that human self-divinization is ubiquitous.

"Then [the god] Enlil went up into the ship. . . . Standing between us, he touched our foreheads and blessed us: 'Hitherto Utnapishtim has been but a man; But now

---

104. Popper, *Three Worlds*, 144.
105. Niebuhr, *Christ and Culture*, 5.
106. Brunk, "Why Are So Many," 26, 29–30.

Utnapishtim and his wife shall be like unto us gods'!" (*Epic of Gilgamesh*, third millenium BCE).[107]

"Therefore, having become calm, subdued, enduring and collected, one sees the [universal] Self in the self. Everything one sees is the Self. Evil does not overcome him; he overcomes all evil. Free from evil, free from impurity, free from doubt, he becomes a brahman" (*Brhadaranyaka Upanishad*, sixth century BCE).[108]

"And next, in an orderly manner, they ascend to the parent and personally hand themselves over to become powers, and by becoming powers they come to be within God. Such is the good end of those who possess acquaintance: to become God" (*Poimandres*, second century CE).[109]

"I gazed upon [al-Lah] with the eye of truth. . . . Then he changed me out of my identity into His Selfhood. . . . He said, 'I am through Thee, there is no god but Thou'" (*Sufi Abu Yazid Bistami*, ninth century CE).[110]

"Nothing was left to them but God. . . . One of them said, 'I am God (the Truth).' Another said, 'Glory be to me! How great is my glory,' while another said, 'Within my robe is naught but God.'" (*Sufi Abu Hamid al-Ghazali*, twelfth century CE).[111]

"In that very instant I saw myself received in union by the One who sat there in the abyss upon the circling disk,[112] and there I became one with him in the certainty of unity" (*Hadewijch of Brabant*, thirteenth century CE).[113]

"In a sense I am God. I see the future, plan the Universe, save mankind; I am utterly and completely immortal; I am even male and female. . . . I am in a sense identical with all spirits from God to Satan. I reconcile Good and Evil and create light, darkness, worlds, universes" (*John Custance*, 1951 CE).[114]

Chaos and the Human Spirit

A third and crucial aspect of the human covenant with Leviathan is that it allowed chaos to deaden the human spirit. Chaos is the unwinding and dissolution of creation; and by definition it's the abode of Leviathan and his cohorts. To worship or to be in league with Leviathan is to give oneself over therefore to the realm of chaos and death. To be infected with chaos is to enter the wasteland (Isa 45:19) and in fact to be sucked into uncreation itself (Jer 4:23–25). Indeed, the second death (Rev 2:11; 20:6; 20:14;

---

107. Heidel, *Epic of Gilgamesh*, tablet XI, lines 193–94.
108. Arbman, *Ecstasy or Religious Trance*, 522.
109. Layton, "Poimandres," 458.
110. Newberg et al., *Why God Won't Go Away*, 105.
111. Merkur, "Unitive Experiences," 142.
112. A winged solar disk associated with the Egyptian god Horus.
113. Merkur, "Unitive Experiences and the State of Trance," 137.
114. Custance, *Wisdom, Madness, and Folly*, 51.

21:8) is not God's punishment but is a bald description of destiny as the person's body, mind, and spirit are darkened until nothing of the original God-image is left.

Therefore the presence of chaos everywhere in creation is the real reason sin transmits across the generations. Though it sounds oxymoronic, this condition might be labeled as disordered lawfulness at the chaoplexic structural level. Sin as a multigenerational parameter in deep-level self-organizing moral systems throws these systems into irreversibly skewed death patterns. As a result, we dispense with awkward doctrines of original sin which lead into a genetic-transmission cul-de-sac and convoluted illogic to explain Jesus' exemption from this factor.

This has direct impact on sin's invasion of the human spirit. Our minds are hierarchical, open, multi-agent systems which relate dynamically with their spirit agents. In such systems, structures are capable of dynamically changing as various agents interact.[115] As a new parameter created by the covenant agreement with Satan and death, sin enters the mind's multiple agent system. This changes the structure of the spirit agent by upward causation. We can say furthermore that what especially changes are the goals and purposes which drive the spirit agent. This is because in dynamic multi-agent systems, output of one level of agents is designed to be other agents' goals and desires.[116] Inevitably, therefore, the spirit will also be dead in trespasses and sins, as the Epistle to the Ephesians puts it. Conversely, by Holy Spirit-aided downward causation, a spirit-agent can reorder its mind agents.

---

115. Sycara, "MultiAgent Systems," 79.
116. Ibid., 81.

6

THE UNIVERSAL COVENANT

In Daniel Defoe's *Robinson Crusoe*, Man Friday stumps the castaway Crusoe with this question: "If God much strong, much might as Devil, why God no kill the Devil, so make him no more do wicked?"[1]

Man Friday's pidgin English doesn't obscure the fact that, like the Greek philosopher Epicurus more than two thousand years earlier,[2] he's flummoxed by evil in creation. Theories about evil's persistence in the face of a good and strong God are lumped together as the doctrine of theodicy. As Man Friday demonstrates, the key question about creation's moral governance asks why a God worthy of the title doesn't eradicate evil. I first raised this question in the prologue and now it's time to examine theodicy in more detail.

Previously we learned that the physical creation references, not itself, but God, who is the external Other. This creation-Other relationship is called "covenant." Now we must grapple with Man Friday's dilemma and expand the covenant principle to moral and ethical evil. This is a global enterprise which includes all human and terrestrial life. I will argue also that it includes the angelic realms and demons.

Let's begin with a question asked by philosophers of law. Supposing there was a society of sinless angels,[3] would a fundamental governing code still be required? The answer is "yes," since if individuals truly exercise free will, even angelic communities require coordination and procedures to settle legitimate disputes which arise. In other words, sinlessness, whether angelic or human, cannot preclude the need for structures to guide interpersonal relationships. Furthermore, such communities require

---

1. Defoe, *Robinson Crusoe*, 172.
2. Lactantius, "Of the Advantage and Use," 564–65.
3. Shiner, "Justice in the Garden," 301.

The Universal Covenant

that acknowledged norms and values preexist the system.[4] Given such mores, God's presence as the authoritative outside adjudicator (the Other) guarantees that justice isn't *ad hoc*.

Judeo-Christian sources acknowledge such a foundational moral compact in both traditional and canonical writings. For instance, in 1 Enoch 6:3, Samyez, the leader of the angelic revolt, fears that he alone will be held culpable. Obviously, though, culpability requires a preexisting code. Later in 1 Enoch (41:5; 69:13) the existence of a pre-primeval moral code is reaffirmed in the reference to the Great Oath which binds the forces of creation. Similarly, Louis Ginzberg notes the Jewish legend which says that the first thing that God created was the Torah.[5]

That angelic realms actually are subject to such code boundaries is clear from biblical texts asserting that Christians will judge angels (1 Cor 6:3), that "God puts no trust even in his holy ones" (Job 15:15), and that God "charges error" against his angels (Job 4:18). In a nutshell, these texts presuppose the basic moral framework for which we are searching. Logic tells us that as the Jewish legend implies, this covenant "document" was indeed primordial since all creation contents must cohere with it.

In light of *The Leviathan Factor's* emerging thesis that creation is chaoplexic from top to bottom, then theodicy resolves itself into a profoundly different issue than what Man Friday could ever visualize. On the one hand, creation's foundational structure is a cellular automaton. On the other hand, self-organizing systems are its operational machinery. In addition, the rules required to drive these systems—including morality and ethics—are fully grounded in God as outside creator. Whatever Friday's answer is in detail, it's law-based within these structures.

From a functional perspective, the inclusion of a moral code, agents, and their actions speaks to Edward Fredkin's concern for the missing workload in the automaton. He noted that only a tiny proportion of the automaton is needed for operating physics from the big bang until the present.[6] Now we see that much of the additional capacity has been allocated to a platform for personal and collective moral agency. In fact, we might speculate further that a key benefit of the automaton is that its logic-space operation offers unlimited resources for the moral platform's pre-universe operations right through to its eternal future.

In any event, in neural network terms, God relates to creation as top-end feed downward causation and creation relates to God via the feed upward causation. God's downward causation consists of blessings and curses which act on the system to establish equilibrium. Angelic and human causation consists of (dis)obedience to the system specifications. Incidentally, since in such a dynamic network system God is active in it by definition, we no longer have to knock down the straw man of illicit divine

---

4. Ibid., 306–7.
5. Ginzberg, *Legends of the Bible*, 1.
6. Fredkin, "New Cosmogony," 116–21.

interventions in creation. God operates in the system, but the system is a dynamic dualism, not monism.

In the remainder of the chapter, I will focus first on Genesis, ANE, and Sinai covenants. Their historical grounding offers a solid basis from which we may analyze creation's moral structure. Then I turn to the four major parameters which drive moral chaoplexity: *lex talionis*, the covenant *rîb*-lawsuit, the kinsman redeemer, and covenant restoration. I will argue that these four system components operate in both cosmic and terrestrial realms. That this is so hopefully will become clearer as the chapter unfolds. For the moment we may affirm that these realms can interact only if each is subject to the same system rules.

I. THE COVENANT IN ANE CONTEXT

The first full-blown nonbiblical covenant treaty comes from Lagash in Sumer in the mid-third millennium BCE.[7] If covenant is defined to include the temple pillars and stelae on which ancient kings set forth their laws, then the date regresses even more to the fourth millennium BCE.[8] Turning to the Bible, we find the primitive (or proto) universal covenant in Genesis 1–11.[9] As the unchanging structure of the divine-human relationship, this is God's core compact with all creatures.

While successive revelation unfolds increasing degrees of God's plans and purposes, this doesn't conflict with the proto covenant. Instead, successive revelation fleshes it out. It's important that we not lose sight of this covenant continuity because the key foundation stone—the kinsman redeemer—is envisioned in Genesis, archetyped in Sinai, described in Isaiah, named in Daniel, revealed in the gospels, explained theologically in the Pauline writings, and worshiped in Revelation.

The sequence of covenant features in Genesis 1–11 reflects the natural story line of the toledoth tablets[10] (family histories) which comprise the source documents of this section. The glimpses we get are significant because they build a theological bridge from Adam and Eve to the election of Israel. The generic ANE covenant form includes a preamble or title, historical prologue, stipulations, deposit of the document in the sanctuary, periodic public reading, witnesses, curses for breaking the treaty, and blessings for keeping it.[11] Though not all of these elements are present in early Genesis, we can trace how the telling of prehistory is fashioned around several key components of covenant.

Even before we learn who God is, Gen 2:5, 8 presents the out of/into salvation motif which we find throughout all of the Bible. We are most familiar with its application to God's call of Israel out of Egypt. In this instance, Egypt is an analogy for chaos

---

7. Hillers, *Treaty-Curses*, 13.
8. Lundquist, "Temple, Covenant, and Law," 300.
9. Vogels, *God's Universal Covenant*, 11.
10. Wiseman, *Ancient Records*, 59–73.
11. Kitchen, *Ancient Orient*, 92–93.

and wilderness while the promised land is a metaphor for God's rest. However, the Exodus from Egypt isn't the prototype of the wilderness-to-promised land movement. The original idea is in Gen 2, where God forms humanity out of dust and brings them into the garden. In covenant structural terms, this is the *historical prologue.*

Then, in Gen 4:26, after the intimacy afforded by the tree of life was gone, "people began to invoke the name of the LORD." With these words the Great King presents himself by name, a *preamble* identification feature which normally precedes the historical prologue. Next we encounter God's command to till (*abad*) and keep (*samar*) the ground. Walter Vogels argues that both verbs are found throughout Exodus where they mean servitude and submission to the covenant respectively.[12] This would define *abad* and *samar* as a covenant *request for submission*. However, as we have seen earlier, to keep the ground carries a guardianship meaning and therefore also can be characterized as a *covenant stipulation*.

Vogels also draws out the similarity between Abel's acceptable sacrifice of the first fruits of the flock and the fat portions for YHWH, each anticipating later Mosaic stipulations. Furthermore, he observes that Noah took seven pairs of clean animals on the ark (versus one pair of the unclean) thus providing for both food and sacrifice from the clean. *Blessings and curses* are centered on Gen 2:15–17 and its specific warning that humans will die if the covenant is broken.

At the conclusion of Noah's family genealogy in Gen 11, we move quickly into the story of Abram's covenant with God. While God's original call and promise of blessing came in ch. 12, it's in the Genesis 15 account that we meet the strangeness of ANE treaty practices. We are told that Abram was to supply for this covenant ceremony a heifer, female goat, and ram, all three years old, as well as a turtledove and young pigeon. The animals were cut into two halves and after sundown "a smoking firepot and a flaming torch passed between these pieces." Just as in the later wilderness wanderings the pillar of cloud and fire signified God's presence, the smoking pot and flaming torch here indicate that YHWH himself moved between the animal pieces.

The backdrop to this story is that parties to a legal kinship agreement in the ANE presented young purebred animals to be cut in halves representing the two signatories. In fact, the Hebrew term for making a covenant, *bĕrīt*, literally means to cut a covenant. An Old Aramaic inscription illustrates the warning that the cutting conveyed, "Just as this calf (young bull) is cut up, so may this same [treaty-maker] Mati'il be cut up."[13] A biblical parallel, Jer 34:18, is quite explicit, spelling out YHWH's warning to covenant-breakers, "I will make [them] like the calf when they cut it in two and passed between its parts." In other words, to pass between the cut animal was a personal oath accepting dismemberment for breaking the terms of the covenant.

Such dismemberment is spoken of in several biblical texts: the grandsons of Saul by the Gibeonites (2 Sam 21:6); the chiefs of the people at the Peor heresy (Num 25:6); the

---

12. Vogels, *God's Universal Covenant*, 20–24.
13. Cross, "Brief Excursus," 266.

Levite who dismembered his concubine (Judg 19:29); and likely also Nahash the Ammonite who exacted a condition of gouging out an eye for noncompliance (1 Sam 11:2). We do well to keep *běrīt* in a corner of our mind pending further discussion below and in chapter 12. As a prelude now, we can say that at Calvary Jesus accepted dismemberment on behalf of the covenant default entrapping both the human race and the whole creation.

Throughout this book, we have seen that the OT biblical text has deep roots in its ANE environment, and the theology of covenant is no different. The discovery of Ashurbanipal's library of one hundred thousand volumes at Nineveh in 1853 seemed to trigger a cavalcade of other archaeological finds. These included the Tell el-Amarna tablets (1887), Nippur cuneiform (1889), Boghazköy (Hittite) archives (1906), Nuzu tablets (1925), Ugarit texts (1929), the Mari archives (1936), and the Qumran scrolls (1947).[14] These materials have helped to place the Sinai covenant in the period around 1446 BCE.[15] An earlier treaty between Samsi-Adad I of Assyria (1748–1716 BCE) and Yasub-Addu contained mutual oaths, an arrangement paralleling Deut 26:16–19,[16] thus implying an early date for Deuteronomy. This correlation may be tested by matching the typical structure[17] of many ANE curse treaties[18] with the Sinai covenant[19] as follows.

---

14. Harrison, *Old Testament Times*, 15–16.

15. Harris, *Leviticus*, 288–91.

16. Cross, "Brief Excursus," 268.

17. Kitchen, *Ancient Orient*, 92–94.

18. Hillers identified some two dozen 15th–13th ANE curse treaties from Hattusas and Ugarit. See Hillers, *Treaty-Curses*, 7.

19. Kitchen, *Ancient Orient*, 96–97.

Table 6.1
ANE and Sinai Covenants

Second Millennium ANE Curse Treaties	Sinai Covenant
Preamble or title—identifies the author of the covenant	Preamble—Exod 20:1
Historical Prologue—statement of previous relations and the benefits conferred by the suzerain	Historical Prologue—Exod 20:2
Stipulations—the vassal's obligations	Stipulations—Exod 20:3–17
Deposition—the covenant is placed in the vassal's sanctuary	Deposition of Text—Exod 25:16
Periodic Public Reading—the covenant is read to the people	Public Reading—Deut 31:10–13
	Blessings and Curses—Deut 28–30
Witnesses—a long list of the gods invoked as witness to the covenant	Witnesses—since there were no pagan deities, these could be memorial stones (Exod 24:4), Moses' song (Deut 31:16), the lawbook itself (Deut 31:26), or the people (Josh 24:22)
Curses—invoked if the vassal breaks the treaty	
Blessings—invoked if the vassal keeps the treaty	
Oath—a formal oath of obedience	Oath and Ceremony—indications in Exod 24:1–11; there's also the procedure for action against a faithless vassal (the covenant lawsuit or *rib* pattern, Deut 32)
Ceremony—a solemn initiation ceremony	
Enforcement—a procedure for acting against rebellious vassals	

In comparing these, we find that in the Hebrew covenant the order of blessing, curse, and witness is exactly reversed from the late second millennium ANE treaties, but otherwise the order is the same. However, ANE curse treaties were completely restructured between the second and the first millennium BCE. Consequently the treaty pattern above was replaced with a form which had only the preamble or title and the stipulations and curses, which were either succeeded or preceded by the divine witnesses. Since the Sinai covenant parallels the more sophisticated ANE form prior to its restructuring, the Sinai covenant must date from the second millennium.

Hence the highly structured Sinai covenant has nothing in common with Julius Wellhausen's prophet-authored theory of the covenant. ANE treaty data has rendered Wellhausen untenable.[20] In hindsight, we can see that Wellhausen's hermeneutics, borrowed from Vatke's German idealism and romanticism, as well as from Protestant antinomianism, led him astray.[21]

A final comment on the Sinai covenant's early date relates to the idea that Israel read its experience back into the Genesis proto-covenant as a prophecy based on past events.[22] The data leads us to affirm the opposite. Genesis is not anachronistic but introductory, revealing crucial parts of God's hidden patterns which were first

---

20. Hillers, *Treaty-Curses*, 2.
21. Cross, "Kinship and Covenant," 15.
22. Vogels, *God's Universal Covenant*, 16.

embedded in nature and then made manifest through revelation in Eden and later covenant disclosures.

II. FEATURES OF THE UNIVERSAL COVENANT

Now, leaving aside questions of ANE covenant forms, what can we say about the more important issue of the universal covenant's content? As I indicated earlier, four aspects of the covenant structure are especially prominent parameters in the relationship between God and the angelic/human realms.

Lex Talionis

To modern readers, perhaps the most unfamiliar aspect of the Sinai covenant is its use of *lex talionis*. In literal terms, this is the law of equivalence of retaliation which in its most recognizable form limited retribution to an eye for an eye. Obviously this much of the idea has been popularized. The part which is unfamiliar to us is the fact that *lex talionis* controls moral law in all creation. This macro structure is the basis of the universal covenant and further specified by the Sinai covenant, which, being promulgated as a legal document, carried the force of law. We recall that all second millennium covenants included stipulations, the core of which for Israel consisted of the Decalogue in Exod 20:3–17. At Sinai, YHWH, as the suzerainty treaty's superior party, required Israel, as the vassal signatory and inferior partner to the agreement, to keep the Decalogue. This is followed by consequence sections labeled *blessings* and *curses* and the whole thing is wrapped up with detailed penalties for breach of contract.

The book of Deuteronomy records a covenant renewal as the Israelites waited to enter Canaan. Our present interest is directed toward the reciprocal pairing of blessings (28:3–6) and curses (16–19). For example, the first blessing is, "Blessed shall you be in the city, and blessed shall you be in the field" (3). The corresponding curse is, "Cursed shall you be in the city, and cursed shall you be in the field" (16). Another direct couplet is, "Blessed shall be your basket and your kneading bowl" (5), and "cursed shall be your basket and your kneading bowl" (17). The overall format is chiastic after the style of A,B,C,D,E,E^1,D^1,C^1,B^1,A^1, though the exact structure depends on what categories are used as curse and blessing headings.[23] In any event, a thematic equivalency holds for the whole chapter.

What is impressive, however, is the degree to which, apart from the opening synopsis, blessings and curses are allocated grossly unequal space. Of the chapter's sixty-eight verses in the English translations, fourteen are blessings and fifty-four are curses. This strikes us as out of whack, but in fact this imbalance is typical of other ANE curse

---

23. Christensen, *Deuteronomy*, 670–71.

treaties. In the Lipit-Ishtar laws, curses outnumber blessings by about three to one, and in Hammurabi's code, the ratio is around twenty to one.[24]

There is a practical reason for this imbalance. The combination of human sin and spiritual immaturity predisposes people to wrongdoing and thus the need for warning is commensurately greater. "Don't touch the stove or you'll burn yourself" needs to be repeated for infants more than the promise, "If you don't touch the burner, your fingers will work normally when you're eighty years old."

Even so, Israel did receive the old-age promise that YHWH would show love to the thousandth generation of those who keep his commandments (Exod 20:6). The blessings are international in scope, as YHWH will make Israel the head and not the tail, only above and not beneath the peoples of the earth (Deut 28:13). As sojourners, Israel had no land but the literal promise of v. 11 is, "The Lord will cause you to have an excess of prosperity." Most of all, the blessing would reveal God's glory and revere his name rather than pointing to Israel's merit.

On the other hand, every basic expression of God's covenant love is reversed when the covenant is broken.[25] In Egypt, God brought diseases on the Egyptians but in the curse, these would be brought upon Israel. In the blessing, Israel's small numbers had grown but in the curse, they would shrink again until they were at last destroyed. In the blessing, Israel anticipated the land but in the curse, they would be removed from it. In the blessing, others would fear Israel but in the curse, they would fear the nations. The blessing was long life but the curse was life's unpredictability from one moment to the next. The fullness of the covenant lay in serving God while the emptiness would lay in serving idols. Most despairingly of all, in the blessing, Israel left Egypt but in the curse, it would return to slavery. Theologically, all of this is *lex talionis*, where historical outcomes reflect an equivalency based on the degrees of obedience and disobedience to the covenant.

As enactors of *lex talionis*, curses function on several strata. At a community level, the curse guaranteed that YHWH's judgment would fall on anyone profaning what was sacred.[26] The story of Achan exemplifies this. We recall how, after the fall of Jericho, Achan stole and hid in his tent certain spoils of war which God had devoted to destruction because they carried spiritual pollution (Josh 7:1–26). Achan and his family were destroyed so that purity boundaries could be maintained.

At a second level, curses are a method by which God enacts moral judgment among the chosen people as a whole. The salient fact here is that God's correction—whether we call it *lex talionis* or not—always begins with the household of faith. The OT prophetic word is that God will judge and that the chosen people are not exempt from historical disaster. In fact, a prominent theme in the holy war tradition is that

---

24. Kitchen, *Ancient Orient*, 97n41.
25. This paragraph is summarized from Craigie, *Book of Deuteronomy*, 351.
26. Ross, "Curse of Canaan," 232.

God warred against Israel because the people broke covenant with God. This same principle may be observed in the *Hittite Annals*.[27]

The prophets were keenly aware that the holy war principles whereby Israel cleansed peoples from the land could equally well be turned against her. This two-way dialectic[28] meant that Israel was subject to God's holy war through the nations according to the same principles as YHWH dealt with the Gentiles on behalf of Israel. The result for Israel was exile, but the OT depicts God as generally judging all nations who elevate themselves before heaven and/or pollute their land with evil and idolatry.

Such moral corrections were occasionally carried out by the angel of the Lord. A prime illustration, of course, was the expulsion of Adam and Eve from the Garden by the cherubim with the flaming sword (Gen 3:24). Another is King David's disastrous census in 2 Sam 24:16 which resulted in God ordering the angel of the Lord both to kill seventy thousand throughout Israel and then to refrain from destroying Jerusalem.

If the angel of the Lord executes divine curses, does God directly use demonic spirits in actualizing covenant retribution? There seems little doubt that the answer is "yes."

Joel 2:1–11 is a classic instance of covenant reversal, with the prophet warning that the same type of locust plague which befell Egypt is on the verge of annihilating Mt. Zion. In a physical sense such desert locusts, which can move in columns one hundred feet wide and four miles long, desiccate everything in their path.[29] However, the locusts in Joel are of a supernatural character[30] and hence they transcend nature, history, and its empires, signaling instead the return of chaos. Similar supernatural locusts reappear in Rev 9:3–11 as the destroyers from the bottomless pit, and here they are explicitly demonic. These locust demons underscore a major difficulty which we have with chaos' role in the universal covenant. Namely, God uses the very chaos that Jesus' atonement is designed to obliterate. It would seem that the demonic serves as God's unwilling and unwitting agents of consuming, purifying, and retributive fire. This is the very point of the locust attack in Joel 2:3, "Fire devours in front of them, and behind them a flame burns."

Finally, the curse as a negative system parameter is one-half of the two tools, blessings being the other one, by which God tries to bring the dynamic covenant attractor back to equilibrium. History—and here I include the angelic realms—is composed of self-organizing network processes.[31] Charles Hampden-Turner illustrated a negative parameter, though he didn't call it a curse, by analyzing Nazism as a cybernetic (neural network) system. In his reconstruction, the positive variable was the Nazi promise that daunting courage would bring total security. The normal negative feedback loop

27. Lind, *Yahweh Is a Warrior*, 33, 111–13.
28. Soggin, "Prophets on Holy War," 67–71.
29. Mounce, *Book of Revelation*, 194.
30. Childs, "Enemy from the North," 197.
31. Brunk, "Why Are So Many Important Events Unpredictable?," 25–44.

of codes and laws was repressed by the Nazis in order to promote greater obedience to the führer. This weakened negative loop could not control the positive variable, which became a runaway self-exciting system. Daunting courage ceased to be life-giving and became a way of death.[32] To say that a process carries the seeds of its own destruction therefore really refers to its systemic self-organizing nature.

In theological terms, God can shift attractor values as a way to correct the network process. This principle is at work in God's judgment of the divine council in Ps 82:1. The operative words are, "God has taken his place in the divine council; in the midst of the gods he holds judgment." Subsequent verses take the gods to task for their failure to execute justice and then the scene switches to earth where the same message of judgment is spoken. The question is, what's going on here? A mock trial meant to underscore God's sovereignty?[33] A mythopoetic borrowing from Canaanite theology?[34] Or an actual representation of the power structure in creation?[35] Congruent with what I have been arguing, I think we are led to the third possibility. God, in calling the gods (Watchers) to account, is actively intervening to keep both cosmic and terrestrial history in equilibrium. The philosophers' utopian society of angels does indeed require a normative code and an objective external adjudicator.

The Covenant Lawsuit

In both ANE profane treaties as well as in the Sinai covenant, persistent or major *lex talioni* in covenant-breaches are closely related to ancestral sin. If unrepaired, such fractures would lead the superior signatory to sue for breach of promise. In technical terms, this is called the *rîb*-pattern or covenant controversy.

Two forms of the covenant lawsuit were described by Hermann Gunkel and Joachim Begrich in 1933.[36] The first form has the scene of judgment, the speech of the plaintiff, appointment of heaven and earth as judges, the summons to the defendant or judges, an address in the second person to the defendant, the accusation in question form to the defendant, refutation of the defendant's possible arguments, and a specific indictment. In this version, YHWH is the plaintiff, Israel is the defendant, and heaven and earth are the judges.[37] In the second form the defendants are the foreign gods and YHWH is judge.

Though the framework of the covenant lawsuit is straightforward, its contents raise some discomfiting conceptual issues.

---

32. Hampden-Turner, "Authoritarianism," 174–77.
33. VanGerneren, *Psalms*, 533.
34. Dahood, *Psalms*, 269.
35. Smick, "Mythopoetic Language," 96.
36. Huffmon, "Covenant Lawsuit," 285–86.
37. Ibid., 286. See, e.g., Ps 50; Isa 1:2–3; 3:13–15; Jer 2:4; Mic 6:1; Isa 1:2–3, "Hear, O heavens, and give ear, O earth . . ."

Accountability Tension

To begin with, there's tension between personal and ancestral responsibility for wrongdoing. Though a variety of OT texts teach the doctrine of personal accountability,[38] it's especially helpful to look at Ezek 18 because the chapter considers both sides of the question. Verse 2 focuses on the intergenerational proverb, "The parents have eaten sour grapes, and the children's teeth are set on edge." However, v. 4 reverses this accountability: "It is only the person who sins that shall die." In vv. 14–20, Ezekiel massages accountability in some detail, considering the various ethical permutations which might arise from righteous parents and offspring, and the reverse of each. Then he declares again in v. 20, "A child shall not suffer for the iniquity of a parent." However, v. 14, directly between the two assertions of personal accountability, states a crucial caveat to the principle. It says that the consequences of the father's sins are not passed to the son *if the son sees his father's sins and does not do likewise*. In other words, even with personal accountability, the ancestral connection is cut only when a following generation repents.

The doctrines of both multigenerational guilt and personal accountability were present from Israel's earliest history.[39] The ancestral theology wasn't a late add-on[40] or an allegation that God is unjust for unfairly punishing people today for the sins of one's ancestors.[41] It wasn't even a throwing up of one's hands to say that if all depends on our ancestors, how can our decisions change anything?[42] The doctrine simply says that ancestral sin really does play a huge role in bringing a people to a state of divine judgment. This principle was well-apprehended within Israel across many centuries of its history.[43]

Mixed Spiritual Loyalties

Second, in our modern age of pluralistic cultural values, we may fail to appreciate the crucial role played by mixed spiritual loyalties in creating negative multigenerational spiritual consequences. A pre-exilic example is Josiah, who asked Huldah the prophetess if the Mosaic covenant principles of blessings and curses still pertained. God's answer came through Huldah in 2 Chron. 34:24–25. "I will indeed bring disaster upon

---

38. E.g., Gen 18:23; Job 21:19–30; Jer 31:29–30.
39. Gray, "Individual Responsibility and Retribution," 453–59.
40. Harrison, *Introduction to the Old Testament*, 852–53.
41. Block, *Book of Ezekiel*, 559–60.
42. Allen, *Ezekiel 1–19*, 272.
43. Historical examples include David and Bathsheba (2 Sam 12:14); Saul and the Gibeonites (2 Sam 21:1); David's military census (2 Sam 24); Jeroboam's apostasy (1 Kgs 14:1–18); Ahab and Naboth (1 Kgs 21:17–24); Manasseh's Asherah worship and bloodshed (2 Kgs 21:1–16); Jeremiah and Shemaiah (Jer 29:32); and Amaziah's false testimony against Amos (Amos 7:10–17). Additional doctrinal statements include Ezek 9:6–7; Neh 9:2; Ps 79:8a; Ps 106:6; Lam 5:7; Matt 23:32, 36.

this place and upon its inhabitants, all the curses that are written in the book. . . . Because they have forsaken me and have made offerings to other gods my wrath will be poured out on this place and will not be quenched."

Another instance of mixed loyalties comes from Ezekiel. He first pronounced oracles against Israel's blatant idolatry and the false prophets and prophetesses who promised deliverance. This was followed by the statement that Jerusalem's abominations were deeply rooted in its Amorite and Hittite parental lineage (Ezek 16:1–4). Using the images of umbilical cord and afterbirth, he continued, "On the day you were born your navel cord was not cut, nor were you washed with water to cleanse you." Israel suffered from a congenital birth defect inherited from the pollution of the former inhabitants of the land. Due to intermarriage and other boundary breaches, Israel harbored a spiritual contaminate which had never been cleansed. Her claim to the land stemmed from the fact that the Canaanites had been dispossessed when their cup of guilt overflowed.[44] The ironic corollary was that even Israel's ANE predecessors were well aware that spiritual adultery resulted in guilt and outcomes which transcended generational boundaries.[45]

What were some of these ANE idolatries? A central pagan practice was the invoking of spirits from the underworld. As early as the *Gilgamesh Epic*, there are references to digging a sacrificial pit to serve as the doorway to the underworld. Various offerings (loaves, cheese, butter, honey mixed with milk, oil, honey, wine, beer, and sacrificial blood), silver fetishes (a model of the human ear, breast ornaments, and a miniature ladder), and even sacrificial animals were lowered into the pit.[46] Depending on whether it was in or out of the pit, the animal was sacrificed so that its blood entered the lip or depths of the hole.

The ear signified the officiant's desire to hear from the underworld; the ladder was for the spirit to ascend; and the ceremony was carried out at night using black sacrificial animals like dogs or pigs. The pit may well have been deified as *DA-a-bi*, the god of the underworld, which belongs to the same class of deities as the earth spirit *tarpis*. In turn, this is likely related to the Hebrew *teraphim*, the household gods that Rachel stole when she and Jacob fled from her father Laban (Gen 31:19).[47]

Just such a pit procedure was arguably involved when Saul inquired of the witch of Endor and she saw Samuel coming up and looking like a god (*elohim*, 1 Sam 28:13). Similar theology is at work in a late thirteenth-century Hittite source from the royal library. It depicts a lamb being sacrificed to the underworld to annul blood guilt curses which might be operating against the household. The inscription reads, "They slaughter it and let the blood run into a clay vessel and place it before the [image of the] God

---

44. This evil-eviction linkage is made in Lev 18:24; Lev 20:23; Deut 9:4–5; 1 Kgs 21:26; 2 Kgs 17:7–16, etc.
45. Malamat, "Doctrines of Causality," 1–12.
46. Hoffner, "ארב 'ōbh," 131–32.
47. Ibid., 132.

of Blood, and he [the officiant] says: 'Anunnaki, whatever blood guilt is in this house, take it and give it to the God of Blood, let him take it down to the dark Underworld and there peg it down fast.'"[48]

Blood rites take a darker turn with sparagmos, tearing a living being apart, and omophagia, eating its flesh raw, whose purpose was to access spiritual power.[49] These practices date from the Mycenaean age in Ugarit[50] and may be illustrated by a curse delivered against Ugarit by a prophet of Dagan (Dagon):

> An ecstatic of Dagan came to me and thus he said: "Surely I shall eat something that belongs to [King] Zimri-Lim! Give me a lamb so I may eat it!" I gave him a lamb. He ate it alive in front of the great gate. I assembled the elders in front of the great gate of Sagaratum and thus he said: "A plague has been ordained. Demand from the towns that they return the consecrated property. He who committed an assault should be expelled from the town. And for the well-being of thy lord Zimri-Lim, clothe me with a garment."[51]

The word for eat, *akalu*, is from the same root as the word for pestilence, *ukultum*, so the prophet linked the act of eating with the threatened pestilence.[52] The plague would come unless consecrated property (likely stolen gods) was returned. We have here a clear precursor of the Philistines' anxiety to return the ark to Israel when plague broke out in each town where the ark was placed beside Dagon (1 Sam 5:2). The reference to eating the lamb "in front of the city gate" is significant too, because this is where ANE (including biblical) elders and prophets held court. Abraham Malamat pointed out that references to the city gates in Mari and Terqa depict them as the prophesier's area, as do Isa 29:21 and Amos 5:10 for Israel. In both Babylon and Mari the palace gates also functioned in this way.[53] So a curse was pronounced directly to and on the highest authorities of Sagaratum.

Time Lapse

Covenant lawsuits also have the problem of time lapse. The reality of multigenerational sin, guilt, and their consequences is taught by an interlocking set of OT creedoformula[54] texts.[55] The texts' common affirmations are that God blesses those obedient to his covenant to the thousandth generation but that disobedience produces guilt to

---

48. Gurney, *Some Aspects of Hittite Religion*, 29.
49. Astour, "Sparagmos, Omophagia," 2.
50. Ibid., 1.
51. Ibid., 2.
52. Ibid.
53. Malamat, "Secret Council," 232.
54. Krašovec, "Is There a Doctrine."
55. Exod 20:5–6 (parallel Deut 5:9–10); Exod 34:6–7; Deut 7:9–10; Num 14:18; Jer 32:18.

the third and fourth generations. However, the idea that sin, or guilt, or consequences transfer to the third and fourth generations predictably raises questions. R. Alan Cole claims the phrase is a Semitic term indicating continuity and is not arithmetical.[56] M. H. Pope says the third and fourth generation is a soft number because the Hebrews used two consecutive numbers to indicate approximation.[57] *The Interpreter's Bible* cites a rather witty unnamed authority, "There would be no fifth generation—they would all be insane."

Let's illustrate the problem of multigenerational transmission of blood guilt. Catholic healer Francis MacNutt described a Sunday School teacher who wanted prayer for her anger problem. When they began, her face twisted in rage and she began speaking in an altered voice. An intercessor with the gift of discernment of spirits said, "This all started in a black mass said in England hundreds of years ago, when her family was consecrated to Satan." As soon as the person said this, the spirit responded indignantly, "Who told you that!"[58]

In modern counselors' experience, ten generations (300 years) seems to push the limits for multigenerational sin and guilt to track family lines.[59] Why did this particular woman and not all of the presumably thousands of other descendants of their common sinning ancestor suffer from this spirit? As a matter of fact, it's quite possible that the whole set of descendants were emotionally afflicted by demons. But to answer the question directly, we found in Ezekiel 18 that multigenerational transmission depends on whether a descendant has restored covenant with God. This is done by turning away from the practice and affirming absolute loyalty to the triune God.

The black mass which launched the demonic attachment to MacNutt's counselee almost certainly involved a threefold denial of Jesus Christ. Therefore a specific threefold renunciation of that triggering consecration and a threefold expression of loyalty to Jesus Christ must be made to cancel the commitments made to Satan. The primary question then is whether anyone in the woman's direct family line has reversed the Satanic covenant made in the black mass. Whether the precipitating deed can, after some ten generations, go into absolute remission depends on whether someone reactivates the original sin-curse by repeating it.

The MacNutt anger account is relatively straightforward. What about multi-factorial manifestations of covenant fracture? As an example, consider Léonie, a patient of pioneer psychiatrist Pierre Janet. Her family history of epilepsy and insanity was followed in her own life by childhood hysteria, seizures, and anesthesia of the left side and sometimes of the whole nervous system. These had subsided in adulthood, but animal magnetism, an early version of therapeutic touch, performed by other doctors

---

56. Cole, *Exodus*, 156.
57. Pope, "Number, Numbering, Numbers," 563–64.
58. MacNut, *Deliverance from Evil Spirits*, 108.
59. Koch, *Occult Bondage and Deliverance*, 70.

had reactivated them. In addition to all this, when Léonie came to Janet in the 1880s she was apparently dissociated with three alters and was subject to trance states.[60]

This cluster of history and symptoms implies several things. Let's begin with the classic white light vision experienced by one of Léonie's alters.[61] I'll demonstrate in chapter 9 that such white light visions signal demonic spirit-contact. As to the mesmerism, lower level animal mesmerism functions as psychological autosuggestion and higher mesmerism as demonic *psi*.[62]

While either could be the sole cause of her epilepsy and seizures, it's very likely that both aspects were in play. Then finally, the hysteria, bodily anesthesia, and DID point to adolescent trauma of some graphic sort. Current studies indicate that if DID research is controlled for trauma, there's no other relevant fostering pattern involved.[63] So summing up, Léonie's experiences and the family background of mind disorders both point to ancestral covenant-breaking and demonic incursion according to Deut 28:28, 61, 65–67.

Blood Guilt

We move on to a fourth difficult concept in the covenant lawsuit, the principle of blood guilt. Scripture talks about blood guilt in both doctrinal and historical terms. In Deut 21:1–9 we find the covenant procedure for cleansing the land of blood guilt when a person has been anonymously murdered. Unless a suitable method is available to atone for this guilt, it otherwise attaches to the land and the people. Hammurabi's code, which predates the Sinai covenant by three centuries, dealt with this situation by providing for payment to the family of the victim of an unsolved murder. Hittite laws held the property owner liable but if there was none, then the community was accountable. In all these ANE cases, guilt attached and had to be discharged.[64]

There are several biblical instances of blood guilt. For example, after Joab murdered Abner, David stated that he and his kingdom were forever guiltless in the matter. That is, no one has a *go'el* (kinsman redeemer) right to come after David to redress the crime by a *lex talionis* equivalent killing. Furthermore, this guiltlessness extends across the generations to come (2 Sam 3:28). Another example is the 2 Sam 21 narrative of Saul's murder of some Gibeonites, an act which led to three years of famine. When David inquired of the Lord, the answer was, "There is blood guilt on Saul and on his house." This was due to a covenant Joshua had made with Gibeon (Josh 9:15) which Saul had broken. According to ANE treaty terms, Israel therefore was subject to *běrīt* dismemberment equivalent to that suffered by the Gibeonites. There was a

60. Janet, "Les Actes Inconscients," 241n1.
61. Myers, *Human Personality*, 1:326.
62. Kaptchuk, "Historical Context," 38.
63. Ross and Pam, *Pseudoscience in Biological Psychiatry*, 270.
64. Kalland, *Deuteronomy*, 130.

continuing moral guilt that required discharge (*kipper*, atone, 2 Sam 21:3). This was done through the deaths of seven of Saul's offspring. Their executions satisfied the demands of both justice (expiation) and restitution (propitiation) imposed by Saul's blood guilt.[65]

Blood guilt may be summed up in the following crucial principle. Guilt for the original specific sin does not pass down the generational line though, of course, social and other consequences of the sin might. This is because the one who sinned is guilty for his/her own sin. However, *the condition of covenant-rupture which the sin has caused, and which in biblical terms is blood guilt, does pass down the generational line.* Descendants must acknowledge the initiating sin and have God reverse the covenant-breach through confession, renunciation, and forgiveness.

A powerful way to connect blood guilt with chaoplexic law builds on the importance of memory in self-organizing systems. At any point in time, a self-organizing system with its many variables is a direct outcome of the past history of that system. As Gregory Brunk puts it, the size of a forest fire doesn't depend on throwing a larger cigarette out the car window to start it.[66] Instead, we know that it will have everything to do with the wind direction and speed, natural firebreaks, rainfall, numbers of firefighters, and so on—all parameters in the system which constitute the fire's history.

Now, applied to blood guilt, a triggering sin like murder is required to shift the system out of equilibrium just as a forest fire needs a cigarette butt. However, once blood guilt has entered (or begun) the dynamic system, it no longer depends on the initiating sin but continues creating its own history.

This axiom allows us to refine what was said in chapter 3 about Lucifer's transformation into Leviathan. His metamorphosis injected blood guilt into creational systems which ever since has forced them into configurations they weren't meant to have. In addition, when Adam in turn broke covenant with God, he injected a blood guilt parameter into Popper's worlds two and three (mind and culture) which changed these systems and then inevitably deadened peoples' spirits. These combined disequilibria are massive, the kind that disrupt at every structural level and which make sense of the biblical statement that we are dead in our trespasses and sins (Eph 2:1–2). We are in the disrupted systems, both cosmic and terrestrial, and they are in us for the simple reason that this is how network feedback works for agents in the systems. Therefore we cannot escape death's dilemma. Apart from a complete covenant re-creational process we are dead and we will stay dead. This is original sin and it's far more lethal and pervasive than anyone could have believed.

As I already stated in chapter 5, original sin therefore is not conveyed by genetics. Here I simply reiterate that blood guilt, either in the limited sense of MacNutt's counselee or in the global terrestrial sense of Adamic blood guilt, functions as parameters at the chaoplexic moral level within both impersonal systems and people.

---

65. Youngblood, *2 Samuel*, 1053, citing Paul Garnet.
66. Brunk, "Why Do Societies Collapse?," 209.

This realization releases theology from all kinds of awkward and erroneous physicalist theories.

These various *rîb* lawsuit factors bring us to the possibility of repairing covenant breaches through a kinsman redeemer.

The Kinsman Redeemer

The early nineteenth-century tendency to see both the biblical and secular covenants as legislative documents was conditioned by European developments in nation-state building and law codification.[67] However, more recent understanding of the covenant has focused on its character as a kinship treaty. In this model, the covenant was "with each family, if not with each individual.... This meant that each Israelite family was thus placed under the direct protection of God, and could be attacked only at the risk of incurring the enmity of God."[68]

To see through kinship lenses offers an extraordinarily powerful window into the Sinai covenant. In ANE cultures, the kinship relationship was the paramount tie among people.[69] When Jacob met Laban, the latter greeted him as his bone and flesh (Gen 29:14). Similarly, tribesmen greeting David said that they were his bone and flesh (2 Sam 5:1). The near kin had special responsibilities to uphold the welfare of the fellow, being obliged to love the other as his own soul. This explains why Joab accused David of loving those who hate him and hating those who love him (2 Sam 19:6). Joab was charging David with reversing kinship relational loyalties.

Given these kindred ties, we can appreciate why the blood family has responsibility to act as redeemers. The governing principle is that kinsfolk ought to be, not demanding of strict equivalency, but loving, just, and generous to one another. Therefore, in practice, several obligations were stated, though not enforced. A kinsman redeemer was expected to buy back property (Lev 25:25–28), redeem one sold into debt slavery (Lev 25:47–55), marry the widow of a brother or near kin to secure his line (Deut 25:5–10), and loan without interest or rental charge (Lev 25:36). Most of all, though, he was the blood avenger who was required to kill the killer of his kinsman (Num 35:19, 21). Hence Ronald B. Allen stated, "The *goʾel* is principally the 'protector of family rights.'"[70] I'll return to this point in a moment.

As these obligations show, kinship loyalties were deep and lasting. The Masoretic text uses a term which means "lover" to describe the friendship covenant between Solomon and Hiram of Tyre (1 Kgs 5:1).[71] Perhaps reacting to this degree of intimacy,

---

67. Mendenhall, "Ancient Oriental and Biblical Law," 32.

68. Ibid., 39.

69. I have taken important parts of this kinship summary from Cross, "Kinship and Covenant," 3–5.

70. The verb is *gaʾal* and the noun *goʾel*. See Allen, *Numbers*, 1002.

71. Shanks, "God as Divine Kinsman," 33.

English translators soften the word to "friend."[72] Whatever the precise rendering of the Solomon-Hiram treaty, in the larger ANE picture covenant relationships build on such kinship love language. Consequently, Ammon is called kindred of their god Milkom (*am Milkom*) and Moab is called kindred of their god Chemosh (*am Kemos*).[73] Obviously, of course, Israel is called the kindred of YHWH (*am YHWH*). This is a profoundly personal relationship with several dimensions to it. On one level, Israel becomes God's adoptive son. A second level employs metaphors of marriage and fealty oaths. Most importantly, YHWH goes to war against Israel's enemies.[74] He is Israel's kinsman redeemer.

YHWH's OT role as kinsman redeemer is multifaceted.

First of all, God battles chaos on both cosmic and historical fronts.[75] In the Song of Moses which celebrates the Red Sea crossing, (Exod 15), elements like Pharaoh, the sea, and the wind each have a cosmic analogue in Leviathan, the deep, and the blowing Spirit of God (Gen 1:2). Earth and heaven coincide again in the sounds of the celestial hosts marching against the Philistines in the tops of the balsam trees (2 Sam 5:24). They're present together when Elisha's servant sees God's fiery chariots surrounding them when the Syrians attack (2 Kgs 6:15–19). Joel 3:11 links the two realms with its plea that God bring down from heaven his warriors for the Day of the Lord when God will judge the nations. Later, in the dawning of the Persian and intertestamental period, YHWH's battle increasingly morphs into a struggle against the forces of chaos and darkness.[76] In Daniel's vision of the four beasts from the sea (chs. 7–8), the sea is the catchword for chaos and the deep. The beasts are simultaneously historical kingdoms and cosmic powers.

Then second, YHWH's holy war against chaos and the deep answers Man Friday's question, "Why God no kill the Devil?" If we analyze the judgment pronounced on the serpent in Eden, we find that there would be "enmity" between the woman and the serpent (Gen 3:15). Careful word study shows that this enmity, *'eyvah*, is forensic and applies specifically to the hatred in murder. The general meaning is that a killing with malice aforethought is described by *'eyvah*.[77] Since in the OT an animal can be guilty of murder—for instance, an ox that gores—Stanley Rosenbaum links this to the serpent's identity as a mortal enemy of humans. He concludes that what happened in Eden was premeditated homicide. "By robbing Adam and Eve of immortality the snake and its descendants are the murderers of our ancestors and, by extension, of ourselves as well."[78] The serpent is guilty of the double capital crimes of murder and

---

72. Patterson and Austel, *1 Kings*, 57.
73. Cross, "Kinship and Covenant," 12.
74. Ibid., 13.
75. Collins, "Mythology of Holy War," 599.
76. Ibid., 601–3.
77. Rosenbaum, "Israelite Homicide Law," 148–49.
78. Ibid., 150.

theft of immortality. According to the universal covenant laid out with Abram, it's quite clear that the one who breaches it is to be dismembered. Leviathan's crimes broke the universal covenant and he must be drawn and quartered.

So the serpent must be dismembered. How is YHWH as kinsman redeemer to accomplish this? When we work out all the details, God has three functions to perform: (1) The chaoplexic disruption which has thrown creation out of structural equilibrium has to be corrected. This will allow God to retrieve his own family property (creation), and so fulfill his kinsman redeemer responsibility in this area. (2) Then, although Adam is certainly complicit for his own sin of trying to ascend to God's throne, God must deal with Leviathan's double crimes and in particular, his murder of human immortality. This carries implications for human salvation given the OT idea that the murderer is in control of the dead person's blood, which really means his soul.[79] (3) Finally, God has to bring humans back into covenant relationship in fulfillment of the original goal of creating immortal offspring. These three imperatives must all be accomplished in the context of a dualism between God and creation.

God's response in determining how these objects are to be fully accomplished is constrained by the crucial stipulation that a kinsman redeemer has to be of the same blood—that is, identity—as the victim. To see this more clearly, we recall that Adam and Eve were created respectively as a son and daughter of God (Luke 3:38) and given the earth for their domain (Gen 1:26).[80] Therefore when Adam sinned and made a covenant with Leviathan, the property rights passed out of human hands to him, an ownership claim Satan reaffirmed during Jesus' temptations (Luke 4:6). Because of the covenant dualism, YHWH could not redeem this property directly. It had to be the nearest human kinsman (Lev 25:25) who could be in solidarity[81] with the human family. Hence when he agreed to fully discharge YHWH's *go'el* responsibility Jesus also was agreeing to share the same human blood as we have (Heb 2:14). Consequently, the core explanation of Jesus' incarnation is that he entered creation as the second Adam to become kinsman redeemer. He is charged with retrieving that which Leviathan plundered from the first Adam.

I will return to the questions of human immortality, atonement, and dismembering Leviathan in future chapters. For the moment, we may summarize the kinship aspect of covenant by stressing that YHWH was Israel's redeemer. With Sinai, the proto covenant found in Genesis has been renewed and pinpointed so that it's through Israel's blood line that Jesus Christ will enter creation to become the cosmic *go'el*.

---

79. Daube, *Studies in Biblical Law*, 124.
80. Sauer, *King of the Earth*, 82.
81. Denton, "Redeem, Redeemer, Redemption," 21–22.

The Universal Covenant

Restoring the Covenant

As just mentioned, YHWH has appointed Jesus of Nazareth to be creation's kinsman redeemer. In accomplishing this mandate, Jesus inherited three tasks focused on Leviathan: to correct his chaoplexic disruption which has thrown creation out of structural equilibrium; to reverse his destruction of human immortality and dismember him for his double murder; and to restore the human covenant with God. We will deal with these questions separately, starting here with the restoration of the divine-human covenant relationship. The Leviathan-centered issues will be dealt with in chapter 12.

Curse Reversal

The doctrine of covenant restoration through curse reversals was unique to Israel among the nations.[82] The practice can be found at personal, community, and national levels. For example, Judg 17:1–3 tells the story of a mother who reversed her curse on the thief who stole her silver when her own son confessed to the crime. An instance of community-level curse reversal occurs with the tribe of Levi. Jacob cursed Levi's and Simeon's chronic violence, exemplified in their indiscriminate slaughter of Schechemite males (Gen 49:5–7). Later, by rallying to YHWH after Israelite idolatry and killing three thousand Israelites at Moses' behest, this curse was reversed and Levi was blessed by being named the priestly tribe (Exod 32:26–29). Finally, national curse reversal is best exemplified by Israel's return from Babylonian exile.

The operative principle for such examples is found in texts like Lev 26:40–46; Deut 30; and Hos 2:16–25. These texts, which describe covenant *rîb* lawsuit processes, specify that upon Israel's confession of both personal and ancestral sin and mending of ways, God will again bless the covenant people. Earlier we learned that personal guilt for sin is assigned to those who commit the sin. However, the blood guilt triggered by gross sin does pass down multigenerationally. It is this blood guilt which must be dealt with in covenant restoration.

Federal Headship

The centrality of the blood guilt principle merits comment in light of traditional federal headship theology. This theory holds that in his sinlessness Adam was head of all humans and on probation for us. Subsequent to his sin, we are treated as though guilty of it personally. "Bound by the covenant between God and Adam, all of mankind are treated as if they had actually and personally committed what Adam as their representative had done."[83]

---

82. Wolf, "Transcendent Nature," 320–23.
83. Pretorius, "Justification," 44.

It's true that representational headship operates in certain situations. For instance, it's reflected in the Levites' one-for-one substitutional role for all Hebrew males in the OT sacrificial system. Representational headship also seems to be present in the ability of a Christian spouse to "make holy" one's unbelieving partner and children (1 Cor 7:14).

In the larger picture, though, the Adamic federal headship theory misunderstands the nature of covenant blood guilt. True blood guilt theology denies that we are guilty of whatever Adam did (unless we also do it!). The doctrine simply states that ever since Adam broke the universal covenant, all humans begin life in a state of alienation from God according to the covenant stipulations. This distinction can be illustrated by demonic inhabitation in a person. If a murder five generations ago triggered demonic attachments to a family line, the living are not guilty of that murder any more than they are of Adam's sin. In each case, though, they are partially (due to a family murderer) or completely (due to Adam's sin) in a state of alienation from God because of covenant blood guilt. Notice that headship is still involved—but not to "impute" the original sin to descendants. Rather the one who committed the trigger sin started an actual law-based chaoplexic process which unfolds in history. Furthermore, the degree of covenant fracture differs. Adam's blood guilt is absolute and controls our eternal destiny while ancestral murder is not absolute and controls our earthly rest (see below).

General Revelation

As we examine covenant restoration further, it's useful to ask a basic question. To what extent does general revelation alert people that they are in a state of covenant blood guilt, alienated from God, and in need of covenant restoration?

Consider the prophecies of Isaiah. Chapters 1–12 prophesy against Judah and Jerusalem; chapters 13–23 are oracles against some dozen surrounding nations; and in 24–27 we encounter pronouncement of judgment on the whole world. Then Isaiah includes the cosmic powers in God's judgment, "On that day the Lord will punish the host of heaven in heaven, and on earth the kings of the earth" (24:21). The climax comes in 27:1 with the prophecy that Leviathan the fleeing, twisting serpent, the dragon in the sea, will be destroyed. In light of the doctrine of the universal covenant, we're especially interested in the oracles against the nations: "The earth lies polluted under its inhabitants; for they have transgressed laws, violated statutes, broken the everlasting covenant" (24:5). The logic is that peoples who possess only general revelation are aware of sin and thus merit judgment.

Although the Gentile nations didn't have the Sinai law,[84] it's incorrect to say they had nothing in written form. As we have seen already, Egyptian theology stressed *ma'at*, the need for right order. An example of a written Egyptian code is found in

---

84. Grogan, *Isaiah*, 152.

The Instruction of Ptahhotep, an Old Kingdom text (ca. 2200 BCE): "Great is justice [*ma'at*], lasting in effect, Unchallenged since the time of Osiris. One punishes the transgressor of laws, Though the greedy overlooks this; Bareness may seize riches, Yet crime [*isft*, disorder] never lands its wares; In the end it is justice [*ma'at*] that lasts."[85]

Turning to Mesopotamia, we encounter Hammurabi's code from the eighteenth century BCE. Its prologue stated that the gods had commissioned Hammurabi to "make righteousness shine forth in the land, to destroy the wrongdoer and the wicked man ... and to illumine the land."[86] These principles were then spelled out in three hundred-odd subsections.

In any event, written codes are only part of the equation. The more basic fact is that every human has a built-in unwritten moral and ethical compass. According to philosopher and apologist J. Budziszewski this compass registers from five directions. These are conscience, Godward longing, creation's glory, the moral laws of cause and effect, and human physical and emotional design. Budziszewski illustrates the principle with the example of emotional design: "No one celebrates a D&C, but everyone celebrates a birth."[87]

However, even for Budziszewski the moral compass is limited. General revelation may make people aware of their state of covenant alienation from God. But can it reverse this human blood guilt? Given the stipulations of the universal covenant, there can be only one answer: "No, it can't." Some human has to complete the terms of the covenant.

Jesus and Restoration

Jesus of Nazareth is unique in having done precisely this. Because he has kept the universal covenant perfectly, he is now qualified to be the kinsman stand-in for anyone who asks. Compared to the Levitical priests, whose stand-in role was symbolic, Jesus' stand-in function means that those who link themselves to him are no longer liable to dismemberment. In all of this, Jesus is functioning as kinsman redeemer to remove blood guilt from the human clan.

There are three aspects of Jesus' restoration of the universal covenant which are germane here.

The first emerges from God's promise in Lev 26:42 to remember the land. When repentance occurs, then in a divine act of Jubilee one is returned to one's original possession.[88] This condition is called God's rest. For Israel, God's rest meant a safe

---

85. Bricker, "Innocent Suffering in Egypt," 86.
86. Harrison, *Old Testament Times*, 59.
87. Budziszewski, "Revenge of Conscience," 139–40.
88. Hubbard, "Go'el in Ancient Israel," 12.

dwelling-place in the land (Exod 33:14), freedom from war (Josh 23:1), domestic security in marriage (Ruth 1:9), and freedom from work on the Sabbath (Exod 20:10).[89]

However, the principle of rest is given a significant twist in Ps 95:11. Although various explanations of this rest have been offered,[90] the text itself links God's rest to creation. Hebrews 3–4, which build on Ps 95, are usually interpreted to say that after finishing creation God rested and presumably continues to do so.[91] This misses the point. God's real work wasn't designing and enacting creation but demolishing the demonic (Herbert May, "dragonic"[92]) blockade which we discussed in chapter 3. It's from the struggle to achieve this victory that God rested.

Consequently, for Israel to enter God's rest really meant release from slavery to the Canaanite and other ANE nature gods. Such demonic usurpers continue today to dog humans whose loyalty lines to God and the universal covenant are blurred or nonexistent. Therefore a result of Jesus' covenant restoration is that, based on his own victory over the gods through his life, death, and resurrection, there's now the possibility to evict them from their human hosts. This is called deliverance.

A second aspect of God's rest is tied to the cessation of hostility when the *rib* lawsuit is reversed. God promises, "I will make a covenant of peace with them [people in covenant default]; it shall be an everlasting covenant. . . . I will be their God and they shall be my people" (Ezek 37:26–27). On the one hand, that this peace is most fully realized in the age to come is borne out by the application of Ezekiel's words to the New Jerusalem in Rev 21:3. Conversely, the lack of peace in peoples' personal and social relationships in the present age suggest that, professions of faith notwithstanding, their own covenant lawsuit is unresolved. In this respect critics justifiably point to the sorry track record by which religious people fail to manifest the peace which their faith claims to produce.[93] One is reminded of Chesterton's remark that the problem is not that the Christian ideal has been tried and found wanting, but that it has been found difficult and left untried.

Finally, if Jesus is the unique kinsman redeemer, what of those who live without this knowledge? The solution is as follows. At the final judgment, there will be three classes of people (but see below): those who have heard and believed in Jesus; (note that this is a volitional choice: "I acknowledge Jesus as my stand-in, so restoring my covenant with God from whom I am otherwise eternally alienated"); those who have heard and rejected Jesus as their personal stand-in; and those who have never heard and/or understood the gospel word about Jesus. In the latter case, they will be judged according to their works (Rom 2:12–16).

---

89. Campbell, "Rest," 37.
90. See four possible meanings of rest in Enns, "Creation and Re-creation," 269.
91. Bruce, *Epistle to the Hebrews*, 74.
92. May, "Some Cosmic Connotations," 11–12.
93. Dawkins, *God Delusion*, 262–63.

A crucial part of these works will be God's evaluation of each person's heart intent, namely, what their response to the word of Jesus would have been had they heard. Readers will recognize this as the principle of counterfactuals we encountered in chapter 2. Critics who object that God cannot know such counterfactual information[94] assume that each person has libertarian freedom. This defines free will as independent of any prior internal or external causal chain. However, in a creation rooted in the automaton, there's no such absolutely independent freedom. Because humans, as agents in the automaton, actually experience bounded freedom, God can extrapolate various individual futures based on heart intent. The net result of the Molinist principle is that the third class of people also resolves itself into two. There will be those who if they had heard ultimately would have chosen Jesus as kinsman redeemer and those who wouldn't have. At the judgment, no one will be able to claim unjust treatment. They will have chosen their destiny whether they had knowledge of Jesus or not.

III. THE UNIVERSAL COVENANT AND CREATION'S STRUCTURE

With the addition of the universal covenant we are finally able to describe the full structure of creation (table 6.2). We have achieved this by starting with the physical realm and reverse engineering step-by-step until we have arrived at God. In chapter 1 we noted the conceptual confusion resulting from the competing models of top-down emanationalism and bottom-up evolutionism. I think it's now clear that in a creation related to God in bidirectional network systems both metaphors are needed. The principles of growth and development demanded by the automaton and its self-organizing systems push us strongly to a bottom-up symbolization. Conversely, God alone grants the top-down information input which is indispensable for complexification and creation's development. In deference to modern sensibilities, though, I have ordered table 6.2 according to the evolutionary bottom-up metaphor.

---

94. Corrigan, "Could God Know," 44.

Table 6.2
Fundamental Ontologies

Ontological Category	Ontological Status	Structural Status
humans	law-constituted community of embodied spirits	embodied spirit-agents in moral and physical automaton
nature	constellation of laws	automaton with moral and physical code
Leviathan	law-constituted spirit	spirit agent in automaton
heaven	"stones of fire"	automaton with moral code
universal covenant	God's spoken word	yes-no first distinction
God	I Am	self-existent spirit

I want to emphasize the universal covenant's key structural feature. Namely, the covenant's opening sentence (so to speak) can be conceptualized as Spencer-Brown's first distinction. In creating the original yes-no distinction God determined that all that would follow in creation was therefore separated from divine identity. This underscores the crucial point that creation is dualistic, not monistic. Of this principle's various ramifications, let me cite just two.

In terms of fundamental ontology, God is neither within creation or creation's body, nor is creation inside God. All of these are theories held by versions of pan(en)theism. To the contrary, God is "The Other." While this dualistic structure can be expressed in various ways, consistent with the argument that creation is rooted in the automaton and is chaoplexic, I suggest that Carlo Beenakker's limit approach is especially relevant. God, he says, has unlimited computational ability while creation has finite computational ability.[95]

Conversely, Leviathan is within creation and limited. This means that we should be able to see his activities in human affairs as one who opposes God's actions. Given that this is the agenda of the next several chapters, I will lay the necessary groundwork in chapter 7 by asking how Leviathan relates to natural law.

---

95. Beenakker, "Hempel's Dilemma," 69.

7

LEVIATHAN AND NATURE

ONE OF THE MOST notorious books in Western history is *Malleus Maleficarum*, published in 1485. Pope Innocent VIII had authorized it in support of efforts to root out suspected witches in several German districts. The title's English translation, *The Witch Hammer*, conveys the fear with which supposed devilish manifestations were regarded and the felt urgency to eradicate any and all such behaviors. Witches were accused of causing hailstorms, lightning and wind; performing distance seeing; inducing emotions like love and hate; demonstrating predictive powers; performing astral travel; interfering with sexual and re-creative processes; and especially practicing devil sacrifice and worship.[1]

A key worldview issue raised by *Malleus Maleficarum* was the relationship between various supernatural powers and nature's governance. Who did what? Is there creational freedom for angels and demons to use natural law? In turn, is it possible for humans to harness fundamental natural law through devilish magic as witches were accused of doing?

For medievalists such questions related directly to their received worldview. Creation's conceptual structure was the Great Chain of Being which emanated from the Absolute or God. This principle joined Plato's heavenly templates and descending realms to Aristotle's natural ascending gradations. In particular, the Great Chain included celestial realms with spiritual powers who lived and operated in them. As a result, in *Malleus Maleficarum* we read that "the whole mechanism of the world and all corporeal creatures are administered by Angels . . . in this visible world nothing can be disposed except by an invisible creature. Therefore all corporeal matters are governed by the Angels."[2]

---

1. Kramer and Sprenger, *Malleus Maleficarum*, ix, 3, 99.
2. Ibid., 125.

In turn it was believed that devils can cause real physical defects and infirmities, though they cannot override the influence of the stars. This limitation is because the stars are of a higher realm than the region of lower mists where the demons operate. Since the stars are governed by the angels the general good order of the universe would suffer if devils could cause alteration in the functioning of this higher realm.[3] The intermixing of causations meant that it was important to determine whose powers were at work when miracle healings or similar phenomena occurred.

As the Renaissance dawned, opinions were still divided on demonic versus divine causation and of how possession symptoms looked in practice. Pierre Le Loyer said that if illness strikes the brain as epilepsy, mania, melancholy, and so on, the devil takes advantage of this affliction, and, with God's permission, produces insanity.[4] Conversely, Reginald Scot critiqued demonism and while he formally kept natural magic in his system, he decided that demons are either metaphorical and beyond human comprehension or are really psychological disorders and physical diseases.[5] A generation later, John Cotta addressed the more general issue of nature's boundaries by saying that the devil can use natural law but not be its master.[6]

Regardless of such nuances, all of these philosophers shared a common worldview in which natural magic and demonic magic were separated not by specific phenomena but by their proximate causes. While both magics accessed the higher laws of nature, in natural magic humans manipulated the laws through sympathetic ritual. Conversely, diabolical magic was mediated through witchcraft connection with demons.

Notwithstanding the Renaissance, Enlightenment, and the rise of science, the persistence of paranormal phenomena until today forces us to address the same root question as did Innocent VIII. Though we abhor his final solution of witch-burning, we can't avoid asking how Leviathan interacts with nature.

To help orient us to the issues I have chosen four stories.

> On the night of May 8, 1967, Philadelphia attorney Sidney Margulies and one of his firm's typists, psychic Ted Owens, were watching a rainstorm. Although there had been no lightning, Margulies asked Owens, who claimed ability to control weather, to make lightning strike the nearby bridge leading to Camden, NJ. So Owens pointed a hand at the bridge and concentrated on making lightning strike it. Within a few moments a bolt of lightning struck the bridge. According to Margulies' signed affidavit, "there was no other bolt of lightning either before or after the experiment."[7]

---

3. Ibid., 115.
4. Anglo, "Melancholia and Witchcraft," 218.
5. Ibid., 220.
6. Clark, "Scientific Status," 360.
7. Mishlove, *PK Man*, 91–92.

During one of her conversations with the Beyond, when Hildegarde Schaefer asked, "*Was machst du im Jenseits?*" ("What are you doing in the Beyond?"), she was astonished to hear, "*Ich beschaeftige mich mit Fernsehen.*" ("I occupy myself with television.") Further light was shed on September 30, 1985 when medium Klaus Schreiber toggled together a TV monitor, a video camera, and other components. The camera pointed at the TV screen so that they functioned like mirrors facing each other. Images of relatives and other people, both dead and living, started to appear. These receptions continued for many months and some were demonstrated live on German TV.[8]

Due to an injury, Carol Herkimer couldn't sit on the floor cushions with the other New Yorkers with whom she was taking a spirit-boat shamanic journey. She had to sit in a chair with bent tubular metal legs. When the group returned to ordinary reality, people described what they had encountered. "Carol had travelled through a sea of fire.... When she came back, the floor was smoking under her chair, and the bent aluminum tubular leg on one side had burned a channel into the floor, but she hadn't gotten burned. The people who owned the studio were quite upset, and to this day the burned channel is still there."[9]

On July 1, 1999 Sufi dervish Jamal N. Hussein came from Amman, Jordan to a radiology facility in Cleveland, OH. Having signed a liability waiver, he inserted an unsterile metal skewer through both cheeks while being videotaped by a professional crew and watched by several scientists, health-care professionals, and emergency medical technicians. The skewer was .38 cm in diameter and about 25 cm long. The scientists and doctors present confirmed that the left facial puncture healed within two minutes after the skewer was removed. The right was three-quarters healed after eight hours and completely healed after ten, leaving no scar tissues.[10]

These accounts raise many questions about the nature of physical law, its relationship to spiritual powers, and whether such paranormal events are possible.

We begin our assessment with a basic issue: what is nature's control system?

I. NATURE'S CONTROL SYSTEM

The Language of Creation

If Leviathan can interact with nature then he must be able to speak the language of creation. What is this? The near-unanimous conviction that creation is best described by mathematics dates from Plato and Pythagoras. However, this belief comes in competing flavors.

8. Schaefer, "Klaus Schreiber and Martin Wenzel," 203–21.
9. Harner and Horrigan, "Shamanic Healing."
10. Hall et al., "Scientific Study," 205.

The Greek model, traditionally called Platonism and often now realism, says that mathematical truths exist as forms independently of human minds and are universally and eternally true. Theologian Alvin Plantinga puts it this way: "God hasn't *created* the numbers; a thing is created only if its existence has a beginning, and no number ever began to exist."[11] As did Philo and Augustine,[12] Plantinga located these forms in God's mind, making them a part of God's core nature. Hence the human concept of number derives from observed mathematical interrelationships—like *phi*—in our physical environment.

Logicism and formalism, two schools of thought which are related to each other, focus on argument structure divorced from content. Their goal is to approach mathematics as "a carefully crafted, but ultimately meaningless, game played according to rules that, ideally, can be shown never to lead to a formal contradiction."[13] As we have seen, Gödel destroyed such arguments by showing the self-referential illogic of pure mathematical systems.

A fourth approach, intuitionism, more or less reverses Platonism. If the Greeks believed that perception verified the heavenly form, intuitionism says that "perception of something is not the reason for it being true but recognizing the truth of something actually suggests its perceptibility."[14]

I suggest we interpret mathematics as a language. For example, the actual English phrasing in Newton's *Principia* was, "The change of motion is proportional to the motive force impressed; and is made in the direction of the right line in which that force is impressed." This has been reduced to "force is equal to mass times acceleration" and further symbolized by $F = ma$. Sundar Sarukkai summarizes this sequence by noting that the first defining characteristic of mathematics isn't its application to the world as such but to other language(s). Mathematics as language is confirmed by the fact that it can be used to describe worlds that contradict the world we live in.[15] In this respect we recall modern science's many wildly differing cosmologies, all of which are couched in formally coherent mathematical equations.

The upshot is that mathematics is an artifact of creation. Hence we cannot assert that numbers are eternal universals whose existence God affirms. This is tantamount to saying that there's an Absolute which is superior to God. How does this principle apply to Leviathan? Very simply, in a creation whose structural language is mathematics, Leviathan must speak the language.

---

11. Plantinga, *Does God Have a Nature?*, 142–43, italics original.
12. Byl, "Theism and Mathematical Realism," 34.
13. Bridges, "Reality and Virtual Reality," 227.
14. Sarukkai, "Revisiting the 'Unreasonable Effectiveness,'" 416–17.
15. Ibid., 419–20.

Creation and Chaoplexity

I noted in chapter 1 that chaoplexity covers a wide range of phenomena. It will be helpful to review two key examples of these which bear directly on how Leviathan interacts with nature: agents and self-organizing criticality (SOC).

We met agents in chapter 4 where I showed how they are integral to the formation of the human mind and spirit. In chapter 8 I'll explore their role in the disordered mind, but at this stage I want to reiterate the centrality of rule-sets. I will illustrate this point with the software program called "Growing Artificial Societies."

The program generates an artificial intelligence environment where agents must acquire sugar food to thrive. The agent society exists on a two-dimensional grid fifty spaces square similar to a cellular automaton grid. Agents are randomly scattered to begin and have a set of four recurrent (repeating) rules which boil down to a single directive, "From all positions within your view, find the nearest unoccupied position of maximum sugar, go there and collect the sugar."[16] This simple algorithm can generate highly skewed distributions of sugar wealth.

The point of this illustration is twofold. First, agents depend exclusively on their rule-sets. Second, Leviathan is an agent within the systems of creation and therefore is bounded by his rule-sets. The question with which we must wrestle is the nature and degree of these boundaries.

Leviathan therefore operates in chaoplexic systems, especially those which lead to self-organizing criticality (SOC). SOC has been called "more basic than physics" and as such stands behind physics as one of the key logical and organizing principles in creation.[17] Indeed, some have speculated that the big bang itself is the ultimate example of SOC.[18]

When we encountered it earlier in its biological guise, I argued that self-organization demands an external rule-giver. Now we will focus on SOC's superintendent role over other creational processes. Gregory Brunk illustrates this claim by pointing out that SOC is present in processes as wide-ranging as "landslides, avalanches, earthquakes, the background static of AM radios, acoustic emissions from volcanic rocks, solar flares, forest fires, the distribution of galaxies, the meandering pattern of river deltas, sudden flashes in luminosity of the glowing radium-coated hands of a 1950s clock."[19]

A good way to get a handle on SOC is to go back to the original work done by Glenn Held and his colleagues at IBM.[20] They performed an experiment in which grains of sand were dropped one at a time onto a slowly growing pile on a surface with

---

16. Epstein and Axtell, *Growing Artificial Societies*, 21–25.
17. Buchanan, *Ubiquity*, 95.
18. Laughlin and Pines, "Theory of Everything," 29.
19. Brunk, "Why Do Societies Collapse?," 204.
20. Held et al., "Experimental Study," 1120–23.

edges. The pile would grow until it reached the edge and then spill so that it had a size limit. The state in which the pile is balanced at its boundary and could tumble at any moment is called criticality.[21] Researchers were especially interested in the fluctuations that the pile would undergo as it got higher and steeper, and then collapsed in an avalanche before rebuilding.

Both the physical experiment and follow-up computer modeling showed that there is no typically sized avalanche. One grain or millions might tumble. However, Per Bak and his colleagues took a further step and programmed the computer to color grains green if the pile was relatively flat and red if it looked ready to avalanche. The pile at first was green but as it grew the red began filtering in until a dense skeleton of instability ran throughout. This gave a clue to the avalanche: a grain falling on a red spot had a higher chance to trigger a slide than if it fell on the green.

Now here's the kicker. When the number of avalanches are cross-tabulated by size ranges a regular pattern appears. It didn't matter where researchers started their grain count. However many grains they began with, if they doubled the avalanche size an avalanche was 2.14 times less likely to occur. This relationship is called a power law and it takes the general form, "The log of the frequency of events is an inverse linear function of the log of their magnitudes $[log\,(F) = -log\,(M)]$."[22] This relationship wasn't a brand new discovery, as linguist George K. Zipf of Harvard applied power law analysis to alphabet and natural language word distributions in 1949.[23] In fact, eight years before that, Lewis Richardson modeled wars and "other fatal quarrels" as an inverse logarithmic process.[24]

If we ask whether every example of a power law yields a number of 2.14 ratio, the answer is "no." Power laws reflect the fact that there are many classes of aggregate phenomena. Earthquake frequency versus size has a power law number of about 4.0;[25] the distance between magnets and their magnetic alignment, 1.19;[26] forest fire frequency versus area, 2.48;[27] the frequency of biological extinctions versus their size, 4.0;[28] stock market price change versus numbers of transactions, about 16.0[29] and the number of war deaths versus number of wars, 4.0.[30] So it's obvious that the exact number varies greatly but in all these cases the particular system is subject to underlying statistical and mathematical rules.

---

21. Cited in Bak and Chen, "Self-Organized Criticality," 46–47.
22. Brunk, "Why Do Societies Collapse?," 204.
23. Li, "Zipf's Law Everywhere," 16.
24. Richardson, "Frequency of Occurrence of Wars," 598.
25. Buchanan, *Ubiquity*, 38.
26. Ibid., 77.
27. Ibid., 88.
28. Ibid., 112.
29. Ibid., 140.
30. Ibid., 191.

SOC expresses itself in network structures at every stage of creation. At the macro level, the universe is a self-regulating network system poised in a critical state between chaos and rigidity. A fundamental example of this is that the acceleration of the universe's expansion due to dark energy is balanced by feedback from collapsing fields of matter.[31] In terms of terrestrial examples, the involvement of network processes in SOC can be seen in ecological loops. Over varying periods of time, natural processes go through cycles of growth, accumulation, restructuring, and renewal.[32] In chapter 2 we met a case of such dynamic feedback loops in the predator-prey fluctuations described by Lotka and Volterra. For humans, networks are especially important in neural functions and therefore will be central to our discussion of mind and the demonic in chapter 8.

The sum of the matter is that the various mechanisms within chaoplexity subsist the four physical forces. Even as gravity, electromagnetism, and the two nuclear forces operate, their specific functions are guided by subterranean chaoplexity. An earthquake is subject to all the forces of plate tectonics, friction, and heat, but it follows a power law. A lightning bolt depends on convection currents and charged air, water, and ice molecules, yet its underlying geometry is fractal and it's a self-organizing system.[33] Birds flying in flocks keep formation by following agent rules even as they exercise individual volition.[34] Scholars who freely refer to another writer's work become part of a citation graph which follows a power law.[35]

Consequently, for Leviathan to engage the four forces of nature, he must know how to influence chaoplexic self-organizing systems. In the next section we turn our attention to how Leviathan as an agent in the system might use mathematical language and chaoplexity to manipulate natural law.

II. LEVIATHAN AND PHYSICAL LAW

Complementarity

To show how Leviathan manipulates natural law, we begin with the principle of complementarity. Consistent with this idea, Klaus Mainzer has made the remarkably prescient comment that dynamic networks could be applied to "angelic organisms from still unknown star systems."[36] Mainzer's idea is echoed by Ervin Laszlo's suggestion that a variety of nonlinear systems may be modeled independently of their "material substance, types of linkages, and natural, artificial, or even psychological

---

31. Mbonye, "Constraints on Cosmic Dynamics."
32. Holling, "Understanding the Complexity," 392.
33. Iudin et al., "Fractal Dynamics," 016601.1.
34. Reynolds, "Flocks, Herds, and Schools," 25–26.
35. An Yuan et al., "Characterizing the Citation Graph," 99.
36. Mainzer, *Thinking in Complexity*, 169.

origin."[37] It's immaterial whether either Mainzer or Laszlo actually believes in alien angelic organisms, since the underlying principle to which they point is creational complementarity.[38] This allows us to take known laws and extrapolate them into new environments. I have argued throughout this book that we have definite experience of Leviathan. Therefore complementarity of known physical and moral laws allows us to intuit Leviathan's character and actions.

Nobel physicist Richard Feynman puts complementarity in a nutshell in his discussion on finding a new law. "First we guess it. Then we compute the consequences of the guess to see what would be implied if this law that we guessed is right. Then we compare the result of the computation to nature, with experiment or experience, to see if it works. If it disagrees with experiment, it is wrong."[39]

Comparing the demonic hypothesis with Popper's worlds of nature, mind, and culture pretty much sums up this book. I have taken the Leviathan account and shown that it explains the origin and intractability of evil and death. Later we shall see that these can be tied to dynamical mechanisms operating in Leviathan: self-directed intelligent agency, manipulated negative feedback loops, catastrophic failure, and irreversible bifurcations. (These will be explained as we meet them in ch. 12.) I will argue that these were all to be found in Lucifer and actually are fundamental in understanding what he did and why. But to draw these relationships between creation and Leviathan depends on the principle of complementarity.

In specific terms, I propose to show here how Leviathan synchronizes with logic space mathematical forms and uses this connection to influence parameters in chaoplexic systems. A first step is to illustrate that these forms actually underlie various creational events.

Examples of Mathematical Forms

Consider the famous slit-screen photon experiment in quantum mechanics. A photon gun fires a single particle at two slits in a panel which has a projection screen behind it. If the photon acts as a particle, it could not possibly go through both slits simultaneously—yet that is what apparently happens. The individual particle is observed on the detector screen, but not as a single hit. Rather, it appears as an interference pattern similar to waves propagating through water. The interference pattern is not of the physical particle with itself, but of higher-dimensional probability waves which have propagated through both slits. In other words, the particle in its wave function is a mathematical form.

Mathematical forms are also logical candidates to explain the paradox of quantum non-locality. When a pair of entangled particles travel off in opposite directions

---

37. Laszlo, "Systems and Structures," 177.
38. Kelso, "Complementary Nature," 364.
39. Feynman, *Character of Physical Law*, 156.

they must have exactly equal momentum in these directions. Yet observing the momentum of either of these particles is statistical. Once an observation is made, the experimenter knows with similar accuracy the momentum of the other particle which theoretically may even be on the other side of the universe. Though experiments to date show particle entanglement only to a distance of around ten kilometers,[40] quantum theory says that whenever two particles interact, they stay connected thereafter even across the universe.

The riddle is that particles across the universe from each other cannot possibly know when the other is observed or undergoes a state change if the information must be transmitted physically. However, if we locate the communication in nonphysical logic space the situation is different. In Karl Svozil's words, we then "consider the automaton as 'a computational substratum which is nonlocal from the very beginning.'"[41] Nonlocality is a rule, not a physical function, and informational patterns link at a logical level.

A third instance of mathematical forms will surprise or even shock us. Though we may not know much else about physics, most of us learn early on that the universe's speed limit is the velocity of light. Thus it's disconcerting to find out that this speed limit has been exceeded in the lab. In one experiment the velocity of light for a short period was infinite before regressing to a slower velocity.[42] Other work has found velocities ranging from 4.7[43] to 8.0[44] times faster than light over longer lab distances. As in quantum nonlocality, these results are physically impossible but make sense when we understand that the operations involved are occurring at the automaton logic level.

A final example is photon teleportation. Scientists have applied the wave function principle to teleport a photon by quantum entanglement.[45] It's particularly crucial to note that the structural information contained in its wave function is teleported but not the particle itself.[46] This implies that the fresh rose bouquet that Théodore Flournoy saw on the séance table was a clone of an original physical version elsewhere. In this case structural information at the form level was used to conform physical particles already present in the room.

Leviathan's Use of Chaoplexity

For simplicity, let's reduce to the lowest denominator the problem of how Leviathan uses logic space mathematical forms: how do machines synchronize with each other?

40. Tittel et al., "Violation of Bell Inequalities," 3563–66.
41. Svozil, "Computational Universes," 850.
42. Recami, "Superluminal Tunnelling," 917.
43. Nimtz and Haibel, "Basics of Superluminal Signals," 1–5.
44. Aichmann et al., "Demonstrating Superluminal," 605.
45. Jennewein et al., "Experimental Nonlocality."
46. Hiley, "Active Information and Teleportation," 113–26.

A first step is to say what we mean by synchronization. The experimental roots of synchronization derive from Dutch astronomer and physicist Christiaan Huygens. While recovering from an illness in 1665, he noticed that two of the large pendulum clocks in his room were beating in unison. Despite how they were started, stopped, or disturbed, they always returned to this synchronized pattern. Nowadays typical machine-to-machine synchronizations include coupled chaotic signal generators, solid state lasers, and communication devices.

In the general case, synchronization means that two or more chaotic systems "adjust a given property of their motion to a common behavior, due to coupling or forcing. This ranges from complete agreement of trajectories to locking of phases."[47] Since chaotic systems intrinsically defy synchronization, a sufficiently strong forced coupling is needed. Such coupling can result in a complete agreement of attractor trajectories, a locking of phases, or other variations between these.[48] The key point, though, is that synchronization fundamentally occurs in logic space even when it manifests in physical systems.[49]

Machine-to-machine synchronization obviously depends on outside human control to select or create the necessary conditions. For example, as a prelude to synchronizing it with a master basin, a researcher may observe a target attractor basin and fully discover its dynamical parameters even if knowing only a few of its variables or functions.[50] Another instance of human oversight is found in the synchronization method called complete replacement. In this a signal from the master system is sent to the target and becomes a component. Everywhere in the target where this component appears it is replaced with the original signal from the first system until they are synchronized. A third illustration involves noise. It arises naturally in neural networks and often represents time lag between feed-forward excitatory firing and inhibitory back-propagation firing response via a feedback loop. Noise is necessary to maintain attractor equilibrium but reducing or adding to it changes system dynamics since basins are finely pre-tuned at the edge of instability.[51] Noise can be used to partially synchronize attractors which are structurally chaotic and nonequivalent.[52] (Systems are defined as nonequivalent if they are mismatched in more than 50 percent of their parameters.)

With this theoretical background, let's consider how Leviathan uses synchronization to produce levitation. In a famous case in 1928 Iowa, a woman named Emma Schmidt underwent exorcism. When the rite began she immediately levitated over

---

47. Boccaletti et al., "Synchronization of Chaotic Systems," 3.
48. Ibid., 3.
49. Pecora et al., "Fundamentals of Synchronization," 520.
50. Ibid., 531.
51. Milton et al., "Controlling Neurological Disease," 136.
52. Boccaletti et al., "Synchronization of Chaotic Systems," 60–62.

the door and even significant force could barely bring her back down.[53] How did Leviathan synchronize with natural law to put her above the door against the pull of gravity?

To answer this we first need to digress into the history of gravity research. During the 1920s, Albert Einstein developed a unified field theory linking electromagnetism and gravity. In understated words, he wrote, "According to this theory, the separation of the gravitational and electromagnetic field seems arbitrary."[54] At about the same time, Townsend Brown discovered that when he charged a capacitor plate to a high voltage, the plate moved in the direction of its positive pole.[55] Brown and later researchers found that various types of radial spin plates[56] used in combination with oppositely charged electrodes[57] actually seemed to block gravity. This whole field of research, known as electrogravitics, was explicitly aimed at antigravity (termed counterbary).

By 1956 Britain's Gravity Research Group listed a who's who of aeronautical firms claiming to have antigravity test rigs: Douglas, Hiller, Sperry-Rand, Glenn Martin, Sikorsky, Clarke Electronics, General Electric, Bell, Convair, and Lear. Those doing research included Curtiss-Wright, Lockheed, Boeing, and North American plus several European firms and American universities.

From Germany's side of things, by the end of WWII Nazi scientists had test-flown conventionally powered flying saucers. They also had experimented with early versions of antigravity propulsion. Post-war, scientists and saucer technology went to various countries on both sides of the cold war divide, with the United States and perhaps others apparently getting the antigravity aspects.[58] In any event, when the UFO craze broke out in 1947, high-ranking American generals already were aware of man-made saucer objects. With great prescience the generals even speculated that these could be the work of a highly secret American project.[59]

Contemporary conventional science is finally trying to make up for eighty years of neglect of Einstein's work tying electromagnetics to gravity. For example, experimenters have demonstrated levitation with diamagnetic materials like water, protein, diamond, DNA, plastic, wood, and other entities. Magnets are able to cancel gravity's

---

53. Vogl, *Begone Satan!*, 13.

54. Einstein, "Unified Field Theory" (translation of "Neue Möglichkeit").

55. Loder, "Outside the Box."

56. Spin plates induce torsion fields which have the capacity to shield gravity. See Wen et al., "Torsion Field Effect and Zero-Point Energy."

57. Gravity Research Group, "Report GRG-013/56."

58. Cook, *Hunt for Zero Point*, 174–80, 198–99, 223–24.

59. Secret report from US Army Air Force Lieutenant General Nathan Twining, head of the Air Material Command, to Brigadier General George Schulgen in Washington, Sept. 23, 1947. See Cook, *Hunt for Zero Point*, 35.

effect and levitate objects like blobs of water, plants, and frogs. So far objects up to fifteen cms have been levitated with a power requirement of a few amps.[60]

The real cutting edge in antigravity theory, though, is rooted in the zero point energy which fills the vacuum. Particles arise from and disappear into the vacuum and energy fields in it continuously fluctuate about their baseline values. Because this fluctuation activity remains even at absolute zero, the energy is called zero-point energy (ZPE) and the fluctuations zero-point fluctuations (ZPF).

The obvious question is, where does this energy come from? H. E. Puthoff offers two possible answers. On the one hand, it might just be a boundary condition of the universe. If this is so, there's no further issue to discuss. Puthoff favors a solution in which ZPE arises from its interaction with matter.[61] Of course, since ZPE energy is the source of matter this creates a tautology of which Puthoff is well aware. He states, "The ZPF spectrum is dynamically generated by the motion of charged particles which are themselves undergoing ZPF-induced motion, as part of a self-consistent cosmic feedback cycle."[62] This isn't logically incoherent if we grant that such a synergistic relationship is possible as long as it's specified by the controlling rules. (This was explained in the prologue as a function of the God-GUT network.) Puthoff's construction is particularly welcome from the perspective of this book's emphasis that network feedback systems are fundamental in creation.

As did Andrei Sakharov in a pioneering article in 1968, Puthoff proposes that gravity can be explained as an induced effect brought about by the interaction of the electromagnetic ZPE energies with matter. Puthoff writes:

> A particle sitting in the sea of electromagnetic zero-point fluctuations develops a "jitter" motion, or ZITTERBEWEGUNG as German physicists have named it. When there are two or more particles, they are each influenced not only by the fluctuating background field, but also by the fields generated by the other particles, all similarly undergoing Zitterbewegung motion. The coupling between particles due to these fields produces the attractive gravitational force.[63]

So the circle closes. Einstein wrote unified field equations linking electromagnetism and gravity. Real-world science has produced levitation by electromagnetics. Modern theory proposes that these phenomena are defined in the automaton's cells at the informational level. Can we relate these factors to the question of how Leviathan might have levitated Emma Schmidt?

This may be easier than we might expect. I mentioned above how Townsend Brown stumbled upon the connection between a charged capacitor and object movement. The principle is that if two sides of an object are given opposite charges of

---

60. Simon and Geim, "Diamagnetic Levitation," 6200–202.
61. Puthoff, "Source of Vacuum Electromagnetic Zero-Point Energy," 4857.
62. Ibid.
63. Puthoff, "Everything for Nothing," 54.

sufficient energy, gravity is reduced or even totally blocked locally. A modern example is the American B-2 bomber which uses this technology on its wing leading edges and in the exhaust stream to produce about 30 percent more lift.[64]

In Emma's case, all Leviathan had to do was synchronize with electromagnetism at the level of its informational self-organizing structure, induce charge differentials, and presto, gravity blocking and levitation result. Leviathan broke no physical law in this but merely directed its expression. No moral or spiritual law is broken since, by definition, Leviathan can only interfere in specific situations when human permission through covenant breach with God has been granted.

If Leviathan can direct electromagnetism, might it be possible to correlate electromagnetic effects with various authenticated *psi* activities? If so, then perhaps we could extrapolate demonic interaction with nature beyond electromagnetism to the general case. Links between paranormal *psi* and electromagnetism were first suggested over one hundred years ago[65] but we need to take into account three factors.

First, of course, earth has a background electromagnetic field so any measurement related to alleged *psi* artifacts must account for this. Having said that, comparison of background levels with *psi* events from 1868–1980 in Britain found a weak statistical link between lower geomagnetic levels and clairvoyance and telepathy, and between higher levels and poltergeist psychokinesis (moving objects) and hauntings.[66] In the reputedly haunted Hampton Court Palace in Surrey, England, research found significant variations within rooms' magnetic fields. These variations were correlated with the numbers of haunting phenomena reported.[67] Furthermore, anomalous electromagnetic readings have been recorded in a localized area of poltergeist activity for one minute after the event.[68]

Second, the human body generates a small electric current. Kirlian photography, for instance, isn't *psi* but a perfectly normal physical result of body moisture, charge, barometric pressure, and mind emotional state. These combine to produce an ionized gas aura which can be photographed. If the picture is taken in a vacuum with no ionized gas, there's no aura present.[69] On the other hand, the famous Russian psychic Nina Kulagina generated strong electrostatic and electromagnetic force fields nearly four meters from her body,[70] implying a paranormal demonic force.

A third factor is simply that by definition demonically triggered electromagnetism in cases like a lightning bolt will produce no atypical readings. This is because

---

64. Cook, *Hunt for Zero Point*, 135.
65. Eichler, "To Be or Not to Be!," 38.
66. Wilkinson and Gauld, "Geomagnetism and Anomalous Experiences," 305–6.
67. Wiseman et al., "Investigation into Alleged 'Hauntings,'" 202.
68. Roll, "Poltergeists," 83.
69. Hines, *Pseudoscience and the Paranormal*, 352.
70. Mishlove, "Nina Kulagina."

the anomalous aspect is in the timing and circumstances rather than in the physical event itself.

In questions of control of nature, we must bear in mind the flip side. In the same decade as Schmidt was being levitated, a Shanghai man's body mass was compared to cast iron and could only be lifted by seven other men. This happened during an exorcism conducted by a Taoist monk.[71] Therefore the demonically triggered process must be able to produce both weight cancellation and increase.

To illustrate the problem of bidirectional influence further, let's digress for a moment into organic life processes. Two generations ago, Franklin Loehr tested prayer as a technique to influence plant growth and claimed that plants receiving positive prayer (blessing) grew 8.7 percent faster than those receiving negative prayer (cursing).[72] Can a curse or its equivalent regress a plant into its seed form? The ability to both stimulate and regress plant growth would be equivalent to the levitation-weight increase process. According to Jeffrey Mishlove, psychic Uri Geller was handed a sprouted mung bean without warning and told to make time run backward. Geller closed his fist on the bean and concentrated for a few minutes. When he opened his hand, he supposedly held a sproutless, intact bean seed.[73]

To sum up, the demonic can use chaoplexic processes to manipulate electromagnetism. In turn, the wide range of paranormal phenomena reported across the centuries would then imply that via the electromagnetic doorway Leviathan might well intervene in the other forces in nature.

The Fifth Force

One of the debates in contemporary culture concerns the claim that there exists another physical force alongside gravity, electromagnetism, and the strong and weak nuclear forces. Since at least 1986,[74] scientific experiments have been designed to locate a fifth force and on at least one occasion it has been claimed that such a force has been found. In this case, the apparent evidence was subjected to replication testing. Subsequently, the claim was falsified.

However, neognostic ideology claims that *psi* subtle energy is this fifth force. As such, it becomes the explanation *du jour* for all manner of paranormal physical phenomena, not just levitation. One thinks of other exotica like seeing and hearing through solid barriers,[75] reading with the body's surface skin,[76] spontaneous

---

71. Betty, "Growing Evidence," 16.
72. Kraemer, "Power of Prayer on Plants," 244–45.
73. Mishlove, *PK Man*, 24.
74. Fischbach and Talmadge, "Ten Years of the Fifth Force."
75. Owens, "Zen Buddhism," 175.
76. Esdaile, *Mesmerism in India*, 124–25.

combustion of the human body,[77] and human translocation through solid walls,[78] not to mention the long list of *psi-gamma* (mind) phenomena.

A major stumbling block to subtle energy's claim to be a true natural fifth force is that, contrary to chaoplexity's experimental confirmations, subtle energy has only ever been observed via clairvoyant vision[79] and paranormal effects. It has never been sensed by proper instruments[80] and does not replicate like the four real forces of nature.[81] Though phenomena—not an underlying energy—can be detected in lab experiments like J. B. Rhine's at Duke University, they can't be predictably repeated across time and location.

This was famously confirmed with work Jacques Benveniste prepared for publication in *Nature*. He spent four years testing an anti-immune antibody solution which seemed to verify the claims of homeopathy. At *Nature's* request, labs in Israel, Italy, and Canada replicated his results prior to publication.[82] When journal representatives came to his lab, though, Benveniste was unable to replicate the results in their presence.

A generation earlier, Jung had also noticed the subjective aspect of *psi* phenomena. Referring to J. B. Rhine's work, Jung, who was a deep believer in a higher realm of lawful psychoid energy, asserted, "In each series of experiments the first attempts yielded a better result than the later ones. The falling off in the number of hits scored was connected with the mood of the subject. An initial mood of faith and optimism makes for good results. Scepticism and resistance have the opposite effect, that is, they create an unfavourable disposition."[83]

Fifth-force beliefs include a Christianized gnostic element. Many Christians, apparently because they are unaware of this connection, remain convinced that the soul has preternatural *psi* powers. These abilities were allegedly given to Adam at creation and survived the fall. Over the centuries, certain schools of thought therefore have believed that Adam had near-messianic primeval powers. The third century CE *Hermetica* portrayed him as the archetypal primal man who assumes godlike powers over nature.[84] In rabbinic gnosticism, Adam was an enormous, near-supernatural, world-spanning golem. This was a being who encompasses good and evil, mediates human possibilities (including sexual) and is "a symbol of the ultimate wholeness of humankind . . . an incarnation of the wholeness of the physical cosmos."[85] The Renais-

---

77. Gromb et al., "Spontaneous Human Combustion," 29–31.
78. Gersi, *Faces in the Smoke*, 182.
79. Slater, "Toward an Understanding," 219.
80. Quinn, "Therapeutic touch," 44, 48.
81. Benor, *Healing Research*, 116–21.
82. Davenas et al., "Human Basophil Degranulation," 818.
83. Jung, "Appendix: On Synchronicity," 524.
84. Layton, *Gnostic Scriptures*, 452.
85. Niditch, "Cosmic Adam," 142.

sance magician Agrippa saw Adam as "lord and master of Creation and master of all the forces of the created world."[86]

The doctrine that humanity has residual *psi* creational powers has persisted until the present. In the early twentieth century, Watchman Nee argued that "in Adam's fall God had not withdrawn from him that 'supernatural' power which he once possessed. Instead, this power fell with him and became imprisoned in his body."[87] We could hardly imagine a more explicit commitment to gnostic theology than this doctrine of spirit imprisonment in flesh. According to Nee, because these powers are still latent in every person, Satan is trying to achieve control over them and turn their use against people.

For Nee, soul power included clairvoyance, retrocognition, remote sensory abilities of seeing, hearing, feeling and tasting, and mind healing. This last one he called "pathetism" but he actually meant *psi* mesmerism.[88] He saw paranormal mesmerism as an explicit example of the release of creational soul powers.[89]

Nee's beliefs have been echoed by people from various Christian communions. The Welsh revivalist Jessie Penn-Lewis referred specifically to the "animal magnetism which is inherent in every human frame."[90] Rudolf Otto, a Lutheran, argued that Jesus' intense healing powers of will fit alongside suggestion and hypnotism, telepathy, distance *psi*, and animal magnetism.[91] The Cistercian monk Alois Weisinger thought that the residual roots of Adam's preternatural powers can be accessed via trance or hypnosis.[92]

We can draw two conclusions about the relationship of fifth-force subtle energy to creation. First, its non-replicability denies it scientific status; and second, its subjective aspect points to personal causation. In other words, it's the kind of power that came to be known as the Wolfgang Pauli Effect. Physicists joked that whenever the Nobel Prize winner was around, various equipment would randomly explode or otherwise come to grief. Pauli even mentions this himself.[93] I suggest that fifth-force subtle energy falls outside God's created intentions for people and is merely another term for the operation of personal demonic powers who interfere in creation.

---

86. Nauert, *Agrippa and the Crisis*, 279.

87. Nee, *Latent Power*, 26.

88. Ibid., 27. Pathetism is one term of many which were applied to Mesmer's fluid. Others included Mental or Animal Electricity, Mesmerism, Neurology, Etherology, Psychodunamy, and of course, Animal Magnetism.

89. Ibid., 38.

90. Penn-Lewis, *Soul and Spirit*, 25.

91. Otto, "Signs Following," 214.

92. Weisinger, *Occult Phenoman*, 95.

93. Pauli, *Atom and Archetype*, 33–34.

This contradicts the neognostic claim[94] that—whether we call the power *psi*, subtle energy, animal magnetism, innate soul force, or whatever—it's the same power as Jesus' manifestation of *dunamis* (power).

The gnostic meaning which is attributed to *dunamis* was borrowed from Egyptian thought via pre-Christian Greek philosophers like Poseidonius. In these cases, it did mean "cosmic principle" and hence stood for manistic (preternatural) ideas and powers.[95] But this is not the meaning of Jesus' exercise of *dunamis*. There is no hint of an innate vital force or cosmic principle empowering Jesus' healings. To the contrary, it is extremely significant that his healing miracles were manifest only after his baptism in the Holy Spirit and his wilderness refusal to worship Satan. On the one hand, Jesus' healings were direct functions of Holy Spirit empowerment and on the other of explicit rejection of the illicit powers which are rooted in Leviathan and chaos. Consequently Jesus' healings were not signs of a universally accessible subtle power flowing through all people. They signified the continuation of God's battle with the demonic beings who inhabit chaos.[96] The conclusion is inescapable that genuine subtle energy manifestations are nothing less than demonic phenomena.

III. LEVIATHAN'S BOUNDARIES

As was the case with *Malleus Maleficarum*, the modern question is how creation mediates between the competing principles of God's sovereignty and Leviathan's ability to use natural law. In the following remarks I argue that God has imposed a single boundary condition which I call moral permission. This has a double meaning. From a cosmological point of view, Leviathan's rebellion and loss of authority limits this permission to terrestrial affairs. It's actually possible that God, in apportioning the "stars of heaven" (angels), had assigned Lucifer to earth from the beginning to be responsible for humans when they (we) eventually arrived. His fall from heaven confirmed this territory, removed him from heaven's councils, and defined him henceforth as humans' adversary rather than enabler. The second sense from a terrestrial perspective is that as Leviathan his freedom of operation is bounded by human vicegerency. Now as adversary, he must obtain human permission to operate in people and our affairs.

Let's begin evaluating Leviathan's moral permission boundary by considering his computational ability. As we saw earlier, creation's self-organizing systems follow equations which are very complicated. Indeed, at present science lacks the mathematics needed to design chaotic sources which reproduce systems with specific properties.[97] It's currently impossible, for instance, to model earthquake prediction. In spite of the new understanding that earthquakes are SOC systems, it's questionable whether

---

94. Wipprecht, "Healthy Alternative," 11. See also Miller, "Pastorate," 93, 102.
95. Grundmann, "δυναμαι," 287–91.
96. Sarantis, "God, Miracles and Quantum Mechanics," 131.
97. Abarbanel et al., "Blending Chaotic Attractors," 214.

experts will ever be able to predict when a specific earthquake of a given strength will strike, let alone preemptively trigger a controlled release quake.

However, the weather may be a different matter. Futurists already are talking about global weather control and the social, political, and ecological effects of such actions.[98] Even now, the most powerful supercomputers are able to model significant climate phenomena such as the vortices caused by the trade winds interacting with the Hawaiian Islands. With processor speeds of up to 51.9 trillion floating-point operations per second (teraflops),[99] NASA's supercomputer successfully predicted the tracks of hurricanes Frances, Ivan, and Jeanne in 2004.

Modern *psi* apologists believe in weather control just as much as did the authors of *Malleus Maleficarum*. Ted Owens, the same psychic credited with triggering lightning on the Camden, New Jersey, bridge, also reputedly controlled hurricanes via his "nonhuman intelligences." On August 22, 1979, he claimed that he would create a hurricane that would strike Florida. One emerged in a few days which he proceeded to "direct" toward the state. When it became David, a category five storm, he was implored to halt it from wreaking untold destruction. This he supposedly did on September 2. The storm mysteriously dissipated the next day, leaving Neil Frank of the National Hurricane Center saying that it was one of the most dramatic changes he had seen in twenty years of hurricane tracking.[100]

This account prompts two remarks concerning Leviathan's computational limits. In his global weather control vision, Ross Hoffman notes that computing power vastly greater than today's capacities will be required to master such operations.[101] Let's assume that the NASA super-computer's capacity of 51.9 trillion operations per second is a base line for such exponential computing growth. Indeed, by 2015 supercomputer speeds had increased to 150 teraflops.[102] Then we can begin to see the demonic power involved in synchronizing with the SOSs by which David was created in order to compute and direct their future development.

Second, if Owens really did call up demonic powers who controlled hurricane David, it's natural to ask how far we can scale up Leviathan's computational ability. As a scenario let's consider whether Leviathan could have caused any of the celestial warfare which is celebrated in ancient annals. Prior to the nineteenth-century victory of the evolutionary, uniformitarian worldview, philosophers of science routinely ascribed heavenly battles to Mars, Venus, other planets, the sun, comets, and earth. This perspective was resurrected by Immanuel Velikovsky in his book *Worlds in Collision*.[103] Although he was mercilessly ridiculed at the time, Velikovsky won the intellectual war

98. Hoffman, "Controlling the Global Weather," 241–48.
99. Shen et al., "0.125 degree."
100. Mishlove, *PK Man*, 129.
101. Hoffman, "Controlling the Global Weather," 246.
102. Storm, "Need to Crunch 150 Teraflops."
103. Velikovsky, *Worlds in Collision*.

to revive catastrophism. For example, science nowadays routinely discusses major life extinctions in terms of Apollo-class asteroid impacts with earth.[104]

Apollo objects have orbits which bring them inside that of earth's orbit, opening the door for collisions. At least one, Ganymed, is about thirty-nine kms in diameter and would wreak vast destruction on a planetary scale if it hit earth. In fact, just such a blast—though relatively small-scale—occurred in 1907 in Siberia when a meteoroid estimated to be equivalent to a 10–40 megaton hydrogen bomb hit the Tunguska River basin.[105]

Astronomers Victor Cluba and Bill Napier proposed[106] that similar Apollo-class asteroid collisions produced the phenomena during the Exodus which Velikovsky ascribed solely to Venus and Mars. Calculations suggest that a typical asteroid of about one km diameter and a mass of 2.77×10^{12} kgs would even change earth's rotational axis if it impacted at the proper angle. Actually, a smaller one would do the job. "We can realistically suppose that an object of half that size is enough to develop a torque of sufficient value for a huge shift of the poles."[107] An asteroid-triggered pole-upheaval therefore has been proposed as the plausible backdrop for several ancient reports. During the Battle of Gibeon, for instance, Joshua requested the sun to stand still and huge stones fell from heaven (Josh 10:12–13). The Greek philosopher Herodotus said that in historical times the sun had twice risen in the east and twice in the west.[108] In addition to these, the first-century CE Roman writer Pomponius Mela repeated Egyptian temple references to sunrise reversals.[109]

Could Leviathan have caused interstellar disruptions? We learned in chapter 3 that ancient Near Eastern documents clearly point to a struggle in the heavens. In Ugaritic theology, the god Ashtar (Lucifer/Venus) attempted to sit on the throne of Baal (the Sun). So given that Leviathan changed the Nile to "blood" when implored by the Egyptian magicians, it's reasonable to wonder whether he also has the computational ability to operate in the heavenly regions. Might he be able to direct Apollo-class asteroid fragments into earth's path to produce cosmic upheavals which beggar our human imaginations?

The answer is "yes, but." We shall discover in chapter 12 that Leviathan had enough computational ability to think that he could extricate himself from his eternal covenant with God. In principle, then, he likely would be able to influence cosmological events. However, Lucifer's rebellion had resulted in his loss of status within creation; after all, this is how he became Leviathan. In Jesus' words, Lucifer was cast from heaven to earth (Luke 18:10; Rev 12:7–9). This delineates a loss, not of spatiality,

---

104. Morrison et al., "Dealing with the Impact Hazard," 741.
105. Clube and Napier, *Cosmic Serpent*, 140.
106. Ibid., 218–23.
107. Barbiero, "On the Possibility," report DMSIA 7/97.
108. Herodotus, *Histories*, bk. 2, ch. 142, sec. 4.
109. Pomponius, *De Situ Orbis*, I, 59.

but of authority. ANE theology accurately understood Lucifer's attempted coup d'état and read the celestial swordplay of comets, planets, and asteroids as representations of Lucifer's (Ashtar's) revolt. However, Leviathan's loss of authority suggests that the cosmic fireworks which humans saw on the heavenly stage were God's object lessons and not Leviathan's direct interferences.

Loss of authority equates to the second aspect of the boundary condition governing Leviathan. While he has the computational ability to interfere with cosmological events, he has been restricted to activity which has a uniquely terrestrial focus. Even then, Leviathan doesn't have completely free rein on earth since Adam's vicegerency of earth remains as a hierarchical power order. Although Leviathan's disorder led God to create a universe with entropy and death, Adam still was granted conditional immortality and was told to guard the garden. That is, he was warned that disorder lurked in and behind the structures. If he was tempted to manipulate natural law to try to guarantee immortality, death would inevitably result for him just as it had for Leviathan. God was very clear with Adam; "you are in charge—vicegerent—of certain aspects of planet earth's moral and physical systems. Don't relinquish control of these structures to the serpent." It's intriguing that Ted Owen's demonic masters acknowledged the truth of vicegerency. In Owen's words, "[The alien intelligences] have to have human choice. The law is that they can't make a move on their own unless they have human choice tied up or involved in it."[110]

The sum of all this is that the power to control nature via demonic powers is implied by the text, "now they have become like us" (Gen 3:22). The human covenant with Leviathan leads to illicit attempts to control nature via the gods' powers.

Bearing this in mind, what are we to make of testimony that, like Ted Owens, Christian healer Agnes Sanford also claimed to control hurricanes? Agnes and a prayer partner began praying for hurricanes to quiet down and go to sea. Radio announcers would say that the storm was going to sea and there would be little or no damage after all. Then they realized that this might cause drought![111] Once when she and a friend were in a seashore motel, a great wind arose which the newspapers said reached 100 mph. It was throwing small stones against the plate glass window, so Agnes crossly shouted at the wind, "Okay, *that's enough! Quiet down!*" She wrote, "Suddenly, the wind was still. I cannot explain this, nor do I recommend it! It happened, that's all."[112]

Taken literally, Owens and Sanford return us to *Malleus Maleficarum* and its conviction that humans on each side of the cosmic struggle can manipulate nature. But is this really the biblical picture? Though Jesus did control the winds more than once, it's hard to avoid concluding that Sanford blundered into forbidden territory. Here's why.

The question of mixed structures and competing authorities lands us squarely in the center of OT theology and its central concern over the nature gods. The

---

110. Mishlove, *PK Man*, 74.
111. Sanford, *Sealed Orders*, 233.
112. Ibid., 309, italics original.

exclusionary clause of the first commandment, "You shall have no other gods before me" (Exod 20:3), literally set in stone the nonnegotiable foundation of biblical faith. We're not surprised, then, to turn to the holiness legal code and find that its core concern is the intermixing of authentic Yahwism with nature god worship.

Commentators have construed the Mosaic holiness laws in terms of public hygiene, theocratic moral teaching, separation from sin, and religious ritual. However, in 1984 Mary Douglas initiated a new line of interpretation which focuses on holiness and impurity boundaries. She pointed out that because holiness is part of God's identity, "this is a universe in which men [sic] prosper by conforming to holiness and perish when they deviate from it."[113] While justice and moral goodness may "illustrate holiness and form part of it . . . holiness embraces other concepts as well."[114] Specifically, holiness is separation, wholeness, and completeness, principles evident in the physical perfection required of people and animals presented at the tabernacle (Lev 11–15).

Furthermore, holiness and pollution extend to species and categories so that anathema is pronounced on "hybrids and other confusions." For instance, in Lev 18:23 bestiality is labeled "perversion" (*tebhel*), a rare Hebrew word which Douglas says instead ought to be rendered "mixing or confusion."[115] The same concern for hybrids is in Lev 19:19, where the mixing of seeds, cattle, and clothing materials is prohibited. That these hybrid prohibitions are concerned with covenant holiness is strongly implied by even more ancient ANE records. A nineteenth-century BCE inscription from Mari describes the same practices as we see in the "covenant of cutting" of sacrificial animals in Gen 15:7–21. The Mari covenant sacrifice, termed "slaying of the ass,"[116] required a purebred animal (rather than an ass/mare cross which produces a mule) just as did the later Jewish regulations from Sinai.

The argument also applies to the dietary laws. The general principle is that each shall conform fully to its class. "Those species are unclean which are imperfect members of their class, or whose class itself confounds the general scheme of the world." Any class of creature which doesn't move according to the right locomotion for its class is unclean. We recall in this regard Lucifer's descent from flying seraphim to crawling serpent, a movement-mix which confirmed his uncleanness. In contrast, creationally clean four-legged land animals walk, hop, or jump; two-legged birds fly with wings; and scaly fish swim with fins.[117]

All of these impurity laws are prefaced by, "Be holy for I am holy." The argument may be summarized in these words, "Holiness means keeping distinct the categories of creation."[118] This was echoed by Kalinda Stevenson, "That which is clean is

113. Douglas, *Purity and Danger*, 50.
114. Ibid., 51.
115. Ibid., 53.
116. Noth, "Old Testament Covenant Making, 111.
117. Douglas, *Purity and Danger*, 55.
118. Ibid.

in its proper place with the boundaries established by God in creation. That which is unclean is something *out of place*. The *sphere* of the ordinary is the common, while the *realm* of the divine is the holy."[119]

The conclusion to which we are led is that the essence of evil is the total rejection of order, lawfulness, proper station, and function. To be disordered and mixed—whether as demon, human, animal, fish, or fowl—is to be impure and unclean. When we apply the principle to the deep-level self-organizing systems in nature, we conclude that for humans to call upon demonic powers to manipulate these laws is to be mixed, impure, and to break creational boundaries. In fact, the holiness principle which rejects hybridization is simply theological language which stands for the paradox of double-marking that we have found to be at the core of evil.

The holiness principle therefore outlaws the human-demonic hybrid which is central to *psi* control of nature. To the contrary, the biblical dictum is that humans interact with nature through direct physical labor. A dam built to control flooding is theologically pure; demonically empowered prevention of drenching rainstorms which produce flooding is impure. The rare nature control exceptions—Moses, Joshua, Elijah, Jesus—only underscore that there's no conceptual difference between people who control hurricanes spiritually and, say, the Findhorn community in Scotland and its reliance on devas, elves, and the god Pan to grow improbable vegetable gardens.[120]

IV. SUMMARY

I have focused on Leviathan's access to and misuse of physical law, and illustrated this mixed reality with levitation and weather control. The goal has been to establish Leviathan's status within creation's legal framework. With this preparatory work in hand, we can turn our attention to a variety of other ways in which Leviathan's disorder manifests in and through lawful systems. The next three chapters will explore specifically how Leviathan works within the human mind to produce various psychological, cultural, and spiritual phenomena.

---

119. Stevenson, *Vision of Transformation*, xix, italics original.
120. Hawken, *Magic of Findhorn*, 57.

8

THE DISORDERED MIND

IN JANUARY, 1959, MATHEMATICIAN John Forbes Nash Jr. walked into a common room at Princeton. Holding a copy of the *New York Times,* he announced that the paper contained encrypted messages from outer space that were meant only for him.[1] An associate asked how Nash could believe he was being recruited by aliens from outer space to save the world. Nash replied that he believed these to be messages from supernatural beings because they came to him the same way that his mathematical ideas did.[2] Furthermore, the messages not only came in the *Times* but as internal voices as well. "I started to think I was a man of great religious importance, and to hear voices all the time. I began to hear something like telephone calls in my head."[3]

By April of that year, Nash's wife Alicia had him involuntarily committed to McLean Hospital near Boston.[4] This launched a twenty-five-year struggle which Nash ended by deciding "to think conventionally" again so that his work would be socially acceptable. Interestingly, though, in his official Nobel Prize autobiographical sketch, he said, "Rationality of thought imposes a limit on a person's concept of his relation to the cosmos."[5] With these polite words he dismissed the social consensus that paranoid schizophrenia is an illness. Instead he implied that it's an aspect of human consciousness that transcends science.

Nash's schizophrenia is one case of the more general class of mind disorders. My goal in this chapter is to show first, mind disorders' chaoplexic structure and second, how demons use chaoplexity to attach to people. The following brief overviews set the stage by describing the theoretical postures taken by materialism, neognosticism, and

1. Nasar, *Beautiful Mind,* 241.
2. Ibid., 11.
3. O'Connor and Robertson, "John Forbes Nash."
4. Nasar, *Beautiful Mind,* 252–54.
5. Nash, "John F. Nash."

biblical realism toward the disordered mind. In the remainder of the chapter I develop a detailed biblical realist analysis of mind disorders.

For evolutionary materialists, mind disorders are adaptive responses to the struggle for survival. Hence schizophrenia is necessary for creativity to flourish[6] and depression produces a social incapacity which otherwise would result in physical powerlessness or death.[7] Similar benefits are claimed for over-activated stress responses resulting from child abuse. Even though such stress leads to severe impairments like dissociation, hysteric conversion, and post-traumatic stress disorder, it provides short term survival.[8] Ironically, though, altruism is a problem for evolutionary materialism. Because standard theory insists that there must be a direct benefit to the person,[9] genuine altruism among unrelated people presents a major challenge.[10] Evolutionary psychology answers that in this case altruism produces community adaptation and survival.

In contrast to materialism, neognosticism has a transcendent eschatology. By presuming a spiritual dimension to people, neognosticism (holism) speaks of human renewal and change. An acute psychotic episode therefore is primarily spiritual and discloses to the person their deeper relationships to the cosmos.[11] Though his words were carefully chosen, that's what Nash said in his Nobel essay. Altered states and abnormal perceptual, emotional, cognitive, and psychosomatic functioning, defined as pathological in conventional psychiatry, are growth opportunities in the holistic view. Phenomena like voices, visions, NDEs, OBEs, *psi*, mystical union, and cosmic consciousness all signal the presence of this spiritual frontier.[12] Ultragnostic worldviews even envision self-divinization of the race and transcendence of our physical embodiment.[13]

In stark contrast to these perspectives, the biblical realist worldview says that mind disorders are part of the human malaise caused by breaking covenant with God (Deut 28:28). On the legal level, this is expressed as *lex talionis*—as you personally or ancestrally do it shall be done to you. On the relational level, the broken covenant in Eden caused loss of attachment to God. As we saw in chapter 5, attachment refers to a long-term tie with a unique and non-interchangeable partner from whom inexplicable, involuntary separation would cause grief.[14] This is a precise description of our loss of attachment with God. Attachment fracture led to the loss of system homeo-

6. Andreason, *Brave New Brain*, 200.
7. Price and Sloman, "Evolutionary Model," 211.
8. Teicher, "Scars That Won't Heal," 75.
9. Lehmann and Keller, "Evolution of Cooperation and Altruism," 1374.
10. Fehr and Fischbacher, "Nature of Human Altruism," 785.
11. Miller, "Mental Illness and Spiritual Crisis," 29–47.
12. Ibid., 39.
13. Hubbard, *Revelation*, 76, 86, 112, etc.
14. Coleman and Watson, "Infant Attachment," 297.

stasis (rebalancing) by which God upheld the regulation of body, mind, and spirit for perpetual life and well-being.

In conceptual terms, then, *lex talionis* and attachment loss are the moral and psychological descriptors for how Eden opened the doorway to mind disorders. According to one's ancestral inheritances, personal choices, and life traumas a person passes through those doorways into the realm of disorders.

In the following sections I begin with a chaoplexic model of the mind's structure; then I relate this to mind disorders; and finally I show how the demonic penetrates the human mind to mimic and/or cause mind disturbances.

I. THE ORDERED MIND

In its higher functions, the mind is designed to express qualia (sensation and emotion) and awareness. It operates as a transducer or converter between the brain and spirit just as the brain serves as a transducer between the environment and the mind. To appreciate how the mind functions, we can look at the brain. This is because it operates as the lower end of the brain-mind feedback network and therefore exactly reflects the mind's control rules operating in logic space.

To understand this system, therefore, we build from the bottom up, starting with individual neurons in the brain. They transmit ions in electrical pulses which, when they are graphed over time, look like spikes. Neuron firing also takes a form called bursting in which the voltage rises slowly to a particular threshold and then the neuron fires a rapid series of spikes. As the burst fades, the spikes relapse from near-periodic patterns into what seems a chaotic regime before shutting off. In higher organisms, since the neural networks are more complex and inherently chaotic, the chaos is suppressed by feedback from the inhibitory neural circuits. Otherwise, the neurons would all quickly degenerate into erratic behavior. The upshot is that the neural cell assemblies are designed to operate right on the brink of their boundary with chaotic behavior.[15]

System rules which combine syntactic (process) and semantic (meaning) aspects translate the brain's sensory data into mathematical forms or objects which occupy this logic space.[16] The objects—like mathematics as a whole—are analogous to platonic forms[17] insofar as they have reality but not instrumentally detectable physicality. The protocols by which neural net signals are transduced into mathematical objects are technically labeled deterministic finite-state automata or DFAs. The more usual term and hence that already used in this book is agent but regardless of title, the structure is a cluster of recurrent neural network rules.[18] Recurrent rules specify that the

15. Dartnell, "Chaos in the Brain."
16. Duch, "Platonic Model of Mind," 499.
17. Penrose, *Emperor's New Mind*, 94–98.
18. Omlin and Giles, "Extraction of Rules," 41.

processing of network data inputs begins where the previous input cycle has finished. In this way, the network remembers its previous state as the basis for transforming into a new state. As forms are created and laid down, they trace out a trajectory in logic space which is bounded by the values contributed by the various input parts of the network. This bounded area is called an attractor basin.

How many attractor basins might actually be at work creating mathematical mind objects? The mind theory called computationalism requires that any neural synapse be used for a single function. This places an extremely low ceiling on the number of basins. Christopher Cherniak published a much-cited calculation of this sort. He assumed that there are 5×10^{13} synapses and that each cognitive/perceptual element of information requires one megabyte (1,000 neurons) at the rate of one million synapses per mb. Including organizational indices, he stated that this allows for three million (3.0×10^6) motor/cognitive elements without relying on what he called "Cartesian nonspatial substance."[19]

The impossibly tiny neural resources of Cherniak's linear model pale in comparison to those offered by chaoplexity whose system dynamics are virtually without constraint. Nonlinearity's descriptive equations by definition have at least two variables (called degrees of freedom) with exponent values involving infinite decimal expansion (numbers like *pi*). In principle, such a system can create near-limitless mathematical objects because its mind contents' storage capacity is not fixed by physical limits. As a result, attractor basins are a resource-rich method of offering great choice which is constantly present during every neural net cycle at every hierarchical level.

As mentioned above, the mathematical forms have inherent correspondences by creational fiat. They are semantic (purposeful) from one perspective and syntactic (formally structured) from another.[20] This syntactic/semantic relationship may be illustrated by Fechner's law,[21] which determines the neural dynamics by which sensory impressions are received, processed, and distributed throughout the brain. The law may be stated in natural English as follows, using hearing as the example sense:

> Let neural local cell assemblies transduce (convert) external sound waves into mathematical objects and let the mind recognize these objects as sound of varying loudness and pitch. Let this transduction be a nonlinear multiplicand of the magnitude of the sound stimulus, the differential threshold between sound and no sound, and the just-noticeable difference in incremental changes in stimulus.[22]

19. Cherniak, "Undebuggability and Cognitive Science," 405.
20. Jonker and Treur, "Modelling Multiple Mind-Matter Interaction," 182.
21. Norwich and Wong, "Unification of Psychophysical Phenomena," 930.
22. Ibid. The syntactic aspect is expressed in the equation $L = \frac{1}{2}k \ln(I+y'In)$ where L is loudness, I is the intensity of sound expressed as a power, and k, y' and n are constants representing subjective magnitude of stimulus, subjective just-noticeable difference in sound, and the differential threshold between sound and no sound.

In order for people to experience both sensory and emotional qualia, it is crucial that the mathematical objects function as virtually limitless self-organizing DFAs instead of binary computations. To see why this is so, consider the tractability (doability) problem with qualia and cognition when computation and storage are binary only. Models invoking more than perhaps three lines of binary if/then (yes/no) truth tables are essentially unfeasible—the demand on neural processing is too heavy for real life. Cherniak illustrates the truth table dilemma by showing how the brain-as-computer cannot "evaluate even the truth table for 138 independent propositions [yes/no choices, thus 2^{138} different decisions] during the interval from the big bang to the present."[23] Leonid Perlovsky makes the same point by saying that a truth table with 100 lines [and 100 columns] represents more choices to compute (100^{100}) than there are elementary particles in the entire universe.[24] Nonetheless, many theoreticians still treat mind algorithms in terms of constraint-free brain-based if/then rules.[25]

In contrast, the inherent flexibility and capacity of the chaoplexic mind may be illustrated by emotions. The crux of emotional arousal and sensory qualia is that they are enabled by attractor structure. The mind is designed to determine and respond to great variations from midline equilibrium as an attractor's orbits move from criticality toward either fixed periods or into chaos.[26] Włodzisław Duch's graph of rat fear and joy presents a pair of 3-D attractor basins where the number of emotional mind objects is represented by the density of lines in the chart.[27] Heavy density produced by extreme emotions like panic states of mind correspond to chaos in the dynamical system.[28] In this case panic puts the points' orbits at the attractor basin's boundary, and if it's truly catastrophic, a new basin may form or noncompatible basins may synchronize. In psychopathological language, such an outcome might be perceived by an observer as some form of hysteric conversion.

Attractor operation can be illustrated in mental function, too. Consider Ben Goertzel's fictional friend Jane, who's labeled paranoid delusional because "they" are trying to poison her. Jane thinks she's being followed and she can tell who her pursuers are by the color of their clothes. Her behavior and indeed her whole mental fabric follows this governing pattern. The set of psychological processes combine to form a powerful attractor.[29] Out of all the possible states her mind might create, this specific pattern depicts her system. In the bigger conceptual picture, Jane's paranoid control pattern resides in a self-organizing system located in abstract higher-dimensional phase space and rooted in the automaton.

23. Cherniak, "Undebuggability and Cognitive Science," 403.
24. Perlovsky, "Physical Theory of Information," 38.
25. Albus, "Engineering of Mind," 25.
26. Eliasmith, "Moving Beyond Metaphors," 502, though he attributes this ability to the brain.
27. Duch, "Computational Physics," 151.
28. Ibid., 148.
29. Goertzel, "Belief Systems," 124–25.

The complexity of chaoplexic mind operations doesn't preclude the use of simple logic trees in some cognitive processes. These fast and frugal heuristics may be as simple as just one directive like choosing a recognized option over those which are not recognized. For example, when subjects were given conflicting information about the size of cities, 92 percent of participants made their inference about city size based on name recognition. In fact, too much knowledge actually decreases accuracy, a point illustrated by ignorance-driven stock market recognition which can match and often beat professional market advisors.[30] In any event, simple choices function for simple tasks while more complex learning is a nonlinear function.[31]

As an adjunct to Fechner's psychophysical law of sensory transmission, to which I have added transduction, I propose the semantic law of qualia. With a matching syntactic equation, it describes the general regime that governs the experience of the five senses and emotions. "Let those mind objects which are physical sensations and emotional feelings be experienced as 'qualia' (Q), and let the strength of emotion proportionally govern the degree of attractor orbit movement from criticality towards either periodicity (lessor Q) or into chaos (greater Q)."

Qualia emerge from the associational areas in the brain. These include the visual, orientation, attentional, and verbal/conceptual association areas. The attentional area, for instance, is connected to all the sensory modalities—vision, hearing, touch, taste, and smell—although it has only a few linkages with the primary sensory areas. Qualia are a function of both hierarchical and distributed (interconnected) processes. As an example, the monkey visual system has fourteen hierarchical levels. These involve twenty-five neocortical areas that are predominantly or exclusively visual in function, plus an additional seven that are visual association areas. These areas have 302 interconnections, representing about 31 percent of the total pathways if all areas were to be interlinked.[32]

In humans, local cell assemblies synchronize with distant assemblies to form transient patterns which emerge and disappear on time scales of around 100–300 msecs. For example, occipital, parietal, and frontal regions form such synchronies during face recognition, while a hand motion simultaneously produces gamma waves in the frontal cortex and beta waves in the parietal cortex.[33]

That the associational area is a crucial stage in the transduction and manipulation of mind objects is confirmed by what happens when things don't work right.

Synesthesia (Gr. *syn*, together, and *aisthesis*, perception) is just such an instance. For about one person in two hundred,[34] sensory modalities become mixed or scrambled. The most common types are number/color, letter/color, words and music/color,

30. Todd and Gigerenzer, "Précis of Simple Heuristics," 732.
31. Mayer-Kress et al., "What Can We Learn," 463.
32. Felleman and Van Essen, "Distributed Hierarchical Processing," 1.
33. Varela et al., "Brainweb," 235–36.
34. Ramachandran and Hubbard, "Synaesthesia," 6.

musical taste and smell, visual smell, and shaped or auditory pain. V. S. Ramachandran described a man who, when pricked with a needle, would say that he felt the pain. However, the pain felt funny like a tickle so he would start laughing uncontrollably.[35] If St. Paul had been a synesthete, we might say that during his Damascus Road vision he heard a bright light.

From a neurological perspective, a primary cause of synesthesia is improperly cut connections between local cell assemblies. These may reflect universal early childhood connections which didn't get cut. Such cross-modality linkages exist in kittens, ferrets, and hamsters in their first few weeks.[36] From a mind attractor perspective, if, as an example, the synesthesia happens to be the music/color type, an auditory circuit and a color circuit combine their signals so that their two attractors synchronize and produce a new attractor with a blended output. It's very important to understand this synchronization problem since psychiatric disorders can involve improperly coupled or decoupled attractors.

What's the route from qualia to awareness? Physicalist science camouflages its ignorance with labels: quantum gravity in neural microtubules, a sub-quantum anomalous passage from mind to matter, or physical-to-mental phase changes. Perhaps inadvertently acknowledging this theoretical void, Walter Freeman refers to "the nonrational and nonlogical construction from which consciousness emerges."[37] Thus he, like all other physicalists, believes that consciousness mysteriously self-creates from material processes.

In opposition to all of these proposals, I suggest that awareness results from the lawful interaction of newly experienced qualia with indexed memories. How are memories indexed? One is apt to think of movies like *Bruce Almighty* where actor Jim Carey discovers that his life is recorded in a linear filing cabinet whose open drawer stretches endlessly into the distance. In reality, memory is likely indexed according to a different metaphor, fractal geometry (similar shape regardless of scale).

Włodzisław Duch argues that mind objects are recognized by locational proximity in their logic space: "Objects are associated with each other, or are judged to be similar, if they are close in the mind space."[38] (The corollary obviously is that properly integrated memories will be close together in logic space.) Memory-based learning makes roughly the same point in saying that syntactic patterns in a database let one solve classification and decision problems.[39] The upshot for awareness is that an incoming qualia is instantly compared to memory objects in mind space by a nearest-match geometric heuristic (ordering principle), and when an identification is made, the respective attractors synchronize.

35. Ramachandran, "Phantoms in the Brain."
36. Radeau, "Auditory-Visual Interactions."
37. Freeman, "Three Centuries of Category Errors," 1181.
38. Duch, "Computational Physics," 15.
39. Stanfill and Waltz, "Toward Memory-Based Reasoning," 1216.

Nearest-match is nicely illustrated by J. Piaget's "A-not-B Error." In this experiment, a six- to eight-month-old baby is shown a desirable toy which is then hidden under cover "A." After several repetitions, the infant learns to reach for the hidden toy. At this point the child is given a visual cue and the toy is put under another cover "B." If there is a short delay so that short-term memory loses "B," the infant uses a nearest-match heuristic and reaches back to "A." This is proven by the fact that having the child stand changes their viewing angle and they correctly choose "B" because now there is no nearest-match.[40]

Similar nearest-match heuristics are used by all people for every incoming qualia in the process of generating composite awareness.

Let us hypothesize then that the highest level of mind forms in continuity with what we have seen for the lower; and that it might even be relatively straightforward to describe. In fact, Peter Todd and Gerd Gigerenzer say that "higher-order cognitive mechanisms can often be modeled by simpler algorithms than can lower-order mechanisms."[41] For example, a single nonlinear equation models language acquisition.[42] In terms of how awareness manifests, let us suppose that the associational areas' qualia together with objects in mind storage form recurrent networks by invoking downward transduction to neural circuitry. The system is driven by rule-sets whose syntactics may be expressed as a differential equation, and whose semantics produce awareness. The very top of the mind hierarchy therefore may well be a simple law of awareness. "Let the qualia output from each associational area combine with all mind space memories to which they are indexed and through downward transduction form a mathematical object which combines with all other associational networks to produce a composite output which is experienced as awareness."

Let's summarize our model of the mind.

The mind is a law-generated set of mathematical objects residing in logic space and rooted in the automaton as a subset agent of the human agent. The process by which mind objects are created involves local neural cell assemblies, obeying Fechner's law at sensory levels and then a law of qualia and a law of awareness at mid and upper levels respectively. These laws blend within themselves syntactic and semantic correspondences, and they have a common theoretical structure at all levels.[43] In the three-part structure of human personality, the mind acts as a bridge between the body and brain, and the human spirit. As we anticipated in chapter 4, this model enables us to extrapolate from the mind upwards to the human spirit by inferring a law of spirit. It is at the level of the spirit that we encounter that which makes us truly human: our will, truth, beauty, justice, conscience, sense of eternity, and relationship with God.

---

40. Smith and Thelen, "Development as a Dynamic System," 345.
41. Todd and Gigerenzer, "Précis of Simple Heuristics," 740.
42. Abrahamsen and Bechtel, "Phenomena and Mechanisms," 180.
43. Nieder and Miller, "Coding of Cognitive Magnitude," 149–50.

While this primer sketches only the briefest of theoretical frameworks, it's sufficient to lay the groundwork for the following discussion of mind disorders.

II. THE DISORDERED MIND

Table 8.1
Mind Disorders' Prevalence, Percent of Population

Disorder (adults)	2012 USA[A]	2002 Canada	2005 Europe[B]
Anxiety (combined totals)	18.1	12.2[C]	14.2 median
Depression	6.9	4.5[D]	6.9 median
Post Traumatic Stress Disorder	3.5	2.4[E]	1.1[F]
Panic	2.7	1.6[G]	1.8 median
Bipolar	2.6	0.2–0.6[H]	0.9 median
Schizophrenia	1.1	0.3[I]	
Obsessive-compulsive Disorder	1.0	1.8[J]	0.7 median
Epilepsy	0.8[K]	0.5[L]	0.6[M]

    A. National Institute of Mental Health, "Prevalence of Any Mental Illness." Numbers have been combined from individual tables.
    B. Wittchen and Jacobi, "Size and Burden," 365.
    C. Public Health Agency of Canada, "Report on Mental Illnesses," table 1.1.
    D. Van Ameringen et al., "Post-Traumatic Stress Disorder," 171–81.
    E. Ibid.
    F. Storr, "Epidemiology of Stress," 52.
    G. Statistics Canada, "Canadian Community Health Survey."
    H. Van Ameringen et al., "Post-Traumatic Stress Disorder," 171–81.
    I. Ibid.
    J. Public Health Agency of Canada, "Report on Mental Illnesses," table 4.1.
    K. Zahran et al., "Epilepsy Surveillance."
    L Tellez-Zenteno et al., "National and Regional Prevalence," 1623–29.
    M. Forsgren et al., "Epidemiology of Epilepsy," 245–53.

The US National Institute of Mental Health claimed that in 2012 nearly one in five American adults suffered from some form of mental illness.[44] These conditions are thoroughly (!) presented in the *Diagnostic and Statistical Manual of Mental Disorders (DSM)* which is (in)famous for its classification proliferation. Though DSM-5 lists about 330 diagnostic categories,[45] I have summarized in table 8.1 above some selected mind disorders' prevalence rates as reported in Canada, the United States, and Europe. Note that the sources of these numbers do not represent standardized classifications or data input style for median, range, or totals. Epilepsy, which is included here, is usually classed as a neurological disease even though most seizures are

    44. National Institute of Mental Health, "Prevalence of Any Mental Illness."
    45. Grohol and Tartakovsky, "DSM-5 Resource Guide."

neither organic nor lesional (see below). The table is admittedly a cherry-picking that gives only a very rough general look at the prevalence rates of typical conditions from which people suffer.

In any event, my ultimate focus here isn't on prevalence rates *per se* but rather on two foundational aspects of mind disorders: the issue of upward versus downward causation and the chaoplexic structure of mind disorders.

Upward versus Downward Causation

In 1879 Richard von Krafft-Ebing published *Lehrbuch der Psychiatrie auf klinischer Grundlage für practische Aerzte und Studierende*, which appeared in English in 1905 as *Textbook of Insanity*. On the first page he wrote that mental illness is an organic disease of the brain, a principle which neurologists followed until the rise of psychoanalytic therapy in the first half of the twentieth century. By mid-twentieth century the introduction of drugs swung the pendulum again and only recently has the mind seriously reentered the equation.

In modern terms, Krafft-Ebing focused on the upward causation end of the brain-mind network loop(s). At this stage I want to develop an upward/downward causation model in light of current knowledge. I will do so by examining epilepsy and schizophrenia but before embarking on the journey, two quotes will help define the terms. "Bottom-up mechanisms are initiated by stimulation of various somato-, viscero-, and chemo-sensory receptors that influence central neural processing and mental activities via ascending pathways from the periphery to the brainstem and cerebral cortex."[46] And "top-down causation applies whatever level is chosen as the reference level. . . . Top-down causation by information control is the way a higher level instance exercises control of lower level causal interactions through feedback control loops."[47]

Epilepsy

Neurobiology attributes epileptic seizures to recurring excitation of pyramidal cells in either the cerebral cortex or hippocampus, or to the reverberation of oscillations within the thalamus and cerebral cortex.[48] Traditional medicine asserts that these runaway electrical storms result from any of more than fifty sources of brain damage. Major culprits cited include injury at birth, drug or alcohol abuse, severe head injury, infection, tumor, family history of seizures, toxic fumes, and low blood sugar. Conventional medicine considers these factors to be basic pathophysiologies in epilepsy.[49]

---

46. Taylor et al., "Top-Down and Bottom-Up Mechanisms," 31.
47. Auletta et al., "Top-Down Causation," 1160.
48. McCormick and Contreras, "On the Cellular and Network Bases," 838.
49. Reeves, *Disorders of the Nervous System*, 112.

The reality is, though, that only about one-quarter of upward causation epileptic seizures involve an actual organic lesion[50] and the remainder, known as idiopathic epilepsy, result from officially unknown causes. This includes isolated seizures, acute symptomatic seizures, situation-related seizures, or what more generally are termed pseudo-seizures.[51] Even organic seizures ultimately may be outcomes of childhood physical, sexual, and emotional abuse which changed the brain's neural development.

This is evident in a case mentioned by pioneering neurosurgeon Wilder Penfield, who more than fifty years ago had made the connection between trauma and epilepsy. He astutely noted that a fourteen-year-old patient's seizures had a focal point in an area where a lesion seemed to date from a hemorrhage following infant general anesthetic.[52] However, he also discovered that the girl's seizures were fear-based and rooted in an event when she was terrified at age seven by a strange man. Her seizures always reenacted the meadow scene where the man accosted her.[53]

In spite of early work like this, physicalist biases pulled research away from an integrated model. This has led to confusion as exemplified by the statement that non-epileptic seizures fully resemble epileptic seizures except that they have no identifiable physiological cause.[54] By this logic only organically triggered seizures are truly epileptic. Then what about the 75 percent with no officially known causes?

It turns out that these unknown causes are most often trauma of various kinds. Research has shown a strong abuse factor in seizures;[55][56][57] in fact an abuse correlation exists in just over one-half of psychiatric patients who experience temporal lobe epilepsy symptoms.[58] This forces physicalists to say the glass is half-full; due to "their medical condition, subjects with epilepsy share symptoms often attributed to trauma-related phenomena."[59] The reality is the exact reverse: trauma-triggered epilepsy sufferers have related medical conditions.

Other emotional factors also play a role. Of those with complex partial epilepsy, about 50 percent of their seizures are uncontrolled.[60] A study-set of eleven of these persons found that every one of them had emotional triggers related to lack of personal power, anger, and their social environments.[61] Another study of twenty people

---

50. Agamanolis, "Cerebral Ischemia and Seizures."
51. Semah et al., "Is the Underlying Cause," 1257.
52. Penfield, "Psychical Hallucinations," 464.
53. Ibid., 465.
54. Rosenberg et al., "Comparative Study," 447.
55 Salmon et al., "Childhood Family Dysfunction," 695–700.
56 Greig and Betts, "Epileptic Seizures," 269–74.
57 Bowman and Markand, "Contribution of Life Events," 70–88.
58. Teicher, "Scars That Won't Heal," 70.
59. Fleisher et al., "Comparative Study," 661–62.
60. Reiter and Andrews, "Neurobehavioral Approach," 198.
61. Ibid., 199, 200–202. Data collated from tables 1a and 4.

with intractable epilepsy found that they also had emotionally centered triggers: conflict, disappointment, feelings of neglect, fear and rage, or pressure to perform.[62] Both of these smaller studies showed that intractable epilepsy can be treated by training sufferers. Christiane Schmid-Schönbein concluded that learned self-control could "directly interrupt or 'arrest' a beginning seizure, or measures to avoid, compensate for, or actively eliminate provoking factors."[63] Reiter and Andrews, whose patients took from six to thirty-six months to learn the self-control techniques, likewise said:

> Post-treatment seizure frequency was zero per month for the nine patients who experienced less than four seizures per month prior to treatment and less than two seizures per month for the two patients who experienced greater than 12 seizures per month prior to treatment. AED [anti epilepsy drug] medication was either reduced or unchanged except for one patient who started on a previously untried AED medication.[64]

In other words, downward causation control techniques wherein the mind influences the organic lower end of hierarchical network systems can be extremely significant in treating epilepsy.

Schizophrenia

Psychiatry has organized schizophrenia's symptoms according to positive and negative criteria. Positive refers to the presence of something which should be absent and negative to the absence of something which should be present. Positive symptoms are hallucinations, delusions, disorganized speech, disorganized behavior, and inappropriate emotions. Negative symptoms are loss of language and thought fluency, emotional deadness, inability to express pleasure, inability to start things and follow through, and inability to focus attention.[65]

As with epilepsy, the traditional mainstream consensus in schizophrenia has favored upward causation via organic triggers. These triggers include: "hereditary encephalopathy, predilection to environmental injury, infection or postinfectious state, damage from an immunologic disorder, perinatal trauma or encephalopathy, toxin exposure early in development, primary metabolic disease, 'or other early developmental events.'"[66]

By 2001, though, Nancy Andreason, who at the time was editor-in-chief of the *American Journal of Psychiatry*, acknowledged the lack of evidence for a specific schizophrenia gene. This was in spite of "a diligent search by many talented neuroscientists"

---

62. Schmid-Schönbein, "Improvement of Seizure Control," 264.
63. Ibid., 262.
64. Reiter and Andrews, "Neurobehavioral Approach," 202.
65. Andreason, *Brave New Brain*, 196.
66. Gottesman, "Blind Men and Elephants," 68.

for "functional genomics" (the transfer of gene influence to brain abnormalities in any single place) which "has not identified any such specific regional abnormalities or nerve cell lesions."[67] Her comment was underscored by a computer survey covering the years 1961–2001. Researchers John Read et al. found that of 33,648 studies, for every study on the relationship between child abuse and schizophrenia there were thirty on the biochemistry and forty-six on the genetics of schizophrenia.[68]

Shortly after, in 2003, the American Psychiatric Association (APA) defended biogenetic science in a carefully worded statement. In it the APA claimed that schizophrenia reveals reproducible abnormalities of brain structure but that there aren't readily discernible pathologic lesions or genetic abnormalities. The APA also admitted that schizophrenia may be triggered by adverse environmental influences, that is, traumatic events.[69]

The upshot has been a dawning recognition that deterministic genetic factors are only a small part of the story. Instead, genetic factors consist of a "complex multigene trait, with common risk alleles in the general population that may have relatively weak individual effects."[70] In fact, schizophrenia is just one of a stable of mind disorders which have nonspecific genetic factors. In 2013 researchers used 33,332 cases and 27,888 controls to conduct a genome-wide analysis. It was designed to test for the shared risk factors that would link autism spectrum disorder, attention deficit hyperactivity disorder, bipolar disorder, major depressive disorder, and schizophrenia. In the report's words, "Scores for a broad set of common [genetic] variants showed cross-disorder effects for all the adult-onset disorders (bipolar and major depressive disorder, and schizophrenia) and nominally between autism spectrum disorders and both bipolar disorder and schizophrenia." Elsewhere the authors stated that "genome-wide studies have identified rare copy-number variants that confer risk of several neuropsychiatric disorders including autism, attention deficit-hyperactivity disorder, epilepsy, intellectual disability, and schizophrenia."[71] (Note that epilepsy replaced bipolar in the second listing.) There's no smoking gun gene for schizophrenia but instead a cluster of genes each of weak influence which together increase risk for a collective broad cross-section of disorders.

What about downward causation which has been launched by environmental factors? At first this sounds counterintuitive since the environment enters the body-brain, mind, and spirit systems bottom-up. However, unlike a bottom-up viral infection which is organic, trauma, while it may have an initial bottom-up component, quickly transduces into emotional qualia and then begins its reciprocal downward causation action.

67. Andreason, *Brave New Brain*, 206.
68. Read et al., "Contribution of Early Traumatic Events," 321.
69. APA, "Statement on Diagnosis."
70. Pearlson and Folley, "Schizophrenia, Psychiatric Genetics," 722.
71. Cross-Disorder Group, "Identification of Risk Loci," 1371–79.

There's now no doubt that trauma of various kinds constitutes the largest factor by far in triggering childhood, adult-onset, and ancestral schizophrenia. Trauma "include[s] events involving direct threat of death, severe bodily harm, or psychological injury, which the person at the time finds intensely distressing or fearful. Common types of trauma include various forms of violent victimization such as rape and assault, combat exposure, natural disasters, the witnessing of or being threatened with bodily harm."[72]

Other forms of trauma which may trigger schizophrenia in risk-prone people include paternal age at conception (older is worse);[73] infections during pregnancy;[74] famine (e.g., the 1944 Dutch famine);[75] maternal stress from warfare and violence at conception or gestation (e.g., during the Israeli Six-Day War in June 1967);[76] holocaust child survivors subjected to persecution;[77] early childhood physical or sexual abuse (the most significant);[78] combat;[79] and natural disasters (e.g., earthquakes).[80]

Quite apart from direct life-experience triggers of mind disorders, ancestral transmission is crucial. The anecdotal knowledge of multigenerational conveyance of schizophrenia now has emerging research support. As illustration, forty currently schizophrenic Swedes were found from within an eighteen-family pool which all traced their roots to one couple twelve generations earlier.[81] A similar Norwegian study analyzed a community of fifty-two farm households dating from 1665 to the present. They tabulated mental health outcomes of the descendants born from 1846 forward. All cases of hospital-treated psychosis and suicide in that time can be traced back to three mental illness founders who were the household heads in the 1665 population."[82]

Downward causation, whether ancestral or present, depends on a control mechanism called epigenetics. Formally defined, "Epigenetics generally refers to the heritable, but modifiable, regulation of genetic functions that are mediated through non-DNA-encoded mechanisms."[83] These functions are both heritable and reversible; and to many neo-Darwinists' dismay, validate Jean-Baptiste Lamarck's proposal of such processes two centuries ago.[84]

72. Mueser et al., "Trauma, PTSD," 124.
73. Perrin et al., "Critical Periods," 8–13.
74. Malaspina, "Acute Maternal Stress."
75. Lumey et al., "Cohort Profile," 1–2.
76. Malaspina et al., "Acute Maternal Stress."
77. Reulbach et al., "Late-Onset Schizophrenia," 315.
78. Read et al., "Childhood Trauma," 334.
79. Chahine and Chemali, "Mental Health Care," 1596, 1598.
80. Watson et al., "Prenatal Teratogens," 457.
81. Ekholm, *Diagnostic Evaluation*, 27.
82. Andersen and Hynnekleiv, "Hospital-Treated Psychosis," 26.
83. Toyokawa et al., "How Does the Social Environment," 67–74.
84. Barry, "Lamarckian Evolution," 224.

Physicalism assumes that epigenetics' molecular mechanisms explain the process. However, the fundamental factor is nonphysical algorithm-driven logic which mediates the informational interaction between environmental influence and genetic expression. Paul Davies has called this informational process a virtual object, "Expressed more starkly, *the epigenome is a virtual object* . . . its non-existence as a specific physical entity is deeply significant."[85] This epigenetic process explains the multigenerational transferal of mental illness in the preceding Swedish and Norwegian families. In specific terms, starting with the crisis of the initial traumatic event(s), each succeeding generation transferred their mental illness trigger(s) as information which had been absorbed into mind forms, or, in Davies' words, virtual objects.

There remains one vital aspect of schizophrenia's presentation. While positive and negative emotional symptoms characterize part of schizophrenia, the essence for many people is constituted by voices and visions. Here the terrain is tricky. The core voice-and-vision roster as described in Colin Ross' Schneiderian listing is: voices commenting, voices arguing, thoughts ascribed to others, made [forced] feelings, made acts, audible thoughts, made impulses, delusions, thought withdrawal, external influences and thought broadcasting.[86]

These manifestations can have any of three sources. First, some schizophrenics' voices and visions are the result of synesthesias in the associational level wherein qualia are cross-linked in the mind. These can be from birth or induced by trauma flashbacks as in Penfield's patient. Second, since there's extensive co-morbidity between schizophrenia and Dissociative Identity Disorder (DID), voices can be present as alters in a person with multiplicity. The third category is demonic voices and visions. These must be diagnosed by the ethical/moral/emotional contents being promoted and particularly by the theology being promulgated. In addition, the demonic spirits behind these psychological phenomena are responsible for the paranormal *psi* powers which usually accompany their presence.

Mind Disorders as Chaoplexic Processes

The centrality of chaoplexic structures means that it's important to explore network dynamics in understanding mind disorders. Earlier I noted that local cell assembly linkages are both hierarchically and horizontally interconnected, therefore including both local subsystems and long-distance connections. These neural networks employ both upward and downward causation as they operate in criticality on the edge of chaos. The basic idea is that the appearance of mind pathologies always indicates a shift of attractors from criticality toward either highly periodic or chaotic states. This design accommodates perturbations which originate in either the internal or external environment without disturbing the homeostasis of the central nervous system as a

---

85. Davies, "Epigenome," 42–48, italics original.
86. Ross et al., "Schneiderian Symptoms," 113, table 1.

whole. If a network reaches a dynamically switchable point, its attractor's behavior may change qualitatively or discontinuously in an unpredictable manner.[87]

The mind's dynamic structures manifest differently according to the modules involved and the degree of noise impacting parameters in the self-organizing systems. For instance, noise in the form of three carefully clocked neural time-delay perturbations can switch attractors[88] and produce totally different behaviors. As attractors split (bifurcate), blend (synchronize), and self-destruct (im- or explode), these dynamic processes are manifest in the psychological symptoms people experience: flipping between mania and depression, positive and negative schizophrenia, and the occurrence of various types of seizures. In all cases these are manifestations of the same basic chaoplexic operations appearing in different mind modules and hence association areas.

Chaoplexity's neurological importance may be illustrated in the various disorders. Some epileptic research found that in a time frame ranging from minutes to hours in the pre-seizure period there was a transition from chaos to order.[89] Conversely, other findings suggest that the onset of generalized seizures of any type represents a bifurcation from damped to strongly nonlinear behavior.[90] This has been described as a single variable spontaneously switching between attractors.[91] Yet other work shows that pseudoseizures' EEG spikes between seizures (called interictal) are chaotic[92] and point to underlying improper synchronization of both neural circuits and their transduced mind objects. The explanation for all these anomalous results may be that the chaoticity—a state of things in which chance is supreme—of EEG signals is highest during the post seizure state, lowest during the seizure discharge, and intermediate in the pre-seizure state.[93]

Schizophrenia's interregional connections differ from epilepsy's more regional nature. Nonetheless it too produces seemingly contradictory data. On the one hand, schizophrenia's reality-distortion is correlated with decreased frontal-temporal alpha coherence. This implies that there's an attractor evolution toward chaos. Conversely, intrahemispheric coherence is greater for schizophrenics than for healthy subjects.[94] This equates to a movement toward periodicity.

These contradictory attractor behaviors may be compared to normal people. In a test where subjects were asked to predict whether a randomly presented stimulus would appear on the left or right on a computer display, schizophrenics were

87. Toro et al., "Chaos Theories and Therapeutic Commonalities," 239.
88. Milton et al., "Controlling Neurological Disease," 132.
89. Sackellares et al., "Epilepsy," 112–33.
90. Breakspear et al., "Unifying Explanation."
91. Milton et al., "Controlling Neurological Disease," 124.
92. Slutzky et al., "Manipulating Epileptiform Bursting," 559.
93. Lasemidis and Sackellares, "Chaos Theory and Epilepsy," 122.
94. Breakspear et al., "Disturbance of Nonlinear Interdependence," 467.

intermittent, being both highly predictable and unpredictable during the same session. By comparison, normal people are "neither completely random nor completely fixed and deterministic."[95] In schizophrenia, qualia attractors in different associational and brain areas drift in opposing directions from their points of normality and produce strongly intermittent and opposite experiences. This is why the condition expresses with positive and negative symptoms. Normals [Paulus' and Braff's word] tend to remain in equilibrium and show neither extreme attractor behavior.

Equivalent abnormalities arise with other mind disorders as well. Alzheimer's is correlated with a decrease in interregional synchronization.[96] Conversely, Parkinson's, tinnitus, neurogenic pain, and major depression all demonstrate synchronized hemispheric-wide gamma waves which originate in the thalamus.[97] In Parkinson's resting tremor, thalamus and basal ganglia neurons appear to "fire synchronously at a frequency similar to that of the tremor."[98] S. N. Sarbadhikari and K. Chakrabarty found a similar shift toward wave regularity in depression and in fact state that depression, Parkinson's, and cardiac arrhythmia all have improperly coupled circuits. They further state that all mechanical interventions function by deactivating dysfunctional neural [and therefore attractor] couplings.[99] Toro et al. agree that both depression and Parkinson's are related to perturbations pushing the CNS out of homeostasis. They too believe that every mechanical therapeutic intervention—surgery, electroconvulsive therapy, electrical stimulation, sleep deprivation, repetitive transcranial magnetic stimulation, medications for serotoninergic and noradrenergic neurotransmission (depression), and for dopaminergic neurotransmission (Parkinson's)—works to the extent that it helps the CNS neutralize the dysfunctional coupling between subsystems.[100]

In light of all this, it's clear that any discussion of network stabilization must immediately refer to the underlying chaoplexic components. This implies that such regulatory recurrent breakdowns can be generalized to explain mind disorders as a whole regardless of particular triggering events. It then follows that events like epileptic seizures are pathological efforts to recover regulation, that is, to re-establish proper recurrent (feedback) behavior.[101] Likewise bipolar mood swings are a failure of feedback mechanisms to maintain homeostatic equilibrium;[102] and schizophrenia

---

95. Paulus and Braff, "Chaos and Schizophrenia," 7.
96. Breakspear, "'Dynamic' Connectivity," 217.
97. Llinás et al., "Thalamocortical Dysrhythmia," 15224–25.
98. Tass, "Effective Desynchronization," 6.
99. Sarbadhikari and Chakrabarty, "Chaos in the Brain," 452.
100. Toro et al., "Chaos Theories," 240.
101. Lorenzo and Pérez-Muñuzuri, "Influence of Low Intensity Noise," 372.
102. Koutsoukos and Angelopoulos, "Mood Regulation," 9.

is a fundamental breakdown in the regulatory functions in the recurrent loops of the neural networks.[103]

These ideas may be applied directly to the postulate that Adam and Eve were created with conditional immortality. As a part of their mind agents' self-regulatory feedback systems, attractors originally were able to decouple themselves from high-level destructive synchronicities or to recouple after descent into chaos. If so, then the post-Eden inability of mind attractors to handle life's psychological stresses and physical insults to the brain literally represents death's invasion as a parameter in the neural network code which manifests as mind disorders.

Whatever the specifics, we know that mind disorders have been present ever since ancient times. Indeed, mind illness does not measure health as an either/or condition, but as a continuous range in which death's latent symptoms are present in everyone.[104]

III. LEVIATHAN AND THE HUMAN MIND

In this section our goal is to understand how demons synchronize with the human mind. I will apply the same family of chaoplexic principles here as was used in developing our model of mind disorders. Consistent with the argument of the book so far, therefore, we might expect that demonic attachment to human minds occurs at the level of mathematical mind objects. That is, by coupling with human mind attractor basins, demons are able to influence mentally, interfere emotionally, and—in severe cases—virtually "possess" the human host.

"Cross-Species" Synchronization

The principle that demons can attach to human minds by mathematical synchronization is supported by a rather surprising chain of real world evidences.

We encountered the principle of complementarity in chapter 7 with Klaus Mainzer. Here we note what he calls mind object translation. He first commented that the mathematical expressions of dynamic networks "may be simulated by neurobiological brains or silicon computers or angelic organisms from still unknown star systems."[105] Then later he said, "We may even be able to translate representations from one complex system into an alien one. As the representations in both systems are not exactly the same, we would not exactly feel like our neighbour, an animal, or another alien system." He concluded by stating that such a transfer would give some knowledge or a theory about such alien feelings or thoughts.[106] Using his logic, there's no

---

103. Tononi and Edelman, "Schizophrenia," 392, 394.
104. Os, "Is There a Continuum," 245.
105. Mainzer, *Thinking in Complexity*, 169.
106. Ibid., 173.

inherent reason to think that an alien system called a demon cannot synchronize with the human mind. Moreover, it turns out that self-other dynamic linkages involving different system ontologies already have been demonstrated in various contexts.

Before considering that issue, though, let's review familiar examples of synchronization.

Network and attractor synchronization means that two or more chaotic systems adjust a given property of their motion to a common behavior. In fact, certain types of chaotic synchronization result in a perfect matching of every parameter.[107] We met Christiaan Huygens in chapter 7 and saw how his wall clocks synchronized with each other by mechanical vibration. Nowadays machines synchronize at electronic levels. In a common example, one may take two chaotic signal generators and join the actual hardware via output terminals. When signal coupling between them becomes sufficiently strong the chaotic oscillations synchronize.[108] These principles operate in laser arrays which use synchronization in applications like optical communication systems, compact disk, CD/DVD-ROM units, bar code readers, and laser printers.[109]

Synchronization also operates in human-to-human relationships. In infant-parent attachment, synchronization results as parents respond over time to even small changes in their baby's arousal states and meet their needs based on these signals.[110] Recently this relationship has been modeled as a dynamic dyad. The dyadic method treats actions, emotions, learning, and communication as collectively generated dynamic patterns complete with attractors.[111] This use of the concepts and language of attractors also has led to more general analyses of human relationships as nonlinear systems. Adult couples' relationship conflict, for example, has been modeled by nonlinear equations.[112]

Actual cross-ontology synchronization may be illustrated by machine-human photosensitive epilepsy, human-robot shared learning, and machine network memory transfer to humans.

Photosensitive epilepsy is a condition which both the sun and artificial light sources can initiate. It is based on the fact that neural assemblies in the visual cortex synchronize their responses to the frequency of flickering stimuli. Any resulting paroxysm most often produces predominantly generalized tonic-clonic seizures.[113]

A sensational incident of machine-induced epilepsy happened in Japan in December 1997. Some 685 youngsters viewing the *Pokemon* cartoon on TV experienced spasms, nausea, dizziness, blurred vision, seizures, or unconsciousness. The effects

107. Boccaletti et al., "Synchronization of Chaotic Systems," 4.
108. Abarbanel et al., "Blending Chaotic Attractors," 214.
109. Garcia-Ojalvo et al., "Coherence and Synchronization," 2225.
110. Hsu and Fogel, "Stability and Transitions," 1062, 1077.
111. Lavelli et al., "Using Microgenetic Designs," 44.
112. Gottman, "Observing Gay, Lesbian, and Heterosexual," 65–91.
113. Bhattacharya et al., "Nonlinear Dynamics," 2702.

were caused by a rapid strobing technique that flashed red and blue lights on the screen, to make an explosion look "virtual."[114] At least one study has concluded that compared to controls' nonlinear function a patient suffering from photosensitive epilepsy demonstrates linear mind operations.[115] The Pokemon episode is consistent with the fact that mind pathologies are characterized by an attractor shift. The major points in this example are, first, the presence of attractor shift toward chaos; second, the speed with which an external signal produced violent attractor and biological responses; and third, the relatively small amount of perturbation required to bring about these consequences.

Human-machine synchronization also takes place when a robot is programmed to both follow and lead a human in shared learning tasks. In a typical experiment, as a subject moves a joystick signals are sent to a robotic recurrent network. The network begins to predict the joystick movement and give feedback so that the operator experiences less or more resistance based on the degree to which the human and machine track together. When the joystick moves freely, bounded attractors form and when the subject chooses a movement which generates net resistance (that is, when the robot has to learn), a strange attractor forms.[116]

Although this experimental set-up is designed so that both the human and robot learn, synchronization can be produced in both bidirectional and slave-master systems. In the latter, "one subsystem evolves freely and drives the evolution of the other. As a result, the response system is slaved to follow the dynamics (or a proper function of the dynamics) of the drive system, which, instead, purely acts as an external but chaotic forcing for the response system."[117]

It's important to remember this idea, since in the case of demonic synchronization with human mind objects, the relationship may also be master-slave. In this scenario a demon functions as the master system which enslaves the human system.

A third area of direct machine-to-human synchronization involves test patterns and false memories in humans. In an experiment, a trained computer neural network generated sequences called pseudo patterns. Human subjects were presented with a second set of test patterns selected to suggest a third category of control patterns. Thus there were pseudo, test, and control patterns in play. The goal of this confusing and complex process was to see if people would choose computer-generated patterns with which they had no familiarity. If so, then the artificial neural network was deemed to be actually transferring pattern information directly to the human subjects as false memory. This is in fact what happened. The researchers summarized their findings,

---

114. Plunkett, "Banned Pokémon Episode."
115. Bhattacharya et al., "Nonlinear Dynamics," 2714.
116. Tani and Ito, "Interacting," 125.
117. Boccaletti et al., "Synchronization of Chaotic Systems," 3.

"The originality of this research is to show that a network's memory is transported to human participants and affects their behavior."[118]

Machine-to-machine connection merely establishes the principle of synchronization. Person-to-person synchronization applies this to human dyads. However, the *Pokemon* epilepsy and human-robot learning events introduce a yet higher level of operation. In the machine-to-person events, people were aware that certain things were happening to them. However, that a neural net can secretly implant false memories in folks is a radically different principle. This experiment's procedure differed from conventional subliminal messaging buried in video or audio which can be isolated and retrieved. In this case, there was no sensory recapture possible yet without the participant's knowledge, the machine actually restructured part of the mind's nearest-match geometry into a new configuration. In any event, the collective thrust of these data is that for demons to interface with the human mind they need only use the same math language as they use to act on nature. A further implication is that this process can operate at a subterranean level beneath the cognitive awareness of the human half of the dyad.

Finally, attractors can be desynchronized as required by mind healing and exorcism. Consider a simple single-basin artificial network system trained by a learning algorithm. After many iterations it will produce a set of attractors. To reverse this one merely changes the attractor equation to a negative exponent so that re-iteration runs everything backward.[119] More sophisticated highly coupled demon-human mind linkages can be desynchronized via network feedback timing (noise).[120] A variation combines noise strength adjustments and timing to gain control of attractors in larger systems like memory.[121]

Human versus Demonic Causation

Brain mechanisms and chaoplexic mind control systems function according to their design whether their inputs are environmental, internally generated mind activity, or demonic introjects. The obvious question is how one distinguishes a mind disorder of strictly human origin from one which is demonically triggered. For instance, Mitchell Liester argues that voices experienced by the truly deranged are due to misfiring brains. Such folks, he says, are incarcerated in state hospitals because they can't distinguish their own thoughts from peoples' voices around them. He cites imprisoned cultist serial murderer David Berkowitz (Son of Sam) in support of the point.[122]

---

118. Musca et al., "Creating False Memories in Humans," 1577.
119. Meeter, "Control of Consolidation," 59.
120. Lorenzo and Pérez-Muñuzuri, "Influence of Low Intensity Noise," 372.
121. Willeboordse and Kaneko, "Externally Controlled Attractor Selection," 4.
122. Liester, "Inner Voices," 3.

But what does Berkowitz say about his voices? Even when he was a small child, "It was like something came upon me. . . . And I would just go berserk in the apartment. I know that now, after I became a Christian, and many years later, I realized that this was a demonic power that had his hand on my life . . . even back then." Berkowitz was asked about the voices' connection to the cult killings. "After some rituals, initiations, and things I went through, I began to experience [things that] . . . were like hallucinations. And Satan had come upon me with his power. They were like audio-visual things that came, and so forth."[123] So who's right, Liester or Berkowitz? And how do we decide?

In chapter 9, "The Transcendent Light," I deal in more detail with the question of identifying demonic activity, so here I will make only a few introductory comments. The basic dilemma is that both mind and demonic disorders manifest through the same brain and chaoplexic systems. Confronted by people who claim to be demonically oppressed, mainstream psychiatry has few diagnostic options. I believe that the following approaches can help us to revision diagnostic criteria.

First of all, conventional psychiatry conceptualizes mind disorders as upwardly caused by genetic triggers. However, only Huntingdon's is primarily genetic.[124] The research shows that for mind disorders generally genetics play a modest role at best.[125]

This confusion is reflected in how nonspecific medications are labeled for a host of ailments. The US Food and Drug Administration approved selective serotonin reuptake inhibitors (SSRIs) for eight separate psychiatric diagnoses ranging from social anxiety disorder to obsessive-compulsive disorder to premenstrual dysphoric disorder.[126] This is even more startling when we learn that antipsychotic drugs clinically offer no significant benefit over placebos in the first place.[127]

Instead of focusing primarily on upward causation, diagnosis needs to view the body-mind relationship as a chaoplexic feedback network. Depression and anxiety illustrate disorders that have been modeled as systems which include symptoms, emotions, beliefs, and social interactions. These combine to show the brain is a relay station and not a monolinear cause.[128] Thus psychotherapy is targeted to mind-initiated top-down cortical change and drugs to brain initiated subcortical bottom-up change.[129]

Chaoplexity revisions the role of genetics. Just as the brain is plastic so too are genes. It's well known that stress decreases immune response. Recent data shows that

---

123. Ross, "Son of Sam."
124. Andreason, *Brave New Brain*, 33.
125. Maier, "Psychiatric Genetics," 4–7.
126. Lacasse and Leo, "Serotonin and Depression," 1211.
127. Kirsch et al., "Emperor's New Drugs," article 23.
128. Fuchs, "Neurobiology and Psychotherapy," 481.
129. Ibid., 480.

such influence also may be observed at the level of gene expression.[130] Both brain and genes are molded top down by virtue of being a part of network systems.

What all of this means is that top-down mind causation rather than bottom-up organic causation deserves the higher profile in explaining mind disorders. Furthermore, demonic infiltration which functions in logic space will often attach precisely on top-down influence of mind code.

A second factor in identifying a demonic presence in mind disorders involves ego breaches. William James, in commenting on the possibility that demonic possession might really occur, said in his Lowell Lectures of 1896, "If there are devils, if there are supernatural powers, it is through the cracked self that they enter."[131] Personal breaches can be signaled by one's own history of recurrent, severe, and fluctuating mood states. Ancestral breaches supply equal if not more useful information in diagnosing mood disorders. Obvious indicators are family histories of schizophrenia, manic-depression, epilepsy, and suicide.[132]

As with the first diagnostic criterion, this history acquisition needs a much broader perspective than organic issues. Specifically it will focus on initiating trauma,[133] both personal and ancestral. Trauma sometimes may include organic damage, but more often it will be rooted in emotional woundedness or explicit covenant disobedience. Any and all ego breaches offer an opportunity for the demonic to synchronize with the mind.

In recognition of these basic facts, Richard MacKarness, at the time assistant psychiatrist at Park Prewett Hospital in Hampshire, England, wrote, "To me, demoniac possession enters into the differential diagnosis of every disturbed person I see, and I make it routine to inquire, while taking the history, whether any dabbling in the occult has preceded the onset of the illness."[134] With these words, MacKarness acknowledges the correlation between the false god worship involved in occult activity and the onset of mind disorders.

This point prompts a natural segue to a final key issue in identifying demonic activity in the mind, namely the theological content of the phenomena. We began the chapter by highlighting John Forbes Nash and it's fitting to consider this final point with reference to him. In many ways, he's a quintessential poster boy for mind disorders. His mental fog controlled him for decades. His social alienation, inability to express emotion, and blank face and empty eyes are textbook-evocative of schizophrenia's negative symptoms. All of these are faulty attractor synchronizations and can be caused either by ancestral trauma or explicit ancestral *lex talionis* infractions. At the height of his disorder in the late 1960s, he experienced a combination of religious

---

130. Glaser et al., "Psychological Stress-Induced Modulation," 707.
131. Kenny, "Multiple Personality and Spirit Possession," 341.
132. Jamison, *Touched with Fire*, 195.
133. Ross, "Conclusion: A Trauma Model," 270.
134. MacKarness, "Occultism and Psychiatry," 366.

grandeur and fears. On the one hand, he saw himself as the Prince of Peace and the Left Foot of God. At the same time, his fears reflected core terror of rejection and being cast away like the biblical Esau, who lost his birthright.[135]

By the early 1990s Nash was functioning in a rational fashion. Those around him, including some familiar with schizophrenic diagnoses, viewed him as completely recovered. In light of current knowledge about drug toxicity and ineffectiveness, his refusal to take antipsychotic drugs during most of the 1960s when he wasn't hospitalized, and absolutely after 1970, was wise. He thereby avoided tardive dyskinesia and its potential for irreversible brain damage[136] which results from prolonged use of antipsychotics.

Nonetheless, in his constant struggle to recognize and reject paranoid thoughts, Nash himself has referred to his improvement as akin to dieting, presumably a forced and therefore tenuous change. His semi-lucid dreams which were the stuff of his irrational days persisted.[137] He was still plagued by voices although the noise level had been turned way down.[138]

This is worth a comment since we've seen that internal voices can have several sources. There are intense memory scripts such as those triggered by top-down cathartic abreaction (replay) in hysteria, or electrodes or brain-state altering chemicals, both bottom-up brain activation of mind objects. Otherwise voices must be human alter personalities, demons, or, much less frequently, the Holy Spirit. Nash gave no evidence of hysteric conversion or dissociation; he rejected Christianity; and the content of his religious delusions is classic neognostic theology. Therefore, whatever the doorway was, we are left with a finding that the voices were probably demonic. This is reflected in his own original reference to messages from space aliens, uncannily the same tag as Ted Owens used for his spirit masters.

A final note.

We have been considering mind disorders according to medically assigned labels. In fact, though, these disorders often manifest in conjunction with paranormal events, *psi* experiences, religious ecstasies, and various other psychological and spiritual phenomena. Having sketched a picture of how the mind is constituted, works (or not), and is demonically oppressed, it's time to turn our attention to this larger milieu.

---

135. Nasar, *Beautiful Mind*, 326–27.
136. Ibid., 353.
137. Ibid., 389.
138. Ibid., 351.

9

THE TRANSCENDENT LIGHT

CHRISTIAN HEALER WILLIAM M. Branham (1909–1965) was born in a small dirt-floored log cabin in the hills of Kentucky. When his grandmother midwife opened a shuttered window to let morning light in suddenly a "light come whirling through the window, about the size of a pillow, and circled around where I was, and went down on the bed." This light appeared again at his conversion and when he conducted his first baptisms in the Ohio River. He recounted, "Here come that Light, shining down. Hundreds and hundreds of people on the bank right at two o'clock in the afternoon, in June." Of other appearances of the light, perhaps the most dramatic was during a personal retreat when he determined to get to the bottom of his frequent trances. "When I looked back, the light was spreading out on the floor, becoming wider . . . as I looked up, there hung that great star . . . [it] looked more like a ball of fire or light shining."[1]

Branham had no doubts that this was an angelic visitation. In fact, in his adult ministry he didn't begin a healing service until he was conscious "of the presence of the Angel with him on the platform." Without that, "he seemed to be perfectly helpless."[2] However, I shall argue in this chapter that the transcendent light experienced by countless people across the centuries continues to be one of Leviathan's most cunning and dangerous stratagems to deceive the unwary.

Transcendent radiant light as a numinous experience is part of a mystical tradition which is common across all cultures and historical eras.[3] The vision of numinous light with its apparent transcendence and deity is a core paranormal phenomenon. It's experienced by people during near death events, drug-induced altered states, deep

---

1. Weaver, *Healer-Prophet*, 22–35.
2. Ibid., 72.
3. McClenon and Nooney, "Anomalous Experiences," 52.

meditation, and out-of-body travels. Psychic healers see the light, as do witnesses of Catholic Marian visions, Christian healers, and practitioners of esoteric occultism.

Tabulations of incidence rates of people who perceive the light are a bit iffy. This is due to variations in survey sample sizes, participant self-selection, and definitions of the light. However, with all these caveats in mind, what do we find?

To begin with, 1 percent have seen light sufficient to enable one to see clearly in a dark room.[4] The prominent near death experience (NDE) researcher Bruce Greyson found that 7 percent of the population claims to have seen internal lights and colors.[5] A survey of 392 American university students found a rate of 11 percent who had perceived "lights or energies."[6] Alister Hardy in the United Kingdom conducted the largest study (3,000 general population respondents) and found 14 percent who had seen a "glowing" or "particular" light.[7]

The light is not mere symbol or abstraction but it manifests as a literal, intense, awe-inspiring experience. Those who have seen it mostly use descriptive words like shining, shimmering, white light, celestial, brilliant light, calm and gracious light, intense, god light, beings of light, and brilliant, golden light. The persistent reports of transcendent light have spurred scholars to create labels to describe the numinous phenomena people experience. One such list includes: Clear Light, Cosmic Consciousness, Deautomatization, *Fana*, Flow Experience, God Experience, Intensity Experience, Inward Light, Living Flame of Love, Love-Fire, Mystic Experience, the Numinous, Objective Consciousness, the Peace of God (which passes all understanding), Peak-Experience, *Samadhi*, Shamanic Ecstasy, the Silence Beyond Sound, and Subliminal Consciousness.[8]

The following accounts describe perceptions of the light in several psychological, philosophical, and religious contexts of various witness categories.

In Western culture, the light historically manifested in Catholic cloisters, hermetic, and esoteric circles. Emanuel Swedenborg, as an example of the esoteric stream, was very notable as a counter-enlightenment mystic. He wrote, "I myself can bear witness. Its brightness and brilliance are beyond description. What I have seen in heaven I have seen in that light, and therefore more clearly and distinctly than what I have seen in this world."[9]

Seventy-five years later, Swedenborg's esoteric legacy served as one of the occult influences imbibed by Mormon founder Joseph Smith.[10] The latter described his first encounter with the angel Moroni in 1823, "I discovered a light appearing in my

---

4. Buckley and Galanter, "Mystical Experience," 283–84.
5. Greyson, "Near-Death Experiences," 285.
6. Gómez Montanelli and Parra, "Are Spontaneous Anomalous," 4, table 1.
7. Hardy, *Spiritual Nature*, 34.
8. Levin and Steele, "Transcendent Experience," 90.
9. Swedenborg, *Heaven and Hell*, 70.
10. Owens, "Joseph Smith and Kabbalah," 120.

room, which continued to increase until the room was lighter than at noonday, when immediately a personage appeared at my bedside, standing in the air, for his feet did not touch the floor."[11]

In his discussion of yoga, Arthur Koestler described the light as the last stage prior to *samadhi*, the mystical union with Brahmin. This stage may begin with a kaleidoscope of colors followed by single colors. Then, often, a brilliant white light manifests which seems to wipe the mind completely blank.[12]

John was a disillusioned young medical doctor looking for meaning in life when he visited the Divine Light Mission. On his second visit he was astonished when the woman presenter emanated a glowing golden halo which filled the room and then entered into him. This gave him the sense of uniting with the Divine presence and time seemed to stand still. The experience convinced him that the Mission had the Truth and that its founder Guru Maharaji was God incarnate.[13]

Barbara Ann Brennan, in her book on psychic healing, told how to center the energy systems of "Healer, Patient and [Spirit] Guides" by aligning with "the Christ and the universal forces of light. . . . The person channeling simply keeps aligned with the white light or Christ light."[14]

For people anticipating their past-life regression session, "this beautiful visit to your own legacy," Sylvia Browne advised, "I want you to surround yourself with the white light of the Holy Spirit and then, in a magnificent aura around that white light, a glow of deep purple, the royal color of the God who created you."[15]

Hiroshi Motoyama described a dramatically different experience in an intense, even frightening, account of the light. During meditation, the light appeared "as a round blackish-red light like a ball of fire about to explode in the midst of a white vapor." An incredible power levitated his body, terrifying him.[16]

Timothy Leary, after ingesting DMT (N-dimethyltryptamine), said, "Suddenly I opened my eyes and sat up. . . . The room was celestial, glowing with radiant illumination . . . light, light, light. . . . The people present were transfigured . . . God-like creatures. . . . We were all united as one organism. . . . Beneath the radiant surface I could see the delicate wondrous body machinery of each person."[17]

The themes of light, healing, and even redemption are featured in Rita Klaus' story. She had experienced a bright-light NDE at age nine when she nearly drowned. As a very religious adult she was bitter toward God because of her multiple sclerosis. Then she had a strange experience during prayer, "I didn't see people anymore, or the

---

11. Smith, *Pearl of Great Price*, ch. 1, sec. 29–30.
12. Koestler, *Lotus and the Robot*, 99–100.
13. Buckley and Galanter, "Mystical Experience, Spiritual Knowledge," 283–84.
14. Brennan, *Hands of Light*, 203.
15. Browne, *Blessings from the Other Side*, 54.
16. Jourdan, "Near Death Experiences," 177–200.
17. Kleinman et al., "Comparison of the Phenomenology," 566.

priest. There was just this white light, a feeling of absolute love like I'd never felt coursing through me. I felt forgiven and at peace."[18]

In a final illustration light was experienced during a non-orgasmic sexual altered state:

> The light was just going through me. I didn't know what it was part of, but it was definitely a physical feeling going through me and shooting out of the top of my head. I had feelings of white lights shooting out of the top of my head. The lights were really brilliant. The brightness of the lights was incredible. You think of sunlight or lightning, but nothing like this! It was radiant white light brighter than anything I'd seen in nature.[19]

Invariably, those who have witnessed or experienced the light are certain of the integrity of the phenomena beyond any iota of doubt. If the issue is pushed, the reasons offered in favor of a God-did-it thesis seem to boil down to several key defense motions. Through thought transfer the being or light implied it was deity; the person therefore was convinced in the core of their being that they have met God; the individual found their life totally changed spiritually and ethically; and accompanying signs and wonders seem self-validating and obviously from God. In the context of this book, two interrelated questions inevitably arise: are such experiences psychological anomalies, valid human transcendence, demonic manifestations, or divine manifestations? and, what are the criteria which would help us distinguish one causation from another?

Accordingly, in this chapter I aim to conduct a test of such phenomena. While the discussion will orbit fairly widely, the main focal point will be the light. The ultimate goal is that the findings be applicable to other extraordinary phenomena which people claim are from God.

I. NEUROLOGY OF THE LIGHT

In analyzing the mystic light in these accounts, it's obvious that people see it as a real percept. Consequently it must manifest in some way through the apparatus of the brain's visual association system as well as in the controlling mind agents. This means that we should be able to at least start with some basic neurological facts.

Neuropsychology research generally locates mystical experience in the temporal lobes and especially the right lobe. Eugene G. D'Aquili and Andrew B. Newberg,[20] Michael A. Persinger and Katherine Makarec,[21] Vernon M. Neppe and Lewis A. Hurst,[22]

---

18. Morse, *Where God Lives*, 126.
19. Wade, *Transcendent Sex*, 22.
20. D'Aquili and Newberg, *Mystical Mind*, 44.
21. Persinger and Makarec, "Temporal Lobe Epileptic Signs," 179–95.
22. Neppe and Hurst, "Psi, Genetics and the Temporal Lobe," 35–55.

Melvin Morse,[23] R. Joseph,[24] and others[25] all agree on this. Based on their imaging research with Carmelite nuns M. Beauregard and V. Paquette have expanded the range to include eleven brain regions.[26] Joseph regards the amygdala, hippocampus, and inferior temporal lobe as the key areas which "provide the foundations for mystical, spiritual, and religious experience, and the perception, or perhaps the hallucination, of ghosts, demons, spirits, and sprites and belief in demonic or angelic possession."[27] He also notes that the amygdala has a large number of opiate receptors which enkaphelins can use to induce rapture and euphoria. These structures are involved in memory storage and retrieval, receive visual input, and contain neurons sensitive to the upper visual fields.[28] D'Aquili and Newberg agree: "Overall, it appears that the amygdala, hippocampus, and neocortex of the temporal lobes are highly involved in the production of vivid hallucinatory experiences. Further, it seems likely that these structures are involved in visionary mystical experiences."[29]

In earlier chapters I have argued that percepts must be grounded in sources external to the brain-mind complex and that this results in an objective character to symbol formation. As we wrestle with *psi* though—for instance, a golden, glowing Satsung light which some see and others don't—what do we mean by the word percept?

In materialist neurophysiology, a percept is a sensory experience which has an external, physical stimulation. When there is no external object, then the percept is labeled an hallucination. William James stated the mainstream definition, "An hallucination is a strictly sensational form of consciousness, as good and true a sensation as if there were a real object there. The object happens not to be there, that is all."[30] Using this definition, many prominent people experienced hallucinations: Socrates, Joan of Arc, Mohammad, Luther, Swedenborg, Blake, Bunyon, Raphael, Schumann, Goethe, Byron, Samuel Johnson, and a host of others.

Visual images presented to the brain for its computational manipulation can arise externally or internally. In the latter case, the eyes' rods and foveal cones can look backward (or inward), and the retinal pigment and choricacapillary circulation can be seen.[31] When I speak here of internal percepts, I am referring to those which call upon memories that have been laid down previously. This is illustrated by some of Wilder Penfield's subjects who saw themselves in the visual images that resulted from Penfield's electrode stimulations.

23. Morse, "Right Temporal Lobe."
24. Joseph, "Limbic System and the Soul," 105–36.
25. E.g., Nicholson, "Response," 273–83.
26. Beauregard and Paqette, "Neural Correlates of a Mystical Experience," 188.
27. Joseph, "Limbic System and the Soul," 106.
28. Ibid., 117.
29. D'Aquili and Newberg, *Mystical Mind*, 44.
30. Medlicott, "Inquiry into the Significance of Hallucinations," 664.
31. Scheibel and Scheibel, "Hallucinations," 17.

In commenting on Penfield's results, Mardi J. Horowitz et al. state that "other than memories of self-perception in a mirror or photograph, this could not be derived from an actual perception that was laid down directly as an engram [embedded pattern]. Rather, it was derived from a reconstruction of various actual perceptions into imaginative images."[32] This reconstruction process explains why a memory retrieval may not necessarily reproduce representations as exact images. On the other hand, a person who takes LSD cannot manufacture representations from nothing. There must be some previous external symbol grounding.

Suppose that instead of a white light a person has a vision of Superman on the planet Krypton. We do not dismiss this as a complete internal fabrication caused by neuronal misfiring. Instead, the fact that all symbols must be environmentally grounded in some way means that we treat Superman on Krypton as a reconstruction of previous sensory input, even if it seems irrationally blended. This leads to the conclusion that "it seems likely that the mechanisms underlying hallucinations are the same as, or at least are overlapping with, the mechanisms that mediate other imaginal states such as dreams, eidetic (near-photographic, lifelike) images, intense memory images, etc."[33]

Inner percepts then result from combinations of external sensory information with internal memory. This causal sequence for percepts has implications for the generation of visual stimuli which are well-known to result from a wide range of triggers which effectuate no-object viewing. These stimuli include not only psychedelic drugs, which may require a pre-conditioning of the person,[34] but a whole palette of non-chemical techniques like manipulated breathing, chanting, drumming, monotonous dancing, sensory overload and deprivation, fasting, isolation, sleep deprivation, aqua tanks, high-G centrifugal force, fever, brain trauma, seizure, surgical manipulation, and several others.[35] In every case, the kaleidoscope of images are firmly rooted in a mix of preexisting memory objects, or, in Karl Pribram's language, memory frames.[36]

This ability to internally organize data from the external unlabeled world has been called our most basic mental activity.[37] Therefore the picture is greatly muddied when internal percepts are generated which apparently have no memory patterns upon which to draw for reference.

An influential such case involved Jung. In 1909, Jung's associate J. J. Honegger had a male patient diagnosed as paranoid schizophrenic.[38] This man invited Jung to

---

32. Horowitz et al., "Visual Imagery," 470.
33. Scheibel and Scheibel, "Hallucinations," 15.
34. Gilbert, "Pseudo Mind-Expansion," 187.
35. Grof, *Adventure of Self-Discovery*, xii.
36. Pribram, "Brain and the Composition of Conscious Experience," 33.
37. Van Der Kolk and Van Der Hart, "Intrusive Past," 169.
38. Jung attributed the case to Honegger in part 1 of the 1911 ed. of *Wandlungen und Symbole der Libido*. Stevens notes that the event happened in 1909, not 1906 as Jung said. See Stevens, "Critical

look at the sun with him and see the sun's penis. A year later Jung learned of the Mithraic text in which the author describes a similar tube wherein the wind functions as the procreative pneuma.[39] Jung was satisfied that the man had no previous knowledge of the historical context of the vision. This sort of data was critical in leading Jung to postulate that individuals tap into a collective unconscious. He hypothesized that this connection gives knowledge or experience of things which one could not have learned by conventional means. As we shall see in due course, Jung's explanation for such phenomena was wrong.

II. THE PSYCHOLOGY OF PARANORMAL EXPERIENCE

Meanwhile, to say where and even how the brain presents the mind's experience of *psi* and mystical phenomena definitely does *not* explain the origins of such manifestations. Vernon Neppe of the Pacific Neuropsychiatric Institute illustrated the point with out-of-body experiences (OBEs). He says that a person who finds himself outside his body such that he could see it but not move it would be said by a parapsychologist as having had an OBE. Conversely, materialist psychiatry would term the event extreme ego-splitting with sleep paralysis.[40] More generally, materialist neuroscience simply labels such abnormal manifestations as psychopathologies.[41]

Depth psychology wishes to call on Dr. Freud to argue that the psychopathologies in question are projections from peoples' own subconscious. However, Freud actually entertained some doubts on this score. He wanted to believe that phenomena like omens, prophetic dreams, telepathy, and other preternatural forces don't exist. However, he accepted that the amount of solid evidence coming from people of intellectual prominence demanded further investigation. His real hope was that anomalous paranormal data could be explained by present knowledge of unconscious psychic processes without having to make radical worldview changes.[42]

Freud's remarks must be seen in the context of later nineteenth-century models of human personality. The attempts to map paranormal psychology included double personality (Pierre Janet), subliminal self (F. W. H. Myers), repressed memories and exteriorization (Freud himself), collective unconscious (C. G. Jung), ancestral spirits (Carl Wickland), and demonism (John Nevius). Freud struggled with the whole issue of paranormal powers, going so far as to say that if he were starting his career again, he would forgo his sexual theory of erotic energies in favor of the occult theory of subtle energies. After he had been invited to join the advisory council of the American Psychical Institute in the 1920s, Freud wrote to its director, Hereward Carrington, "I

Notice," 671–89.

39. Jung, "Archetypes of the Collective Unconscious," 50.
40. Neppe, "Psychiatric Interpretations," 6.
41. Frith, "Pathology of Experience," 239–42.
42. Freud, *Psychopathology of Everyday Life*, 312.

am not one of those who, from the outset, disapprove of the study of so-called occult psychological phenomena as unscientific, as unworthy, or even dangerous. If I were at the beginning of a scientific career, instead of, as now, at its end I would perhaps choose no other field of work, in spite of the difficulties."[43]

Freud actually had become a corresponding member of the British Society of Psychical Research in 1911, and was made an honorary fellow of the American Society in 1915, and of the Greek Society in 1923. It's doubtless out of his concern to negate this type of "incriminating" data that Freud's biographer Ernest Jones followed such a strict materialist grid in interpreting him.[44]

Analytic psychology, of course, defers to Jung's concept that voices and visions put one in touch with the archetypes of the collective unconscious. However, since by later life Jung saw archetypes as equivalent to spirits, by definition the experient is in touch with a nonphysical realm. Modern transpersonal psychology believes in the Jungian collective unconscious but adds that the phenomena are signs of spiritual transformation, and perhaps even of the hero's mythic journey.[45]

Other branches of the neognostic movement simply define *psi* and the paranormal as nonconsensual perceptions. These are regarded as part of clairvoyant reality,[46] which refers to paranormal events for which the Western scientific paradigm has no genuine explanation. For instance, Emma Schmidt's levitation was nonconsensual according to materialistic science. There is no common consensus that such phenomena fit within the scientific paradigm. However, from the perspective of contemporary neognosticism, levitation is the manifestation of subtle energy or it's a special case of the operation of middle-realm disincarnate spirits.

With these preliminary points in mind, let's return to our question. How do we explain mystical light percepts which apparently have no external object foundations? Certainly, neither denial of the experiences nor supercilious labeling of them as neural disorders is the right response. We accept instead that the events have been internally experienced and we try to account for them.

Near death experiences (NDEs) furnish a prime example of percepts which demand explanation. In his book *Recollections of Death: A Medical Investigation*, cardiologist Michael B. Sabom lists mainstream explanations for NDEs which include semi-consciousness, fabrication, depersonalization, autoscopy, drugs, endorphin release, temporal lobe seizure, altered states of consciousness, and hypercarbia (excessive carbon dioxide).[47] However, all of these require proper sight to even be considered as theoretical possibilities.

---

43. Fodor, *Freud, Jung, and Occultism*, 84.
44. Jones, *Sigmund Freud*, 402–8.
45. Lukoff and Everest, "Myths of Mental Illness," 124.
46. LeShan, *The Medium, the Mystic, and the Physicist*, 28–39.
47. Sabom, *Recollections of Death*, 153–78.

Suppose, though, that the visual association areas have been destroyed and a person still has an NDE? Such was the case for Vicki Umipeg, whose premature birth had resulted in the destruction of her optic nerves and damage to the retinas of her eyes.[48] This was diagnosed as retrolental fibroplasia, a condition caused by excessive oxygen in the incubator. In NDEs at ages twelve and twenty-two, objects were perceived from a distance. In her second NDE, she watched events from near the ceiling during attempts at resuscitation. Since Vicki's optic nerves were destroyed, there is no question that she saw via blindsight and its use of visual subsystems.[49] Her visual association areas had never received nor could they ever receive light stimulation, yet she saw light during the NDE. There simply were no visual frames from either external objects or from memory, so the light—not to mention the resuscitation attempts—which was perceived during the NDEs logically must have had a nonphysical source. This event-description is supported by other cases of NDEs experienced by the blind.[50]

Furthermore, suppose the person has had no brain function for extended periods of time and still has an NDE? In a provocative case Pam Reynolds was brain dead for about forty-five minutes while having surgery for an aneurysm. Yet Reynolds reported a classic NDE where she met deceased relatives and correctly gave observations of her operation.[51] Similarly, a ten-hospital Dutch study of cardiac survivors was published in the prestigious medical journal the *Lancet*.[52] The authors surveyed 344 consecutive patients who had been clinically dead according to their EEGs. Sixty-two (18 percent) reported an NDE and of these, 23 percent saw a light, with the rest experiencing a variety of other paranormal events. For instance, one-half of the sixty-two NDE experients were aware of being dead. The researchers followed up the survivors and their NDE experiences after two and eight years.

In its conclusions, the Dutch study states that true NDEs are different than events induced by brain probes, chemicals, and other artificial means. It continues, "An unknown mechanism causes NDE by stimulation of neurophysiological and neurohumoral processes at a subcellular level in the brain." The authors sum up by saying that lacking a brain-localized cause for NDEs, questions of transcendence arise: "How could a clear consciousness outside one's body be experienced at the moment that the brain no longer functions during a period of clinical death with flat EEG?" They wonder if the answer might involve a transcendent change of state.[53]

This opinion is shared by Kenneth Ring and Sharon Cooper, who, based on their research with the blind, also infer that NDEs are the result of human consciousness

---

48. Ring and Cooper, *Mindsight*, 22–28, 41–59.

49. Stoerig and Cowey, "Blindsight," 536–39.

50. Accounts of 31 blind persons who experienced NDEs are found in Ring and Cooper, *Mindsight*, 15–19.

51. Sabom, *Light and Death*, 37–51. See also Parker, "What Can Cognitive Psychology," 237.

52. Lommel et al., "Near-Death Experiences," 2039–45.

53. Ibid., 2044.

operating outside the physical brain. In reviewer Harvey Irwin's words, "The most fundamental implication of . . . [Ring's and Cooper's] . . . finding of NDEs in congenitally totally blind people . . . [is] that the perceptual-like impressions in NDEs and OBEs evidently are not perceptual at all."[54]

III. TESTING TRANSCENDENCE: ASTRAL TRAVEL

If NDEs have transcendent sources, what are they? The studies just cited assert human consciousness, or in traditional terms, the soul. This term immediately imposes some confusion since soulishness, defined here primarily as the organism's ability to make conscious decisions, appears on an ascending scale in earth's tree of life. If NDEs result from consciousness divorced from the body (astral travel), can higher animals also do it? This is not an irrational question in a day when people expect to see their pets in the next life and serious theologians respond by discussing the possibility of animals in heaven.[55] To avoid confusion, I suggest that in the following discussion we mentally substitute the term spirit for each occurrence of soul. This recognizes the traditional distinction between animal and human life.

To return to our question, the light is associated with several other NDE experiences. Bruce Greyson's list is representative,[56] including a sense of having left one's body, transcending of the ego and the boundaries of space and time, accelerated thought processes, a life review, intense feelings of peace and joy, a vision of future events (precognition), and encounters with deceased relatives. Some researchers put the light at the very core of the NDE, so that meetings with deceased relatives, out-of-body states, and panoramic memories are all manifestations of the transcendent light.

Therefore, if the soul really channels this array of *psi* phenomena during NDEs, several conclusions would follow. The soul indeed would have access to powers which exceed those of the physical world (preternatural powers); other realms exist and are accessible to humans; astral travel is true; and there's survival after death. In fact, stripped of academic hedging, the NDE and OBE community believes in all of these.[57]

Since the light is seen by people who are not having an NDE or OBE, it's reasonable to think that there's a common mechanism for all its manifestations. Because Greyson's list links light with leaving one's body, an examination of astral travel might let us use reverse engineering to explain white light and hence *psi* in general. Our lens will be the three paradigms which are guiding this book: scientific materialism, neognosticism, and biblical realism. The last of these will be the focus of the whole of part 4 of the chapter.

---

54. Irwin, "Mindsight," 112.
55. Lewis, *Problem of Pain*, 124.
56. Greyson, "Dissociation in People," 461. See also Kohr, "Near-Death Experiences," 160–69.
57. Badham, "Death-Bed Visions," 269–75.

Let's begin with scientific materialism and astral travel. Here's what a hypnotized medium saw during an OBE. "After I had observed myself sufficiently, I looked at the bystanders. They were all transparent. Then I looked at my surroundings, but instead of seeing impenetrable furniture and walls, I saw purely transparent things, all was as glass. . . . Without leaving my body out of sight, I moved from one end of Paris to the other as fast as one can shift his thought from one object to another."[58]

A couple of points need to be made here. In the first place, psychiatry labels the ability to see one's own double (doppelgänger) as autoscopy. For instance, an article on autoscopy in a mainstream journal refers to a Mrs. A. She saw her double who was identically dressed and moved in sync with herself. She also saw that her double's legs were misty and transparent.[59]

Now of course such stories, whether in mainstream journals or not, merely beg the question as to what autoscopy is. In neurological terms, the orientation association area is near the top of the parietal lobe in the brain. This area monitors the body's spatial imaging by which the individual locates (him)herself with respect to the environment. In particular, the right orientation association area creates a three-dimensional image of the body in space, and can compare the internally felt position to the co-ordinate system of the outside world.[60] However, it's difficult to explain how circuitry which, like a gyroscope, internally orients the body spatially with respect to the outside world, creates the sort of accurate external video productions seen in autoscopy.

In assessing percepts theoretically, an OBE is the reciprocal of autoscopy. In an OBE, a person perceives their body from outside it. In autoscopy, the person perceives an exterior double body.[61] The implication in either case is that they share the same causation, whatever that might be.[62]

In addition, we notice that transparent physical objects aren't restricted to autoscopy. In a case where a patient was observing her open heart surgery, she looked down from above, "I could look through those that I didn't choose to see what they were doing. . . . I saw them, but I could look through them. My vision was able to penetrate the two doctors and the table."[63] Energy healers—now self-labeling as medical intuitives—are also familiar with the *psi* ability to see into and through the body or to see internal body parts as if they were on T.V.[64] Various other accounts depict peoples' abilities to see into their own body, through solid matter like tables and walls, and

58. Koch, *Christian Counseling and Occultism*, 73.
59. Lukianowicz, "Autoscopic Phenomena," 200.
60. D'Aquili and Newberg, *Mystical Mind*, 33.
61. Blackmore, "Out-of-Body Experiences," 615.
62. Devinsky and Luciano, "Psychic Phenomena," 101.
63. Lawrence, "Paranormal Experiences," 125.
64. Shealy, *Occult Medicine*, 189–91.

even to see a whole scene as transparent matter.[65] Seemingly autoscopy is a percept with no external object and visualization of the interior of another person's body or of transparent scenes is a percept which penetrates the external object.

It seems clear that OBEs and NDEs cannot be dismissed as psychiatric phenomena labeled as autoscopy and that autoscopy cannot be a brain-based function.

What about holism and neognostic theory? The root Greek word *gnosis* actually suggests the act of knowing. It consequently points to experience rather than cognitive information and especially to verification by the inner eye.[66] Ken Wilber describes the inner eye: "Understand that spiritual knowledge itself—gnosis—is the most direct, clear-cut, impactful knowledge imaginable—it simply transcends conceptualization and therefore resists neat hypothetical categorizations and mental mappings."[67] Anthropologist shaman Michael Harner says, "What I don't consider to be fantasy is what I've seen for myself."[68] He is even more explicit about spirits: "In NOR [non-ordinary reality], shamanic practitioners routinely see, touch, smell, and hear spirits; for they find them as real as fellow humans they interact with in OR [ordinary reality]."[69]

The following case combines non-ordinary reality and astral travel. Swami Dadaji, a practiced astral adept, came from his prayer room in Allahabad, India one day. He asked someone to check with the Mukherjee family four hundred miles away in Calcutta to corroborate that he'd been seen there. In due course, they confirmed that a figure looking like Dadaji had been seen sitting in a chair in a room whose other door was locked and barred from the inside. The apparition had asked the Mukherjee daughter, Roma, for some tea and when the figure disappeared, the tea had been one-half drunk, part of a biscuit eaten, and Dadaji's cigarette brand was still burning on the table.[70]

According to traditional subtle body theory, the reason why Dadaji could astral travel is related to the structure of the person. The gross physical body is merely the surface shell for other inner subtle bodies.[71] While the number and labeling of inner body sub-components varies according to the school of thought, for convenience I will use a simplified theosophic setup. This model typically includes the lowest mental body which carries physical memories; the next higher is the detachable emotional body, also called astral; and finally there's the etheric body.[72]

Now, setting aside the loaded question about the integrity of inner eye data, we must ask whether a divisible and detachable mind-soul structure accords with our

---

65. Greene, "At the Edge of Eternity's Shadows," 227–28.
66. Bultmann, "Ginōskō," 119.
67. Wilber, *Eye to Eye*, 70.
68. Mishlove, "Way of the Shaman."
69. Harner, "Science, Spirits, and Core Shamanism."
70. Osis and Haraldsson, "OOBEs in Indian Swamis," 147–50.
71. Zimmer, *Philosophies of India*, 324.
72. Woolger, "Past Life Therapy."

present knowledge. In my view the following three arguments render absolutely untenable the theory of a divisible and traveling subtle mind-soul.

First, in an it-from-bit creation everything—spirit, mind, body—is ultimately formed of mathematical objects which are structured with syntactic and semantic values according to their function and ontology. These exist in nested hierarchies in which systems are in dynamic network loops. Therefore the chaoplexic mind as a whole cannot be detached from the brain during life because of the integral it-bit relationship. This state is only broken at physical death in which the brain is subtracted from the mutually interdependent feedback system.

Second, consciousness results when mind agents interact with each other but they cannot do this apart from using the brain as their transduction device. This is clearly demonstrated in cases of DID. Alters have unique EEG signatures[73] so we know that they really do use different neurological configurations. Consequently, when alters integrate at the mind level there may be bodily reactions like tingling, heat, jerks, and residual headaches. This is because the relevant mind agents are processing the union through neurological networks and their related central nervous system functions. Mind agents cannot interact to produce coherent memory of astral travel because they lack the brain's transduction.

Finally, the corollary of the preceding is that the chaoplexic mind cannot interact with the environment apart from brain transduction of sensory inputs. Thus in brain-dead NDEs like Pam Reynolds' or in any circumstance where there's a complete cessation of neurological activity the mind cannot have observed the environmental events which people report.

As a result, swami Dadaji didn't astral travel. Hence, who or what did the Mukherjee family see? The answer is that as a well-known, if infrequently observed event,[74] bilocation is a demonic paranormal power practiced by adepts.

At this point, it will be helpful to review the chain of argument again. We determined that the light reported in mystical experiences, NDEs, and OBEs does not need external sensory sources. This is substantiated by congenitally blind people who see the light and by NDE survivors who were brain dead at the time they saw it. This data has led researchers to infer a transcendental light source, which they identify as human consciousness, the soul, or the Higher Self. We evaluated such a self's transcendent preternatural powers by asking whether it can split from the body and travel in astral realms. The answer is no. Since the human mind and spirit are part of non-reducible chaoplexic network systems involving the body, any alleged *psi* astral travel must be due to nonhuman sources. Therefore we infer the general conclusion that mystical light experiences and ultimately all *psi* also are due to such nonhuman agents. The task now is to determine the identity of this transcendent power.

---

73. Ludwig, "Psychobiological Functions of Dissociation," 95.
74. Gersi, *Faces in the Smoke*, 183–84.

IV. UNVEILING THE LIGHT

Logic tells us that if the light's source is not human but transcendent then it's from the angelic or demonic realms, or from God. Our ability to differentiate these sources depends on comparing the light's theological content to the biblical mainstream. In this overview, I will test light theology in terms of its claims about the identity of Jesus, human divinity, and sin and redemption.

The Identity of "Jesus"

Peoples' visions of the light and their belief that Jesus appeared in, as, or with it is our starting-point. In chapter 1 we learned out that there can be no mental symbolic construction without grounding in the physical experiential world. In evaluating the following Jesus-in-the-Light phenomenon, it becomes clear very quickly that people's own psychological contents, including memory frames, are reflected in the vision they see.

Hence one person encountered a traditional Jesus, "a man figure in flowing white clothing, very bright, and [with] the most kind, loving look you've ever seen."[75] George Ritchie's Jesus was like God the Ancient of Days in Dan 7:9, "I was propelled up and off the bed. Out of the brilliant light at the head of the bed stepped the most magnificent Being I had ever known. . . . I was in the presence of the One who said, 'I am the Alpha and Omega who is and who was and who is to come, the sovereign Lord of all.'"[76] One of Michael Sabom's cardiac survivors said Jesus had jet-black hair, a very black, short beard, extremely white teeth and scars where the nails had pierced his hands.[77]

Jung's vision of Jesus was very different. Awakening one night, he saw a bright light at the foot of the bed and the figure of Christ on the cross. It wasn't quite life-size and the body was made of greenish gold.[78] Jung had been thinking about the alchemists' transmutation of baseness, accounting for the greenish-gold Jesus. However, he had not been thinking about base metal transmutation, but of psychic re-creation. He thus interpreted the dream as Christ being a symbol of this self-transformation.

The theme of repressed sexuality and subsequent erotic visions of Jesus runs throughout several of the famous Christian mystics. Ann Lee's vision was low-key, although its community application as spiritual and not physical intercourse ultimately destroyed the Shakers which she had founded. "I saw the Lord Jesus, and met with him as a lover, and walked with him, side by side."[79] This next erotic account was previously quoted in chapter 5, "Eden." "My beloved Saviour began to make Himself

---

75. Sabom, *Recollections of Death*, 215.
76. Ritchie, *Ordered to Return*, 32.
77. Sabom, *Recollections of Death*, 76.
78. Jung, *Memories, Dreams, Reflections*, 210.
79. Sasson, *Shaker Spiritual Narrative*, 22.

manifest to me.... He extended Himself beside me, pressed me so closely that I could feel His crown of thorns and the nails in his feet and hands, while He pressed his lips over mine, giving me the most ravishing kiss of a divine spouse, and sending a delicious thrill through my entire body."[80]

The celebrated Saint Marguerite Marie (Sacred Heart of Jesus) initially saw Jesus in his flagellated condition. Later he appeared as "the handsomest, the richest, the most powerful, the most perfect and accomplished of lovers." Marguerite wrote that while he was crushing her with the weight of his love, he said, "Let me do my pleasure. There is a time for everything. Now I want you to be the plaything of my love, and you must live thus without resistance."[81]

These stories remind us of *hieros gamos*, the union of human and god consummated by incubus and succubus intercourse. The appearance of such sexual content in these visions of Jesus is a conclusive indicator that the visions are not of God but are lies from Leviathan. The Jesus encountered is a false persona adopted by a demon which is only too happy to use the sexual vulnerabilities in its human partner.

The vision of Jesus can come in a very sophisticated guise. During an OBE healer Agnes Sanford found herself in a green valley with low bushes which seemed to be alien, literally neither heaven nor earth. She continues, "Jesus walked down the valley past the folded hills, and as He came, every fold filled up with light. I saw Him with the eyes of the spirit, but not in bodily form. Then he spoke to me, though not in words. ... He intended to send me down to the planet earth, not in a body, but in a spirit only. ... He was sending me out like a spy going into a very far country."[82]

After an interim scene set in ancient Sparta where a boy was being sacrificed, she returned to the valley and heard these words, "Now you have seen the very worst that can happen upon the planet earth. Would you then be willing to go down there, when I deem it best, and to be born and live on that planet for the purpose of relieving suffering?"[83]

This vision is noteworthy for four things.

First, we cannot help but notice the messianic flavor of Sanford's willingness to leave eternity to go to earth to do God's will. Second, we have seen that in any event the human spirit isn't preexistent and doesn't proceed fully formed from heaven but is created in history. Third, the vision perfectly fits the classic OBE otherworld journey where the pioneering adventurer returns from an inner psychic exploration to give a message of salvation to the rest of us.[84] This OBE pattern is actually a distinguishing mark of a demonic source, and has repeated itself in history ever since Gilgamesh's prototypical psychic journey around 3200 BCE. Fourth, the Sparta scene is a direct re-

---

80. Nisbet, *Insanity of Genius*, 248.
81. Leuba, *Psychology of Religious Mysticism*, 111–13.
82. Sanford, *Sealed Orders*, 281–82.
83. Ibid.
84. Campbell, *Hero with a Thousand Faces*, 30.

play of a childhood vision in which Sanford also seemed to have slipped back through time.[85] However, such replays do not indicate that she was present for the original event (if there even was one), either in a previous or current body or soul. It attests that the information came from a demonic familiar spirit which could have been present at the scene.

Leviathan is indeed subtle, as a review of Sundar Singh's experience confirms. On the one hand, the vision which convinced him of the truth of Jesus Christ came with a strange light and the form of Jesus. The words spoken were like those spoken to Saul, "How long will you persecute me? I have come to save you; you were praying to know the right way."[86] These contents were sufficient to lead to his apparent conversion.

On the other hand, Singh regarded his subsequent ecstatic visions of the Third Heaven as a place visited by only a few—including him—during their earthly lives. When we analyze these visions, we'll discover a very peculiar thing, "Christ on his throne is always in the middle, a figure ineffable and indescribable."[87] This is disconcerting because in scripture Jesus virtually never takes the center position.[88] To illustrate, when Stephen was murdered and was given a vision of heaven, he saw Jesus standing at God's right hand (Acts 7:56). The center is reserved for God the Father, although a rare exception in Rev 7:17 has the Lamb at the center of the throne. Christ-in-the-center conflicts with the doctrine of his exaltation which puts him at the right hand of God. It's antichrist who takes his seat in the center-place of the Most High (Isa 14:13–14; 2 Thess 2:4). In fact, the Bible emphasizes the doctrine of self-emptying (*kenosis*) for both the Father and Son. In Jesus' case, *kenosis* climaxes on the cross, not on heaven's throne. In effect, the vision depreciates Jesus' atonement, a theme which is crucial for making a theological assessment of the light and its doctrinal contents.

Demonic impersonations of the holy Trinity are entirely consistent with the Jesus, Lord Jesus, Father, and Holy Spirit demons whose false fronts must be detected and uncovered by deliverance healers.[89] Demonic impersonation is the very essence of apparent cases of reincarnation,[90] ancestral spirits,[91] dead family members allegedly met during NDEs,[92] and cases where afflicted people seem to assume the character of other people, whether living or dead.[93]

---

85. Sanford, *Sealed Orders*, 17.
86. Streeter and Appasamy, *Sadhu*, 6.
87. Ibid., 117.
88. Ps 110:1; Mark 16:19; Luke 22:69; Acts 2:36; 5:31; Eph 1:20; Phil 2:9; Heb 1:3, 13; 8:1; 10:12; 12:2. See Hay, *Glory at the Right Hand*.
89. Hochstetler, "The God We Serve."
90. Stevenson has done several studies, including "American Children," 742–48.
91. Otis, *Twilight Labyrinth*, 205.
92. Badham, "Death-Bed Visions," 270–72.
93. Rogo, *Infinite Boundary*, 14–50.

Human Divinity

A biblical dualistic worldview of creation may be synopsized as follows. The first act of God the Father was to establish a logical reality, other than the Trinity, called not-God or the Other (the first distinction). The Son acted next, speaking the automaton into existence in this Other with heaven, its first structure, being designed as the domicile of spirit beings. The Son then created the quantum vacuum and out of it the physical universe with its life and people. The third and ultimate goal of God's trinitarian creational actions is theosis, the work of the Spirit in transforming covenant people into God-likeness.

However, present-day radiant light experiencers promote a diametrically opposed monistic doctrine. In each of Eastern, esoteric, and neognostic Western theology, creation isn't separate from God but is integrally part of God. Humans therefore are also a part of divinity.

Three quotations will clarify this theology in action. The first is a description given by a participant in a Stanislav Grof holotropic (breathing-and-drumming-induced altered states') session:

> I was flooded with the divine light of supernatural radiance and beauty whose rays were exploded into thousands of exquisite peacock designs. From this brilliant golden light emerged a figure of a Great Mother Goddess who seemed to embody love and protection of all ages. She spread her arms and reached toward me, enveloping me into her essence. I merged with this incredible energy field, feeling purged, healed, and nourished. . . . Then the figure of the goddess gradually disappeared. . . . It became clear to me that what I was experiencing was the merging with and absorption into the Universal Self, or Brahma.[94]

This next account comes from P. M. H. Atwater, who's investigated over three thousand near death experiences and who herself has had three NDEs:

> I can positively affirm that being bathed in The Light on the other side of death is more than life changing. You know it's God. No one has to tell you. You know. You can no longer believe in God, for belief implies doubt. There is no more doubt. None. You now know God. And you know that you know. And you're never the same again. And you know who you are . . . a child of God, a cell in The Greater Body, an extension of The One Force, an expression from The One Mind. No more can you forget your identity, or deny or ignore or pretend it away. There is One, and you are of The One.[95]

In this third example the person had ingested a high dose of LSD:

---

94. Grof, "Psychology of the Future."
95. Atwater, *Beyond the Light*, 142.

On another level, I became the entire universe; I was witnessing the spectacle of the macrocosm with countless pulsating and vibrating galaxies and was it at the same time ... During the undisturbed episodes of fetal existence, I experienced feelings of basic identity and oneness with the universe; it was the Tao, the Beyond that is Within, the Tat tvam asi (Thou art That) of the Upanishads. I lost my sense of individuality; my ego dissolved, and I became all of existence. ... I spent most of this time feeling one with nature and the universe, bathed in golden light that was slowly decreasing in intensity.[96]

Respondents in an earlier NDE study by Kenneth Ring reported neognostic opinions—though not labeled as such—following an NDE in which they saw the light. They didn't especially attend church or participate in formal religious worship more often afterwards. Rather, there was a heightened inward religious feeling which made conventional religious observances seem irrelevant. Some had an indifference or even contempt for organized religion. There was an "overall tolerance for all ways of religious worship ... there is no one religion or religious denomination which is superior or 'true.'" Respondents instead regarded all religions as expressions of a single truth and emphasized their ethical teachings rather than dogma. Finally, Ring, calling this a *post-hoc* comment, said experiencers were statistically more likely to believe in the possibility of reincarnation.[97]

In his interpretation of the respondents' experience of the light, Ring dismissed the idea that they encountered the "Lord of the Universe." Instead, he thought it more reasonable to assume that it was each one's higher Self which "is an aspect of the divine," thereby indicating his own commitment to monistic theology.[98]

The feelings of merging into and being absorbed by the universal self, the One Mind or the universe described in the preceding quotations are only part of the story. It's now known that NDE and OBE light experiencers also find themselves in hellish situations. Often the person identifies loss of ego control as the terrifying aspect of the experience; they also experience nothingness or existing in an eternal featureless void; and blatant hellish images often begin with a sense of falling down into a dark pit.[99] Atwater rejects hell as merely "a peculiar idiom in the Aramaic language that used the name of a city dump where trash was burned." Nonetheless she reported peoples' NDE experiences of hell as "cold, clammy, icy hard, foggy or grayish, hellish scenarios, shunning, fight for continued existence, pain, surges of fear/anxiety, themes of good and evil, angels and devils."[100]

The primary take-away point is that experiences of the radiant light do not confirm that humans have inherent divinity. We will find in chapter 11 that a similar logic

---

96. Grof, "Psychology of the Future."
97. Ring, "Religious Aspects," 108–9.
98. Ibid., 113.
99. Greyson and Bush, "Distressing Near-Death Experiences," 98–99.
100. Atwater, "Is There a Hell?," 152, 154.

is employed to use a few peoples' alleged past-life memories to prove reincarnation. In the present context the mix of heavenly and hellish experiences recalls the classic gnostic dilemma over evil. If humans are inherently divine, how does evil fit with God and is there judgment? These questions are the focus of the next section.

Sin and Redemption

George Ritchie was transformed by his vision of Jesus. Though he became a Presbyterian elder, he now believes that Christian orthodoxy—what he calls negative religion—tells people at communion that they are dogs not fit to come to Jesus' table. The real truth, says Ritchie, is that "if God is our Father and Jesus is our brother, then we also have to be gods and not lowly worms."[101]

If, in Teilhard's words, we are moving inexorably toward a full union with God at a universal Omega point, then apparently Ritchie's right. Everyone is in process of becoming a god. Teilhard foresaw Omega either arriving in peace with evil reduced to a minimum, or in conflict where evil grows also. If the latter is the case, the noosphere, Teilhard's term for mind zone, will split into two territories, "each attracted to an opposite pole of adoration," but still curving toward each other.[102] The only logical construction to be placed on this idea is enantiodromia's belief in the resolution of opposites in each other. Surely, though, this begs the two-sided question: can moral opposites in fact cancel each other like arithmetic? and would zeroing out evil against good serve justice for those who have suffered at the hands of evil? If, as Christian orthodoxy does, one introduces Jesus' cross to zero out evil, then we no longer are in a universal oneness creation but one where Jesus is sin-bearer and not avatar (master teacher).

Jesus-light theology blithely ignores this dilemma. In her comments on NDE theological content, Carol Zaleski points out that there is almost never a sense of sin or penalty, though there may be pangs of regret for missed opportunities and misdeeds. Guilt has no place.[103] To illustrate, we may cite this compilation of light teaching given to Jayne Smith:

> This white light began to infiltrate my consciousness. It came into me. It seemed I went out into it. I expanded into it as it came into my field of consciousness. There was nothing I was aware of except this brilliant white light.
>
> I knew that I was immortal, that I was eternal, that I was indestructible, that I always had been, that I always will be, and that there was no way in this world I could ever be lost.

---

101. Ritchie, *Ordered to Return*, 165–66.
102. Chardin, *Phenomenon of Man*, 317.
103. Zaleski, *Otherworld Journeys*, 125, 132.

I said to him [man in purple] again, "Everything that has happened to me since I crossed over is so beautiful. Everything is so perfect. What about my sins?"

He said, "There are no sins, not the way you think of them on Earth. The only thing that has any meaning here is what you think."

Then he asked me a question. "What is in your heart?"

Then in some incredible way that I don't understand at all, I was able to look deeply inside myself, really into the very core of me to my essence. I saw that what was there was love, nothing else. My core was perfect love, loving perfection. I had complete love and acceptance for everything. I saw my own gentleness, tenderness, harmlessness. I simply was perfect and loving.[104]

The same teaching came to Barbara Marx Hubbard, whose spirit guide insisted upon the doctrine of innocence and dictated this to her: "Remember, dearly beloved, that humanity is innocent. Your consciousness defect is not caused by your own intent."[105]

Physician-researcher Raymond Moody commented that the modern NDE life review exchanges the reward-punishment model for "a vision which features not unilateral judgment, but rather cooperative development towards the ultimate end of self-realization." Death is not a final reckoning in which accounts are closed. Progress can continue after death even for eternity.[106]

The logical outcome of this theology of sin and judgment is an openness to universalism. As I wrote above, NDE researcher Kenneth Ring found NDE universalist theology in which people view all religions as expressions of a single truth.[107] His respondents therefore felt no moral judgment from the presence sensed within the light.[108] Christ light visions typically depreciate the historical Jesus because for neognosticism his function was merely to model how the Christ principle incarnates in every person who is truly given over to God. There is no historic redemption which occurred on Jesus' cross. We each recapitulate Jesus' self-transformation. The anonymous Ramala wrote, "The Nazarene's life was intended to show what Humanity can achieve and what Humanity may do when it, too, is Christed. . . . The Christ expression exists in all of you, and the light which you shine, the Christ light, will vary according to your point of consciousness, your soul knowingness.[109]

104. Williams, "Jayne Smith's Near-Death Experience."
105. Hubbard, *Revelation*, 230.
106. Zaleski, *Otherworld Journeys*, 131.
107. Ring, "Religious Aspects," 109.
108. Ibid., 109, 112.
109. Anonymous, "Revelation of Ramala," 275–76.

These sin-denying visions and voices at first sight stand in stark contrast to the testimony of a missionary who asked God how he saw her. "Was she Mary Magdalene weeping at Jesus' feet or the one whose righteousness is as filthy rags?" After some time, she looked up and saw a picture between the wardrobe and window:

> It showed a narrow dusty, uphill road, and along the road came a child, a little girl. She was not a happy child . . . she did not see the beautiful figure waiting for her at the end of the road, the figure of Christ. . . . He had the loveliest smile and was robed in shimmering white. . . . "You are that child still travelling on life's way. My child, I shall wipe away the soil and dust of sin, and all the tears."[110]

On the face of it, the missionary's vision conforms more closely to the biblical teaching of Jesus as sin-bearer. Nonetheless, we note that Christ only promises to wipe away the soil and dust of sin, analogous to the tears which he'll also wipe away. Dust, however, is a surface and not interior condition. When scripture speaks of fundamental cleansing, it's of washing the heart. So we're left with ambiguity at best and lies at worst, which, being demonic trademarks, imply such a spirit as the source.

Indeed, transcendent light theology has demoted Jesus Christ from his role as the incarnate Second Person of the Trinity who obtained salvation from sin. Now he's merely an ascended middle realm avatar healer who's available for house calls. In comparison note that in Eph 4:9 Paul wrote, "When it says, 'He ascended,' what does it mean but that he had also descended into the lower parts of the earth?" That is, Christ's ascension to the right hand of God followed his descent from heaven to become the incarnate redeemer.

The neognostic conversion of Jesus Christ from redeemer to avatar is manifest in those circles where demons are acknowledged and Jesus is regarded as a power-name. Judith Miller, who specializes in rehabilitation of people diagnosed with schizophrenia, made an astounding statement. Calling herself agnostic, she tells clients who are invaded by Satan that they ought to call on their power source, whether that be Jesus, a shamanistic animal, or even an extraterrestrial. Pray to Jesus, she says, "who's much stronger than Satan." In one case, parents brought their young son who was suffering from an invasion by Satan. After telling the boy to pray to Jesus, he came back in a week with everything cleared up![111]

Another neognostic healer likewise conceded the power of Jesus' name. William Baldwin was a pioneer in spirit release therapy, which assumes that oppressing spirits are frequently lingering deceased humans who need help to go to the light. However, Baldwin acknowledged that "dark energy beings seem to exist and conform to historic descriptions and classic behavior attributed to demons." He found that these dark

---

110. Hardy, *Spiritual Nature of Man*, 34.
111. Miller, "Mental Health, Mental Illness."

spirit beings distort the answer and avoid confirmation when asked to state, "Jesus Christ is my Lord and Master."[112]

These stories, of course, raise an obvious question. If Jesus is merely a symbol of the divine Christ light or spark which indwells everyone and is known as the Self, why would "dark energy beings" obey when ordered in his name to leave a person?

V. SUMMARY

To sum up, the transcendent radiant light, which at its most powerful is the unitive experience in which the individual seems to be one with creation and God, is found across many cultures, religions, and historical periods. Although the light's ideological contents reflect these variations, the core insistence that humans may trigger our inherent divinity is the same. The light, the transcendent beings, and the voices, visions and other *psi* that accompany these phenomena therefore contradict biblical assertions of sin and salvation. In spite of reassurance that it's the unmistakable sense of God's presence,[113] every form of such light ultimately denies Jesus' atonement. Consequently, the light and all of its associated phenomena must be regarded as extremely potent and duplicitous demonic activities. This light is nothing less than the Satanic light of 2 Cor 11:14.

It's essential to realize that in testing the spirits, Christians' theoretical framework has an inadequate appreciation of three crucial dimensions. We've failed to understand that in our natural state we're alienated from God, in covenant with Satan, and living in Holy Spirit-restrained chaos. This structural confusion enables the demonic to use Popper's worlds two and three as access points to every human mind. Furthermore, we have been unaware that access becomes near-inevitable entry when combined with a sufficient breach of *lex talionis* in individuals and family lines. Finally, we have not appreciated the depth of counterfeiting which Satan produces. The truth is that there is no apparently divine mental activity or bodily phenomena which Leviathan will not ape.

Jesus taught that at the last judgment, many people will stand before the Son of Man claiming to have walked in his paths and will learn to their horror that they never knew him. The preternatural miracle experiences which they offer as proof of their righteousness and relationship with Jesus will turn out to be the fruit of false light. They believed the lies of Satan, the father of lies. Jesus left no doubt that such false belief, action, and misplaced loyalty will cause one to be thrown into outer darkness (Matt 25:30). Therefore, we must take his warnings absolutely seriously and uncover the nature and operation of Leviathan's false transcendent light.

---

112. McGregor, review of *Spirit Releasement Therapy*.
113. Van Beeck, "Unanticipated Inner Experiences," 7.

10

ECSTASY

THERE'S A PARTICULARLY RIVETING TV bite from the 1990s.

A church in Florida was in the midst of a holy laughter revival. Of the people on stage, the leader was merely standing, smiling, and offering an occasional exhortation. A couple of folks who had been slain in the spirit (purportedly rendered unconscious by the Holy Spirit) were prone on the platform floor. Another man was standing absolutely motionless and totally unresponsive in what looked like a catatonic trance. The audience, including the senior pastor and his wife, were in the pews howling with laughter.

None of this religious ecstasy was surprising to the people present. This is because the leader in charge, evangelist Rodney Howard-Browne, was known for conducting exactly these kinds of meetings. He has described his own introduction to ecstatic experiences.

> Suddenly, the fire of God fell on me. It started on my head and went right down to my feet. His power burned in my body and stayed like that for three whole days. . . . In the fourth day, I am not praying, "O Lord, send your glory," I am praying, "Please lift it off me so that I can bear it . . ."
>
> My whole body was on fire. . . . Out of my belly began to flow a river of living water. I began to laugh uncontrollably and then I began to weep and then speak with other tongues.
>
> I was so intoxicated on the wine of the Holy Ghost that I was literally beside myself.[1]

Howard-Browne obviously had no doubts that God was the source of his visitation. However, that is precisely the assumption that I want to examine, though in its general case. I will argue that relatively little ecstatic phenomena is from God. Much of

---

1. Howard-Browne, *Touch of God*, 74.

it comes from Leviathan, greatly augmented from human social-psychological sources. To those who set store by such phenomena, this judgment may seem harsh. From a theological point of view, though, it merely reflects Jesus' words. The kingdom's wheat and Leviathan's weeds grow together in the field until the end of the age (Matt 13:25). Meanwhile, how do we tell them apart in history?

In chapter 9 we explored mystical experience by focusing on the transcendent radiant light. Now I will use speaking in tongues (glossolalia, ermeneglossia, and xenoglossia) and holy laughter to examine ecstasy. Tongues and laughter have played central roles in post-reformation religious renewals and each has stirred up intense controversy. Glossolalia has been welcomed as the unique sign of Holy Spirit baptism while modern holy laughter renewals have been compared to "something from the history books."[2] Indeed, as Howard-Browne testifies, they often occur together as part of a collection of phenomena.[3]

I. GLOSSOLALIA IN HISTORY

I must preface our discussion of glossolalia by making it clear that I regard tongues as a valid, continuing gift of the Holy Spirit for the church today. I will not defend this conviction except to simply note that to me the primary Pauline teaching texts in 1 Cor 12 and 14 are conclusive in this stance. My deeper concern is whether particular tongues are genuine or false. I will approach the question by briefly surveying the various ways in which tongues have manifested in Western history and then use a linguistic, cultural, and theological framework to assess the experience.

There are scattered reports of possible glossolalia in ancient pre-Christian histories.[4] In the Christian era apart from the early church, glossolalia was known as far abroad as the Later Han Dynasty in China (25–220 CE). Second-century gnostics practiced tongues and left behind a few examples of "distorted Greek formulations in Coptic context."[5] According to the historian Eusebius, Montanus, a leader in the second century charismatic movement, babbled and uttered strange prophecies in a manner contrary to church tradition. Early church Fathers like Novation (d. ca. 257) and Ambrose of Milan (d. 397) defended tongues. Pachomius (d. 346), who never learned Latin, reportedly once prayed earnestly for three hours and then conversed with a visitor from the west in that language.[6] Three centuries later, Caedmon (ca. 670) acquired the ability to swiftly render teachings from scripture into Anglo-Saxon

---

2. Duin, "Praise the Lord," 24.

3. See Malony and Lovekin, *Glossolalia*, 103, for the correlation between laughter and tongues speaking.

4. May, "Survey of Glossolalia," 75.

5. Williams and Waldvogel, "History of Speaking in Tongues," 65.

6. Ibid., 69.

religious poems. He quoted these in a chant, a technique which he had never learned and was only present during this recitation.[7]

A variation of this is found in Hildegard of Bingen (1098–1179). Though she knew both Latin and German, she sang concerts in a strange language which was neither but seemed a peculiar combination of both.[8] This close-but-not-quite identification echoes the findings of some modern linguists who have tried to identify certain glossolalic utterances.[9] Several other instances of clerics speaking unlearned languages (*xenoglossia*) come from the thirteenth century, as do cases of audiences evidently understanding a Latin sermon as though it were delivered in their native dialect (*ermeneglossia*). Both glossolalia and xenoglossia continued during the Reformation and Counter Reformation. Examples of Roman Catholics who exhibited xenoglossia include Louis Bertrand and Francis Xavier.

Physicians were enough aware of these phenomena that several mentioned them in books or dissertations. Lemnius (1628) thought that people exhibiting melancholy, frenzy, and other maladies sometimes will speak strange unlearned tongues and yet not be possessed by the devil. Schmilauer (1608) believed that a boy who spoke in a foreign language was using Latin or other foreign words he had heard, presenting them in a gibberish-like conversation. On the other hand, Gerstmann (1652) held that knowledge of unlearned languages implied demonic powers.[10]

With the Camisards (French Huguenots, also called the Prophets of Cévenne), a new twist entered the tongues scene. Among the charismatic manifestations in the Huguenot community were special linguistic abilities given to preliterate infants. In one recorded case in 1701, a child about fourteen months of age "'which had never of itself spoken a Word, nor could it go alone,' in a loud childish voice began exhorting 'to the Works of Repentance.'"[11] Historian Henry M. Baird wrote, "From the mouths of those that were little more than babes came texts of Scripture, and discourses in good and intelligible French, such as they never used in their conscious hours."[12] Subsequent glossolalic utterances were experienced among the Jansenists and the Moravians around 1730.

For their part, Camisard refugees arrived in England in time for the Wesleyan revival. A laughter attack suffered by the Wesley brothers (see below) may have been in Charles' mind the night he shared a room with a Camisard prophet. "The man gobbled like a turkey-cock," Charles said, so that he began exorcising, "thou deaf and dumb devil." He summed up, "Nor did I sleep very sound with Satan so near me."[13]

7. Van Beeck, "Unanticipated Inner Experiences," 8–9.
8. Williams and Waldvogel, "History of Speaking in Tongues," 70.
9. Bennett, "Gifts of the Holy Spirit," 29–30.
10. Diethelm, "Medical Teaching," 4, 7.
11. Williams and Waldvogel, "History of Speaking in Tongues," 76.
12. Baird, *Huguenots*, 187.
13. Williams and Waldvogel, "History of Speaking in Tongues," 80.

By the end of the eighteenth century, Enlightenment rationalism had generated a powerful religious counter impulse ranging from German pietism to Swedborgianism to English romanticism. As part of this reflex, glossolalia reappeared with Gustav von Below in Prussia (1817), the Irvingites in England (1830), and the Mormons in United States (ca. 1830). Modern Pentecostal historians have argued that in many cases nineteenth-century tongues speaking went unreported because observers either didn't recognize its significance or couldn't distinguish it from other physical phenomena.[14]

Tongues appeared at the turn of the nineteenth century in frontier camp meetings. For instance, after a period of intense intercessory prayer tongues broke out at the conclusion of a revival rally in North Carolina in 1801.[15] They were recognized in part because the Shakers had already brought the practice to the United Sates in 1774. In 1833, when the Mormon movement was on fire, secular media were well aware of tongues. The *Western Courrier* of Ravenna, Ohio, wrote in August of that year that "the 'unknown tongues' [of the Mormons] are getting out of fashion. Their prophecies, like signs of rain, fail in dry weather."[16] Later, between 1854 and 1900, there were many accounts of sporadic outbreaks of tongues and healings.[17] Tongues obviously were known but their practice was often controversial and in the case of Mormons outside the pale of orthodoxy.

Mormon glossolalia was no fly-by-night affair. When the Kirtland, Ohio, temple was dedicated in 1836, hundreds of elders spoke in tongues. Singing in tongues was not unusual. Over time, though, and especially in the later nineteenth and then twentieth centuries, xenoglossia designed to foster communication with non-English speakers became the real focus. One such incident involved Brigham Young himself. Witnesses certified that he spoke an unlearned Indian language with Chief Black Hawk near Kanab, Utah:

> This is to certify that the undersigned, in connection with Jacob Hamblin and Ammon Tenney, were located at Kanab, Utah, as missionaries, when President Brigham Young, in connection with Jesse W. Fox Sr., visited the town. Black Hawk, an Indian Chief, also some other chiefs were camped near there.... President Young commenced to talk to them in their own tongue, and continued to do so for a period of time estimated by me to be 20 or 30 minutes. This incident was quite a surprise to all of us, as we knew that President Young did not know their language.[18]

In 1847, Mormon missionaries to Wales claimed that they taught a Hindu from Bengal, India, in "eight different languages of the east," and astonished him by singing

14. Synan, *Holiness-Pentecostal Movement*, 25n29.
15. See Johnson, "Revival Movements," 30.
16. Copeland, "Speaking in Tongues," 21.
17. Frodsham, *With Signs Following*, 9–17.
18. Quoted in Hardy, "Brigham Young," 432.

in Malabar and Malay.[19] All of this raised embarrassing questions for holiness Christians, some of whom held that if glossolalia ever returned to the church, it would be miraculous xenoglossia and not some unknown tongue. They were evidently unaware of the Mormon claim to have practiced xenoglossia for generations and of the implications this had for the spiritual origin of the practice.

In the larger secular picture, William James reported that he encountered tongues in the mid 1870s. A woman had come from the country to Boston to get help from learned men regarding "the unknown language which her lips were irresistibly impelled to utter."[20] James didn't recall what had triggered this in her, but spiritualism was in vogue. The trances evoked by mediums mimicked those experienced by many in the various revivals who were slain in the spirit. It's telling that when Pentecostal pioneer Charles F. Parham discussed false tongues in 1911, he specifically linked them to Christian Science, hypnosis, and spiritualism. "May God help us to try every message-giver, interpreter, trance medium, and wizard that mutters and peeps, and only honor such as are truly of God."[21]

Two cases in the 1890s illustrate the link between tongues and spiritualism. As we saw in chapter 1, Théodore Flournoy spent several years studying the medium Élise-Catherine Müller (Hélène Smith). Flournoy called her "a veritable museum of all possible phenomena," including table-rapping, voices, visions, hallucinations, automatic writing, somnambulism, catalepsy, and trance.[22] What this list omits is her glossolalia, which purported to be in the Martian language.[23] This claim, of course, was no more (or less) spurious than Joseph Smith's declaration that Brigham Young's glossolalia was the pure Adamic language.[24]

Meanwhile, back in the United States, William James had been consulting since February, 1895 with a Mr. Le Baron (a pseudonym). The previous summer Le Baron had visited a camp of spiritists, where his participation in their séances resulted in possession. This invasion manifested in "*another's voice*—unearthly, awful, loud, and weird" and nearby clairvoyants said they saw "phantasms of ancient Egyptian sages" standing over him.[25]

A few months later, Le Baron says that he was talking with his inner voice when it suddenly "changed abruptly off from English into unintelligible sounds resembling a foreign tongue."[26] Upon Le Baron's request this "psycho-automatism" then gave a translation which referred to Le Baron as son of the Nile, son of Egypt, and son of Ra.

---

19. Copeland, "Speaking in Tongues," 22.
20. Le Baron, "Case of Psychic Automatism," 143.
21. Parham, *Everlasting Gospel*, 72, 120–21.
22. Shamdasani, "Encountering Hélène," xix.
23. Flournoy, *Des Indes à la Planète Mars*, 188.
24. Copeland, "Speaking in Tongues," 16.
25. Le Baron, "Case of Psychic Automatism," 147.
26. Ibid., 156.

In his efforts to find a real linguistic basis for them, Le Baron transcribed his original utterances into English phonetics.

Given this nineteenth-century backdrop of various glossolalic phenomena, Agnes Ozman's tongues on January 1, 1901, at Bethel Bible College in Topeka, Kansas, was in hindsight totally unsurprising. Ozman couldn't speak English for three days—speaking "Chinese" instead—and soon the Topeka newsboys were shouting, "Pentecost, Pentecost, Pentecost, read all about the Pentecost." Twelve ministers simultaneously sang "Jesus Lover of My Soul," supposedly in six known languages which observers claimed to understand.[27]

Mormons had claimed for seventy years that they had the gift of xenoglossy and now the Pentecostals made the same assertion. Topeka offered no new manifestations, but there was, however, a new justification—tongues were the unique proof of baptism in the Holy Spirit. Building on the holiness tradition, Parham taught a three-part sequence of divine infilling consisting of conversion, sanctification, and Holy Spirit baptism.

In retrospect, twentieth-century North American experiences of glossolalic phenomena may be divided into two parts. The first was institutional and produced pentecostal-charismatic denominational consolidation. The second was glossolalia's expansion into non-charismatic Christian circles beginning around 1960. This produced movements rather than churches: Latter Rain, Kansas City prophets, Third Wave, the Toronto Blessing (i.e., Kingdom Now), Fourth Wave, and the like. Though these continue to have theological reverberations today, no new phenomena appeared during the century.

II. ANALYZING GLOSSOLALIA

The truth or error of tongues has proven to be contentious throughout church history. In the following comments I will address some of the issues which have rendered glossolalia so problematic.

Is Glossolalia a Real Language?

In 1911 Emile Lombard called glossolalia's nonsensical utterances *phonations frustes*, or unpolished sounds. Do these sounds reflect true linguistic structures? I invite the reader to take the self-administered test found in table 10.1 below. I have listed a series of *phonations frustes* in the left-hand column. The right-hand column is in a scrambled order and contains the speaker or origin of the statements. The reader is invited to match up the sounds and sources. All except two are utterances of native English speakers. (Note that diacritic letter marks have been mostly removed.)

---

27. Parham, "Latter Rain," 51–55.

Ecstasy

Table 10.1
Phonations Frustes

1. "stimele inkepe. Surume tome lete skiru. Istepe tompo dere ombo luto lutoston."[A]	a. Allegedly a dead son speaking to his mother in a French séance.
2. "ichtiou, gao, itivare, gibastow, ovede."[B]	b. J. Lee Grady, Editor, *Charisma* magazine.
3. "'vasta loito 'rakiri memto, stela'toro, 'tan tala, vasaito, la'porto,"[C]	c. Transcribed from the Irvingite movement in 1831.
4. "Un te a tiki, un se; un se, un se; te a tiki un se."[D]	d. Spoken by a male at a Full Gospel Businessmen's Fellowship International meeting.
5. "Keil ama tondo ramala indiksia. Ilia tondi lam atra silia contira sa ma."[E]	e. A person labeled schizophrenic.
6. "Au, au, sixarda kavda! sivda, vnoza, mitta minogam, kalandi, indi, yakutasma bitas, okutomi mi nuffan, zidima."[F]	f. Artificially composed tongues representing a typical glossolalist utterance.
7. "tewa tura alda phobaratina estero dato itenarassu delemeric alcadinema mon tet."[G]	g. Albert Le Baron upon being possessed during spiritualist séances.
8. "Hey amei hassan alla do hoc alors loore Has heo massan amor ho ti prov his aso me.[H]	h. A spell from an unidentified language.
9. "ginga aris phelantros aruna du ma pri qui mar shan di brig-."[I]	i. Spoken by a graduate student who had been told to create a pseudolanguage as part of a class experiment.
10. "i mod mété modé modé iné palette is ché péliché ché chire né ci ten ti vi"[J]	j. Automatic writing from a 32-year-old female Methodist who had studied German and Spanish.

A. Le Baron, "Case of Psychic Automatism," 159.
B. Sechehaye, *Autobiography of a Schizophrenic Girl*, 92.
C. Malony and Lovekin, *Glossolalia*, 32.
D. Kildahl, "Psychological Observations," 127.
E. Grady, "What It's Like to Speak in Tongues."
F. Jacobson, *Selected Writings*, 639.
G. Samarin, "Evolution in Glossolalic Private Language," 58.
H. Drummond, *Edward Irving and His Circle*, 170.
I. Goodman, "Glossolalia and Single-Limb Trance," 102.
J. Flournoy, *Des Indes à la Planète Mars*, 188. Flournoy's medium translated this utterance from the "Martian" to French as "O mère, tendre mère, mère bien-aimée, calme tout ton souci, ton fils est près de toi," which equates to "Oh mother, tender mother, well-loved mother, calm all your anxiety, your son is near you," a reference to a deceased man purportedly being channeled through the medium.

In checking the correct linkages we find that these utterances derive from five categories of speakers. Three represent typical Christian glossolalists (3d, 5b, 8c). Three (one of which was a French speaker) resulted from séances or during a self-induced trance state (1g, 9j, 10a). Two were deliberately fabricated, one as a classroom pseudolanguage experiment (7i) and another as a deliberate aping of typical Christian glosssalalia (4f). One is an unknown spell (6h) and one is from a person labeled schizophrenic who was also native French speaking (2e).

Glossolalia often has a lineal arrangement in which new or additional sounds alliteratively imitate previous sounds. An example of sound alliteration is in utterance number 10, *ché péliché ché chire né ci ten ti vi*, which happens to be from the native French speaker who was in a séance-generated trance. Another illustration is the prayer phrase, *koyentrey piyliysiy gamboy yamboy hamboy zddriy* (not in the list of utterances).[28] This alliterative arrangement is seen not only in tongues but in Wernicke's aphasia.[29] In the latter condition—resulting from a stroke, for instance—there is a loss of the brain function which attaches meaning to the signals. The person loses the ability to speak because they have lost the meaning of language.

Another trait is a tonal structure of the utterance which apparently holds true across cultures and languages. This has been synopsized as "a threshold of onset, a brief rising gradient of intensity, a peak, and a final, often precipitous decay."[30] A common tonal range may parallel William J. Samarin's finding of interregional continuity of sounds. Such commonalities could even imply an original universal tongue, sometimes called *Ursprache* the speech of Ur. Table 10.2 shows some correlations derived from tongues speakers' survey responses.

Table 10.2
Tonal Structure vs. Geographical Location

(ka) shun di	Washington State
schone do (ka)	California
shan-da	Michigan
shawn-dye	Connecticut
shandah	North Carolina
shanda	New York

When all is said and done, however, it seems that though *phonations frustes* have pattern and form they are not themselves developed human language. Charismatic John Sherrill played forty-plus recordings for six linguists from graduate institutions in New York.[31] Three were on staff at Columbia University, two at Union Theological Seminary, and one at General Theological Seminary. Two were specialists in modern languages, three in ancient languages, and one in the structure of language. They couldn't identify any languages but did easily spot two cases of made-up gibberish that Sherrill included. In the 1970s, a group of US government linguists listened to a

---

28. Samarin, "Glossolalia as Regressive Speech," 80.
29. Ibid., 80.
30. Goodman, "Phonetic Analysis of Glossolalia," 227.
31. Sherrill, *They Speak with Other Tongues*, 100–101.

tape of Harold Bredesen speaking in tongues. He claimed that he spoke in Polish and Egyptian Coptic, but they found no resemblance to any known language. One hundred and fifty linguists in Toronto also heard his tongues speech and concluded that it was highly improbable that it was any human language. Similar results have been obtained by others. Findings like these underlay arguments that no direct research confirmation exists that glossolalists have spoken more than a few words or phrases of modern languages currently being spoken.[32]

What Is the Physical Mechanism for Glossolalia?

The most attractive explanation of glossolalia is that it's a speech regression which employs early-childhood phonetics. On this view, *phonations frustes* "is a stream of speech produced unconsciously with early-acquired rules of phonation"[33] (sound production).

We may measure this suggestion against the case of a girl with delayed speech acquisition due to a left-hemisphere lesion. At forty-four months of age, though she had a word and grammar comprehension of a thirty-month-old child, she only vocalized incomprehensible spontaneous speech.[34] We are reminded here of the *Nettalk* speech synthesizer which went through a babbling phase as it learned to recognize human speech.

The fact that some glossolalists need coaching[35] to learn tongues and must practice[36] their tongues indicates that these speakers are exhibiting a willful element of self-induction. These learning practices may be compared with the Jesus Prayer ejaculations of Hesychist monks. They repeat the prayer so often that it becomes programmed as a form of subliminal speech which continues autonomously during conversation and sleep.[37] Self-induced tongues may also be compared to actors and actresses who learn turkey talk, nonlinguistic verbalizations which are meant to convey emotional contents.

Furthermore, the regression explanation accommodates those forms of glossolalia which accompany a trance experience. Severe dissociation involves a switch from left hemisphere to right hemisphere dominance, with the degree of splitting controlling the depth of trance. For instance, radical corpus callosum surgery results in split-brain patients who demonstrate the existence of separate minds.[38] In a hypnosis study of Finnish high-schoolers, about 7 percent were able to shut down their

---

32. Malony and Lovekin, *Glossolalia*, 28.
33. Samarin, "Glossolalia as Regressive Speech," 77, 85.
34. Pizzamiglio et al., "Language Disorder in a Child," 309.
35. Kildahl, "Psychological Observations," 131.
36. Samarin, "Evolution in Glossolalic Private Language," 58.
37. Williams and Waldvogel, "History of Speaking in Tongues," 69.
38. Joseph, "Dual Mental Functioning," 770.

left hemisphere to the point where they produced an age-regressed self-conscious personality.[39] These personalities said they were human, gave their name, the place where they lived, and could describe their personality and social environment. This seems to be a clear instance of selective access of the right hemispheres similar to certain surgical anesthesias.

Regardless of the precise mechanism, all three spirit sources—human, demonic, divine—are able to manifest glossolalia through the mind/body language systems. The key is the source spirit's ability to access early-age phonetic memory frames. Since any given case of nonsense glossolalia could have any one of three sources, the sounds themselves cannot be used to identify their source. Authenticity must be tested by the spiritual rules laid down in scripture.

What about Xenoglossia and Ermeneglossia?

Ever since sixteen linguistic nations at Pentecost each heard Peter's message in their own tongue (Acts 2:9–11), xenoglossia (speaking an unknown language) and its reciprocal ability ermeneglossia (understanding an unknown language) have been ticking cross-cultural time bombs for Christian theology. The essential problem is that these abilities extend across religious boundaries. Let's consider the issue further, beginning with the following illustration from J. S. Slotkin:

> Recently a Winnebago sitting next to me sang a song with what I heard as a Fox text (Fox is an Algonquian language closely related to Menomini, the language I use in the rite), sung so clearly and distinctly I understood every word.
>
> When he was through, I leaned over and asked, "How come you sang that song in Fox rather than Winnebago (a Siouan language unintelligible to me?)"
>
> "I did sing it in Winnebago," he replied. The afternoon following the rite he sat down next to me and asked me to listen while he repeated the song; this time it was completely unintelligible to me because the effects of Peyote had worn off.[40]

Here is a clear case of Native American ermeneglossia. Nels Charles' account of speaking the Wintu language is similar. "I can't even talk Wintu well, but when a spirit enters me the spirit talks and they say I talk Wintu perfectly well. It is just like talking with unknown tongues and getting the spirit in the Pentecostal church."[41] Carlyle May adds that "in African religions xenoglossia has a wide geographical distribution and is a rather frequent occurrence."[42] As a result, even if witnesses confirm that Christian

---

39. Kampman, "Hypnotically Induced Multiple Personality," 220.
40. Slotkin, "Peyote Way," 485.
41. Jennings, "Ethnological Study," 12.
42. May, "Survey of Glossolalia," 84.

charismatics like Dennis Bennett have spoken in an unlearned foreign language,[43] the spirit source of the utterance is unknown without confirmatory testing.

As the following non-tongues anecdote shows, the question of source is not to be taken lightly. Carroll Jay was a Methodist minister who had been practicing hypnosis since 1954 as a way to relieve pain for family and friends. In the late sixties he began experimenting with previous-life regression of subjects. On May 10, 1970, after hypnotizing his wife, Dolores, for back treatment, he asked, "Does your back hurt?" To his surprise the answer was "*nein*" (no). Three days later when he tried to evoke this personality again it identified itself, "*Ich bin Gretchen*" (I am Gretchen).[44]

Investigator Ian Stevenson, a psychiatrist at the University of Virginia, interviewed nineteen people from Dolores' past, went to her childhood community, and had her take a lie detector test. In the end, he was convinced that this personality spoke passable though imperfect German even though Dolores knew no German. Furthermore, he believed that the contents of her conversations placed her at age sixteen in Chancellor Bismarck's time.[45] If his reconstruction is correct, the issue is stark. Either humans survive death in a near-earth realm as spiritualism holds, and/or reincarnation is true, or a familiar demonic spirit has impersonated a now-deceased girl named Gretchen.

So let's take a quick tally. Brigham Young, who claimed to be head of the true restored church of Jesus Christ, is certified to have spoken an unlearned Native American tongue. A witness informed Episcopalian priest Dennis Bennett that he prayed in Japanese, a language unknown to him. Methodist Dolores Jay submitted to hypnosis and an alien personality emerged speaking German, a language she had never contacted. J. S. Slotkin heard a song in the Fox dialect, which he knew, although it was really sung in Winnebago, which he didn't know.

The conclusion to which we are driven is that the preternatural ability to speak or understand unlearned languages does not of itself guarantee that the Holy Spirit is the empowering agent. In fact, the opposite conclusion is the norm—that the miraculous tongue is a powerful indicator of Leviathan's presence. There is no justification whatsoever for assuming such abilities are of the Holy Spirit unless other spiritual checks confirm that they are.

Ought Every Christian to Have the Spiritual Gift of Tongues?

Does God intend that every Christian have the gift of tongues? I am here using tongues in its inclusive meaning and not merely in reference to nonsense utterances. Prior to Parham and Topeka, this question was never on the theological agenda but since then much ink has been spilled in answering it. In real life testing, it turns out

43. Bennett, "Gifts of the Holy Spirit," 27–29.
44. Stevenson, "Case of Gretchen," 8.
45. Ibid., 11–13, 17, 70.

that something under 10 percent of tongues spoken by Christians are from the Holy Spirit. Gerald McGraw calls more than 90 percent of tongues false.[46] A. E. Ruark kept notes for four hundred case studies of which around 19 percent involved tongues. "Only about one in ten . . . is not demonic. Of course, the majority of those who speak in tongues refuse testing."[47] Another healer, George Birch, is even more pessimistic about tongues, reporting that of 207 persons he tested, only three had tongues not clearly demonic—and these three were still inconclusive as to their origin.[48] These residual three may have been self-generated tongues much like those described above and by other healers.[49]

In addition, interpreters of tongues would do well to be tested also. In this respect John Kildahl has drawn attention to a man who had been raised in Africa by missionary parents. He attended worship where he was a complete stranger and spoke the Lord's Prayer in the African dialect he had learned as a youth. When he sat down, an interpreter offered the meaning, reporting that it was a message about the imminent second coming of Christ.[50]

In October of 1906 Parham was invited to speak at the Azusa revival and then quickly "disinvited." The reasons included his Ku Klux Klan involvements, rumors of sodomy with boys (he was actually arrested but charges were dropped), and his authoritarian style of leadership. In spite of these moral blots, he nonetheless understood very well the ability of Satan to counterfeit tongues:

> Many hundreds, in seeking Pentecost, were taught to yield to any force, as God would not permit them to be misled; under those conditions they were ripe for hypnotic influence, often practiced by workers or spooks. Two thirds of the people professing Pentecost are either hypnotized or spook-driven, being seized in the first place with a false spirit or coming under the control of one afterward. We cannot be too careful to try or test the spirits, and any person unwilling to have their experience tested by going to God for themselves or with the brethren, reveal the fact that they are demon-controlled; and the demon seeks this subterfuge to continue his damaging operations. Often in casting out these false controls they have cried out of individuals, "Don't dishonor the Holy Spirit by doubting that this is His power that so mightily uses us"; but they come out in the mighty name of Jesus, leaving the person free to exercise a sane, enthusiastic service for God, baptized in the Holy Spirit and speaking in a clear language.[51]

---

46. McGraw, "Tongues Should Be Tested," 5.
47. Ruark, "Falsities of Modern Tongues," 159.
48. Birch, *Deliverance Ministry*, 149–50.
49. Hochstetler to Lawrence E. Burkholder, personal correspondence.
50. Kildahl, "Psychological Observations," 137.
51. Parham, *Everlasting Gospel*, 72.

At another level, we must ask why, apart from Topeka-style assertions of universality, we would expect that many or all Christians would have the gift of tongues. If we compare the gift of tongues to those of pastor or evangelist, surveys show that the latter spiritual gifts are present in about 3–6 percent and 10 percent of Christians respectively.[52] It's true that Paul wished us all to speak in tongues (1 Cor 14:5). He also wished that we all were single (1 Cor 7:7)! One is reminded here of A. M. Hills, a critic of holiness spirituality. In his response to a woman who had claimed six Holy Spirit baptisms, right up to the so-called dynamite and lyddite types promoted by holiness leader B. H. Irwin, Hills said, "This poor soul should have sought for and received one more baptism, 'the baptism of common sense.'"[53] Biblical common sense should lead us to expect that only a small minority of Christians will speak in genuine tongues.

III. ECSTATIC LAUGHTER

With ecstatic (holy) laughter we enter very different territory. Scripture doesn't teach holy laughter as a spiritual gift and its appearance in history is virtually absent until the eighteenth century. It therefore falls into the category of religious innovation rather than biblical continuity. A few historical snapshots will lay a sufficient foundation for evaluation of the spiritual validity of this practice.

It's well-known that the Methodist revival was often opposed by ecclesiastical Anglicanism. However, the Wesley brothers themselves found the appearance of uncontrolled laughter vexatious. In his journal for May 9, 1740, John described a manifestation which was strong enough that it immobilized both himself and Charles:

> Part of Sunday my brother and I then used to spend in walking in the meadows and singing Psalms. But one day, just as we were beginning to sing, he burst out into a loud laughter. I asked him, if he was distracted; and began to be very angry, and presently after to laugh as loud as he. Nor could we possibly refrain, though we were ready to tear ourselves in pieces, but we were forced to go home without singing another line.[54]

Wesley was ambivalent about the source of psychological manifestations. On the one hand, he was keenly aware of the true demonic oppressions of people who hear malevolent inner voices.[55] Conversely, he was ready to assign certain phenomena to emotional disorders. He described Methodists who spoke of "feeling the Blood of Christ running upon their Arms, or going down their Throat, or poured like warm

---

52. Wagner, *Your Spiritual Gifts*, 177.
53. Synan, *Holiness-Pentecostal Movement*, 58.
54. Wesley, *Works*, 1:304.
55. Lavington, *Enthusiasm*, vol. 2, pt. 3, 66.

Water on their Breast, or Heart." In his journal he wrote that these were "the mere empty Dreams of an heated Imagination."[56]

As we learn from his lament of June 18, 1759, Wesley regarded the laughter outbreaks as demonic. "While I prayed with them many crowded into the house, some of whom burst into a strange, involuntary laughter, so that my voice could scarce be heard, and when I strove to speak louder a sudden hoarseness seized me. Then the laughter increased."[57] According to his journal, he regarded these disturbing harassments as Satanic laughter that interfered with peoples' attempts to worship God:

> [Several broke] into horrid Fits of laughter;—buffeted by Satan by such a Spirit of Laughter, as they could in Wise resist, though it was Pain and Grief unto them:—one laughing, till almost strangled:—some were offended, and would not believe but they could help laughing, if they would:—but God suffered Satan to teach them better. They were suddenly seized in the same Manner, laughing almost without ceasing. Thus they continued for two Days, a Spectacle to all.[58]

When holy laughter broke out in Edward Irving's London church in the 1830s, it was interpreted by its critics as not just personal but collective emotionalism. An observer described the scene for Thomas Carlyle, "Whereupon the whole congregation got into foul uproar, some groaning, some laughing, some shrieking, not a few falling into swoons—more like a bedlam than a Christian church." When Carlyle and his wife Jane visited Irving's home, likely in the fall of 1831, he said they saw a woman prophesying, "raving like one possessed . . . talking as sensibly as one would do with a pint of brandy in his stomach."[59]

Laughter also appeared in the 1830s American frontier. "The subject appeared rapturously solemn, and his laughter excited solemnity in saints and sinners. It is truly indescribable."[60] As with Howard-Browne's meetings, various bodily phenomena accompanied the laughter: barking, being slain in the spirit, singing, and jerks. Kentucky's Cane Ridge revival featured bodily contortions. "Sometimes the head would fly every way so quickly that their features could not be recognized. I have seen their heads fly back and forward so quickly that the hair of females would be made to crack like a carriage whip, but not very loud."[61]

Three generations later, laughter was back for an encore in the Azusa Street revival and its North American diaspora. A report from Portland, Oregon, gushed that "the Lord wonderfully blest in the service, and one precious sinner was saved,

---

56. Ibid., 69.
57. Wesley, *Works*, 2:562.
58. Ibid., 305.
59. Drummond, *Edward Irving*, 169.
60. Stone, "Piercing Screams," 15.
61. Galli, "Revival at Cane Ridge," 13.

sanctified and baptized with the Holy Ghost. The Lord filled her mouth with holy laughter and she spoke in new tongues and has been under His power ever since."[62] In a harbinger of what was to occur ninety years later, the Azusa laughter also appeared in Toronto:

> One young woman who was very nice and precise in the world was marvelously saved. She had been under deep conviction for days. When once surrendered, she seemed to sweep with one bound from the altar of burnt offering into the most holy place, from the cross to the Pentecostal chamber, sealed with the Bible evidence. (Acts 10:46) She laughed incessantly for hours and hours. Sometimes she speaks in a tongue while at her work.[63]

A contemporary example of holy laughter comes from the late twentieth-century Fourth Wave movement. We will return to this theology below, but for the moment I will simply note the consistent pattern of laughter outbreaks which reappear in Toronto, Pensacola (FL), Brownsville (TX), and elsewhere. The following is a typical account given by a certain Belma Vardy:

> I assured her that she was safe. "Nothing will happen to you. I've been going for weeks and, nothing has happened to me by way of the manifestations . . .
> We burst into uncontrollable laughter. It overwhelmed us and we just howled with laughter. No matter how hard we tried, we couldn't stop—it was totally out of our control. . . . My girlfriend was lying across the seats and crawling along them like a worm, laughing hysterically. . . . To us it seemed like there was a wall of silence around us; we could see someone speaking, but we couldn't hear him.[64]

When we compare these women with the Wesley brothers, we find exactly the same process at work as each case begins. People who have absolutely no intention of being bowled over find themselves conquered by a behavior over which they have no control. However, there's a major difference of interpretation. John Wesley called their experience Satanic; Torontonian Belma Vardy said theirs was the river of life from the throne of God.

IV. ANALYZING HOLY LAUGHTER

Psychosocial Interpretations

Psychosocial interpretations include psychiatric pathologies, group emotional dynamics, and altered states. Both psychiatric and altered states' explanations by definition

---

62. Prentiss, "Pentecost in San Jose and Portland," 22.
63. Copley, "Pentecost in Toronto," 4.
64. Chevreau, *Catch the Fire*, 178–79.

focus on individuals and to account for group outbreaks therefore must also assume a social component. However, for this analysis I will accept this tension.

Wesley's Anglican critic Bishop George Lavington saw the Methodist manifestations as emotional outbursts, calling them a species of Delirium and Distemper. Hypochondria, he said, operates in the spleen, which is the "principal Ingredient of Enthusiasm" and is "called by some the Organ of Laughter; whence laughing people are said to vent their Spleen."[65]

Modern psychiatry treats Lavington's shopping list of delirium, distemper, and enthusiasm as emotional and mental pathologies which may have various organic roots. Eugen Bleuler, who coined the term schizophrenia in 1911, noticed that some parathymia—bizarre laughter, joy, or sorrow in schizophrenia—is marked by unprovoked or inappropriate bursts of laughter. Psychiatry also associates unseemly laughter with certain bulbar palsies, post-gelastic seizure fits, chemical hallucinogens,[66] hysteria, and schizophrenia.[67] It occurs in connection with epilepsy[68] and has actually been called laughter epilepsy.

However, symptom associations do not prove causation nor define an actual illness. According to Nancy Andreason, a leading member of the American Psychiatric Association, the boundaries selected in defining mental disorders have no inherent biological meaning but mostly have to do with social functioning.[69] This is old hat; ninety people were committed to Bedlam by their relatives from 1772–95 with diagnoses of enthusiasms and Methodism.[70]

The tricky task of discerning whether a given behavior is socially deviant, pathological, or demonic (or perhaps all three!) is well-illustrated by Oliver Cromwell. On September 2, 1650, Cromwell's exhausted English army took advantage of a tactical lapse by Scottish forces to win a massive victory at the Battle of Dunbar. As Cromwell walked among the three thousand Scottish battlefield dead, he was seized with a laughing attack. According to an eyewitness:

> Oliver Cromwel certainly had this Afflatus. One that I knew, that was at the Battle of Dunbar, told me that Oliver was carried on with a Divine Impulse; he did Laugh so excessively as if he had been drunk; His Eyes sparkled with Spirits. He obtained a great Victory; but the action was said to be contrary to Human Prudence. The same fit of Laughter seiz'd Oliver Cromwel just before the Battle of Naseby; as a Kinsman of mine, and a great Favourite of his, Colonel J. P. then present, testifi'd.[71]

65. Lavington, *Enthusiasm*, vol. 1, pt. 2, 72.
66. Schultes and Hofmann, *Plants of the Gods*, 26.
67. Black, "Pathological Laughter," 68.
68. Devinsky and Luciano, "Psychic Phenomena," 104.
69. Andreason, "Linking Mind and Brain," 1587.
70. Copestoke and Malony, "Adverse Effects," 237.
71. Aubrey, *Miscellanies*, 87.

In labeling Cromwell's laughter as an Afflatus (spirit) and Divine Impulse, commentator John Aubrey quoted Cicero to drive home the point, "No-one anywhere has ever been a great hero without a divine spirit."[72] With these words he affirmed that Cromwell's laughter manifestations were from God. The reason for Aubrey's identification reflected an inherited Greco-Roman theology of daemons (daimons). They were thought to be minor gods or deceased human heroes who function as soul-guides and give audible inspiration. For instance, Socrates' daemon spoke to him as an inner voice and warned him against participating in an assassination plot. Socrates called this his "accustomed divine sign."[73] The emperor Augustus who reigned when Jesus was born asked, "Who is found more divine [daimonic] than I?"[74]

Aubrey's daimon assessment was far from unanimous, though. For starters, George Lavington couldn't decide whether Cromwell needed counseling or committing, "'Tis a Question undecided, whether Oliver was more of the Enthusiast, or the Hypocrite: and I presume the Fits are no Proof of a good Cause either in the Protector, or the Methodist."[75] For their part, Royalists accused Cromwell, a Freemason, of having been trained in the practice of witchcraft by Menasses Ben Israel of Amsterdam. It was further alleged that Cromwell's familiar (demonic helping spirit) was "a tall dark man with a sour frowning face. His name was Grimoald."[76]

In the second place, social hysteria is a recognized phenomenon and is particularly epitomized in Western history by Dancing Mania. Also called the Dance of St. John or Dance of St. Vitus, it appeared in 1374 at Aix-la-Chappelle in people who had come from Germany. The general consensus was that the dance was maniacal, with some dancers even laughing or crying themselves to death.[77] Priests exorcised many dancers in Liege, a response generated by what they observed:

> They formed circles hand in hand, and appearing to have lost all control over the senses, continued dancing, regardless of the bystanders, for hours together, in wild delirium.... While dancing they neither saw nor heard, being insensible to external impressions through the senses, but were haunted by visions, their fancies conjuring up spirits whose names they shrieked out; and some of them afterwards asserted that they felt as if they had been immersed in a stream of blood.... Others, during the paroxysm, saw the heavens open and the Saviour enthroned with the Virgin Mary.[78]

---

72. Aubrey, *Miscellanies*, 87.
73. Myers, "Automatic Writing," 540.
74. Ferguson, *Demonology*, 37.
75. Lavington, *Enthusiasm*, vol. 1, pt. 2, 73.
76. Summers, *Witchcraft and Black Magic*, 47.
77. Bartholomew, "Tarantism," 287.
78. Hecker, *Epidemics of the Middle Ages*, 87–88.

A more conventional social hysteria occurred in 1787 England. It was triggered when a female cotton mill worker put a mouse down the bodice of another who dreaded mice. The workers, however, blamed poisoned cotton and within four days, twenty-three women and one man contracted anxiety, strangulation, and strong convulsions which required five or six people to restrain.[79] The psychological origin of the phenomenon was confirmed when symptoms ceased after assurances were given that no cotton was poisoned.

Hysteric laughter has aspects which are triggered and controlled by social dynamics. Such factors as TV sound tracks, the presence of other people, larger audiences, higher densities of people, and the presence of a stimulus person have all been shown to influence the generation of laughter.[80] Factors like these may have helped foment a laughter outbreak in the Bukoba district of Tanganyika from 1962–64. It started in a Catholic convent school and spread to fourteen other schools, forcing their closures. Eventually some one thousand persons were affected. "The laughing girls were initially sent home whereupon their mothers became affected and soon after other female relatives. . . . Some patients required hospitalization because of exhaustion. No organic process could explain this happen-stance."[81]

However, the Bukoba laughing outbreak involved certain psychological effects which seem to transcend social dynamics. For instance, victims thought things were moving around in their heads, with many saying that they were frightened of something and that they feared that someone was chasing them. A man who felt sorry when he saw some of the afflicted nearby returned to his hut and shortly afterward "he felt something telling him to laugh and cry and shout. This he continued to do for most of the night."[82] As in tarantism and dancing mania, one explanation of these symptoms is that demons superimposed themselves on hysteric dynamics to exacerbate the social and emotional distress people experienced.

Finally we come to modern holy laughter and its conceptualization as an altered state of consciousness (ASC). Within a theological context, this puts it alongside other phenomena like spirit trances (being slain in the Spirit) and some glossolalia. Mark Cartledge, who adopted this model, located holy laughter in the halfway house between wakefulness and sleep. In other words, it belongs with hypnagogia, which he mentions in a note, daydreams, and waking visions (lucid dreams). He thinks that ASCs are part of Christianity's historical traditions, and that though Quaker silence, Catholic liturgy, and Pentecostal music are different means of ASC induction, they have similar worship outcomes.[83] Therefore, although the laughter is a natural human capacity, God mysteriously shows up in the midst of this psychological event.

79. Ibid., 140.
80. Freedman and Perlick, "Crowding, Contagion, and Laughter," 295–303.
81. Black, "Pathological Laughter," 69.
82. Rankin and Philip, "Epidemic of Laughing," 167–69.
83. Cartledge, "Interpreting Charismatic Experience," 131.

This proposal opens before us a Pandora's box, and not merely because of the great range of psychological conditions which shelter under the ASC umbrella. (Erika Fromm, for instance, lists four minor and seven major altered states.)[84] The real issue is in Cartledge's claim that God shows up in the context of altered states. When we recall the various witnesses' description of their daimon—Socrates, Cromwell, Jung, and others—they all agree that this presence, known via powerful inner promptings and voices, is capable of overwhelming them. To quote Jung, "There was a daimon in me and in the end its presence proved decisive. It overpowered me and if I was at times ruthless it was because I was in the grip of the daimon."[85] We see, then, that the question of what superhuman power comes to inspire and control, Satan or God, is extremely crucial, not merely for holy laughter, but for any paranormal phenomena. I will approach this problem in terms of several aspects of biblical theology.

Theological Considerations

Spiritual assessments attribute holy laughter in part or in whole to either God or Satan. Several factors bear on our interpretation.

First of all, there's only a half-dozen possible allusions to prophetic ecstasy in the pre-biblical ANE.[86] In Israel itself, prophets expressed themselves differently. While David danced ecstatically before the Lord as the ark entered Jerusalem (2 Sam 6:14), he, along with Samuel, Saul, and the whole company of prophets (1 Sam 10:10–13; 19:23–24) also went about naked. Nakedness as a sign of judgment is evident in Isaiah, who walked naked through the streets for three years (Isa 20). This was a dramatic warning about the impending exile of Egypt and Ethiopia to Assyria. While the Hebrew prophets appeared strange to their community, though, they didn't strive to alter their consciousness. Quite to the contrary, their goal was to soberly speak God's word even though it might come via dream, vision, or inner voice. On the other hand, we see in Elijah's Baal-worshipping opponents (1 Kgs 17:18–40) the ANE pattern of inducing altered states through nervous system activation. The intent was to open the personality to spirit-possession and thus to demonic empowerments.

A second consideration focuses on biblical norms of worship and practice. The simplest of these is the affirmation that things ought to be done decently and in order (1 Cor 14:40), and in the fear of God. What about the interrupted preaching experienced by Wesley, on the American frontier, and in the modern Fourth Wave revivals? Laughter apologists like Episcopalian priest Hugh Williams explain this as "God distracting us from our routine ways and concentrating our attention on Him."[87] In one way the principle is fine—who can object to God's freedom to upset human

---

84. Fromm, "Nature of Hypnosis," 83.
85. Jung, *Memories, Dreams, Reflections*, 356.
86. Isbell, "Origins of Prophetic," 62–80.
87. Duin, "Praise the Lord," 28.

applecarts?—but the logic presupposes that holy laughter is of God. However, this is the very question we're trying to answer.

A third, more difficult problem is that laughter which interrupts preaching short-circuits essential truth. Senior pastor John Arnott's original expectations of the Toronto Airport Vineyard were that God would "save the lost, heal the sick, and expand the kingdom." When strange manifestations came instead, Arnott and Randy Clark, a St. Louis Vineyard pastor, decided that God meant to start with a party and not with a heavy message of holiness.[88] Rodney Howard-Browne says that "one night I was preaching on hell when laughter just hit the whole place. The more I told people what hell was like, the more they laughed."[89] Uncontrolled laughter in response to a sermon on hell is not fear of God, nor is the fun, partying, and sneering at sobriety of which some laughter apologists boast.[90]

Fear of hell cuts both ways, though. Jonathan Edwards defended the unusual manifestations which accompanied New England's Great Awakening, one of which was terror of hell. He asked, why wouldn't there be cries, groans, and tears if one sees oneself being dangled over hell from the hand of God, whom they "see to be exceedingly provoked"? "No wonder they are ready to expect every Moment when this angry God will let them drop."[91]

However, Edwards' terror was no more biblical than is sneering laughter. Writing in response to the Welsh Revival, Jessie Penn-Lewis distinguished true concepts of God's holiness from false. The false produces terror of God which either drives people away or forces them into actions of slavish fear. Conversely, the true "produces worship, godly awe and hatred of sin. God draws near based on Calvary but does not terrorize."[92] Consequently fear of hell itself can be of human, demonic, or Godly origin, but there will be dramatic differences among these.

A fourth biblical imperative is that all phenomena must be tested to determine its spiritual source. This transitions us from holy laughter to a broader consideration of ecstatic phenomena.

Mick Brown's story is salutary. A *Telegraph* magazine writer, he did a feature on the Toronto Blessing and ended his article with a description of being lightly touched by John Arnott on the forehead. Brown says he fell to the ground "as if my legs had been kicked away from underneath me. I hit the floor—I swear this is the truth—laughing like a drain."[93]

Nevertheless, Brown subsequently stated that his experience didn't change in any way his reservations about fundamental Christianity. "It didn't make me think that

---

88. Hanegraaff, *Counterfeit Revival*, 54–55.
89. Duin, "Praise the Lord," 24.
90. Tillin, "Toronto Phenomenon."
91. Edwards, *Distinguishing Marks*, 18.
92. Penn-Lewis, *War on the Saints*, 306–7.
93. Brown, "Unzipper Heaven, Lord," 30.

Buddhism, Hinduism, Islam, Red Indian Shamanism or whatever other kind of manifestation of faith could go out with the bathwater."[94] In other words, the true work of the Holy Spirit testifying to Jesus Christ was absent at the time of his article.

If nothing changed for Brown because of his Toronto experience, everything did change for Claire Myers Owens during her Zen Buddhist zendo repentance:

> Suddenly such powerful repentance and desire to expiate seized me that my very body shook uncontrollably. Sobs tore up from the depths of my being. It was like tearing up the roots of my ego, annihilating life-long delusions of my own goodness. This emotional storm continued hour after hour. I was oblivious, blind to everything and everybody in the zendo.
>
> After five hours two monitors came and lifted me up. My body was so heavy and my legs so weak I was unable to walk.[95]

Myers Owens says that "the enlightened man emerges from this overwhelming experience a new person. A transformation of his character, behavior, and hierarchy of values has occurred. A new life style arises without his volition, astounding no one so much as the person to whom it happens. His ego has mysteriously disappeared."[96]

If we placed this same testimony in a Christian church so that zendo became evangelistic meeting and transformation became conversion, would the account read differently? I suspect that virtually any Christian evangelist would be overjoyed to hear words like Myers Owens spoke. Since genuine repentance is always honored by God (Luke 18:13–14), was Owens' experience therefore of God? The answer becomes "no" when we learn that the episode climaxed with her receiving the power to see through the wall and watch two men sitting on the other side. By now we have seen enough *psi* data to recognize this as demonic power at work. Therefore no spiritual feelings or experiences outside of biblical guidelines can ipso facto be assumed to be of God.

Consider these further examples. A forty-five-year-old man suffered from seizures which all began with a feeling of happiness. He could only describe them as being "completely out of this world" and like being in heaven.[97] In chapter 9 I told the story of Rita Klaus' white light redemption. Her spiritual feelings bear repetition: "[There was] a feeling of absolute love like I'd never felt coursing through me. I felt forgiven and at peace."[98] A kundalini participant said of the purported inner serpent uncoiling inside her, "I was experiencing very blissful orgiastic feelings.... I felt such incredible love toward the world and toward other people that I wanted to get up

---

94. Taylor, "What Happened Next?," 1, 8.
95. Owens, "Zen Buddhism," 174–75.
96. Ibid., 156.
97. Subirana and Oller-Daurella, "Seizures with a Feeling," 248.
98. Morse with Perry, *Where God Lives*, 126.

and give a big hug to everybody."[99] Michael Harner describes the shamanic universe, "When you go there, what do you find? You find cosmic unity, you find a sense of love, you find what's called shamanic ecstasy, where tears of joy exist. It's the same world of the Christian mystics of the medieval times. It's the same world of the great Eastern saints."[100]

Counterintuitive though it may feel, every spirit must be tested (1 John 4:1–3). Traditional charismatic, Kingdom Now, and Fourth Wave apologists ought to be very concerned about the eat now, check later theology espoused by the movements. In urging people to open themselves to the Holy Spirit, John Arnott says, "I don't want you to even entertain the thought that you might get a counterfeit." He explains that the Toronto Blessing's leaders' original grid was that the manifestations were demonic. But now? "If he [the recipient] thinks it's God and he likes it, let him enjoy it! Because you can test the fruit later."[101]

This is a potentially catastrophic response. Sociologist Margaret Poloma describes herself as a full participant in the pentecostal-charismatic movement[102] and wrote in part as a sympathetic apologist for the Toronto Blessing. In discussing exactly those manifestations which Arnott recommends that recipients uncritically enjoy, Poloma said, "It is likely that intense worship and prayer have the power to bring forth a natural power (called *chi* in some cultures, *kundalini* in others, *prana* in still others), including a release of human emotions that in turn contribute to increased mental and physical health."[103]

Two things are noteworthy in these remarks. First, Poloma acknowledged that manifestations are not necessarily of the Holy Spirit and second, she attributed these to purely natural forces. However, *chi, kundalini, and prana* are only three of at least ninety-five worldwide labels for this psychic power. Other terms more-or-less recognizable to Westerners include *mana, ki, life force, élan vital, entelechy, etheric force, synchronicity,* and *bioplasma.*[104] These all refer to the same *psi* demonic powers which are not natural in the least. As to *kundalini* specifically, it's the process whereby these demonic powers manifest as the uncoiling serpent who rises through the seven chakras in turn. Even kundalini's teachers warn that the unwary can die during the unleashing of these dark powers. We must conclude that if Poloma accurately represented Fourth Wave theology, it—as does Christianity generally—stands in desperate need of education about the realities of Satan's deceptions.

---

99. Grof, *Adventure of Self-Discovery*, 115.
100. Mishlove, "Way of the Shaman."
101. Hanegraaff, *Counterfeit Revival*, 52.
102. Poloma, "Toronto Blessing," 258.
103. Ibid., 267.
104. White and Krippner, "X Energy," 550–55.

V. SUMMING UP

Throughout Christian history ecstatic and mystical experiences often have been contrasted with prophetic action as competing views of spirituality. However, this is not the only way to frame ecstatic phenomena. A better understanding of unusual religious experience which also fits perfectly with chaoplexity is to evaluate ecstasy according to the historical center line.

In Augustinian theology, the church is a mixture of good and evil, *simul justus et peccator*, that is at once justified and sinner. As history unfolds, the city of God jousts with the city of earth, so that Augustinianism actually tries to preserve the purified center line of salvation. Consequently, Augustinianism emphasizes moral and ethical concerns. By claiming to stand in continuity with the proven and biblical historical core, Christian orthodoxy in this tradition automatically questions the spiritual legitimacy of novel phenomena.

A second view of church history is the Joachimite. For Joachim of Fiore (1135–1202), history proceeds sequentially according to eras marked by the activities of Father, Son, and Holy Spirit. In every historical period, renewal movements have adopted this view to justify ecstatic phenomena and its accompanying novel teaching. This is not a "return to 'go' but progress, providence."[105] If we're convinced God wants to do a new work, then why wouldn't we too speak like Holy Ghost Bartender Howard-Browne? He told God, "Either you come down here and touch me, or I'm going to come up there and touch You."[106]

The current North American Joachimite version is Kingdom Now and Fourth Wave theologies. These movements stand in the tradition of Latter Rain eschatology which asserts an unprecedented outpouring of spiritual gifts, empowerment, and paranormal phenomena prior to Christ's return. The tongues and laughter movement is innovationist and Joachimite. It sees the renewal wing of the modern church as true to the age of the Holy Spirit and expects new things not experienced formerly. Progress dictates newness, whether of universal tongues, laughter, or any other experience with potentially preternatural overtones. This is the case especially since new manifestations of the Spirit are visualized as harbingers of the great end-times evangelistic in-gathering.

Both Augustinian and Joachimite historiography really represent the two extremes sitting on either side of the historical centerline. The overall system may be characterized as a self-organizing feedback network which guides history. The various influences in laughter, for instance—self-learning, group hysteria, person-to-person dyadic transactions, demonic manipulation—are each parameters in the system.

At first blush, to locate the demonic as a parameter in history sounds a bit like the demonic-as-social structure theory. This idea was popularized by writers like

---

105. Yoder, "Anabaptism and History," 255.
106. Howard-Browne, *Touch of God*, 73.

Heinrich Schlier,[107] Hendrik Berkhof,[108] John Howard Yoder,[109] and Walter Wink.[110] They argued that the demonic is merely an impersonal zeitgeist which impels the system. Wink, for instance, defined this driving force as a dominant in the Jungian collective unconscious, and likened it to German *Volk* culture. A moment's reflection, though, tells us that the impersonal zeitgeist is just gussied-up language for Richard Dawkins' memes, the ideas which operate subterrainly in culture. In reality, demons are actual personal agents who enter the system and synchronize with it. Thereafter the system follows a new course based on the degree to which the demonic synchronization has shifted the attractor(s) which organize it.

Recognizing the chaoplexic nature of ecstatic phenomena helps us to understand why they recur throughout history. As self-organizing systems they are part of the actual fabric of historical processes. In this view, Joachimite innovationists push the social-religious network toward chaos and Augustinian traditionalists pull it back toward rigid periodicity. As these two forces interact, the systems build toward an avalanche which frequently is marked by frenetic emotional, physical, and spiritual phenomena. Though some contest the view that history is self-organizing,[111] the evidence suggests[112] that the avalanche process which explodes in viral bronchitis, the lab sand pile, or the stock market is no different than that observed in the laughter and tongues revival.

Summing up, then, although religious communities usually regard ecstasy as of divine origin, tongues outbreaks and especially holy laughter manifestations are classic examples of self-organizing phenomena. Any genuine Holy Spirit activity seems peripheral at best.

---

107. Schlier, *Principalities and Powers*, 25.
108. Berkhof, *Christ and the Powers*, 69.
109. Yoder, *Politics of Jesus*, 135–62.
110. Wink, *Naming the Powers*, 104–48.
111. Reisch, "Chaos, History, and Narrative," 1–20.
112. Brunk, "Why Are So Many Important Events Unpredictable?," 34.

11

THE FINAL FRONTIER

HALL OF FAME BASEBALL player Ted Williams died in 2002 at age eighty-three. Unfortunately, instead of being quietly gathered to his fathers, his remains were subjected to a viciously contested burial which became the stuff of tabloid headlines. While his daughter wanted to spread his ashes in the Everglades his son intended to freeze him so that his DNA could be cloned and bring Williams back from the dead.[1]

It must be admitted that, just as at first glance NASA proposals to achieve worldwide weather control seem incredibly presumptuous, so too do arguments that death could be overcome. Nonetheless, the human drive to overcome death is taken very seriously. Techniques like cryogenics (freezing) or generalizing cancer cells' replicational immortality[2] are mere tips of the iceberg in beating death. Scientific efforts to eradicate disease and reverse aging[3] show that defeating death is regarded as humanity's final frontier.

Given this milieu, it's important to reexamine immortality in light of the Genesis trees of the knowledge of good and evil, and of life. The flow of the chapter is as follows. Section 1 relates immortality to creation's underlying death structures and processes. An important addendum in section 2 is the belief that death is actually permeable, with the dead inhabiting a near-earth realm. The tree of the knowledge of good and evil in section 3 lets us assess two modern immortality "trees": exotic technologies and spiritual transcendence. A close relative to transcendence, reincarnation, completes the tree of knowledge in section 4. The final section recreates the immortalizing sequence in Eden's tree of life and leads to a concluding discussion of resurrection as the culmination of the tree of life in the eschaton.

---

1. CBC, "Family Feud."
2. O'Hare et al., "Conditional Immortalization," 646–51.
3. De Grey et al., "Is Human Aging," 667–76.

I. IMMORTALITY AND THE LOSS OF HOMEOSTASIS

It's been clear for some time that the laws of physics and chemistry are not the fundamental code of created life.[4] Remarking on this, chemist Michael Polyani says that "the organism is shown to be, like a machine, a system which works according to two different principles: [1] its structure serves as a boundary condition [2] harnessing the physical-chemical processes by which its organs perform their functions."[5] These comments point to the fact that creation's laws are layered. Therefore without suitable control systems the physical structures would be organically inert. This repeats what we learned in chapter 4 about the four levels of law—*aphar* (dust, i.e., physics and chemistry), *basar* (animated flesh), *nephesh* (soul), and *ruah* (wind/spirit)—which are required for people to exist as humans.

In addition, the fundamental structure by which all these levels cohere is the massive informational system called the automaton. The automaton's nodes are the seat of the various chaoplexic processes which we observe upstream in Popper's three worlds. It's reasonable to expect then that the immortalizing tree of life will be expressed within the matrix of self-organizing system theory. The tree of life may be visualized as a network control structure working to regulate and balance overall well-being. In systems terms this principle of regulation is called homeostasis.

The question quickly becomes one of determining where and how homeostasis both exercises and loses its general oversight.

One answer is that homeostasis operates by balancing energy inputs and expenditures. In kinetic terms, living organisms are thermodynamic systems which extract energy from the environment for bodily metabolism and thereby reduce bodily entropy. Conversely, although no one energy factor like metabolism's toxic by-products characterizes all diseases, bodily systems nonetheless decline at the rate of about 1 percent a year.[6] Therefore in conceptual terms they reflect the general movement toward entropy in the universe. As a result, over the course of a life-span the body's energy inputs lose the race to rebalance the increasing inefficiencies of the homeostatic systems. The gradual lifetime increase in entropy results in disease, aging, and eventually death.

A second possibility is that humans are programmed for death. Evolutionary theory predicts that the miracle which initiated life ought to have produced eternal youth and immortality. Instead death prevails. Why? August Weismann (1834–1914) suggested that there's a genetic program which limits the number of cell divisions during a life-span. This later became known as the (Leonard) Hayflick limit and was first confirmed experimentally by H. Earle Swim in 1959.[7] The current thinking is that

---

4. Polyani, *Personal Knowledge*, 390.
5. Polyani, "Life's Irreducible Structure," 124.
6. Bortz, "Aging as Entropy," 324.
7. Gavrilov and Gavrilova, "Evolutionary Theories of Aging," 343.

an internal clock counts down from birth to death and places a numerical limit on the number of cell replications to be allowed. This restricts the number of times cells can be replaced to maintain bodily well-being. The clock is tied to the telomeres which cap the ends of chromosomes to protect against degradation and end-fusion. When the telomeres wear down from repeated replication cycles, a signal stops them from further replications.[8]

A third hypothesis views disease and aging as the loss of information complexity. In particular, many healthy bodily functions and components reflect a chaoplexic fractal design. We will recall that fractals—a snowflake is a familiar example—have a repeating design no matter how close in we zoom to view segments. This structure appears with the heart beat, walking gait, and the tracheobronchial tree, among others. In the case of pulmonary tube function, this design is reflected in disease response. Consequently, if the bronchial tubes are plugged with moisture, the clearing occurs in avalanches of air intake, the size of which follows a nonlinear power law characteristic of self-organizing criticality.[9]

When a bodily system loses enough informational complexity, the adaptive capabilities of the individual will be reduced.[10] A particularly damaging outcome will result when a system's homeostatic regulation has been seriously thrown out of adjustment through physical, psychological, or spiritual trauma. In dynamic terms, the phase state trajectory has crossed from the original attractor basin to another one. The question then is whether intervention can enable a reversal or correction of this crossover. Ultimately, homeostasis may be unable to reset the system to its original baseline.[11]

In these three cases of entropy increase, programmed death, and complex information loss, the materialist position is that deterioration of organic function causes the control structure to break down and homeostasis to be lost.[12] However, since the physics and chemistry of organic processes are actually subservient to the deeper layered structures, the physical phenomena of localized entropy, replicational ceilings, and complexity loss are secondary factors.

The question of lawful prior cause is the basic theoretical issue, and as we saw with mind disorders in chapter 8, plays out at every level. Ervin Laszlo made the same point in different words, commenting that disturbances to bodily systems are buffered by self-regulation, "which enables the cells and molecular components of the body to adjust." Feedbacks are guided by what Laszlo calls inherent norms[13] but which are more accurately called rule-sets. Regardless of labels though, while biological cell,

8. Aviv et al., "Growth, Telomere Dynamics," 830.
9. Suki et al., "Fluctuations, Noise and Scaling," R2.
10. Goldberger et al., "What Is Physiologic Complexity," 23.
11. Nesse, "Natural Selection," 91.
12. Azzone, "Disease as Instability," 84.
13. Laszlo, "Systems and Structures," 183.

molecular, and control system failure happen interactively, the ultimate oversight responsibility lies with the underlying dynamic structural relationships.

Although entropy increase, internal cell death programming, and complexity loss each offers valuable insights into disease and aging, we still must ask whether they have the ability either singly or collectively to explain the loss of system-wide homeostasis. What we're really looking for is an inclusive feedback network paradigm that enfolds gene expression, biochemical pathways, developmental and physiological variables, individual behavior, social relationships, and even cultural and spiritual values.[14]

Zoologist Alfred Emerson echoed this larger search horizon with these words, "Homeostasis may be a delicate regulation by means of subtle mechanisms, as well as a grosser and more obvious control. It may be psychological as well as physiological. It may involve activation or inhibition. Homeostatic effects are often web effects with many negative feedbacks. There may be homeostasis of homeostatic mechanisms."[15]

As a result, the problem of death is reduced to finding a way to reverse or overcome loss of homeostasis.

II. AN INTERMEDIATE REALM?

In the preceding discussion of creational law, entropy, and immortalization, I have made the tacit assumption that human death is a one-way street, an absolute disconnect from earthly life. In so doing, I have taken at face value the OT teaching about Sheol and the NT doctrines of Hades and Paradise. In the OT, Sheol is the place to which all people go upon death, while in the NT, the theology of death had evolved so that the unjust go to Hades and the righteous to Paradise. I have also accepted verbatim the biblical statement that death is the final enemy (1 Cor 15:26).

However, many people question or even reject these premises in part or in whole. Surveys show that up to 8 percent of the general population believe that they have communicated with the dead; or that they have been controlled or possessed by a spirit of the dead; or that they have knowledge of past lives.[16] People hear voices, see spirits, perform automatic writing, and experience direct spirit control of their voices, including xenoglossy and ermenoglosssy, the speaking and understanding of unlearned languages. Indeed, such beliefs and experiences are general throughout human history.[17]

People fit these paranormal events into various niches but a common uniting thread is a belief that the spirits of dead humans operate in an intermediate realm.

---

14. Nesse, "Natural Selection," 89.

15. Emerson, "Dynamic Homeostasis," 142.

16. Charlottesville, VA, 8%. See Palmer, "Community Mail Survey," 232; Winnipeg, MB, around 4%. See Ross and Joshi, "Paranormal Experiences," 358; Hardy, *Spiritual Nature of Man*, 47, found 8%.

17. Bourguignon, "World Distribution and Patterns."

The Final Frontier

For instance, some believe in reincarnation (see section 4), which presupposes by definition that souls recycle between history and non-history until a final release is achieved. Others think that there is a life-death-resurrection linear progression but that there are way stations. The Roman Catholic way station is called purgatory; I shall return to this in the next chapter. Still others hold to a neoplatonic philosophy which regards inner voices as ancestral souls stuck in transit in an intermediate realm. Given the various phenomena and claims attributed to an intermediate realm, it's timely to re-examine whether death in fact is the final frontier.

To set the table, it will be helpful to briefly review basic intermediate realm theory.

Neoplatonism divided reality into four ascending zones, the terrestrial, intermediary, celestial, and the Infinite. The intermediary plane which concerns us is the home of all disincarnate human spirits such as ghosts, departed souls in transit, spiritists' controls, and our own subtle bodies if they disengage from our gross body when we're asleep. In addition, though, there are angels, demons, heaven, and hell.[18] This eclectic mix is the source of great confusion and a recipe for deception for those who accept this model and encounter inner voices in themselves or others.

Several examples will illustrate the neoplatonic model.

An influential event in the modern era was the exorcism of Gottliebin Dittus in Möttlingen, Germany, between December 1841 and Christmas Eve 1843.[19] One of the phenomena Gottliebin experienced was an apparition which spoke through her and which claimed to be that of a recently deceased neighbor. It's crystal clear from pastor Johann Blumhardt's own words that he came to believe that the spirit really was the deceased woman. Blumhardt writes, "I posed a few questions, addressing them to the voice, which I assumed belonged to the dead widow."[20]

> Blumhardt—Is there no peace in the grave?
> Voice—No.
> Blumhardt—Why not?
> Voice—It is the reward for my deeds.
> Blumhardt—Have you not confessed everything?
> Voice—No. I murdered two children and buried them in a field.
> Blumhardt—Do you not know where to get help? Can you not pray?
> Voice—I cannot pray.
> Blumhardt—Do you not know Jesus who can forgive sins?
> Voice—I cannot bear the sound of that name.
> Blumhardt—Are you alone.
> Voice—No.
> Blumhardt—Who is with you?
> Voice—[Hesitatingly, but then with a rush] The most wicked of all.

---

18. Smith, *Forgotten Truth*, 47.
19. Krüger, "Johann Christoph Blumhardt," 430–31.
20. Zuendel, *Awakening*, 39.

After citing Luke 8:30, where Jesus asked the spirit speaking through the Gadarene demoniac its name, Blumhardt categorically stated that Jesus' personal question proved that demons are departed human spirits.[21]

Ancestral spirits marched to a quite different drumbeat with Harry Edwards. He was a noted healer whose career began during WWI and was enlarged after he attended a séance in 1936. Edwards believed that healing is built into creational law and is actualized by departed human spirits who learn how to become "spirit doctors" after death.[22] Said Edwards, "Every one of these healings is super-normal according to medical practice. Each one is a planned act, administered by a superior intelligence to that of man."[23] At his peak he claimed six thousand healings in four years, primly pointing out that Lourdes required more than a century to record sixty-five out of millions of visitors.[24] In 1954, Edwards presented evidence to the Archbishops' Commission on Healing and after several years of deliberations, Archbishop Lang's committee voted 8–3 that communication with spirit was verifiable.[25]

For a third account we turn to Jung. His first cousin Hélène Preiswerk served as the case study in his doctoral dissertation on spirit possession and mediumship.[26] The controlling spirit identified itself as Jung's and Preiswerk's grandfather Samuel. A Swiss Reformed pastor and denominational church leader, Samuel had been a spiritualist. In fact, he kept a chair in his study for the spirit of his first wife, with whom he had intimate weekly conversations. Jung's own mother was often required to stand behind his chair to keep the spirits away while Samuel prepared his sermons.[27] Although Jung eventually decided that Hélène was tapping into her own psychic fragments, by the 1920s he was investigating séances with Albert von Schrenk-Notzing and Eugen Bleuler. These explorations led Jung to say, "I do not hesitate to state that I have observed a sufficient number of such phenomena to be completely convinced of their reality. They are inexplicable to me."[28] It shouldn't surprise us then that in later years, Jung turned about face and committed to a spirit viewpoint.

So, is death permeable?

As we observed earlier with the mystical transcendent light, demonic spirits produce all genuine paranormal events. These include such things as levitation, psychic healing, electromagnetic disturbances, precognition, clairvoyance, clairsentience, induction of lightning and rain, bilocation and astral travel, other-world journeys, and

---

21. Ibid., 39–41.
22. Edwards, *Healing Intelligence*, 141–45.
23. Ibid., 130.
24. Ibid., 138.
25. Ibid., 102.
26. Jung, "On the Psychology and Pathology," 17–24.
27. Jaffé, "Details about C. G. Jung's Family," 39–40.
28. Jaffé, "Psychic World of C. G. Jung," 195.

so forth. As paranormal phenomena, the presumption of ancestral spirits therefore must be interpreted in the light of this commonality.

A way of doing this for ancestral spirit ideology is to apply Occam's razor to see which of the following solutions best explains the data. On the one hand, we might hypothesize that after death humans somehow transcend creation's covenant boundaries to acquire and use *psi* powers to influence the living. In addition, these departed humans seize control of natural law to produce localized unnatural phenomena. Or, alternatively, demons, who already have such paranormal powers by virtue of their participation in creation's structural systems, deceptively manifest them within nature and human affairs. I suggest that the demonic explanation is a hand-in-glove fit.

Three points, one scientific, one biblical, and a third theological, impress themselves on us in any summary evaluation of the intermediate realm.

First, creation is fundamentally dualistic and therefore covenantal. From Gödel's falsification of creation's self-reference, to Spencer-Brown's first distinction, to creation's need for an automaton programmer—all of these demand that God be external to creation. The neoplatonic system with the All emanating downwards in continuous fashion from one monistic realm to the next does not reflect reality. Instead, that which connects one element of creation to the other is their mutual membership in the automaton's rule-set structures. But all of these structures are distinct from God.

Second, death in the Bible has impermeable boundaries. People go to Sheol in the OT, or to hades and paradise in the New Testament. There are only a select few exceptions which prove the rule. Samuel's appearance after death (1 Sam 28:19) and Jesus' transfiguration where he met Moses and Elijah (Mark 9:4) are scant grounds to prove that the deceased linger in some hypothetical near-earth realm. Even when Samuel was called up from Sheol by the Witch of Endor, what did he tell Saul? "Tomorrow you'll be joining me here." There would be no hanging around to tidy up unfinished business. We are forced to the conclusion that all manifestations of ancestral spirits in every culture are really demons who have synchronized previously with human mind memory attractors.

Finally, we must challenge any theology which appeals to a supposed intermediate realm as an avenue for help for the dead or intercession with God for the living. For tribal, folk, and Eastern religions, this means ancestral worship as a means of guaranteeing community security. For neognostics, it embraces spirit guide energy healing as well as spirit regression therapy which purports to take people through their past lives to secure healing of current traumas. For the Catholic communion, this means appeal to Mary and the saints. All are anathema.

III. THE TREE OF KNOWLEDGE

I have said more than once that in order to control his immortality Adam covenanted with Leviathan to use demonic *psi* powers to manipulate natural law. In light of the argument so far, we may phrase this as the attempt to maintain homeostasis through demonically empowered synchronization with self-organizing systems. However, human reliance on demonic manipulation of natural law is not restricted to the direct application of *psi* power as in subtle energy healing.[29]

Today modern science also postulates immortalization via exotic technologies. For its part, neognosticism visualizes a spiritual transcendence of death. To appreciate how Adam's attempt to subvert nature are recapitulated in these two ideas, we need to probe them in greater detail.

Secular Exotic Technologies

The following proposals have been urged as technological ways to defeat death.

- The simplest form is tissue engineering. This medical advance forgoes prosthetics and transplants in favor of regeneration of organs and by implication, of whole bodies. The ultimate goal is to develop the technology to the point that emergence of the body from its underlying forms can be done perpetually.[30] Ironically the idea resurrects Hans Driesch's form-object work which he rooted in vitalism.

- Conventional biology wants to recreate extinct species. Japanese and French scientists apparently hope to combine 3,700-year-old mammoth DNA with sperm from a living elephant. By the third repeat of putting sperm into the new female creature which results each time, the animal would be 88 percent original.[31]

- Leading-edge immortality theoretician Pierre Baldi of the University of California has bigger dreams. He projects that in a few centuries, it will be possible to sequence the genome of every living person. This would lead to statistical models to narrow genome possibilities and then this data would be used to recreate the DNA of dead people.[32]

- Then there's panspermia, a 2,500-year-old theory rooted in the idea that life came to earth from the wider universe.[33] The concept that humans might reverse this and plant life elsewhere has secured interest from scientists like DNA Nobel winner Francis Crick.[34] An esoteric version argues that future human existence can be secured by interbreeding with alien life forms. It's more or less the modern *coitus redux* of the immortal/mortal interpretation of Gen 6:1–4 in which the

---

29. Burkholder, "What's the 'Subtle Energy,'" 109–13.
30. Cooper, *Bodily Transformation*.
31. Baldi, *Shattered Self*, 81–82.
32. Ibid., 83.
33. Wickramasinghe et al., "Progress towards the Vindication of Panspermia," 403–13.
34. Crick and Orgel, "Directed Panspermia," 341–46.

Sons of God married the daughters of man. In modern fringe mythology this takes the form of UFO-based sexual experimentation on human abductees.[35]

- With the final anthropic point physicists take the ultimate step. A far-distant future is envisioned when humans will have exited from an uninhabitable earth and will have become immortalized as virtual software agents.[36]

All of these suggestions fit under the umbrella of physical eschatology, meaning that they attempt to circumvent death through the laws of the physical universe. However, as we learned in chapter 3, death is programmed into the universe. Therefore physical eschatologies are doomed from the start since they fail to deal with this structural roadblock.

Spiritually Driven Immortalization

Classic gnosticism taught stages on the path of the soul's ascent; and modern neognostics follow this pattern regardless of the labels attached to their schools of thought. Wouter J. Hanegraaff makes the astute observation that holists view the personality contents of the first stage after death as virtually identical to the experiences people have in altered states of consciousness.[37] One is reminded here of how absolutely certain Ken Wilber and Michael Harner are about the truth they perceive in nonconsensual reality. If one already believes that the friends, ancestors, angels, kaleidoscopic landscapes, and ethical neutralities one meets in a mystical trance or during an NDE are what one will encounter after death, then death has no sting. Indeed, this is pretty much what NDE survivors say. Immortality is just around the corner.

Barbara Marx Hubbard's spirit master told her to "read through the New Testament for the vision of the future. You have neglected Christ." However, she didn't accept orthodox Christian theology but viewed scripture as an evolutionary map of human potential. This interpretation led her to assert that humans can co-create the future and can experience real resurrection within history. This will be possible because we are empowered by the same inner Christ Self as was Jesus. Hubbard literally means that our mammalian bodies will soon perish and be transcended.[38] Others have given her idea specific form with the proposal that spiritual evolution over a lifetime can enable living human flesh to self-transform into a radiant celestial body via DNA's plasticity.[39]

Oddly enough, victory over death within history also appears in Christian Kingdom Now beliefs. As a subset of Latter Rain eschatology, this fringe element believes

---

35. Holden and French, "Alien Abduction Experiences," 164.
36. Prince, "Simulated Worlds," 204–10.
37. Hanegraaff, *New Age Religion*, 259.
38. Hubbard, *Revelation*, 65–69.
39. Kelleher, "Retrotransposons as Engines," 10.

that the glorified body is possible now.[40] Therefore the Church's mission is to conquer death within history. "We who are alive and remain are left here for one ultimate purpose: to conquer the last enemy which is death. God has left us here to take dominion over death."[41]

Teilhard, on the other hand, takes us to a post-historical eschaton. He argued that entropy is handled by the transformation of physical energy into spiritual energy. Humans are part of evolution's ascent toward consciousness and its culmination in a supreme consciousness outside space and time called the Omega Point.[42]

Except for Kingdom Now, spiritually driven immortalization is rooted in a monistic worldview. In particular, it depends on the assumption that God inherently lives in each person via the divine higher Self. However, we have seen repeatedly that creation is actually dualistic, functioning as a God/human relational feedback network. From a chaoplexic perspective the I-Thou relationship functions just like human dynamic systems. In particular, human interpersonal relationships are characterized by a relatively small number of attractors that tend to be stable during normal system operations.[43]

In dynamic terms, Adam's choice to break covenant with God and to eat of the tree of knowledge caused a catastrophic bifurcation in his core system. God's general covenant to provide for humankind—colloquially, rain for the just and unjust—still existed. However, the reciprocal network which linked God and Adam in personal relational attachment was rendered inoperative since God was no longer a parameter. The God attachment was replaced by a new attractor basin which linked Adam to Leviathan and chaos. This new system operated within Adam alongside the original "God basin" which had become self-referencing. Biblical theology expresses the totality of the disaster in these words: "You were dead through the trespasses and sins in which you once lived, following the course of this world, following the ruler of the power of the air, the spirit that is now at work among those who are disobedient" (Eph 2:1–2).

We may press the point even further. The structural outcome of the human covenant with Leviathan led to the loss of conditional immortality as chaos and order vied for the same phase space. This echoed what Spencer-Brown showed in his calculus of logic. Consequently, death was not a punitive but a logical outcome of a fundamental confusion of structure. This may be traced in the corruption sequence triggered in Adam by this disarray. It started with the loss of relational attachment to God and followed with atrophied emotional selfhood; genome decay and misdirection of genetic expression; deterioration of immune, endocrine and neural homeostatic systems; physiological morbidity (disease); and finally death.

40. Gardiner, *Radiant Glory*, 75.
41. Paulk, *Satan Unmasked*, 265.
42. Chardin, *Phenomenon of Man*, 297.
43. Lavelli et al., "Using Microgenetic Designs," 48.

In summing up the tree of knowledge, it's clear that immortality can only be addressed through regeneration of fundamental self-organizing systems. However, humans cannot undo catastrophic deep-level systemic bifurcations. The confusion of structure at the root of disease and death requires divine restoration of correct structure. Suffice it to say that the tree of knowledge doesn't lead to immortality but leaves us dead.

IV. REINCARNATION

When we combine ancestral spirit phenomena with peoples' belief in reincarnation, it's clear that a lot of people accept an intermediate realm and a permeable death. Though the numbers vary, about 20 to 25 percent of Euro-Americans believe in reincarnation.[44] This finding is paralleled in Canada where 26 percent of general respondents and 32 percent of fifteen- to nineteen-year-olds believe they'll be reincarnated. In contrast, even though three-quarters of Canadians claim at least nominal Christian affiliation, only 20 percent expect to be resurrected.[45] Since Western populations have low percentages of citizens with explicit Eastern cultural roots—2 percent in the United Kingdom[46]—the vast majority of those believing in reincarnation do so from choice rather than from inherited belief.

The traditional argument put forward on behalf of reincarnation is that karma is the most rational cosmic moral law. Three aspects of this claim deserve our attention. To begin with, apologists claim that karma ensures a precise and likely linear relationship between one's actions and their consequences. These principles hold both within history and across multiple incarnations of the person. It doesn't matter if it takes millions of births;[47] karma will guarantee that everyone (even demons) will balance their scales and be reunited with God. Furthermore, in the late nineteenth-century an argument based on genetics emerged. It was an era when intergenerational social ills were blamed on genetic inheritance and reincarnation offered an alternative answer. It said that many aspects of personality are indeed inherited but non-genetic. One apologist put it this way: "The Ego on rebirth picks up the threads of its mental and moral 'make-up' pretty much where it dropped them, say fifteen or twenty centuries ago."[48] In the bigger picture, a third element is that karma can even be applied to the rise and fall of nations at the collective level.

Therefore, karma and reincarnation seem to provide an answer to theodicy's perennial question: how come bad things happen to good people? Past-life wrong-doing as the source of present-life outcomes is double-edged though. For instance, we're

44. Walter and Waterhouse, "Very Private Belief," 187.
45. Bibby, *Unknown Gods*, 126–27.
46. Walter and Waterhouse, "Very Private Belief," 188.
47. Ram and Achari, *Cosmic Game*, 30.
48. Fawcett, *Case for Reincarnation*, 16.

forced to explain what the inmates of Auschwitz and Buchenwald did in a past life that was so evil that they merely got what they deserved. We can add other examples from today's headlines: what evil was committed by those who starve in a famine, are tortured by despots, are victims of brain cancer, or who burn to death in a house fire?[49]

Whitley Kaufman asks another cogent question: how did the karmic process begin and who was the first sufferer? If we reply that the process has no beginning, we commit the error of infinite regression and offer a nonanswer. It brings to mind the famous and perhaps apocryphal story of the woman who explained that creation rested on a turtle. When asked what was next down, the answer was, another turtle. Each question was answered the same way and finally in exasperation she said, "It's turtles all the way down!"

Kaufman also argues that contrary to its claims karma disallows moral responsibility. He notes that people have no recollection of the actions which are supposedly the cause of their karmic reward or pain. However, personal awareness is at the heart of legal justice; a person guilty of a crime must know why (s)he is being punished.[50] This is the exact test in defining cases of criminal insanity.

In the end, it's hard to avoid the conviction that belief in karma has no supporting evidence whatsoever. This judgment fits the findings of anthropologist Agehananda Bharati. In assessing Hindu and Buddhist psychic phenomena, he offers a real-life perspective on karma, "As a young monk, I walked through India, visiting some 250 villages; virtually without exception, villagers told me, unsolicitedly, about harm caused to them by evil spirits, witches and discontented local divinities. Hardly anyone spoke about the effects of bad *karma*, except as an afterthought."[51]

What about reincarnation's claim that people remember past lives? There are two main types of data put forth here.

On the one hand we have the childhood-memory class of evidence. The following illustration is typical of this argument.

Emilia was the second child and oldest daughter in the Lorenz family in Brazil. As an unhappy girl, she told several siblings (but not her parents) that if there was such a thing as reincarnation, she'd come back as a man. She made several suicide attempts and finally died of cyanide poisoning on October 12, 1921. Some while later, her mother received three separate messages at séances stating that Emilia was returning but as a boy. Mr. Lorenz was incredulous at this gender change suggestion although ready to believe Emilia might return. In due course, Mrs. Lorenz delivered a son and he was named Paulo.

In writing up this case, psychiatrist Ken Stevenson delineated seventeen parallels between Emilia and Paulo. For instance, each had the habit of breaking off corners of new loaves of bread; each preferred one sibling, Lola; Paulo stated that he had taken

---

49. Kaufman, "Karma, Rebirth, and the Problem of Evil," 21.
50. Ibid., 22–23.
51. Bharati, "Ontological Status," 230.

sewing lessons from DoZa Elena, which Emilia had done too. Unfortunately, each also ended their life in suicide.[52]

As of the year 2002, Stevenson had three thousand such childhood memories' cases in his files. Most of them came from just a few countries, including India, Sri Lanka, Burma, Thailand, Turkey, Lebanon, Syria, West Africa, and northwest native North America.[53] These cases usually followed a pattern: (1) an elderly person predicted they would be reborn and often indicated the parents; (2) after their death a relative or someone near had a dream in which the deceased announced their return; (3) the new baby had birthmarks which corresponded to scars or wounds on the deceased person; (4) when the child could speak (before the age of five) they described aspects of the deceased person's life with increasing detail; (5) and the child displayed attitudes and behaviors foreign to the birth family but similar to those of the deceased person.[54] Interestingly, after about age five, the child gradually would forget all of these memories. The implication was that as the child's ego differentiates, whatever process had been manifesting the so-called memories was curtailed.

The second type of memory data comes from adult memories retrieved through hypnotic regression. Following are reports from three therapists who use the regression technique.

Sylvia Browne stated that she has hypnotically regressed tens of thousands of people, and that this has proven to her that we've all lived before. It's worth relating a pivotal event which led her to pursue life regression and spirit release therapy. A client who had an insomnia problem

> suddenly started babbling, in the present tense, about his hard life as a pyramid builder, and then lapsed into several minutes of the goofiest-sounding nonsense syllables I'd ever heard. I thought he was having a psychotic breakdown right before my eyes. . . . I sent a tape of the session to a psychology-professor friend at Stanford, expecting him to agree with my suspicion that this poor client needed psychiatric help. Instead, he called back three days later, almost breathless with excitement, to tell me that after considerable research, he and his colleagues were in unanimous agreement that those goofy-sounding syllables were actually my client speaking fluent seventh-century-B.C. Assyrian, a language that would have been very popular among pyramid builders.[55]

An earlier clinician, Helen Wambach, recruited 1,088 volunteers whom she hypnotically regressed. Most claimed past-life memory recall. One of her star witnesses was Bob. He had learned self-hypnosis in his early twenties when he was in a Veteran's Hospital dying of tuberculosis. His condition gradually improved until he was well

---

52. Stevenson, *Twenty Cases*, 179–90.
53. Gupta, "Reliving Childhood?," 38.
54. Ibid.
55. Browne with Harrison, *Blessings from the Other Side*, 44–45.

enough to be discharged, after which he realized he was having psychic flashes. These led him to volunteer as a subject in Wambach's research. When in the trance state, Bob spoke unlearned foreign languages (xenoglossy) and could write hieroglyphics. In total, Helen and Bob supposedly uncovered fourteen previous lives dating back to 2000 BCE Egypt, excluding an unregressed gap from 100–1300 CE.[56] Commenting on Bob and on another key witness, Shirley, Wambach said that she could find no karmic purpose or pattern in their rebirth sequences.

A third regression practitioner is psychiatrist Shakuntala Modi. Based on eleven years of work with hundreds of clients, she has made astounding claims about their past life memories. These memories include peoples' current lives, all past lives, and between-life experiences in heaven. "Many of my patients have even regressed to the time of their creation and to the creation of the universe and beyond."[57] Consistent with these claims many patients recalled their birth by God the Mother. According to Modi, "Most of our feelings of inferiority, inadequacy, imperfection, fear, depression, rejection, and separation anxiety have their roots when we were first created by God. . . . They [the clients] find themselves being thrust out as a separate soul from the core of God (the mother), but still connected to God with a silver cord (like a cosmic umbilical cord)."[58] The theological claim that clients were part of Mother God from whom they were birthed explains why they insisted they had memories from creation or before.

Space prohibits a point-by-point rebuttal of these reports, so I will briefly comment only on the core claim that childhood memories and adult hypnotic regression prove that reincarnation is true.

As it turns out, basic arithmetic highlights a major problem with such a claim. The incidence of alleged past lives memories is thrown into sharp relief when we consider the number of *Homo sapiens spiritus* who have ever lived. Assuming a date for Adam of at least ten thousand years ago, some 98–100 billion humans have been born during the last ten millennia.[59] Therefore the question is, if people really are reincarnated, why is the ratio of memory recall—a mere few thousands out of this astronomical database—so low?

More fundamentally, nature itself destroys reincarnation's central cosmological assumption. The doctrine of rebirths depends on an eternal cycle in which each universe in turn emanates from the godhead and returns to the godhead in a pointless cosmic game.[60] However, creation neither emanates from God nor is it oscillating between sequential existences. The data shows that it's actually expanding at an

---

56. Wambach, *Reliving Past Lives*, 70–76.
57. Modi, *Remarkable Healings*, 183.
58. Ibid., 89.
59. Haub, "How Many People," 3–4.
60. Ram and Achari, *Cosmic Game*, 28.

accelerating rate and will not collapse into itself.[61] This unidirectional arrow of time along with the irreversible increase in entropy means that this creation is destined to die, not devolve and recreate.

V. THE TREE OF LIFE

I said earlier that death is loss of homeostasis. How did the tree of life solve this problem?

The roots of the solution have been stated already in earlier chapters when I said that our loss of child attachment to God in Eden cut us off from the tree of life. Therefore we must be able to connect our loss of attachment to God to our loss of homeostasis.

The principle has been powerfully illustrated on the human level by French analyst Marguerite Sechehaye. She described a young woman, Renee, who suffered from intense unreality and voices. Sechehaye helped Renee regress to infancy and as we read the story now it's quite obvious that Renee suffered from loss of mother attachment. Renee called Sechehaye Mama, who in turn filled the role, up to and including substituting apples for the missing mother's breasts. "She put the piece in my mouth, and with my eyes closed, my head against her breast, I ate, or rather drank, my milk. A nameless felicity flowed into my heart."[62] Renee's mind disorder began to abate from that very moment of reattachment.

So our argument is that in Eden relational intimacy or attachment with God was how the regulation of body, mind, and spirit was upheld to produce conditional immortality. To see how God's relational intimacy with Adam generated immortalization, I will extrapolate backward from still-existing systems. For this reconstruction to be valid, the necessary connections among the emotional environment, physiological well-being, and loss of the human-divine emotional dyad must be demonstrated. The appeal of this proposal is that a great deal of modern evidence has been uncovered which underscores how belief, emotion, and relationships influence somatic functioning.

Mind Control of Body Physiology

Starting with two historical cases, the following illustrations are a surface sampling of evidences for various psychosomatic functions.

In 1784, the French Academy set up history's first placebo experiment to test Mesmer's animal magnetism.[63] Investigators told a boy that one tree on an estate was

---

61. Cirkovic, "Anthropic Arrow of Time," 44.
62. Sechehaye, *Autobiography*, 79.
63. Kaptchuk, "Powerful Placebo," 1722–25.

magnetized and then took him to four trees in order. He sweated at the first, began tremors at the second, and by the fourth, he collapsed into convulsions. However, at no time had he been near any tree that actually had been magnetized. He produced all the symptoms within himself.[64] In another case of autosuggestion in the 1880s, French physician Dr. Henri Bourru of Rochefort medical school traced a client's name on his arms with the dull point of an instrument. He told him that at 4 p.m. his arms would bleed along the lines and his name would appear. Accordingly, the client fell asleep at the appointed hour. "On his left arm the letters stood out in bright red relief, and in several places there were drops of blood. The letters were still visible three months afterwards, although they had grown faint."[65]

The mind's ability to think something into being is also seen in dissociative identity disorder (DID). Many dissociated people have alters with completely different physiologies which change almost instantaneously. One such example is of a person who broke out in hives whenever a particular alter drank orange juice. The hives would appear if personalities changed while drinking and subside if the alters changed again while still drinking.[66]

Similar emotion-based phenomena manifest in hysteric conversion reactions. Josef Breuer and Sigmund Freud described a girl whose hypnagogic vision involved a terrifying (demonic?) hallucination. Her right arm having gone to sleep at the same time, she developed contracture and anesthesia, and for eighteen months she was unable to speak her native language.[67]

Antidepressant medications are especially fertile ground for demonstrating connections between belief and physiological responses. Between 1987–99 manufacturers marketed several new antidepressant drugs, including Prozac, Paxil, Zoloft, Effexor, Serzone, and Celexa. A meta-study was performed on the forty-seven clinical trials which were submitted to the US Food and Drug Administration prior to the drugs' approval. The results? Patients given these drugs statistically showed only a small response—in fact tiny enough to be deemed clinically negligible.

As a result, the authors concluded that these antidepressants may be little more than active placebos and that "there may be little justification for the clinical use of these medications."[68] In other words, the patients' faith in the medication—whether placebo or active—was the crucial variable. In fact, drug therapy tests show that placebos operate on the same brain areas as do the actual active drugs to which they are experimentally linked. As an example, in patients with Parkinson's the placebos

---

64. Harrington, "Many Meanings," 184.
65. Hudson, *Law of Psychic Phenomena*, 153.
66. Chopra, *Quantum Healing*, 122.
67. Breuer and Freud, "On the Psychical Mechanism," 4.
68. Kirsch et al., "Emperor's New Drugs."

directly shadowed the true drug-response pattern.[69] To reiterate, the patients' belief in the therapy is the key aspect.

Some research has suggested that implantation of human embryonic dopamine neurons into Parkinson's patients ameliorates some of the symptoms of the condition. However, double blind sham surgery showed just one difference between controls and real surgery recipients. Namely, sham patients reported more social contact after four months although both groups had a significant improvement in physical functioning during the year's follow-up. The more important finding was that there were several significant differences in outcomes which were based on patient beliefs. Those who thought they received real implants improved whether or not they actually received the neural material.[70]

What about hard-core organic diseases like cancer? A study of mental imagery was done of 159 cancer patients who were expected to die within a year. Sixty-three were alive two years later, of whom 22.2% showed no cancer, 19.1% were in remission, and 31.8% were stabilized. As a comparison, healthy subjects who imagined white cells attacking germs had "increased neutrophil adherence, lymphocyte counts and salivary immunoglobin A concentration." The researchers concluded that probability of remission seems related to the ability to do imaging.[71]

One of the most famous cases of psychosomatic healing was told by *Saturday Night* editor Norman Cousins. Suffering from a rare degenerative disorder called ankylosing spondylitis, he put himself on a regimen of laughter, Vitamin C, and a positive attitude. Cousins' story became a cultural phenomenon and he received thousands of letters from doctors who thanked him for showing them the value of mind/body healing.[72]

Emotions and Genetic Expression

The mind is deeply implicated in bodily health and therefore homeostasis. Well and good. The next link in the chain of evidence is to show how this relationship is connected to emotional direction of gene expression.

For more than half a century animal researchers have known that the emotional environment directly affects how genes express themselves. Early studies at McGill University[73] demonstrated that rat strains bred to be bright and dull regressed or improved respectively in direct correlation to their emotional environment. Later research used mice inbred for fear, cognitive dullness, and hyperactivity (the BALBc strain) and for phlegmatic character (the C57 strain). When BALBc young were raised

---

69. Goldapple et al., "Modulation," 38.
70. McRae et al., "Effects of Perceived Treatment," 415.
71. Sheikh et al., "Somatic Consequences," 149.
72. Harrington, "Many Meanings," 189.
73. Meaney, "Nature, Nurture, and the Disunity of Knowledge," 56–57.

from birth by C57 mothers, they developed into animals that are very much like C57 adults. Geneticist John Crabbe offers a third example of the connection between emotional environment and gene expression. He led a multi-lab gene stability study using mice with designed identical genes. The expectation was that mice from the same inbred lines would exhibit the same anxiety behaviors. To the researchers' great surprise, behaviors fluctuated within lines which had the same genes. The conclusion was that the mice responded directly to the emotional states of their handlers.[74] The research also demonstrated that effective parenting is crucial in how experience shapes gene expression (epigenetics).[75]

How does the emotional environment impact on human gene expression and brain plasticity?

A wide-ranging set of information bears on the connections between human emotional interactions and physiological systems. The ability of the emotional environment to shape and change neural growth and gene expression starts in infancy and continues throughout life.[76] This relationship is manifest in connections between stress and childhood brain development,[77] infant attachment and disease,[78] early childhood abuse and adult mental pathology,[79] in stress and wound healing of caregivers,[80] in impaired immune systems,[81] and in a variety of psychosomatic conditions and their associated protein changes.[82]

There's simply no gainsaying the intimate connection among mind, neural plasticity, gene expression, and emotional environment.[83] Ever since Donald Hebbes' groundbreaking work, it's been known that the brain has remarkable plasticity. This means that neurons have great flexibility in establishing new synoptic connections when healing organic or psychological injury. This is typically seen in a sufferer who is highly motivated and wills self-healing.[84]

What is significant is a new appreciation of the degree to which emotional systems rooted in the mind mediate gene behaviors. I have focused mostly on parent-infant attachment relationships. (While Daniel J. Siegel and others expand the infant attachment bond to caregivers other than biological parents, the evidence for in utero

---

74. Goleman, *Social Intelligence*, 243–44.
75. Hammond and Young, "Microsatellite Instability," 1630–34.
76. Fuchs, "Neurobiology and Psychotherapy," 480.
77. Teicher, "Scars That Won't Heal," 71–75.
78. Schore, "Effects of a Secure Attachment," 12–17.
79. Read et al., "Contribution of Early Traumatic Events," 327–30.
80. Kiecolt-Glaser et al., "Slowing of Wound Healing," 1194–96.
81. Glaser et al., "Psychological Stress-Induced Modulation," 707–12.
82. Kiecolt-Glaser et al., "Emotions, Morbidity, and Mortality," 84–90.
83. Davidson et al., "Emotion, Plasticity, Context, and Regulation," 904.
84. Nicholson, "Building a Better Brain," 22–29.

bonding still argues for the necessity of the blood parent.[85]) However, even near-total strangers like new college room-mates begin to show significant similarity in their emotional experience when they live together for several months.[86] Dating couples with a relationship history of several months show even more dramatic similarities. These partners converge in values, attitudes, verbal and social skills, cognitive complexity and mental abilities, eating and drinking habits, and perceptions of others.[87]

The conclusion is inescapable. In the integrated complex of phase space mind objects and their neural network correlates, interpersonal emotional transactions are a fundamental mechanism of gene expression in the individual.

The Human-Divine Dyad

I have argued that Leviathan corrupted the feedback circuit between Adam and God, thereby introducing death into *Homo sapiens spiritus*. It should be possible for us to tease out something of the functioning of the primal system even if its original harmony no longer exists in humanity. In overview, the trees of life and knowledge, and their influence and functioning, may be represented as dynamic attractors. The tree of life and proper order stands for human relationship to God and it enabled synchronization with God. Conversely, the tree of knowledge stands for human relationship to nature. After being co-opted by Leviathan, it incorporated chaos and disorder.

The dynamic attractor driving the tree of life network was the divine/human bilateral covenant relationship. God granted unlimited entrée for Adam to consume relationship, a partaking which confirmed to him that he belonged to God. Belonging is rooted early in the Genesis account where we see Adam naming the animals (Gen 2:19). Walter Russell Bowie writes in *The Interpreter's Bible* that "when Adam named the animals he determined what they should be like and how they should behave."[88] This refers to the ANE concept that the essential nature of the one who names is reflected by the name-bearer.[89]

The principle is expanded into the divine/human realm in God's naming of all the families on earth (Eph 3:15). Adam's ability to name the animals was to be exercised as stewardship of their well-being. Likewise, God's naming-and-owning of Adam points to his perpetual renewal of Adam's life. In sum, the animals belonged to Adam and Adam belonged to God. It's remarkable how well this primeval naming-and-owning coheres with our modern understanding of the universal and innate human need to

---

85. Siegel, "Toward an Interpersonal Neurobiology," 69.
86. Anderson et al., "Emotional Convergence," 1061.
87. Ibid., 1054.
88. Bowie, "Exposition," 498.
89. Abba, "Name," 500.

belong.[90] On the other hand, it's sobering to realize that hell defines the state of all those creatures who ultimately refuse to belong to God.

Since chaos and disorder were originally absent within Adam his mind and spirit were unadulterated. However, by living in our specific universe, Adam was physically subject to lack of energy replacement at a rate commensurate with the universe's increase in entropy. Therefore God's naming-and-owning of Adam was not a mere theological cliché. It was a profound and continual homeostatic physical rebalancing of Adam.

This rebalancing relied on the connection between information input and energy replacement. At a fundamental level, information and entropy are quantitatively related to the amount of knowledge an observer can obtain. Physicist Basilio Catania explains, "[If] a mole of nitrogen has 10^{28} bits of entropy, it means that we *lack* 10^{28} bits of information to *know* all the states of that volume of gas . . . when we say that we *have* 10^{10} bits of information . . . it means that we *know* all 10^{10} binary microstates that describe that object or event."[91]

From the context of this energy and information relationship, we may then ask how God confronted entropy and preserved homeostasis in Adam. The answer is that, just as God knows for the universe at large, God knew informationally for Adam the initial and all possible subsequent states of the dynamic structures ordering his physical systems. God's synchronization with the attachment module in Adam's spirit exerted downward causation on Adam's mind, shifting his emotional system attractors. At the mind stage the informational process became an energetic process and via the sequence described earlier neutralized entropy and maintained homeostasis in Adam's self-organizing network systems.

Resurrection

I have shown how conditional immortality functioned in the past. Our challenge now is to interpret the tree of life in terms of the universe's ultimate heat death and the future of humans. In distinction to exotic technologies, spiritually driven victory over death in history, and reincarnation, true immortalization depends on resurrection. There are two complementary aspects to resurrection, that of the universe and that of humans.

Present cosmological understanding combines the universe's open nature with the prediction of heat death in the remote future. If humans are to be bodily resurrected then the universe as host must overcome this dead-end future and assume an entropic/negentropic equilibrium. For the universe to achieve this, structures at the level of the automaton require reversing and/or remaking. Since creation, including

---

90. Baumeister and Leary, "Need to Belong," 499.
91. Catania, "Physics of the Boolean Observer," italics original.

the universe, is a self-organizing system,[92] entropy can only be reversed and the physical universe immortalized by amending or adding parameters in the automaton. Given that the automaton is designed to instantiate any rule-set, it meets Robert John Russell's criterion that "if God is to transform the universe, it follows that God must have created the universe such that it is transformable."[93]

Entropic reversal logically will begin in the same node to which Roger Penrose unknowingly pointed in his comment about the creator's phase space fine-tuning of the big bang.[94] In fact the node may contain a single binary choice in which the original "no" produced a universe with entropy. The "yes" choice sits waiting to trigger a universe with no entropy but with an eternal steady-state equilibrium. If this instantiation conceptually replicates the big bang, it would produce the sort of cataclysmic reconfiguration described by the NT remark that heaven will pass away with a loud noise and the elements with fire (2 Pet 3:10).

The human aspect of resurrection must begin with a clarification of the term. Specifically, resurrection isn't resuscitation of people who regain life after being declared clinically dead. An example is George Rodonaia, a vocal communist dissident in Tbilisi, Georgia. In 1976 he was run over twice by a car as part of a KGB assassination attempt. After three days in the morgue where he was supposedly quick-frozen, he was revived as the first incisions of his post-mortem began.[95]

True resurrection is death followed by restored embodiment in the new creation. This rules out theories of spiritual resurrection which echo platonic ideas of soul ascent into immortality. Here it's helpful to review the NT accounts which describe Jesus' resurrection embodiment. The gospels tell us that (1) Mary Magdalene and the "other Mary" grabbed Jesus' feet (Matt 28:9); (2) Philip felt the wounds (John 20:27); (3) Jesus ate fish (Luke 24:13); (4) Jesus cooked fish for the disciples (John 21:13); and (5) he walked to Emmaus and ate supper with Cleopas and his friend (Luke 24:30). These are all physical, hands-on things so whatever the precise nature of his spiritual body, it was able to function in the physical world.

However, re-created embodiment as just stated is only part of the resurrection story. In our earlier discussion of physical eschatologies, there was no hint of a vision beyond that of perpetuating existing human life. Here's the problem, though, as put to us by Leon Kass.

Suppose we lived for even a quarter life-time more, what would be the result? Using his examples, do pro tennis players want to play 25 percent more matches? Do parents who've finished raising their children want to extend this ten years? Would Don Juans who'd seduced a thousand women be more fulfilled after seducing 1,250? Kass undercuts life extension's basic assumption, saying that at root people long "not

---

92. Mbonye, "Cosmology with Interacting Dark Energy," 117–34.
93. Russell, "Eschatology and Scientific Cosmology."
94. Penrose, *The Large, the Small and the Human Mind*, 47–48.
95. Atwater, *Beyond the Light*, 74.

so much for deathlessness as for wholeness, wisdom, goodness, and godliness—longings that cannot be satisfied fully in our embodied earthly life, the only life, by natural reason, we know we have."[96]

In other words, if immortalization were to be granted to us as we presently are with our innate evil, self-centeredness, and inability to love our neighbor, eternity would be unbearable. So resurrection must deal first of all with the core identity of human personality.

At this juncture, we find that the road forks dramatically. The terms *perennial philosophy*, *prisca theologia*, *prisca philosophia*, and *primordial tradition* all refer to the ancient conviction that humans can self-regenerate. We can transcend evil by returning to the beginning to recreate ourselves and so dispel chaos. Mircea Eliade summed up modern neognostic historical recapitulation: "Initiatory death abolishes Creation and history and delivers us from all failures and 'sins.'"[97]

The *Alchemy Journal* offers a current example of this ideology. "All blockages, suppressed negative emotions need to be released. When issues are not processed in a lifetime, they can follow a soul into the next life . . . *for we must be cleansed before we can exist in the same vibration as the Messiah.*"[98] The message is clear: we transform ourselves. In this ancient theory masquerading as progressive modern theology, God, Jesus Christ, and the Holy Spirit are happy to have us once we've reintegrated our core splitness.

On the other hand, the biblical witness states categorically that humans are dead in sin (Rom 3:23, etc.), a conclusion at which we also arrived in chapter 3. Structurally speaking, since Eden humans have been suffering from an irreversible split in the attractor systems governing the intimate relationship with God. In technical language, the dynamic sequence that is involved is called an explosive bifurcation or blowup[99] and its aftermath is "a complete restructuring of the system, a chaostrophic discontinuity."[100] This catastrophe is humankind's basic problem, and, to put it bluntly, we cannot return to Go and fix it. This structural reality gives a context for the biblical teaching on transformation. According to St. Paul, if a person is in Christ there is a new creation (2 Cor 5:17). The conclusion is that human resurrection begins in history with revivification of the spirit as covenant with God is restored. Then, also within history, we can pursue a resurrection journey which enables us to progressively take on a purified mind which functions like Jesus' mind does (Rom 12:1–2; 1 Cor 2:16). Finally, at the end of the age, the resurrection body is set free of the death trap and both humans and our host universe will be immortalized.

---

96. Kass, "L'Chaim and Its Limits," 21, 23.
97. Eliade, *Forge and the Crucible*, 157.
98. Hamblen, "Jesus as Alchemist," italics mine.
99. Galaktionov and Vazquez, "Problem of Blowup," 400.
100. Rosser, "Aspects of Dialectics," 320.

12

FROM ETERNITY TO ETERNITY

> The devil, Satan, will be overcome. Infused with love, his task as selector will be rendered loving. He will not have to be buried in the bottomless pit. He will be released from his anger and reunited with God. . . . "Original sin" will be forgiven.[1]

BARBARA MARX HUBBARD'S SPIRIT guide was the source of this promise that Leviathan would be reunified with God in the eschaton. As the natural, indeed necessary, conclusion to a monistic theology, these words state exactly what Jung wrote years earlier when, by calling Satan God's shadow side, he turned the Trinity into the quaternity.[2]

Throughout the book, though, I have shown how Leviathan's demonic evil is rooted in a dualistic creation. Now we must answer a hard question. In spite of creation's dualistic structure, are Jung, Teilhard, Hubbard, and countless others of like persuasion right in claiming that everyone, both human and demonic, somehow ends up in the Omega Point, New Jerusalem, Planetary Pentecost, or whatever one calls the eschaton? Even if they have clearly told God they want to jump ship? In other words, what happens to free-willed beings if creational choice really allows one to opt out? Forever?

These are the questions we must address. To do so, I will reconstruct Leviathan's biography according to the principles which govern his personality structure. So far we've seen how Leviathan caused chaos and how this plays out in some areas of human experience. As the book concludes, I want to retell Leviathan's biography in terms of his primordial past and eternal future. These two segments are bisected by Jesus' atonement as the pivotal point within the cosmic drama set in motion by Leviathan. This lets us weave things together with a simple *aba*[1] literary structure.

---

1. Hubbard, *Revelation*, 235.
2. Jung, "Psychological Approach," 165–80.

I. LUCIFER'S TRANSFORMATION INTO LEVIATHAN

We have seen how the Four Senses hermeneutic can integrate the various levels of historical, allegorical, spiritual, and eschatological information in Isa 14, Ezek 28, and the book of Job. Out of those earlier discussions, we learned that Lucifer, the shining one, is the Latin Vulgate equivalent of the LXX *eosphorus* and the Hebrew *helel*. He was formed as a cherub, walked on the holy mountain, attended the heavenly altar, reflected the light of Jesus the pre-incarnate Word, became full of his own grandeur, determined to live autonomously, and finally lost his heavenly status. Lucifer was now Leviathan and appears everywhere in the ANE records as the serpent or dragon monster.

In addition to Leviathan, the OT calls the dragon by many names. These include Tannin, Rahab, Tiamat, Nahash Bariah, and Nahash Aqalathon. Leviathan captures the meaning of all of these titles. In the following remarks I will use the names Lucifer and Leviathan interchangeably depending on whether the reference is to the dragon's pre- or post-transformation period.

According to Job 41:4, God put a rhetorical question to Job, "Will it [Leviathan] make a covenant with you [as it did with me] to be taken as your servant forever?" This question directly tells us that Leviathan, the first created being, had made a covenant to be God's eternal servant. To grasp the deeper aspects of what transpired in this covenant we turn to ANE protocols for slaves who chose perpetual servanthood.

A slave had no genealogy, being a person without a name. (S)he was a piece of property and usually marked with a sign, as, for instance, in Egypt, where captives of war were branded and stamped with the name of the king. The brand in ancient Babylonia could be a mark on the forehead, a special haircut, or even a clay or metal tablet suspended by a chain from the neck, wrist, or ankle. In the neo-Babylonian period the custom was to tattoo the owner's name on the wrist. For our present discussion it's important to note that temple slaves were usually marked with the symbol of the god or goddess in whose temple they served.[3] As an example, Philo said that the Jewish high priest wore the name YHWH on his forehead. "The high priest wore a golden plate showing a name that only the purified may speak, and 'that Name has four letters.'"[4] (Note that elsewhere Philo quoted the root text, Exod 28:36, directly. It reads that the high priest had on his head "a rosette of pure gold" engraved with "Holy to the LORD.")[5]

Someone who consented to perpetual slavery after their six years of mandatory service expired was required by Mosaic law to have their ear pierced with an awl (Exod 21:6; Deut 15:17). The hole may have been for a ring or cord with a clay or metal tag on it, although this wouldn't preclude a tattoo as well. The principle of

---

3. Mendelsohn, "Slavery in the OT," 385.
4. Philo, "On the Life of Moses," 503–4.
5. Philo, "On the Migration of Abraham," 103.

marking a person for ownership is found with Cain (Gen 4:15), Israel (Isa 44:5; 49:16), and God's elect (Ezek 9:4). The formal ceremony for perpetual slavery required that the owner bring the slave into the Presence of God at the sanctuary and even maybe to the altar. The slave would repeat a formal renunciation of freedom. Consequently the door post to which the slave's ear was fixed was likely that of the sanctuary, though it could have been the owner's house. Regardless of specific details, the ceremony was a public indication of permanent slavery.[6]

Perpetual slavery confirmed by covenant at the heavenly altar is the backdrop to God's question to Job: "Will Leviathan make a covenant with you as he did with me to be taken as your servant forever?" This is a double-edged rhetorical question, first since we know—but Job apparently does not—that Leviathan began as Lucifer; and second because the answer can only be "no."

Leviathan will *not* make a servant covenant with people; to the contrary, he is our sworn enemy. The church father Olympiodorus acknowledged this in his commentary on Job 41:4. He interpreted God as asking whether Leviathan will offer humans a covenant of peace, and "stop fighting his war against you?"[7]

The sum of the matter is that Lucifer willingly entered into perpetual (eternal) servanthood to God; he received YHWH's mark of possession; and then he attempted to renege on the commitment, becoming the enemy of God and eventually of humans.

So far our analysis has used conventional historical and biblical tools. Now, using the principles of self-organizing network theory, my intent is to throw further illumination on Lucifer's transformation into Leviathan.

Lucifer's Intelligent Agency

Recent work in artificial intelligence has shown how agents can, given the appropriate operating instructions, develop their own goals. These may even include desires,[8] a movement toward emotional qualities which appears in agent systems like *Pandemonium*. In such simulators, the artificial agents have been given evaluation criteria which enable them to choose actions based on feelings.

This becomes especially interesting when the agents have at least some limited foreknowledge, including that of their own death. Jim Doran, the developer of one such system, explained, "An agent with foreknowledge may be reliably aware of (some of) its own future actions and decisions, even though these are yet to be chosen."[9] Doran noted further that

---

6. Durham, *Exodus*, 321.
7. Simonetti and Conti, *Ancient Christian Commentary*, 213.
8. Pezzulo and Calvi, "Pandemonium Can Have Goals," 240.
9. Doran, "Agents with Exact Foreknowledge," 528.

a rational agent will act having due regard to its goals and to what it knows and believes about the world. One particular type of rational agent uses predictive planning, that is, it predicts alternative futures, selects a future which it judges attainable and compatible with its goals and tries to bring that particular future about, striking a balance between conflicting objectives as may be appropriate.[10]

Now, what happens when we apply these findings to Lucifer, who was real and not virtual? I suggest that Lucifer was so constituted as to have some ability to forecast his future according to choices yet to be made. I argue additionally that he tried to break his servanthood vow in such a way that he would escape the universal covenant's pre-set consequence of death. This attempted escape from his perpetual servanthood, an indentureship which he swore at the door post of the heavenly altar, followed Lucifer's own modeling of possible alternative futures.

The reason for these actions is clear from our earlier discussions. Namely, at some critical point prior to the formation of the universe, Lucifer became pridefully consumed with his grandeur and functions. He was convinced that he was more than a perpetual servant and that he could be autonomous. He expected to escape creational boundaries and exist independently, even to the point of ascending to God's place outside creation, and perhaps even forcing the Trinity to absorb him and morph into a quaternity (as Jung asserted). This would put him with God on heaven's throne.

Lucifer's Manipulation of His Control Systems

From a self-organizing systems perspective, we are able to explore this decision a bit further. A dynamic system consists of variables which interact so that although they look disordered, they are fundamentally deterministic underneath.[11] In complex networks, subsystems often include a control variable which is itself influenced either directly by the first subsystem or through a chain of other linked subsystem components. By manipulating these subsystem feedback loops a system can influence its own control parameters. In neural network terms, the feedback loops are called negative since they moderate the unfettered expression of the main positive variables driving the system. It's worth repeating F. D. Abraham's comment which first appeared in the prologue:

> All living and psychological systems are self-organizational. That is, they can control their own control parameters, giving them the capacity to make bifurcations [forced splits] within their own dynamical schemes and complex dynamical systems. Sentient beings can thus learn their own response diagrams,

---

10. Ibid., 530.
11. Faure and Korn, "Is There Chaos in the Brain?," 775.

so to speak, can learn to navigate them, and can imagine extrapolations of those diagrams and test a new universe of self.[12]

Psychologists have debated why behavioral self-regulation does or doesn't work in people. One interpretation pins the blame on personal failures like false assumptions, too much emotion, and lack of strength. It assumes that a person wants to meet the demands of the feedback behavioral loop but can't. Against this, some argue that the problem is rooted in misdirected personal goals and desires. "After all," says one wit, "it takes proficient self-regulation to be a successful burglar."[13]

Lucifer was like the second case. The negative feedback loop built into his covenant with God wasn't too weak but he was too intent on voiding it. Specifically, the positive variable driving his system was that he walked among the stones of fire (Ezek 28:14, 16) and the negative feedback loop was his status as God's servant forever (Job 41:4). In this case, excessive pride in the positive variable drove Lucifer to analyze ways to repress the negative control loop and so end his perpetual servanthood to God. The natural question which arises is how he repressed his servanthood control loop.

Neural networks lose self-regulation in several ways. However, the most effective means of both causing and correcting this loss is by adjusting the negative feedback loop timing. The principle may be illustrated by comparing performance efficiencies in speech recognition software. An electronic neural network system with just eleven nodes (that is, neurons) and thirty links but based on pulse *timing* far outperforms one using one thousand nodes and ten thousand interconnections and based on conventional pulse *strength* variation.[14]

Any delay by Lucifer in performing a command from God automatically constituted an intrusion in the feedback loop. Done skillfully and repeatedly, it would lead to drag and system change. Lucifer's constant goal in this was to direct the change very carefully to break out of the servanthood attractor, leave intact his selfness, and avoid death. F. D. Abraham makes the point that a system may attempt to time itself to favor the locus of a trajectory at the moment of bifurcation.[15] I think that this aptly describes Lucifer's action.

Luciferian feedback delay forces us to think about time. I have argued that Lucifer's transformation into Leviathan occurred prior to the creation of the physical universe. This being so, we must consider the relationship of his feedback loop delay to the creation of time.

For example, we might visualize time prior to the universe as meta-time or kairos (opportune) time defined as a simple before-after sequence. Such kairos time may

---

12. Abraham, "Introduction to Dynamics," 46.
13. Bandura, "Failures in Self-Regulation," 204.
14. USC, "Novel Neural Net."
15. Abraham, "Introduction to Dynamics," 45.

actually even have a mathematical correlate which agents running in a computer simulation might be able to model.[16] This reminds us of Doran's artificial intelligence agents with foreknowledge of their own death, a principle which he too roots in meta-time.[17]

This meta-time operates within the cellular automaton so that all supernatural beings and heaven itself function according to it. It follows that time began when the automaton was given its start command and began computing its next states in sync with its clock cycle, not when the physical universe began. Therefore Lucifer's self-organizing system feedback delay occurred within automaton time which predated the physical universe.

Lucifer's Catastrophic Failure

What actually happened when Lucifer took control of his own negative feedback loop(s)? I will address this first with a brief comment on logic and then more fully in dynamic terms.

We recall that Kurt Gödel found that self-referencing arithmetical statements and their linguistic (semantic) equivalents lead to paradox. H. Martyn Cundy illustrated this with St. Paul's quotation of the Cretan poet Epimenides. The statement, "Cretans are always liars," if true, makes Epimenides a liar who is telling the truth (Titus 1:12).[18] The only way to avoid such logical contradiction is for an outside observer, that is, a non-Cretan, to make the statement. Otherwise statements will be true and false at the same time. This points to our need for God to authenticate creational systems from the outside; in fact, this is the rock-bottom truth of the universal covenant. Therefore when Lucifer tried to self-authenticate from inside creation he fell into paradox.

Paradox returns us to chapter 1 where we met Spencer-Brown and his discovery that marked and unmarked states eventually occupy each other's space in reentry logic. This double occupancy results when reentry data is unmoderated by new outside information as in the feedback loops of networks. In other words, Spencer-Brown's reentry data was identical to original input data. His solution was that the double occupancy was possible due to oscillating states which sequentially occupied the same logic space.

However, let's consider the explanation Spenser-Brown rejected, namely that marked and unmarked states simultaneously occupy the same logic space. When a neural network—whether electronic or in the minds of sentient beings—operates according to its rules, it forms logic space trajectories. A trajectory to which others tend is called an attractor. Now suppose that we define Spencer-Brown's simultaneous state as a new, blended mind object which has been created by the synchronization

---

16. Stone, "Time as Chronos and Kairos."
17. Doran, "Agents with Exact Foreknowledge," 531.
18. Cundy, "Gödel's Theorem in Perspective," 36.

of diametrically opposed chaotic attractors.[19] We've already encountered this concept in chapter 8 in the discussion of how demons link with human minds. In the present context, I suggest two implications of this logic space confusion.

First, it becomes a powerful statement of Lucifer's refusal of external covenant data from God, whose function was to correct Lucifer's own false reentry valuations. Lucifer in the most literal sense imaginable was a liar from the beginning of his attempt to self-regulate (John 8:44). Second, the simultaneous state-space occupation by marked and unmarked states actually offers a rather dramatic definition of the ANE sea. In moral terms, it's the ultimate ambiguity of the simultaneous presence of good and evil such that an observer inside the system cannot distinguish one from the other. From the human perspective, this offers a clear reason why we are enjoined to walk by faith and not by sight (2 Cor 5:7). We are observers inside our own system; our minds have been subjected to reentry marking by chaos; and it's impossible for us to truly discern good and evil for ourselves.

With the addition of one more factor we will have traced the dynamic transformation of Lucifer into Leviathan. Let's consider Lucifer and his walking among stones of fire as the dominant chaotic attractor A, and his perpetual covenant with God as the feedback-control chaotic attractor B. Over time Lucifer's actions generated trajectories for each of these so that basins of attraction for A and B were formed. Between these two basins there was a region of indecision, called the separatrix or saddle.

A characteristic of dynamic systems is that maximum freedom of choice requires that attractors operate close to the edge of instability.[20] Using this freedom, Lucifer entered his own system(s) and via feedback loop time delays he caused A and B to approach each other at the separatrix. We infer this movement because, given his intent to change attractors—as any thinking being can do[21]—each system was required to go outside its basin boundaries into a chaotic regime. To move toward rigid periodicity at the attractors' loci would have locked him into the original attractors with decreased decision-making ability. Consequently, he shifted the attractors toward disequilibrium, A and B collided, both attractors disappeared and a new attractor discontinuous to them formed in the dominant A basin. The sequence is called an explosive bifurcation or blowup[22] and its aftermath is "a complete restructuring of the system, a chaostrophic discontinuity."[23]

In the final section when we consider the question of Leviathan's ultimate destiny it will be necessary to return to this chaostrophic discontinuity. In the meantime, I shall move on in the next part to the central pivot-point in our reconstruction of cosmic history.

19. Boccaletti et al., "Synchronization of Chaotic Systems," 16.
20. Milton et al., "Controlling Neurological Disease," 136.
21. Abraham, "Introduction to Dynamics," 45.
22. Galaktionov and Vazquez, "Problem of Blowup."
23. Rosser, "Aspects of Dialectics," 320.

II. JESUS' ATONEMENT: THEOLOGICAL AND STRUCTURAL DYNAMICS

Under the proper conditions, a chaotic disturbance can grow in amplitude and converge toward the center of its logic or phase space.[24] If likened to a stone thrown in a pond, the disturbance can produce local reverberations which like a ripple folds at the bank and reappears elsewhere in the pond. Lucifer's transformation into Leviathan was the ripple which began disruption within the angelic ranks and creation itself. Furthermore, this disturbance, chaos, is an irrevocable process which leads to death. The problem before us now is to understand how the life, death, and resurrection of Jesus addresses this fundamental problem.

Because Lucifer fractured the universal covenant, creation and humanity are now in bondage to Leviathan and chaos. Therefore Jesus' mission was to mend the torn covenant, destroy Leviathan, and eradicate chaos. I will tackle these questions by looking first at some theological aspects of Jesus' atonement and second at the fundamental chaoplexic processes that are involved.

The Theology of Atonement

As Herbert Wolf has reminded us, Israel was unique in the ANE in having provision for a covenant curse reversal.[25] We recall that the main features of suzerainty treaties included performance stipulations, blessing and curse provisions for (dis)obedience, and procedures for an enforcement lawsuit (*rîb*) if the covenant has been abrogated. In this context, the two operative verbs are *bĕrīt*, to cut a covenant and *kipper*, to atone. They are the bookends which describe how a covenant was sealed to begin with and how it was restored when broken. In each case, the sacrificial animal was cut asunder, in *bĕrīt* as curse and in *kipper* as restorative blessing.

Kipper is often translated with words like cover, reconcile, expiate, purge, and secure pardon, terms which are interpreted as the removal of past guilt. A cognate word, *koper*, symbolically means redemptive price, bribe, ransom, or satisfaction. However, its root meaning is to cover or seal over with pitch or bitumen as in Gen 6:14 where Noah sealed the cracks in the ark.[26] This meaning is consistent with Mary Douglas' argument that atone "means to cover or recover, cover again, to repair a hole, cure a sickness, mend a rift, make good a torn or broken covering."[27] More generally,

---

24. Peat, "Chaos," 368.

25. Wolf, "Transcendent Nature," 320–23.

26. The word כפר which Gen 6:14 translates as pitch or bitumen is found only here in the OT. The cognate Akkadian *kupru* means bitumen and is used in the Gilgamesh epic. See Wenham, *Genesis 1–15*, 173.

27. Douglas, "Atonement in Leviticus," 117–18.

the *kpr* group of Hebrew words implies restoration of the original order of relationship between humans and God.[28]

The biblical pattern for understanding *kipper* is the Day of Atonement in Lev 16. Aaron first sacrificed a bull for himself and his household, and then the goat devoted to YHWH for the people. In each case, blood was sprinkled seven times on the cover (*kapporet*) of the ark which contained the Testimony or Ten Words of the Covenant. The area in front of the ark (tent of meeting) and the four horns of the altar were likewise purified. Therefore each area from the inner sanctuary on outwards was purified in turn. This first act of atonement removed the guilt stemming from the uncleanness, transgressions, and sins of the Israelites, but left death unresolved.

This incompleteness involved the second goat, Azazel. The operative text is Lev 16:21, "Then Aaron shall lay both his hands on the head of the live goat, and confess over it all the iniquities of the people of Israel, and all their transgressions, all their sins, putting them on the head of the goat, and sending it away into the wilderness by means of someone designated for the task."

What was Azazel?

Jewish sources record at least nine linguistic variations for Azazel although the biblical term is only in Lev 16. Azazel may mean scapegoat, serve as a term for destruction or entire removal, refer to a desolate region or precipice, or it could be the name of a demon.[29] There are several arguments favoring the last option.

To begin with, scholars cite the parallelism in Lev 16:8 where lots are cast on the two goats. "One lot for the LORD and the other lot for Azazel" is a correspondence of living beings which is lost if Azazel is a place, animal, or idea. One supernatural being, YHWH, demands another, Azazel.

Second, the Azazel element in Leviticus finds echoes in impurity disposal texts in Mesopotamia. A typical example is the Babylonian *Akitu* Festival during which the god Marduk's Esagila temple was cleansed. The exorcist first purified the temple with water from the Tigris and Euphrates rivers, and its doors with cedar oil. He offered incense on a silver censor and the carcass of a decapitated ram was used to swipe the temple to pick up the evil. After incantations, the carcass was taken to the river and thrown in while the exorcist faced west. To finish the ritual, the exorcist, accompanied by the slaughterer with the ram's head; went to the open country (wilderness) where they remained from days five to twelve.[30]

However, ANE linguistic comparisons link Azazel not merely with moral impurity like that of the *Akitu* Festival but with Mot the Canaanite god of death.[31] This suggests that on the day of Jewish atonement the second goat Azazel then represented death (Mot) being evicted from the sanctuary and sent to the wilderness. Indeed, in

---

28. Lang, "פפר *kipper*," 292.
29. Selms, "Scapegoat," 1066. See also Harrison, "Azazel," 375; and Wright, "Azazel," 536–37.
30. Wright, *Disposal of Impurity*, 62–64.
31. Tawil, "Azazel the Prince of the Steppe," 59.

the ANE wilderness was a catchword for chaos, the netherworld, and the place of demons. The function of ANE exorcism was to chase demons back to the netherworld taking with them disease, sickness, destruction, and death. "From the body of the sufferer go away. O all evil, arise and depart to the place of Ereškigal, take away the skin of the scapegoat from the body of the sufferer . . . so that all evil return to the netherworld."[32] The conclusion is that Azazel, Mot, and Leviathan are one and the same, and that on the day of atonement the goat devoted to Azazel symbolized Leviathan conveying (or accompanying) sin and death to the place of demons. This was a graphic prophecy of the ultimate destiny of Satan and death in the lake of fire (Rev 20:10, 14). To summarize this aspect of the Day of Atonement theology, the sacrificial goat removed covenant-breach guilt while the Azazel goat removed chaos and death.

In the third place, a variety of later Jewish and Christian sources identify Azazel as demonic. These sources include 1 Enoch, Apocalypse of Abraham, the Talmud, various Midrashes, and some church fathers. The second-century BCE Jewi sh text 1 Enoch 10:4–5 connects Azazel, the wilderness, and judgment: "The Lord said to Raphael, 'Bind Azaz'el hand and foot [and] throw him into the darkness! And he made a hole in the desert which was in Duda'el [about twenty kms east of Jerusalem][33] and cast him there.'" The church fathers concurred. Irenaeus referred to "Azazel, that fallen and yet mighty angel"[34] and Origen wrote that the goat Azazel was the serpent, Satan. "Moreover (the goat), which in the book of Leviticus is sent away (into the wilderness), and which in the Hebrew language is named Azazel, was none other than this [serpent]."[35]

Some church fathers symbolized both the sacrificial and Azazel goats as types of Jesus.[36] One can see that the combination of a living goat and a dead goat on the Day of Atonement is reflected in NT atonement theology and Christian doctrine. The question then and now is whether the death, life, or both of the sacrificial victim(s) is the important aspect of atonement?[37] This uncertainty is reflected in the major theories of Jesus' atonement throughout Christian history.

The classic Christus Victor model was developed by the early church fathers, who held that Eden's sin gave Satan moral and legal rights which transferred the human race into his jurisdiction. "For at the first Adam became a vessel in his (Satan's) possession, whom he did also hold under his power."[38] Consequently, salvation is defined as Jesus' victory over the demonic powers. Justin Martyr described Jesus' mission, "For He was made man also, as we before said, having been conceived according to

---

32. Ibid., 51.
33. Ibid., 45n14.
34. Irenaeus, "Against Heresies," 674.
35. Origen, "Against Celsus," 1173.
36. E.g., Barnabas, "Epistle of Barnabas," 263.
37. Morris, *Apostolic Preaching of the Cross*, 110–22.
38. Irenaeus, "Against Heresies," 909.

the will of God the Father, for the sake of believing men, and for the destruction of the demons."[39] Jesus' death as a sinless human became the means of victory over Satan, who held the power of death, because it authorized Jesus to take back that which Satan had stolen.

In *Cur Deus Homo* (Why Did God Become Man?),[40] Anselm of Canterbury (1033–1109) outlined the theory of legal satisfaction. Right moral order in the universe not only prevents God from arbitrarily remitting peoples' sins, but demands the death of every sinner as the only way to discharge guilt.[41] Since Jesus is more than human, his meritorious death is sufficient and can substitute for all.

The third major view, first stated by Peter Abelard (1079–1142), is atonement as ethical transformation. It stresses that Jesus' example of love motivates our reciprocal love for God, an action which leads to our ethical and moral improvement. In his exposition of Rom 3:19–26, Abelard wrote, "We have been justified through the blood of Christ and reconciled to God in this way . . . led by such a gift of divine grace . . . true charity should not now shrink from enduring anything for him."[42]

These viewpoints all have elements of truth as well as inadequacies.[43] However, in the abbreviated form in which I have presented them, they still leave unresolved the question of whether the universal covenant has been mended by Jesus' death, life, or both.

A strict interpretation of *lex talionis* clearly specifies a life for a life with the consequence that each party suffers equal loss (Exod 21:23). Is the universal covenant therefore structured so that if God suffers loss, creation must also? This was Anselm's position with his argument that since God lost honor due to human rebellion, humans must lose life.

However, suppose the question is reversed to ask whether, if creation suffers loss, must God also? It would seem so; God's feelings about Israel's covenant breach and being spurned by her are summed up in the phrase, brokenness of heart. "Those of you who escape shall remember me among the nations where they are carried captive, how I was crushed by their wanton heart that turned away from me" (Ezek 6:9). This is not a loss of honor but of relationship.

Indeed, we see mutual loss in God's covenant with Abram in Genesis 15. Referring to the ritual's sacrificial animals, Thomas Finger very aptly puts words in God's mouth, "Let me be torn in pieces if I do not perform this covenant."[44] Finger leaves unsaid the equally important fact that the same fate awaits Abram if *he* breaks the covenant. I wrote in chapter 11 that death following breach of the universal covenant

---

39. Justin Martyr, "Second Apology," 353.
40. Anselm, *Cur Deus Homo*, 178.
41. Ibid., 203.
42. Abailard, "Exposition," 283.
43. See Reichenbach, "By His Stripes," 560n18.
44. Finger, *Christian Theology*, 34.

wasn't a punitive but a logical outcome of a fundamental confusion of structure. This automatically brought loss of relationship to both God and creation. Hence the logic of covenant breach was and is about accountability for the relationship, not about creating a system designed for failure.

In John 8:44, Jesus called Satan a murderer and liar from the beginning. Therefore as our *go'el* (kinsman redeemer), Jesus avenged Leviathan's blood guilt for the murder of both creation and humanity. He did this as creation's "first born." This refers, not to his human birth in Bethlehem, but to his headship as the preeminent one, the sovereign heir, and destined ruler of all (Col 1:15).[45] As head of creation, he alone can carry responsibility to destroy the works of Satan (Heb 2:14). Jesus' kinsman redeemer blood vengeance was undertaken to uphold objective *lex talionis* standards of cosmic justice.

From the perspective of the torn and dismembered ANE kinsman redeemer we begin to see how immense was Jesus' emptying (*kenosis*) of himself to descend into human flesh (Eph 4:9). His crucifixion represented the cutting or tearing in pieces which was required of humans for Adam's covenant breach. Jesus discharged the *běrīt* formula with his own sinless life in which he was obedient unto death (Phil 2:8). Furthermore, covenant equivalency meant that Jesus had to make atonement as a human and not as God. If he had sacrificed himself as God this would have left the human obligation untouched. This denies Anselm's argument that it was because of his divinity that Jesus' merit is enough for all. The *běrīt* view is that a human broke the covenant and a human had to complete the obligations. With his death on the cross Jesus brought to a conclusion the covenant with Adam. From then on the covenant would be written on the heart by the Holy Spirit (Ezek 36:26–27).

A multi-part atonement process is reflected in 1 Cor 15:17 and paralleled by similar ideas in Rom 4:25 and 5:10. In each case, we infer the discharge of *běrīt* by *kipper* to produce forgiveness from sin, but apart from Jesus' resurrection, we remain dead. In other words, death can discharge guilt but cannot produce life. This is exactly what we saw in chapter 3: death leads to a chaoplexic dead end and there can be no recovery from it.

Almost a century ago the dilemma was put in a rather pungent question in the *Critical and Exegetical Commentary*: "How can a dead Christ save others from death?"[46] More recent literature[47] echoes the idea that Jesus' resurrection adds a component to salvation which his death alone fails to accomplish. In other words, to the question, does atonement rest on Jesus' life, death or both? the answer is "all of the above." His human sinlessness qualified him to cancel the Adamic curse with his death and his resurrection as the new Adam was the precursor of the general resurrection of the dead.

---

45. Kooy, "Jesus as First-Born," 272.
46. Robertson and Plummer, *Critical and Exegetical Commentary*, 349.
47. Kistemaker, *First Epistle to the Corinthians*, 326.

At this stage we might well ask why Jesus was crucified rather than executed by some other means. If the key factor is that expiation blood literally must be shed then several other techniques were available to the Romans and all likely produced more blood. These included drawing-and-quartering, beheading, fighting with lions, being sawn in two, and impaling.

The reason Jesus was crucified is theological. This method echoed the ANE world tree which signified the connection between God and humanity. Jesus hanging on the cross stood for the reunion of God and humanity, and for the mending of the universal covenant. God took the very symbol which gnostics across the centuries have claimed as the basis for connection to deity and affirmed that it is so—provided Jesus was on it in history. An early church father, Irenaeus, referred to the world tree: "The Son of God was also crucified in these [length, breadth, height, depth] imprinted in the form of a cross on the universe."[48]

Jesus' Atonement and Chaoplexity

Expressed in dynamic terms Leviathan's works produced a structural disorder in creation wherein good and evil have come to occupy the same moral state space. This confusion must be reordered. The following reconstructions are inferred from the scientific and theological principles with which we have become familiar in this book.

By definition the covenant is a feedback network linking God and creation. Lucifer's revolt produced cascading cataclysmic covenant impacts on himself, heaven, the physical universe, and humans. Originally Lucifer had the same reciprocal covenant relationship with God as did creation as a whole. However, because he triggered an explosive bifurcation in his dynamic system, his positive and negative attractors disappeared and were replaced by a single discontinuous attractor which was self-referential. At this stage, as Leviathan he had no covenant connection with God. Consequently he no longer served the heavenly altar though he did retain access to heaven.

Heaven, like the rest of creation, is a self-organizing network in covenant with God. The covenant's master positive attractor expresses God's correction, sustenance, and blessing. The negative slave attractor expresses heaven's obedience and vitalization. In the original creation state, these attractors were in balance (homeostasis). In technical terms, this means that over time the sum of their states perpetually converge to zero so that the system is kept in equilibrium.[49]

However, Leviathan and his demons had shifted heaven's self-organizing systems (SOSs) past criticality into chaos, introducing death into them. To cleanse heaven there was a double challenge: to correct/purify its SOSs and to rid it of the rebels.

Let's consider the purification issue in light of Jesus' atonement.

---

48. Irenaeus, *Proof of the Apostolic Preaching*, 70.
49. Sundarapandian, "Global Chaos," 692.

The Leviathan Factor

I noted above that Jesus is the first born of creation (Col 1:15), meaning that he's creation's sole head and representative before God. As such, he therefore qualified as a parameter in the macro obedience feedback system directly linking heaven with God. Jesus generated a primary life attractor just as Leviathan's rebellion had produced a death attractor. Due to its instability, Leviathan's death attractor trajectory collided with the life attractor. Following chaotic boundary crisis rules,[50] the self-referencing death attractor which had infiltrated the heaven/God network was destroyed and the network was corrected. The caveat here is that such boundary crisis events are marked by residual chaotic system activity.[51] Therefore Leviathan's death SOSs will continue apart from heaven until they dissipate, or are dynamically nullified, or he leaves creation.

The second issue in cleansing heaven was to rid it of the rebels. Was Jesus' atonement required to evict them from heaven? The answer is "no"; the rebels were in covenant default and hence in a *rîb* lawsuit with God. The preset outcome of ultimate covenant fracture is death/dismemberment and/or exile. Consequently Michael and his angels threw Satan (Leviathan) and his devils out of heaven and down to earth (Rev 12:7–9). This eviction is actually the first part of a three-stage demonic exile in Revelation: from heaven to earth (12:9), earth to the abyss (20:2), and the abyss to the lake of fire (20:10). Note that each of these evictions is merely a sequential stage in the legal penalty of the original *rîb* lawsuit.

The inevitability of exile and/or death doesn't preclude us from noting the dynamic process involved. A helpful metaphor is the sword-bearing cherubim who closed the "east gate" of Eden (paradise) to humans (Gen 3:24). In structural terms, this implies that both Eden and heaven were rendered off-limits ("Then war broke out in heaven") by angelic instantiation of a new logical boundary condition embedded in a control algorithm.

This brings us to consider the universe. In chapter 11 I suggested that the automaton has one logic node containing a single binary choice of "no" (death, entropy) and "yes" (life, no entropy). When creating the present universe, death's presence prompted God to bypass the "yes" option in favor of "no." This choice is like the simple if/then logic function used in computer software: if(condition;x;y). In this case, the condition was that the universal covenant be in equilibrium. If it was not—as was the case when the universe was created—then the function would return an entropic universe. If the condition would have been met then the function would have returned a non-entropic universe. So the issue was whether Jesus' atonement nullified the non-equilibrium death condition which led to the entropic universe.

Jesus was incarnated into the death system and died at Calvary because of it. In theological terms, (1) he "became sin" on our behalf (2 Cor 5:21) and (2) paradoxically, with his sinless death he discharged the *rîb* lawsuit penalty of death under

---

50. Ott, "Crises," 1700.
51. Grebogi and Ott, "Crises," 181–82, 199.

which creation labored. As we all know, though, death continues to hold sway in the universe. How do we account for these conflicting outcomes in dynamic terms?

If the entropic universe were internally reversible, then macro control could be switched from the death setting to the life setting using either an externally applied noise or an internal property in an already-noisy system.[52] However, the old (present) universe isn't reversible; it can only be destroyed. This is because it's path dependent, meaning that the system is fully controlled by its own history.[53] Jesus' sinless death did not and cannot arbitrarily reverse death inside the entropic universe since the root issue is that the universal covenant is unbalanced. Consequently, Jesus' atonement needed to first correct this imbalance. As I wrote in the prologue, the grand unified theory (GUT) is the ultimate network connection between creation and God. A properly functioning GUT would result in the universal covenant being balanced so that there would be no death. Jesus' atonement from within creation allowed him to synchronize with God the Father, the Other, outside creation. This reactivated God's option to choose the non-entropic life-sustaining universe. Now in covenant with God, in the eschaton the new universe will be empowered to grow, bringing "order [which] acts back upon order in the production of more order."[54]

In summary, Jesus' atonement, and specifically his resurrection, initiated the new universe. It only awaits God's fullness of time to be fully instantiated. In the meantime, Leviathan's residual chaotic system activity means that death continues until the eschaton fully comes.

Finally, how did Jesus' atonement affect humans?

In the primal human negative feedback to God's positive blessing, obedience followed a sequential chain: $A \to B \to C \to D \to \ldots$ Readers will recall that the primal sin was a synchronization (*hieros gamos*, heavenly marriage) between Satan's mind and those of Adam and Eve. The synchronization with Leviathan broke human loyalty to and connection with God. This forced the chain to close in on itself: $A \to B \to C \to D \to \ldots O \to P \to A \to B \to C \to D \ldots$[55] That is, the system became self-referential. Francis Heylighen notes that when a system settles into this type of negative feedback regime, it's "impervious to external disturbances. The system has now become responsible for its own maintenance, and consequently become largely independent from the environment. It is also 'closed' against influences from the outside."[56] In biblical language, Adam and Eve had become "dead through the[ir] trespasses and sins . . . following the ruler of the power of the air" (Eph 2:1–2). In spite of all this, though, the potential covenant link still existed.

---

52. Pasemann and Stollenwerk, "Attractor Switching," 14.
53. David, "Path Dependence," 92.
54. Swensen, "Autocatakinetics, Yes—Autopoiesis, No," 208.
55. Heylighen, "Science of Self-Organization," sec. 3.6.
56. Ibid.

Consequently, Jesus' mission as the race's sole head and representative was to break the self-reference loop and restore covenant feedback to God. In light of Heylighen's comment, external influences could not correct Adam's disobedience SOS. At this point, the feedback chain had to be restored by "a contingent event like the one that produces the path-dependent sequence in the first place."[57] In other words, Jesus had to enter history with its antecedent contingencies and be a true human within the same negative feedback system that Adam had forged.

Jesus' sinless obedience even to death at Calvary did two things for humankind as a class. It broke the connection with Leviathan and it restored the network feedback with God. Together these constituted the "contingent event" which reversed the disobedience-based Adamic SOS path-dependencies. In parallel with how he enabled the new universe the resurrected Jesus initiated the new person Christ SOS. Since this SOS switch is for humankind as a class, we must consider how specific individuals may leave the disobedience/death SOS and enter the obedience/life SOS.

The complementarity principle lets us assume that like the mind, spirit structures are distributed and hierarchical. Within this environment, the will is a dynamic module composed of self-regulation goals.[58] For our discussion the most germane of these is directional change or reprioritization. The will employs both feed backward and feed forward loops to enable historical learning and futures modeling when making choices.

The will dialogues with and is influenced by an associated subsystem which we have encountered in earlier chapters as the God attachment module. For an individual to enter the life SOS initiated by Jesus, the will must first want and choose to exit the death SOS. In theological language, this directional change is called repentance. However, the person cannot actuate this choice alone because the death SOS is self-referential. Therefore the human decision must be enabled by the Holy Spirit, who synchronizes as a parameter in the person's self-reference feedback loop. Using noise perturbation laws of attractor switching,[59] the Holy Spirit shifts the person's Adamic SOS attachment attractor to the attachment attractor in the Christ SOS. With the person's if/then switch now obedience-selected, the Holy Spirit synchronizes[60] with the person's attachment attractors.

It's crucial to state the fine print.

First, the Holy Spirit synchronizes with the person's spirit attachment module but not with their will module. God absolutely refuses to infringe upon a person's will. Second, both death (the biblical old nature) and life SOSs continue to function within the Christ-SOS person. The kingdom of Leviathan and the kingdom of God are

---

57. Mahoney, "Path Dependence," 521.
58. Karoly, "Mechanisms of Self-Regulation," 25, 30.
59. Milton et al., "Controlling Neurological Disease," 120–32.
60. Abarbanel et al., "Blending Chaotic Attractors," 214.

intermixed and overlapping, as Oscar Cullmann pointed out some years ago.[61] Third, humans are not inherently connected to God; nor can people self-ascend to God; nor does anyone or anything restore people to God apart from Jesus Christ.

In chaoplexic terms, Jesus' victory over Leviathan may be summarized as follows. Calvary is the point in cosmic history where the Man from Heaven reversed the systemic self-referencing paradox initiated by Lucifer the Morning Star and introduced to humans by the Man from Earth. This paradox reversal enabled God to renew covenant relationship with humans and in due course to launch the new creation. The functioning of these lawful processes explains why the Son of God was incarnated. A creational system reversal could only be accomplished by a parameter—Jesus of Nazareth—within a creation whose dissonance was originally caused by Leviathan as an agent within that same creation.

III. LEVIATHAN'S FUTURE

From our discussion of the universal covenant stipulations we recall that whomever breaches it carries blood guilt and is liable to dismemberment. When we apply this principle to Leviathan we encounter several issues, some of which actually pertain to both Leviathan and humans. A key springboard for both categories is the connection between dismemberment and the biblical terms "first death" and "second death." A corollary to this, uniquely attuned to human destiny, is whether purgatory exists as a Christianized intermediate realm between the two deaths. Finally there's the matter of whether annihilation might be the meaning of dismemberment, and if not, what, why, and where hell is.

First Death

In the earlier OT texts first death is the termination of human earthly life as one joined his/her ancestors. It's likened metaphorically to a shattered pitcher (Eccl 12:6), a snare with cords (Ps 18:4), waves that encompass (2 Sam 22:5), and so on.[62] As biblical revelation unfolds, though, death begins to acquire a more distinct spiritual dimension. By the intertestamental period Sheol was no longer just a dusty, silent, shadowy void but had become the nether world and the place of perdition or destruction (*abaddon*). This is epitomized by the new word *Gehenna*, a transliteration of the Aramaic Valley of Hinnom,[63] which appears suddenly in the second century BCE. Reflecting Persian

---

61. Cullmann, *Christ and Time*.
62. Myers, "Death," 899–900.
63. Jeremias, "γέεννα," 657.

influence,[64] *Gehenna* was pictured as "a place of judgment for the wicked" with "frequent mention of fire, darkness, and dread."[65]

When we turn our attention to Leviathan we find that in the larger ANE context he's partnered with Mot. On occasion these are each personified and equated.[66] Ambiguity creeps in, though, since at other times Leviathan and even Baal himself are depicted as being subject to Mot.

For instance, in the Ugaritic texts, Baal smites Leviathan but the result is that Baal must descend into Mot's jaws. "Verily thou must come down into the throat of Mot son of El, into the miry gorge of the hero loved of El."[67] Mot, as Death, has the ability to swallow Baal. Death's grasp is cosmic, with "[jaws reaching] to earth, lips to heaven [and] a tongue to the stars, [so that] Baal will enter his stomach [and] go down into his mouth."[68] All of these metaphors are echoed in Jesus' descent into death.

As to the OT, the idea that death swallows the living appears in several texts like Prov 1:12, Hab 2:5, and Isa 5:14. The latter reads, "Therefore Sheol has enlarged its appetite and opened its mouth beyond measure; the nobility of Jerusalem and her multitude go down." However, Isaiah turns the whole logic on its head with the further affirmation in 25:7 that YHWH will swallow death forever (cf. Rev 20:14). This cosmic reversal has been labeled as hoisting Mot on his own petard![69]

Given that people are physically embodied and that Leviathan is not, how does the idea of first death apply to Leviathan? I suggest that his first death was the loss of covenant reciprocity, that is, denial of access to the tree of life. This loss of covenant produced alienation from God, transformation into Leviathan, and his fall into chaostrophic discontinuity. These combined constitute Leviathan's first death. First death for people begins with the loss of relational reciprocity with God. It produces a hybridized mind linked with chaos which exacerbates or causes mind disorders and ends with physical death.

Since the first death is loss of covenant reciprocity and Jesus has restored the possibility of this covenant relationship with God for humans, the question of Leviathan's destiny also arises. If people may reenter relationship with God, might Leviathan also? Is it possible that Lucifer's transformation into Leviathan is reversible so that Leviathan might return to his previous angelic status?

---

64. Myers, "Death," 900.
65. Scharen, "Gehenna in the Synoptics," 328.
66. Kline, "Death, Leviathan, and the Martyrs," 235.
67. Driver, *Canaanite Myths and Legends*, 103, Baal I.i, lines 1–8.
68. Ibid., 105. I.ii, lines 1–7.
69. Sarna, "Epic Substratum," 16n14.

Satan/Lucifer/Leviathan Restored?

I have previously said that Leviathan/Satan is destined for the lake of fire. Yet his possible salvation is the epicenter of the doctrine of *apokatastasis*, the belief that all things will be restored to their primal condition. The Greek word translated as restoration is a verb in Acts 3:21, although the NRSV gives it a noun construction, "universal restoration." Other texts cited by universalists include Mal 4:6 (Elijah will return to restore the hearts of fathers and children to each other), 1 Cor 15:22–8 ("all will be made alive" so that "God may be all in all"), as well as Rom 8:19, 21; 11:32; Eph 1:10; and Col 1:20.

Fire is at the heart of *apokatastasis*, being visualized as both a cleansing agent as well as a punitive one. In the NT the theology of purifying and penalizing fire was rooted in John the Baptist's proclamation that Jesus' coming would be a baptism of fire (Matt 3:11). Jesus himself is quoted in Mark 9:49, "Everyone will be salted with fire," and in Luke 12:49, "I came to bring fire to the earth, and how I wish it were already kindled." These salting and burning functions have been called antithetical and paradoxical operations.[70] Alternatively, though, they might describe a sequence within the same purification process. This second interpretation seems to have been the thinking of those early church fathers who asserted that salting fire is both purification and penal.[71] As purification, it refines the character and punitively it burns up useless works. In the latter case, the fire consumes itself as it cleanses until nothing is left to burn (1 Cor 3:15).

Jean Daniélou summarizes the argument for *apokatastasis*, "In the end God's patient love will succeed in making all his creatures weary of their unfaithfulness. The most stubborn will eventually give in and consent to love him."[72] Various theologians throughout church history have been inclined to the doctrine. These include Clement, Origen, Jerome, Gregory of Nyssa, John Chrysostom, John Scotus Erigena, Hans Denck, Friedrich Schleiermacher, and several lessor figures in the modern period.[73]

As Daniélou's remark shows, *apokatastasis* holds that every sin ultimately can and will be discharged by God's limitless grace. As a result, after a sufficiently long detoxification in God's hellfire re-education camp, Leviathan will qualify to return to his angelic status. The early church father Gregory of Nyssa put it this way, "In the same way when death, and corruption, and darkness, and every other offshoot of evil had grown into the nature of the author of evil, the approach of the Divine power, acting like fire, and making that unnatural accretion to disappear, thus by purgation of the evil becomes a blessing to that nature, though the separation is agonizing."[74]

---

70. Lang, "πῦρ," 944.
71. Jeremias, "γέεννα," 658.
72. Daniélou, *Origen*, 287.
73. Patrides, "Salvation of Satan," 467–78.
74. Gregory of Nyssa, "Apologetic," 950, ch. 26.

In spite of such universalist arguments, though, any Christian theology of *apokatastasis* which includes Satan has been no more than a minority view. Thomas Aquinas probably spoke not only for the medieval orthodox majority but for non-universalists across the centuries. "Consequently, such an opinion must be considered erroneous, and in accord with Catholic Faith it must be held firmly both that the will of the good angels is confirmed in good, and that the will of the demons is obstinate in evil."[75] In other words, says Aquinas, Satan and his demons are not redeemable, an opinion underscored at the Earling healing. Lead exorcist Theophilus Riesinger asked a demon, "What would you do, if God made it possible for you to atone for your injustice to Him?" The answer came, "Are you a competent theologian?"[76]

Aquinas' analysis exemplifies how discussions of Leviathan and *apokatastasis* generally have taken place on biblical, theological, and philosophical grounds.[77] However, the argument in sections one and two builds a new and different foundation under Aquinas' conclusion. We found that the prior and controlling fact is that Leviathan destroyed his covenant attractor of walking among stones of fire. This means that *there literally is no covenant relationship to which he can return*. The core aspect of his nature which was designed to facilitate relationship with God was destroyed as an objective outcome of dynamically structured processes in creational law. Leviathan cannot reverse his entrapment in the first death.

Apokatastasis and the Dead

Given that Leviathan is irredeemable, what about human *apokatastasis*? In chapter 11 I considered an intermediate realm and its connection to the possible human triumph over death; here I want to evaluate post-death spiritual and moral restoration. The idea that the dead might have three destinations—heaven, hell, and some third realm—dates in various forms from pre-Christian Hindu, Iranian, and Greek thought.[78]

Apparently relying on Plato, the Orphics, and the Pythagoreans,[79] Origen believed that there's no sinner so essentially incorrigible that (s)he can't be completely purified and allowed into Paradise. Thus for Origen hell became purgatory and salvation universal. Augustine was more circumspect and referred to in-between states. These he called the not completely wicked (*mali non valde*), and the not completely good (*boni non valde*). Though these were perhaps metaphorical, by the twelfth century Christian scholastics like Werner II, abbot of Saint-Blaise, were arguing for a more concrete purgatorial purification for people. It's best, he said, to finish one's cleansing work here

---

75. Aquinas, "Question LXIV," 604.
76. Vogl, *Begone Satan!*, 17.
77. See Beougher, "Are All Doomed to Be Saved?," 6–24.
78. Le Goff, *Birth of Purgatory*, 18–23.
79. Le Goff, *Birth of Purgatory*, 55.

on earth but as long as one has started, it can be finished after death. Otherwise, "Your crimes will burn in you until they are consumed."[80]

According to Jacques Le Goff, by the fourteenth century purgatory's residents had begun to receive power to assist the living: "The system of solidarity between the living and the dead instituted an unending circular flow, a full circuit of reciprocity."[81] The ability to communicate with ancestors implied a porous intermediate realm in that prayers for the dead could purify the just and prayers to the dead could assist the living.[82] Purgatory was now the post-death means by which *apokatastasis*, the restoration of all things, could be achieved.

This theology may be put into a larger interfaith context. Purgatory's basic conceptualization is little different from other doctrines in which the deceased inhabit or transit post-death realms. For example, in pre-Christian Greek thought, the earth's structural elements are in strife with each other. When a person dies, (s)he must slough off attachments to these earthly rudiments that otherwise would prevent their ascent through the heavens.[83] In similar manner, the eighth-century CE Tibetan *bardos* have a four-stage ascent to liberation or rebirth. Deceased people move through these *bardos* during a maximum period of forty-nine days.[84]

Moreover, although the presenting language differs, there's really no substantive underlying doctrinal disparity among various cultures' prayers for and guidance from the dead. To illustrate this, let's compare the examples below.

The first one is addressed to the Roman Catholic Saint Blaise. "Dear Bishop and lover of souls, you willingly bore heavy crosses in faithful imitation of Jesus. Similarly, with Christlike compassion, you cured many sufferers. Then after undergoing horrible tortures you died as a martyr for Christ. Obtain a cure for these (name the illnesses here) ills if this is agreeable to God. Amen."[85]

The second is a traditional Islamic quote from a companion of Mohammed. "Messenger of Allah! I have been dutiful toward my parents. Are there any duties I owe them after their deaths? The Prophet said, 'Yes, to pray for them, to ask forgiveness for them, to accomplish for them those things that they were not able to accomplish in their lives.'"[86]

A third one comes from African Christian theologian Gabriel M. Setiloane. After he was pick-pocketed on the train but found his money on the floor, his fellow passengers said to him, "Your ancestors are by your side." Acknowledging his own ancestral

---

80. Ibid., 140.
81. Ibid., 356–57.
82. Bermejo, "Purgatory," 2937.
83. Schweizer, "Slaves of the Elements," 456–57.
84. Langerfeld, "Dead Arise," 41.
85. "Prayer to Saint Blaise."
86. Arimi, "Honoring One's Ancestors."

attachments he wrote, "The dead are not dead; they are ever near us.... They chide us when we go wrong, Bless us and sustain us for good deeds done."[87]

The foundational questions with *apokatastasis* for the dead involve both metaphysics and biblical theology.

We may illustrate the metaphysical problem with an example. During Christian prayer healing, Celeste, as part of a larger revelation, had a vision of her ancestors in a cave in Barbados. These men professed Christianity but practiced voodoo. Due to Celeste's prayers, "Jesus" appeared to them in the cave and after he revealed his love to them, they fell at his feet in tears and adoration.[88] Both Celeste in the present and her ancestors in the past received spiritual healing. In addition, Celeste's inherited condition of fibroid tumors went into remission.

Suppose this vision is assumed to be literally true (*veridical*, meaning it fully conforms to real facts) as many charismatic or Fourth Wave participants are wont to do with such exotica. Then in a classic time warp Jesus of Nazareth appeared to the ancestral idolaters in Barbados when Celeste received her vision and prayed. There seem to be two theoretical possibilities for this interpretation to be true. Healer Patricia Smith described the first: God sees all history as one panorama and can enter into it at any point.[89] If this is so, then all ideas of past, present, and future are merely constructs of the human mind.[90] In these metaphysics all space-time points have equal value.

However, we have seen how the automaton's continuous computing function produces both sequential development and previous-state memory. Creation's arrow of time is real and unidirectional,[91] meaning that space-time points do not have equal value. While God can indeed see beginnings from endings, this doesn't mean that God is free to break time's creational boundaries and change that which has already been. Smith's metaphysics and theology are very wrong; no-one, contrary to the demonic vision she saw, can expect God to redo the ancestral past. What God can do is cut off the curses from that past which intrude into the present.

Alternatively, we might hypothesize that at the time of the cave events, God invoked counterfactual knowledge of what Celeste would pray in the future. From Celeste's perspective, such a past-directed prayer isn't a request that God change the past but a request "for God to *have done* something at a time prior to the time of the prayer."[92] Put more forcefully, past-directed prayer becomes part of the original causal sequence for historical events. Thus in *Miracles*, C. S. Lewis wrote:

> The event has already been decided—in a sense it was decided "before all worlds." But one of the things taken into account in deciding it, and therefore

87. Setiloane, "How the Traditional World-View Persists," 34.
88. Smith, *From Generation to Generation*, 112–13.
89. Ibid., 69–70.
90. Isham and Polkinghorne, "Debate over the Block Universe," 135.
91. Castagnino et al., "Cosmological Origin," 370.
92. Timpe, "Prayers for the Past," 308.

> one of the things that really cause it to happen, may be this very prayer that we are now offering. Thus, shocking as it may sound, I conclude that we can now at noon become part causes of an event occurring at ten o'clock [in the morning]. . . . My free act [of prayer] contributes to the cosmic shape. That contribution is made in eternity or "before all worlds"; but my consciousness of contributing reaches me at a particular point in the time-series.[93]

This counterfactual argument might appeal to some since it purports to explain how a present-day vision could become part of past causations. However, it also smacks of philosophical parlor games by opening the door to logical and anachronistic time paradoxes. Such time loops are the staple of science fiction movies, TV shows, and novels—not of Christian theology.

In sum, Celeste's vision echoes one experienced by Agnes Sanford, part of which I related in chapter 9. According to Sanford, as a young teen voices began assaulting her after she entered a Buddhist temple and repeated the same chant as used by the monks, "O-me-to-fu." Subsequently she had a waking vision which, she said, "was as if I had slipped back through time and seen this particular episode [in Sparta]."[94] The truth is that Celeste's and Agnes' visions were conceptually no different than alleged time slips experienced by people during spirit release regression therapy. All of them are demonic counterfeits.

So much for metaphysics.

In biblical theology the intermediate realm question seems to be "Which one?" The NT sends the dead to either hades (Luke 16:23) or paradise (Luke 23:43), and to these the Roman church added purgatory (officially) and infant limbo (unofficially). Limbo, in fact, was further subdivided into limbo of the patriarchs (*limbus patrum*) and limbo of infants (*limbus infantium*). In 1905 Pope Pius X made a definitive (but not infallible) declaration confirming the existence of limbo for unbaptized children.[95] Within a century (2007) the International Theological Commission relaxed this by calling the theory of limbo "a possible theological opinion."[96] On the whole, one gets the impression of a celestial round-about with traffic angels busily directing the dead into the proper exit.

The Protestant option can be described metaphorically as a T-intersection where at death the unrighteous turn left into hell and the righteous take a right into heaven. This is theologically unclear, though, since the terms are applied to both temporary post-death and final post-judgment destinations. For example, the NT refers to the righteous dead as "asleep in Christ" (1 Thess 4:14 and elsewhere), leading to arguments about whether they are conscious, in soul sleep, or nonexistent and awaiting true re-creation at the resurrection.

93. Lewis, *Miracles*, 179.
94. Sanford, *Sealed Orders*, 14, 17.
95. Robinson, "Catholic Statements."
96. International Theological Commission, "Hope of Salvation."

To all these we may add Mormonism's double meaning for hell. On the one hand, it's a temporary zone from which even the unrighteous may eventually escape. Conversely, this hell precedes the last-judgment hell reserved for the truly reprobate.[97]

In trying to find our way through this tangle, I will focus on a couple of key questions. The first deals with the evidence for a morally cleansing intermediate realm and the second with whether there is post-death personality progress.

Though the stage had been set by the various influences mentioned earlier, the Roman doctrine of purgatory emerged out of paranormal NDEs. An early example (ca. 700 CE) of this is Drythelm's vision. He was a pious Northumberland family man who saw "an enormous valley with fire on one side and ice on the other, which is not hell, but a place of temporary torment."[98] Drythelm was ordered in the vision to return and describe this purgatorial realm to the living.

It's critically important to realize that such revelatory visions, signs, and wonders can be neither self-authenticating nor the basis on which to (re)shape biblical theology. Emanuel Swedenborg, Joseph Smith (Mormonism), Andrew Jackson Davis (spiritualism), and Ann Lee (Shakers)—all of these false prophets spawned aberrant movements directly based on their visions. Unfortunately, all too often today's prophetic deviations are to be found in Third and Fourth Wave Christianity. An example from the Fourth Wave Toronto Blessing was cited by a disenchanted former Vineyard pastor: "I became disconcerted by the prophetic words that came forth especially one by Carol Arnott in which she had her bride experience where she was taken into the very presence of Jesus and said that the love that she experienced was even better than sex!"[99] Arnott's close parallels with *hieros gamos* throughout history is staggering. The deep conviction that such visions are true and from the Lord is irrelevant. Comparable conviction is equally present in contemporary movements like shamanism[100] and transpersonal psychology.[101]

The self-authentication claim is both illusory and dangerous. Even when signs and wonders seem true, they may be falsely rooted. Jung provides an excellent case study of this principle. In October 1913, he had a vision of a monstrous, bloody flood which covered Europe from the lowlands to the Alps. Two weeks later the vision recurred even more vividly with the blood even more pronounced. An inner voice spoke, "Look at it well, it is wholly real and it will be so. You cannot doubt it." In spring and early summer 1914, he had a thrice-repeated dream in which an arctic cold wave froze the whole region into ice. Finally, on August 1, war broke out.[102] The prophetic visions were accurate. However, given Jung's rejection of biblical faith, we

97. Peterson, "What Is the Meaning," 36–38.
98. Zaleski, *Otherworld Journeys*, 31.
99. Gowdy, "Toronto Pastor Speaks."
100. Harner, "Science, Spirits, and Core Shamanism."
101. Grof, "Ervin Laszlo's Akashic Field."
102 Jung, *Memories, Dreams, Reflections*, 175–76.

reference the implication of Deut 13:1 that false gods have the power to manipulate the conditions under which their prophecies can be fulfilled.

In turning to the Bible, the answer we get about an intermediate realm depends on the question we ask. If we ask for the biblical evidence in support of purgatory, both Roman Catholic[103] and Protestant[104] scholars use words like "meager" and "fanciful." The only actual reference which links prayers for the dead with atonement for their sins is 2 Macc 12:39–45, which in any case most Protestants reject as scripture. Other core citations are 2 Tim 1:18, which some argue is a past-tense prayer for Onesimus who's dead; and Matt 12:32, which is Jesus' statement that sin against the Holy Spirit cannot be forgiven in this age or the age to come. Catholic scholar A. M. Bermejo calls both of these inconclusive. As to the famous passage in 1 Cor 3:13–15, this refers to burning, subtraction, and loss at the judgment and not to an interim refining meant to fit one for paradise. Judgment eschatology explains why commentators like Friedrich Lang write that some will be saved only by the skin of their teeth.[105]

However, if we ask whether a non-purgatorial intermediate realm is taught in scripture the answer is a strong "yes." In the OT Sheol is the place of the dead but as the intertestamental period unfolded, two further aspects emerged. Sheol became an intermediate realm and then eventually, along with Gehenna and Tartarus, places of final punishment, with the latter reserved for rebel angels.[106] In the NT hades replaces Sheol and occurs eleven times.[107] It is equivalent to Tartarus in 2 Pet 2:4, to Sheol in Acts 2:27, and to the abyss in Rom 10:7, Luke 8:31, and Rev 20:1–3. At the judgment, the unrighteous dead leave Hades and it will be thrown into the lake of fire (Rev 20:13–14). Therefore Hades and hell are distinct.

Paradise is the intermediate realm of the righteous dead. The word was borrowed from Persia and originally meant park, enclosure, or garden. It appears three times in the NT, most famously in Luke 23:43 where Jesus tells the penitent thief, "Today you'll be with me in Paradise."

Heretofore, we have examined *apokatastasis* in terms of prayers to and for the dead. Now we turn our attention to the possibility of post-death progress.

I have shown in previous chapters that human persons are agents in the automaton, creation's fundamental structure. The automaton consists of a near-infinite multidimensional grid containing logic cells. These cells contain rule-sets which specify all the relationships which science calls laws. We also learned that, in OT language, an agent operates under the control of four categories of rule-sets. These are *aphar* (dust), *basar* (animated flesh), *nephesh* (soul), and *ruah* (wind or spirit). A*phar* refers to the laws of physics and chemistry, *basar* to the laws sustaining organic life, *nephesh*

---

103. Bermejo, "Purgatory," 2938.
104. Wright, *For All the Saints?*, 29.
105. Lang, "πῦρ," 944.
106. Scharen, "Gehenna in the Synoptics," 327.
107. Matt 11:23; 16:18; Luke 10:15; 16:23; Acts 2:27, 31; 1 Cor 15:55; Rev 1:18; 6:8; 20:13, 14.

to laws of emotions and mind, and *ruah* to laws which constitute the seat of covenant with God. Human persons develop from conception to death as these rule-sets are activated sequentially through interaction with one's environment. Therefore the question before us is whether post-death development is possible when the sequence is prematurely halted in life.

In wrestling with a Christian response to disability, theologian Burton Cooper has stated a perhaps-traditional position that it's the person formed by their history that enters heaven:

> The term "resurrected body" would then express our total personality, spiritually transformed. It would point not so much to our identity at one moment in our life—namely, the moment of our physical death—but to what we have become, given our physical and mental potentialities, our socio-historical environment, and our experiences, values, commitments, and decisions.[108]

However, this avoids life's hard issues. An example of premature personality halting is fetal wastage. Research shows that about 8 percent of normal pregnancies spontaneously miscarry and a further 8 percent do so without the woman's knowledge.[109] In addition, to take the Canadian province of Ontario as an example, in 2011 there were about thirty-three deliberately induced abortions per one hundred live births.[110] Apart from fetal wastage, there are other cases where truncated mental development might be supposed to obstruct spiritual growth. These include comas, various organic diseases, degenerative illnesses, developmental disabilities , and genetic syndromes. A large grab bag of syndromes and diseases cause retardation conditions with IQs less than fifty[111] and with profound retardation IQs of about 20–25. If personhood begins when egoic self-awareness emerges then it's natural to ask whether there's a progressive development after death for all the preceding which results in maturity in Christ (Eph 4:15).

To begin with, the NT plumb line is that a post-death moral transformation is not in the cards. People are to sanctify (*hagiasmos*) themselves within history. Whether it's Jesus urging us to be complete (perfect, Matt 5:48) or Paul teaching that we are to be mature with the full stature of Christ (Eph 4:13) or James commanding that we should be mature (perfect) and complete (Jas 1:4), the emphasis is present tense. A recent joint statement from a number of leading Roman Catholics and evangelical Protestants emphasized this. The document states that this-world purification and transformation is paramount over mere intellectual assent to doctrine.[112]

---

108. Cooper, "Disabled God," 181.

109. Parazzini et al., "Trends of Spontaneous Abortions," table 1. See also Whittaker et al., "Unsuspected Pregnancy," 1126.

110. Johnston, "Historical Abortion Statistics."

111. McGuffin et al., "Mental Retardation," 66, 71–72, 77.

112. "Salvation, The Gift of," 21.

Therefore to postulate post-death psychological growth immediately puts us into conflict with the general this-world moral principle. The only way to proceed would be to assume that moral and psychological growth represent different categories. From this stance, the conjectures which follow for truncated development are presented as possible but not necessary or exclusive options.

First—Any genetically human organism which has not reached a psychological "I-ness" has no spirit. In this it resembles Adam prior to God breathing spiritual life into him. Such an organism will enter neither heaven nor hell nor dwell in any limbo. It isn't resurrected but simply ceases to be.

Second—God will evaluate each genetically human organism and counterfactually determine what their earthly personality growth would have been with normal development. A similar counterfactual determination of their spiritual choices results in outcomes where some inherit hell and some heaven. The elect will be granted resurrection bodies.

Third—All genetically human organisms with a functioning cerebral cortex will be granted resurrection bodies with mind and spirit at the level they achieved in life. Their spiritual innocence gains all of them heaven.

Fourth—All creation is made new. The eschaton is open-ended[113] and growth will happen at every level for all those in relationship with God. Genetically human organisms will be part of this. God's desire for relationship results in their personality completion. This builds on the analogical principle that "our constitution is not what makes us special; rather, it is necessary so that we can be special."[114]

In all cases, mentally limited people who have responded to God in love rather than knowledge are kingdom citizens and will find their heavenly place accordingly. This reflects the principle that nothing can separate us from God's love (Rom 8:38–39). It also reflects the requirement that God's love is for creatures with personality who can reciprocate that love.

In the end, it may be wisest to affirm the absolute justice and wisdom of God in these matters, and to accept that the possibility of post-death psychological growth remains in mystery.

So, putting aside intermediate realms, let's try to summarize Leviathan and first death.

The chaoplexic view of Leviathan is fundamental to a proper theological understanding of his first death. To the long-standing question about whether Satan and his demons can repent, the conclusive answer is "no." The reasons are twofold. First, as a function of creational laws governing self-organizing network systems, Leviathan's chaostrophic discontinuity is dynamically irreversible. Second, these catastrophic events were triggered by Lucifer's deliberate free choice. God will absolutely not infringe on creaturely free choice to restore to covenant relationship those who have

---

113. Wheeler, "Toward a Process-Relational Christian Eschatology," 230.
114. Bjork, "Artificial Intelligence and the Soul," 99.

clearly shown that they prefer autonomy. As an addendum, we may note that the same conclusions hold for humans who have tasted the heavenly gift and then fallen away (Heb 6:4). Persistent rejection of the universal covenant over time leads to an irreversible system bifurcation. Return (repentance) is absent from possible future system outcomes in such cases.

Annihilation as Second Death?

If Satan/Lucifer/Leviathan cannot be restored, will he be eternally tormented or annihilated? This question leads us to the biblical doctrine of the second death, designated by Rudolf Bultmann as definitive death.[115] As a term, second death appears four times in Revelation (2:11; 20:6; 20:14; 21:8) and nowhere else in the NT. In addition, it is found in the Aramaic version (Targums) of OT texts: "Let Reuben live in eternal life and not die the second death" (Deut 33:6);[116] The prophet said, "With my ears I was hearing when this was decreed before the Lord God of Hosts: 'Surely this sin shall not be forgiven you until you die the second death,' says the Lord of hosts" (Isa 22:14).[117] Targum Isa 65:5–6 integrates Gehenna with the second death: "Their retribution is in Gehenna where the fire burns all the day. Behold, it is written before me: 'I will not give them respite while they live, but theirs is the retribution of their sins; I will hand over their bodies to the second death.'"[118] To these quotes we may add the Targums' varied rendering of second death, from "a second death,"[119] to "the death that the wicked die in the world to come,"[120] to "the second death which the wicked die in the world to come."[121]

When we try to actually state what the second death is, we run into problems. To begin with, in the normal use of language, death means cessation, termination, finality, and ending. Therefore, if the second death is other than complete annihilation or absolute erasure then we must go further and ask what is left of sentient personality after the second death.

In his assessment of this issue, Gregory Boyd returns to Karl Barth's idea of *das nichtige*, or nothingness. Because of his belief in fundamental philosophical opposites (enantiodromia), Barth stated that whatever God willed demanded other choices to which God said no. Boyd has taken this and contended that if agents of free will can choose that which God negates, then *das nichtige* has the potential to become actualized within creation. However, when the eschaton comes virtually all that opposes

---

115. Bultmann, "θάνατό," 17.
116. Grossfeld, *Targum Onqelos to Deuteronomy*, 109.
117. Chilton, *Isaiah Targum*, 44.
118. Ibid., 123–24.
119. Grossfeld, *Targum Onqelos to Deuteronomy*, 104.
120. Clarke, *Targum Pseudo-Jonathan*, 98.
121. McNamara, *Targum Neofiti*, 165.

God, including the content of *das nichtige*, becomes nothing, since only God's reality is now allowed.[122] I say "virtually" since Boyd permits an apparent exception, a residual will which is "the last remnant of the original dignity of self-determination that God gave the creature."[123]

We may applaud Boyd for trying to mediate between a punitive fiery hell which horrifies human sensibilities and annihilation which makes a mockery of unpunished evil. Still, he leaves important questions unanswered. For starters, is cosmic justice served if, as he asserts, "the entire content of what is willed against God is exposed as nothingness?"[124] Is sin committed against God really a mere choosing of nothingness? Instead of Leviathan being a willful murderer, liar, and destroyer who is held accountable for the evil perpetrated on creation, he is reduced to a misguided cherubim or seraphim who chose nothingness. Surely, though, his rampage through creation cannot be written off as merely choosing that which God negated.

We must also grapple with whether a residual will persists after the second death. If the actions of every being within creation have a moral content which is salted by fire (Mark 9:42), the biblical evidence is that this process is an internal psychological burning, as the abbott Werner said. Isaiah 33:1 makes the astonishing statement that one's own spirit (*ruach*) can be a consuming fire. Ezekiel 28:18 echoes this: "I brought out fire from within you; it consumed you."

Here again our knowledge of chaoplexic processes is helpful. For creatures who have broken covenant with God the fire may be interpreted as a fixed negative attractor locked rigidly into place. As we saw earlier, the term negative points to its function as an attractor which attempts to re-regulate. In this case, biblical burning means it's bounded so that it never approaches its focus nor exceeds its perimeter. In fact its trajectories have infinite capacity to never go through the same phase space point twice.[125] There is no possibility of correction, growth, reversibility, or change of any kind because there is no longer fresh outside information to modify the system. All relatedness is gone and this burn attractor is literally a perpetual motion device. In biblical language, its worm never dies nor does the fire go out (Isa 66:24).

All in all, it would be astonishing if demonic and human choices produced an anti-God, anti-covenant personality which was erased leaving only the will which had made the choices. In such an event, there would be an eternal torment consisting of one's will endlessly contemplating the nothingness it has chosen in light of what it might have chosen. Let us assume alternatively that each creature really is paid according to its works (Rev 20:12), that God truly is impartial to all beings (Acts 10:34), and that the freely chosen character formed within cosmic history constitutes the continuing nature of every being in the eschaton. This leads to the conclusion that God

---

122. Boyd, *Satan and the Problem of Evil*, 342.
123. Ibid.
124. Ibid.
125. Slutzky et al., "Deterministic Chaos," 607. See also Kentridge, "Modularity of Mind," 3.

has irreversibly ceded some measure of true eternal self-existence to everyone who rejects covenant relationship. Continuing self-awareness seems borne out in Jesus' teaching about weeping and gnashing of teeth among those entering outer darkness (Matt 8:12, etc.).

Therefore the creature has some continuing existence in the second death but experiences final divorce from divine law and God's rulership, and expulsion from creation. Consequently we are led to wonder where such a separated realm is. C. S. Lewis, for example, suggested that hell "is in no sense parallel to heaven; it is 'the darkness outside,' the outer rim where being fades away into nonentity."[126] To locate hell on a fence-sitting rim of creation may be an understandable tactic in trying to answer the question in human spatial terms. Nonetheless, any solution which puts hell even on the rim of the new creation is unsatisfactory. This is because any doctrine of hell must start with the New Jerusalem as God's cleansed temple.

Readers will recall the extensive discussion of Eden as a sanctuary. At that time, we especially focused on the ANE traditions of the cosmic axis, the mountain of the gods, the individual as Eden, and Adam as priest/king. Now we need to expand our horizons to include the larger concept of creation itself as sanctuary. This produces an all-encompassing perspective of God's sanctuary being the place of his dwelling at any and all levels of creation. The Jewish midrash *Tanhuma Leviticus* laid out the logic of the centrality for all reality of God's sanctuary:

> Just as the navel is positioned in the centre of a man, thus is the land of Israel positioned in the center of the world. . . . And the Temple is in the center of Jerusalem, and the Great Hall is in the center of the Temple, and the Ark is in the centre of the Great Hall, and the Foundation Stone is in front of the Ark, and beginning with it the world was put on its foundation.[127]

Perhaps the most astonishing biblical reference to creation as God's sanctuary is to be found in the book of Revelation. The New Jerusalem, we are told, will come down out of heaven to earth, but contrary to the *Midrash Tanhuma*, there is no temple at the center (Rev 21:22). Instead we encounter a cube-shaped city of 1,200 stadia or about 1,500 miles per side. It turns out that the only other cube-shaped biblical objects in a similar setting are the holy of holies in the tabernacle and Solomon's temple.

Furthermore, not only is John the Apostle drawing our attention to the complete city as the holy of holies, he intends that we realize that the city's dimensions equate to the extent of the then-known Greek world. This means that the whole world is the holy of holies.[128] New meaning is lent to texts like Isa 6:3 where the seraphim worship God, proclaiming that the whole earth is full of his glory. Indeed, Jon Levenson has made a good case that the word in the AV translated full, being a noun, should really

---

126. Lewis, *Problem of Pain*, 115.
127. Midrash Tanhuma, *Leviticus, Kedoshim 10*, cited in Levenson, "Temple and the World," 283.
128. Watts, "Making Sense of Genesis 1," 1–12.

be rendered fullness. Then Isa 6:3 would read, "The fulness of the whole earth is his glory."[129]

This theology is reflected in Philo's idea that the whole universe is God's sanctuary. He described the cosmos as the true temple wherein the angels serve as priests and the earthly temple's blueprint is symbolic of the universe.[130] In this Philo is repeating the tradition that the pattern Moses saw on the mountain was intended to be a cosmic map. Josephus made the same argument: "If anyone do without prejudice, and with judgment, look upon these things [tabernacle appointments], he will find they were every one made in way of imitation and representation of the universe."[131]

The crucial point in all of this is that in the New Jerusalem, God does something never before seen. God leaves the realm of deepest darkness which heretofore was the triune deity's residence[132] and enters creation to take up permanent homesteading. All darkness is swept away in the New Jerusalem (Rev 21:23–24), which in its positive form says that God is the city's light. It's also a negative warning that all polluting things—the cowardly, faithless, polluted, murderers, fornicators, sorcerers, liars, and idolaters—are denied entry (Rev 21:8). One and all, these are not ethical but spiritual idolatry labels describing those who have rejected unqualified allegiance to the Lamb. They will not be invited to his marriage feast (Rev 19:9).

Remember the demon Azazel's exile from the sanctified temple to the wilderness? Its eschatological meaning is that hell and its God-rejecting residents cannot be within the purified New Jerusalem nor even on its rim. The only solution which retains sanctuary purity demands that hell be outside the New Jerusalem beyond the city wall (Rev 21:27) in outer darkness. Hell is literally nowhere since outside creation there is nothing. Outer darkness has no spatiality or any of the features which accompany created order within the automaton. Since time is a function of created order, there is consequently neither chronological advance nor regression and thus no awareness of time. The creature, whether demonic or human, is locked into a perpetual self-only awareness whose content exactly reflects its personal history and development within creation.

In the end, God grants each creature who inherits the second death what it has most wanted in life—complete autonomous selfism without relationship to God whatsoever. God, who originally dwelt in deepest darkness, has entered the new creation (Rev 21:3–4; 22–23) and abandoned outer darkness to those who choose eternal autonomy over covenant relationship. They have made a decision God accommodates but does not desire. As a result, hell isn't so much punishment as the only thing God could do to provide for those who will not live in covenant. Leviathan and his followers will enter final exile in the ultimate Babylon of outer darkness and the rebel whose legs were too short will truly ascend to the (erstwhile) throne of God

---

129. Levenson, "Temple and the World," 289.
130. Davila, "Macrocosmic Temple," 4.
131. Josephus, *Antiquities*, bk. III, ch. 7, para. 7.
132. 1 Kgs 8:12; Ps 18:11; 97:2.

GLOSSARY

Agent	In computer terms, an agent is an autonomous software system which can sense its environment, pursue its own agenda, and bring this about in the future. In human terms, agents are the mathematical objects which are the core of mind/brain network operations.
Artificial Neural Network	An artificial neural network is designed to processes information the way the brain does through interconnected neurones or nodes. As input data is processed its output is compared to the target output and an error is computed. This error is then fed into (back- or forward-propagated) to the neural network and used to adjust it.
Bilocation	A person's body is apparently present in two different locations at once.
Cellular Automaton	A cellular automaton is a collection of cells on a multidimensional grid that evolves through discrete time steps according to a set of rules based on the states of neighbouring cells. (S. Wolfram).
Chaoplexity	The term chaoplexity was coined by John Horgen to show that complexity theory and chaos theory represent aspects of the same family of dynamic systems' phenomena.
Chaos - Mathematical	Mathematical chaos is rooted in certain nonlinear equations. These are deterministic though random in appearance and their evolution as systems is very sensitive to changes in their initial parameters. Their future states are virtually impossible to predict.

Glossary

Chaos - Theological	An ancient Near Eastern term referring to the primordial formless wasteland which blocked creation of the universe. At bottom it represents a morally skewed aspect of mathematical chaos.
Complexity Theory	The correlated interaction between a system's parts based on rules or algorithms that guide its operation. The more complex a system is, the less its' probability to be so. The coordinated system manifests properties not carried by, or dictated by, individual parts.
Consensus Reality	Perception of reality according to the normal sensory and scientific processes.
Downward-Upward Causation	A loop system in networks with ascending levels of hierarchy which utilize feedbacks. With proper rules, higher and lower levels can produce effects on each other.
Dualism	In ordinary usage, dualism distinguishes between matter and spirit (and therefore body and mind). Theological dualism signifies first the relationship between God and creation and second between the principles of good and evil.
Dynamic Systems	Dynamic systems are characterized by how they change over time. The focus is on how changes at the micro level of relationships among a system's constituents give rise to new patterns of behavior at macro levels.
Fractal	Fractals are infinitely complex patterns that are self-similar across different scales.
Mimesis	From the Greek "to imitate," it means the attempt to imitate or reproduce reality.
Monism	Monism is the philosophical system which merges all apparent distinctions between body and soul, matter and spirit, object and subject, matter and force into a single higher unity.
Neo-Darwinism	Neo-Darwinism postulates that natural selection acts on the heritable (genetic) variations within individuals in populations and that mutations (especially random copying errors in DNA) provide the main source of these genetic variations. .

Glossary

Neognosticism	Neognosticism, also called holism, adds layers of Jung's collective unconscious and science's quantum nonlocality to the ancient gnostic theology.
Neural Network	A neural network is a set of interconnected processing elements (neurones or nodes) working together to solve specific problems.
Nonlinear System	A nonlinear system is any problem where the variable(s) to be solved for cannot be written as a linear sum of independent components.
Paranormal	Paranormal describes any phenomena whose explanation exceeds what is physically possible though conventional laws of nature.
Phase (Platonic, state, logic) space	The abstract mathematical space in which every possible state of an equational system is depicted.
Power Law	A power law deals with classes of aggregate phenomena. In the general case, the log of the frequency of events is an inverse linear function of the log of their magnitudes, i.e., $log(F) = -log(M)$.
Psi	*Psi*, the 23rd letter of the Greek alphabet, refers to paranormal processes: extrasensory perception like clairvoyance or clairsentience (*psi-gamma*) or psychokinesis, actions on matter (*psi-kappa*).
Self-Organizing Systems	Dynamic systems whose control rules have the capacity to produce new configurations of greater complexity if one or more of their control parameters are changed by external input.
Semiosis	Literally "sign relations," semiosis is the process in which specific objects and ideas are given symbolic meaning so they can be generalized to a universal meaning.
Synchronization of Chaotic Systems	Synchronization of chaos is a process wherein two (or many) chaotic systems (either equivalent or nonequivalent) adjust a given property of their motion to a common behavior, due to coupling or forcing. This ranges from complete agreement of trajectories to locking of phases. (S. Boccaletti).

Glossary

Transpersonal Realm	The theory that at a deep mental level one connects to the imagery and realities of the larger mystical, spiritual universe. These realities include disincarnate spirits and *psi* abilities.
Trichotomy of Personality Structure	Trichotomy visualizes human personality as body, soul, and spirit.

BIBLIOGRAPHY

Aaronson, Scott. Review of *A New Kind of Science*, by Stephen Wolfram. *Quantum Information and Computation* 2 (2002) 410–23.
Abailard, Peter. "Exposition of the Epistle to the Romans (an Excerpt from the Second Book)." In *A Scholastic Miscellany: Anselm to Ockham*, edited and translated by Eugene R. Fairweather, 276–87. Philadelphia: Westminster, 1956.
Abarbanel, Henry D. I., et al. "Blending Chaotic Attractors Using the Synchronization of Chaos." *Physical Review E* 52 (1995) 214–17.
Abba, Raymond. "Name." In Buttrick, *Interpreter's Dictionary*, 3:500–508.
Abel, David L. "Is Life Reducible to Complexity." In *Fundamentals of Life*, edited by Gyula Palyi et al., 57–72. Paris: Elsevier, 2002.
Abel, David L., and Jack T. Trevors. "Self-Organization vs. Self-Ordering Events in Life-Origin Models." *Physics of Life Reviews* 3 (2006) 211–28.
Abraham, F. D. "Chaos, Bifurcations, & Self-Organization: Dynamical Extensions of Neurological Positivism & Ecological Psychology." *PsychoScience* 1 (1995) 85–118.
———. "Introduction to Dynamics: A Basic Language; A Basic Metamodeling Strategy." In *Chaos Theory in Psychology* edited by Frederick D. Abraham and Albert R. Gilgen, 31–49. Westport, CT: Greenwood, 1995.
Abrahamsen, Adele, and William Bechtel. "Phenomena and Mechanisms: Putting the Symbolic, Connectionist, and Dynamical Systems Debate in Broader Perspective." In *Contemporary Debates in Cognitive Science*, edited by R. Stainton, 159–86. Oxford: Blackwell, 2006.
Abramowitz, Mortimer, et al. "Human Vision and Color Perception." *Molecular Expressions: Science, Optics & You*. http://micro.magnet.fsu.edu/optics/lightandcolor/vision.html.
Agamanolis, Dimitri P. "Cerebral Ischemia and Seizures." *Neuropathology*. http://www.neuropathology-web.org/chapter2/chapter2dseizures.html.
Aichmann, H., et al. "Demonstrating Superluminal Signal Velocity." In *Proceedings of the International Symposium on Quantum Theory and Symmetries. Goslar, Germany July 18–22, 1999*, edited by H. D. Doebner et al., 605–11. Singapore: World Scientific, 2000.
Albanese, Catherine L. "The Magical Staff: Quantum Healing in the New Age." In *Perspectives on the New Age*, edited by James R. Lewis and J. Gordon Melton, 68–84, 307–10. Albany: State University of New York Press, 1992.
———. "The Subtle Energies of Spirit: Explorations in Metaphysical and New Age Spirituality." *Journal of the American Academy of Religion* 67 (1999) 305–25.
Albright, W. F. "The Goddess of Life and Wisdom." *American Journal of Semitic Languages and Literatures* 36 (1920) 258–94.

Bibliography

Albus, J. S. "The Engineering of Mind." In *From Animals to Animats 4: Proceedings of the Fourth International Conference on Simulation of Adaptive Behavior*, edited by P. Maes et al., 23–32. Cambridge: MIT Press, 1996.

Alexander, Samuel. *Space, Time, and Deity*. Vol. 2. London: Macmillan, 1927.

Alland, D. S., and J. B. Delair. *Cataclysm! Compelling Evidence of a Cosmic Castrophe in 9500 B.C.* Santa Fe: Bear, 1997.

Allen, Leslie C. *Ezekiel 1–19*. Dallas: Word, 1994.

Allen, Ronald B. *Numbers*. In *Genesis–Numbers*, edited by Frank E. Gaebelein et al. Expositor's Bible Commentary 2. Grand Rapids: Zondervan, 1992.

Alonso-Sanz, Ramon, and Margarita Martin. "Reversible Cellular Automata with Memory: Two-Dimensional Patterns from a Single Site Seed." *Physica D: Nonlinear Phenomena* 175 (2003) 1–30.

Amen, Daniel G. *Healing the Hardware of the Soul*. New York: Free, 2002.

American Psychiatric Association. "American Psychiatric Association Statement on Diagnosis and Treatment of Mental Disorders." Release no. 03-39. September 26, 2003. http://www.critpsynet.freeuk.com/APA.htm.

———. *Diagnostic and Statistical Manual of Mental Disorders*. 3rd ed. Revised. Washington, DC: 1987.

———. *Diagnostic and Statistical Manual of Mental Disorders*. 4th ed. Washington, DC: American Psychiatric Association, 1994.

Anand, B. K., and G. S. Chhina. "Investigations of Yogis Claiming to Stop Their Heart Beats." *Indian Journal of Medical Research* 49 (1961) 90–94.

Anand, K. J. S. "A Scientific Appraisal of Fetal Pain and Conscious Sensory Perception." Written testimony offered to the Constitution Subcommittee of the US House of Representatives, US House Committee on the Judiciary, 109th United States Congress.

Andersen, Jan E., and T. Hynnekleiv. "Hospital-Treated Psychosis and Suicide in a Rural Community (1877–2005). Part 2: Genetic Founder Effects." *Acta Psychiatrica Scandinavica* 116 (2007) 20–32.

Anderson, Cameron, et al. "Emotional Convergence between People over Time." *Journal of Personality and Social Psychology* 84 (2003) 1054–68.

Andreason, Nancy C. *Brave New Brain: Conquering Mental Illness in the Era of the Genome*. New York: Oxford University Press, 2001.

———. "Linking Mind and Brain in the Study of Mental Illnesses: A Project for a Scientific Psychopathology." *Science* 275 (1997) 1586–93.

Anglo, Sydney. "Melancholia and Witchcraft: The Debate between Wier, Bodin, and Scot." *Folie et Déraison à la Renaissance*, edited by A. Gerlo, 209–22. Brussels: Edition de l'Université de Bruxelles, 1976.

Annegers, John F., et al. "A Population-Based Study of Seizures after Traumatic Brain Injuries." *New England Journal of Medicine* 338 (1998) 20–24.

Anonymous. *The Revelation of Ramala*. Saffron Waldon, UK: Daniel, 1978.

Anselm. "Cur Deus Homo." *Saint Anselm Basic Writings*. Translated by S. W. Deane. La Salle, IL: Open Court, 1962.

Aquinas, Thomas. "Question 64. The Punishment of the Demons: Second Article, 'Whether the Will of the Demons Is Obstinate in Evil?'" In *Basic Writings of Saint Thomas Aquinas*, edited by Anton C. Pegis, 1:600–608. New York: Random House, 1945.

Arbman, Ernst. *Ecstasy or Religious Trance*. Vol. 2. Uppsala: Svenska Bokförlaget, 1968.

Bibliography

Arecchi, F. T. "Why Science Is an Open System: Implying a Meta-Science." In *The Science and Theology of Information*, edited by Christoph Wassermann et al., 108–18. Geneva: Labor et Fides, 1992.

Arimi, Jiro. "Honoring One's Ancestors under Islam." Article originally published in the July–September 2007 issue of *Dharma World*. http://www.rk-world.org/dharmaworld/dw_2007jshonoring.aspx.

Arnold, Clinton. *The Colossian Syncretism: The Interface between Christianity and Folk Belief at Colossae*. Grand Rapids: Baker, 1996.

Arzy, Shahar, et al. "Speaking with One's Self: Autoscopic Phenomena in Writings from the Ecstatic Kabbalah." *Journal of Consciousness Studies* 12 (2005) 4–30.

Astour, Michael C. "Sparagmos, Omophagia, and Ecstatic Prophecy at Mari." *Ugarit-Forschungen* 24 (1992) 1–2.

Athanasius. "Athanasius to Adelphius." In *Nicene and Post-Nicene Fathers*, series 2, vol. 4, edited by Philip Schaff, 1320, letter 60. Albany, OR: Ages Software (ver. 1.0), 1997.

———. "Four Discourses Against the Arians: Texts Explained; Eleventhly, Mark 13:32 and Luke 2:52." In *Nicene and Post-Nicene Fathers*, series 2, vol. 4, edited by Philip Schaff, 1001, chapter 28. Albany, OR: Ages Software (ver. 1.0), 1997.

———. "On the Incarnation." In *Nicene and Post-Nicene Fathers*, series 2, vol. 4, edited by Philip Schaff, 328, chapter 54. Albany, OR: Ages Software (ver. 1.0), 1997.

Atwater, P. M. H. *Beyond the Light*. New York: Birch Lane, 1994.

———. "Is There a Hell? Surprising Observations about the Near-Death Experience." *Journal of Near-Death Studies* 10 (1992) 149–60.

Aubrey, John. *Miscellanies upon the Following Subjects*. London: Castle, 1696.

Auletta, Gennaro, et al. "Top-Down Causation by Information Control: From a Philosophical Problem to a Scientific Research Programme." *Journal of the Royal Society Interface* 5 (2008) 1159–72.

Aviv, Abraham, et al. "Growth, Telomere Dynamics and Successful and Unsuccessful Human Aging." *Mechanisms of Ageing and Development* 124 (2003) 829–37.

Ayala, Francisco J. "Human Nature: One Evolutionist's View." In *Whatever Happened to the Soul? Scientific and Theological Portraits of Human Nature*, edited by Warren S. Brown et al., 31–48. Minneapolis: Augsburg Fortress, 1998.

Azusa Papers. *Jesus the Light of the World*. http://www.apostolicfaith.org/Library/Index/AzusaPapers.aspx.

Azzone, Giovanni F. "Disease as Instability, Error and Entropy." *Modern Trends in BioThermoKinetics* 3 (1994) 81–85.

Bacchetti, S., and C. M. Counter. "Telomerase: A Key to Cell Immortality." *International Journal of Oncology* 7 (1995) 423–32.

Badham, Paul. "Death-Bed Visions and Christian Hope." *Theology* 83 (1980) 269–75.

Baines, John. "Temple Symbolism." *Royal Anthropological Institute of Great Britain and Ireland* 15 (1976) 10–15.

Baird, Henry M. *The Huguenots and the Revocation of the Edict of Nantes*. Vol. 2. New York: Scribner, 1895.

Bak, Per, and Kan Chen. "Self-Organized Criticality." *Scientific American* 264 (1991) 46–53.

Baker, Anthony D. "Theology and the Crisis in Darwinism." *Modern Theology* 18 (2002) 183–215.

Baldi, Pierre. *The Shattered Self: The End of Natural Evolution*. Cambridge: MIT Press, 2001.

Bandura, Albert. "Failures in Self-Regulation: Energy Depletion or Selective Disengagement?" *Psychological Inquiry* 7 (1996) 20–24.

Banerjee, Chandra. "Archbishop: Mother Teresa Had Exorcism." *Seattle Times*, September 6, 2001. http://community.seattletimes.nwsource.com/archive/?date=20010906&slug=teresa06.

Barbiero, F. "On the Possibility of Very Rapid Shifts of the Poles." *Report DMSIA* 7/97. University of Bergamo, 1997. http://scholar.googleusercontent.com/scholar?q=cache:iW2dBTTnCI8J:scholar.google.com/+On+the+possibility+of+very+rapid+shifts+of+the+poles&hl=en&as_sdt=0,5.

Barker, Margaret. *The Gate of Heaven*. London: SPCK, 1991.

Barlow, David A., et al. "Gender Identity Change in a Transsexual: An Exorcism." *Archives of Sexual Behaviour* 6 (1977) 387–95.

Barna Group. "Americans Draw Theological Beliefs from Diverse Points of View." October 8, 2002. https://www.barna.org/component/content/article/5-barna-update/45-barna-update-sp-657/82-americans-draw-theological-beliefs-from-diverse-points-of-view#.V7YQ4ZMrLOQ.

———. "Most American Christians Do Not Believe That Satan or the Holy Spirit Exist." April 13, 2009. https://www.barna.org/barna-update/faith-spirituality/260-most-american-christians-do-not-believe-that-satan-or-the-holy-spirit-exis#.V7YRGpMrLOR.

Barnabas. "Fasting, and the Goat Sent Away, Were Types of Christ." In "The Epistle of Barnabas," in Roberts and Donaldson, *Ante-Nicene Fathers*, 1:262–63. Albany, OR: Ages Software (ver. 2.0), 1997.

Barr, James. "Pre-scientific Chronology: The Bible and the Origin of the World." *Proceedings of the American Philosophical Society* (1999) 379–87.

Barrow, John D., and John K. Webb. "Inconstant Constants." *Scientific American* 292 (2005) 56–63.

Barry, Guy. "Lamarckian Evolution Explains Human Brain Evolution and Psychiatric Disorders." *Frontiers in Neuroscience* 7 (2013) 224. http://www.ncbi.nlm.nih.gov/pmc/articles/PMC3840504.

Barth, Karl. *Church Dogmatics*. III.3, *The Doctrine of Creation*. Translated by G. W. Bromiley and R. J. Ehrlich. Edinburgh: T. & T. Clark, 1960.

Bartholomew, Robert E. "Tarantism, Dancing Mania and Demonopathy: The Anthropolitical Aspects of 'Mass Psychogenic Illness.'" *Psychological Medicine* 24 (1994) 281–306.

BaruÆss, I. "Failure to Replicate Electronic Voice Phenomenon." *Journal of Scientific Exploration* 15 (2001) 355–67.

Baumeister, Roy F., and Mark R. Leary. "The Need to Belong: Desire for Interpersonal Attachments as a Fundamental Human Motivation." *Psychological Bulletin* 117 (1995) 497–529.

Beal, Vangie. "Internet." *Webopedia*. http://www.webopedia.com/TERM/I/Internet.html.

Beatrice, Pier Franco. "The Word 'Homoousios' from Hellenism to Christianity." *Church History* 71 (2002) 243–72.

Beauregard, M., and V. Paqette. "Neural Correlates of a Mystical Experience in Carmelite Nuns." *Neuroscience Letters* 405 (2006) 186–90.

Beenakker, Carlo. "Hempel's Dilemma and the Physics of Computation." In *Knowledge in Ferment: Dilemmas in Science, Scholarship and Society*, edited by Adriaan in 't Groen, 65–70. Leiden: Leiden University Press, 2007.

Beghi, L. Forsgren, et al. "The Epidemiology of Epilepsy in Europe—A Systematic Review." *European Journal of Neurology* 12 (2005) 245–53. http://onlinelibrary.wiley.com/doi/10.1111/j.1468-1331.2004.00992.x/abstract;jsessionid=7ED4A188EEFBADB0B883E441206E5ED4.f03t02.

Behe, Michael. *Darwin's Black Box: The Biochemical Challenge to Evolution.* New York: Free Press, 1996.

Bennett, Dennis J. "The Gifts of the Holy Spirit." In *The Charismatic Movement*, edited by Michael P. Hamilton, 15–32. Grand Rapids: Eerdmans, 1975.

Benor, Daniel T. *Healing Research.* Vol. 1, *Holistic Energy Medicine and Spirituality.* München: Helix, 1992.

Bentzen, Aage. *King and Messiah.* London: Lutterworth, 1955.

Beougher, Timothy K. "Are All Doomed to Be Saved? The Rise of Modern Universalism." *Southern Baptist Journal of Theology* 2 (1998) 6–24.

Berkhof, Hendrik. *Christ and the Powers.* Scottdale, PA: Herald, 1977.

Bermejo, A. M. "Purgatory." In *Encyclopedic Dictionary of Religion*, vol. 3, *O–Z*, edited by Paul Kevin Meagher et al., 2937. Washington, DC: Corpus, 1979.

Bertalanffy, Ludwig von. "Chance or Law." In *Beyond Reductionism*, edited by Arthur Koestler and John R. Smythies, 56–84. London: Hutchinson, 1969.

Bettenson, Henry, ed. *Documents of the Christian Church.* London: Oxford University Press, 1963.

Bettini, Stefano. "Anthropic Reasoning in Cosmology: A Historical Perspective." *Journal of Physics* 59 (1991) 1069–76.

———. "A Cosmic Archipelago: Multiverse Scenarios in the History of Modern Cosmology." October 12, 2005. http://www.arxiv.org/abs/physics/0510111.

Betty, Stafford. "The Growing Evidence for 'Demonic Possession': What Should Psychiatry's Response Be?" *Journal of Religion and Health* 44 (2005) 13–30.

Bharati, Agehananda. "The Ontological Status of Psychic Phenomena in Hinduism and Buddhism." In *Parapsychology and Anthropology*, edited by Allan Angoff and Diana Barth, 223–40. New York: Parapsychology Foundation, 1974.

Bhattacharya, Joydeep, and Hellmuth Petsche. "Universality in the Brain while Listening to Music." *Proceedings of the Royal Society of London B* 268 (2000) 2423–33.

Bhattacharya, Joydeep, et al. "Nonlinear Dynamics of Evoked Neuromagnetic Responses Signifies Potential Defensive Mechanisms against Photosensitivity." *International Journal of Bifurcation and Chaos* 14 (2004) 2701–20.

Bibby, Reginald. *Unknown Gods.* Toronto: Stoddard, 1993.

Bilaniuk, P. B. T. "Traducianism." In *Encyclopedic Dictionary of Religion*, vol. 3, *O–Z*, edited by Paul Kevin Meagher et al., 3555. Washington, DC: Corpus, 1979.

Bindra, Satinder. "Archbishop: Mother Teresa Underwent Exorcism." *CNN New Delhi*, September 7, 2001. http://edition.cnn.com/2001/WORLD/asiapcf/south/09/04/mother.theresa.exorcism.

Birch, George A. *The Deliverance Ministry.* Camp Hill, PA: Horizon, 1988.

Bishop, R. K. "James Ussher." In *The Concise Evangelical Dictionary of Theology*, edited by Walter A. Elwell, 532. Grand Rapids: Baker, 1991.

Biti-Anat, Lilinah. "Ba'al Battles Mot." Part 4 of *The Ugaritic Myth of Ba'al.* 1995–1997. http://www.library.jbsheets.com/babylonian/Baal.txt.

Bjork, Russell C. "Artificial Intelligence and the Soul." *Perspectives on Science and Christian Faith* 60 (2008) 95–102.

Black, Donald W. "Pathological Laughter: A Review of the Literature." *Journal of Nervous and Mental Disease* 170 (1982) 67–71.

Blackmore, Susan. "Out-of-Body Experiences in Schizophrenia: A Questionnaire Survey." *Journal of Nervous and Mental Disease* 174 (1986) 615–19.

Blakeslee, Sandra. "The Christmas Tree in Your Brain." *Toronto Star*, December 21, 2003.

Block, Daniel I. *The Book of Ezekiel: Chapters 10–24*. Grand Rapids: Eerdmans, 1998.

———. *The Book of Ezekiel: Chapters 25–48*. Grand Rapids: Eerdmans, 1998.

Bloom, Howard. *The Lucifer Principle: A Scientific Expedition into the Forces of History*. New York: Atlantic Monthly, 1995.

Bobrow, Robert S. "Paranormal Phenomena in the Medical Literature Sufficient Smoke to Warrant a Search for Fire." *Medical Hypotheses* 60 (2003) 864–68.

Boccaletti, S., et al. "The Synchronization of Chaotic Systems." *Physics Reports* 366 (2002) 1–101.

Borchert, Donald M. "Beyond Augustine's Answer to Evil." *Canadian Journal of Theology* 8 (1962) 237–43.

Bortz, Walter M. "Aging as Entropy." *Experimental Gerontology* 21 (1986) 321–28.

Bourguignon, Erika. "World Distribution and Patterns of Possession States." In *Trance and Possession States*, edited by Raymond Prince, 3–34. Proceedings of the second annual conference of the R. M. Bucke Memorial Society. Montreal: R. M. Bucke Memorial Society, 1966.

Bowie, Walter Russell. "Exposition." In *The Interpreter's Bible*, vol. 1, *Genesis*, edited by George A. Buttrick. Nashville: Abingdon, 1952.

Bowman, Elizabeth S., and Philip M. Coons. "The Differential Diagnosis of Epilepsy, Pseudoseizures, Dissociative Identity Disorder and Dissociative Disorder Not Otherwise Specified." *Bulletin of the Menninger Clinic* 64 (2000) 164–80.

Bowman, Elizabeth S., and Omkar N. Markand. "The Contribution of Life Events to PseudoSeizure Occurrence in Adults." *Bulletin of the Menninger Clinic* 63 (1999) 70–88.

Boyd, Gregory A. *God at War*. Downers Grove: InterVarsity, 1997.

———. *Satan and the Problem of Evil: Constructing a Trinitarian Warfare Theodicy*. Downers Grove: InterVarsity, 2001.

Boyd, Jeffrey H. "One's Self-Concept and Biblical Theology." *Journal of the Evangelical Theological Society* 40 (1997) 207–27.

Bracht, John. "Natural Selection as an Algorithm: Why Darwinian Processes Lack the Information Necessary to Evolve Complex Life." *Perspectives on Science and Christian Faith* 54 (2002) 264–69.

Bradley, Walter L. "Information, Entropy, and the Origin of Life." In *Debating Design: From Darwin to DNA*, edited by William A. Dembski and Michael Ruse, 331–51. Cambridge: Cambridge University Press, 2004.

———. "Is There Scientific Evidence for the Existence of God? How the Recent Discoveries Support a Designed Universe." 1995. http://www.leaderu.com/offices/bradley/docs/scievidence.html.

Braude, Stephen E. *The Limits of Influence: Psychokinesis and the Philosophy of Science*. New York: Routledge and Paul, 1986.

———. "Psi and Our Picture of the World." *Inquiry* 30 (1987) 277–94.

Braun, Bennett G. "Psychophysiologic Phenomena in Multiple Personality and Hypnosis." *American Journal of Clinical Hypnosis* 26 (1983) 124–37.

Breakspear, M. "'Dynamic' Connectivity in Neural Systems: Theoretical and Empirical Considerations." *Neuroinformatics* 2 (2004) 205–26.

Breakspear, M., et al. "A Unifying Explanation of Primary Generalized Seizures through Nonlinear Brain Modeling and Bifurcation Analysis." *Cerebral Cortex* 16 (2006) 1296–1313. http://cercor.oxfordjournals.org/content/early/2005/11/09/cercor.bhj072.full.pdf.

Breakspear, M., et al. "A Disturbance of Nonlinear Interdependence in Scalp EEG of Subjects with First Episode Schizophrenia." *NeuroImage* 20 (2003) 466–78.

Brennan, Barbara Ann. *Hands of Light: A Guide to Healing through the Human Energy Field.* New York: Bantam, 1988.

Breuer, Josef, and Sigmund Freud. "On the Psychical Mechanism of Hysterical Phenomena: Preliminary Communication." In *Complete Psychological Works of Sigmund Freud*, edited by James Strachey, 2:3–17. London: Hogarth, 1955.

Bricker, Daniel P. "Innocent Suffering in Egypt." *Tyndale Bulletin* 52 (2001) 83–100.

Bridges, Douglas S. "Reality and Virtual Reality in Mathematics." *Bulletin of the European Association of Theoretical Computer Studies* 78 (2002) 221–30.

Brown, George Spencer-. *Laws of Form*. New York: Bantam, 1973.

Brown, Mick. "Unzipper Heaven, Lord: Ha-Ha, Ho-Ho, Hee-Hee." *Telegraph Magazine*, December 3, 1994.

Brown, Schuyler. "'Begotten, Not Created': The Gnostic Use of Language in Jungian Perspective." In *The Allure of Gnosticism: The Gnostic Experience in Jungian Psychology and Contemporary Culture*, edited by Robert A. Segal et al., 70–83. Chicago: Open Court, 1995.

Browne, Sylvia. *Blessings from the Other Side*. With Lindsay Harrison. New York: Dutton, 2000.

Bruce, F. F. *Epistle to the Hebrews*. Grand Rapids: Eerdmans, 1964.

Brueggemann, Walter. "From Dust to Kingship." *Zeitschrift für die Alttestamentliche Wissenschaf* 84 (1972) 1–18.

Brunk, Gregory G. "Why Are So Many Important Events Unpredictable? Self-Organized Criticality as the 'Engine of History.'" *Japanese Journal of Political Science* 3 (2002) 25–44.

———. "Why Do Societies Collapse? A Theory Based on Self-Organized Criticality." *Journal of Theoretical Politics* 14 (2002) 195–230.

Buchanan, Mark. *Ubiquity*. London: Weidenfeld & Nicolson, 2000.

Buchheim, Anna, et al. "Measuring Adult Attachment Representation in an fMRI Environment: Concepts and Assessment." *Psychopathology* 39 (2006) 136–43.

Buckley, Peter. "Mystical Experience and Schizophrenia." *Schizophrenia Bulletin* 7 (1981) 516–21.

Buckley, Peter, and M. Galanter. "Mystical Experience, Spiritual Knowledge, and a Contemporary Ecstatic Religion." *British Journal of Medical Psychology* 52 (1979) 281–89.

Budziszewski, J. "The Fallen City." In *The Revenge of Conscience: Politics and the Fall of Man*, 136–46. Dallas: Spence, 1999.

Bugslag, James. "Material and Theological Identities: A Historical Discourse of Constructions of the Virgin Mary." *Théologiques* 17 (2009) 19–67.

Bultmann, Rudolf. "Ginōskō, Gnōsis, Epiginōskō, Epignōsis." In *Theological Dictionary of the New Testament*, edited by Gerhard Kittel and Gerhard Friedrich, abridged in 1 vol. by Geoffrey W. Bromily, 119–23. Grand Rapids: Eerdmans, 1985.

———. "θάνατ, θνήσκω, αποθνήσκω, συναποθνήσω." In *Theological Dictionary of the New Testament*, edited by Gerhard Kittel et al., 7–25. Grand Rapids: Eerdmans, 1964–1976.

Burkholder, Lawrence E. "What's the 'Subtle Energy' in Energy Healing?" *Perspectives on Science and Christian Faith* 55 (2003) 104–16.

Buttrick, George A., ed. *Interpreter's Dictionary of the Bible*. 4 vols. Nashville: Abingdon, 1962.

Byl, John. "Theism and Mathematical Realism." *Proceedings of the Association of Christians in the Mathematical Sciences*, Grand Rapids, 2001, 33–48.

Caetano-Anollés, Gustavo. "Evolved RNA Secondary Structure and the Rooting of the Universal Tree of Life." *Journal of Molecular Evolution* 54 (2002) 333–45.

Campbell, J. Y. "Rest." In Buttrick, *Interpreter's Dictionary*, 4:37–38.

Campbell, Joseph. *The Hero with a Thousand Faces*. Princeton: Princeton University Press, 1949.

Canadian Broadcasting Corporation. "Family Feud over Ted Williams Body." http://www.cbc.ca/sports/baseball/family-feud-over-ted-williams-body-1.326374.

Capra, Fritjof. *The Tao of Physics: An Exploration of the Parallels between Modern Physics and Eastern Mysticism*. 3rd ed. Boston: Shambhala, 1991.

Carroll, Sean M. "Is Our Universe Natural?" *Nature* 440 (2006) 1132–36.

Carruthers, Peter. "The Case for Massively Modular Models of Mind." In *Contemporary Debates in Cognitive Science*, edited by R. Stainton, 205–25. Oxford: Blackwell, 2005.

Cartledge, Mark J. "Interpreting Charismatic Experience: Hypnosis, Altered States of Consciousness and the Holy Spirit." *Journal of Pentecostal Theology* 13 (1998) 117–32.

Cassian, John. "Conference 14, 8." In *John Cassian Conferences*, translated by Colm Luibheid, 160–61. Mahwah, NJ: Paulist, 1985.

Cassuto, Umberto. *A Commentary on the Book of Genesis, Part 1*. Translated by Israel Abrahams. Jerusalem: Magnes, 1961.

———. *The Documentary Hypothesis and the Compilation of the Pentateuch*. Translated by Israel Abrahams. Jerusalem: Magnes, 1961.

Castagnino, Mario, et al. "The Cosmological Origin of Time Asymmetry." *Classical and Quantum Gravity* 20 (2003) 369–91.

Catania, Basilio. "The Physics of the Boolean Observer." International Symposium on Communication, Meaning and Knowledge vs. Information Technology, Lisbon, September 13, 1989. http://www.chezbasilio.org/immagini/Lisbon.pdf.

Chahine, L. M., and Z. Chemali. "Mental Health Care in Lebanon: Policy, Plans and Programmes." *Eastern Mediterranean Health Journal* 6 (2009) 1596–612.

Chaitin, Gregory J. "Gödel's Theorem and Information." *International Journal of Theoretical Physics* 22 (1982) 941–54.

Chardin, Pierre Teilhard de. *The Future of Man*. New York: Harper, 1964.

———. *The Phenomenon of Man*. Translated by Bernard Wall. London: Collins, 1959.

Cherniak, Christopher. "Undebuggability and Cognitive Science." *Communications of the ACM* 31 (1988) 402–12.

Chevreau, Guy. *Catch the Fire*. Toronto: HarperCollins, 1995.

Childs, Brevard S. "The Enemy from the North and the Chaos Tradition." *Journal of Biblical Literature* 78 (1959) 187–98.

———. "Garden of Eden." In Buttrick, *Interpreter's Dictionary*, 2:23.

———. "Tree of Knowledge, Tree of Life." In Buttrick, *Interpreter's Dictionary*, 4:695–97.

Chilton, Bruce D. *The Isaiah Targum*. Wilmington, DE: Glazier, 1987.

Chopra, Deepak. *Quantum Healing: Exploring the Frontiers of Mind/Body Medicine.* New York: Bantam, 1989.

Christensen, Duane L. *Deuteronomy 21:10—34:12.* Word Biblical Commentary 6b. Nashville: Nelson, 2002.

Arraj, James, and Tyra Arraj. *Christian Prayer and Contemplation Forum,* newsletter 2, April 1995. http://www.innerexplorations.com/forum/2.htm.

Cirkovic, Milan M. "The Anthropic Arrow of Time and Realistic World Models: On Price and a Temporal Universe." *Serbian Astronomical Journal* 164 (2001) 41–52.

Civil, M. "The Sumerian Flood Story." In *Atra-Hasīs: The Babylonian Story of the Flood,* edited by W. G. Lambert and A. R. Millard, 138–45. Oxford: Clarendon, 1969.

Clark, R. T. Rundle. *Myth and Symbol in Ancient Egypt.* London: Thames and Hudson, 1959.

Clark, Stuart. "The Scientific Status of Demonology." In *Occult and Scientific Mentalities in the Renaissance,* edited by Brian Vickers, 351–74. Cambridge: Cambridge University Press, 1984.

Clarke, Ernest G. *Targum Pseudo-Jonathan: Deuteronomy.* Collegeville: Liturgical, 1998.

Cleland, Carol E. "Methodological and Epistemic Differences between Historical Science and Experimental Science." *Philosophy of Science* 69 (2002) 474–96.

Clifford, Richard J. *The Cosmic Mountain in Canaan and the Old Testament.* Cambridge: Harvard University Press, 1972.

Clines, David J. A. *The Theme of the Pentateuch.* Sheffield: JSOT, 1982.

Clube, Victor, and Bill Napier. *The Cosmic Serpent: A Catastrophist View of Earth History.* London: Faber & Faber, 1982.

Coate, Morag. *Beyond All Reason.* London: Constable, 1964.

Coghlan, Andy. "Craig Venter Close to Creating Synthetic Life." *New Scientist,* March 13, 2013. https://www.newscientist.com/article/dn23266-craig-venter-close-to-creating-synthetic-life.

Cole, R. Alan. *Exodus: An Introduction and Commentary.* Downers Grove: InterVarsity, 1973.

Coleman, Priscilla, and Anne Watson. "Infant Attachment as a Dynamic System." *Human Development* 43 (2000) 295–15.

Collins, John J. "The Mythology of Holy War in Daniel and the Qumran War Scroll: A Point of Transition in Jewish Apocalyptic." *Vetus Testamentum* 25 (1975) 596–612.

———. "Patterns of Eschatology at Qumran." In *Traditions in Transformation,* edited by Baruch Halpern and Jon D. Levenson, 351–75. Winona Lake, IN: Eisenbrauns, 1981.

Cook, Nick. *The Hunt for Zero Point.* New York: Broadway, 2002.

Cooper, Burton. "The Disabled God." *Theology Today* 49 (1992) 173–82.

Cooper, Melinda. *Bodily Transformation—Tissue Engineering and the Topological Body.* Global Biopolitics Research Group Working Paper 12, June 2006. http://www.kcl.ac.uk/sspp/departments/politicaleconomy/research/biopolitics/publications/workingpapers/wp12.pdf.

Copeland, Lee. "Speaking in Tongues in the Restoration Churches." *Dialogue: A Journal of Mormon Thought* 24 (1991) 20–23.

Copestoke, David R., and H. Newton Malony. "Adverse Effects of Charismatic Experiences: A Reconsideration." *Journal of Psychology and Christianity* 12 (1993) 236–44.

Copley, A. S. "Pentecost in Toronto." *Apostolic Faith* 1 (1908) 4. Paper # 5. http://www.apostolicfaith.org/Library/Index/AzusaPapers.aspx.

Corning, Peter A., and Stephen Jay Kline. "Thermodynamics, Information and Life Revisited, Part I: To Be or Entropy." *Systems Research and Behavioral Science* 15 (1998) 273–93.

Corrigan, Richard H. "Could God Know What I Would Freely Do? Molinism and the Grounding Objection." *Philosophical Frontiers* 3 (2008) 43–57.
Couliano, Ioan Petru. *Out of This World: Otherworldly Journeys from Gilgamesh to Einstein*. Boston: Shambhala, 1991.
Craigie, Peter C. *The Book of Deuteronomy*. Grand Rapids: Eerdmans, 1976.
Cranfield, C. E. B. *The Epistle to the Romans*. Edinburgh: T. & T. Clark, 1975.
Crick, Francis, and L. E. Orgel. "Directed Panspermia." *Icarus* 19 (1973) 341–46.
Cross-Disorder Group of the Psychiatric Genomics Consortium. "Identification of Risk Loci with Shared Effects on Five Major Psychiatric Disorders: A Genome-Wide Analysis." *Lancet* 381 (2013) 1371–79.
Cross, Frank Moore. "A Brief Excursus on *bĕrīt*, 'Covenant.'" In *Canaanite Myth and Hebrew Epic*, 265–73. Cambridge: Harvard University Press, 1973.
———. *Canaanite Myth and Hebrew Epic*. Cambridge: Harvard University Press, 1973.
———. *From Epic to Canon: History and Literature in Ancient Israel*. Baltimore: Johns Hopkins University Press, 1998.
———. "The Tabernacle." *Biblical Archaeologist* 10 (1947) 45–68.
Cullmann, Oscar. *Christ and Time: The Primitive Christian Conception of Time and History*. Translated by Floyd Filson. London: SCM, 1951.
Cundy, H. Martyn. "Gödel's Theorem in Perspective." *Science and Christian Belief* 3 (1991) 35–49.
Cuneo, Michael. "Of Demons and Hollywood: Exorcism and American Culture." *Studies in Religion/Sciences Religieuses* 27 (1998) 455–65.
Curtis, A. H. W. "The 'Subjugation of the Waters' Motif in the Psalms: Imagery or Polemic?" *Journal of Semitic Studies* 23 (1978) 245–56.
Custance, John. *Wisdom, Madness, and Folly: The Philosophy of a Lunatic*. London: Gollancz, 1951.
Cyranoski, David, and Sara Reardon. "Chinese Scientists Genetically Modify Human Embryos." *Nature*, April 22, 2015. http://www.nature.com/news/chinese-scientists-genetically-modify-human-embryos-1.17378.
D'Aquili, Eugene G., and Andrew B. Newberg. *The Mystical Mind: Probing the Biology of Religious Experience*. Minneapolis: Fortress, 1999.
Dahood, Mitchell. *Psalms*. Vol. 2. Anchor Bible. Garden City: Doubleday, 1966–1970.
Daniélou, Jean. *Origen*. Translated by Walter Mitchell. London: Sheed and Ward, 1955.
Darr, Katheryn Pfisterer. "The Book of Ezekiel." In *The New Interpreter's Bible*, vol. 6, edited by Leander E. Keck. Nashville: Abingdon, 2001.
Dartnell, Lewis. "Chaos in the Brain." *Plus* 35 (2005). http://www.plus.maths.org/issue35/features/dartnell.
Daube, David. *Studies in Biblical Law*. Cambridge: Cambridge University Press, 1947.
Davenas, E., et al. "Human Basophil Degranulation Triggered by Very Dilute Antiserum Against IgE." *Nature* 333 (1988) 816–18.
David, Paul A. "Path Dependence: A Foundational Concept for Historical Social Science." http://link.springer.com/article/10.1007/s11698-006-0005-x.
Davidson, Richard J., et al. "Emotion, Plasticity, Context, and Regulation: Perspectives from Affective Neuroscience." *Psychological Bulletin* 126 (2000) 890–909.
Davies, Paul. *The Cosmic Blueprint*. New York: Touchstone, 1988.
———. *The Edge of Infinity*. London: Dent, 1981.

———. "The Epigenome and Top-Down Causation." *Interface Focus* 2 (2012) 42–48. http://rsfs.royalsocietypublishing.org/content/2/1/42.

———. "The Intelligibility of Nature." In *Quantum Cosmology and the Laws of Nature: Scientific Perspectives on Divine Action*, edited by Robert John Russell et al., 145–61. Vatican City: Vatican Observatory, 1993.

———. *The Mind of God*. New York: Simon & Schuster, 1992.

———. "Multiverse or Design? Reflections on a 'Third Way.'" Unpublished lecture, Center for Theology and the Natural Sciences, Berkeley, March 22, 2003.

———. "Universe from Bit." In *Information and the Nature of Reality from Physics to Metaphysics*, edited by Paul Davies and Niels Henrik Gregersen, 65–91. Cambridge: Cambridge University Press, 2010.

———. "Where Do the Laws of Physics Come From." http://www.thebookofbeginnings.com/sources/15/WhereDotheLawsofPhysicsComeFrom.pdf. Print version in *Visions of Discovery: New Light on Physics, Cosmology and Consciousness*, edited by Raymond Y. Chiao et al., 689–708. Cambridge: Cambridge University Press, 2008.

Davila, James R. "The Macrocosmic Temple, Scriptural Exegesis, and the Songs of the Sabbath Sacrifice." *Dead Sea Discoveries* 9 (2002) 1–19.

Dawkins, Richard. *The God Delusion*. New York: Houghton Mifflin, 2008.

———. *The Selfish Gene*. Oxford: Oxford University Press, 1978.

Day, Allan J. "Adam, Anthropology and the Genesis Record: Taking Genesis Seriously in light of Contemporary Science." ISCAST Online Journal Pre-2005, Vol. 0. May 7, 2015. http://www.iscast.org/journal/articles/Day_A_2000-01_Adam_Anthropology.pdf.

Day, John. *God's Conflict with the Dragon and the Sea: Echoes of a Canaanite Myth in the Old Testament*. Cambridge: Cambridge University Press, 1985.

De Grey, Aubrey D. N. J., et al. "Is Human Aging Still Mysterious Enough to Be Left Only to Scientists?" *BioEssays* 24 (2002) 667–76.

Deecke, L., and H. H. Kornhuber. "An Electrical Sign of Participation of the Mesial 'Supplementary' Motor Cortex in Human Voluntary Finger Movement." *Brain Res* 159 (1978) 473–76.

Deem, Rich. "Quotes from Scientists regarding Design of the Universe." *GodAndScience.org*. June 21, 2007. http://www.godandscience.org/apologetics/quotes.html.

Defoe, Daniel. *Robinson Crusoe*. London: Penguin, 2001.

Delitzsch, Franz. *A New Commentary on Genesis*. Vol. 1. Translated by Sophia Taylor. Minneapolis: Klock & Klock, 1978. Originally printed Edinburgh: T. & T. Clark, 1888.

Dembski, William A. *No Free Lunch: Why Specified Complexity Cannot Be Purchased without Intelligence*. Lanham, MD: Rowman & Littlefield, 2002.

Denton, Michael J., et al. "Physical Law Not Natural Selection as the Major Determinant of Biological Complexity in the Subcellular Realm: New Support for the Pre-Darwinian Conception of Evolution by Natural Law." *BioSystems* 71 (2003) 297–303.

Denton, R. C. "Redeem, Redeemer, Redemption." In Buttrick, *Interpreter's Dictionary*, 4:21–22.

Devinsky, Orrin, and Daniel Luciano. "Psychic Phenomena in Partial Seizures." *Seminars in Neurology* 11 (1991) 100–109.

Dewar, Elaine. *The Second Tree: Of Clones, Chimeras and Quests for Immortality*. Toronto: Random House, 2004.

Dewhurst, Kenneth, and A. W. Beard. "Sudden Religious Conversions in Temporal Lobe Epilepsy." *British Journal of Psychiatry* 117 (1970) 497–507.

Diethelm, Oskar. "The Medical Teaching of Demonology in the 17th and 18th Centuries." *Journal of the History of the Behavioral Sciences* 6 (1970) 3–15.

Dluge, Robert. "My Interview with a Powwower." *Pennsylvania Folklife* 21 (1972) 39–42.

Dolev, Shahar, and Avshalom C. Elitzur. "Biology and Thermodynamics: Seemingly-Opposite Phenomena in Search of a Unified Paradigm." *Einstein Quarterly: Journal of Biology and Medicine* 15 (1998) 24–33.

Donoghue, John F. "The Fine-Tuning Problems of Particle Physics and Anthropic Mechanisms." In *Universe or Multiverse?*, edited by Bernard Carr, 231–46. Cambridge: Cambridge University Press, 2007.

Donovan, Gill. "Archbishop Denies Exorcism Performed on Mother Teresa." *National Catholic Reporter*. September 14, 2001. http://www.thefreelibrary.com/Archbishop+denies+exorcism+performed+on+Mother+Teresa.-a078728710.

Doran, Jim. "Agents with Exact Foreknowledge." In *Mechanizing Mathematical Reasoning*, edited by Dieter Hutter and Werner Stephan, 528–42. Berlin: Springer, 2005.

Dorsey, David A. *The Literary Structure of the Old Testament: A Commentary on Genesis-Malachi*. Grand Rapids: Baker, 1999.

Douglas, Mary. "Atonement in Leviticus." *Jewish Studies Quarterly* 1 (1993–94) 109–30.

———. *Purity and Danger: An Analysis of the Concepts of Pollution and Taboo*. London: Ark, 1984.

Driver, G. R. *Canaanite Myths and Legends*. Edinburgh: T. & T. Clark, 1956.

Drummond, Andrew Landale. *Edward Irving and His Circle*. London: Clarke, 1934.

Duch, Włodzisław. "Computational Physics of the Mind." *Computer Physics Communications* 97 (1996) 136–53.

———. "Platonic Model of Mind as an Approximation to Neurodynamics." In *Brain-like Computing and Intelligent Information Systems*, edited by S-i. Amari and N. Kasabov, 491–512. Singapore: Springer, 1997.

Duin, Julia. "Praise the Lord and Pass the New Wine." *Charisma* 20 (1994) 21–24, 26, 28.

Dumont, Matthew P. "The Nonspecificity of Mental Illness." *American Journal of Orthopsychiatry* 54 (1984) 326–34.

Durham, John I. *Exodus*. Waco, TX: Word, 1987.

Easterbrook, Gregg. "The New Convergence." *Wired*, December 1, 2002. http://www.wired.com/2002/12/convergence-3.

Ebeling, Gerhard. "The New Hermeneutics and the Young Luther." *Theology Today* 21 (1964) 34–46.

Eccles, John C. *How the Self Controls Its Brain*. Berlin: Springer-Verlag, 1994.

———. "The Human Person in Its Two-Way Relationship to the Brain." In *Research in Parapsychology 1976*, edited by J. D. Morris et al., 252–61. Metuchen, NJ: Scarecrow, 1977.

Edis, Taner. "Darwin in Mind: 'Intelligent Design' Meets Artificial Intelligence: What's Wrong with the Information Argument Against Evolution?" *Sceptical Inquirer* 25 (2002) 35–39.

Edwards, Harry. *The Healing Intelligence*. New York: Taplinger, 1971.

Edwards, Jonathan. *The Distinguishing Marks of a Work of the Spirit of God*. Boston: Cooper, 1741.

Eichler, James E. B. "To Be or Not to Be! A 'Paraphysics' for the New Millennium." *Journal of Scientific Exploration* 15 (2001) 33–56.

Einstein, Albert. "Neue Möglichkeit für eine Einheitliche Feldtheorie von Gravitation und Elektrizität." *Preussische Akademie der Wissenschaften, Phys.-math. Klasse*,

Sitzungsberichte (1928) 322–6. English version, "Unified Field Theory of Gravitation and Electricity." Translated by A. Unzicker and T. Case. http://arxiv.org/pdf/physics/0503046v1.

Ekholm, Birgit. *Diagnostic Evaluation of Schizophrenia for Genetic Studies*. Umeå, Sweden: Department of Clinical Sciences, Umeå University, 2005.

Eliade, Mircea. *The Forge and the Crucible*. Translated by Stephen Corrin. 2nd ed. Chicago: University of Chicago Press, 1962.

———. *Shamanism: Archaic Techniques of Ecstasy*. Translated by Willard R. Trask. Princeton: Princeton University Press, 1964.

———. "Spirit, Light, and Seed." *History of Religions* 11 (1971) 1–30.

Eliasmith, Chris. "Moving Beyond Metaphors: Understanding the Mind for What It Is." *Journal of Philosophy* 100 (2003) 493–520.

Ellenberger, Henri. *The Discovery of the Unconscious*. New York: Basic, 1970.

Ellis, G. F. R. "The Theology of the Anthropic Principle." In *Quantum Cosmology and the Laws of Nature: Scientific Perspectives on Divine Action*, edited by Robert John Russell et al., 368–405. Vatican City: Vatican Observatory, 1993.

———. "Top-Down Causation and Emergence: Some Comments on Mechanisms." *Interface Focus* 2 (2012) 126–40.

Emerson, Alfred E. "Dynamic Homeostasis: A Unifying Principle in Organic, Social, and Ethical Evolution." *Zygon* 3 (1968) 129–68. Originally published in *Scientific Monthly* 78 (1954) 67–85.

Emmeche, Claus, et al. "Levels, Emergence, and Three Versions of Downward Causation." In *Downward Causation: Minds, Bodies and Matter*, edited by Peter Bøgh Andersen et al., 13–34. Århus: Århus University Press, 2000.

Enns, Peter E. "Creation and Re-Creation: Psalm 95 and Its Interpretation in Hebrews 3:1—4:13." *Westminster Theological Journal* 55 (1993) 255–80.

Epstein, Joshua M., and Robert Axtell. *Growing Artificial Societies: Social Science from the Bottom Up*. Cambridge: MIT Press, 1996.

Esdaile, James. *Mesmerism in India and Its Practical Application in Surgery and Medicine*. London: Longman, Brown, Green, and Longmans, 1846.

Etzold, Eckhard. "Does Psi Exist and Can We Prove It? Belief and Disbelief in Psychokinesis Research." *Proceedings of the Parapsychological Association Convention*, 2004, 367–77.

Evarts, Edward V. "A Neurophysiologic Theory of Hallucinations." In *Hallucinations*, edited by Louis Jolyon West, 1–14. New York: Grune & Stratton, 1962.

Faivre, Antoine. *Access to Western Esotericism*. Albany: State University of New York Press, 1994.

Faure, Philippe, and Henri Korn. "Is There Chaos in the Brain? I. Concepts of Nonlinear Dynamics and Methods of IInvestigation." *CR Academy of Science, Paris Sciences de la vie / Life Sciences* 324 (2001) 773–93.

Fawcett, E. Douglas. *The Case for Reincarnation*. Adyar Pamphlet 102. Madras: Theosophical Publishing House, 1919. Originally published 1889 as, "The Case for Metempsychosis," *Lucifer* 5.

Fee, Gordon D. *The First Epistle to the Corinthians*. Grand Rapids: Eerdmans, 1987.

Feenstra, Ronald J. "Reconsidering Kenotic Christology." In *Trinity, Incarnation and Atonement*, edited by Ronald J. Feenstra and Cornelius Plantinga, 128–52. Notre Dame: University of Notre Dame Press, 1989.

Feferman, Solomon. "Are There Absolutely Unsolvable Problems? Gödel's Dichotomy." *Philosophia Mathematica*, series 3, 14 (2006) 134–52.

Fehr, Ernst, and Urs Fischbacher. "The Nature of Human Altruism." *Nature* 425 (2003) 785–91.

Feldman, Ruth, and Arthur I. Eidelman. "Parent-Infant Synchrony and the Social-Emotional Development of Triplets." *Developmental Psychology* 40 (2004) 1133–47.

Felleman, D. J., and D. C. Van Essen. "Distributed Hierarchical Processing in the Primate Cerebral Cortex." *Cerebral Cortex* 1 (1991) 1–47.

Ferguson, Everett. *Demonology of the Early Christian World*. New York: Mellon, 1984.

Feynman, Richard. *The Character of Physical Law*. Cambridge: MIT Press, 1990.

Finger, Thomas. *Christian Theology: An Eschatological Approach*. Vol. 1. Scottdale, PA: Herald, 1985.

Fischbach, Ephraim, and Carrick Talmadge. "Ten Years of the Fifth Force." *XXXI Recontres de Moriond*. June 5, 1996. http://www.arxiv.org/pdf/hep-ph/9606249v1.pdf.

Fitzmyer, Joseph. *Romans*. Anchor Bible. New York: Doubleday, 1992.

Fleisher, William, et al. "Comparative Study of Trauma-Related Phenomena in Subjects with Pseudoseizures and Subjects with Epilepsy." *American Journal of Psychiatry* 159 (2002) 660–63.

Flew, Antony, and Gary Habermas. "My Pilgrimage from Atheism to Theism: A Discussion between Antony Flew and Gary Habermas." *Philosophia Christi* 6 (2004) 197–212.

Flournoy, Théodore. *Des Indes à la Planète Mars*. Paris: Éditions du Seuil, 1983.

———. *From India to the Planet Mars*. Translated by Daniel B. Vermilye, 1901. Princeton: Princeton University Press, 1994.

Fodor, Nandor. *Freud, Jung, and Occultism*. New York: University Books, 1971.

Foerster, W. "*Echthrós* [hostile], *échthra* [hostility]." In *Theological Dictionary of the New Testament*, edited by Gerhard Kittel and Gerhard Friedrich, abridged in 1 vol. by Geoffrey W. Bromily, 285–86. Grand Rapids: Eerdmans, 1985.

Forrest, Peter. "The Incarnation: A Philosophical Case for Kenosis." *Religious Studies* 36 (2000) 127–40.

Forster, Peter. "Ice Ages and the Mitochondrial DNA Chronology of Human Dispersals: A Review." *Philosophical Transactions of the Royal Society of London B* 359 (2004) 255–64.

Fox, Matthew. *The Coming of the Cosmic Christ: The Healing of Mother Earth and the Birth of a Global Renaissance*. San Francisco: Harper, 1988.

Fradkov, Alexander L., and Robin J. Evans. "Control of Chaos: Survey 1997–2000." In *Proceedings of the 15th IFAC World Congress*, 2002, edited by Luis Basañez and Juan A. de la Puente. http://www.ipme.ru/ipme/labs/ccs/alf/fe_ifaco2.pdf.

Francis, Matthew. "First Planck Results: The Universe Is Still Weird and Interesting." *Ars Technica*. http://arstechnica.com/science/2013/03/first-planck-results-the-universe-is-still-weird-and-interesting.

Franklin, Stan, and Art Graesser. "Is It an Agent, or Just a Program? A Taxonomy for Autonomous Agents." In *Proceedings of the Third International Workshop on Agent Theories, Architectures, and Languages*, 21–35. London: Springer-Verlag, 1996.

Fredkin, Edward. "Digital Mechanics: An Informational Process Based on Reversible Universal Cellular Automata." *Physica D* 45 (1990) 254–70.

———. "Finite Nature." Proceedings of the 27th Recontre de Moriond, 1992. http://52.7.130.124/wp-content/uploads/2015/07/finite_nature.pdf.

———. "A New Cosmogony." In *Proceedings of the Physics of Computation Workshop*, 116–21. Institute of Electrical and Electronic Engineers. October 2–4, 1992. http://www.leptonica.com/cachedpages/fredkin-cosmogony.html.

Freedman, Jonathan L., and Deborah Perlick. "Crowding, Contagion, and Laughter." *Journal of Experimental Social Psychology* 15 (1979) 295–303.

Freeman, Anthony. "God as an Emergent Property." *Journal of Consciousness Studies* 8 (2001) 147–59.

Freeman, Walter J. "Three Centuries of Category Errors in Studies of the Neural Basis of Consciousness and Intentionality." *Neural Networks* 10 (1997) 1175–83.

Freud, Sigmund. *Psychopathology of Everyday Life*. London: Benn, 1930.

Frith, Chris. "The Pathology of Experience." *Brain* 127 (2004) 239–42.

Frodsham, Stanley H. *With Signs Following*. Springfield, MO: Gospel, 1946.

Fromm, Erika. "The Nature of Hypnosis and Other Altered States of Consciousness: An Ego Psychological Theory." In *Hypnosis: Developments in Research and New Perspectives*, edited by Erika Fromm and Ronald E. Shor, 81–103. New York: Aldine, 1979.

Fuchs, Thomas. "Neurobiology and Psychotherapy: An Emerging Dialogue." *Current Opinion in Psychiatry* 17 (2004) 479–85.

Fuller, Robert C. "Unorthodox Medicine and American Religious Life." *Journal of Religion* 67 (1987) 50–65.

Galaktionov, Victor A., and Juan L. Vazquez. "The Problem of Blowup in Nonlinear Parabolic Equations." *Discrete and Continuous Dynamical Systems* 8 (2002) 399–443.

Galli, Mark. "Revival at Cane Ridge." *Christian History* 14 (1995) 9–14.

Garcia-Ojalvo, Jordi, et al. "Coherence and Synchronization in Diode-Laser Arrays with Delayed Global Coupling." *International Journal of Bifurcation and Chaos* 9 (1999) 2225–29.

Gardiner, Gordon P. *Radiant Glory: The Life of Martha Wing Robinson*. 6th ed. Brooklyn: Bread of Life, 1982.

Gavrilov, Leonid A., and Natalia S. Gavrilova. "Evolutionary Theories of Aging and Longevity." *Scientific World Journal* 2 (2002) 339–56.

Gawain, Shakti, with Laurel King. *Living in the Light: A Guide to Personal and Planetary Transformation*. Rev. ed. Novato, CA: New World, 1998.

Gerber, Richard. *Vibrational Medicine: New Choices for Healing Ourselves*. Santa Fe: Beast, 1988.

Gibbs, W. Wayt. "The Unseen Genome: Gems among the Junk." *Scientific American* 289 (2003) 26–33.

Gilbert, Albin R. "Pseudo Mind-Expansion through Psychedelics and Brain-Wave Programming versus True Mind-Expansion through Life Conditioning to the Absolute." *Psychologia* 3–4 (1971) 187–92.

Gillespie, Richard. "Dating the First Australians." *Radiocarbon* 44 (2002) 455–72.

Ginzberg, Louis. *Legends of the Bible*. Old Saybrook, CT: Konecky & Konecky, 1909–1956.

Glaser, Ronald, et al. "Psychological Stress-Induced Modulation of Interleukin 2 Receptor Gene Expression and Interleukin 2 Production in Peripheral Blood Leukocytes." *Archives of General Psychiatry* 47C (1990) 707–12.

Gödel, Kurt. "Some Basic Theorems on the Foundations of Mathematics and Their Implications." 1951. In *Kurt Gödel: Collected Works*, vol. 3, *Unpublished Essays and Lectures*, edited by Solomon Feferman et al., 304–23. New York: Oxford University Press, 1995.

Goertzel, Ben. "Belief Systems as Attractors." In *Chaos Theory in Psychology and the Life Sciences*, edited by Robin Robertson and Allan Combs, 123–34. Mahwah, NJ: Erlbaum, 1995.

Goldapple, Kimberly, et al. "Modulation of Cortical-Limbic Pathways in Major Depression." *Archives of General Psychiatry* 61 (2004) 34–41.

Goldberger, Ary L., et al. "What Is Physiologic Complexity and How Does It Change with Aging and Disease?" *Neurobiology of Aging* 23 (2002) 23–26.

Goldstein, Jeffrey. "The Construction of Emergent Order, Or, How to Resist the Temptation of Hylozoism." *Nonlinear Dynamics, Psychology, and Life Sciences* 7 (2003) 295–314.

Goleman, Daniel. *Social Intelligence: The New Science of Human Relationships*. Large print ed. New York: Random House, 2006.

Gómez Montanelli, Daniel E., and Alejandro Parra. "Are Spontaneous Anomalous/Paranormal Experiences Disturbing? A Survey among Undergraduate Students." *International Journal of Parapsychology* 13 (2002–2005) 1–14. http://www.alipsi.com.ar/investigaciones/pdf/montanelli_parra_ijp.pdf.

Good, Roger. "The Parts of Man in Translation." *Affirmation and Critique* 2 (1997) 47–50. http://www.affcrit.com/pdfs/1997/04/97_04_gl.pdf.

Goodman, Felicitas. "Phonetic Analysis of Glossolalia in Four Cultural Settings." *Journal for the Scientific Study of Religion* 8 (1969) 227–39.

Gordis, Robert. "The Knowledge of Good and Evil in the Old Testament and the Qumran Scrolls. *Journal of Biblical Literature* 76 (1957) 123–38.

Gordon, Cyrus. "Leviathan: Symbol of Evil." In *Biblical Motifs: Origins and Transformations*, edited by Alexander Altmann, 1–9. Cambridge: Harvard University Press, 1966.

Gordon, Robert P. "(*Twb*), Be Good, Do Well, Act Rightly." In *New International Dictionary of Old Testament Theology and Exegesis*, edited by Willem A. VanGemeren, 2:354. Grand Rapids: Zondervan, 1997.

Görres, Joseph von. *La Mystique Divine, Naturelle, et Diabolique Tome 1*. Translated from German by M. Charles Sainte-Foi. Paris, 1861–1862.

Gottesman, Irving I. "Blind Men and Elephants: Genetic and Other Perspectives on Schizophrenia." In *Genetics and Mental Illness: Evolving Issues for Research and Society*, edited by Laura Lee Hall, 51–77. New York: Plenum, 1996.

Gottman, John Mordechai. "Observing Gay, Lesbian, and Heterosexual Couples' Relationships: Mathematical Modeling of Conflict Interaction." *Journal of Homosexuality* 45 (2003) 65–91.

Gowdy, Paul. "Toronto Pastor Speaks on Deception." https://same.wordpress.com/2008/05/31/toronto-speaks-on-deception.

Grady, J. Lee. "What It's Like to Speak in Tongues." *Beliefnet*. 2003. http://www.beliefnet.com/Faiths/Christianity/2003/06/What-Its-Like-To-Speakin-Tongues.aspx.

Gravity Research Group. "Report GRG-013/56 February 1956: Electro-Gravitics Systems: An Examination of Electrostatic Motion, Dynamic Counterbary and Barycentric Control." http://www.padrak.com/ine/INE24.html.

Gray, Herbert G. "Individual Responsibility and Retribution." *Hebrew Union College Annual* 32 (1961) 107–20.

Grebogi, Celso, and Edward Ott. "Crises, Sudden Changes in Chaotic Attractors, and Transient Chaos." *Physica D: Nonlinear Phenomena* 7 (1983) 181–200.

Greene, F. G. "At the Edge of Eternity's Shadows: Scaling the Fractal Continuum from Lower into Higher Space." *Journal of Near-Death Studies* 21 (2003) 223–40.

Greenhill, Eleanor Simmons. "The Child in the Tree: A Study of the Cosmological Tree in Christian Tradition." *Traditio* 10 (1954) 323–71.

Gregory, Anita Kohsen. Introduction to *Possession: Demonical and Other*, by T. K. Oesterreich, v–xvi. Seacaucus, NY: University Books, 1966.

Gregory of Nyssa. "IV. Apologetic: The Great Catechism." In *Nicene and Post-Nicene Fathers*, series 2, vol. 5, edited by Philip Schaff, 950, chapter 26. Albany, OR: Ages Software (ver. 2.0), 1997.

Greig, Emma, and Tim Betts. "Epileptic Seizures Induced by Sexual Abuse: Pathogenic and Pathoplastic Features." *Seizure* 1 (1992) 269–74.

Greyson, Bruce. "Dissociation in People Who Have Near-Death Experiences: Out of Their Bodies or Out of Their Minds?" *Lancet* 355 (2000) 460–63.

———. "Near-Death Experiences and the Physio-Kundalini Syndrome." *Journal of Religion and Health* 32 (1993) 277–90.

Greyson, Bruce, and Nancy Evans Bush. "Distressing Near-Death Experiences." *Psychiatry* 55 (1992) 95–110.

Grof, Stanislav. *The Adventure of Self-Discovery*. Albany: State University of New York Press, 1988.

———. "Ervin Laszlo's Akashic Field and the Dilemmas of Modern Consciousness Research." http://www.stanislavgrof.com/wp-content/uploads/pdf/Ervin_Laszlo.pdf.

———. "Psychology of the Future: Lessons from Modern Consciousness Research." http://www.stanislavgrof.com/wp-content/uploads/pdf/Psychology_of_the_Future_Stan_Grof_long.pdf.

Grogan, G. W. "The Old Testament Concept of Solidarity in Hebrews." *Tyndale Bulletin* 49 (1998) 159–73.

Grohol, John M., and Margarita Tartakovsky. "DSM-5 Resource Guide." *PsychCentral*. http://www.psychcentral.com/dsm-5.

Gromb, S., et al. "Spontaneous Human Combustion: A Sometimes Incomprehensible Phenomenon." *Journal of Clinical Forensic Medicine* 7 (2000) 29–31.

Grossfeld, Bernard. *Targum Onqelos to Deuteronomy*. Collegeville: Liturgical, 1988.

Grosso, Michael. "Jung, Parapsychology, and the Near-Death Experience: Toward a Transpersonal Paradigm." *Anabiosis* 3 (1983) 3–38.

Grünbaum, Adolf. "The Pseudo-Problem of Creation in Physical Cosmology." *Philosophy of Science* 56 (1989) 373–94.

Grundmann, W. "δυναμαι, δυναμις." In *Theological Dictionary of the New Testament*, edited by Gerhard Kittel et al., 2:287–91. Grand Rapids: Eerdmans, 1964–1976.

Guénon, René. *Symbolism of the Cross*. Translated by Angus Macnab. London: Luzac, 1975.

Gupta, Akhil. "Reliving Childhood? The Temporality of Childhood and Narratives of Reincarnation." *Ethnos* 67 (2002) 33–56.

Gurney, O. R. *Some Aspects of Hittite Religion*. Oxford: Oxford University Press, 1977.

Habel, Norman C. "Ezekiel 28 and the Fall of the First Man." *Concordia Theological Monthly* 38 (1967) 516–24.

Hall, Howard, et al. "The Scientific Study of Unusual Rapid Wound Healing: A Case Report." *Advances in Mind-Body Medicine* 17 (2001) 203–9.

Hamblen, Collins. "Jesus as Alchemist." *Alchemy Journal* 5 (2004). http://www.alchemylab.com/AJ5-3.htm.

Hameroff, Stuart. "'Funda-Mentality'—Is the Conscious Mind Subtly Connected to a Basic Level of the Universe?" *Trends in Cognitive Science* 2 (1998) 119–27.

Hamilton, Victor P. *The Book of Genesis: Chapters 1–17*. Grand Rapids: Eerdmans, 1990.

Hamming, R. W. "The Unreasonable Effectiveness of Mathematics." *American Mathematical Monthly* 87 (1980) 1–7.

Hammond, Elizabeth, and Larry Young. "Microsatellite Instability Generates Diversity in Brain and Sociobehavioral Traits." *Science* 308 (2005) 1630–34.

Hampden-Turner, Charles. "Authoritarianism, Schismogenesis and the Self-Exciting System: Bateson and Nevitt Sanford." In *Maps of the Mind*, 174–77. London: Beazley, 1981.

Hanegraaff, Hank. *Counterfeit Revival*. Dallas: Word, 1997.

Hanegraaff, Wouter J. *New Age Religion and Western Culture*. Leiden: Brill, 1996.

Haran, Menahem. "The Ark and the Cherubim: Their Symbolic Significance in Biblical Ritual." *Israel Exploration Journal* 9 (1959) 30–38, 89–94.

Hardy, Alister. *The Spiritual Nature of Man: A Study of Contemporary Religious Experience*. Oxford: Clarendon, 1979.

Hardy, L. G. "Brigham Young and the Gift of Tongues." *Improvement Era* 37 (1934) 432–33. https://archive.org/stream/improvementera3707unse/improvementera3707unse_djvu.txt.

Harkavy, Allan Abraham. *Human Will: The Search for Its Physical Basis*. New York: Lang, 1995.

Harnad, Stevan. "Artificial Life: Synthetic vs. Virtual." In *Artificial Life III*, edited by Christopher G. Langton, 539–52. Proceedings of the Santa Fe Institute Studies in the Sciences of Complexity 17. Reading, MA: Addison-Wesley, 1994.

Harner, Michael. "Science, Spirits, and Core Shamanism." *Shamanism* 12 (1999). http://www.mcs.ca/vitalspark/2020_schools/313shamo1.html.

———. "Shamanic Healing: We Are Not Alone." With Bonnie Horrigan. *Shamanism* 10 (1997). http://www.shamanism.org/articles/article01.html.

Harpur, Tom. "Bible's Literal Interpretation Is Outdated." *Toronto Star*, August 3, 2003.

———. "Symbols Are about Reality." *Toronto Star*, January 4, 2004.

Harrington, Anne. "The Many Meanings of the Placebo Effect: Where They Came From, Why They Matter." *Biosocieties* 1 (2006) 181–93.

Harris, R. Laird. *Leviticus*. In *Genesis–Numbers*, edited by Frank E. Gaebelein et al. Expositor's Bible Commentary 2. Grand Rapids: Zondervan, 1990.

Harrison, R. K. "Azazel." In *International Standard Bible Encyclopedia*, vol. 1, *A–D*, edited by G. W. Bromiley et al., 375. Grand Rapids: Eerdmans, 1979.

———. *Introduction to the Old Testament*. Grand Rapids: Eerdmans, 1969.

———. *Old Testament Times*. Grand Rapids: Eerdmans, 1970.

Hartle, James, and Stephen Hawking. "The Wave Function of the Universe." *Physical Review D* 12 (1983) 2960–75.

Hartley, John. *Leviticus*. Waco, TX: Word, 1992.

Hartman, Louis F. "Sin in Paradise." *Catholic Biblical Quarterly* 20 (1958) 26–40.

Haub, Carl. "How Many People Have Ever Lived on Earth?" *Population Today*, November/December 2002, 3–4. http://www.prb.org/Publications/Articles/2002/HowManyPeopleHaveEverLivedonEarth.aspx.

Hausdorff, Jeffrey M., et al. "Is Walking a Random Walk? Evidence for Long-Range Correlations in Stride Interval of Human Gait." *Journal of Applied Physiology* 78 (1995) 349–58.

Hawken, Paul. *The Magic of Findhorn*. New York: Bantam, 1976.

Hawking, Stephen. "Gödel and the End of Physics." http://www.damtp.cam.ac.uk/strings02/dirac/hawking.

Hawking, Stephen, and Neil Turok. "Open Inflation Without False Vacua." *Physics Letters B* 425 (1998) 25–32.

Hay, David M. *Glory at the Right Hand: Psalm 110 in Early Christianity*. Nashville: Abingdon, 1973.

Hecker, J. F. C. *The Epidemics of the Middle Ages*. Translated by B. G. Babington. London: Woodfall, 1844.

Heidel, Alexander. "Epic of Gilgamesh." In *The Gilgamish Epic and Old Testament Parallels*. Chicago: University of Chicago Press, 1946–1973.

Held, G. A., et al. "Experimental Study of Critical-Mass Fluctuations in an Evolving Sandpile." *Physical Review Letters* 65 (1990) 1120–23.

Hendriksen, William. *Romans*. Grand Rapids: Baker, 1980/81.

Hepper, P. G., and S. Shahidullah. "The Beginnings of Mind: Evidence from the Behaviour of the Fetus." *Journal of Reproductive and Infant Psychology* 12 (1994) 143–54.

Herodotus. *The Histories*. Translated by A. D. Godley. Cambridge: Harvard University Press, 1920.

———. "The Persian Wars, Book II: Euterpe." In *The Greek Historians*, edited by Francis R. B. Godolphin. New York: Random House, 1942. http://mcadams.posc.mu.edu/txt/ah/Herodotus/Herodotus2.html.

Hesse, F. "*Chriō, christós, antichristos, chrisma, christianós*." In *Theological Dictionary of the New Testament*, edited by Gerhard Kittel and Gerhard Friedrich, abridged in 1 vol. by Geoffrey W. Bromily, 1322–24. Grand Rapids: Eerdmans, 1985.

Heylighen, Francis. "The Science of Self-Organization and Adaptivity." http://www.redfish.com/research/EOLSS-Self-Organiz.pdf.

Hiley, B. J. "Active Information and Teleportation." In *Epistemological and Experimental Perspectives on Quantum Physics*, edited by Daniel Greenberger et al., 113–26. Dordrecht: Kluwer Academic, 1999. DOI: 10.1007/978-94-017-1454-9_8.

Hill, Carol A. "The Garden of Eden: A Modern Landscape." *Perspectives on Science and Christian Faiith* 52 (2000) 31–46.

Hillers, Delbert R. *Treaty-Curses and the Old Testament Prophets*. Biblica et Orientalia 16. Rome: Pontifical Biblical Institute, 1964.

Hines, Terence. *Pseudoscience and the Paranormal*. 2nd ed. Buffalo: Prometheus, 2003.

Hippolytus. "Apostolic Tradition." In *The Treatise on the Apostolic Tradition of St. Hippolytus of Rome*, edited by Gregory Dix and Henry Chadwick. London: Alban, 1992.

Hochstetler, Dean. "The God We Serve Is Able to Deliver Us." Unpublished paper. Nappanee, IN. September 12, 1998.

———. Hochstetler to Lawrence E. Burkholder. Personal correspondence. September 18, 2005.

Hodder, Ian. "Women and Men at Çatalhöyük." *Scientific American* 290 (2004) 77–83.

Hoffman, Ross N. "Controlling the Global Weather." *Bulletin of the American Meteorological Society* 83 (2002) 241–48.

Hoffner, Harry. "אוב *'ôbh*." In *Theological Dictionary of the Old Testament*, edited by G. Johannes Botterweck et al., 1:130–34. Grand Rapids: Eerdmans, 1974–2006.

Holcombe, A. D. "Christ-Consciousness, Kundalini & Spirit-Energy." *Journal of Religion and Psychical Research* 16 (1993) 90–93.

Holden, Katharine J., and Christopher C. French. "Alien Abduction Experiences: Some Clues from Neuropsychology and Neuropsychiatry." *Cognitive Neuropsychiatry* 7 (2002) 163–78.

Holling, C. S. "Understanding the Complexity of Economic, Ecological, and Social Systems." *Ecosystems* 4 (2001) 390–405.

Horgan, John. "The End of Science Revisited." *Computer* 37 (2004) 37–43.

Horowitz, Mardi J., et al. "Visual Imagery on Brain Stimulation." *Archives of General Psychiatry* 19 (1968) 469–86.

Howard-Browne, Rodney. *The Touch of God*. Tampa: Revival Ministries International, 1992.

Hoyle, Fred, and Chandra Wickramasinghe. *Evolution from Space*. London: Dent, 1981.

Hoyle, Fred, and J. V. Narlikar. "A Radical Departure from the 'Steady State' Concept in Cosmology." *Proceedings of the Royal Society* A290 (1966) 162–76.

Hsu, Hui-Chin, and Alan Fogel. "Stability and Transitions in Mother-Infant Face-to-Face Communication during the First 6 Months: A Microhistorical Approach." *Developmental Psychology* 39 (2003) 1061–82.

Hubbard, Barbara Marx. *The Revelation: Our Crisis Is a Birth*. Greenbrae, CA: Foundation for Conscious Evolution, 1993.

Hubbard, Robert L., Jr. "The Go'el in Ancient Israel: Theological Reflections on an Israelite Institution." *Bulletin for Biblical Research* 1 (1991) 3–19.

Hudson, Thomson Jay. *The Law of Psychic Phenomena*. Chicago: McClurg, 1901.

Huffmon, Herbert B. "The Covenant Lawsuit in the Prophets." *Journal of Biblical Literature* 78 (1959) 285–95.

Ingvar, D. H. "On Ideation and 'Ideography.'" In *The Principles of Design and Operation of the Brain: Proceedings of a Study Week Organized by the Pontifical Academy of Sciences, Vatican City*, edited by John C. Eccles and Otto Creutzfeldt, 433–53. Berlin: Springer-Verlag, 1990.

International Theological Commission. "The Hope of Salvation for Infants Who Die without Being Baptised." 2007. http://www.vatican.va/roman_curia/congregations/cfaith/cti_documents/rc_con_cfaith_doc_20070419_un-baptised-infants_en.html.

Irenaeus. "Against Heresies." In Roberts and Donaldson, *Ante-Nicene Fathers*, 1:909.

———. *Proof of the Apostolic Preaching*. Translated by Joseph P. Smith. New York: Paulist, 1952.

Irwin, Harvey. "Mindsight: Near-Death and Out-of-Body Experiences in the Blind." *Journal of Parapsychology* 64 (2000) 107–13.

Isaacs, T. Craig. "The Possessive States Disorder: The Diagnosis of Demonic Possession." *Pastoral Psychology* 35 (1987) 263–73.

Isbell, Charles D. "The Origins of Prophetic Frenzy and Ecstatic Utterance in the Old Testament World." *Wesleyan Theological Journal* 11 (1976) 62–80.

Isham, Christopher J., and John C. Polkinghorne. "The Debate over the Block Universe." In *Quantum Cosmology and the Laws of Nature: Scientific Perspectives in Divine Action*, edited by Robert John Russell et al., 135–44. Vatican City: Vatican Observatory, 1993.

Iudin, D. I., et al. "Fractal Dynamics of Electric Discharges in a Thundercloud." *Physical Review E* 68 (2003) 016601.1–016601.11.

Jacobs, Irving. "Elements of Near-Eastern Mythology in Rabbinic Aggadah." *Journal of Jewish Studies* 28 (1977) 1–11.

Jacobson, Roman. *Selected Writings*. Vol. 4. The Hague: Slavic Epic Studies, 1966.

Jaffé, Aniela. "Details about C. G. Jung's Family." *Spring* (1984) 35–43.

———. *From the Life and Work of C. G. Jung.* Translated by R. F. C. Hull. New York: Harper & Row, 1971.

———. "The Psychic World of C. G. Jung." In *Freud, Jung, and Occultism*, edited by Nandor Fodor, 187–203. New York: University Books, 1971.

Jamison, Kay Redfield. *Touched with Fire: Manic-Depressive Illness and the Artistic Temperament.* New York: Free Press, 1993.

Janet, Pierre. "Les Actes Inconscients et la Mémoire pendant le Somnambulisme." *Revue Philosophique* 25 (1888) 238–79.

Jeeves, Malcolm. "Brain, Mind, and Behavior." In *Whatever Happened to the Soul? Scientific and Theological Portraits of Human Nature*, edited by Warren S. Brown et al., 73–98. Minneapolis: Augsburg Fortress, 1998.

Jennewein, Thomas, et al. "Experimental Nonlocality Proof of Quantum Teleportation and Entanglement Swapping." University of Vienna Institute for Experimental Physics, February 9, 2008. http://www.arxiv.org/pdf/quant-ph/0201134.pdf.

Jennings, George J. "An Ethnological Study of Glossolalia." *Journal of the American Scientific Affiliation* 20 (1968) 5–16.

Jeremias, Joachim. "γέεννα." In *Theological Dictionary of the New Testament*, edited by Gerhard Kittel et al., 1:657–58. Grand Rapids: Eerdmans, 1964–1976.

Johnson, Alan F. *Revelation.* In *Hebrews–Revelation*, edited by Frank E. Gaebelein et al. Expositor's Bible Commentary 12. Grand Rapids: Zondervan, 1981.

Johnson, Guion G. "Revival Movements in Ante-Bellum North Carolina." *North Carolina Historical Review* 10 (1933) 21–43.

Johnston, Wm. Robert. "Historical Abortion Statistics, Ontario (Canada)." http://www.johnstonsarchive.net/policy/abortion/canada/ab-canada-ON.html.

Joines, Karen Randolph. "The Serpent in Gen 3." *Zeitschrift für die Alttestamentliche Wissenschaf* 85 (1975) 1–11.

Jonas, Hans. "Myth and Mysticism: A Study of Objectification and Interiorization in Religious Thought." *Journal of Religion* 49 (1969) 315–29.

Jones, Ernest. *Sigmund Freud: Life and Work.* Vol. 3, *The Last Phase.* London: Hogarth, 1957.

Jones, Philip. "Embracing Inana: Legitimation and Mediation in the Ancient Mesopotamian Sacred Marriage Hymn *Iddin-Dagan A*." *Journal of the American Oriental Society* 123 (2003) 291–302.

Jonker, C. M., and J. Treur. "Modelling Multiple Mind-Matter Interaction." *International Journal of Human-Computer Studies* 57 (2002) 165–214.

Jordan, Paul. *Neanderthal.* Phoenix Mill, UK: Sutton, 1999.

Joseph, R. "Dual Mental Functioning in a Split-Brain Patient." *Journal of Clinical Psychology* 44 (1988) 770–79.

———. "The Limbic System and the Soul: Evolution and the Neuroanatomy of Religious Experience." *Zygon* 36 (2001) 105–36.

Josephus. *Antiquities of the Jews.* Grand Rapids: Kregel, 1960.

Jourdan, J. P. "Near Death Experiences and Transcendental Experiences: Neurophysiological Correlates and Hypotheses." *Journal of Near Death Studies* 12 (1994) 177–200. http://dr.jp.jourdan.pagesperso-orange.fr/Articles/Near-Death%20Experiences%20and%20Transcendental%20Experiences.pdf.

Jung, C. G. "Appendix: On Synchronicity." In *The Structure and Dynamics of the Psyche*, Complete Works 8, Bollingen Series XX, 520–31. New York: Pantheon, 1960.

———. "Archetypes of the Collective Unconscious." In *Complete Works 9,i*, 3–50. Princeton: Princeton University Press, 1968.

———. "Christ, a Symbol of the Self." In *Complete Works 9,ii, Bollingen Series XX*, 36–71. New York: Pantheon, 1959.

———. "Foreword to Quispel: 'Tragic Christianity.'" In *Complete Works 18, Bollingen Series XX*, 651–53. Princeton: Princeton University Press, 1950–1976.

———. "Jung and Religious Belief." In *Complete Works 18, Bollingen Series XX*, 702–4. New York: Pantheon, 1950–1976.

———. *Letters 2: 1951–1961, Bollingen Series XCV*. Princeton: Princeton University Press, 1953–1975.

———. *Memories, Dreams, Reflections*. Edited by Aniela Jaffé. Translated by Richard and Clara Winston. New York: Vantage, 1989.

———. "On Psychic Energy." In *Complete Works 8, Bollingen Series XX*, 3–66. New York: Pantheon, 1960.

———. "A Psychological Approach to the Dogma of the Trinity." In *Complete Works 11, Bollingen Series XX*, 165–80. Princeton: Princeton University Press, 1953–1978.

———. "On the Psychology and Pathology of So-Called Occult Phenomena." In *Complete Works 1*, 17–24. New York: Pantheon, 1957.

———. "Transformation Symbolism in the Mass." In *Complete Works 11, Bollingen Series XX*, 201–96. Princeton: Princeton University Press, 1954.

Jusczyk, Peter W. "How Infants Begin to Extract Words from Speech." *Trends in Cognitive Sciences* 3 (1999) 323–28.

K. Stigler, et al. "An Empirical Investigation of the Discriminability of Reported Mystical Experiences among Religious Contemplatives, Psychotic Inpatients, and Normal Adults." *Journal for the Scientific Study of Religion* 32 (1993) 366–72.

Kaiser, Walter, Jr. *The Book of Leviticus*. Nashville: Abingdon, 1994.

Kalland, Earl S. *Deuteronomy*. In *Deuteronomy–2 Samuel*, edited by Frank E. Gaebelein et al. Expositor's Bible Commentary 3. Grand Rapids: Zondervan, 1992.

Kampman, Reima. "Hypnotically Induced Multiple Personality: An Experimental Study." *International Journal of Clinical and Experimental Hypnosis* 24 (1976) 215–27.

Kaneko, Kunihiko. "Chaos as a Source of Complexity and Diversity in Evolution." In *Artificial Life: An Overview*, edited by Christopher C. Langton, 163–77. Cambridge: MIT Press, 1995.

Kaptchuk, Ted J. "Historical Context of the Concept of Vitalism in Complementary and Alternative Medicine." In *Fundamentals of Complementary and Alternative Medicine*, edited by Marc S. Micozzi, 35–48. New York: Churchill Livingstone, 1996.

———. "Powerful Placebo: The Dark Side of the Randomized Controlled Trial." *Lancet* 351 (1998) 1722–25.

Karoly, Paul. "Mechanisms of Self-Regulation: A Systems View." *Annual Review of Psychology* 44 (1993) 23–52.

Kass, Leon R. "L'Chaim and Its Limits: Why Not Immortality?" *First Things* 113 (2001) 17–24.

Kaufman, Whitley R. P. "Karma, Rebirth, and the Problem of Evil." *Philosophy East & West* 55 (2005) 15–32.

Keel, Othmar. *The Symbolism of the Biblical World: Ancient Near Eastern Iconography and the Book of Psalms*. Translated by Timothy J. Hallett. New York: Seabury, 1978.

Keil, C. F., and F. Delitzsch. *Old Testament Commentaries: Genesis to Judges 6:32*. Grand Rapids: Associated Publishers and Authors, n.d.

Kelleher, Colm A. "Retrotransposons as Engines of Human Bodily Transformation." *Journal of Scientific Exploration* 13 (1999) 9–24.

Keller, Helen. *Teacher: Anne Sullivan Macy; A Tribute by the Foster-Child of Her Mind.* New York: Doubleday, 1955.

———. *The World I Live In.* London: Hodder and Stoughton, 1904.

Kelly, Kevin. "God Is the Machine." *Wired*, December 1, 2002. http://www.wired.com/wired/archive/10.12/holytech.html.

Kelso, J. A. Scott. "The Complementary Nature of Co-ordination Dynamics: Self-Organization and Agency." *Nonlinear Phenomena in Complex Systems* 5 (2002) 364–71.

Kennedy, J. E. "Do People Guide Psi or Does Psi Guide People? Evidence and Implications from Life and Lab." *Journal of the American Society for Psychical Research* 94 (2000) 130–50.

Kenny, Michael. "Multiple Personality and Spirit Possession." *Psychiatry* 44 (1981) 337–38.

Kentridge, Robert William. "Modularity of Mind, Cerebral Localisation and Connectionist Neuropsychology." Review of *Subsymbolic Natural Language Processing: An Integrated Model of Scripts, Lexicon, and Memory*, by R. Miikkulainen. *Psycoloquy* 5 (1994). http://www.cogsci.ecs.soton.ac.uk/cgi/psyc/newpsy?5.87.

Kiecolt-Glaser, J., et al. "Emotions, Morbidity, and Mortality: New Perspectives from Psychoneuroimmunology." *Annual Review of Psychology* 53 (2002) 84–90.

———. "Slowing of Wound Healing by Psychological Stress." *Lancet* 346 (1995) 1194–96.

Kiefer, Heather Mason. "Divine Subjects: Canadians Believe, Britons Skeptical." *Gallup*, November 16, 2004. http://www.gallup.com/poll/14083/divine-subjects-canadians-believe-britons-skeptical.aspx.

Kildahl, John P. "Psychological Observations." In *The Charismatic Movement*, edited by Michael P. Hamilton, 124–42. Grand Rapids: Eerdmans, 1975.

Kirilyuk, Andrei P. "Universal Symmetry of Complexity and Its Manifestations at Different Levels of World Dynamics." *Proceedings of the Institute of Mathematics of the NAS of Ukraine* 50 (2004) 821–22.

Kirsch, Irving, et al. "The Emperor's New Drugs: An Analysis of Antidepressant Medication Data Submitted to the U.S. Food and Drug Administration." *Prevention & Treatment* 5 (2002). http://www.alphachoices.com/repository/assets/pdf/EmperorsNewDrugs.pdf.

Kistemaker, Simon J. *First Epistle to the Corinthians.* Grand Rapids: Baker, 1993.

Kitchen, K. A. *Ancient Orient and Old Testament.* Chicago: InterVarsity, 1966.

Kleinman, J. E., et al. "A Comparison of the Phenomenology of Hallucinogens and Schizophrenia from Some Autobiographical Accounts." *Schizophrenia Bulletin* 3 (1977) 560–86.

Kline, Meredith G. "Death, Leviathan, and the Martyrs: Isaiah 24:1—27:1." In *A Tribute to Gleason Archer*, edited by Walter C. Kaiser Jr. and Ronald F. Youngblood, 229–49. Chicago: Moody, 1986.

Knight, Douglas A. "Cosmogony and Order in the Hebrew Tradition." In *Cosmogony and Ethical Order*, edited by Robin W. Lovin and Frank E. Reynolds, 133–55. Chicago: University of Chicago Press, 1985.

Koch, Kurt. *Christian Counseling and Occultism.* Grand Rapids: Kregel, 1965.

———. *Occult Bondage and Deliverance.* Grand Rapids: Kregel, 1972.

Koestler, Arthur. *The Lotus and the Robot.* New York: Macmillan, 1961.

Kohr, Richard. "Near-Death Experiences, Altered States, and Psi Sensitivity." *Anabiosis* 3 (1983) 160–69.

Kolodiejchuk, Brian. *Mother Teresa: Come Be My Light*. New York: Doubleday, 2007.

Kooy, V. H. "First-Born." In Buttrick, *Interpreter's Dictionary*, 2:270–72.

Koutsoukos, Elias, and Elias Angelopoulos. "Mood Regulation in Bipolar Disorders Viewed through the Pendulum Dynamics Concept." *International Journal of Bipolar Disorders* 2 (2014) 9. http://www.journalbipolardisorders.com/content/2/1/9.

Kovach, Stephen D., et al. "A Defense of the Doctrine of the Eternal Subordination of the Son." *Journal of the Evangelical Theological Society* 42 (1999) 462–77.

Kraemer, C. E. S. "The Power of Prayer on Plants." *Interpretation: A Journal of Bible and Theology* XIV (1960) 244–5.

Kramer, Heinrich, and James Sprenger. *Malleus Maleficarum*. Translated by Montague Summers. London: Bracken, 1928, 1996.

Krašovec, Jože. "Is There a Doctrine of 'Collective Retribution' in the Hebrew Bible?" *Hebrew Union College Annual* 65 (1994) 35–89.

Krüger, Günter. "Johann Christoph Blumhardt (1805–1880): A Man for the Kingdom." *Currents in Theology and Missions* 23 (1996) 427–41.

Kurucz, Robert L. "Elementary Physics in the Cellular Automaton Universe." http://arxiv.org/abs/astro-ph/0605467.

Kurzweil, Raymond. *The Age of Intelligent Machines*. Cambridge: MIT Press, 1990.

———. "Reflections on Stephen Wolfram's *A New Kind of Science*." http://www.kurzweilai.net/reflections-on-stephen-wolfram-s-a-new-kind-of-science.

Kutchins, Herb, and Stuart A. Kirk. *Making Us Crazy*. New York: Free Press, 1997.

Kwon, Jun Soo, et al. "Gamma Frequency—Range Abnormalities to Auditory Stimulation in Schizophrenia." *Archives of General Psychiatry* 56 (1999) 1001–5.

L'Engle, Madeleine. *The Wind in the Door*. New York: Farrar, Straus and Giroux, 1973.

Lacasse, Jeffrey R., and Jonathan Leo. "Serotonin and Depression: A Disconnect between the Advertisements and the Scientific Literature." *PLoS Medicine* 2 (2005) 1211.

Lactantius. "Of the Advantage and Use of the World and of the Seasons." In "A Treatise on the Anger of God," in Roberts and Donaldson, *Ante-Nicene Fathers*, 7:562.

Lang, B. "פפר *kipper*; כפרה *kappōret*; כפר *kōper*; כפרים *kippurîm*." In *Theological Dictionary of the Old Testament*, edited by G. Johannes Botterweck et al., 7:292. Grand Rapids: Eerdmans, 1974–2006.

Lang, Friedrich. "πῦρ." In *Theological Dictionary of the New Testament*, edited by Gerhard Kittel et al., 6:928–52. Grand Rapids: Eerdmans, 1964–1976.

Langdon, Stephen. *Semitic*. Mythology of All Races 5. New York: Cooper Square, 1964.

———. *Sumerian Liturgical Texts*. Publications of the Babylonian Section 10. Philadelphia: University of Pennsylvania Museum, 1917.

Lasemidis, L. D., and J. C. Sackellares. "Chaos Theory and Epilepsy." *Neuroscientist* 2 (1996) 118–26. http://citeseerx.ist.psu.edu/viewdoc/download?doi=10.1.1.40.7741&rep=rep1&type=pdf.

Langerfeld, Joseph K. "The Dead Arise: Cases of Death and Return in Tibet." *School for International Training Occasional Papers* 3 (2002) 40–54.

Laszlo, Ervin. "Systems and Structures—Toward Bio-Social Anthropology." *Theory and Decision* 2 (1971) 174–92.

Laughlin, R. B., and David Pines. "The Theory of Everything." *Proceedings of the National Academy of Science* 97 (2000) 28–31.

Lavelli, Manuela, et al. "Using Microgenetic Designs to Study Change Processes." In *Handbook of Research Methods in Developmental Science*, edited by D. G. Teti, 40–65. Oxford: Blackwell, 2005.

Lavington, George. *The Enthusiasm of Methodists and Papists Compared.* Vol. 1, pt. 2. London: Knapton, 1749.

———. *The Enthusiasm of Methodists and Papists Compared.* Vol. 2, pt. 3. London: Knapton, 1754.

Lawrence, Madeleine M. "Paranormal Experiences of Previously Unconscious Patients." In *Parapsychology and Thanatology*, edited by Lisette Coly and Joanne D. S. McMahon, 122–48. New York: Parapsychology Foundation, 1995.

Layton, Bentley. *The Gnostic Scriptures: A New Translation with Annotations and Introductions.* New York: Doubleday, 1987.

Le Baron, Albert. "A Case of Psychic Automatism, Including 'Speaking with Tongues.'" In *Essays in Psychical Research*, by William James, 143–66. Cambridge: Harvard University Press, 1986.

Lechler, Alfred. "Occult Bondage and Deliverance." In *Christian Counseling and Occultism*, by Kurt Koch, 140–68. Grand Rapids: Kregel, 1965.

Leger, Theodore. *Animal Magnetism or Psychodunamy.* New York: Appleton, 1846.

Le Goff, Jacques. *The Birth of Purgatory.* Translated by Arthur Goldhammer. Chicago: University of Chicago Press, 1981.

Lehmann, L., and L. Keller. "The Evolution of Cooperation and Altruism—a General Framework and a Classification of Models." *Journal of Evolutionary Biology* 19 (2006) 1365–76.

Leiber, Justin. "Nature's Experiments, Society's Closures." *Journal for the Theory of Social Behaviour* 27 (1997) 325–43.

León, Carlos A. "'El Duende' and Other Incubi: Suggestive Interactions between Culture, the Devil, and the Brain." *Archives of General Psychiatry* 32 (1975) 155–62.

LeShan, Lawrence. *The Medium, the Mystic, and the Physicist.* New York: Viking, 1974.

Leuba, James H. *The Psychology of Religious Mysticism.* New York: Harcourt, Brace, 1925.

Levenson, Jon D. *Creation and the Persistence of Evil: The Jewish Drama of Divine Omnipotence.* New York: Harper & Row, 1988.

———. "The Temple and the World." *Journal of Religion* 64 (1984) 275–98.

Levin, Janna, et al. "The Topology of the Universe: The Biggest Manifold of Them All." *Classical and Quantum Gravity* 15 (1998) 2689–97.

Lewis, C. S. *Miracles.* New York: Collier, 1947.

———. *The Problem of Pain.* London: Collins, 1940.

Lhermitte, Jean. "Visual Hallucination of the Self." *British Medical Journal* 1 (1951) 431–34.

Libet, Benjamin. "Cerebral Processes That Distinguish Conscious Experience from Unconscious Mental Functions." In *The Principles of Design and Operation of the Brain*, edited by John C. Eccles and Otto Creutzfeldt, 185–211. Berlin: Springer-Verlag, 1990.

Lichtenstein, Benyamin B. "A Matrix of Complexity for Leadership: 14 Disciplines of Complex Systems Leadership Theory." In *Complex Systems Leadership Theory*, edited by J. Hazy et al., 285–304. Boston: ISCE, 2007.

Liester, Mitchell B. "Inner Voices: Distinguishing Transcendent and Pathological Characteristics." *Journal of Transpersonal Psychology* 28 (1996) 1–30.

Lind, Millard. *Yahweh Is a Warrior: The Theology of Warfare in Ancient Israel.* Scottdale, PA: Herald, 1980.

Lindars, Barnabas. "Ezekiel and Individual Responsibility." *Vetus Testamentum* 15 (1965) 453–59.

Lindquist, John M. "What Is a Temple? A Preliminary Typology." In *The Quest for the Kingdom of God: Studies in Honor of George E. Mendenhall*, edited by H. B. Huffman et al., 205–19. Winona Lake, IN: Eisenbruns, 1983.

Lineweaver, Charles H., and Chas A. Egan. "Life, Gravity and the Second Law of Thermodynamics." *Physics of Life Reviews* 5 (2008) 225–42.

Linkenkaer-Hansen, Klaus. "Self-Organized Criticality and Stochastic Resonance in the Human Brain." PhD diss., Helsinki University of Technology Laboratory of Biomedical Engineering, 2002.

Llinás, Rodolfo R., et al. "Thalamocortical Dysrhythmia: A Neurological and Neuropsychiatric Syndrome Characterized by Magnetoencelaphography." *Proceedings of the National Academy of Sciences USA* 96 (1999) 15222–27.

Lloyd, Seth. "Computational Capacity of the Universe." *Physical Review Letters* 88 (2002) 237901.1.

Loder, Theodore C., III. "'Outside the Box' Space and Terrestrial Transportation and Energy Technologies for the 21st Century." Presented at 40th AIAA Aerospace Sciences Meeting and Exhibit, Reno, 2002. http://www.stealthskater.com/Documents/Loder_01.pdf.

Lommel, Pim van, et al. "Near-Death Experiences in Survivors of Cardiac Arrest: A Prospective Study in the Netherlands." *Lancet* 358 (2001) 2039–45.

Lorenzo, M. Nieves, and Vicente Pérez-Muñuzuri. "Influence of Low Intensity Noise on Assemblies of Diffusively Coupled Chaotic Cells." *Chaos* 11 (2001) 371–76.

Lovejoy, Arthur O. *The Great Chain of Being.* Cambridge: Harvard University Press, 1942.

Luckinbill, Daniel David. *Ancient Records of Assyria and Babylonia.* Vol. 2. New York: Greenwood, 1927.

Ludwig, Arnold M. "The Psychobiological Functions of Dissociation." *American Journal of Clinical Hypnosis* 26 (1983) 93–99.

———. "Witchcraft Today." *Diseases of the Nervous System* 265 (1965) 288–91.

Lukianowicz, N. "Autoscopic Phenomena." *AMA Archives of Neurology and Psychiatry* 80 (1958) 199–220.

Lukoff, David. "The Diagnosis of Mystical Experiences with Psychotic Features." *Journal of Transpersonal Psychology* 17 (1985) 155–81.

Lukoff, David, and Howard C. Everest. "The Myths of Mental Illness." *Journal of Transpersonal Psychology* 17 (1985) 123–53.

Lumey, L. H., et al. "Cohort Profile: The Dutch Hunger Winter Families Study." *International Journal of Epidemiology* (2007) 1–9.

Lundquist, John M. "Temple, Covenant, and Law in the Ancient Near East and in the Old Testament." In *Israel's Apostasy and Restoration: Essays in Honor of Roland K. Harrison*, edited by Avraham Gileadi, 293–305. Grand Rapids: Baker, 1988.

———. "What Is a Temple? A Preliminary Typology." In *The Quest for the Kingdom of God: Studies in Honor of George E. Mendenhall*, edited by H. B. Huffman et al., 205–19. Winona Lake, IN: Eisenbruns, 1983.

Luther, Martin. "The Magnificat." In *Martin Luther's Writings: Sermons, Commentary & Other Works.* http://www.godrules.net/library/luther/NEW1luther_c5.htm.

———. *Luther's Works.* Vol. 21. Saint Louis: Concordia, 1956.

Maahs, Kenneth H. "Chaos." In *International Standard Bible Encyclopedia*, edited by G. W. Bromiley et al., 1:633. Grand Rapids: Eerdmans, 1979.

MacKarness, Richard. "Occultism and Psychiatry." *Practitioner* 212 (1974) 363–66.

MacNutt, Francis. *Deliverance from Evil Spirits: A Practical Manual*. Grand Rapids: Chosen, 1995.

Mahoney, James. "Path Dependence in Historical Sociology." *Theory and Society* 29 (2000) 507–48.

Maier, Wolfgang. "Psychiatric Genetics." In *Psychiatric Genetics: Methods and Reviews*, edited by Marion Leboyer and Frank Bellivier, 3–21. Totawa, NJ: Humana, 2003.

Mainzer, Klaus. *Thinking in Complexity: The Computational Dynamics of Matter, Mind, and Mankind*. 4th ed. Berlin: Springer-Verlag, 2004.

Malamat, Abraham. "Doctrines of Causality in Hittite and Biblical Historiography: A Parallel." *Vetus Testamentum* 5 (1955) 1–12.

———. "The Secret Council and Prophetic Involvement in Mari and Israel." In *Prophetie und geschichtliche Wirklichkeit im alten Israel: Festschrift für Siegfried Hermann*, edited by Rüdiger Liwak and Siegfried Wagner, 231–36. Stuttgart: Kohlhammer, 1991.

Malaspina, Dolores, et al. "Acute Maternal Stress in Pregnancy and Schizophrenia in Offspring: A Cohort Prospective Study." *BMC Psychiatry* 8 (2008). http://www.biomedcentral.com/content/pdf/1471-244X-8-71.pdf.

Malony, H. Newton, and A. Adams Lovekin. *Glossolalia*. New York: Oxford University Press, 1985.

Mann, Robert B. "Inconstant Multiverse." *Perspectives on Science and Christian Faith* 57 (2005) 302–10.

Marais, M. A. "Information Concepts in the Science-Theology Dialogue." In *Design, Information and Complexity in Creation*, edited by C. W. Du Toit, 25–58. Unisa: Research Institute for Theology and Religion, University of South Africa, 2003.

Markopoulou, Fotini. "The Internal Description of a Causal Set: What the Universe Looks Like from the Inside." *Communications in Mathematical Physics* 211 (2000) 559–83. http://www.arxiv.org/abs/gr-qc/9811053.

Marks-Tarlow, Terry. "The Observer in the Observed: Fractal Dynamics of Re-entry." *Dynamical Psychology* (2002). http://www.goertzel.org/dynapsyc/2002/ObserverObserved.htm.

Marsella, S. C., et al. "PsychSim: Agent-Based Modeling of Social Interactions and Influence." In *Proceedings of the International Conference on Cognitive Modeling*, 36:243–48. Pittsburg, July 30–August 1, 2004. http://citeseerx.ist.psu.edu/viewdoc/download?doi=10.1.1.126.9185&rep=rep1&type=pdf.

Martyr, Justin. "Names of God and of Christ, Their Meaning and Power." In "The Second Apology of Justin Martyr," in Roberts and Donaldson, *Ante-Nicene Fathers*, 1:353.

Masters, Robert E. L., and Jean Houston. *The Varieties of Psychedelic Experience*. New York: Holt, Rinehart and Winston, 1966.

May, Herbert G. "Some Cosmic Connotations of MAYIM RABBÎM, 'Many Waters.'" *Journal of Biblical Literature* 74 (1955) 9–21.

May, L. Carlyle. "A Survey of Glossolalia and Related Phenomena in Non-Christian Religions." *American Anthropologist* 58 (1956) 75–96.

Mayer-Kress, Gottfried J., et al. "What Can We Learn from Learning Curves?" In *Unifying Themes in Complex Systems: Proceedings of the Second International Conference on Complex Systems*, vol. 2, edited by Yaneer Bar-yam and Ali Minai, 455–64. Boulder: Westview, 2003.

Mbon, Friday. "Deliverance in the Complaint Psalms: Religious Claim or Religious Experience?" *Studia Biblica et Theologica* 12 (1982) 3–15.

Mbonye, Manasse R. "Constraints on Cosmic Dynamics." Rochester Institute of Technology. 2003. http://scholarworks.rit.edu/cgi/viewcontent.cgi?article=1412&context=article.

———. "Cosmology with Interacting Dark Energy." *Modern Physics Letters A* 19 (2004) 117–34.

McCabe, Gordon. "The Structure and Interpretation of Cosmology: Part II—The Concept of Creation in Inflation and Quantum Cosmology." *Studies in History and Philosophy of Science Part B: Studies in History and Philosophy of Modern Physics* 36 (2005) 67–102.

McCartney, Dan G. "*Ecco Homo*: The Coming of the Kingdom as the Restoration of Human Vicegerency." *Westminster Theological Journal* 56 (1994) 1–21.

McCasland, S. V. "Spirit." In Buttrick, *Interpreter's Dictionary*, 4:434.

McClenon, James, and Jennifer Nooney. "Anomalous Experiences Reported by Field Anthropologists: Evaluating Theories Regarding Religion." *Anthropology of Consciousness* 13 (2002) 46–60.

McCormick, David, and Diego Contreras. "On the Cellular and Network Bases of Epileptic Seizures." *Annual Review of Physiology* 63 (2001) 815–46.

McCoy, Brad. "Chiasmus: An Important Structural Device Commonly Found in Biblical Literature." *Chafer Theological Seminary Journal* 9 (2003) 18–34.

McCrone, John, "The Theory Vacuum." *Dichotomistic*. http://www.dichotomistic.com/mind_readings_quantum%20mind.html.

McCullough, Lori. "Dimensions of the Temple Account in I Kings 5–9 Compared with Ancient Near Eastern Temple Paradigms." MA thesis, Vanderbilt University, 2007.

McFadden, T. M. "Canonization and Beautification (Western Church)." In *Encylopedic Dictionary of Religion*: *A/E*, edited by Paul Kevin Meagher et al., 616. Washington: Corpus, 1979.

McGraw, Gerald E. "Tongues Should Be Tested." *Alliance Witness* 109 (1974) 3–6.

McGregor, Cecil. Review of *Spirit Releasement Therapy: A Technique Manual*, 2nd ed., by William J. Baldwin. Terra Alta, WV: Headline, 1992. Original source of review is no longer available.

McGuffin, Peter, et al. "Mental Retardation." In *Seminars in Psychiatric Genetics*, 66–86. London: Royal College of Psychiatrists, 1994.

McGuire, William, ed. *Analytical Psychology: Notes of the Seminar Given in 1925*. Princeton: Princeton University Press, 1989.

McKenna, Terence. *Food of the Gods*. New York: Bantam, 1992.

McNamara, Martin. *Targum Neofiti 1: Deuteronomy*. Collegeville: Liturgical, 1997.

McRae, Cynthia, et al. "Effects of Perceived Treatment on Quality of Life and Medical Outcomes in a Double-Blind Placebo Surgery Trial." *Archives of General Psychiatry* 61 (2004) 412–20.

Meadows, Donella H. "Places to Intervene in a System." *Whole Earth* (1997). http://center.sustainability.duke.edu/sites/default/files/documents/system_intervention.pdf.

Meaney, J. "Nature, Nurture, and the Disunity of Knowledge." *Annals of the New York Academy of Sciences* 935 (2001) 50–61.

Medlicott, R. W. "An Inquiry into the Significance of Hallucinations with Special Reference to Their Occurrence in the Sane." *International Record of Medicine* 171 (1958) 664–77.

Meeter, Martijn. "Control of Consolidation in Neural Networks: Avoiding Runaway Effects." *Connection Science* 15 (2003) 45–61.

Meir, C. A., ed. *Atom and Archetype: The Pauli/Jung Letters, 1932–1958*. Princeton: Princeton University Press, 2001.

Mendelsohn, I. "Slavery in the OT." In Buttrick, *Interpreter's Dictionary*, 4:385.

Mendenhall, George E. "Ancient Oriental and Biblical Law." *Biblical Archaeologist* 17 (1954) 26–46.

Merkur, Daniel. "Unitive Experiences and the State of Trance." In *Mystical Union and Monotheistic Faith: An Ecumenical Dialogue*, edited by Moshe Idel and Bernard McGinn, 125–53, 175–83, 230–41. New York: Macmillan, 1989.

Meyer, Stephen C. "The Origin of Biological Information and the Higher Taxonomic Categories." *Proceedings of the Biological Society of Washington* 117 (2004) 213–39.

Michel, Denis. "Life Is a Self-Organizing Machine Driven by the Informational Cycle of Brillouin." *Origin of Life and Evolution of Biospheres* 43 (2013) 137–50.

Midrash Tanhuma. *Leviticus, Kedoshim 10*. In Jon D. Levenson, "The Temple and the World," *Journal of Religion* 64 (1984) 275–98.

Millard, A. R. "The Etymology of Eden." *Vetus Testamentum* 34 (1984) 103–6.

Miller, John. "The Pastorate and New Age Healing." *Pastoral Psychology* 27 (1978) 91–104.

Miller, Judith. "Mental Health, Mental Illness and Consciousness." Unpublished lecture from Second Inter-Professional Conference on Spirituality and Health-Care, University of Toronto, October 25, 2002.

———. "Mental Illness and Spiritual Crisis: Implications for Psychiatric Rehabilitation." *Psychosocial Rehabilitation Journal* 14 (1990) 29–47.

Miller, Stanley L. "A Production of Amino Acids under Possible Primitive Earth Conditions." *Science* 117 (1953) 528–29.

Milton, J. G., et al. "Controlling Neurological Disease at the Edge of Instability." In *Quantitative Neurosciences: Models, Algorithms, Diagnostics, and Therapeutic Applications*, edited by P. M. Pardalos and J. C. Sackellares, 119–45. Boston: Kluwer, 2004.

Mintz, Elizabeth E., and Gertrude R. Schmeidler. *The Psychic Thread: Paranormal and Transpersonal Aspects of Psychotherapy*. New York: Human Sciences, 1983.

Mishlove, Jeffrey. "Nina Kulagina: Unusual Powers of Mind over Matter." http://www.williamjames.com/Folklore/MINDOVER.htm.

———. *The PK Man*. Charlottesville, VA: Hampton Roads, 2000.

Mishlove, Jeffrey, and Michael Harner. *The Way of the Shaman*. Berkeley: Intuition Network. http://www.intuition.org/txt/harner.htm.

Modi, Shakuntala. *Remarkable Healings*. Charlottesville, VA: Hampton Roads, 1997.

Mohit, A. "Mental Health and Psychiatry in the Middle East: Historical Development." *Eastern Mediterranean Health Journal* 7 (2001) 336–47.

Monson, John. "The New 'Ain Dara Temple: Closest Solomonic Parallel." *Biblical Archaeology Review* 26 (2000) 20–35, 67.

Moo, Douglas. *The Epistle to the Romans*. Grand Rapids: Eerdmans, 1996.

Moor, Johannes C. de. "East of Eden." *Zeitschrift für die Alttestamentliche Wissenschaf* 100 (1988) 105–11.

Morgan, C. Lloyd. *Emergent Evolution*. London: Williams and Norgate, 1921.

Morris, Leon. *The Apostolic Preaching of the Cross*. Grand Rapids: Eerdmans, 1976.

———. *The Gospel according to John*. Grand Rapids: Eerdmans, 1971.

Morrison, David, et al. "Dealing with the Impact Hazard." In *Asteroids III*, by W. F. Bottke, 739–54. Tucson: University of Arizona Press, 2002.

Morse, Melvin. "The Right Temporal Lobe and Associated Limbic Structures as the Biological Interface with an Interconnected Universe." *Network* 12 (1999). http://www.spiritualscientific.com/yahoo_site_admin/assets/docs/THE_RIGHT_TEMPORAL_LOBE_AND_ASSOCIATED_LIMBIC_LOBE_STRUCTURES.67184922.pdf.

———. *Where God Lives: The Science of the Paranormal and How Our Brains Are Linked to the Universe*. With Paul Perry. New York: Cliff Street, 2000.

Mosher, Loren. "Letter of Resignation." *Psycho-Spiritual Dialogue* 2 (2002) 16–17.

"Mother Teresa Was Not Exorcised, Archbishop Says." *Zenit.org News Agency*, September 10, 2001. http://www.ewtn.com/vnews/getstory.asp?number=18682.

Mounce, Robert H. *The Book of Revelation*. Grand Rapids: Eerdmans, 1979.

Mousseau, Jacques. "Freud in Perspective." *Psychology Today* 6 (1973) 50–60.

Mowinkel, Sigmund. *The Psalms in Israel's Worship*. Vol. 1. Translated by D. R. Ap-Thomas. Oxford: Blackwell, 1967.

Mueser, Kim T., et al. "Trauma, PTSD, and the Course of Severe Mental Illness: An Interactive Model." *Schizophrenia Research* 53 (2002) 123–43.

Munday, John C. "Eden's Geography Erodes Flood Geology." *Westminster Theological Journal* 58 (1996) 123–54.

Murphy, Nancey. "Scientific Perspectives on Christian Anthropology." *CTI Reflections* 8 (2004/2005) 82–100.

Musca, Serban C., et al. "Creating False Memories in Humans with an Artificial Neural Network: Implications for Theories of Memory Consolidation." In *Proceedings of the 27th Annual Meeting of the Cognitive Science Society*, edited by B. G. Bara et al., 1576–81. Mahwah, NJ: Erlbaum, 2005.

Myers, Allen C. "Death." In *International Standard Bible Encyclopedia*, edited by G. W. Bromiley et al., 1:899–900. Grand Rapids: Eerdmans, 1979.

Myers, Carol L. *The Tabernacle Menorah: A Synthetic Study of a Symbol from the Biblical Cult*. Missoula: Scholars, 1976.

Myers, Frederic W. H. "Automatic Writing. IV. The Daemon of Socrates." *Proceedings of the Society for Psychical Research* 5 (1888–89) 522–47.

———. *Human Personality and Its Survival of Bodily Death*. Vol. 1. Reprint. New York: Arno, 1975.

———. *Human Personality and Its Survival of Bodily Death*. Vol. 2. Reprint. New York: Arno, 1975.

Myss, Carolyn. *Anatomy of the Spirit*. New York: Random House, 1996.

Nagel, Thomas. "The Psychophysical Nexus." In *Concealment and Exposure and Other Essays*, edited by Thomas Nagel, 194–236. New York: Oxford University Press, 2002.

———. "What Is It Like to Be a Bat?" *Philosophical Review* 83 (1974) 435–50.

Nagy, D., et al. "The Effect of Disorder on the Hierarchical Modularity in Complex Systems." *Fractals—Complex Geometry Patterns and Scaling in Nature and Society* 14 (2006) 101–10. http://arxiv.org/pdf/cond-mat/0506395v2.

Nasar, Sylvia. *A Beautiful Mind*. New York: Simon & Schuster, 1998.

Nash, John Forbes. "John F. Nash—Biographical." Nobelprize.org. 2014. http://www.nobelprize.org/nobel_prizes/economic-sciences/laureates/1994/nash-bio.html.

National Institute of Mental Health. "Any Mental Illness (AMI) among U.S. Adults." National Institute of Mental Health. http://www.nimh.nih.gov/health/statistics/prevalence/any-mental-illness-ami-among-us-adults.shtml.

Nauert, Charles G., Jr. *Agrippa and the Crisis of Renaissance Thought.* Urbana: University of Illinois Press, 1965.

Nee, Watchman. *The Latent Power of the Soul.* New York: Christian Fellowship, 1972.

Neiman, David. "Gihon and Pishon: Mythological Antecedents of the Two Enigmatic Rivers of Eden." In *Proceedings of the Sixth World Congress of Jewish Studies, August 13–19, 1973,* 1A:321–28. Jerusalem: World Union of Jewish Studies, 1977.

Neppe, Vernon M., and Lewis A. Hurst. "Psi, Genetics and the Temporal Lobe." *Parapsychological Journal of South Africa* 2 (1981) 35–55.

———. "Psychiatric Interpretations of Subjective Paranormal Perception." *Parapsychological Journal of South Africa* 3 (1982) 6–16.

Nesse, Randolph M. "Natural Selection and the Regulation of Defenses: A Signal Detection Analysis of the Smoke Detector Principle." *Evolution and Human Behavior* 26 (2005) 88–105.

Newberg, Andrew, et al. *Why God Won't Go Away.* New York: Ballantine, 2001.

Nicholson, Philip. "Response." *Subtle Energies and Energy Medicine Journal* 7 (1996) 273–83.

Doige, Norman. "Building a Better Brain." *Saturday Night,* May 1, 2001, 22–29. http://www.arrowsmithschool.org/arrowsmithprogram-background/pdf/building_a_better_brain.pdf.

Niditch, Susan. "The Cosmic Adam: Man as Mediator in Rabbinic Literature." *Journal of Jewish Studies* 34 (1983) 137–46.

Niebuhr, H. Richard. *Christ and Culture.* New York: Harper & Row, 1951.

Nieder, Andreas, and Earl K. Miller. "Coding of Cognitive Magnitude: Compressed Scaling of Numerical Information in the Primate Prefrontal Cortex." *Neuron* 37 (2003) 149–57.

Nimtz, G., and A. Haibel. "Basics of Superluminal Signals." *Annals of Physics* 11 (2002) 163–71. http://arxiv.org/pdf/physics/0104063.

Nisbet, J. F. *The Insanity of Genius.* 4th ed. Folcroft, PA: Folcroft Library Editions, 1973.

Norwich, Kenneth H., and Willy Wong. "Unification of Psychophysical Phenomena: The Complete Form of Fechner's Law." *Perception & Psychophysics* 59 (1997) 929–40.

Noth, Martin. "Old Testament Covenant Making in the Light of a Text from Mari." In *The Laws in the Pentateuch and Other Studies,* by Martin Noth, translated by D. R. Ap-Thomas, 108–17. Edinburgh: Oliver & Boyd, 1966.

O'Connor, J. J., and E. F. Robertson. "John Forbes Nash." http://www-history.mcs.st-andrews.ac.uk/Biographies/Nash.html.

O'Hare, Michael J., et al. "Conditional Immortalization of Freshly Isolated Human Mammary Fibroblasts and Endothelial Cells." *Proceedings of the National Academy of Sciences USA* 98 (2001) 646–51.

Oepke, T. "κενὸν." In *Theological Dictionary of the New Testament,* edited by Gerhard Kittel et al., 3:659. Grand Rapids: Eerdmans, 1964–1976.

Oesterreich, T. K. *Possession: Demonical and Other.* Seacaucus, NY: University Books, 1966.

Omlin, Christian W., and C. Lee Giles. "Extraction of Rules from Discrete-Time Recurrent Neural Networks." *Neural Networks* 9 (1996) 41–52.

Ontario Consultants on Religious Tolerance. "Limbo: The Destination of Unbaptized Newborns and Infants if They Die?" ReligiousTolerance.org. December 19, 2010. http://www.religioustolerance.org/limbo.htm.

Origen. "Against Celsus." In Roberts and Donaldson, *Ante-Nicene Fathers,* 4:1173.

Orr, William F., and James Arthur Walther. *I Corinthians.* Anchor Bible. Garden City: Doubleday, 1976.

Os, Jim van. "Is There a Continuum of Psychotic Experiences in the General Population?" *Epidemiologia e Psichiatria Sociale* 12 (2003) 242–52.

Osis, K., and E. Haraldsson. "OOBEs in Indian Swamis: Sathya Sai Baba and Dadaji." In *Research in Parapsychology 1975*, edited by J. D. Morris et al., 147–50. Metuchen, NJ: Scarecrow, 1976.

Ostling, Richard N. "There Is a God, Atheist Believes." *Toronto Star*, December 10, 2004.

Ostoma, Tom, and Mike Trushyk. "What Are the Hidden Quantum Processes behind Newton's Laws? EMQG, CA Theory, Quantum Inertia, and Newtonian Physics." http://www.arxiv.org/abs/physics/9904036.

Oswalt, John N. *The Book of Isaiah Chapters 1–39*. Grand Rapids: Eerdmans, 1986.

———. "The Myth of the Dragon and Old Testament Faith." *Evangelical Quarterly* 49 (1977) 163–72.

Otis, George. *The Twilight Labyrinth*. Grand Rapids: Chosen, 1998.

Ott, Edward. "Crises." *Scholarpedia* 1 (2006) 1700. http://scholarpedia.org/article/Crises.

Otto, Rudolf. "Signs Following." Appendix 7 of *The Idea of the Holy*, by Rudolf Otto, translated by John W. Harvey. London: Oxford University Press, 1925.

Owens, Claire Myers. "Zen Buddhism." In *Transpersonal Psychologies*, edited by Charles T. Tart, 153–202. New York: Harper & Row, 1975.

Owens, Lance S. "Joseph Smith and Kabbalah: The Occult Connection." *Dialogue: A Journal of Mormon Thought* 27 (1994) 117–94.

Paczuski, Maya, and Per Bak. "Self-Organization of Complex Systems." June 5, 1999. http://www.arxiv.org/abs/cond-mat/9906077v1.

Pagels, Heinz. *Perfect Symmetry: The Search for the Beginning of Time*. London: Penguin, 1992.

Pahnke, Walter N., and William A. Richards. "Implications of LSD and Experimental Mysticism." *Journal of Religion and Health* 5 (1966) 175–208.

Palmer, John. "A Community Mail Survey of Psychic Experiences." *Journal of the American Society for Psychical Research* 73 (1979) 221–50.

Parazzini, Fabio, et al. "Trend of Spontaneous Abortions in Italy 1980–1991." *Human Reproduction* 11 (1996) 914. humrep.oxfordjournals.org/content/11/4/914.full.pdf.

Parham, Charles F. *The Everlasting Gospel*. Baxter Springs, KS: Apostolic Faith Bible College, 1911.

———. "The Latter Rain." In *The Life of Charles F. Parham*, by Sarah Parham, 51–58. New York: Garland, 1985. Original: Joplin, MO: Tri-state Printing, 1930.

Parker, Adrian. "What Can Cognitive Psychology and Parapsychology Tell Us about Near-Death Experiences?" *Journal of the Society for Psychical Research* 65 (2001) 225–40.

Pasemann, Frank, and Nico Stollenwerk. "Attractor Switching by Neural Control of Chaotic Neurodynamics." *Max-Planck-Institute for Mathematics in the Sciences Preprint 7 D-04103*. Leipzig, 1998. http://www.mis.mpg.de/preprints/1998/preprint1998_7.pdf.

Patrides, C. A. "The Salvation of Satan." *Journal of the History of Ideas* 28 (1967) 467–78.

Patterson, R. D., and Hermann J. Austel. *1 Kings*. In *1 Kings–Job*, edited by Frank E. Gaebelein et al. Expositor's Bible Commentary 4. Grand Rapids: Zondervan, 1988.

Paulk, Earl. *Satan Unmasked*. Atlanta: K Dimension, 1984.

Paulus, Martin P., and David L. Braff. "Chaos and Schizophrenia: Does the Method Fit the Madness?" *Biological Psychiatry* 53 (2003) 3–11.

PBS. "Secret of the Wild Child." March 4, 1997. http://www.pbs.org/wgbh/nova/transcripts/2112gchild.html.

Peacocke, Arthur. "The Sciences of Complexity: A New Theological Resource?" In *Information and the Nature of Reality from Physics to Metaphysics*, edited by Paul Davies and Niels Henrik Gregersen, 249–81. Cambridge: Cambridge University Press, 2010.

Pearlson, Godfrey D., and Bradley S. Folley. "Schizophrenia, Psychiatric Genetics, and Darwinian Psychiatry: An Evolutionary Framework." *Schizophrenia Bulletin* 34 (2008) 722–33.

Peat, F. David. "Chaos: The Geometrization Of Thought." In *Chaos Theory in Psychology and Life Sciences*, edited by R. Robertson and A. Combs, 359–72. Mahwah, NJ: Erlbaum, 1995.

Peck, M. Scott. *People of the Lie*. New York: Simon & Schuster, 1983.

Pecora, Louis M., et al. "Fundamentals of Synchronization in Chaotic Systems, Concepts, and Applications." *Chaos* 7 (1997) 520–43.

Penfield, Wilder. "Psychical Hallucinations." In *Epilepsy and the Functional Anatomy of the Human Brain*, edited by W. Penfield and H. H. Jasper, 452–69. Boston: Little, Brown, 1954.

Penn-Lewis, Jesse. *Soul and Spirit: A Glimpse into Bible Psychology*. Poole, UK: Overcomer, n.d.

———. *War on the Saints*. With Evan Roberts. 9th ed. New York: Lowe, 1973.

Penrose, Roger. *The Emperor's New Mind*. Oxford: Oxford University Press, 1989.

———. *The Large, the Small and the Human Mind*. Cambridge: Cambridge University Press, 1999.

Perazzo, Carlos A., et al. "Large Scale-Invariant Fluctuations in Normal Blood Cell Counts: A Sign of Criticality?" *Fractals* 8 (2001) 279–83. http://arxiv.org/pdf/physics/0005029.

Perlovsky, Leonid I. "Physical Theory of Information Processing in the Mind: Concepts and Emotions." *SEED* 2 (2002) 36–54.

Perrin, Mary Karine Kleinhaus, et al. "Critical Periods and the Developmental Origins of Disease: An Epigenetic Perspective of Schizophrenia." *Annals of the New York Academy of Sciences* 1204 (2010) 8–13. http://www.ncbi.nlm.nih.gov/pmc/articles/PMC4180658.

Persinger, Michael A., and Katherine Makarec. "Temporal Lobe Epileptic Signs and Correlative Behaviors Displayed by Normal Populations." *Journal of General Psychology* 114 (1987) 179–95.

Peters, Ted. *Playing God: Genetic Determinism and Human Freedom*. New York: Routledge, 1997.

Peterson, H. Donl. "What Is the Meaning of the Book of Mormon Scriptures on Eternal Hell for the Wicked?" *Ensign* (1986) 36–38. https://www.lds.org/ensign/1986/04/i-have-a-question?lang=eng.

Petrov, Plamen. "The Church-Turing Thesis as an Immature Form of the Zuse-Fredkin Thesis (More Arguments in Support of the 'Universe as a Cellular Automaton' Idea)." http://citeseerx.ist.psu.edu/viewdoc/download?doi=10.1.1.127.7634&rep=rep1&type=pdf.

Pezzulo, Giovanni, and Gianguglielmo Calvi. "A Pandemonium Can Have Goals." In *Proceedings of the Sixth International Conference on Cognitive Modeling*, 237–42. Mahwah, NJ: Erlbaum, 2004. http://iccm-conference.org/2004/proceedings/papers/Pezzulo.pdf.

Philo. "On the Life of Moses." In *Philo VI*, translated by F. H. Colson, bk. 2, sec. 114, 503–4. Cambridge: Harvard University Press, 1984.

———. "On the Migration of Abraham." In *Philo VI*, translated by F. H. Colson, sec. 191, 103. Cambridge: Harvard University Press, 1984.

Pigliucci, Massimo. "Design Yes, Intelligent No: A Critique of Intelligent Design Theory and Neocreationism." *Sceptical Inquirer* 25 (2001) 34–39.
Pizzamiglio, et al. "Language Disorder in a Child with Early Left Thalamic Lesion." *Neurocase* 10 (2004) 308–15.
Plantinga, Alvin. *Does God Have a Nature?* Milwaukee: Marquette University Press, 1980.
Plato. "Timaeus." In *Plato in Twelve Volumes*, translated by W. R. M. Lamb, vol. 9. Cambridge: Harvard University Press, 1925. http://www.perseus.tufts.edu/hopper/text?doc=Perseus%3Atext%3A1999.01.0180%3Atext%3DTim.%3Asection%3D30c.
Plunkett, Luke. "The Banned Pokémon Episode That Gave Children Seizures." *Kotaku*. October 20, 2015. http://www.kotaku.com/5757570/the-banned-pokemon-episode-that-gave-children-seizures.
Poe, Edgar Allan. *Eureka—A Prose Poem*. Urbana: University of Illinois Press, 2004.
Polkinghorne, J. C. *Belief in God in an Age of Science*. New Haven: Yale University Press, 1998.
———. "Creatio Continua and Divine Action." *Science and Christian Belief* 7 (1995) 101–8.
———. *Reason and Reality*. Philadelphia: Trinity, 1991.
———. *Science and the Trinity*. New Haven: Yale University Press, 2004.
———. "Theological Notions of Creation and Divine Causality." In *Science and Theology: Questions at the Interface*, edited by Murray Rae et al., 225–37. Edinburgh: T. & T. Clark, 1994.
Poloma, Margaret M. "The 'Toronto Blessing': Charisma, Institutionalization, and Revival." *Journal for the Scientific Study of Religion* 36 (1997) 257–71.
Polyani, Michael. "Life's Irreducible Structure." *Journal of the American Scientific Affiliation* 22 (1970) 123–31.
———. *Personal Knowledge: Towards a Post-Critical Philosophy*. London: Routledge & Paul, 1958.
Pomponius Mela. *De Situ Orbis*. Translated by E. Spedicato, Appendix 1, 59. In "On the Reversal of the Rotational Momentum of Earth: A Derivation and Analysis of the Herodotus Equation," by E. Spedicato. http://www.unibg.it/dati/bacheca/63/21825.pdf.
Pope, Alexander. "Essay on Man." In *Project Gutenberg eBook*, edited by Henry Morley, Epistle I, VIII. http://www.gutenberg.org/files/2428/2428-h/2428-h.htm.
Pope, Marvin H. *Job*. Anchor Bible. Garden City: Doubleday, 1983.
———. "Number, Numbering, Numbers." In Buttrick, *Interpreter's Dictionary*, 3:563–64.
Popper, Karl. *The Logic of Scientific Discovery*. London: Hutchinson, 1959.
———. *Three Worlds: The Tanner Lecture on Human Values*. Ann Arbor: University of Michigan Press, 1978. http://tannerlectures.utah.edu/_documents/a-to-z/p/popper80.pdf.
Porteous, N. W. "Image of God." In Buttrick, *Interpreter's Dictionary*, 2:683.
Portnoy, Stephen L., and David L. Petersen. "Genesis, Wellhausen and the Computer: A Response." *Zeitschrift für die Alttestamentliche Wissenschaf* 96 (1984) 421–25.
Posner, M. I., et al. "Localization of Cognitive Operations in the Human Brain." *Science* 240 (1988) 1627–31.
"Prayer to Saint Blaise." Eternal Word Television Network. https://www.ewtn.com/Devotionals/novena/blaise.htm.
Prentiss, Henry. "Pentecost in San Jose and Portland." *Apostolic Faith* 1 (1907) 22. Paper # 8. http://www.apostolicfaith.org/Library/Index/AzusaPapers.aspx.
Pretorius, Mark. "Justification as It Relates to Adam and Christ within the New Covenant." *Conspectus* 1 (2006) 43–64.

Prewitt, Terry J. *The Elusive Covenant: A Structural-Semiotic Reading of Genesis.* Bloomington: Indiana University Press, 1990.

Pribram, Karl H. "Brain and the Composition of Conscious Experience." *Journal of Consciousness Studies* 6 (1999) 19–42.

Price, John S., and Leon Sloman. "The Evolutionary Model of Psychiatric Disorder." *Archives of General Psychiatry* 41 (1984) 211.

Prince, N. H. E. "Simulated Worlds, Physical Eschatology, the Finite Nature Hypothesis and the Final Anthropic Principle." *International Journal of Astrobiology* 4 (2005) 204–10.

Pritchard, James B. "The Myth of Zu." In *Ancient Near Eastern Texts Relating to the Old Testament,* edited by James B. Pritchard, 112–13. 2nd ed. Princeton: Princeton University Press, 1955.

Proctor, M. T. "The God Attachment Interview Schedule: Implicit and Explicit Assessment of Attachment to God." PsychD diss., University of Western Sydney, 2006. http://researchdirect.uws.edu.au/islandora/object/uws%3A2388/datastream/PDF/view.

Public Health Agency of Canada. "A Report on Mental Illnesses in Canada." Table 1.1 http://www.phac-aspc.gc.ca/publicat/miic-mmac/chap_1-eng.php.

Puthoff, Harold E. "The Energetic Vacuum: Implications for Energy Research." *Speculations in Science & Technology* 13 (1990) 47–57.

———. "Everything for Nothing." *New Scientist* 1727 (1990) 52–55.

———. "Source of Vacuum Electromagnetic Zero-Point Energy." *Physical Review A* 40 (1989) 4857–62.

Quenette, P. Y., and J. F. Gerard. "Why Biologists Do Not Think like Newtonian Physicists." *Oikos* 68 (1993) 361–63.

Quinn, Janet F. "Therapeutic Touch as Energy Exchange: Testing the Theory." *Advances in Nursing Science* 6 (1984) 42–49.

Radday, Yehuda T., et al. "Genesis, Wellhausen and the Computer." *Zeitschrift für die Alttestamentliche Wissenschaf* 94 (1982) 467–81.

Radeau, Monique. "Auditory-Visual Interactions in Spatial Scene Analysis: Development and Neural Bases." In *Third Annual Auditory-Visual Speech Processing Conference December 4–6, 1998,* edited by Denis Burnham et al., 97–102. Terrigal: New South Wales, Australia. http://www.isca-speech.org/archive_open/archive_papers/avsp98/av98_097.pdf.

Rahner, Karl. *Theological Investigations.* Vol. 5, *Later Writings.* Translated by Karl-H. Kruger. Baltimore: Helican, 1966.

Rakestraw, Robert V. "Becoming Like God: An Evangelical Doctrine of Theosis." *Journal of the Evangelical Theological Society* 40 (1997) 257–69.

Rakova, Marina. *The Extent of the Literal: Metaphor, Polysemy and Theories of Concepts.* Basingstoke, UK: Palgrave Macmillan, 2003.

Ram, Pandit Sri, and Ramanuja Achari. *The Cosmic Game: A Comparative Study between Hinduism & Christianity.* Sydney: Simha, 2005.

Ramachandran, V. S., and E. M. Hubbard. "Phantoms in the Brain." *2003 Reith Lecture.* BBC Radio, April 2, 2003. http://www.bbc.co.uk/radio4/reith2003/lecture1.shtml.

———. "Synaesthesia—A Window into Perception, Thought and Language." *Journal of Consciousness Studies* 8 (2001) 3–34.

Rankin, A. M., and P. J. Philip. "An Epidemic of Laughing in the Bukoba District of Tanganyika." *Central African Journal of Medicine* 9 (1963) 167–70.

Read, J., et al. "Childhood Trauma, Psychosis and Schizophrenia: A Literature Review with Theoretical and Clinical Implications." *Acta Psychiatrica Scandinavica* 112 (2005) 330–50.

Read, John, et al. "The Contribution of Early Traumatic Events to Schizophrenia in Some Patients: A Traumagenic Neurodevelopmental Model." *Psychiatry* 64 (2001) 319–245.

Recami, Erasmo. "Superluminal Tunnelling through Successive Barriers: Does QM Predict Infinite Group-Velocities?" *Journal of Modern Optics* 51 (2004) 913–23.

Reeves, Alexander G. *Disorders of the Nervous System: A Primer*. Chicago: Year Book Medical, 1981.

Reichenbach, Bruce. "By His Stripes We Are Healed." *Journal of the Evangelical Theological Society* 41 (1998) 551–60.

Reisch, George. "Chaos, History, and Narrative." *History and Theory* 30 (1991) 1–20.

Reiter Joel M., and Donna Joy Andrews. "A Neurobehavioral Approach for Treatment of Complex Partial Epilepsy: Efficacy?" *Seizure* 9 (2000) 198–203.

Renggli, Franz. "The Sunrise as the Birth of a Baby: The Prenatal Key to Egyptian Mythology." *Journal of Prenatal and Perinatal Psychology and Health* 16 (2002) 215–35.

Reulbach, Udo, et al. "Late-Onset Schizophrenia in Child Survivors of the Holocaust." *Journal of Nervous and Mental Disease* 195 (2007) 315–19.

Reynolds, Craig W. "Flocks, Herds, and Schools: A Distributed Behavioral Model." *Computer Graphics* 21 (1987) 25–34.

Richardson, Lewis Fry. "Frequency of Occurrence of Wars and Other Fatal Quarrels." *Nature* 148 (1941) 598.

Richet, Charles. *Thirty Years of Psychical Research*. London: Collins, 1923.

Rifkin, Jeremy. *Algeny*. New York: Viking, 1983.

Ring, Kenneth, and Sharon Cooper. *Mindsight: Near-Death and Out-of-Body Experiences in the Blind*. Palo Alto, CA: William James Center for Consciousness Studies, 1999.

———. "Religious Aspects of Near-Death Experiences: Some Research Findings and Their Implications." *Journal of the Academy of Religion and Psychical Research* 3 (1980) 105–14.

Ringach, Dario L. "Spontaneous and Driven Cortical Activity: Implications for Computation." *Current Opinion in Neurobiology* 19 (2009) 439–44. http://www.ncbi.nlm.nih.gov/pmc/articles/PMC3319344.

Ritchie, George G. *Ordered to Return: My Life After Dying*. Norfolk, VA: Hampton Roads, 1998.

Robertson, Archibald, and Alfred Plummer. *A Critical and Exegetical Commentary on the First Epistle of St. Paul to the Corinthians*. Edinburgh: T. & T. Clark, 1911.

Robertson, Robin. *Jungian Archetypes: Jung, Gödel, and the History of Archetypes*. York Beach, ME: Nicolas-Hayes, 1995.

Robinson, B. A. "Catholic Statements about the Fate of Unbaptized Newborns, Infants, etc., During the 20th Century." *Ontario Consultants on Religious Tolerance*. http://www.religioustolerance.org/limbo2a.htm.

———. "Satan: Diversity of Beliefs about Satan by the General Public." *Ontario Consultants on Religious Tolerance*. http://www.religioustolerance.org/chr_sat4.htm.

Rogo, D. Scott. *The Infinite Boundary: A Psychic Look at Spirit Possession, Madness, and Multiple Personality*. New York: Dodd, Mead, 1987.

Rohl, David. *Legend: The Genesis of Civilisation*. London: Century, 1995.

Roland, P. E., et al. "Supplementary Motor Area and Other Cortical Areas in Organization of Voluntary Movements in Man." *Journal of Neurophysiology* 43 (1980) 118–36.

Roll, William G. "Poltergeists, Electromagnetism and Consciousness." *Journal of Scientific Exploration* 17 (2003) 75–86.

Rosenbaum, Stanley N. "Israelite Homicide Law and the Term 'Enmity' in Genesis 3:15." *Journal of Law and Religion* 2 (1984) 145–51.

Rosenberg, Gregg H. "Rethinking Nature: A Hard Problem within the Hard Problem." *Journal of Consciousness Studies* 3 (1996) 76–88.

Rosenberg, Harriet J., et al. "A Comparative Study of Trauma and Posttraumatic Stress Disorder Prevalance in Epilepsy Patients and Psychogenic Nonepileptic Seizure Patients." *Epilepsia* 41 (2000) 447–52.

Ross, Allan P. "The Curse of Canaan." *Bibliotheca Sacra* 137 (1980) 228–40.

Ross, Colin A. "Conclusion: A Trauma Model." In *Pseudoscience in Biological Psychiatry: Blaming the Body*, edited by Colin A. Ross and Alvin Pam, 273–78. New York: Wiley, 1995.

Ross, Colin A., and Shaun Joshi. "Paranormal Experiences in the General Population." *Journal of Nervous and Mental Disease* 180 (1992) 357–61.

Ross, Colin A., and Alvin Pam. *Pseudoscience in Biological Psychiatry: Blaming the Body*. New York: Wiley, 1995.

Ross, Scott. "Son of Sam Becomes Son of Hope." *Christian Broadcasting Network*. http://www.cbn.com/700club/scottross/interviews/SonofSam.aspx.

Rosser, J. Barkley, Jr. "Aspects of Dialectics and Nonlinear Dynamics." *Cambridge Journal of Economics* 24 (2000) 311–24.

———. "On the Complexities of Complex Economic Dynamics." *Journal of Economic Perspectives* 13 (1999) 169–92.

Ruark, A. E. "Falsities of Modern Tongues." In *Quiet Warrior*, by Dorothy Brotherton, 153–67. Beaverlodge, Alberta: Spectrum, 1991.

Ruse, Michael. "Is Evolution a Secular Religion?" *Science* 299 (2003) 1523–24.

Russell, Jeffrey Burton. *Lucifer: The Devil in the Middle Ages*. Ithaca: Cornell University Press, 1984.

Russell, Robert John. "Eschatology and Scientific Cosmology: From Conflict to Interaction." *Witherspoon Lecture*. Princeton: Center of Theological Inquiry, 2004. http://static1.1.sqspcdn.com/static/f/38692/411739/1254137183593/Eschatology+and+Scientific+Cosmology+-+From+Conflict+to+Interaction.pdf?token=WLkwYtvqz9PDyhBd1hjtFpsBhSY%3D.

———. Introduction to *Quantum Cosmology and the Laws of Nature: Scientific Perspectives on Divine Action*, 1–31. Vatican City: Vatican Observatory, 1993.

Sabom, Michael. *Light and Death*. Grand Rapids: Zondervan, 1998.

———. *Recollections of Death: A Medical Investigation*. New York: Harper & Row, 1982.

Sackellares, J. Chris, et al. "Epilepsy—When Chaos Fails." In *Chaos in the Brain*, edited by K. Lehnertz and C. E. Elger, 112–33. Singapore: World Scientific, 2000. http://citeseerx.ist.psu.edu/viewdoc/download?doi=10.1.1.42.650&rep=rep1&type=pdf.

Salatin, Joel. *Folks, This Ain't Normal*. New York: Center Street, 2011.

Salmon, Peter, et al. "Childhood Family Dysfunction and Associated Abuse in Patients with Nonepileptic Seizures: Towards a Causal Model." *Psychosomatic Medicine* 65 (2003) 695–700.

"Salvation, The Gift of." *First Things* 79 (1998) 20–23.

Samarin, William J. "Evolution in Glossolalic Private Language." *Anthropological Linguistics* 13 (1971) 55–67.

———. "Glossolalia as Regressive Speech." *Language and Speech* 16 (1973) 77–89.

———. *Tongues of Men and Angels: The Religious Language of Pentecostalism*. New York: Macmillan, 1972.

Sanella, Lee. *Kundalini—Psychosis or Transcendence?* San Francisco: Dakin, 1976.

Sanford, Agnes. *Sealed Orders*. Plainfield, NJ: Logos International, 1972.

Sarantidis, Constantine. "God, Miracles and Quantum Mechanics." In *Health and Faith: Medical, Psychological and Religious Dimensions*, edited by John T. Chirban, 127–33. Lanham, MD: University Press of America, 1991.

Sarbadhikari, S. N., and K. Chakrabarty. "Chaos in the Brain: A Short Review Alluding to Epilepsy, Depression, Exercise and Lateralization." *Medical Engineering and Physics* 23 (2003) 445–55.

Sarna, Nahum. "Epic Substratum in the Prose of Job." *Journal of Biblical Literature* 76 (1957) 13–25.

Sarukkai, Sundar. "Revisiting the 'Unreasonable Effectiveness' of Mathematics." *Current Science* 88 (2005) 415–23.

Sasson, Diane. *The Shaker Spiritual Narrative*. Knoxville: University of Tennessee Press, 1983.

Satinover, Jeffrey. *The Quantum Brain*. New York: Wiley, 2001.

Sauer, Erich. *The Dawn of World Redemption*. London: Paternoster, 1964.

———. *The King of the Earth: The Nobility of Man according to the Bible and Science*. London: Paternoster, 1962.

Sauer, J. A. "The River Runs Dry—Creation Story Preserves Historical Memory." *Biblical Archaeology Review* 22 (1996) 52–57, 64.

Saussure, Ferdinand de. *Course in General Linguistics*. Translated by Wade Baskin. London: Owen, 1964.

Saver, Jeffrey L., and John Rabin. "The Neural Substrates of Religious Experience." *Neuropsychiatry* 9 (1997) 498–510.

Schaefer, Hildegard. "Klaus Schreiber and Martin Wenzel and their Video Images." In *Bridge between the Terrestrial and the Beyond: Theory and Practice of Transcommunication*, translated by Heidemarie Hallmann, 203–21. Freiburg im Breisgau: Bauer, 1989. http://www.worlditc.org/c_04_s_bridge_content.htm.

Scharen, Hans. "Gehenna in the Synoptics, Part 1." *Bibliotheca Sacra* 155 (1998) 324–37.

Scheibel, Madge E., and Arnold B. Scheibel, "Hallucinations and the Brain Stem Reticular Core." In *Hallucinations*, edited by Louis Jolyon West, 15–35. New York: Grune & Stratton, 1962.

Schlier, Heinrich. *Principalities and Powers in the New Testament*. New York: Herder & Herder, 1961.

Schmidhuber, Jürgen. "In the Beginning was the Code." Transcript of TEDx talk, Belgium, March 15, 2013. http://www.kurzweilai.net/in-the-beginning-was-the-code.

Schmid-Schönbein, Christiane. "Improvement of Seizure Control by Psychological Methods in Patients with Intractable Epilepsies." *Seizure* 7 (1998) 261–70.

Schore, Allan N. "Effects of a Secure Attachment Relationship on Right Brain Development, Affect Regulation and Infant Mental Health." *Infant Mental Health Journal* 22 (2001) 12–17.

Schultes, Richard Evans, and Albert Hofmann. *Plants of the Gods: Origins of Hallucinogenic Use*. New York: McGraw-Hill, 1979.

Schwartz, Hans. "Modern Scientific Theories of the Future and Christian Eschatology." *Word and World* 16 (1996) 473–81.

Schweizer, Eduard. "Slaves of the Elements and Worshipers of Angels: Gal. 4:3, 9 and Col. 2:8, 18, 20." *Journal of Biblical Literature* 107 (1988) 455–68.

Searle, John R. "Consciousness." *Annual Review of Neuroscience* 23 (2000) 557–78.

Sechehaye, Marguerite. *Autobiography of a Schizophrenic Girl*. Translated by Grace Rubin-Rabson. New York: Grune & Stratton, 1951.

Seife, Charles. *Alpha & Omega: The Search for the Beginning and End of the Universe*. New York: Viking, 2003.

Selms, A. van. "Scapegoat." In *New Bible Dictionary*, edited by J. D. Douglas, 1066. Downers Grove: InterVarsity, 1996.

Semah, F., et al. "Is the Underlying Cause of Epilepsy a Major Prognostic Factor for Recurrence?" *Neurology* 51 (1998) 1256–62.

Setiloane, Gabriel M. "How the Traditional World-View Persists in the Christianity of the Sotho-Tswana." *Pula: Botswana Journal of African Studies* 1 (1978) 27–42. https://archive.lib.msu.edu/DMC/African%20Journals/pdfs/PULA/pula001001/pula001001003.pdf.

Shamdasani, Sonu. "Encountering Hélène: Théodore Flournoy and the Genesis of Subliminal Psychology." In *From India to the Planet Mars*, by Théodore Flournoy. Original translation (1901) by Daniel B. Vermilye, xix–li. Princeton: Princeton University Press, 1994.

Shanks, Hershel. "God as Divine Kinsman: What Covenant Meant in Ancient Israel." *Biblical Archaeology Review* 25 (1999) 32–33, 60.

Shattuck, Roger. "Afterward: A Mind of One's Own." In *The Story of My Life*, by Helen Keller, 429–54. New York: Norton, 2003.

Shaw, Sandy, and Paul Shapshak. "Fractal Genomics Modeling: A New Approach to Genomic Analysis and Biomarker Discovery." In *3rd International IEEE Computer Society Computational Systems Bioinformatics Conference, August 16–19, 2004*, 9–17. Stanford, CA: IEEE Computer Society, 2004.

Shealy, Norman. *Occult Medicine Can Save Your Life*. With Arthur S. Freese. New York: Dial, 1975.

Sheikh, Anees A., et al. "Somatic Consequences of Consciousness." In *The Science of Consciousness: Psychological, Neuropsychological and Clinical Reviews*, edited by Max Velmans, 140–61. London: Routledge, 1996.

Sheldrake, Rupert. *A New Science of Life*. London: Bland & Briggs, 1981.

Shen, B.-W., et al. "The 0.125 Degree Finite-Volume General Circulation Model on the NASA Columbia Supercomputer: Preliminary Simulations of Mesoscale Vortices." *Geophysical Research Letters* 33 (2006). http://onlinelibrary.wiley.com/doi/10.1029/2005GL024594/full.

Sherrill, John. *They Speak with Other Tongues*. New York: McGraw-Hill, 1964.

Shiner, Roger A. "Justice in the Garden of Eden." *Philosophy* 63 (1988) 301–16.

Shubin, Neil H., and Charles R. Marshall. "Fossils, Genes, and the Origin of Novelty." In *Deep Time: Paleobiology's Perspective, Supplement to Vol. 26, No. 4*, edited by Douglas H. Erwin and Scott L. Wing, 324–40. Lawrence, KS: Paleontological Society, 2000.

Siegel, Daniel J. "Toward an Interpersonal Neurobiology of the Developing Mind: Attachment Relationships, 'Mindsight,' and Neural Integration." *Infant Mental Health Journal* 22 (2001) 67–94.

Sikkema, Arnold E. "A Physicist's Reformed Critique of Nonreductive Physicalism and Emergence." *Pro Rege* 33 (2005) 20–32.

Simon, M. D., and A. K. Geim. "Diamagnetic Levitation: Flying Frogs and Floating Magnets." *Journal of Applied Physics* 87 (2000) 6200–204.

Simonetti, Manlio, and Marco Conti, eds. *Ancient Christian Commentary on Scripture, Old Testament VI: Job*. Downers Grove: InterVarsity, 2006.

Simpson, Cuthbert A. *Genesis*. Vol. 1 of *Interpreter's Bible*. Nashville: Abingdon, 1980.

Sipper, Moshe, and Marco Tomassini. "Generating Parallel Random Number Generators by Cellular Programming." *International Journal of Modern Physics C* 7 (1996) 181–90. http://citeseerx.ist.psu.edu/viewdoc/download?doi=10.1.1.21.870&rep=rep1&type=pdf.

Slater, Eliot, and A. W. Beard. "The Schizophrenia-like Psychoses of Epilepsy, i. Psychiatric Aspects." *British Journal of Psychiatry* 109 (1963) 95–112.

Slater, Victoria E. "Toward an Understanding of Energetic Healing, Part I: Energetic Structures: The Quantum Field and Chaos Theory." *Journal of Holistic Nursing* 13 (1995) 209–24.

Slotkin, J. S. "The Peyote Way." In *Reader in Comparative Religion: An Anthropological Approach*, edited by William A. Lessa and Evon Z. Vogt, 513–17. Evanston, IL: Row, Peterson, 1958.

Sluhovsky, Moshe. "The Devil in the Convent." *American Historical Review* 107 (2002) 1379–411.

Slutzky, Marc W., et al. "Deterministic Chaos and Noise in Three *In Vitro* Hippocampal Models of Epilepsy." *Annals of Biomedical Engineering* 29 (2001) 607–18.

Slutzky, Marc W., et al. "Manipulating Epileptiform Bursting in the Rat Hippocampus Using Chaos Control and Adaptive Techniques." *IEEE Transactions on Biomedical Engineering* 50 (2003) 559–70.

Smedes, Taede. "Chaos: Where Science and Religion Meet? A Critical Evaluation of the Use of Chaos Theory in Theology." In *Studies in Science & Theology 8: Yearbook of the European Society for the Study of Science and Theology 2001-2002*, edited by N. H. Gregersen et al., 277–94. Århus: Århus University Press, 2002.

Smick, Elmer. *Job*. In *1 Kings–Job*, edited by Frank E. Gaebelien et al. Expositor's Bible Commentary 4. Grand Rapids: Zondervan, 1988.

———. "Mythopoetic Language in the Psalms." *Westminster Theological Journal* 44 (1982) 88–98.

Smith, Huston. *Forgotten Truth: The Primordial Tradition*. New York: Harper & Row, 1976.

Smith, Linda B., and Esther Thelen. "Development as a Dynamic System." *Trends in Cognitive Sciences* 7 (2003) 343–48.

Smith, Mark S. *The Ugaritic Baal Cycle*. Vol. 1. Leiden: Brill, 1994.

Smith, Norman Kemp. *Hume's Dialogues on Natural Religion*. 2nd ed. Edinburgh: Nelson, 1947.

Smith, Patricia A. *From Generation to Generation*. Jacksonville, FL: Jehova Rapha, 2001.

Smith, Richard. "The Revival of Ancient Gnosis." In *The Allure of Gnosticism: The Gnostic Experience in Jungian Psychology and Contemporary Culture*, edited by Robert A. Segal et al., 204–23. Chicago: Open Court, 1995.

Smolin, Lee. "Atoms of Space and Time." *Scientific American* 290 (2004) 66–75.

———. *The Life of the Cosmos*. New York: Oxford University Press, 1997.

———. "Scientific Alternatives to the Anthropic Principle." In *Universe or Multiverse?*, edited by Bernard Carr, 323–66. Cambridge: Cambridge University Press, 2007.

———. "The Self-Organization of Space and Time." *Philosophical Transactions: Mathematical, Physical and Engineering Sciences* 361 (2003) 1081–88.

Soggin, J. Alberto. "The Prophets on Holy War as Judgement against Israel." In *Old Testament and Oriental Studies*, 67–71. Rome: Biblical Institute Press, 1975.

Speiser, E. A. *Genesis*. Garden City: Doubleday, 1985.

Sperry, Roger. "Changed Concepts of Brain and Consciousness: Some Value Implications." *Zygon* 20 (1985) 41–57.

Spitzer, Robert L., et al. *DSM-IV-TR Casebook*. Washington: American Psychiatric Publications, 2002.

Stanfill, Craig, and David Waltz. "Toward Memory-Based Reasoning." *Communications of the ACM* 29 (1986) 1213–20.

Staples, W. E. "The 'Soul' in the Old Testament." *American Journal of Semitic Languages and Literatures* 44 (1928) 145–76.

Stapp, Henry P. "The Hard Problem: A Quantum Approach." Theoretical Physics Group, Lawrence Berkeley Laboratory, University of California, November 21, 1995. http://citeseerx.ist.psu.edu/viewdoc/download?doi=10.1.1.143.8730&rep=rep1&type=pdf.

Statistics Canada. "Canadian Community Health Survey: Mental Health and Well-Being." *Daily*, September 3, 2003. http://www.statcan.gc.ca/daily-quotidien/030903/dq030903a-eng.htm.

Steinhart, Eric. "Digital Metaphysics." In *The Digital Phoenix: How Computers Are Changing Philosophy*, edited by Terrell Ward Bynum and James H. Moor, 117–34. Malden, MA: Blackwell, 1998.

Stenger, Victor. "Nuthin' to Explain." *Huffington Post*, April 22, 2012. http://www.huffingtonpost.com/victor-stenger/physics-outer-space_b_1443869.html.

Stevens, Anthony. "Critical Notice: A Review of Richard Noll's Jung Cult and Aryan Christ." *Journal of Analytical Psychology* 42 (1997) 671–89.

Stevenson, Ian. "American Children Who Claim to Remember Previous Lives." *Journal of Nervous and Mental Disease* 171 (1983) 742–48.

———. "The Case of Gretchen." In *Unlearned Languages: New Studies in Xenoglossy*, 7–71. Charlottesville: University Press of Virginia, 1984.

———. *Twenty Cases Suggestive of Reincarnation*. New York: American Society for Psychical Research, 1966.

Stevenson, Kalinda Rose. *Vision of Transformation: The Territorial Rhetoric of Ezekiel 40–48*. Atlanta: Scholars, 1996.

Stoerig, Petra, and Alan Cowey. "Blindsight in Man and Monkey." *Brain* 120 (1997) 535–59.

Stone, Anthony P. "Time as Chronos and Kairos: Physical and Metaphysical Time." *Physical Interpretations of Relativity Theory (PIRT) Conference IX: London: September, 2004*. http://homepage.ntlworld.com/stone-catend/PIRT-IX-APStone-FullText.pdf.

Stone, Barton W. "Piercing Screams and Heavenly Smiles." *Christian History* 14 (1995) 15–17.

Storm, Darlene. "Need to Crunch 150 Teraflops per Second? Meet First-of-a-Kind Supercomputer." *Computerworld*, May 7, 2014. http://www.computerworld.com/article/2476236/high-performance-computing/need-to-crunch-150-teraflops-per-second—meet-first-of-a-kind-supercomput.html.

Storr, Carla L. "Epidemiology of Stress Disorders." Johns Hopkins Bloomberg School of Public Health, 2011. http://ocw.jhsph.edu/courses/PsychiatricEpidemiology/PDFs/Lecture4.pdf.

Strasburger, Hans, and Bruno Waldvogel. "Sight and Blindness in the Same Person: Gating in the Visual System." *PsyCh Journal* 4 (2015) 178–85.

Streeter, B. H., and A. J. Appasamy. *The Sadhu: A Study in Mysticism and Practical Religion.* London: Macmillan, 1922.

Stringer, Christopher B. "Dating the Origin of Modern Humans." *Geological Society, London, Special Publications* 190 (2001) 265–74.

Subirana, A., and L. Oller-Daurella. "The Seizures with a Feeling of Paradisical as the Onset Manifestation of Certain Temporal Symptomatic Epilepsies." In *Ve Congrès Neurologique International: Lisbonne, 7–12 Septembre, 1953, Volume IV,* 246–50. Lisboa, 1954.

Suki, Béla, et al. "Fluctuations, Noise and Scaling in the Cardio-Pulmonary System." *Fluctuation and Noise Letters* 3 (2003) R1–R25.

Sundarapandian, V. "Global Chaos Anti-Synchronization of Liu and Chen Systems by Nonlinear Control." *International Journal of Mathematical Sciences & Applications* 1 (2011). http://ijmsa.yolasite.com/resources/25-may.pdf.

Summers, Montague. *Witchcraft and Black Magic.* London: Rider, 1946.

Svozil, Karl. "Computational Universes." *Chaos, Solitons & Fractals* 25 (2005) 845–59.

Swensen, Rod. "Autocatakinetics, Yes—Autopoiesis No: Steps toward a Unified Theory of Evolutionary Ordering." *International Journal of General Systems* 21 (1992) 207–28.

Sycara, Katia P. "MultiAgent Systems." *AI Magazine* 19 (1998) 79–92.

Synan, Vinson. *The Holiness-Pentecostal Movement in the United States.* Grand Rapids: Eerdmans, 1971.

Szasz, Thomas. *Insanity: The Idea and Its Consequences.* New York: Wiley, 1987.

Tani, Jun, and Masato Ito. "Interacting with NeuroCognitive Robots: A Dynamical Systems View." In *Proceedings of the Second International Workshop on Man-Machine Symbiotic Systems,* 123–34. Kyoto, November, 2004. http://citeseerx.ist.psu.edu/viewdoc/download;jsessionid=06ECC3534EE9D3ABCE4BFFE6F4F679EA?doi=10.1.1.189.44&rep=rep1&type=pdf.

Targ, Russell, and Harold Puthoff. *Mind-Reach.* Charlottesville, VA: Hampton Roads, 2005.

Tart, Charles T. "Transpersonal Realities or Neurophysiological Illusions: Toward an Empirically Testable Dualism." Presented at the meeting of the American Psychological Association, Toronto, 1978. http://www.csp.org/experience/docs/tart-trans_real.html.

Tass, Peter A. "Effective Desynchronization with Bipolar Double-Pulse Stimulation." *Physical Review E* 66 (2002) 1–9.

Tawil, Hayim. "Azazel the Prince of the Steepe [sic]: A Comparative Study." *Zeitschrift für die Alttestamentliche Wissenschaf* 92 (1980) 43–59.

Taylor, Ann Gill, et al. "Top-Down and Bottom-Up Mechanisms in Mind-Body Medicine: Development of an Integrative Framework for Psychophysiological Research." *Explore: Journal of Science and Healing* 6 (2010) 29–41.

Taylor, Mike. "What Happened Next?" *Evangelicals Now* (1995) 1, 8.

Teicher, Martin. "Scars That Won't Heal: The Neurobiology of Child Abuse." *Scientific American* 286 (2002) 68–75.

Tellez-Zenteno, José F., et al. "National and Regional Prevalence of Self-Reported Epilepsy in Canada." *Epilepsia* 45 (2004) 1623–29. http://www.onlinelibrary.wiley.com/doi/10.1111/j.0013-9580.2004.24904.x/full.

Tengström, Sven. "רוּחַ *rûah*." In *Theological Dictionary of the Old Testament,* vol. 13, edited by G. Johannes Botterweck et al., 365–66. Grand Rapids: Eerdmans, 1974–2006.

Terborgh, John, et al. "Ecological Meltdown in Predator-Free Forest Fragments." *Science* 294 (2001) 1923–26.

Terrien, Samuel. "The Omphalos Myth and Hebrew Religion." *Vetus Testamentum* 20 (1970) 315–38.

Thaxton, Charles B., et al. *The Mystery of Life's Origin: Reassessing Current Theories*. New York: Philosophical, 1984.

Thuan, Trinh Xuan. "Cosmic Design from a Buddhist Perspective." *Annals of the New York Academy of Sciences* 950 (2001) 206–14.

Tillin, Tricia. "The Toronto Phenomenon: Laughing in the Spirit; Is It of God? How Can Christians Decide?" 1994. http://www.banner.org.uk/tb/laughsp.html.

Timpe, Kevin. "Prayers for the Past." *Religious Studies* 41 (2005) 305–22.

Tipler, Frank J. *The Physics of Immortality: Modern Cosmology, God, and the Resurrection of the Dead*. New York: Doubleday, 1994.

Tittel, J., et al. "Violation of Bell Inequalities by Photons More Than 10 km Apart." *Physical Review Letters* 81 (1998) 3563–66.

Todd, Peter M., and Gerd Gigerenzer. "Précis of Simple Heuristics That Make Us Smart." *Behavioral and Brain Sciences* 23 (2000) 727–41.

Tononi, Giulio, and Gerald M. Edelman. "Schizophrenia and the Mechanisms of Conscious Integration." *Brain Research Reviews* 31 (2000) 391–400.

Toro, Mauro, et al. "Chaos Theories and Therapeutic Commonalities among Depression, Parkinson's Disease, and Cardiac Arrhythmias." *Comprehensive Psychiatry* 40 (1999) 238–44.

Touryan, Kenell J. "From Objective-Realism to Subjective-Relativism: Can We Find a Golden Mean?" *Perspectives on Science and Christian Faith* 53 (2001) 188–95.

Toyokawa, Satoshi, et al. "How Does the Social Environment 'Get into the Mind'? Epigenetics at the Intersection of Social and Psychiatric Epidemiology." *Social Science & Medicine* 74 (2012) 67–74. http://www.ncbi.nlm.nih.gov/pmc/articles/PMC3246041.

Treumann, Rudolf A. "Evolution of the Information in the Universe." *Astrophysics and Space Science* 201 (1993) 135–47.

Trevors, J. T., and D. L. Abel. "Chance and Necessity Do Not Explain the Origin of Life." *Cell Biology International* 28 (2004) 729–39.

Tryon, Edward P. "Is the Universe a Vacuum Fluctuation?" *Nature* 246 (1973) 396–97.

University of Southern California. "Novel Neural Net Recognizes Spoken Words Better than Human Listeners." *ScienceDaily*, October 1, 1999. http://www.sciencedaily.com/releases/1999/10/991001064257.htm.

Vaas, Rüdiger. "Is There a Darwinian Evolution of the Cosmos? Some Comments on Lee Smolin's Theory of the Origin of Universes by Means of Natural Selection." May 28, 2002. http://www.arxiv.org/abs/gr-qc/0205119.

———. "Time Before Time: Classifications of Universes in Contemporary Cosmology, and How to Avoid the Antinomy of the Beginning and Eternity of the World." http://www.arxiv.org/pdf/physics/0408111.

Van Ameringen, Michael, et al. "Post-Traumatic Stress Disorder in Canada." *CNS Neuroscience & Therapeutics* 14 (2008) 171–81. http://onlinelibrary.wiley.com/doi/10.1111/j.1755-5949.2008.00049.x/full.

Van Beeck, Frans Josef. "Unanticipated Inner Experiences: Three Cases and a Reflection on Discernment." *Toronto Journal of Theology* 19 (2003) 7–23.

Van Cleve, James. "Mind-Dust or Magic? Panpsychism versus Emergence." *Philosophical Perspectives* 4 (1990) 215–26.

Van Der Kolk, Bessel A., and Otto Van Der Hart. "The Intrusive Past: The Flexibility of Memory and the Engraving of Trauma." In *Trauma: Explorations in Memory*, edited by Cathy Caruth, 158–82. Baltimore: Johns Hopkins University Press, 1995.

Van Gelder, David. "A Case of Demon Possession." *Journal of Pastoral Care* 41 (1987) 151–61.

VanGerneren, Willern A. *Psalms*. In *Psalms–Song of Songs*, edited by Frank E. Gaebelein et al. Expositor's Bible Commentary 5. Grand Rapids: Zondervan, 1991.

Varela, Francisco. "A Calculus for Self-Reference." *International Journal of General Systems* 2 (1975) 5–24.

Varela, Francisco, et al. "The Brainweb: Phase Synchronization and Large-Scale Integration." *Nature Reviews Neuroscience* 2 (2001) 229–39.

Velikovsky, Immanuel. *Worlds in Collision*. New York: Dell, 1950.

Veneziano, Gabriele. "The Myth of the Beginning of Time." *Scientific American* 290 (2004) 54–59, 62–65.

Venter, Craig. Interview by Charlie Rose. May 21, 2010. Video and transcript. https://charlierose.com/videos/13900.

Versluis, Arthur. *The Egyptian Mysteries*. London: Arkana, 1988.

Vilenkin, Alexander. "A Measure of the Multiverse." *Journal of Physics A: Mathematical and Theoretical* 40 (2007) 6777. http://arxiv.org/pdf/hep-th/06091933.

Vitzthum, Richard C. "Philosophical Materialism." *The Secular Web*. http://www.infidels.org/library/modern/richard_vitzthum/materialism.html.

Vogels, Walter. *God's Universal Covenant: A Biblical Study*. Ottawa: University of Ottawa Press, 1979.

Vogl, Carl. *Begone Satan!* Translated by Celestine Kapsner. Rockford, IL: Tan, 1973.

Voss, Karen-Claire. "Spiritual Alchemy: Interpreting Representative Texts and Images." In *Gnosis and Hermeticism from Antiquity to Modern Times*, edited by Roelef van den Broek and Wouter J. Hanegraaff, 147–81. Albany: State University of New York Press, 1998.

Wade, J. "Love and Death: The Relationship between Altered-State Sex and Near-Death Experiences." *International Journal of Healing and Caring* 3 (2003) 12–13. https://www.scribd.com/document/25397823/The-International-Journal-of-Healing-Caring-January-2003-January-2004.

Wagner, Peter C. *Your Spiritual Gifts Can Help Your Church Grow*. Ventura, CA: Regal, 1979.

Walker, Larry L. "Tree of the Knowledge of Good and Evil." In *New International Dictionary of Old Testament Theology and Exegesis*, edited by Willem A. VanGemeren, 4:1259–60. Grand Rapids: Zondervan, 1997.

Walker, Sara Imari, and Paul C. W. Davies. "The Algorithmic Origins of Life." *Journal of the Royal Society Interface* 10 (2013). http://rsif.royalsocietypublishing.org/content/10/79/20120869.short.

Wallace, H., et al. "Age-Specific Incidence and Prevalence Rates of Treated Epilepsy in an Unselected Population of 2,052,922 and Age-Specific Fertility Rates of Women with Epilepsy." *Lancet* 352 (1998) 1970–73.

Wallace, Howard N. *The Eden Narrative*. Harvard Semitic Monographs 32. Atlanta: Scholars, 1985.

Walter, Tony, and Helen Waterhouse. "A Very Private Belief: Reincarnation in Contemporary England." *Sociology of Religion* 60 (1999) 187–97.

Waltke, Bruce K. "The Creation Account in Gen. 1:1–3—Part II: The Restitution Theory." *Bibliotheca Sacra* 132 (1975) 136–44.

———. *Creation and Chaos*. Portland: Western Conservative Biblical Seminary, 1974.

Waltner-Toews, David. "An Ecosystem Approach to Health and Its Applications to Tropical and Emerging Diseases." *Cadernos de Saúde Pública* (2001) S07–S36. http://www.scielo.br/scielo.php?pid=S0102-311X2001000700002&script=sci_arttext.

Wambach, Helen. *Reliving Past Lives*. New York: Harper & Row, 1978.

Watson, Jennifer B., et al. "Prenatal Teratogens and the Development of Adult Mental Illness." *Development and Psychopathology* 11 (1999) 457–66.

Watson, Paul. "The Tree of Life." *Restoration Quarterly* 23 (1980) 232–38.

Watts, John D. W. *Isaiah 1–33*. Waco, TX: Word, 1985.

Watts, Rikki. "Making Sense of Genesis 1." *Stimulus* 12 (2004) 1–12.

Weaver, C. Douglas. *The Healer-Prophet: William Marrion Branham; A Study of the Prophetic in American Pentecostalism*. Macon, GA: Mercer University Press, 2000.

Weinberg, Steven. "A Designer Universe?" *New York Review of Books*, October 21, 1999. http://www.nybooks.com/articles/archives/1999/oct/21/a-designer-universe.

———. "Living in the Multiverse." In *Universe or Multiverse?*, edited by Bernard Carr, 29–42. Cambridge: Cambridge University Press, 2007.

———. "Is the Universe a Computer?" *New York Review of Books*, October 24, 2002. http://www.nybooks.com/articles/2002/10/24/is-the-universe-a-computer.

Weisinger, Alois. *Occult Phenomena in the Light of Theology*. Westminster, MD: Newman, 1957.

Weiss, Rick. "Of Mice, Men and In-Between: Scientists Debate Blending of Human, Animal Forms." *Washington Post*, November 20, 2004.

Wen, Xiong-wei, et al. "Torsion Field Effect and Zero-Point Energy in Electrical Discharge Systems." *Journal of Theoretics* 5–6 (Dec. 2003 / Jan. 2004) http://www.free-energy-info.co.uk/jiang.pdf.

Wenham, Gordon J. *Genesis 1–15*. Waco, TX: Word, 1987.

———. "Sanctuary Symbolism in the Garden of Eden Story." In *Proceedings of the Ninth World Congress of Jewish Studies: Division A, The Period of the Bible*, 19–25. Jerusalem: World Union of Jewish Studies, 1986.

Wesley, John. *The Complete Works of John Wesley*. Vol. 1, *Journals 1735–1745*. Albany, OR: Ages Software (ver. 2.0), 1996, 1997.

———. *The Complete Works of John Wesley*. Vol. 2, *Journals 1745–1760*. Albany, OR: Ages Software (ver. 2.0), 1996, 1997.

West, Bruce J., et al. "Multifractality of Cerebral Blood Flow." *Physica A* 318 (2003) 453–60.

Westermann, Claus. *Genesis 1–11: A Commentary*. Translated by John J. Scullion. Minneapolis: Augsburg, 1974.

Wheeler, David L. "Toward a Process-Relational Christian Eschatology." *Process Studies* 22 (1993) 227–37.

Wheeler, John Archibald. "Information, Physics, Quantum: The Search for Links." In *Feynman and Computation*, edited by Anthony J. G. Hey, 309–36. Cambridge, MA: Perseus, 1999:

Wheelwright, Philip. *The Presocratics*. New York: Odyssey, 1966.

White, John, and Stanley Krippner. "The X Energy: A Universal Phenomenon." Appendix 1 in *Future Science: Life Energies and the Physics of Paranormal Phenomena*, edited by John White and Stanley Krippner. New York: Anchor, 1977.

Whitehead, Alfred North. *Process and Reality: An Essay in Cosmology*. New York: McMillan, 1929.

Whitfield, Charles L. *The Truth about Mental Illness*. Deerfield Beach, FL: Health Communications, 2004.

Whittaker, P. G., et al. "Unsuspected Pregnancy Loss in Healthy Women." *Lancet* 321 (1983) 1126–27.

Wickramasinghe, N. C., et al. "Progress Towards the Vindication of Panspermia." *Astrophysics and Space Science* 283 (2003) 403–13.

Widengren, Geo. "The King and the Tree of Life in Ancient Near Eastern Religion." *King and Saviour IV*. Uppsala: A.-B. Lundequistka Bokhandeln, 1951.

Wigner, Eugene. "The Unreasonable Effectiveness of Mathematics in the Physical Sciences." *Communications on Pure and Applied Mathematics* 13 (1960) 1–14.

Wilber, Ken, *Eye to Eye: The Quest for the New Paradigm*. Garden City: Anchor, 1983.

Wilcox, David L. "Establishing Adam: Recent Evidences for a Late-Date Adam (AMH@100,000 BP)." *Perspectives on Science and Christian Faiith* 56 (2004) 49–54.

Wilkinson, H. P., and A. Gauld. "Geomagnetism and Anomalous Experiences, 1868–1980." *Proceedings of the Society for Psychical Research* 57 (1993) 275–310.

Willeboordse, Frederick H., and Kunihiko Kaneko. "Externally Controlled Attractor Selection in a High-Dimensional System." *Physical Review E* 72 (2005) 1–7.

Williams, George H., and Edith Waldvogel. "A History of Speaking in Tongues and Related Gifts." In *The Charismatic Movement*, edited by Michael P. Hamilton, 61–113. Grand Rapids: Eerdmans, 1975.

Williams, Jay G. "Genesis 3." *Interpretation: A Journal of Bible and Theology* 35 (1981) 274–79.

Williams, Kevin. "Jayne Smith's Near-Death Experience." International Association for Near-Death Studies. http://www.near-death.com/smith.html.

Winiwarter, Peter. "Autognosis: The Theory of Hierarchical Self-Image Building Systems." In *Proceedings of the International Conference on Mental Images, Values and Reality*, vol. 1, edited by John Andrew Dillon. Salinas, CA: Intersystems Publications, 1986. http://www.bordalierinstitute.com/autognosis.pdf.

Wink, Walter, *Naming the Powers: The Language of Power in the New Testament*. Philadelphia: Fortress, 1984.

Wiseman, P. J. *Ancient Records and the Structure of Genesis*. Nashville: Nelson, 1985.

Wiseman, Richard, et al. "An Investigation into Alleged 'Hauntings.'" *British Journal of Psychology* 94 (2003) 195–211.

Wittchen, Hans-Ulrich, and Frank Jacobi. "Size and Burden of Mental Disorders in Europe—A Critical Review and Appraisal of 27 Studies." *European Neuropsychopharmacology* 15 (2005) 357–76.

Wolf, Herbert M. "The Transcendent Nature of Covenant Curse Reversals." In *Israel's Apostasy and Restoration*, edited by Avraham Gileadi, 319–25. Grand Rapids: Baker, 1988.

Woolger, Roger J. "Body Psychotherapy and Regression: The Body Remembers Past Lives." In *Body Psychotherapy*, edited by Tree Staunton, 172–201. London: Brunner-Routlege, 2002.

Wouter J. Hanegraaff, ed. *Gnosis and Hermeticism from Antiquity to Modern Times*. Albany: State University of New York Press, 1998.

Wright, David F. *The Disposal of Impurity*. Atlanta: Scholars, 1987.

Wright, David P. "Azazel." In *Anchor Bible Dictionary*, vol. 1, edited by David Noel Freedman, 536–37. New York: Doubleday, 1992.

Wright, N. T. *For All the Saints? Remembering the Christian Departed*. Harrisburg, PA: Morehouse, 2003.

Wright, Robert. "Did the Universe Just Happen." *Atlantic* 261 (1988) 29-44.
Yardin, L. *The Tree of Light: A Study of the Menorah.* London: Horovitz, 1971.
Yoder, John H. "Anabaptism and History, 'Restitution' and the Possibility of Renewal." In *Umstrittenes Taufertum 1525-1975*, edited by H. J. Goertz, 244-58. Gottingen: Vandenhoeck & Ruprecht, 1975.
———. *The Politics of Jesus.* Grand Rapids: Eerdmans, 1972.
Youngblood, Ronald F. *2 Samuel.* In *Deuteronomy-2 Samuel*, edited by Frank E. Gaebelein et al. Expositor's Bible Commentary 3. Grand Rapids: Zondervan, 1992.
Yuan, An, et al. "Characterizing the Citation Graph as a Self-Organizing Networked Information Space." In *Proceedings of the Innovative Internet Computing Systems: Second International Workshop, Kü Germany, June 20-22, 2002*, 97-107. Berlin: Springer, 2002.
Zahran, Hatice, et al. "Epilepsy Surveillance among Adults—19 States, Behavioral Risk Factor Surveillance System, 2005." *US Department of Health and Human Services, Centers for Disease Control and Prevention.* 2008. http://origin.glb.cdc.gov/Mmwr/preview/mmwrhtml/ss5706a1.htm.
Zaleski, Carol. *Otherworld Journeys: Accounts of Near-Death Experience in Medieval and Modern Times.* New York: Oxford University Press, 1987.
Zimmer, Heinrich. *Philosophies of India.* Princeton: Princeton University Press, 1952.
Zimmer, J. Raymond. "A Possible Natural Complement to the Story of the Fall." *Perspectives on Science and Christian Faith* 54 (2002) 158-69.
Zuendel, Friedrich. *The Awakening.* Farmington, PA: Plough, 1999.
Zuse, Konrad."Calculating Space." MIT Technical Translation AZT-70-164-GEMIT. Cambridge: MIT, 1970. ftp://ftp.idsia.ch/pub/juergen/zuserechnenderraum.pdf.
———. "Rechnender Raum." *Elektronische Datenverarbeitung* 8 (1967) 336-44. Also published as Konrad Zuse, "Rechnender Raum," *Schriften zur Datenverarbeitung, Band 1.* Friedrich Vieweg & Sohn, Braunschweig, 1969.

INDEX

Abraham, F. D., sentient beings can control their own chaoplexic responses, 9, 264–65
Adam
    98–100 billion humans born during last 10,000 years, 252
    and ANE counterparts, 105–7
    and blood guilt, 137, 142
    and chaoplexic nature of covenant fracture, 248–49
    and chaoplexic nature of covenant repair, 276
    and Eve taken from preexisting human population, 102
    and Jesus in responses to Satan/Leviathan, 117
    and Leviathan's boundaries, 166
    and *psi*, 161–62
    and self-divinization, 119
    and the human–divine dyad, 257–58
    as priestly First Man, 108–9, 110
    and Eve and two trees, 75, 102
    expulsion from Eden, 130
    granted conditional immortality, 111, 113, 186
    his self-reference equals 'dead in trespasses and sins,' 275
    his sin discharged by Jesus' dismemberment, 272
    his spirit as divine law clone versus Jesus' spirit shared with the Father and Holy Spirit, 96–97
    immortality via natural law control, 245–46, *see* nature control, 115–17
    loss of vicegerency, 118
    pre-Adamic humans subject to moral law and angelic tutelage, 102
    robbed of immortality, 113, 139–40
Agent
    and consciousness, 205
    and their programmer's purposes, 56
    demonic and synchronization with culture, 238
    dependance on rule-sets, 151
    human mind as math agents, 92, 121, 176
    human spirit as agents, 96, 121
    humans as virtual software agents in far future, 247
    may project own futures including death, 263–64
Algorithm
    adjusted to expel Satan/Leviathan from heaven, 274
    and complex specified information, 45
    and science's resistance to God as programmer, 21–22
    at lowest automaton level are deterministic, 21
    core of human body, mind, spirit, 80, 84, 92, 173, 176, 183, 189
    evolutionary algorithms, 48–49
    linguistic instructions generating life, 8
    statements in the automaton, 7
    teleologically-driven, 49
Altered state(s), 101, 170, 193, 196, 200
    and NDE neognostic experiences, 209–10
    as precursors of post-death realities, 247
    in ecstatic laughter, 232–33
Ancestral spirits, 199
    alleged in Jung's family, 244
    alleged in reincarnation, 249
    as middle realm disincarnate healers, 244
    demons impersonate as, 208, 245
Andreason, Nancy, 82, 180, 230
Animal magnetism
    accepted by Jesse Penn-Lewis, Rudolf Otto, Alois Weisinger, Watchman Nee, 162–63
    and Janet's patient, 135
    as a French placebo test, 253
Anthropology
    and *imago Dei*, 96–97

Index

Anthropology *(continued)*
  creation of Adam and Eve as conditional immortals, 102, 166, 186
  imago Dei and Christology, 97–99
  low god and creation, 54
  NT and tripartite human, 96
  revealed in ANE temple model of tripartite humans, 92–94
  revealed in OT Hebrew terms, 94–95
  Solomon's temple and the human spirit, 95

Astral travel
  and consciousness, 202
  and materialism, 203
  and swami Dadaji, 204
  as demonic phenomena, 244
  as psi, 202–3, 205
  in *Malleus Maleficarum*, 147

Atonement
  Abelard, ethical transformation, 271
  Anselm, legal satisfaction, 271
  by Jesus, and chaoplexity, 274–77
  by Jesus, denied by gnostic theology of humans' inherent divinity, 214
  by Jesus, as a full-blooded human, 98, 272
  Day of, and the cleansing blood of covenant-breach guilt, 269
  gnostic, symbolic death and psychic self-transformation, 29
  Justin, Christus Victor, 270–71

Attractor
  and demonic synchronization with history's SOS processes, 238
  and human repentance, 276
  and Lucifer's rebellion, 265–67, 273–74, 280
  as system dynamics in blessings and curses, 130–31
  defined, 2, 69, 172–74
  God as, 3–4, 17
  in chaoplexity, 19
  in demonic synchronization and desynchronization, 189
  in God–human and human–human relationships, 248, 258, 260
  in synesthesia, 175
  in the trees of Life and Knowledge, 257
  shift in mental pathologies, 183–86, 188

Automaton
  according to Zuse and Fredkin, 20
  allows bounded choice although deterministic, 145
  and meta-time according to its clock cycle, 266
  and the laws sustaining human agents, 285–86
  as a logical grid with control algorithms, 7
  as creation's lowest-level mechanism, 5
  contains algorithmic rules for ethics and morality, 123
  houses human agents with our mind/spirit, 176
  houses various cosmologies, 37
  locus of Leviathan's rebellious actions which skew creation, 60–61, 76–77
  multidimensional, 20
  non-local, 155
  makes information primary in creation, 21–22
  structure linking all creation together, 245
  subsists vacuum, 23
  unused quantum choices exist as system memory, 55–56

Azazel
  Azazel goats as types of Jesus' mission, 270
  death removed by Azazel on Day of Atonement, 269–70
  Leviathan in ANE is equivalent to Azazel and Mot (death), 270, 278

Bak, Per, 21, 152
Barth, Karl, as the nothingness (*das nichtige*) God didn't create, 70, 288–89
Behemoth, as land monster alongside Leviathan, the water monster, 64–65
Berkowitz, David, (Son of Sam) voices and hallucinations he self-labeled Satanic, 190
Biblical realism, 13, 14
  definition, 35
  use of syntactic and semantic techniques, 84
Boyd, Gregory
  and God's counterfactual middle knowledge, 57
  chaos and demonic-in-YHWH theory, 70
Branham, William M., mystical light present at his birth and throughout life, 193
Brennan, Barbara Ann, 25, 195
Brown, Mick, overcome by laughter at Toronto Blessing without converting to Christ, 234–35
Browne, Sylvia
  regression therapy, 251
  white light vision, 195
Brunk, Gregory
  history is self-organizing, 238
  SOCs are ubiquitous and reflect power laws, 151–52
  SOSs depend on past history, 137
Buddhism, 59, 235

Cartledge, Mark, laughter as altered state, 232–33

Index

Cassuto, Umberto, 32, 34, 71
Causation, 21, 48, 148
  and Adam's immortality, 258
  and fifth force, 162–63
  by demons, 189–92
  downward, 50–51, 61, 84, 86, 89–92, 113, 121, 123
  upward, 84, 87–89, 121, 123
Chaos
  and chimeric human minds, 118–19, 278
  and its role in mind pathologies, 171, 173, 183–86
  and Joachimite historiography, 238
  and original sin as disordered chaoplexic structures, 121
  and the deep, 71–72
  as a catchword for the netherworld and place of demons, 270
  as gap theory and first stage of creation, 68
  as OT *tohu wabohu*, 67
  as the serpent, 66
  as Yahweh's primary cosmic and historical battleground, 139–40
  causation and neural networks, 183
  caused by Lucifer as a system bifurcation, 70
  chaostrophic spiritual discontinuity precludes creatures' self-salvation, 260
  claimed by gnostic theology to be reversible by self-transformation, 260
  creation as conflict with chaos (*chaoskampf*), 72–74
  deadened the human spirit, 120, 214, 248
  Egyptian: creation reverts to at time's end, 65
  its destruction part of Jesus' three–part mission, 268
  its double marking precludes self-diagnosis of good and evil, 267
  theological and mathematical chaos share deep-level structures, 67, 69–70
  with periodic rigidity the framework for creation's equilibrium, 153
Chiasm, definition and origin, 34
Christology, Chalcedon and Jesus' two natures, 97–99
Confession, 137, 141
Consciousness
  according to Teilhard and Jung, 86
  and downward causation, 90
  and Paleolithic humans, 101
  as an emergent qualitative change from biological functions, 83–84, 175
  as Hubbard's alleged Christ Self inner voice, 28
  culmination in the Omega Point, 248
  materialist views
  Nagel: need for consciousness conceptual revolution, 80
  pansychism: spirit inherent in matter, 85
  Popper's world two, 56, 118
Creation
  and death due to entropy, 58
  and heaven as an SOC, 273–74
  and Leviathan's ability to exercise macro control, 163–66
  and string theory, 38–39
  as designed, 39–40
  as a feedback network with God acting in downward causation, 61, 123
  demonstrates Leviathan's existence via his causations of death and *psi*, 8–10
  follows its algorithmic rules, 49
  is open and not self-referential, 17
  is computational, 19–23
  laws cannot be annulled but only manipulated, 67
  mathematics as creation's language, 150
  moral dualism in, 10, 209
  morally controlled by *lex talionis*, 128
  opposed by Leviathan and chaos, 72–74
  signals God's existence by his roles as attractor, information source, and life-giver, 2–8
  standard big bang model, 37
Cromwell, Oliver, his laughter, 230–31
Curse(s)
  Adamic, canceled by Jesus' death and resurrection, 272
  as chaoplexic process, 130–31
  as enacter of *lex talionis*, 129–30
  as stipulated in the covenant lawsuit, 133–34
  initiated by ancestral black mass, 135
  initiated by trauma and occult practices, 135–36
  present and ancestral curses reversed via confession and repentance, 141

Darwin(ism)
  and complex specified information, 45
  as Newtonian ideology, 20, 36
  assumptions, 44
  chance and randomness, 45–47
  dismayed by epigenetics' validation of Lamarck, 182
  gradual change versus externally-granted god parameters, 47–48
Darwinism(neo), as Kuhnian collapse, 23
Davies, Paul, 3, 4, 6, 16, 20, 40, 44, 51, 183
Dawkins, Richard, 14, 48, 238

de Chardin, Teilhard, 24–25, 52, 78, 86, 211, 248
de Molina, Luis, middle knowledge and counterfactuals, 57
Death, first
  and original sin, 121, 137, 142, 261
  as *tohu wabohu*; *tehom*; Spencer-Brown's double-marking; L'Engle's un-Naming, 75–76
  blocked creation, 77
  Buddhist, Hindu, multiverse, human sin theories of causation, 59
  due to cell replication limits and/or information loss, 240–41
  entropy as as ultimate root, 58, 166, 240–41
  God as cause via creation's design, 60
  impermeable in Bible, 245
  in humans, 278
  overcome at Teilhard's Omega Point, 248
  rebellious angels as cause, 60–61
  self-referencing denies death as a causative loop, 76–78
  technologies to overcome, 239, 246–47
Death, second, 120, 288–91
Dembski, William, 45, 46, 48
Depression, 177, 184, 185, 190
Divinization, as self-divinization, 119–20, 170; as theosis, 97, 209
Douglas, Mary
  atonement, 268
  essence of evil is rejection of order, 167–68
Driesch, Hans, 15, 246
Drug(s), 79, 91, 178, 192, 198, 200
  and seizures, 180
  ineffectiveness in psychiatric disorders, 190, 254

Eccles, John, 83, 227,
Ecstasy
  as Joachimite and Augustinian theology in chaoplexic conflict, 237–38
  during Zen Buddhism zendo, 235
  in shamanism, 236
  in the OT, 233
Eden
  Adam as priestly First Man, 108
  location, 103–6
  reflection of ANE motifs: cosmic mountain, temple sanctuary, 106–9
Einstein, Albert, 22, 31, 55, 85, 157
Ellis, G. F. R., 30, 31, 40, 61, 68
Emergence
  creates new laws, 84
  evolution as, 50–51
Enantiodromia
  as Teilhard's Omega Point, 211
  phenomena need their opposites, 70
Entropy, 41, 43, 248, 253
  its reversibility in the resurrection, 258–59, 274–75
Epigenetic, virtual object regulation of genetics, 182–83, 256
Epilepsy
  and laughter, 230
  as chaoplexic process, 184
  conventional triggers, 178
  Janet's patient Léonie, 135–36
  learned self-control, 180
  machine induced, 187–88
  prevalence rates, 177
  trauma and emotional triggers as major causes, 179–80

Fechner's Law, 84, 172, 174, 176
Feynman, Richard, 36, 57, 154
Fifth force
  as Christianized gnostic theology, 161–62
  as demonic, 162
  as the source of *psi*, 160–61
Flournoy, Théodore, 14–16, 29, 155, 219
Fourth Wave, 116, 220, 229, 233, 236–37, 282
  bodily phenomena in Fourth Wave, 228
  hell incites laughter in Fourth Wave revival, 234
Fredkin, Edward, 5, 7, 20, 21–22, 55, 123
Free will
  and rejection of covenant, 261
  free will and counterfactuals, *see* Molinism
  God provides human via creaturely agency in the automaton, 54–56, 145
  God refuses to infringe, 276, 287
  in angelic communities, 122
Freud, Sigmund, 199, 200, 254

Gap, creation theory of, 60, 67–68
Genetic
  DNA information coding sequence same as computer and linguistic, 40
  emotions influence gene expression, 255–57
  genetic algorithms preselect according to future goals, 49, 52
  genetic factors are weak and non-specific in many mind disorders, 181
  genetic program limits cell divisions, 240
  original sin non-genetic, 137
God
  and *chaoskampf* as a block to creation, 72–74
  and cosmic mountain, 106–7, 109, cosmic tree, 111

and counterfactual ancestral healing, 282–83
and creation's dualism, 11
and downward causation, 123
and dynamic history, 130–31; blood guilt as dynamic process, 137
and Egyptian anthropology, 91
and enantiodromia in Barth, 70
and entropic universe, 8, 274; entropic reversal in the new creation, 259
and gap theory, 67–68
and nature gods, 166–68
and pre-Adamic sinfulness, 102
and relationship attachment (dyad), 112–13, 117, 248
and the human spirit as sanctuary, 95–96; imago Dei and divine clone, 97
and the Light, 196, 209
and the proto covenant, 124–25
as amoral or immoral due to natural suffering and death, 60
as attractor, information source, life-giver, 3–8
as creation's programmer and designer, 7, 22, 40–41, 53–54
as energy, 25–26; as nature's body (panentheism), 51; as the 'Other,' 51–53, 146; as personal, 53, 113; as demiurge, 54
as source of ecstasy, 215
creator of Behemoth and Lucifer/Leviathan, the cosmic monsters, 64–65
fear of: John Arnott, Rodney Howard-Browne, Jonathan Edwards, Jesse Penn-Lewis, 234
has a broken heart after covenant breach, 271
overcomes Levathian chaos to create universe, 61
refuses to infringe a person's will, 276; overcomes rebellious wills in *apokatastasis* (universalism), 279–80
Goddess
 as energy, 25
 as Paleolithic fertility: Venus of Willendorf, Çatalhöyük, 101
 as Great Mother, 115–16, 117, 209
 dispenser of water of life, 111
Gödel, Kurt, 17, 51, 85, 150, 266
Greyson, Bruce, 194, 202, 210
Guilt, blood
 and ANE sacrificial practices, 133–34, 136; see *curse*, 135
 and chaoplexic processes, 137
 and general revelation, 142–43
 covenant breach requires blood guilt dismemberment, 125
 defined, 137
 humans innocent of Adam's sin but guilty of covenant fracture, 142
 Leviathan's avenged by Jesus, 272
 on the land, Deut 21:1–9, 136; as *lex talionis*, 136
Gunkel, Hermann, *chaoskampf*, 72; *rîb*-pattern covenant lawsuit, 131

Hanegraaff, Wouter
 neognostics equate post-death state with altered states' experiences, 247
 New Agers avoid reality of post-Aquarius heat dead universe, 77–78
Hardy, Alister, 194, 242
Harkavy, Alan, 7, 54
Harner, Michael, 204, 236, 247
Hawking, Stephen, 38, 39, 77
Headship, federal, 141–42
Hell
 and universal restoration, 279–80
 as a fixed negative attractor, 289
 as nothingness, 288–89
 as second death, 288–91
 enantiodromia and hell, 288
 incited fear with Jonathan Edwards, 234
 Leviathan requires a creation with hell for moral accountability, 289
 rejected by neognostic evaluation of NDEs, 210–11
Hermeneutics
 four senses, 34–35, 106, 262
 Jewish, 34
 postmodern, 31
Hieros gamos, 115–16, 207, 275, 284
High god, 54, 63, 66
Higher Self, 27–29, 120, 205, 210, 248
Homeostasis
 and mind pathologies, 183, 185
 as information and attachment in Adam, 258
 as SOSs exerting network control, 240–42, 258
 attempts to maintain via demonic synchronization, 246
 balanced in Adam, 273
Howard-Browne, Rodney
 demanded that God descend to him, 237
 ecstatic experience of the fire of 'God,' 215
Hubbard, Barbara Marx
 and planetary birth with the 'felt' evolved inner Christ, 28

Index

Hubbard, Barbara Marx *(continued)*
  and the planetization of spirit when our mammalian bodies perish, 78
  spirit guide: denial of human sin, 212; spiritual evolution, 247; Leviathan restoration, 247

Immortality
  conferred directly by tree of life, vicariously by tree of knowledge, 115
  manipulation of natural law to preserve his life killed Adam, 166
  provided to Adam and Eve via God-attachment, 113, 253
  serpent is self-proclaimed creator, life-giver, and image of immortality, 65–66
  should be present in our universe or a multiverse, 58–59, 240
  stolen by the serpent, 102, 113, 139, 248
  via exotic technologies, 246–47
  Yahweh must restore, 140
Intermediate realm
  and Harry Edwards' healing work, 244
  and Johann Blumhardt's deliverance experience, 243–44
  and Jung's ancestral inheritance of spiritualism, 244
  as limbo, purgatory, hades, paradise, 283–84
  defined Platonically, 243
  in pop culture, 242

James, William, 191, 197, 219
Janet, Pierre, 135–36, 199
Jesus
  absent during 1995 Toronto signs and wonders outbreak, 235
  accepts us after we've reintegrated our core psychic splitness, 260
  and atonement theories, 270–71
  and dismemberment as the first-born of creation, 272–73
  and his chaoplexic atonement, 274–76
  and his divine-human identity, 97–99
  and power of his name in neognostic therapy, 213
  and the final judgment, 144–45, 214
  as *apokatastasis*, 279
  as kinsman redeemer, 11, 124, 136, 138–39, 143–45; Yahweh as KR, 139–40
  as one model of the universal savior myth, 28
  as second Adam, 140
  as sin-bearer versus avatar healer, 211, 213
  as the ANE Tree of Life, 112
  empowered by the Holy Spirit and not by demonic *dunamis*, 162–63
  his mission: restore the covenant, destroy Leviathan, eradicate chaos, 268
  his resurrection as the type of human restored embodiment, 259
  man from heaven, 99, 277
  versus Adam in nature control, 117
  visions of him by: Mother Teresa, 12, George Ritchie, Carl Jung, Ann Lee, Saint Marguerite Marie, Agnes Sanford, Sundar Singh, apostle Stephen, 206–8, missionary, 213, Celeste, 282
Jung, C. G.
  Christ as symbol of the Self, 27
  collective unconscious, 24, 199–200
  family spiritualism and intermediate realm, 244
  his daimon (spirit guide), 233
  Honegger's Mithraic procreative pneuma, 198–99
  predictive visions of WW 1, 284
  psychoid energy, 25, 86
  subjectivity of Rhine's *psi* experiments, 161
  vision of 'Jesus,' 206

Keller, Helen, 30, 81, 87, 88, 89
Kingdom Now
  and testing spirits, 236
  as Joachimite history, 237
  as movement, 220
  glorified body possible in history, 247–48
  psi healing heat, 13
Kinsman redeemer
  and moral chaoplexity, 124
  in OT, 136, 138–40
  Jesus as, 143–45, 272
Kipper, 29, 137, 268–69, 272
Kundalini, 25, 235, 236

Laszlo, Ervin, 45, 153, 154, 241
Laughter
  215, 228, 229
  analyzing, 229–36
  as demonic: J. Wesley, 227–28
  as Joachimite self-organizing system movement, 238
  at Toronto Blessing, 234–35
Leviathan
  and Adam's original sin as a fall into chaos, 120–21
  and ANE cosmic rebellion mythology, 63
  and asteroid impact, 164–65
  and *hieros gamos* ritual sexuality, 116

and his attendance on God's throne as
    Lucifer, 66
and his claim to divinity as the primeval
    serpent, 65
and his computational limits, 164–65
and his internal paradox as cause of form-
    less waste, 76
and levitation, 156, 159
and nature: examples of his actions, 148–49
and the persistence of his death-generating
    self-organizing systems, 274
and the possibility of restoration: Gregory
    of Nyssa, 279; Aquinas, 280; Riesinger
    demon, 280
as a primary source of religious ecstasy,
    215–16
as cause of paranormal phenomena, 10
as Lucifer covenanted with God to be his
    servant forever, 262–63
as Satan: eviction from heaven, 274
as structural disorder in which good and
    evil occupy the same moral state space,
    273
as the source of psychological transcendent
    light, 193
as the source of sexual visions involving
    'Jesus' as partner, 206–7
boundaries in nature, 163
chaostrophic discontinuity is dynamically
    irreversible, 287
constrained by Adam's vicegerency, 166
creates chimeric human minds after Adam's
    sin, 118, 275
cut loose from humans by Jesus' sinless
    obedience, 276
first death, 278
his reality in clients recognized by an atheist
    therapist, 213
injected blood guilt into creation, 137, 272
known as Leviathan, 1
name first appears in 2400 BCE, 1, 71, and
    in OT, OT apocryphal, intertestamental,
    and NT books, 2
operates in chaoplexic systems, 151, 156
originator of evil, 11
paired with Behemoth in two-monster
    water and land typology, 2, 64–65
people who performed his counterfeit
    miracles will be condemned at the judg-
    ment, 214
reduced to ground-undulating ' dust-eater,'
    64
replaced God in Adam's relational attach-
    ment network, 248, 257
reunified with God in the eschaton, 261

second death, 279–80, 288–91
speaks creation's mathematical language,
    150
thrown from heaven to earth to the abyss to
    the lake of fire, 274
to be drawn and quartered, 140
Lewis, C. S., 202, 282, 290
Lex Talionis
allows demonic entry, 214
blessings and curses drive the system,
    128–29
cases in the OT, 136–37
creation's moral law: equivalence of retalia-
    tion, 128
explains Jesus dismemberment, 272
when creation suffers loss, so too does God,
    271
Light (paranormal)
all manifestations are due to nonhuman
    agents, 205
and dark together comprise God, 60
and darkness in ANE, 64
and right lobe neurological percept, 196–98
as a core paranormal phenomenon seen by
    many, 193–96
as an energetic god, 25–26
as manifestation of divinity within person,
    209–10
denies sin, 211–13
experienced during NDEs, 200–202
present as demonic vision in human alter,
    136
seen with or as vision of Jesus, 206–8
Lucifer
a liar from the beginning, 267
and gap theory, 68
and his chaostrophic discontinuity, 267, 273
and his early biography, 262
and his perpetual covenant with God, 263
and his transformation into Leviathan, 66
and loss of creational status, 165–66
as creator, life-giving, immortal serpent
    demonic enemy of God, 65–66
as Day Star light both attendant at and pre-
    tender to God's throne, 62–63
as origin of chaos, 67, 77
attempts to join trinity by manipulating his
    self-regulation, 264–65
God and restitution, 68
triggered a covenant break with God de-
    signed to avoid death, 9, 264

Ma'at, 61–62, 76, 142–43
Mainzer, Klaus, 82, 84–85, 153, 186
Malleus Maleficarum, 147, 163, 164, 166

INDEX

Manichaean, 9, 60, 70
Mass, black, 135
Materialism, presuppositions, 14
Mbonye, Manasse, 38, 83, 153, 259
Memory
  alleged in reincarnation experiences, 250–52
  and Jesus' preexistence, 98
  as unrealized quantum possibilities in the automaton, 55
  formation in people, 81
  in machine–human synchronization, 187–89
  in SOSs, 137
  involvement in neognostic Light visions, 206
  involvement in both valid and hallucinatory percepts, 197–98
  organized in people by fractal geometry, 175–76
  phonetic memory frames in glossolalia, 224
Meyer, Stephen, 45, 49
Mimesis, 27, 28, 108
Mind disorders
  and attachment loss with God, 171
  and downward causation, 190–91
  and emotional trauma and covenant fracture as demonic access, 191
  and selective serotonin reuptake inhibitors (SSRI) drugs' ineffectiveness, 190
  causation, 178–83
  lex talionis triggers, 171, 191
  materialist explanation of mind disorders, 170
Molinism, free will and counterfactuals, 56–57, 75, 145
Mormon(ism), 194, 218–20, 284
Mot, death in ANE, 73, 269–70, 278
Multiverse
  based on cosmic selection in which all possible universes exist, 41–42
  denied by theory testability, naturalness, and metaphysical rationality, 42–44
  eternal, 16
  fails self-reference test, 19
  non–observation of strings invalidates multiverse, 39
  should produce a universe with immortality, 59
Murphy, Nancey, 83, 92
Myss, Caroline, 33

Nagel, Thomas, definition of consciousness, 80
  humans and bats, 79
Nash, John Forbes, 169, 170, 191–92
Nature gods

  and mixed moral structures, 166
  freedom from is God's rest, 144
  see *hieros gamos*, 115
NDE
  and neognostic theology, 209–10
  contents of, 202
  mainstream explanations, 201
  percepts lacking physical visual functions, 201–2, 205
Neognosticism
  and acute psychosis as spiritual growth, 170, 192
  and *psi* energy as fifth force, 160–63
  as holography, 26, 29
  claims that Jesus used *psi dunamis* (power), 163
  definition and labels, 23–24, 200
  hermeneutics: tree of life in semiotic terms, 33
  religious opinions following an NDE, 210
  rooted in semiotic language, 27–29
  salvation via psychic recapitulation of Jesus' self-transformation, 212, 260
  transitioning from Pisces to Aquarius, 77
  use of collective unconscious and energies as transcendent, 24–25
Network control
  in reversing the universe's entropy, 275
  in shifting Adamic attractor to Christ attractor, 276
  via negative exponent, 189
  via noise strength, 189
  via pulse timing, 7, 18, 156, 184, 189, 265, 267
Nobel Prize, winners, Frances Crick, 246; John Eccles, 83; David Hubbel, 88; Richard Feynman, 36; John Forbes Nash, 169; Wolfgang Pauli, 86; Michael Polyani, 83; Charles Townes, 44; Steven Weinberg, 36; Torsten Wiesel, 88; Eugene Wigner, 53
Non–locality, 24, 154, 155

OBE, as autoscopy, 203
Omega
  neognostic eschatology, 78, 211, 248, 261
  universe's fine-tuning, 40
Oswalt, John, *chaoskampf* in history, 74–75

Parham, Charles, 219–20, 225, 226
Parkinson's, 185, 254, 255
Pauli, Wolfgang, 86, 162
Penn–Lewis, Jesse, 162, 234
Penrose, Roger, 39, 259
Perennial philosophy, 24, 260
Polkinghorne, John, 4, 5, 52, 60, 80, 282

Poltergeist, 10, 159
Polyani, Michael
    life depends on structure and process, 240
    people, not acids, think and are conscious, 50, 83
Popper, Karl
    Adam's sin injected blood guilt into worlds two and three, 137
    demonic access to human mind in world one, 214
    Leviathan and chaos in world three, 119
    three worlds, 56
    world one and Adam's attempt to link with automaton, 118
Power law, 152, 153, 241
Pribram, Karl, 29, 198
Psi
    and electromagnetism, 159–62
    and weather control, 164, 168
    as ancestral spirits, 245
    as new laws, 80, 86
    as nonconsensual reality, 200
    as traditional energies in the Toronto Blessing, 236
    as voices and visions, 13–15
    with alters and light, 136
Purgatory
    and hell, 283–85
    and reincarnation in intermediate realm, 243
    cross-cultural prayers to/for the dead, 281–82
    NDE as medieval source, 284
Puthoff, Harold, 3, 4, 16, 36, 158

Qualia, 84, 92, 171
    and Deterministic Finite Automata (DFAs), 173
    and schizophrenia, 181, 183, 185
    as law of consciousness, 174–76
Quaternity, Satan as member of a four-part godhead, 60, 261, 264

Rahab, 71, 73–75, 262
Regression therapy, 195, 225
Reincarnation
    and Hindu theory of creation, 59
    as a demonic lie, 208
    believed by NDE experiencers, 210
    early childhood and adult previous life memories, 250–52
    Euro-American and Canadian belief in, 249
    karma and theodicy, 249–50
Repentance, 143, 217, 235, 276, 288
Reprogram creation
    by tree of knowledge, 118
    chaos defined as automaton's rules reprogrammed, 61, 76, 77
    Leviathan's revolt reprogrammed natural laws to produce death, 9, 67, 69
Rest, God's, 125, 143–44
    the elect, 144
Resurrection
    embodiment like Jesus' resurrection body, 259
    of body at end of age, 260
    of universe, 258–59
Reynolds, Pam, 201, 205
Ring, Kenneth, 201, 210, 212
Ritchie, George, 206, 211

Sabom, Michael, 200, 206
Sanford, Agnes
    demonic voices, 283
    hurricane control, 166
    OBE 'pre-birth' visions: of Jesus, Sparta, 207
Satan
    a murderer and liar from the beginning, 272
    and a black mass in England 300 years ago, 135
    and his empowerment of 'Son of Sam,' David Berkowitz, 190
    and his legal right to earth, 107
    and his self-referential irreversible system bifurcation which broke covenant with God, 9, 76
    and three renunciations of dedications to the devil, 135
    ANE symbol for immortality, ontologically demonic, self-referencing, 66
    as creationism's cause of prehistoric animal death, 60, and ruler of preprimeval world, 68
    as earth's ruler after Adam's sin, 140, 270
    as the *ha-satan*, adversary, in Job, 64
    belief in, legacy Christian countries, 1
    contrasted with Jesus in nature control, 117
    death in the lake of fire, 270
    fall from heaven, 66, 68
    his *apokatastasis* (restoration) a minority view, 280
    his *apokatastasis* (restoration) is impossible, 287, see Leviathan, 279
    his existence indicated by death and *psi* phenomena, 8
    his power over death, 270
    origin as Lucifer the cherubim, 9
Sauer, Erich, 107, 108, 109
Schizophrenia
    ancestral influence, 182

Index

Schizophrenia *(continued)*
  and laughter, 230
  and neognostic therapeutic power source, 213
  chaoplexic processes, 184–85
  epigenetic causation, 182–83
  minimal biogenetic but major trauma triggers, 180–82
  voices and visions, 183
Schmidt, Emma, 156, 158, 160, 200
Self-reference
  denies closed emergent systems, 85
  and Gödel, Spencer-Brown, Varela, 17–19
  denies panpsychism, 52
  overcome in salvation by Holy Spirit, 276
Semiosis, 27, 28, 35, 108
Smith, Joseph, 195, 219
Smolin, Lee, 18, 20, 21, 39, 42
Somatic control
  in animal magnetism, DID, hysteric conversion, medications, neuronal implants, imagery, 253–55
  via emotional expression, 255–57
  via God-human dyad, 257–58
Sophia, elevated by neognosticism over the Logos, 27
Spencer-Brown, Geo., 18, 51, 66, 69, 76, 146, 248, 266
Spirit, human
  and biblical anthropology, 94–96
  mainstream biblical scholars' physicalist view, 92
  modeled by ANE temple construction, 92–94, 109
  transducer between mind and God, 92
Stevenson, Ian, 208, 225, 250, 251
String theory, 38–39, 42–43
  as the fifth force, 160–63
  faster than light, 24
Svozil, Karl, 9, 21–22, 61, 77, 155
Swedenborg, Emanuel, 194, 284
Synchronize(ation)
  and Leviathan's weather control, 164
  and levitation, 156–59
  and seizures, 184–85
  as cross-connections in synesthesia, 174–75
  between Leviathan and math forms, 154
  cross species, 186–89
  definition, 156
  illegitimate between human mind and automaton nodes, 56
  Jesus' atonement synchronized creation with God the father, 275
  of demons with social systems, 237–38
  of Jesus with creation in the grand unified theory (GUT), 4
  of people with God via the tree of life, 257–58
  tree of life as an attractor enabling synchronization with God, 257
  types, 156

Ted Owens, nature control, 148, 164, 166, 192
Teresa, Mother, 12–13
Tongues
  demons called the source of tongues by Charles Parham, 226
  in Christian history, 216–20
  less than 10 percent Holy Spirit, 225–27
  Leviathan as a primary source of tongues, 225
  phonations frustes, 220–23
  Satan the source of a Camisard's tongues according to C. Wesley, 217
  xenoglossia and ermeneglossia, 224–25
Trance, 9, 10, 136, 162, 193, 215, 219, 222, 223, 232, 247, 252
Tree of Knowledge
  Adam's sin: probationary test, sexuality, 114, including *hieros gamos*, 115–16; illicit wisdom, nature control, 116–17
  its fruit caused a catastrophic bifurcation in Adam, 248
  see chaos, 118
Tree of Life
  and resurrection, 258
  as a network control balancing structure producing homeostasis, 240, 253, 257–58
  as intimate covenant relationship between God and humans, 112
  as symbol grounding in Genesis, 33–34
  in ANE sources, 105–6, 110–11
  in OT, 111
  its loss is the first death, 278
  Jesus as, 112
  primeval king as the Tree or its sanctuary priest/gardener, 107
Trinity, the, 54–53, 98, 99, 208, 209, 213, 261, 264

Varela, Francisco, 17, 18, 51, 69, 76

Waltke, Bruce
  chaos hostile but becomes good, 69
  creation battle with monsters, 72, 73
Weinberg, Steven, 7, 36, 44, 53–54
Wellhausen, Julius, 32, 33, 127
Wheeler, John, 5, 22, 287
Wilber, Ken, 26, 204, 247

Wolf, Herbert, 141, 268
Wolfram, Stephen, 20, 55–56

Yamm, raging sea, 61, 71, 73, 74, 76

Young, Brigham, 218, 219, 225

Zuse, Konrad, 20, 55

www.ingramcontent.com/pod-product-compliance
Lightning Source LLC
Chambersburg PA
CBHW080725300426
44114CB00019B/2493